THE PHONOLOGY OF THE WORLD'S LA

Series Editor: Jacques Durand, Université de Toulouse-le-Mirail

The Phonology of Norwegian

General Editor: Jacques Durand

The Phonology of Danish
Hans Basbøll

The Phonology of Dutch
Geert Booij

The Phonology of Standard Chinese
San Duanmu

The Phonology of Polish
Edmund Gussman

The Phonology of English
Michael Hammond

The Phonology of Norwegian
Gjert Kristoffersen

The Phonology of Portuguese
Maria Helena Mateus and Ernesto d'Andrade

The Phonology and Morphology of Kimatuumbi
David Odden

The Lexical Phonology of Slovak
Jerzy Rubach

The Phonology of Hungarian
Péter Siptár and Miklós Törkenczy

The Phonology of Mongolian
Jan-Olof Svantesson, Anna Tsendina, Anastasia Karlsson, and Vivan Franzén

The Phonology of Armenian
Bert Vaux

The Phonology and Morphology of Arabic
Janet Watson

The Phonology of Catalan
Max Wheeler

The Phonology of German
Richard Wiese

In preparation

The Phonology of Icelandic and Faroese
Kristján Árnason

The Phonology of Tamil
Prathima Christdas

The Phonology of Italian
Martin Krämer

The Phonology of Spanish
Iggy Roca

THE
PHONOLOGY
OF
NORWEGIAN

—

Gjert Kristoffersen

OXFORD
UNIVERSITY PRESS

OXFORD
UNIVERSITY PRESS

Great Clarendon Street, Oxford OX2 6DP
Oxford University Press is a department of the University of Oxford.
It furthers the University's objective of excellence in research, scholarship,
and education by publishing worldwide in

Oxford New York

Athens Auckland Bangkok Bogotá Buenos Aires Calcutta
Cape Town Chennai Dar es Salaam Delhi Florence Hong Kong Istanbul
Karachi Kuala Lumpur Madrid Melbourne Mexico City Mumbai
Nairobi Paris São Paulo Singapore Taipei Tokyo Toronto Warsaw
and associated companies in Berlin Ibadan

Oxford is a registered trade mark of Oxford University Press
in the UK and in certain other countries

Published in the United States
by Oxford University Press Inc., New York

British Library Cataloguing in Publication Data
Data available

Library of Congress Cataloging in Publication Data
Data applied for

Typeset by SPI Publisher Services, Pondicherry, India
Printed in Great Britain
on acid-free paper by
Biddles., King's Lynn, Norfolk

ISBN 978–0–19–823765–5 (Hbk.)   978–0–19–922932–1 (Pbk.)

1 3 5 7 9 10 8 6 4 2

PREFACE

The aim of this book is to provide a comprehensive analysis of the phonology of the variety of Norwegian spoken by the majority of the inhabitants of the most densely populated area of Norway, the south-eastern region surrounding its capital Oslo. Even if the book is written within the framework of Generative Phonology, the main purpose is not to defend a specific theoretical approach, but to present data and propose analyses of a specific phonological system in a (hopefully) clear, concise and coherent manner, so that the reader can judge the merits of and perhaps take issue with the solutions offered. I have therefore chosen to write the book within what I considered to be a fairly mainstream generative approach when I started working on the book some 5 years ago—Lexical Phonology, the basic principles of which I can safely assume to be familiar to the majority of the phonological community.

Given the advent of Optimality Theory, which has enjoyed an enormous interest since it was introduced in 1993, and which today may be said to be the dominant theoretical approach to Generative Phonology, the book may appear as somewhat outdated. But since Optimality Theory has been in a constant flux over the few years that it has existed, and since the main aim of the book is not primarily to put the latest theoretical developments to the test, I have chosen not to make Optimality Theory the theoretical backbone of the book. But it will be referred to at different points, and the reader will notice that the book to a certain extent has been informed by Optimality Theoretic concepts, or at least concepts that have been brought to the foreground by the introduction of Optimality Theory.

Many people have read and commented on earlier versions of the book, or answered questions about data that were not available in the literature. Thanks are due to Geert Booij, Jacques Durand, Rolf Theil Endresen, Thorstein Fretheim, Jan Hognestad, Kristian Emil Kristoffersen, Chantal Lyche, Eric Papazian, Tomas Riad, Helge Sandøy, Arne Torp, and two anonymous reviewers who commented on an early draft of Chapters 1–3 and 5.

I have also been given the opportunity to present aspects of my work to audiences at the University of Utrecht (June 1996), the Free University, Amsterdam (September 1996), University of Leiden (November 1996), at the OUP conference arranged in Pézenas, France in June 1996 as well as at the MONS meeting in Trondheim, Norway in November 1997.

I am grateful for all comments and questions that I have received; they have undoubtedly improved the quality of the book considerably. I am especially grateful to Geert Booij and Tomas Riad, who at different stages read and commented on substantial portions of the manuscript. Of course I am all the same to blame for all remaining shortcomings.

Thanks are also due to Geert Booij for inviting me to spend the year 1996 at the Free University in Amsterdam, and for the excellent working conditions that I was provided with there. I also gratefully acknowledge the financial support from the Norwegian Research Council (NFR) that made my stay in the Netherlands possible. Finally, I am grateful to Magnhild Svenheim, at the University Library in Tromsø, for invaluable help with some last moment reference checking.

G.K.

1999

CONTENTS

ABBREVIATIONS AND SYMBOLS

adj.	adjective	NP	noun phrase
Agr.	agreement	NPA	Nasal Place Assimilation
AP	accent phrase *or* adjectival phrase	obs.	obstruent
		OCP	Obligatory Contour Principle
ap	apical		
appr	approximant	p.	page
asp	aspirated	p.c.	personal communication
bot.	botanical	PP	phonological phrase
C	consonant	pl.	plural
coll.	colloquial	poss.	possessive
cont	continuant	post	posterior
comp.	comparative	Pr	proper noun
CSP	Core Syllabification Principle	prep.	preposition
		pts.	participle
CSR	Compound Stress Rule	PWd	prosodic word
def.	definite	RR	the Retroflex Rule
DN	Dano-Norwegian	sg.	singular
fem.	feminine	SCC	Strict Cycle Condition
FP	focal phrase	SD	structural description
H	high tone *or* heavy syllable	son	sonorant
		SPE	Sound Pattern of English
Hfoc	high focal tone	spr. gl.	spread glottis
H%	high boundary tone	SSP	Sonority Sequencing Principle
Hfoc%	high focal boundary tone		
Hz.	Herz	sup.	superlative
id.	identical (with)	TBU	tone-bearing unit
imp.	imperative	TF	tonal foot
indef.	indefinite	TM	the Trondheim Model (of intonation)
IP	intonational phrase		
IPSR	Initial Primary Stress Rule	UEN	Urban East Norwegian
IU	intonational utterance	V	vowel
L	low tone *or* light syllable	v., V	verb
lat	lateral	VP	verb phrase
lit.	literally	voc	vocoid
masc.	masculine	WbP	Weight by Position
MSR	Main Stress Rule	zool.	zoological
ms.	milliseconds	α	variable ranging over + and −
n., N	noun		
nas	nasal	μ	mora
n.a.	not applicable	σ	syllable

Ø   zero
/ /   phonemic *or* underlying representation
[ ]   phonetic representation
¹   the following syllable has primary stress and accent 1 (in phonetic
           representations)
²   the following syllable has primary stress and accent 2 (in phonetic
           representations)
´   primary stress (in orthographic representations)
`   secondary stress (in orthographic representations)
.   syllable boundary

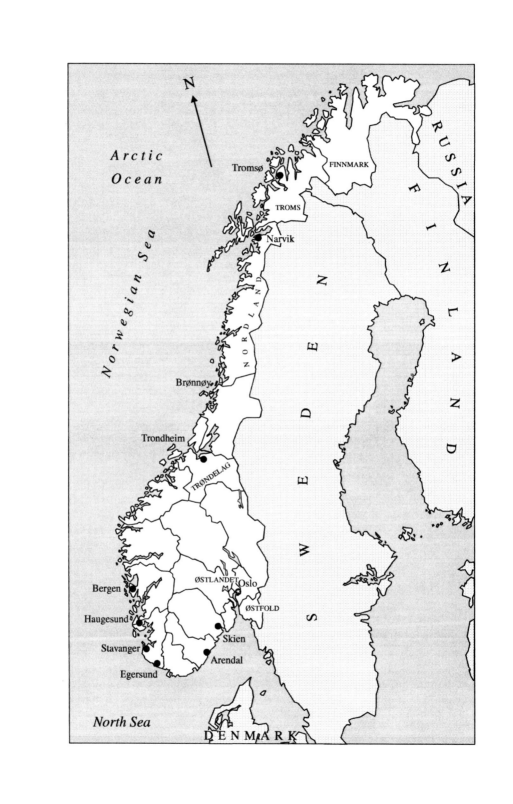

1

INTRODUCTION

1.1 GEOGRAPHICAL AND TYPOLOGICAL REMARKS

Norwegian is the branch of North-Germanic spoken in Norway. The other members of the North-Germanic branch are Swedish, Danish, Icelandic and Faroese. Norwegian is not spoken as a mother tongue outside of Norway, except that it may still be found among older speakers in some Scandinavian settlements in the United States.[1]

Among the North-Germanic languages, Swedish, Danish and Norwegian are particularly close. They are to a large degree mutually intelligible, although amount of previous exposure, education and the accents of the interlocutors will play a certain role.[2] Modern Icelandic and Faroese, which descend from the tongue of the settlers from Norway who came to Iceland and the Faroese islands during the medieval period, are generally not understood by Norwegians.

Typologically, Norwegian, Swedish and Danish today form one distinct group with respect to the two other languages. They can be distinguished from Icelandic and Faroese as Mainland Scandinavian by the fact that they have lost most of the rich inflectional system of the Medieval Scandinavian languages as one can observe it, for example, in Old Norse texts.[3] Old Norse had four nominal cases, marked on nouns, adjectives and pronouns. The verbal inflectional system implied marking of person and number of the subject on the finite verb, and the subjunctive mood was in regular and productive use.

Details apart, this grammatical system is conserved in modern Icelandic, and to a somewhat lesser extent in Faroese, while in mainland Scandinavian there are only remnants of it.[4] Dative is still in use in a fair number of rural dialects of Norwegian and Swedish, but restricted to definite forms. Accusative and genitive have disappeared, but one of the old endings marking genitive case, /-s/, has been transformed into a clitic marking possession, with about the same distribution as its cognate in

---

[1] The majority of the immigrants came from Norway before World War I. The most easily accessible source on Norwegian in the United States is Haugen (1969).

[2] Setting will also play a role. In all three countries, television programs in the two other languages are consistently subtitled. But at least on Norwegian public radio, Danish and Swedish are seldom translated, in contrast with English, which as a rule is translated by the English voice being faded out after a few seconds and supplanted with a Norwegian voice reading a translation.

[3] Old Norse was the language spoken in Norway, Iceland and on the Faroese islands during the Middle Ages.

[4] There is one curious exception to this development. The dialect spoken in Älvdalen in the Dalarna province in Sweden has to this day preserved the old inflectional and conjugational system almost intact. The most comprehensive description of the Älvdalen dialect is Levander (1909).

English. In addition, the pronominal system has preserved a distinction between nominative case forms, used in subject and to a certain extent in predicative forms, and oblique case forms, used in all other syntactic positions. Dialects differ with respect to what extent this distinction is preserved.

1.2 A LANGUAGE WITH TWO WRITTEN NORMS

The linguistic situation in Norway with respect to written as well as spoken norms is special compared to other European countries.[5] This is because Norwegian can be rendered in writing through not one but two official norms, called *Bokmål* (literally 'book language') and *Nynorsk* (literally 'new Norwegian').[6]

The origin of this state of affairs is political and social tensions that developed during the nineteenth century. From being an independent kingdom until the late medieval period, Norway from the fourteenth century on gradually became a province of Denmark. Four centuries later, during the final stages of the Napoleonic wars, this situation was overthrown. As part of the Kiel treaty between Denmark on the one side, and England, Russia and Sweden on the other, signed in January 1814, Norway was transferred from Denmark to the Swedish king, whose crown prince, the former French maréchal Jean Baptiste Bernadotte, was one of the political and military leaders on the winning side. In this situation, before the treaty had taken effect, a constitutional assembly was called, consisting of civil servants, merchants and some representatives from the independent farming class. The constitution, which was signed on May 17th 1814, declared Norway an independent monarchy, and thereby opposed the Kiel treaty.

In the ensuing negotiations between the Norwegian parliament and the Swedish king, the king acknowledged the constitution with some amendments, and the result was a so-called personal union of the two countries under the Swedish king. This meant that the king and foreign service should be common to the two countries, while Norway retained all other institutions pertaining to an independent country, such as for instance a separate king's council and its own monetary system.

Norway was thereby to a considerable extent re-established as a nation, and a question that soon arose was that of a Norwegian written language. The written language used by the educated classes before 1814 was Danish, and the continued use of Danish after 1814 was one of the many ways of expressing and securing the relative independence from Sweden.

---

[5] A good introduction to the history of the Scandinavian languages, and thereby to the interrelationship between them, is Haugen (1976). An introduction to the sociolinguistic situation in Norway and in Scandinavia can be found in Vikør (1995).

[6] It must be emphasized that in principle the two norms are functionally equivalent in the sense that there is no forced choice of norm with respect to situation, topic, etc. Most Norwegians will use only one of them, where geographical background and the urban/rural division are the main deciding factors behind the choice. A rough estimate is that 15% use Nynorsk, while the remaining 85% use Bokmål. Bokmål is therefore clearly the dominant norm. No major newspaper is solely in Nynorsk, and advertising and the popular press is almost exclusively in Bokmål.

From the ensuing tension between the two countries grew a strong nationalism that soon gave rise to voices who wanted to replace Danish by a proper Norwegian (written) language. The spoken language in Norway at that time can be divided into two distinct types. Local dialects were used by people living in rural areas and by the lower socio-economic classes in the towns. The upper class, which consisted of high ranked civil servants, and a small merchant class used a language of which we have little specific knowledge. It must have been distinctly Norwegian, but influenced by written and spoken Danish.[7]

This meant that the written Danish used in the first decades after 1814 did not reflect *either* of the two types very well. Combined with the political tensions outlined above, and the dominant Romantic ideology with its emphasis on history and nationalism, this created a climate where the idea of developing a Norwegian written norm gained increased support.

The first step towards this goal was to decide which type of spoken variety, rural dialect or upper class speech, should be reflected in the new norm.[8] Because the speech of the upper class was associated with Denmark and Danish culture, Danish was controversial among some groups. The dialects therefore presented themselves as a viable alternative, strengthened by the fact that they gradually came to be looked upon as direct descendants of Old Norse, the language of the former period of independence which had also witnessed a rich literary culture.

The two views soon came to oppose each other. Adherents of the national option proposed that a completely new orthographic norm should be construed, built partly on Old Norse grammar, partly on contemporary dialect systems. Adherents of the Danish alternative instead wanted to modify the Danish orthography so that middle and upper class urban pronunciation and lexis, the so called *dannet dagligtale* (lit. 'educated daily speech') would be better reflected.

In the end, the views of *both* camps were upheld. By the turn of the century two norms had been established and officially recognized. *Nynorsk* was construed by Ivar Aasen (1813–1896) around the middle of the nineteenth century, based on his extensive research on Norwegian rural dialects. *Bokmål* is the result of several spelling reforms with Danish as the original starting point.[9]

Let us first take a closer look at Nynorsk. Aasen (1864) is a grammar where his choice of norm for the new language is justified. The connection with Old Norse

---

[7] See Section 1.4 below for a more detailed discussion on the origin and nature of this variety.

[8] I disregard the fact that the relationship between speech sound and graphemic representation must be seen as arbitrary in principle. I assume that in a given speech society which has developed an alphabetical script, most literate speakers will have a set of association rules that link graphemes or groups of graphemes to certain speech sounds, so that writing in fact is looked upon by the language user as a transcription that will render a normal pronunciation for any well-formed string of graphemes.

[9] *Riksmål* and *Landsmål* were the official names of the two norms until 1929, when the names were changed to *Bokmål* and *Nynorsk*. Both the original terms imply that the norms were looked upon as applicable for the whole country, as both *rike* and *land* mean 'country'. The new terms are neutral in this respect, being derived in one case from *bok* 'book' and from the adjective *ny* 'new' in the other. The term *Riksmål* was later retained by the more conservative faction of the Bokmål movement, whose members fiercely opposed the official policy of introducing forms reflecting what was looked upon as lower class speech into Bokmål. For convenience, I shall refer to the two norms as Bokmål and Nynorsk only.

was important to Aasen, who therefore to a considerable extent based his norm on archaic, rural dialects, mostly located in the western and central part of Southern Norway. Aasen's explicit goal was a norm which could be seen as a common denominator of Norwegian dialects. His 1864 grammar reflects his method on this point. When choosing the form of inflectional suffixes, candidate forms taken from different dialects were usually discussed. The one that best met the different requirements defined by Aasen was selected. This was not always the geographically most widespread form. A good example is his choice of suffix form for the def. sg. of so-called 'strong' fem. nouns. The Old Norse ending was /-in/, so that the def. sg. of *bók* 'book' was *bókin*. The /n/ was later truncated, so that the spoken result was a suffix consisting of an oral vowel. But probably due to an intermediary stage of nasalization, this vowel was in many dialects lowered to [e], [ɛ], [æ] and [ɑ].[10] The original high vowel quality was only retained in a few marginal areas. Aasen nevertheless chose *-i* as the orthographic ending, because it exposed a closer relationship with Old Norse, even though the [ɑ] ending was, and still is, far more common in the dialects.

Nynorsk quickly gained support, first among the radical part of the intelligentsia, and was recognized as an official norm in 1885. It expanded steadily until the Second World War, but has declined since then. Nynorsk has never managed to establish itself to a substantial degree in any town, it has remained a norm predominantly used in rural areas. Its stronghold remains in the central and western part of Southern Norway.

Nynorsk has undergone several reforms since Aasen created it. The underlying strategy has been to broaden its dialectal basis by including forms that reflect East Norwegian speech. This created considerable turbulence between the wars, especially in the 1930s. The strategy was nevertheless successful. In 1938 a new norm was introduced where forms considered to be eastern to a considerable degree were established as so-called 'main forms'.[11] These quickly established themselves as the most commonly used, and can be said to represent the unmarked form of Nynorsk today. The conservative subnorm, which is closer to the Aasen norm of 1864, is rarely seen.

We now turn to Bokmål. The main proponent of the reform strategy was Knud

---

[10] Back rounded vowels are also found, but this development cannot be explained by nasalization.

[11] One important feature of all Norwegian spelling reforms has been that old forms are usually not banned, but are allowed as variants along with the new forms. Such variant sets are in some cases divided into a *main form* (*hovedform*) , that is, a form that obligatorily must be used in school text books and by civil servants, and a *secondary form* (*sideform*), which may be used in other contexts, for example by the pupils themselves. In other cases, variants have equal status, in the sense that for example textbook authors can choose the one they prefer. The result of this policy is that both norms can be further subdivided into what are often called radical and conservative subnorms. But the fact that a given form is listed in the dictionaries does not in itself mean that it is in widespread use. Most users of Bokmål tend to use a moderately conservative norm, while most users of Nynorsk seem to avoid the most salient conservative as well as radical forms. This also holds for the language used in the media and other sectors of the public domain. In short one can say that most speakers and institutions steer a middle course. Consistent use of radical or conservative forms is always the result of a premeditated decision on the part of the speaker, newspaper editors, etc.

Knudsen (1812–1895). His aim was to alter the Danish orthography step by step until it reflected the speech of the educated classes. Bokmål (then Riksmål) can be said to have been definitively established as a norm separate from written Danish by the spelling reform of 1907, when the lenited *b*, *d*, *g* of Danish were restored as *p*, *t*, *k* in accordance with Norwegian pronunciation (e.g. Danish *tag* → Bokmål *tak*, 'roof'), and short, stressed vowels were marked by means of gemination of the following consonant grapheme (e.g. Danish *tak* → Bokmål *takk*, 'thank'). By the next reform, of 1917, the goal that the norm should reflect educated, middle-class speech can be said to have been fully achieved.

But by this time, the political climate had changed. Based on democratic ideals, an additional goal was now formulated, which was to take the orthographic conventions further so that they would reflect urban lower class and rural speech. To illustrate this point, we can continue to use the def. sg. of fem. nouns as an example. In Standard Danish, masc. and fem. nouns have merged into one class, with -*en* as the suffix marking def. sg. This system was upheld in Bokmål until 1917, but in accordance with vernacular speech it now became possible to use a separate suffix on fem. nouns, viz. -*a*, while masc. nouns retained the -*en*. This policy was taken even further in 1938.

The new forms were not felt to be part of middle-class urban speech. But when the social-democratic city council of Oslo in 1939 decided that the radical norm should be used in all textbooks to be used in primary schools in Oslo, it caused most publishing houses to shift to this norm in order not to lose their part of the important Oslo textbook market. This sparked a revolt from the upper and middle class in Oslo and other towns, led by the Riksmålsforbundet, which represents the conservative Bokmål norm.[12] The revolt succeeded. In 1954 the Oslo decision to allow only radical forms was revoked, and as a result textbooks started to appear in a more conservative version. Today the radical forms are rarely seen; as mentioned above, most Bokmål users will use a slightly conservative form, usually called *moderat Bokmål*.

(1) gives an example of Danish spelling compared with moderate and radical Bokmål.

(1) (a) Danish: Vi kast-ede bog-en
    (b) Moderate Bokmål: Vi kast-et bok-en
    (c) Radical Bokmål: Vi kast-a bok-a
        Gloss: We throw-PRET book-THE
        Translation: We threw the book away

An additional goal of the spelling reforms of this century, at least up to the 1960s, was gradually to fuse the two norms into one. This goal has always been a contro-

---

[12] In fact, members of the Riksmålsforbundet will claim that they do not represent Bokmål, but a third and separate norm. But apart from the fact that this norm contains a number of conservative spellings that are no longer allowed in the official norms, one can safely look upon Riksmål as a conservative variety of Bokmål.

versial one, and engendered much political dispute, which climaxed in the 1950s. A national commission was set up in 1964, which resulted in the establishment of *Norsk Språkråd* (The Norwegian Language Council) in 1972, where both camps are represented. The main task of the Council is to further the development of the norms, but the explicit goal of creating one norm seems on the whole to have been abandoned, at least for the time being.

1.3 A LANGUAGE WITHOUT AN OFFICIALLY RECOGNIZED SPOKEN NORM

While the actual pronunciation of Norwegian has played a fundamental role in the development of both norms, the existence of two competing written norms has on the other hand prevented the formation of an uncontroversial spoken norm. There is in other words no officially sanctioned way of speaking Norwegian. Norsk Språkråd (see above), whose main function is to develop and maintain the written norms, should normally not occupy itself with pronunciation. This means that even major monolingual Norwegian dictionaries only give spelling, definitions and grammatical information. No pronunciation is given. The official policy underlying this is that any pronunciation that is rooted in a Norwegian speech variety is as acceptable as any other. Hence no single pronunciation should be codified as the more correct one.[13]

However, one must bear in mind that the absence of official norms does not preclude the possibility that unofficial norms may emerge. As we have seen, the written norms, and especially Bokmål, have been construed to reflect certain pronunciation patterns. The speech varieties where these are most consistently found can in turn be claimed to be the spoken realization of the norm.

With this in mind, we can now turn to the question of what is the spoken basis of the most common forms of Nynorsk and Bokmål, respectively. With respect to Nynorsk, one can say that the spoken basis of the most common form is primarily rural dialects of Southern Norway. But these dialects show considerable variation among themselves, so that one cannot identify a single unified dialect system as representing a spoken norm underlying Nynorsk. Hence, the speakers of these dialects cannot be said to *speak* Nynorsk, even if they write it. What one with some justification could call spoken Nynorsk is only found in three environments: in broadcasting, on the stage, and in the formal and even casual speech of some educated persons who actively promote the idea that Nynorsk should have a spoken

---

[13] This policy is not uncontroversial. In both camps there are factions that argue for the establishment of official spoken norms connected with Bokmål and Nynorsk. It is also to a certain degree undermined by the requirement that only a certain percentage of the speech employed in the state-owned broadcasting company may be in dialect. This rule presupposes that there are varieties that are neutral with respect to dialect, be they reading styles or formal speech styles, and which would therefore come close to meeting the requirements for being a standard language.

norm. None of these varieties represents naturally acquired speech, so the question that one often is asked as an expert on Norwegian language, namely how many people in Norway speak Nynorsk, is in my opinion rather meaningless. Nynorsk is by definition not primarily a spoken language, it is a way of *writing* Norwegian that in principle is available to any member of the Norwegian speech society.[14] But the fact that there are marginal contexts where the speech variety employed is recognized as spoken Nynorsk, makes it impossible to reject the notion altogether.

Bokmål on the other hand is in its most common variety looked upon as reflecting formal middle-class urban speech, especially that found in the eastern part of Southern Norway, with the capital Oslo as the obvious centre. One can therefore say that Bokmål *has* a spoken realization that one might call an unofficial standard spoken Norwegian. It is in fact often referred to as *Standard Østnorsk* ('Standard East Norwegian'). In addition to being spoken by a fair proportion of the members of the Norwegian speech society, a fairly conservative version of it is the most commonly used stage language in Norwegian theatres, including those outside Oslo. It is also a variety often used in news readings on radio and TV, and it is the variety most commonly taught to foreigners.[15]

But this variety has never been established as an *official*, national norm, either for Bokmål or in general. Due to the counterweight posed by the Nynorsk movement, social consent about a spoken standard language based on middle-class urban speech has not emerged. As mentioned above, the policy of the authorities, represented by Norsk Språkråd, is that there should not be a standardized spoken norm. Although controversial, and despite the dominance of Standard Østnorsk in some contexts, it is therefore correct to say that the notion of a spoken, national norm has a weaker status in Norway than in most other European countries.

As already noted, the official ideology behind this policy is that all spoken varieties of Norwegian shall be considered of equal status. Everyone should in other words be able to speak his or her own dialect in any context.[16] It must be said at this point that the variation among Norwegian dialects and accents, Standard Østnorsk included, seems small compared to what one finds in other European languages.[17] Speakers of different Norwegian dialects have therefore small problems in understanding each other.

---

[14] The question of how many people speak dialects that are close to Nynorsk is of course a meaningful one, but very difficult to answer in the absence of uncontroversial criteria that decide how spoken Nynorsk is to be delimited.

[15] Representative works are Haugen and Chapman (1982), Strandskogen (1979) and Strandskogen and Strandskogen (1995).

[16] This should not be understood as a situation where all speech varieties have the same amount of prestige. Linguistic prejudice is still widespread, but seems less marked today than it was only a few decades ago.

[17] The Norwegian word *dialekt* covers both the term 'accent' and the term 'dialect', as used for instance in Chambers and Trudgill (1980: 5). Most of the variation found in Norwegian would probably qualify as variation with respect to accent if we go by this distinction.

1.4 THE SYSTEM TO BE DESCRIBED IN THIS BOOK

It is often taken for granted that a description of the phonology of a given language
will be a description of the spoken standard variety of that language, which the
author very often can claim to speak himself. Due to the situation outlined above,
writing an account of Norwegian phonology is somewhat more complicated.

Earlier accounts of Norwegian phonology have nevertheless either explicitly or
implicitly been accounts of Standard Østnorsk.[18] This is the choice that will be
made for this book also, but with one important modification. Given the fact that
spoken Standard Østnorsk has not been officially codified, it is difficult to delimit
it in a precise and uncontroversial way from other urban varieties of the same region.[19] The language system that will be covered in the following chapters will
therefore be urban East Norwegian speech in general.[20]

Standard Østnorsk can be considered a sociolect that has developed as a result
of tension between Danish as the official written, and in some contexts spoken,
language used by the upper class before 1814, and the variety of Norwegian used
by the lower social classes in the towns of Eastern Norway. Even if sources are
scarce, it probably emerged more or less in the form we know today during the first
half of the nineteenth century, at least as an informal speech style among the educated classes.

As noted above, these consisted of a merchant class and the civil servants, of
which the clergy was the dominant group. (For historical reasons, there was almost
no nobility.) Before 1814, members from both groups were continually recruited
from abroad, especially from Denmark, but in the merchant class also from other
North-European countries. In addition, the only university in the kingdom was in
Copenhagen, so all priests, whether they were of Norwegian or Danish stock, had
to spend several of their formative years in Denmark to receive their education there.

The variety spoken by the educated classes during the final half of the nineteenth
century we may for convenience call Dano-Norwegian (DN). DN diverged from
the standard spoken Danish of the time in that it lacks the most salient sound
change that Danish underwent during the middle ages, the radical consonant

---

[18] I myself do not speak Standard Østnorsk, but the accent of my home town on the Southern coast
modified after 25 years of living in other parts of the country. My speech can all the same be seen as
closely related to Standard Østnorsk, especially in more formal situations.

[19] There in fact exist three pronouncing dictionaries that purport to convey the correct Standard
Østnorsk pronunciation, Alnæs (1925), Berulfsen (1969) and Vanvik (1985). None of them enjoy official status. The two former are both rather old, and on several points they must be considered obsolete.
The most recent of the three, Vanvik (1985), is unfortunately the smallest one, and given its limitation
to Standard Østnorsk, it does not cover more colloquial speech styles. The lexical distribution of the
retroflex flap is for example not given (see Chapter 4.3.3), although it is stated in the preface that there
are words where the flap must be considered standard.

[20] But there will all the same be many Norwegian varieties that are left out. The reader is therefore
warned that most Norwegian scholars would look on the present book as one falling far short of what
the title promises. The gravest omission is perhaps the fact that the western and central dialects of southern Norway, on the basis of which Nynorsk was founded, are hardly discussed at all.

weakenings that distinguish Danish from the other Nordic languages today (Skautrup 1944: 229ff.). DN in the nineteenth century showed a certain propensity to soften /p, t, k/ to /b, d, g/, which represented the first stage of the change, but that was as far as it went, and it is uncertain how widespread this was in speech. It may very well have been reading pronunciation, as it is precisely this first stage which is consistently reflected in written Danish. DN also had tonal accents, which standard Danish lacked.

But another phonological feature of Danish, the use of monophthongs where Old Norse and most Norwegian dialects had diphthongs was to a certain extent made part of the DN system. Yet another feature that distinguished DN phonologically from the surrounding Norwegian dialects is the avoidance of the retroflex flap that had developed in East Norwegian dialects. And at least up to the first decades of this century, retroflexes in general, that is, fully assimilated clusters of /r/ + coronal consonant, seem to have been avoided; cf. Alnæs (1925: 12ff.).[21]

Dano-Norwegian is also markedly different from East Norwegian dialects with respect to realization of some morphological features. First of all, it retains the two-gender system that had developed in Danish, and thus does not distinguish feminine and masculine noun endings as is done in the surrounding Norwegian dialects. In the major class of regular verbs, where the vernacular varieties use the suffix /-a/ to mark the preterite and perfect participle and where Danish uses /-ede/ and /-ed/, DN developed a compromise form, /-et/, for both, which today is the most common form used in Bokmål, as illustrated in example (1). This ending is also used in the participle form of irregular verbs, where East Norwegian dialects have a vowel suffix. Another difference is the generalized ending /-ene/ in def. pl. forms in DN, where the dialects have /-a/ on masculine and neuter nouns, and /-ene/ on feminines only. Finally, DN does not have different infinitive endings depending on the quantity of the root syllable in Old Norse, which also is a characteristic feature of East Norwegian dialects.

The tension between these systems resulted in a situation with two main sociolects at each end of an idealized scale. But in actual phonological systems, and hence in actual speech, the two are connected through a set of linguistic variables, where items from one of the sociolects can alternate with their cognates from the other. Most speakers of Østnorsk today will have access to both. This means that all the special features of DN reported above have survived into Standard Østnorsk. But they are no longer the only forms available to its speakers. Thus feminine endings are more common now, vowel endings may alternate with the /-et/ ending in verbs, and the retroflex flap has become more or less acceptable when it can alternate with /l/, (but not when it can alternate with /r/).[22] Urban Østnorsk of today is therefore a mixed system where elements from two formerly different varieties live happily together as variants and where either member of a given variable can be

---

[21] The retroflex series of coronal consonants is further discussed in Sections 2.1.2, 2.3.2.2 and 4.3.
[22] Other retroflexes are fully accepted; scattered and inconsistent remains of split pronunciation of /r/ + coronal clusters are found in stage language only.

called on to different degrees depending on speech style, social and geographical background, etc.

On the whole, it seems that middle-class speech, although it is still largely Standard Østnorsk in the sense given above, is gradually opening up to elements from the other system. It is this development that makes the precise delimitation of the concept Standard Østnorsk problematic, and it is the principal reason why this book will cover urban East Norwegian speech in general. In the following chapters, this variety, or cluster of varieties, will be referred to as UEN, for Urban East Norwegian.

1.5 EARLIER ACCOUNTS OF NORWEGIAN PHONOLOGY

Not much has been published in English, German or French that covers substantial portions of Norwegian phonology. Western (1889) is an early phonetic description of the author's Kristiania (= Oslo) pronunciation. Important structuralist accounts are Borgstrøm (1938), Vogt (1942), Haugen (1942a) and Vanvik (1972, 1973). Early generative accounts are Standwell (1972, 1975) and Weinstock (1970). Haugen (1942a) excepted, all of these works are concerned with Standard Østnorsk only.[23]

Also when we turn to what is published in Norwegian, the account will by no means be impressive, even if there is a continuous tradition going back to the phonetic and neogrammarian scholars of the latter part of the nineteenth century. Bibliographies and a representative collection of articles can be found in Jahr and Lorentz (1981, 1983a), which cover phonology and prosody respectively. Since 1980, things have not changed radically. There has been a steady but limited output, of which the non-generative contributions of Endresen (1985, 1991) deserve to be mentioned.

While some topics have been quite thoroughly discussed in the literature, others have received considerably less attention. Two topics have aroused much and continuous interest from phonologists working on Norwegian. These are the tonal accents and the retroflex segments. As in Swedish, most Norwegian dialects can distinguish two forms minimally by means of different pitch contours. The first author to write about these to my knowledge was Ivar Aasen (Aasen 1864: 48ff.), and as can be seen from the selection of articles in Jahr and Lorentz (1983a), the topic attracted much interest in the century that followed.

The other topic that has attracted much interest is the analysis of the series of retroflex segments that are found in the dialects of Eastern and Northern Norway. Historically they derive from sequences or /r/ + a coronal consonant. Minimal pairs

---

[23] Within the post-SPE paradigms, there is very little published in English. My own doctoral dissertation, Kristoffersen (1991), is perhaps the only work which tries to cover a rather broad field, and the discussions found in the present book will in many respects rely heavily on the analyses presented in the dissertation.

like [ˈkɑʈ] 'map' and [ˈkɑt] 'cat' led many structuralist scholars to conclude that the retroflex consonants should be seen as separate phonemes. How to reconcile this conclusion with the morpho-phonological rule which, without exception, changes underlying clusters of /r/ plus coronal split by a morpheme or word boundary into retroflexes, engendered much discussion among structuralist and early generative scholars. These discussions are well documented in Jahr and Lorentz (1981a).

Other areas, such as stress placement across native and non-native words, voicing assimilations, nasal place assimilations and vowel shortening processes, have not been subject to thorough and comprehensive analyses. The analyses presented in this book will therefore on several points be tentative, because a comprehensive range of data in many cases is not available.

1.6 TRANSCRIPTION CONVENTIONS

Transcriptions are generally in broad IPA, with irrelevant phonetic details omitted. Square brackets denote phonological surface structure; representations belonging to any level more abstract are enclosed in phonemic slashes. Orthographic symbols are written in italics.

1.6.1 Prosody

Syllable boundaries are marked with the conventional dot. Quantity in vowels is marked with the conventional colon, while ambisyllabic consonants are written as geminates divided by a syllable boundary, as in the form [ˈʋɛg.gn̩], veggen 'the wall'. Like all Germanic languages, Norwegian has word stress. In addition, primary stressed syllables may be realized with two different, contrastive pitch contours, called accent 1 and accent 2, as detailed in Chapters 9 and 10. Primary stress and tonal accent are marked by a single symbol. Primary stress and accent 1 is marked by means of a superscript numeral '1' before the stressed syllable, cf. again [ˈʋɛg.gn̩], while primary stress with accent 2 is marked by means of a superscripted '2', as in [²ʋɛg.gɾ], vegger 'walls'.

1.6.2 Vowels

I have chosen to use the same symbol to denote long and short high vowels, although the short might have been transcribed [ɪ, ʏ, ʉ̞, ʊ] instead of [i, y, ʉ, u]. Long and short mid vowels are differentiated, however, the short being transcribed [ɛ, œ, ɔ] and the long [eː, øː/eː, oː]. Note the symbol /ʉ/, which is used for the high, central, round vowel that is often referred to as 'Swedish /u/'.

Diphthongs will be analysed and hence transcribed as sequences of a nuclear short vowel followed by a consonantal glide, the latter being either /j/ or /w/.

In disyllabic words that end in a sequence of schwa plus a coronal sonorant, the schwa will not be transcribed. Instead, the sonorant will be marked as syllabic.

Examples are [¹ʋoː.pn̩], *våpen* 'weapon', [²nœk.kl̩], *nøkkel* 'key' and [¹fet.tr̩], *fetter* 'male cousin'. Even though there normally will be a minimal vocalic transition between the preceding obstruent and the sonorant, this transition will be argued to be purely phonetic in nature.

1.6.3 Consonants

Most of the consonantal symbols used are common stock. Note that /ʋ/ will be used instead of the more common /v/. Phonetically this sound is an approximant more than a fricative, and phonologically it behaves in many respect as a sonorant, see Chapter 2.3.2.3.

Retroflex (apical) consonants will be transcribed as /ʈ, ɖ, ʂ, ɳ, ɭ, ɽ/. Realizations of the /r/ phoneme are phonetically a tap, and will therefore be transcribed as [ɾ].

1.7 OVERVIEW

The book is organized as follows. In Chapter 2, the phonetic and phonological properties of the segment inventory will be discussed. Chapter 3 will deal with the structure of the lexicon and the phonotactic principles that can be defined over lexical items. In Chapter 4, word phonology and its interaction with lexical structure are discussed. The basic principles of syllabification in UEN will be the topic of Chapter 5. In Chapter 6, stress placement in simplex words is analysed, while the topic of Chapter 7 will be cyclic assignment of stress. Chapter 8 will deal with cyclic syllabification and Chapter 9 with the tonal accents that characterize most Norwegian dialects. In Chapter 10, intonation will be analysed. Chapter 11 will deal with connected speech, that is, the postlexical phonology of UEN, and finally, Chapter 12 will be devoted to the relationship between Bokmål orthography and UEN speech.

2

SEGMENTS: INVENTORY AND FEATURE SPECIFICATIONS

In this chapter an analysis of the vowel and consonant segments of UEN will be proposed. The subject of Section 2.1 is the phonetic properties of the segment inventory. Section 2.2 presents the phonological model in terms of the features and feature organization that will be used. Finally, Section 2.3 contains a phonological analysis of the segments and segment classes discussed in Section 2.1. In this section, the main stress will be put on features that are uncommon with respect to other languages. Features that Norwegian has in common with most other Germanic languages will not be commented on in detail.

2.1 PHONEME INVENTORY AND PHONETIC REALIZATION

2.1.1 Vowels and diphthongs

2.1.1.1 Vowel inventory in stressed syllables

The set of surface vowels that can function contrastively in stressed syllables in UEN is presented in (1).

(1) Vowel phonemes
    Long: iː, yː, ʉː, uː, eː, øː, oː, (æː), ɑː
    Short: i, y, ʉ, u, ɛ, œ, ɔ, (æ), ɑ

The set of long vowel phonemes can be established by the following set of minimally contrasting words [²liː.sə], *Lise* woman's name; [²lyː.sə], *lyse* 'to light'; [²lʉː.sə], *luse* 'to delouse'; [²luː.sə], *lose* 'to steer'; [²leː.sə], *lese* 'to read'; [²løː.sə], *løse* 'to solve'; [²loː.sə], *låse* 'to lock'; [²lɑː.sə], *lase* 'rag'.

A corresponding set containing short vowels is [¹sin], *sin* (poss. pronoun; [¹syn], *synd* 'sin'; [¹sʉn], *sunn* 'healthy'; [¹un], *ond* 'wicked'; [¹sɛn], *send* 'to send' (imp.); [¹sœn], *sønn* 'son'; [¹sɔn], *sånn* 'such'; [¹sɑn], *sand* 'sand'.[1]

I do not assume a non-derived distinction between lax and tense vowels, as is for example often assumed for German, for example by Wiese (1996) and Féry (1995) and the sources cited there. The difference in quality indicated by the use of non-

---

[1] *[¹sun] is missing from the list, and has been replaced with the near minimally contrasting [¹un]. This contrasts fully with [¹ʉn] (*Unn*, woman's name) and [¹ɔn] (*ånd*, 'spirit'). But it should be noted that the contrast between short /ʉ/ and /u/ is not common; an older complementary distribution depending on the following consonant is still detectable. In UEN, [u] is prevalent before /m, f, ŋ, k/, see also Chapter 12.3.

identical IPA symbols for corresponding long and short vowel phonemes in (1) is often ascribed to differences in tenseness. But contrary to German, short vowels in open, unstressed syllables will in general not have the 'tenser' quality associated with long vowels, except in hiatus before another vowel. In Norwegian examples such as *kaffe* and *økonomi*, whose German cognates *Kaffee* and *Ökonomie* are cited by Féry (1995: 49) as examples with tense, short vowels, the corresponding vowels are clearly both lax and short. There is in other words no difference in tenseness between short vowels in closed and in open syllables. Tenseness is hence completely predictable from either vowel length or phonotactic environment. As will be argued in Chapters 5 and 6, vowel length should be derived from stress. Tenseness should therefore not be seen as an underlying feature.

2.1.1.2 [æ]: a marginal phoneme

The phonemic status of [æ] is unclear—hence the parentheses in (1) and its absence from the lists of minimal pairs just given. Basically, it patterns as an allophone of /e/, occurring before /r/ and /ʈ/, where [e, ɛ] in general are blocked. Thus we find [²læː.ɾə], *lære* 'to teach' and [¹tʋæɾ], *tverr* 'cross' (adj.), but not *[²leː.ɾə] and *[¹tʋɛɾ], nor *[²læː.tə] and *[¹sæn]. [æ] also occurs before the glides /j/ and /w/ in the diphthongs /ej/ and /ew/, for example in [¹ʋæj], *vei* 'road' and [¹sæw], *sau* 'sheep' (sg.). Neither *[¹ʋɛj] nor *[¹sɛw] is possible in UEN. The relationship between the mid and low unrounded front vowels will be further analyzed in Chapter 4.4.

2.1.1.3 The central vowels

A special feature of the Norwegian vowel system is the presence of four contrastive high vowels, of which three are rounded. While /i/ and /u/ can be regarded as unmarked vowels universally, the presence of a front, rounded vowel [y] in addition to these is rarer, but found in the majority of North European languages. In addition to these three, Norwegian and Swedish have a fourth high vowel, which is commonly referred to as 'Swedish u', and transcribed by the IPA symbol [ʉ]. But even if the same IPA symbol is used, the phonetic realization of this vowel is not identical in UEN and Standard Spoken Swedish. In the latter, it is normally diphthongized and pronounced with what has been described as 'inrounded', or compressed lips (Fant 1973: 193, Malmberg 1956: 316, Lindau 1978: 547f, Lass 1984: 88). It is also regarded as more fronted than the Norwegian vowel (Noreen 1903: 512f, 517f, Danell 1937: 36f, Malmberg 1967: 88, Elert 1970: 67). In UEN, it is monophthongal and pronounced with somewhat protruded lips, although the degree of protrusion may vary.

The majority of the sources seem to agree that UEN [ʉ] is more retracted with respect to tongue body position than [i, y], but more advanced than [u], converging on 'advanced central' as the most common description.[2] But one recent source,

² Relevant discussion can be found in Aasen (1864: 12f.), Storm (1884: 165ff.), Broch & Selmer (1961: 49), Jensen (1969: 42, 46), Sivertsen (1967: 70f.), Vanvik (1972: 127) and Endresen (1991: 112f.). In Ladefoged and Maddieson (1996: 291f.) Norwegian [ʉ] is classified as central, while Swedish [ʉ] is classified as front.

Endresen (1991: 112), interprets [ʉ] as phonetically front, although a little more central than [y]. From an articulatory point of view, [ʉ] can be said to be more central than [y] if the tongue body is more retracted during articulation of the former. But another possible way of differentiating the two may be by degree of lip rounding. Vanvik (1972: 127) says that lip rounding in [ʉ] is made with ". . . practically the same lip-position as /u:/", while in long and short /y/, the lips are protruded and farther apart. This is in accordance with Foldvik (1989: 112), and also in accordance with my own articulation. But contrary to this view, Endresen (1991: 100) claims that Norwegian [y] is *less* rounded than the cardinal vowel [y], while Norwegian [ʉ] has the same degree of rounding as the cardinal vowel.[3] (Recall that this author also classifies [ʉ] as a front vowel, though a little more central than [y].)

In the absence of a representative sample of cine-radiographic data showing tongue position and degree of lip protrusion of the two vowels, it is difficult to evaluate the two opposing claims. Given that tongue retraction and lip rounding both result in a lower second formant (F2), it may very well be that we are dealing with a case of articulatory variation, where two different strategies may be used to obtain the same acoustic effect. The only viable approach is probably to look at how the vowels differ with respect to acoustic properties, since the value of the second formant, F2, can be equated with backness, back vowels having lower values than front vowels. Intermediate values can be taken as evidence for a vowel being central.[4] But since both lip protrusion and tongue retraction lower F2, the question of how this intermediate quality between back and front vowels is produced cannot be answered directly by inspecting formant values.

Very little is published on the formant structure of Norwegian vowels.[5] Values for my own pronunciation of the vowels in (1) are provided in (2) and (3).[6] The second formants of non-low segments have been framed for ease of reference.

---

[3] The same point is made in Haugen (1942a: 71), where [ʉ] is claimed to be 'overrounded' in 'much of eastern Norway', while [y] and [ø] 'have been kept distinct from the others by a partial delabialization'. Haugen's source is Storm (1884: 165n), but it is difficult to see that the text there justifies Haugen's conclusion. As far as I can see, Storm's point is only relevant for the rounding of the back vowels.

[4] One should bear in mind, however, that we are dealing with continua on which the categories front, central and back must be superimposed. The fact that a given vowel has an F2 value intermediate between that of [i] and that of [u], does not mean that this 'centrality' is phonologically relevant. But given the fact that the two vowels in question are contrastive, we would expect to find some clues in the signal as to how this contrast is produced acoustically.

[5] A set of formants for UEN vowels is reproduced in Vanvik (1973), but no table of formant values is provided. Values for Swedish long vowels are provided in Fant (1973: 96), but due to the differences between Standard Swedish and UEN, these cannot be taken as representative for their cognate vowels in UEN.

[6] My vowel pronunciation used in the recordings underlying (2) and (3) is as far as I can judge identical to UEN pronunciation. Each vowel was pronounced six times in the frame l_n, except for [æ], where words with a following /r/ were used, and for [ə], which was pronounced in an open syllable following a stressed one: [²soː.lə]. The glides were produced as part of the diphthongs [æj] and [æw], also inserted in the frame l_n. The mean duration for the long vowels was 251 ms., and that of the short vowels 133 ms. The formant values were extracted by means of LPC-analysis on a KAY Computerized Speech Lab at around the middle point of the vowel span.

(2)   *Formant values of high vowels and glides*

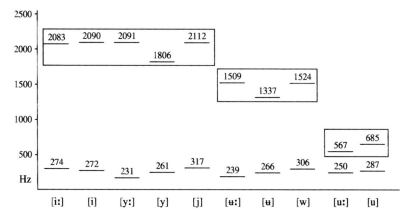

In (2) we see that the putative central segments have markedly lower values than the front vowels and glides.[7] This can be taken as evidence that they will be *perceived* as more back than the front vowels. But it can also be argued that the lower F2 value for [ʉ] most likely derives from a more retracted tongue. We noted above that [y], at least for some speakers, is articulated with more protruded lips than [ʉ]. If lip position alone were responsible for the difference in F2 values, we would therefore expect the former to have the lowest value. The opposite is true, both in (2) and in Vanvik's data reported in footnote 7. We can therefore conclude that at

(3)   *Formant values of non-high vowels*

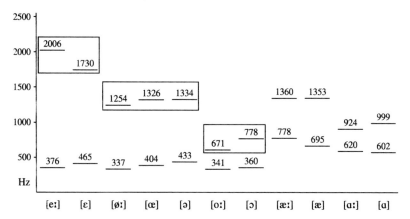

[7] The same difference emerges in spectrographic data provided in Vanvik (1973). I have tried to extract the central tendency of the second formant of [iː, yːʉː], which represent the speech of a 26-year-old man from Oslo. The results are given below. No values are provided here for [uː] because the second formant is not visible in the reproduction of the spectrogram for this vowel. The values, which must be seen as approximations, are as follows: 2. formant for iː, 2150; for yː, 2050; for ʉː, 1600. We see that the fit between these data and my own is quite good.

least for speakers who articulate [ʉ] with less rounding than [y], the lower F2 value must be brought about by retraction of the tongue. The difference is hence a difference in backness also with respect to articulation.

In (4) the above values for the first and second formants have been plotted into a co-ordinate system which shows the distribution within the acoustic vowel space defined by the two formants. We see that among the vowels with first formant values below 500 Hz., three different clusters reflect the differences shown in (2) and (3) with respect to backness interpreted as F2 value. One consists of the vowels usually interpreted as back and rounded in articulatory terms, another of the front high vowels and glide plus the unrounded mid vowels, and a third, central group comprises [ʉː, ʉ, w, øː, œ, ə], that is, the high vowels usually described as central, the glide [w] plus the mid, non-back round vowels and schwa.[8]

That [œ] and [ə] have identical values is somewhat unexpected, and should be checked against a broader set of data. But they are hardly contrastive, because [ə] does not occur in stressed syllables, and [œ] will only occur in unstressed syllables in forms where a stressed syllable in a second compound member has been further reduced due to lexicalization.[9]

(4)   *Vowel space defined by first and second formant values*

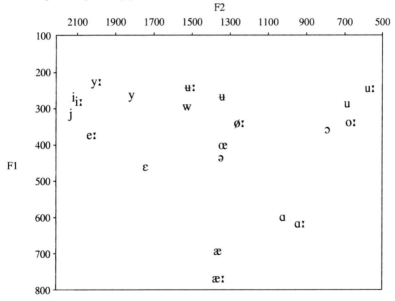

[8] Note that there is no systematic glide corresponding to the back, high vowels.
[9] This has happened in some place names, such as the city name *Tromsø*. If (4) represents the facts correctly, this should rhyme with *homse* 'homosexual (coll.)'. This pair would not normally be considered as rhyming, but this may be due to convention and spelling. Note also that the final vowel in *Tromsø* can be pronounced as more tense in careful pronunciation.

We shall return to the phonological interpretation of the pattern seen in (4) in Section 2.3 below. But before we leave the phonetic realization of vowels, a short comment should be made on the lack of symmetry in the spacing of the vowels in (4). A commonly stated expectation for vowel inventories is that the contrastive members will be spaced symmetrically within the possible acoustic or articulatory space. Such a symmetry is for example exposed in the prototypical five vowel system [i, u, e, o, a], where we find a front–back distinction among high and mid vowels, enhanced by rounding of the back series, and one low, unrounded vowel.

If we look at the distribution in (4), we see that on the front–back dimension, there seem to be three degrees of backness among the non-low vowels, and two among the low. In itself, this can be seen as a simple expansion by one category on all three levels, retaining the basic symmetry. The non-asymmetry of the distribution arises in connection with the distribution of high round vowels, where the odd member appears to be [y]. Except for this vowel, the round vowels are confined to the central and back group. [y] is in other words the only phonetically front vowel that is rounded, and it thereby emerges as the marked member of the set, a fact that is also reflected in its higher degree of lip protrusion.

If we further conjecture that such a skewed distribution is non-optimal due to its lack of symmetry, we would expect it to be prone to change. If we look at the UEN system in isolation, it seems robust and stable. But if we take dialect data into consideration, a more unstable picture emerges.[10]

First of all, there are tendencies to eliminate /y/, the marked member of the set. Some rural dialects of southern Norway are known to have neutralized both long and short /i/ and /y/ into /i/ (Storm 1884: 162, Ross 1905: 25f, Larsen 1894: 90).[11] Other dialects have merged short /y/ and /ʉ/. Several dialects in the southern part of the western coast show this type of merger (Sandvik 1979: 53f, Gabrielsen 1991: 27f.). In some dialects the product is [ʉ], while in others it is [y]. Except for the last type, the result is a symmetrical nine-vowel distribution where round vowels are confined to the central and back group, given that the quality of the mid, non-back round vowel in all dialects corresponds to a central vowel.[12]

Another way to make the distribution more symmetrical would be to introduce central vowels also in the non-high ranges. According to Torp (1982: 56ff.), this actually took place in several East Norwegian dialects. Here, the back short vowels /o/ and /a/ developed central allophones before the retroflex flap. These were subsequently phonemicized due to vowel lengthening. The result was a more symmetric distribution consisting of 11 vowels, but it should be noted that the majority of these systems subsequently have developed into the standard nine-vowel system.

---

[10] These tendencies now seem to have been stalled by the spreading of the inventory described here.

[11] Also short /ø/ could be delabialized, but as this often took place as a neutralization between back /o/ and non-back /ø/ into a centralized [å], it is unclear whether delabialization of [y] and [ø] can be given a unitary explanation.

[12] The fact that /y/, which arose as a product of i-umlaut, has been eliminated in other Germanic languages, such as English and Icelandic as well, weakens the suggstion that its elimination in Norwegian dialects is caused by later fronting of /u/.

2.1.1.4 Diphthongs

As mentioned in Chapter 1.6, diphthongs are analysed as sequences of a short vowel plus a consonantal (non-nuclear) glide. Consisting of a sequence of phonemes, their analysis is therefore a question of identifying the members with the appropriate phonemes, plus a combinatorial analysis. The attested combinations are given in (5). Those specified as marginal occur only in a few loan words. The palatal glide /j/ has the same degree of rounding as the preceding vowel.

(5)   *Diphthong inventory*

    Common: [æj, œj, æw]
    Marginal: [ɔj, ʉj, ɑj]

On the assumption that [j] is the consonantal correspondent of the high front vowel /i/, and that [æ] and [ɛ] are neutralized before glides,[13] we see that the first member of the diphthongs ending in [j] can be any short vowel that is distinct from [j] with respect to place features, except [u].

    The only member of the set that does not end in a palatal glide is [æw]. As mentioned above, this glide is rounded and central, not back. In addition, it is often heard as labiodental [ʋ]. This is a recent change that seems to be spreading in UEN, whereby the /w/ following a vowel is changed into a [–voc] segment. Thus the word ['sæw], *sau* 'sheep' is often heard as ['sæʋ].

2.1.1.5 Vowels in unstressed syllables

Vowels in unstressed syllables, that is, syllables which lack primary as well as secondary stress, are always short.[14] Under stress shift, the short and long vowels in (1) above define corresponding pairs in the sense that when a syllable with a long vowel loses stress, the vowel is reduced to the corresponding short vowel. This is the same vowel that we find in stressed syllables with short vowels. Thus the same alternation that we find between [oː] and [ɔ] when stress shifts, is found in stressed syllables when the vowel is subject to closed syllable shortening, as in [fɔ.'roː.də], *forråde* 'to betray' vs. [fɔ'rɔt], *forrådt* 'betrayed' (pts.).

    Examples of such alternations are given in (6).[15]

(6)   *Vowel length alternations induced by stress shift*

    Symmetric alternations:

    (a) [iː] ~ [i]   [kɑ.'liː.bɽ] *kaliber* 'calibre'   [kɑ.li.'breː.rə] *kalibrere* 'to calibrate'

---

[13] Arne Torp (p.c.) informs me that younger speakers may have a contrast between /ɛj/ and /æj/, in that loanwords such as *tape* and *shake* are pronounced ['tɛjp] and ['ʂɛjk], while native words such as *sleip* 'slimy' and *bleik* 'pale', are pronounced ['ʂl̩æjp] and ['bɽæjk].

[14] The only exception to this are vowels occurring before another vowel, where we find the tense quality of long vowels, and perhaps also greater duration.

[15] By symmetric alternations is meant alternations where only quantity is involved, while asymmetric alternations involve vowel quality as well.

(b) [ʉː] ~ [ʉ]   [ba.ˈʃʉːn] *basun* 'trumpet'   [ˈʉːt.ba.ʃʉ.,neː.rə]
(bibl.)   *utbasunere* 'to proclaim
loudly'

(c) [uː] ~ [u]   [ba.ˈruːn] *baron* (id.)   [ba.ru.ˈniː] *baroni*
'barony'

(d) [oː] ~ [ɔ]   [kɔm.ˈfoːr] *komfort* 'comfort'   [kɔm.fɔ.ˈtɑː.bl̩]
komfortabel 'comfortable'

(e) [ɑː] ~ [ɑ]   [pa.²rɑː.də] *parade* (id.)   [pa.ra.ˈdeː.rə] *paradere*
'to parade'

Asymmetric alternation:

(f) [ɔ] ~ [uː]   [ˈkɑː.nɔn] *kanon* 'canon'   [ka.ˈnuː.nisk] *kanonisk*
'canonical'

Alternations involving /e/

(g) [eː] ~ [ɛ]   [²teː.l̩.,nuːr] *Telenor*   [tɛ.l̩.ˈnuːr] (id. alternative
(name of telephone company)   pronunciation)

(h) [eː] ~ [-]   [mɛ.ˈseːn] *mesén* 'patron'   [mɛ.sn̩.ˈnɑːt] *mesenat* 'pa-
tronage'

(i) [eː] ~ [ə]   [dɛ.ˈkreːt] or [də.ˈkreːt]   [dɛ.kra.ˈteː.rə] *dekretere*
dekret 'decree'   'to decree'

(j) [ɛ] ~ [-]   [a.ˈpɛl] *appell* 'appeal'   [a.pl̩.ˈleː.rə] *appelere*
'to appeal'

(k) [ɛ] ~ [ə]   [bʉd.ˈʂɛt] *budsjett* 'budget'   [bʉd.ʂə.ˈteː.rə]
budsjettere 'to budget'

(l) [ɛ]   [dʉ.ˈwɛl] *duell* 'duel'   [dʉ.we.ˈleː.rə] *duellere*
'to fight a duel'

The asymmetric pattern is confined to unstressed short /o/ before final /n/. When stressed as a result of suffixation, the vowel is raised to /uː/. Other examples are *Pláton* ~ *platónisk* and *Apóllon* ~ *apolónisk*. We also find it in one case involving closed syllable shortening due to inflection, viz. [ˈguː], *god* 'good' vs. [ˈgɔt], *godt* 'good (neuter)'.[16]

The alternation pattern involving [eː], [ɛ], [ə] and zero is more complicated. The distribution can be captured by the following metrical constraints:

- [eː] occurs in stressed, open syllables, and in some stressed final VC-syllables, cf. (g–i), subject to lexical marking; cf. Chapters 6.4.8 and 8.2.
- [ɛ] occurs in
  - closed syllables, stressed and unstressed, cf. (i–j)
  - open syllables when heading a foot not carrying main stress, cf. (i)
  - unstressed syllables lacking an underlying consonant that may serve as onset, cf. (l).[17]

[16] See Chapter 12.4 for a short discussion of the historical origin of the alternation.
[17] The glide in (6l) is not underlying, but the product of Glide Formation; cf. Chapter 5.4.2.

- Syllabic sonorants occur in open syllables in a weak position of a foot or in an unfooted syllable when a coronal sonorant is adjacent to the vowel and there is a consonant preceding the head that can serve as onset, cf. (j).
- [ə] turns up elsewhere, cf. (i) and (k).

An important point about the distribution of schwa in UEN is that stress reduction in Norwegian may not neutralize *all* vowels in schwa, as in English and Dutch; only /e/ may systematically alternate with schwa in stress reduction. This suggests that schwa should not be seen as an independent segment, but as a realizational variant of /e/. The analysis of schwa proposed here therefore differs from that proposed for other Germanic languages such as Dutch (Booij 1995) and German (Wiese 1986), where schwa is seen as a separate entity in the vowel system that can only occur in unstressed syllables.

The fact that the [eː] and [ɛ] can alternate with schwa or a syllabic sonorant, depending on metrical position and environment, suggests that the vowel underlying this set of alternants should be specified without features in the lexicon, that is, as an empty [+voc] position that will be spelled out with respect to feature content only after metrical structure has been assigned. The distribution can be summed up in the following table, where the two factors that seem to influence the realization of the underlying empty vowel, stress level and syllable structure, are combined.

(7)   *Distribution of /e/-allophones*

	Main Stress (primary or secondary)	Other heads of feet	Unstressed syllables	
			No onset	Onset
Open syllables	eː	ɛ	ɛ	ə Syllabic sonorant
Closed syllables	[eː] in some final syllables [ɛ] elsewhere	ɛ	ɛ	ɛ

The distribution of [eː] and [ɛ] in stressed, closed syllables in final position will be further discussed in Chapters 6.4.8 and 8.2. The possibility that [æ] should be analysed as a positional variant of /e/ is discussed in Chapter 4.4, while the realization of unstressed /e/ in word-final position will be taken up in Chapter 11.5.

2.1.2 Consonants

2.1.2.1 Inventory

The phonetic descriptions that follow, are to a large extent built on the analysis in Endresen (1985). The inventory of segments that on the surface can establish minimal pairs is given in (8).

(8)   *Consonant inventory*

	Bilabial/ labiodental	Dental/ alveolar	Retroflex	Palatal	Velar	Laryngeal
Stops	p, b	t, d	ʈ, ɖ		k, g	
Nasals	m	n	ɳ		ŋ	
Fricatives	f	s	ʂ	ç		h
Liquids		ɾ, l	ʈ, ɭ			
Approximants	ʋ, w			j		

2.1.2.2 Oral and nasal stops

The oral stops are divided into two series distinguished by different laryngeal activity. In postvocalic position one series tends to be voiced ([b, d, g]) and the other voiceless ([p, t, k]). In word-initial position and at the beginning of a stressed syllable irrespective of its position in the word, the two series are distinguished phonetically not primarily by voice, but by [p, t, k] being aspirated and [b, d, g] being unaspirated, voiceless or only partially voiced.[18] As in several other Germanic languages, the contrast is neutralized after /s/. Here, only unaspirated, voiceless stops occur.[19]

The dental/alveolar stops are laminal (denti-)alveolars, with the tip of the tongue usually set against the lower teeth, and the blade raised against the (dental-)alveolar area (Endresen 1985: 74ff; 1991: 62).[20] The retroflex stops, as for example in [¹kʰɑʈ], *kart* 'map', are apicals. The descriptions of the precise point of contact vary somewhat. Vanvik (1972: 137f.) suggests that they are alveolar. Endresen (1991: 63) claims that they are postalveolar, while according to Endresen (1985: 76) may vary between postalveolar and alveolar. The latter finds support in palatographic evidence presented in Moen and Simonsen (1997). For reasons of typographical simplicity I shall use the retroflex IPA symbols to refer to these sounds, which therefore must be taken to mean retracted tongue tip, but not necessarily a postalveolar point of contact.

There are three nasal stops, symmetrically patterned with the oral ones. Examples are [¹lam], *lam* 'lamb', [¹lan], *land* (id.) and [¹laŋ], *lang* 'long'. They correspond to these with respect to all articulatory details except for the crucial difference with respect to the position of the velum.

A glottal stop may occur in syllable-initial position of vowel-initial roots. Thus

---

[18] Examples in prevocalic position are [¹biːl], *bil* 'car' vs. [¹pʰiːl], *pil* 'arrow', [¹dɔm], *dom* 'judgement' vs. [¹tʰɔm], *tom* 'empty' and [¹gʉt], *gutt* 'boy' vs. [¹kʰʉt], *kutt* 'cut'. Examples of postvocalic contrasts are [¹jɔb], *jobb* 'job', [¹jɔd], *jod* 'iodine', [¹jɔg], *jogg* 'jog' (imp.), and [²lɛp.pʰə], *leppe* 'lip', [²lɛt.tʰə], *lette* 'to lighten', [²lɛk.kʰə], *lekke* 'to leak'.

[19] There is accordingly no difference in the pronunciation of the two phrases *hans biller* ('his beetles') and *han spiller* ('he plays'); both are pronounced [¹han.²spil.lɾ]. These are distinct from *hans piller* ('his pills'), which is pronounced [¹hans.²pʰil.lɾ]. (The example is from Hovdhaugen 1971: 163).

[20] Vanvik (1972: 136) claims that these sounds are apico-dentals with laminal-alveolar contact. Endresen's arguments against this analysis is in my opinion convincing: the position of the tongue tip seems variable, and it is the laminal contact that constitutes the phonetically regular property of these stops.

the word *alle* 'all' (pl.) is most commonly pronounced as [ˀˀɑl.lə]. Unlike German, the glottal stop is not normally inserted word-medially in stressed syllables. Thus *teater* 'theatre' is normally pronounced [te.ˈɑːtr̥], only in very emphatic pronunciation may [te.ˈˀɑːtr̥] be heard.

2.1.2.3 Fricatives

There are four contrastive oral fricatives, all voiceless. [f], as for example in [ˈfeː], *fe* 'cattle', is basically the same sound as its cognates in other Germanic languages. In addition, there are two coronal fricatives, both strident, and a non-strident palatal. While [s], as for instance in [ˈseː], *se* 'to see', is lamino-alveolar, the precise articulatory properties of [ʂ], as in [ˈʂeː], *skje* 'spoon', are somewhat unclear. The sound has two sources, one historical and one synchronic. As an assimilation product from historical /sj-/ and /skV/, where V in the latter case represents a front vowel, it must be seen as underlying. In these cases, the expected outcome would be a distributed (= laminal), postalveolar [ʃ], given the fact that the trigger was a front, often high vowel. But the sound is also the phonological product of the Retroflex Rule applying on sequences of /rs/, and in this case the expected outcome would be a retracted apical. We would therefore expect two phonetically different non-anterior stridents. Larsen (1907: 41), which is an analysis of the Kristiania [Oslo] vernacular at the turn of the century, describes them as different and as palatalized and retroflex respectively. A much later source, Sivertsen (1967: 79) says that some older speakers will use a slightly retroflex pronunciation when the source is /rs/, while the sound used when the source is /sj, skV/ is slightly palatalized. Vanvik (1972: 146), however, does not make this distinction. In his consonant chart there is no retracted apical sibilant: the only non-anterior sibilant symbol used is [ʃ]. On p. 143f. this is described as a palato-alveolar, which I take to mean a laminal, distributed articulation. The products of the Retroflex Rule are specifically included in this description. Endresen (1985: 77, 1991: 73f.), on the other hand, claims that the most common way of articulating the postalveolar sibilant is apico-postalveolar, that is, [ʂ], irrespective of historical origin. In the following, I shall follow Endresen in assuming that the sound in contemporary UEN is an apical, irrespective of phonological environment and historical origin. It will be transcribed as [ʂ], but lacking a thorough investigation of the articulatory properties of this sound, I do not mean to imply that it will be a retroflex sound for all speakers and in all environments. Assuming that the main mode of realization is retroflex, the two sibilants can be distinguished by characterizing one as being laminal and the other as apical.

The last fricative, a non-strident that phonetically is usually classified as palatal [ç], cf. [ˈçeː], *kje* 'kid', is unstable in many dialects. Endresen (1991: 75f.) says that it is often pronounced as alveolo-palatal [ɕ], and suggests that this pronunciation is gaining ground among speakers of East Norwegian. This fronting process has been taken further in some of the major southern towns, specifically, Bergen, Stavanger and Oslo, where younger speakers tend to merge /ʂ/ and /ç/ into [ʂ] (Papazian 1994).

[h], as in [²hɑ:.gə], *hage* 'garden', is voiceless and similar to English [h]. Whether it should be classified as an obstruent or approximant is unclear, given its lack of supralaryngeal features. Its classification here as a fricative is simply a matter of convenience. Phonologically it does not enter into a natural class relationship with fricatives, nor with approximants.

2.1.2.4 Liquids

There are three liquids, which interact in a very complex manner. One is a true lateral, while the two others phonetically belong to the tap/flap type. The tap [ɾ] is the realization of underlying /r/.[21] Most sources (Endresen 1991: 68, Sivertsen 1967: 85, Foldvik 1977, among others) describe it as alveolar.[22] Unlike the coronal stops, it is an apical, articulated by the tip of the tongue rapidly tapping against the alveoli.

The retroflex flap [ɽ] is found in eastern and northern dialects of Norwegian as well as in a number of Swedish dialects. It is articulated by moving the apex rapidly forward from a retroflexed position, hitting the alveolar ridge momentarily on its way towards the lower teeth. Historically it derives both from Old Norse /rð/ and /l/, the former probably being the environment where it originated due to similarity of articulatory movement. Its phonemic status is precarious. In most roots where it may occur, it can alternate with [ɾ] in words where Old Norse had /rð/ and with [l] where Old Norse had /l/. Examples are [¹buːr]/[¹buːɽ], *bord* 'table' and [¹suːl]/[¹suːɽ], *sol* 'sun'.[23, 24] But there are words that can only be pronounced with [ɽ], such as [¹møːɽ], *møl*,[25] which contrasts minimally with [¹møːr], *mør* 'tender'.

As to the lateral, several sources, such as Vogt (1939) Vanvik (1972: 142f.),

---

[21] An example is [¹raːr], *rar* 'funny'. It can occasionally also be realized as a trill, for instance in emphatic speech. Uvular (or velar) realization may occur in two distinct sub-populations of UEN-speakers. It is used by some older, upper-class Oslo speakers, probably a vestige of an aborted change from apical to uvular pronunciation that seems to have taken place earlier this century. Uvular pronunciation can also be heard among speakers who have not managed to acquire the more complex apical articulation.

[22] In Foldvik (1977) this is supported by a palatogram. Vanvik (1972: 143), however, describes it as postalveolar, but no evidence is presented.

[23] In rural dialects it has a more secure phonemic status, see for example the discussion in Faarlund (1974). Note that this contrast seems to refute the (implicit) claim in Maddieson (1984: 89n) that languages do not distinguish flaps and taps, made explicit in van der Hulst (1995a: 100). The reason why this fact is not recorded in Maddieson (1984), where Norwegian is one of the languages in the data base, is that the variety described in the source, Vanvik (1972), is upper class Oslo speech, where the retroflex flap is not recognized for sociolinguistic reasons—see the following footnote.

[24] There are sociolinguistic constraints on the use of [ɽ], especially strong in words where it can alternate with [ɾ]. Frequency data for use in Oslo speech are presented and analysed in Tanner (1976), Jahr (1981) and Hoftvedt (1980), for example. Unfortunately, [ɽ] alternating with [l], and [ɽ] alternating with [ɾ] are not separated in any of the analyses, apparently due to the low frequency of the latter. But it is explicitly stated that there are instances of both types in the recorded speech data; see for example Hoftvedt (1980: 33).

[25] The word is difficult to translate, but it is a noun that is used in informal speech to characterize things or states of affairs that the speaker strongly dislikes. (If the variety where [ɽ] is absolutely banned for sociolinguistic reasons really exists, words like this are simply not available for the speakers of this variety.)

Papazian (1977) and Jahr (1981: 329, 1988) observe that it is in the process of changing from an denti-alveolar laminal type, which was the normal realization (outside retroflex environments, see Chapter 4.3) earlier in this century, into an alveolar apical. This has led to a neutralization of the unmarked lateral and the one belonging to the retroflex series. The product of the neutralization is described as 'slightly' retroflex by both Vanvik (1972) and Jahr (1981). Endresen (1991: 83f.) describes it as varying between alveolar and postalveolar. I take this to mean that with respect to articulation it corresponds to the retroflex series of the stops and sibilants described above.

There are nevertheless distributional constraints on the development. According to Papazian (1977: 10f.) and Jahr (1981: 329f.), laminal articulation is still *possible* prevocalically, after front and high vowels and after non-coronal consonants. After coronal stops, which are laminal, the laminal lateral will occur obligatorily, as in *Atle* 'man's name'. After non-high, back vowels, and to a lesser degree after [u], one finds a velarized laminal [ɫ].[26]

In summary, the phonetic properties of laterals in UEN are characterized by a division between a laminal and an apical type. The laminal type is in the process of giving way to the apical type in most environments. The two types do not contrast phonemically, however, except after long, back, non-high vowels. This has resulted in neutralization of the contrast between laminal and retroflex articulation that is otherwise found in obstruents and nasals.

To complicate the situation further, laterals in many environments alternate with the retroflex flap. As with the [r] ~ [ɽ] alternation, the retroflex flap is the only possible segment only in a few lexical items.[27] In the following, laterals will be transcribed as [l] when finer distinctions are not relevant.

2.1.2.5 Approximants

As mentioned at the end of the section on vowels above, there are two glides, one palatal, [j], and one labial, [w].[28] They are both articulated without any audible friction, and as shown in (2) and (4) above, their formant structures correspond closely to the vowels [i] and [ʉ]. The labial glide should therefore be transcribed [ɰ], but because no confusion can arise, I shall use the symbol [w].

The labiodental [ʋ] is normally articulated without any a-periodic noise, and should therefore phonetically be classified as an approximant. Its formant structure when produced as an alternant for the glide in the diphthong [æw] is very close to that of both [ʉ] and [w]. Phonologically it behaves as an obstruent in some environments: see Section 2.3.2.3 below.

---

[26] Endresen (1990: 177ff.) claims that there is no velarization involved in this environment with respect to the laminal type, at least in Oslo speech, so that the difference is solely one between laminal and apical articulation.

[27] The pattern is analysed in Chapter 4.3.

[28] The palatal glide is realized as rounded [ɥ] after rounded vowels, see the table under (17) for examples.

2.2 FEATURE GEOMETRY

2.2.1 Introduction

A generative phonological analysis will consist of two main components, a set of representations of phonological structure of which the underlying lexical representations of morphemes and the fully derived surface representations are the two most important, and a set of rules relating these representations.[29] In this section, the principles for representing segment structure that are assumed in this book will be presented.

In Chomsky and Halle (1968), the phonological segment was seen as composed of an unordered set of binary features without further internal structure of phonological significance. The unitary nature of the segment implied in this view was questioned in Goldsmith (1976), who showed that tone may behave in an independent fashion with respect to the other features in a given feature matrix defining a segment. This view, termed Autosegmental Theory, was later extended to other features: see for example the articles collected in van der Hulst and Smith (1982). Taken to its logical conclusion, it implies a complete decomposition of the segment into a set of features which all could act independently of each other. Without further constraints imposed, this implies that any set of features in principle can define a natural class, for example in assimilation processes.

But in works such as Clements (1985), Sagey (1990) and McCarthy (1988) it has been pointed out that this is not in accordance with the facts. The set of attested phonological interactions between groups of features is clearly a subset of the set predicted by an unconstrained, autosegmental model, which was therefore seen as too powerful. There is clearly a need to constrain the theory so that it will predict the set of possible interactions, distinguish between marked and unmarked interactions, and exclude the impossible types. In answer to this need the theory of Feature Geometry was developed, in the works just cited and others. Here features are seen as hierarchically ordered in a tree structure. The underlying idea is that a phonological rule can only target one node in the tree at a time. If this node is a terminal node in the feature tree, the rule will only affect that feature. But if the rule targets a node higher up in the tree, all the features subsumed under that node will be affected. When a phonological process is seen to affect several features, these features should therefore be exhaustively subsumed under a common mother node, which is then the node affected by the rule expressing the process. A rule affecting nodes not organized in this constrained way is predicted to be an impossible, or at least a more marked rule, than one that affects only one node.

The vital question then becomes how such a hierarchy must be constructed in order to account for the wide variety of phonological processes which are attested.

---

[29] Since the advent of Optimality Theory (Prince and Smolensky 1993) this picture has become somewhat more complicated. In this approach rules deriving one canonical surface representation of a given string have been eliminated in favour of a set of competing surface representations which are evaluated by means of a set of ranked, violable constraints.

The organizing principle that was chosen *ex hypothesis* was that the hierarchy should mirror articulation. The mother node on top of the hierarchy is the so-called Root node, defining the segment itself and the point of contact with the prosodic structure that the segment is part of. The featural content of the segment can then be organized either as part of the Root node itself or in different subnodes such as a Laryngeal node and a Place node. Space does not permit a recapitulation of the different proposals that have been put forth with respect to how features should be related to each other within this framework. I shall assume the model outlined in Clements and Hume (1995) as a starting point for the analysis of UEN segment structure in Section 2.3.

Two types of nodes must be distinguished: Class nodes and Terminal nodes. Class nodes are those nodes which are not terminal in the tree, that is, which subsume one or more nodes. Such daughter nodes may define subclasses, which may be Class nodes themselves or Terminal nodes. As their name suggests, Terminal nodes cannot dominate further nodes. They implement specific components of the segment that have a precise phonetic interpretation, and will be written in square brackets. Class nodes, on the other hand, group such components into classes that *ex hypothesis* define natural classes of phonological segments.

While all Class nodes are assumed to be monovalent, terminal features may be binary or monovalent. The question whether a given feature should be seen as monovalent or binary, or whether phonological theory should allow binary features at all, has been subject to much discussion since the mid 1980s—see for example the different views expressed in Pulleyblank (1995), Harris and Lindsey (1995) and van der Hulst (1995a). This question is again closely bound up with the question of underspecification, which we shall return to below.

2.2.2 The Root node

The overall structure of the feature geometry assumed is shown in (9). Laryngeal and Oral Cavity are class nodes that will be further specified below, while the three other dependants of the root are terminal features.

(9) *The Root node*

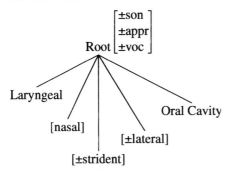

In accordance with Clements (1990) and Clements and Hume (1995: 268f.), the Root node is assumed to be made up of three fully specified binary features, [±sonorant], [±approximant] and [±vocoid]. These are the so-called major class features, which as shown in (10) can combine to form the four major segment classes. These again can be ranked by sonority, with obstruents as least sonorous, and vocoids as most sonorous.

(10)   *The major class features*

[–son, –appr, –voc]:   obstruents (stops and fricatives)
[+son, –appr, –voc]:   nasals
[+son, +appr, –voc]:   liquids
[+son, +appr, +voc]:   vocoids (vowels and glides)

With Clements and Hume (1995: 269) I assume that these features are specified in underlying structure to the extent necessary to drive syllabification processes. By being part of the Root node itself, they will be directly accessible for the building of prosodic structure.

Steriade (1995) assumes [nasal] and [lateral] to be monovalent, as there is scant evidence that the converse sets, non-nasals and non-laterals, form natural classes. However, in order to distinguish the two rhotics among the liquids, /r,ɽ/, from the lateral, it seems necessary to specify them as [–lateral]. I shall therefore assume that [lateral] is binary, but that only coronal approximants can be specified for the feature.[30] I also assume [strident] to be binary because it will be necessary to refer to the class of non-stridents when stating co-occurrence constraints in Chapter 3.

2.2.3 The Laryngeal node

The Laryngeal node is assumed to be organized as shown in (11), also in accordance with Clements and Hume (1995: 269f.). However, I have supplanted [spread glottis] with [asp], for reasons that will become clear in Chapter 4.2.

(11)   *Organization of the Laryngeal node*

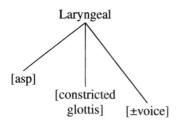

---

[30] This restriction could be stated formally by assuming that [lateral] is a dependant of the Coronal node rather than the Root node. Clements and Hume (1995: 293) cite several problems connected with this assumption, however. Lacking conclusive evidence, I therefore leave the question open.

It will be argued in Chapter 4.2 that a comprehensive and maximally coherent analysis should be based on the assumption that [voice] is binary, with [–voice] being the active value in UEN. I shall in other words argue that recent proposals that this feature should be seen as monovalent, such as Lombardi (1994, 1995) lead to problems with respect to the relevant UEN data.

[asp] will be seen as monovalent. Its phonetic interpretation can be associated with either spread glottis or Voice Onset Time. Iverson and Salmons (1995) argue that [spread glottis] in most Germanic languages functions as carrier of the basic phonological contrast under the Laryngeal node. This hypothesis will also be discussed in Chapter 4.2.

[constricted glottis] is necessary for the specification of glottal stops, given that the feature accounting for closure in the oral stops, [±continuant], is dependent on the Oral Cavity node.

2.2.4 The Oral Cavity node

The Oral Cavity node has two dependants, the Class node Place and the Terminal node [±continuant], as shown in (12).

(12) *Dependants of the Oral Cavity node*

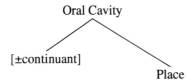

[continuant] is a binary feature. Oral and nasal stops are [–cont], while fricatives and the remainder of the sonorants are [+cont]. Note that I count laterals and the rhotics [r, ɽ] as [+cont]. There are no processes in UEN in which these sounds form a class with oral or nasal stops, and there are processes, such as Nasal Assimilation discussed in Chapter 11.4, where [–cont] seems to be called for in the SD of the rule, but where these sounds must be excluded.

2.2.5 The Place node

The Place node organizes place features for consonants and vowels, and aperture features for vowels. The organization argued for in Clements and Hume (1995) subsumes vowel place and aperture features under the node organizing consonantal place features. This means that vowels and consonants have a common Place node, C-place, while vowels are characterized by having two hierarchically ordered Place nodes, a V-place dominated by C-place. These alternative ways of organizing the Place node are shown schematically in (13), where Place in (12) has been replaced with C-place (Consonantal Place).

The motivation behind this move away from the view that vowels and consonants have only partially overlapping place structure, which had been assumed in earlier work on feature geometry such as Sagey (1990), McCarthy (1988) and Halle (1992), is that interactions between consonants and vowels in place assimilations, such as palatalization of velars in front of front vowels, are easier to analyse within an approach where both classes are assumed to have the same basic structure, see Hume (1994) where this approach is developed and argued for in detail.

In the unmarked case, consonants have a simpler structure with respect to place than vowels. In assimilation processes vowels may spread their place features onto consonants. The result is either that the consonants retain their original place features, but acquire secondary articulations expressed by means of a secondary V-place, or that the original place features are delinked, so that the consonants acquire the features spread from the vowel as their primary features. Secondary articulations are thus created by linking the vocalic features as V-place specifications under the C-place nodes without the underlying main place feature being delinked, while full assimilation can be represented as the vowel features spreading to the C-place node of the consonant with subsequent delinking of the former place specification—see Clements and Hume (1995: 294f.).

(13)   *Structure of the Place node*

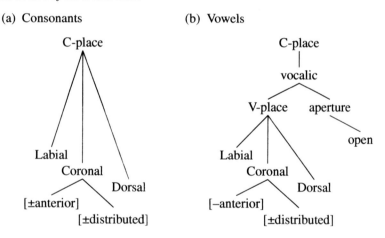

    (a) Consonants   (b) Vowels

In Clements and Hume's theory front vowels are defined as Coronal and back vowels as Dorsal. The feature [±back] is seen as superfluous, on the assumption that palatals are Coronal (Hume 1994, 1996), while central vowels are seen as lacking both a Coronal and a Dorsal node (Clements and Hume 1995: 277, Kenstowicz 1994: 465, Steriade 1995: 151). As we shall see in the following, the latter assumption is difficult to reconcile with UEN data, and I shall therefore argue that it is better to retain [±back] as a dependant of the Dorsal node in order to capture this contrast.

Clements and Hume (1995) analyse vowel height by means of a feature 'open', which can be distributed over several ordered tiers, open 1, open 2 . . . open *n*. Given that the data that support such a solution are yet quite scarce, I adopt the more conservative features [±high] and [±low]. I am not aware of any Norwegian data that clearly bear on the question, so no substantive claims are implied by this choice. The same holds for the retention of the features under a separate aperture node instead of subsuming them under Dorsal, which represents the more traditional view.

These modifications are implemented in the representations shown in (14). For reasons that will become clear in Chapter 4.3, I propose that [±anterior] and [±distributed] be analysed as monovalent [apical] and [posterior].

(14)   *Structure of the Place node, modified*

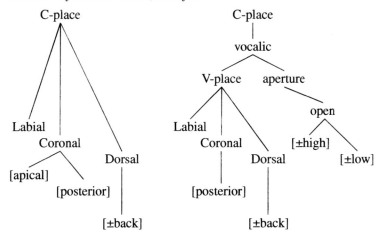

2.2.6 Underspecification

The question whether segments are fully or partly specified for their featural structure in underlying representations has been a much discussed topic within generative phonology. Full specification was assumed to be necessary within the SPE framework, mainly to avoid the use of three contrasting feature values, '+', '−' and 'zero'. But fully specified segments encode a considerable amount of redundant information that therefore can be inserted by redundancy rules. In addition, markedness relations between feature specifications cannot be encoded directly within a framework that relies on fully specified segments in underlying structure. Third, within autosegmental phonology, a spreading rule can be formulated more simply if it fills in structure on a segment unspecified for that feature. Underspecification also allows one to distinguish between phonologically active and inert feature values, whether these are derived from a universal theory of markedness or are language-specific.[31] In the light of such arguments, it was proposed that the

---

[31] Coronals have for example been pointed to as especially prone to assimilation, a fact that may be accounted for if Coronals are seen as the unmarked, and therefore unspecified, place of articulation, see for example the articles in Paradis and Prunet (1991). Other researchers, such as McCarthy and Taub (1992) and Booij (1993) have pointed out problems with this analysis of Coronals.

danger of introducing trivalent features should be circumvented in other ways than by banning any kind of underspecification.[32]

Three main views can be identified: full specification in underlying structure opposed to two views based on some degree of lexical minimality: 'radical' underspecification and 'contrastive' underspecification. The original motivation for full specification was provided in Stanley (1967). It has later been restated in Mohanan (1991) and Steriade (1995).

Radical underspecification   (e.g. Kiparsky 1982, Pulleyblank 1986 and Archangeli and Pulleyblank 1989) assumes that only one value of a given feature, the marked one, is present in underlying structures in environments where it cannot by predicted. The opposite value is filled in by default rules later in the derivation. To block the possibility for rules to refer to three values of a feature, a convention was introduced that filled in the default value no later than the first rule in the phonology that refers to this value. Thus when this rule applies, no segment is left unspecified for the feature in question.

Contrastive underspecification   (Clements 1988, Steriade 1987, Mester and Itô 1989) claims that only non-contrastive feature values should be left unspecified in the lexicon. Thus in cases when a given feature serves to define a lexical distinction between two minimally contrasting lexical items, both values must be specified. Only when a feature value is redundant, that is, predictable by morpheme structure constraints or rules, can it be left unspecified.[33]

Closely linked to the different views on underspecification is the question whether features should be defined as monovalent or binary. If a feature is monovalent, it will either be present or absent, but its absence cannot be ascribed a positive phonological value that can be referred to by rules or constraints. Use of monovalent features therefore derives what is sometimes referred to as 'trivial underspecification'. Within a framework that only allows monovalent features, such as Government phonology (Kaye, Lowenstamm and Vergnaud 1985, Harris and Lindsey 1995), underspecification is therefore not an issue. Also, the issue of whether features are underspecified or not will become less important in frameworks such as Feature Geometry if more features can be reanalysed as monovalent. An inspection of the features employed in the last section will reveal that several features that used to be seen as binary have now been redefined as monovalent. One example are the major place features, where the traditional [±coronal, ±anterior] have been redefined into three monovalent features: Labial, Coronal and Dorsal.

One aspect of underspecification in the traditional sense will be retained, however. Based on the data discussed in Section 2.1.1.5 above, I shall assume in the

---

[32] For more detailed reviews of the issues involved in underspecification, see Archangeli (1988) and Steriade (1995).

[33] It should be mentioned also that phonetic representations, and therefore by implication phonological surface representations, have been argued to be underspecified to a certain extent; see for example Keating (1988) and Pierrehumbert and Beckman (1988).

following section that the vowel inventory contains a segment which lacks place features altogether. This segment will surface as a non-back, mid vowel: see Chapters 4.4 and 11.5 for further discussion.

2.3 PHONOLOGICAL SEGMENT STRUCTURE

2.3.1 Vowels

2.3.1.1 Overview

In (15) the proposed feature specification of the underlying set of vowels is given. /e/ is interpreted as a vowel devoid of place and aperture features. In the morphemes where it occurs, it is underlyingly represented as a segment that is [+voc] only. Its acqusition of coronal features is dependent on metrical structure: see Section 2.1.1.5 above and Chapters 4.4 and 11.5

(15)　*Phonological structure of vowels*

		i	y	ʉ	u	e	ø	o	(æ)	ɑ
V-place:	Labial		✓	✓	✓		✓	✓		
	Coronal	✓	✓						✓	
	Dorsal			✓	✓		✓	✓		✓
	[back]			−	+		−	+		
Aperture:	High	+	+	+	+		−	−	−	−
	Low	−	−	−	−		−	−	+	+

2.3.1.2 The phonological structure of central vowels

In accordance with Clements and Hume (1995) I assume that front vowels are Coronal and back vowels Dorsal. The phonetic evidence presented in Section 2.1 suggested that [ʉ, ɵ] should be seen as neither front nor back, but central. In the following section we shall review the arguments for their being phonologically different from back and front vowels as well. The data presented suggest that they should be phonologically classified as Dorsal. The phonemic contrast between front and non-front vowels is thereby captured by the former being Coronal and the latter Dorsal. With respect to the contrast between central and back vowels, I shall tentatively propose that this be done by maintaining the feature [±back] under the Dorsal node, contra Clements and Hume (1995). [−back] on this interpretation will specify central vowels.

Note that the need for a three-way classification arises only among the high vowels, where there are three labial vowels. In the mid range, the necessary distinctions can be captured by means of Coronal and Dorsal alone, since there are only two labial vowels here, /o/ and /ø/. Because it is the contrast between the high vowels [y, ʉ, u] that is critical, I shall base the analysis on the double need to distinguish them and at the same time to capture any phonological subgrouping among them that is revealed by their patterning in the language.

Assuming that coronal vowels are redundantly posterior, the subfeatures under Coronal cannot be used to specify vowels further along the front–back dimension. A three-way contrast must therefore be captured either by assuming with Clements and Hume (1995: 277), Kenstowicz (1994: 465) and Steriade (1995: 151) that (all) central vowels are unspecified for both Coronal and Dorsal, or by positing an additional subfeature under either Coronal or Dorsal. The assumption that central vowels lack features under Place predicts that they will group positively neither with coronal nor dorsal vowels in any phonological process, since no natural class can be specified which groups the placeless vowels with either of the two groups specified for place. The assumption that central vowels should be specified by means of a subfeature under either Coronal or Dorsal predicts that they will group phonologically with either coronals or dorsals, but not both. If we can find data that show that the central vowels in fact pattern with front or back vowels, this will falsify the hypothesis that they are placeless.

There are data that strongly suggest that /ʉ/ cannot be Coronal. It must therefore either be placeless or Dorsal. It is more difficult to decide between the latter two alternatives, but system internal considerations as well as data from other dialects than UEN suggest that /ʉ/ cannot be placeless.

To see that /ʉ/ is not Coronal, consider first the following distributional pattern. The retroflex flap [ɽ] occurs in free variation with [l] in some environments, among them after a long vowel. Its distribution in this environment is as shown in (16).[34]

(16)   *Alternation between [ɽ] and [l] after long vowels*

Underlying form	Surface form with [l]	Surface form with [ɽ]	Gloss
/mil/	['miːl]	*['miːɽ]	'10 km'
/syl/	['syːl]	*['syːɽ]	'awl'
/stjeɽ/	['stjeːl]	['stjæːɽ]	'steal!'
/søɽ/	['søːl]	['søːɽ]	'mess'
/gʉɽ/	['gʉːl]	['gʉːɽ]	'yellow'
/sʉɽ/	['sʉːl]	['sʉːɽ]	'sun'
/koɽ/	['koːl]	['koːɽ]	'cabbage'
/dɑɽ/	['dɑːl]	['dɑːɽ]	'valley'

We see that [ɽ] is blocked after the class of high, front vowels /i/ and /y/.[35] [eː] is also impossible before [ɽ]; /e/ will obligatorily be realized as [æː] in this context. But after [ʉ] and [ø] both the flap and the lateral can occur. Hence we can make the following generalization if /ʉ/ and /ø/ are interpreted as phonologically [Dorsal: –back]: [ɽ] is blocked after [Coronal: –low] vowels. Since the constraint pertains positively only to coronals, this may of course also be captured in an approach where central

---

[34] Recall that vowel length is not analysed as underlying. The distribution of the retroflex flap is analysed in more detail in Chapter 4.3.

[35] The pattern may be explained phonetically by the fact that the articulation of [ɽ] involves tongue movements that are very different from those involved in articulating non-low front vowels, making the transition from vowel to flap rather complex. Front vowels are articulated by raising the blade of the tongue, while [ɽ] is articulated by raising and drawing the tip of the tongue backwards.

vowels are placeless. What these data show is only that /ʉ/ cannot be Coronal.

/ʉ, ø/ are also distinguished from /i, y, e/ in a process of glide formation in hiatus between a non-low vowel immediately followed by another syllabic peak.[36] This rule, which will be stated formally in Chapter 5.4.2, spreads the features of a vowel onto a following, empty onset position. Examples are given in (17). After /i, y, e/ the resulting glide emerges as coronal (phonetically palatal) [j] or [ɥ], depending on the rounding of the preceding vowel. After all other vowels the glide is labial-velar, [w] or [w̝]. It is important to notice that the pattern cuts across the round/non-round division in the vowels, so it cannot be roundness in itself that governs the choice between the glides.

(17)   *Glide formation*

Underlying form	Surface form	Gloss
/dialyse/	[di.ja.²lyː.sə]	'dialysis'
/syanid/	[sy.ɥa.¹niːd]	'cyanide'
/dʉalisme/	[dʉ.w̝a.¹lis.mə]	'dualism'
/koala/	[ku.¹waː.la]	'koala'
/real/	[²reː.ʲal]	'straightforward'
/røa/	[¹røː.w̝a]	place name

As with the distribution of the retroflex flap after long vowels, we see that the pho-netic grouping of /i, y, e/ vs. /ʉ, ø/ is reflected in the phonology. There must in other words be a phonological feature that will render a coronal glide when Glide Forma-tion applies to /i, y, e/ and a labial–velar glide when it applies to /ʉ, u, ø, o/. Ana-lysing /i, y, e, æ/ as Coronal will make the necessary distinction: spreading a coronal vowel will give a coronal glide, spreading of other vowels will give a labial–velar glide which will be back if the vowel is Dorsal and central if the vowel is placeless.[37]

---

[36] The glides are most audible after high vowels, but can also be heard after mid vowels, at least in emphatic speech. As pointed out by an anonymous reviewer, this may suggest that glide formation should be seen as a phonetic implementation rule; see Chapter 11.1.3 for a short discussion of the dis-tinction between phonological rules proper and phonetic implementation rules. On the assumption that phonetically induced alternations may be phonologized, the distinction between /i, y, e/ and the other vowels is still of phonological interest, even if the rule at hand should prove to be a phonetic one. A similar rule in Dutch is discussed in Booij (1995: 66f.).

[37] Alternative ways of capturing the difference between /y/ and /ʉ/ are certainly conceivable. Analy-ses of the corresponding contrast in Swedish can be found in several sources, and given the close rela-tionship between Norwegian and Swedish, it is conceivable that these may carry over into Norwegian. The most widespread approach involves lip activity instead of tongue position. One has simply trans-formed the descriptions of Swedish /ʉ/ as 'inrounded', or articulated with 'compressed' lips, into a new feature, [±inrounded] (Lass 1984: 88f.) or [±compressed] (Lindau 1978). But whatever its merits with respect to Swedish, the approach is not appropriate for Norwegian, since it does not even capture the phonetic facts. As stated in Section 2.1.1.3 above, most analysts agree that it is [y] which is special in Norwegian, having more extreme lip rounding than [ʉ, u]. A feature based on lip activity should there-fore single out /y/, not /ʉ/. One way this could be done within the present framework is by reintroducing the feature [round] as a possible daughter of the Labial node. /ʉ, u, ø, o/ could then be analysed as Labial only, while /y/ in addition could be specified as [round]. However, while this would formally render /y/ and /ʉ/ distinct, it cannot capture the class /i, y, e/ as opposed to /ʉ/, since it is the latter that formally patterns with /i, e/ as non-round. Since the data in (16) and (17) require that /ʉ/ be distinguished from /i, e/, and that /y/ be grouped with them, use of [round] is empirically inadequate and must be rejected.

Are there data that may decide between the hypotheses that /ʉ, ø/ are either placeless or Dorsal? There are no phonological rules in UEN that I know of which may throw light on the question. But it should be noted that if /ʉ, ø/ are analysed as placeless, they must be grouped with /e/ on the analysis assumed here, since the latter is also assumed to be underlyingly placeless. But while /e/ shows an intricate pattern of realization depending on metrical structure (cf. Section 2.1.1.5 above, Chapter 4.4 and 11.5), and whereas it will acquire a Coronal place node in stressed syllables as well as in closed syllables, but remain placeless in other positions, none of these properties hold of /ʉ, ø/. They will remain placeless independent of metrical structure, and can therefore only be distinguished from /e/ in underlying structure and from schwa in surface structure by their specification as Labial. It seems unlikely that it should be this property alone that allows /ʉ, ø/ to appear in stressed syllables, while the third placeless vowel in surface structure, non-labial schwa, can only appear in unstressed syllables in weak, metrical positions. If it is the lack of features that explains the distribution of schwa, as suggested for example by van Oostendorp (1998), it becomes hard to explain the non-restricted distribution of /ʉ, ø/ with respect to metrical structure.

A piece of evidence from a non-UEN dialect that /ʉ/ must be grouped with /u/ can also be mentioned. This is a process of monophthongization in my own dialect, the southern coast Arendal dialect. It represents a very recent change, perhaps still in progress. Because it depends on a complicated pattern of r-vocalization that itself may be in the process of collapsing, it is difficult to establish reliable data. But according to my own intuitions, the pattern is as displayed in (18).[38]

(18)   *R-vocalization and monophthongization in Arendal*

Underlying form	Gloss	R-vocaliza- tion	Monophthong- ization
/siʀ-nes/	family name (compound)	¹siæ.ˌneːs	n. a.
/syʀne/	'turn sour'	²syæ.nə	n. a.
/tʉʀne/	'do gymnastics'	²tʉæ.nə	²tœː.nə
/tuʀne/	'thorn'	²tʊæ.nə	²tɔː.nə

This change must refer to the class of non-coronal high vowels. But this class is impossible to capture within a framework where /ʉ/ lacks place features, while /u/ is Dorsal. If on the other hand both are Dorsal, and distinguished by /ʉ/ being [–back], the process can simply be characterized as one that targets high, dorsal vowels.

The assumption that Dorsal should include central as well as back vowels entails that central vowels and front vowels cannot form a natural class, and that central

---

[38] Each line should be read as a diachronic development, and not necessarily as steps in a synchronic derivation. Mid vowels may also undergo monophthongization, but because /e/ is consistently lowered to [æ] before /ʀ/ by a well-established, obligatory rule, the surface result will be monophthongs across the board.

vowels will be expected to pattern with back vowels in phonological processes. With respect to the first prediction we have seen that there are indeed processes that support this in that they target coronal vowels only. While I know of no other data that will group /y/ and /ʉ/, there is on the other hand evidence that the mid, non-back round vowel groups with coronal vowels. First there is a restricted, lexicalized alternation between velar stops and palatal continuants, where the set of vowels that occurs after the latter consists of [i, y, e, ɵ, æ]. But as will be argued in Chapter 4.6.2, it is questionable whether this alternation should be analysed synchronically as a rule that spreads Coronal from the vowel onto the consonant. But it nevertheless reflects an older, general palatalization process where the non-back, round mid vowel clearly patterned with the coronal vowels. Going even further back, /y/ and /ø/ arose as part of the phonological inventory in Old Norse as products of i-umlaut applying to high back and mid back vowels respectively. Since this is clearly a process whereby the coronality of /i/ in an unstressed syllable was spread to preceding back vowels in stressed syllables, the output of i-umlaut must clearly have been coronal vowels. This shows that if /ø/ is phonologically central in modern UEN, it has at some stage been reclassified from Coronal to Dorsal. Since there was no other round vowel corresponding to /ʉ/ in the mid range, the consequences for the system as whole were negligible and only detectable in distributional patterns such as those just discussed.

2.3.2 Consonants

In this section an overview of the feature specification assumed for consonants will be given in Sections 2.3.2.1 and 2.3.2.2. The following two sections are devoted to segments that in some way or other represent problems of analysis. Section 2.3.2.3 deals with the status of /v/ with respect to the major class features, while the topic of the final section is the underlying source of the velar nasal [ŋ].

2.3.2.1 Overview

The feature values for consonants are given in (19). As with the vowel specifications in (15), '√' denotes that a monovalent feature is present in the segment in question. Except for the major class features, redundant values of features assumed to be binary have been left out.

The glottal stop is not included. It has the same features as /h/, plus the feature Constricted glottis under the laryngeal node. The motivation for assuming binary [±voice], with [−voice] as the underlying value of the feature that accounts for the voicing contrast, will be given in Chapter 4.2.

The analysis of front vowels as Coronal in Section 2.3.1.1 above entails that the palatal consonants /ç, j/ must be analysed as Coronal as well, in line with Hume (1994). Historically, all instances of /ç/ derive from /k/, and a substantial number of /j/ from /g/ followed by a front vowel (including /j/). The change that seems to be about to take place in major towns today whereby /ç/ and /ʂ/ are merged into /ʂ/ (Papazian 1994), is clearly a change into a coronal consonant, however. If /ç/ is

Coronal already, the change can be accounted for simply as linking of [+strident], which would imply linking of [apical].[39]

(19) *Feature composition of consonants*[40]

	p	b	f	m	ʋ	w	t	d	s	ṣ	n	r	l	ʈ	ç	j	k	g	ŋ	h
ROOT																				
±son	−	−	−	+	±	+	−	−	−	−	+	+	+	+	−	+	−	−	+	−
±appr	−	−	−	−	±	+	−	−	−	−	−	+	+	+	−	+	−	−	−	+
±voc	−	−	−	−	−	+	−	−	−	−	−	−	−	−	−	+	−	−	−	−
±lateral												−	+	−						
nasal				✓							✓								✓	
±strident	−	−	−	−	−	−	−	−	+	+	−	−	−	−	−	−	−	−	−	−
±continuant	−	−	+	−	+	+	−	−	+	+	−	+	+	+	+	+	−	−	−	+
LARYNGEAL																				
±voice	−	−					−		−	−							−	−		−
CONS. PLACE																				
Labial	✓	✓	✓	✓	✓	✓														
Coronal							✓	✓	✓	✓	✓	✓	✓	✓	✓	✓				
posterior														✓	✓	✓				
apical										✓		✓		✓						
Dorsal																	✓	✓	✓	

2.3.2.2 Coronal feature specification

Of the apical series only /r, ʈ, ṣ/ are included in (19). The underlying specifications of coronal, non-vocalic segments with respect to coronal features are shown in (20). Note that the retroflex series has been left underspecified for the [posterior] feature, given the fact that except for /ʈ/, it is redundant. The laminal series is assumed to be unspecified for both Posterior and Apical, while the alveopalatals are specified as Posterior only.

(20) *Coronal segments*

	Laminals					Retroflex							Palatal	
	t	d	s	n	l	t	ḍ	ṣ	ṇ	l	ʈ	r	ç	j
Posterior											✓		✓	✓
Apical						✓	✓	✓	✓	✓	✓	✓		

---

[39] See Kristoffersen (1998) for an analysis of other coronal/palatal relationships in Norwegian.

[40] The glides /w/ and /j/ have been included in the chart, even though their characterization as glides *ipso facto* defines them as non-syllabic vowels. They have partly been included for the sake of completeness, so that (19) rather represents the set of non-syllabic segments. There is also a more substantial motivation, however, since /j/ in some environments behaves like a non-vocalic segment; cf. Chapters 3.2.4.4, 5.2.1 and 5.3.2.

Detailed discussions of the specification and phonological patterning of coronals follow in Chapters 4.3 and 11.3.

2.3.2.3 [υ]: sonorant or obstruent?

I have chosen to classify the /υ/-segment as [±son, ±appr], that is, as both an obstruent and a sonorant, in (19). The reason for this is that it presents a janus-like quality in that in some respects it behaves as a glide, in others as an obstruent.[41]

The fact that /υ/ may precede sonorants in syllable codas, as in ['hɛʊn], *hevn* 'revenge', and ['trɛʊl̩], *trevl* 'shred', suggests that it should be classified as more sonorous than laterals and nasals. Its sonorant properties also reveal themselves in onsets. In the same way as other sonorants it can occur between an initial obstruent and the syllable nucleus, as for example in ['tʊær], *tverr* 'sullen'.

But the form ['ʊrœʊl̩], *vrøvl* 'nonsense' reveals that /υ/ also can occur in the obstruent slot in onsets, followed by /r/ in the sonorant slot. Here it contrasts minimally with the obstruent /f/, as in the minimal pair ['friː], *fri* 'free' vs. ['ʊriː], *vri* 'to twist'.[42]

The same ambiguity emerges in the contrast between the monosyllabic ['ʊrœʊl̩] class and a set of words with comparable segmental structure, but where the final /l/ is syllabic, for example [²stæʊ.ʊl̩], *støvel* 'boot'. This difference in syllabification may be accounted for by assuming that [υ] in the monosyllabic forms represents an underlying sonorant, while [υ] in the disyllabic forms represents an obstruent. Hence the '±' specifications in (19), indicating that we are dealing with a segment that behaves both as a sonorant and as an obstruent, depending on environment.

2.3.2.4 [ŋ]: underlying or derived?

In analyses of other Germanic languages it is often assumed that the velar nasal is not part of the underlying set of consonant segments. Instead, it is derived by spreading of place features from a following dorsal stop, which may or may not delete; see Borowsky (1990) for English, Wiese (1996: 224ff.) for German and Hovdhaugen (1971: 144) for Norwegian. This analysis reflects the fact that [ŋ] historically, and in cases where a following velar segment is absent in present-day language, derives from a nasal + velar stop cluster in Germanic languages. Positing an underlying cluster, where the place specification of the nasal derives from spreading from the following segment, will explain why [ŋ] never occurs after a long vowel. It will also account for cases where a given morpheme surfaces with a cluster in some environments, and with only the velar nasal preserved in others. An example from English is *sing* vs. *singer* (Borowsky 1990: 67ff.), where the velar stop surfaces in the latter, but not in the former.

---

[41] In this it resembles the correspondent segment in Russian, cf. Kiparsky (1985: 104), where it is stated that '[t]he labial fricative /v/ patterns as an obstruent in some ways and as a sonorant in others'.

[42] A curious fact is that while /υ/ can precede only /r/ in onsets, it can precede only the complementary set of coronal sonorants, /l/, /ɽ/ and /n/, in rhymes. It can in other words not precede /r/ in a coda. The word *maur* 'ant' can therefore either be pronounced ['mæwr] or ['mæʊ.ʊɽ], but not as *['mæʊr].

Alternations of this type are extremely rare in Norwegian, however. One example is that between [dif.ˈtɔŋ], *diftong* 'diphthong' vs. [dif.tɔŋ.ˈgeː.ɾə], *diftongere* 'diphthongize'.[43] Here it is conceivable to posit a final /g/ in the underlying form, and a rule that deletes word-final, voiced stops when preceded by nasals, since word-final sequences of this type are banned by the phonotactics of the languages; see Chapter 3.2.4.1.[44] A problem with this solution would be that the final stop does not surface in inflected forms of the words either, only in derivations. We thus find [dif.ˈtɔŋ.n̩n̩], 'the diphthong'. This parallels English, however, and an analysis along the lines of Borowsky (1993) could surely be worked out for Norwegian as well. But given the marginality of this type of alternation in Norwegian, a simpler solution would be to assume lexical allomorphy in the few cases where the alternation is found. The fact that the segment cannot occur after long vowels cannot in itself count as a strong motivation for postulating underlying clusters as long as the last segment hardly surfaces.

I therefore conclude that /ŋ/ should be counted among the underlying segments in Norwegian. A root such as *tang*, 'seaweed', prounounced [ˈtaŋ], should therefore be listed in the lexicon as /taŋ/, not /taŋg/. The related question whether the nasals in words such as *tank* (id.) and *tango* (id.) should be listed with underlying /ŋ/, or an underspecified nasal which will acquire its Place specification from the following stop, will be discussed in Chapter 11.4.

[43] Taking verbs derived by means of the suffix /-ere/ as data, there are no examples in Norsk Termbank (1986) of /mb/ showing this alternation, two involving /nd/ (*vagabond* and *sekund*, where the relation between *sekund* 'second' (= measure of time) and *sekundere* 'to second' (= 'assist') can be questioned on semantic grounds) and three involving /ng/ (*diftong*, *monoftong* and *rang*). That the latter is realized as [raŋ.ˈseː.ɾə], and not *[raŋ.ˈgeː.ɾə], supports the claim that we are dealing with a lexicalized pattern motivated by factors of the lending languages more than by general constraints on Norwegian phonology.

[44] This rule would also account for the alternation between [ˈblɔn], *blond* (id.) and [blɔn.²diː.nə], *blondine* '(a) blonde', and would therefore not be a rule that applies to velars only.

3

PHONOTACTIC CONSTRAINTS

In this chapter the structure of lexical items in terms of segment sequencing will be discussed. It is organized as follows. In Section 3.1 I shall introduce the lexical architecture assumed, and in Section 3.2 I shall go on to discuss the phonotactic principles that constrain segment sequences in the lexicon. Note that this will be done independently of syllabic structure, for reasons that will become clear below. Syllable structure will be discussed in Chapter 5.

3.1 THE STRUCTURE OF THE LEXICON

3.1.1 Word structure

Morphemes are classified in two basic types: *roots* and *affixes*. Roots are minimal, morphologically non-complex units that belong to the major lexical classes, and which can form stems in word formation to which affixes can be added. In Norwegian, roots from all word classes can be zero-derived into well-formed words, that is, derived or inflected into words without any overt morphological marker in the form of an affix being added. Thus a noun can be zero-inflected into its sg. indef. form, and an adjective into the form that is used to modify non-neuter, sg. and indef. nouns. Verbal roots are realized as words in imperatives and in vowel-final infinitives which lack the infinitival suffix. Words that have been zero-derived in this sense will be referred to as *simplex words*.

Complex words are then all words which consist of more than one morphological unit that can be identified with a specific part of the segmental string. I assume that all complex words that are products of non-productive word formation are listed in the lexicon, but with internal morphological structure represented, for example by means of labelled brackets. With respect to words already listed in the lexicon, the word formation rules can therefore be seen as morphological redundancy rules applying across the brackets of the lexical entries. But they can also be used to create new words (Aronoff 1976: 31, Spencer 1991: 198).

Only the results of fully productive morphological rules may be seen as actually built during the lexical derivation.[1] These rules are few in Norwegian, and they comprise the regular inflectional rules plus a few derivational rules. Hence, mor-

---

[1] This does not preclude the possibility that words built by such rules may be idiomized, and thereby lexicalized, as e.g. English *scissors*.

phemes are constituents that lexical entries have been built from, and which are visible through the morphological structure of each entry.

Affixes can be classified into two subtypes by the way they behave when they are prosodified: they may be prosodically cohering or prosodically non-cohering (or prosodically independent). Cohering affixes are incorporated in the same prosodic word as their stem, while non-cohering affixes form prosodic words of their own. Clitics are seen as a type of cohering affixes that are added to their stem in the syntax, i.e. at the postlexical level.

A *stem* is defined as the input for a morphological rule, that is, the unit to which an affix is added or which undergoes some other type of morphological modification. The stem is therefore a relational term; a unit is a stem only with respect to some morphological rule. A word is morphologically well-formed only when it is specified for the morphological categories that pertain to the word class that it belongs to. This means that any member of a word class that is inflected, in Norwegian nouns, adjectives and verbs, must be specified for the relevant inflectional categories.[2] A well-formed noun must therefore bear the morphological features for number and definiteness, an adjective must carry the relevant agreement markers, and a verb must be marked for whether it is an infinitive, a participle, an imperative, etc. As just mentioned, such features can in many cases be realized as zero.

3.1.2 Roots

Roots are minimal lexical entries which form the basic stems of word formation. Being minimal, they do not have any internal, morphological structure. In the following sections I shall outline the segmental structure of two minimal types, monovocalic and bivocalic roots, in order to identify the phonotactic principles that we will expect UEN words to be subject to. Both will illustrate the clustering properties of consonants in prevocalic position. In monovocalic roots we will be able to identify the clustering properties of consonants postvocalically, and in bivocalic roots the constraints which hold on clustering intervocalically will reveal themselves. Examples are provided in (1). For completeness, examples of longer roots, all loan words, are also in provided in (1), but these may be regarded as extensions of the basic types in that no clusters not found in the monovocalic and bivocalic roots are found in longer roots.[3]

---

[2] Pronouns are also inflected, but the system is highly suppletive. Notions like stem and affix are therefore irrelevant for the pronominal system.

[3] The fact that clusters in monovocalic and bivocalic roots will always occur after a stressed vowel might imply that the possibility for complex clusters to occur is more limited after unstressed vowels, even if unstressed syllables clearly may be closed in Norwegian. I have not investigated this hypothesis further.

(1) *Types of lexical roots with respect to segment structure*

	Examples	Lexical repr.[4]	Surface structure
Type 1:	*tak* 'roof'	/tak/	[¹taːk]
Monovocalic roots	*takk* 'thank'	/ta**k**/	[¹tak]
	kalk 'chalk'	/kalk/	[¹kaɽk]
	laks 'salmon'	/laks/	[¹laks]
	larm 'noise'	/larm/	[¹lɑrm]
	laken 'sheet'	/lakn/	[¹lɑː.kn̩]
	sykkel 'bicycle'	/sy**k**l/	[¹syk.kl̩]
	ankel 'ankle'	/ankl/	[aŋ.kl̩]
	hamster 'hamster'	/hamstr/	[¹ham.stɽ]
Type 2:	*kake* 'cake'	/kake/	[²kɑː.kə]
Bivocalic roots[5]	*bakke* 'hillside'	/ba**k**e/	[²bak.kə]
	merke 'mark'	/merke/	[²mær.kə]
	veske 'bag'	/veske/	[²vɛs.kə]
	rangle 'rattle' (toy)	/raŋle/	[²raŋ.ɽə]
	rakle 'catkin' (bot.)	/rak.le/	[²rak.ɽə]
	gammel 'old'[6]	/gamal/	[²gam.mal]
Type 3:	*baryton* 'baritone'	/bariton/	[¹bar.ɾi.tɔn]
Longer roots	*apostel* 'apostle'	/apostl/	[a.¹pɔs.tl̩]
(all loan words)	*elefant* 'elephant'	/elefant/	[ɛ.lə.¹fant]
	anaconda (id.)	/anakonda/	[a.na.¹kɔn.da]
	apokalypse (id.)	/apukalypse/	[a.pu.ka.²lyp.sə]

3.1.3 Non-cohering affixes

The class of non-cohering affixes contains the set of derivational affixes that form their own prosodic domains under syllabification and foot formation. Their surface structure complies with the canonical word form, but unlike roots, they must be joined to a stem in order to surface. I assume that this dependence is expressed by means of subcategorization frames that state the morphological conditions that must be met by the stem that the affix is attached to. Some examples of non-cohering affixes are given in (2).

---

[4] The letters in boldface mean that the segment is moraic in surface structure: see Chapter 5.1.3.

[5] Many loan words correspond to this type, but they may have a full vowel in the final syllable, e.g. *tango*, 'tango'. Corresponding structures can be derived within the native vocabulary by suffixation, e.g. *kaka*, def. sg. of *kake*. The type with a full vowel and final consonant is rare in the native vocabulary, except in personal names. The example given has an alternative form complying with type 1, [²gam.ml]].

[6] Some analysts, e.g. Hagen (1986) argue that the final schwa in this type should be analysed as a suffix, marking indef. sg. Here I shall see them as part of the stem. It is difficult to find compelling arguments deciding between the analyses, but the question has no bearing on the topic at hand, since the result of counting the schwa as a suffix would be that the relevant roots should be classified as monovocalic instead.

(2) *Non-cohering derivational affixes*[7]

Affix	Morphological sub-categorization frame[8]	Examples
/ʉː-/	$[[\_] [X]_{Adj, N}]_{Adj, N}$	[²ʉː.ˌfriː] *ufri* 'unfree'
		[²ʉː.ˌvɛn] *uvenn* 'enemy' (lit. unfriend)
/mis-/	$[[\_] [X]_{Adj, V, (N)}]_{Adj, V, (N)}$	[²mis.fɔ.ˌŋœjd] *misfornøyd* 'discontented'
		[²mis.ˌbrʉː.kə] *misbruke* 'misuse'
/van-/	$[[\_] [X]_{Adj, V, N}]_{Adj, V, N}$	[²van.ˌmɑkt] *vanmakt* 'lack of power'
		[²van.ˌnæːrə] *vanære* 'to disgrace'
/foːre/	$[[\_] [X]_{V}]_{V}$	[²foː.rə.ˌkɔm.mə] *forekomme* 'to occur'
/an-/	$[[\_][X]_{V, N}]_{V, N}$	[¹aŋ.ˌkɔm.mə] *ankomme* 'to arrive'
/-skaːp/	$[[X]_{N} [\_]]_{N}$	[²viː.tŋ.ˌskɑːp] *vitenskap* 'science'
/-naːd/	$[[X]_{V} [\_]]_{N}$	[²søːk.ˌnɑːd] *søknad* 'application'
/-heːt/	$[[X]_{A} [\_]]_{N}$	[¹friː.ˌheːt] *frihet* 'freedom'
/-dom/	$[[X]_{A, N} [\_]]_{N}$	[²uŋ.dɔm] *ungdom* 'youth'
/-som/	$[[X] [\_]]_{Adj}$	[²spɑː.ˌʂɔm] *sparsom* 'thrifty'
/-baːr/	$[[X]_{V} [\_]]_{Adj}$	[²brʉːk.ˌbɑːr] *brukbar* 'fit for use'
/-akti/	$[[X]_{N} [\_]]_{Adj}$	[²drœm.mɑk.ti] *drømmeaktig* 'dreamlike'
/-mesi/	$[[X]_{N} [\_]]_{Adj}$	[²reː.gl̩.ˌmɛs.si] *regelmessig* 'regular'

3.1.4 Cohering affixes

The second type of lexical affixes that are relevant for the analysis of lexical structure consists of the prosodically dependent affixes. This category cuts across the traditional distinction between derivation and inflection. While some derivational affixes belong to the non-cohering type discussed in the previous section, others are prosodically integrated with their host, and must therefore be defined as cohering. All inflectional affixes are suffixes, and all are cohering. (3) gives examples of cohering derivational affixes.

Tables (4) through (6) present the inflectional suffixes, with examples. It should be noted that except for /-sk/, the only place of articulation allowed for consonants in these affixes is coronal. This can be connected with the sequential constraint that will be stated below, which seems general to all Germanic languages, namely that only one postvocalic consonant may have a place of articulation other than coronal. As postvocalic consonants in stems can vary freely over place of articulation (but no more than one), this reduces the degrees of freedom with respect to variation of place of articulation in suffixes to zero.

Verbs   are inflected for tense and to a limited extent for mood (imperative vs.

---

[7] Even if I shall argue in the ensuing chapters that vowel length is not represented as such in underlying representations, I include it here for clarity.

[8] N, A and V represent Noun, Adjective and Verb respectively. Since non-coheringness means that the affix will be realized as a separate phonological word, it has been represented within its own set of morphological brackets.

(3) *Cohering derivational affixes*

Affix	Morphological sub-categorization frame	Examples
/be-/[9]	[_ [X]$_V$]$_V$	[bə.ˈfriː] *befri* 'to liberate'
		[bə.ˈtɑː.lə] *betale* 'to pay'
/for-/	[_ [X]$_V$]$_V$	[fɔ.ˈbeː.drə] *forbedre* 'to improve'
		[fɔ.ˈrɑn.drə] *forandre* 'to change'
/-iŋ/	[[X]$_V$ _]$_N$	[fɔ.ˈrɑn.driŋ] *forandring* 'change'
/niŋ/	[[X]$_V$ _]$_N$	[²byg.niŋ] *bygning* 'building'
/-r/	[[X]$_V$ _]$_N$	[bə.ˈfriː.jɽ] *befrier* 'liberator'
/-rt/	[[X]$_V$ _]$_N$	[ˈduk.kət] *dukkert* 'dip' (in the sea)
/-sk/	[[X]$_N$ _]$_{Adj}$	[ˈhɑtsk] *hatsk* 'hateful'
/-lse/	[[X]$_V$ _]$_N$	[bə.ˈfriː.jl̩.sə] *befrielse* 'liberation'
/-sl/	[[X]$_V$ _]$_N$	[ˈtrif.sl̩] *trivsel* 'well-being'

indicative).[10] They also have an infinitive form, a present participle and a perfect participle. As in other Germanic languages, a considerable number of verbs are characterized by irregular inflection in the form of vowel ablaut. The so-called regular inflection is by suffix.[11] Two main subclasses within the regular verbs can be identified on the basis of the form of the preterite and past participle suffix. The members of the first select the consonant-initial suffixes given in line 1 of (4), while the members of the second take the vowel-initial ones given on the second line.[12]

(4) *Inflectional suffixes on regular verbs*

	Infinitive[13]	Present	Preterite	Present participle	Perfect participle
	/-e/	/-r/	/-te, -de/	/-ne/	/-t, -d/
Example: /bak/ 'bake'	[²bɑː.kə]	[²bɑː.kɽ]	[²bɑk.tə]	[²bɑː.kn̩.nə]	[ˈbɑkt]
	/-e/	/-r/	/-et ~ -a/	/-ne/	/-et ~ -a/
Example: /kast/ 'throw'	[²kɑs.tə]	[²kɑs.tɽ]	[²kɑs.tət]	[²kɑs.tn̩.nə]	[²kɑs.tət]
			[²kɑs.tɑ]		[²kɑs.tɑ]

Nouns are declined for number and definiteness.[14] There are three genders governing agreement relations with adjectives and anaphoric pronouns, and a number of declension classes which to a certain degree correspond to the gender division,

[9] There are a few examples of nouns and adjectives with this prefix, cf. Faarlund *et al.* (1997: 94).
[10] The subjunctive, which is formally identical with the infinitive, is in semi-productive use in (inventive) swearing, but apart from this, appears only in lexicalized phrases.
[11] There are also mixed types where the preterite may be irregular and the past participle regular.
[12] In addition to the syntactic passive which corresponds to the one found in other Germanic languages, there is also a morphological passive, marked by the suffix /-s/, mainly used with infinitives and present forms, and with preterites of the 'bake' class.
[13] A lexically defined subclass can in vernacular speech take /-a/ as infinitive marker.
[14] Morphological case is only manifest as allomorphy within the pronominal system. In some rural dialects, dative is still found, but only in definite forms.

but which also define subgroups and groups cutting across the genders. There are sociolinguistic constraints on the use of the feminine marker /-a/ of def. sg. in upper class speech. The same restriction holds for the other /-a/ endings.[15] (5) shows the different suffixes that can be attached to nouns. The lines in the table roughly correspond to masculines, feminines and neuters, but as just mentioned, the correspondence is not perfect.

(5)   *Inflectional suffixes attaching to nouns*

	−Definite −Plural	+Definite −Plural	−Definite +Plural	+Definite +Plural
Masc.	no ending	/-n/	/-r/	/-ne/ ~ /-ɑ/
Example: /laks/, 'salmon'	[¹lɑks]	[¹lɑk.sn̩]	[²lɑk.sɽ]	[²lɑk.sn̩.nə]
Fem.	no ending	/-n/ ~ /-ɑ/	/-r/	/-ne/
Example: /ʋik/, 'bay'	[¹ʋiːk]	[¹ʋiː.ka]	[²ʋiː.kɽ]	[²ʋiː.kn̩.nə]
Neuter	no ending	/-e/	no ending	/-ne/ ~ /-ɑ/
Example: /tak/, 'roof'	[¹tɑːk]	[¹tɑː.kə]	[¹tɑːk]	[¹tɑː.ka]

Adjectives   take comparative and superlative suffixes, subject to a size constraint on the base, as in English. There is also a defective system of agreement. Attributive adjectives that modify a non-definite singular neuter, and adjectives following singular neuters as predicates irrespective of definiteness, are normally marked with a /-t/. An /-e/ is normally added to an attributive adjective when the noun is definite and/or plural, and to a predicate when the noun is plural. (6) shows the form of the endings that can attach to an adjective.

(6)   *Inflectional suffixes attaching to adjectives*

	−neuter, −plural, −definite	Agr. marker, neuter sg	Agr marker, +plural or +definite	Comp.	Sup.
		/-t/	/-e/	/-re/	/-est/
Example: /stiʋ/ 'stiff'	[¹stiːʋ]	[¹stiːft]	[²stiː.ʋə]	[²stiː.ʋɽ.rə]	[¹stiː.ʋəst]

3.2 PHONOTACTIC STRUCTURE

3.2.1 The relationship between sequential constraints and syllabic constraints

In this section I shall discuss the most important sequential constraints which govern how segments can be combined in morphemes, that is, the set of morpheme

---

[15] As can be seen from the table, the exclusion of /-a/ makes the distinction between the two first lines, i.e. the distinction between masculine and feminine declination, disappear.

sequencing constraints that hold over the set of lexical entries.[16] In Chapter 5, the constraints that govern the syllabification of these strings, and thereby the possible combinations of segments into onsets and rhymes, will be discussed. I assume in other words that in an analysis of the phonotactic principles of a given language, lexical sequencing constraints as well as syllabic constraints are needed.[17] The reason why I choose to state the phonotactic sequencing constraints before syllable structure is that most syllabic sonorants, which are common in UEN, can be seen as arising from sequences of consonants which cannot be accommodated within one syllable due to the Sonority Sequencing Principle; see Chapter 5.1.4. For example, I shall assume that the lexical entries for [ˈpuk.kl̩] *pukkel* 'hump' and [ˈpʉɽk] *pulk* 'small, boat-shaped sleigh' are /pukl/ and /pʉlk/ respectively. Both orders of sonorant and obstruent are hence well-formed in lexical entries, but if the obstruent comes before the sonorant, the latter will be realized as a syllabic head, resulting in a disyllabic output. This entails that while they can be analysed as instantiations of the same basic type of morpheme structure, a monovocalic root, syllabification constraints imply that they will be assigned very different syllabic structures.

There is also another argument for keeping phonotactics and syllabification rules apart. Phonotactic principles defined over a given lexicon can in general be seen as a set of redundancy rules that delimit the kind of structures which occur. The reason for non-occurrence of a given string may be due to its being an accidental gap for diachronic reasons, or it may be due to an active co-occurrence constraint in the language. The set of phonotactic principles defined on lexical structure can tell us which combinations are found and which are not. On the other hand, if we assume that syllable structure is derived by a set of general principles in the form of a set of syllabification rules or as mapping of a segmental string to a syllable template, we would expect these principles to respect the active constraints, but not accidental gaps. A diagnostic for this distinction would be loan words, for instance the pronunciation of foreign names, which cannot always be assumed to be part of a given speaker's lexicon. If these contain sequences that are excluded by the phonotactic principles defined over the lexicon, we would expect speakers to have no problems pronouncing them if they represent accidental gaps, but if they violate active constraints, we would expect speakers to adjust them so that they conform with the constraints.[18]

---

[16] The classic analysis of East Norwegian phonotactics is Vogt (1942). Analyses can also be found in Vanvik (1972) and Endresen (1991). The principles governing the phonotactics of Norwegian, Swedish and Danish are to a considerable degree the same, but a full comparative analysis will exceed the scope of the present book. The most comprehensive analysis of Swedish phonotactic structure is Sigurd (1965). Danish is analysed in Basbøll (1973). Diderichsen (1953) and Spang-Hanssen (1959) are of indirect and perhaps chiefly methodological interest, in that they are primarily concerned with the distribution of graphemes in written Danish.

[17] See also Yip (1991) for arguments along the same lines. Yip distinguishes between coda constraints and cluster conditions, the latter being what is referred to here as sequential constraints or phonotactic constraints.

[18] See Fischer-Jørgensen (1952: 38) for a short discussion along similar lines.

Let me illustrate this with some examples. Due to its non-occurrence word-initially in many languages, /tl/ is often defined as an impossible onset. For English, it can be argued that this is due to an active constraint, because the sequence will be split medially in words like *Atlantic*. According to Kenstowicz (1994: 251) the /t/ in this word is glottalized while an onset /t/ will be aspirated. But in Norwegian, where /tl/ is also not found word-initially, the pronunciation [¹beː.tlɛm] for 'Bethlehem', can be taken as an argument for the accidental gap option. A syllable boundary is normally inserted after a long vowel, and because /tl/ in this word occurs after a long vowel, it can be argued that the sequence here forms an onset. There are in addition no aspects of the pronunciation such as glottalization that argue against this. On the contrary, the sequence in this example is pronounced in exactly the same way as in the man's name *Atle*, [²ɑt.lə], where the /t/ can be argued to be in the coda due to a minimality constraint on stressed syllables that will be discussed in Chapter 5.1.3.

Another example is the English word [ˈbænd], *band* 'group of musicians'. There are three problems with the English pronunciation from an East Norwegian point of view. The vowel [æ] does not normally occur before non-apical consonants, final clusters of nasals + voiced stop do not occur in East Norwegian, and the length of the vowel will be perceived as somewhat indeterminate with respect to the contrast between long and short vowel in Norwegian because of the length induced by the following voiced consonant in English. The most common pronunciation is [¹bæn]. [¹bɑn] and [¹bæːn] may occur, but *[¹bænd] is impossible. This suggests that the written consonant group normally induces a short vowel, and that the ban against nasal + stop clusters is a true constraint in East Norwegian. The almost total absence of [æ] before non-apicals must on the other hand be due to an accidental gap in the synchronic grammar that is slowly being filled by loan words and spelling pronunciations of family names; see the discussions in Chapters 2.1.1.2 and 4.4.

Finally, while /pn/ is absent word-initially, Norwegian speakers have no difficulty pronouncing a word like *pneumatisk* 'pneumatic' with an initial [pn]. On the other hand, the constraint against /sr/ onsets can be argued to be an active constraint. Many Norwegians apparently find it difficult to pronounce *Sri Lanka* by the letter: very often one will hear [si.ri.¹laŋ.kɑ].

The hypothesis that emerges is that only active constraints will govern syllabification, while accidental gaps may be filled by loan words.[19] In order to capture this difference, and also to be able to characterize the inventory of postvocalic consonant sequences in a coherent manner, phonotactic sequencing in roots should be discussed without reference to predictable aspects of metrical structure. However, I shall not refrain from referring to syllable structure when that will benefit the

---

[19] In order to be able to use loan words in testing for this difference, they must be spelled in a way that clearly suggests a pronunciation that is at odds with patterns found in the native vocabulary. For example, since all instances of [ʈ] are spelled *rt* in Norwegian, it is impossible to test by means of loan words whether its absence from word-initial position is due to an accidental gap, since no language from which Norwegian borrows vocabulary today allows this combination prevocalically in writing.

discussion, thus anticipating the analysis of syllabic constituency when appropriate.

3.2.2 Prevocalic sequencing of consonants

In their lexical representation, stems of all the three types defined in (1) may be vowel-initial, or may begin with a maximum of three consonantal segments. Examples of the four possible types are given in (7), where X represents the set of possible postvocalic consonant sequences.

(7)   *Schematic prevocalic consonant sequencing*

Type 0	VX	/oːl/	'eel'
Type 1	CVX	/koːl/	'cabbage'
Type 2a	CCVX	/kroːl/	'crawl'
Type 2b	CCVX	/skoːl/	'saucer'
Type 3	CCCVX	/skroːl/	'shouting'

3.2.2.1 Single prevocalic segments

All the segment types that are listed in (8) in Chapter 2 may function as a single prevocalic consonant, except /w, ɾ, ŋ/. Of these, /w, ŋ/ cannot occur prevocalically at all, while /ɾ/ may occur only in clusters. The absence of /w/ is probably due to a true constraint, since foreign words spelt with an initial *w*, such as *watt*, are pronounced with [ʋ], [ˈʋɑt]. Vietnamese names beginning in the sequence *ng*, which postvocalically signals [ŋ] in Norwegian, are never spontaneously pronounced with initial [ŋ], so this is probably a true phonotactic constraint as well. Apical (retroflex) [ʈ, ɖ, ɳ, ɾ] do not occur word-initially, while [ʂ, ɭ] do; see Chapter 2.1.2. As noted in footnote 19 it is difficult to test by means of loan words whether the absence of the former set is due to an accidental gap or to a true constraint, but it should be noted that [ʈ, ɖ, ɳ] may occur as onsets in non-initial syllables such as [fɔ.ˈʈɛl.lə], *fortelle* 'to tell', [ʋæ.ˈɖiː], *verdi* 'value', [ˈbɑː.ɳɑ], *barna* 'the children' and [ˈsuː.ɾɑ], *sola* 'the sun'. /h/ and /ç/ are restricted to syllables with main stress and to word-initial syllables.

3.2.2.2 Clusters of two and three consonants

Prevocalic clusters with two members fall into two main types: Obstruent + sonorant, and /s/ + stop. The possible combinations of the first type are given in (8), where some rare combinations of sonorant + sonorant have also been included.[20] All the possible three place clusters can be formed by adding an initial /s/ to a subset of the clusters in (8). These have been marked by shading of the relevant cells.

---

[20] The table is based on Endresen (1991: 214), but it has been simplified by elimination of predictable (or near predictable) surface contrasts. /ʂ/ is not included in the obstruent column because it cannot contrast with [s] in these clusters. Recall also that [ç] and [h] cannot occur in prevocalic clusters. Finally, the absence of /w/ and /ŋ/ from the table is also due to their non-occurrence in the environment under discussion.

(8) *Co-occurrence restrictions within (s) + obstruent + sonorant clusters*

Consonant 1	Consonant 2					
	/m/	/n/	/l/	/r/	/j/	/ʋ/
/p/			✓	✓	✓	
/b/			✓	✓	✓	
/t/				✓	✓	✓
/d/				✓	✓	✓
/k/		✓	✓	✓		✓
/g/		✓	✓	✓		
/f/		✓	✓	✓	✓	
/s/	✓	✓	✓			✓
/ʋ/				✓		
/m/					(✓)	
/n/					(✓)	

As can be seen from the numerous empty cells above the line between /ʋ/ and /m/, not all combinations of obstruent + sonorant are possible. Some of the gaps have resulted from assimilation processes that have merged Old Norse velar or coronal obstruents with a following /j/ into palatal segments /ç/ or /j/.[21]

The constraint against /kj-/, /gj-/ and /sj-/can be stated as in (9).

(9) *Dorsal/strident + palatal constraint*

$$* \begin{Bmatrix} \text{[Dorsal]} \\ \text{[+strid]} \end{Bmatrix} \quad \text{[Coronal: posterior, } \neg \text{apical] V}$$

I know of no loan words where this constraint is violated.

Nasals have a very limited distribution as second members of initial consonant clusters. Recall that /ŋ/ cannot occur in prevocalic position at all. If the nasal is /m/, the preceding obstruent can only be /s/. Since the cluster /fm/ is excluded by the Shared Place Constraint; see (11) below, the constraint can be stated as one blocking initial clusters of stops + /m/, as in (10).

(10) *Stop + /m/ constraint*
* # [−son, − cont] m V

The lack of clusters consisting of velar stop + /m/ is likely to be due to an accidental gap, however, since the Cambodian name *Khmer* is pronounced [ˈkmeːɾ] and not,

---

[21] It should therefore be noted that the filled /tj/ and /dj/ cells represent only a few words. The survival, or perhaps reappearance, of these clusters is often attributed to reading pronunciation. Examples are [²tjeː.nɾ] *tjener* 'servant' and [²dje:.ʋl] *djevel* 'devil'. (The latter word has more colloquial forms beginning in /j/ in all dialects, for example [²jæː.ʋl].)

for example, *[kə.ˈmɛːɾ]. But similar examples are difficult to find involving sequences of coronal stop + /m/. It is perhaps significant that the word spelled *astma*,
'asthma' is never heard with the *t* pronounced, the only possible pronunciation is
[ˈɑs.mɑ]. On the assumption that only the first consonant following a short vowel
is syllabified as a coda, cf. Chapter 5.3.4, pronunciation of the stop would result in
the onset of the second syllable being /tm/. The non-occurrence of coronal stops +
/m/ may therefore derive from a true constraint.

If the nasal is coronal /n/, /k, g, f, s/ can occur in the preceding slot. The non-
occurrence of coronal stops + /n/ can be dealt with by the Shared Place Constraint,
see (11) below. Only the non-occurrence of labial stops with /n/, that is, */pn/ and
*/bn/ does not follow from this constraint. However, due to the existence of
[pnæw.ˈmɑː.tisk], *pneumatisk* 'pneumatic', it should probably be seen as an accidental gap.

Only some homorganic obstruent + sonorant clusters are allowed, we do not find
*/tl. . ./, */dl. . ./, */tn. . ./, */dn. . ./, */pv. . ./, */bv. . ./ nor */fv. . ./ in the native
vocabulary. For reasons that we shall return to presently, /s/ and /ʂ/ must be excluded from this constraint. It can be formulated as a constraint against shared
place nodes—an anti-OCP effect, in other words.[22]

(11) *Shared Place Constraint*

While the OCP would block adjacent, identical place nodes, place nodes that have
the same main articulator specification, but non-identical dependent feature specifications, do not seem to be subject to the constraint. This may explain the fact that
/r/ may combine with /t, d/. While the stops lack dependent features under the Coronal node, /r/ is underlyingly specified as [ap]. But this explanation should extend
to clusters of /t,d/ + the retroflex flap /ɽ/, which is also specified as [ap]. The non-
occurrence of such clusters can be seen as deriving from an independent constraint
that blocks combinations of the flap with non-apical coronals, be it consonants or
coronal vowels; see the discussion in Chapter 4.3.3.

But combinations of /s/ + /t/, which are both non-apical, are not subject to (11)
either. This might constitute an argument for [±strident] being a dependent of the
Coronal node, since this would cause /t/ and /s/ to have different structure under the
place node and hence be immune to the constraint.

---

[22] The Obligatory Contour Principle (OCP) says that two adjacent autosegments on a given tier must
be non-identical. This implies that if two adjacent melodic units are identical with respect to their feature
specification on a given tier, this identity must be represented as a many to one association to one
autosegment. See Kenstowicz (1994: 322ff and 532ff.) for further discussion.

An additional problem is that while coronal stops can be combined with /r/ but not with /l/, the inverse relationship obtains for /s/. While /sl/ is allowed, /sr/ is disallowed. If /s/ were uniquely specified as [+strident] under Coronal, we would expect it to combine with all other coronals. In order to exclude /sr/ clusters, I state the constraint in (12).

(12)   /sr/-filter
        * #sr . . .

As noted above, this seems to be a true, phonotactic constraint, since the loan word *Sri Lanka* is very often heard as [si.ri.¹laŋ.ka].

The Shared Place Constraint itself is on the other hand more problematic. In addition to Mexican place names such as *Tlalocula*, where the initial cluster is pronounced without an epenthetic vowel, we have Russian river names such as *Dnepr* and *Dnestr*, which are also pronounced with initial clusters.[23] Also, on the assumption that [¹as.tma] is blocked because of a constraint against /tm/ in onsets, we would not expect to find words such as [²fɛs.tne], *festne* 'to fasten' and [²ɔr.dne], *ordne* 'to put in order' if (11) were a true constraint. At least some of the clusters that are blocked by it may be accidental gaps.

The two sonorant + sonorant combinations, /mj/ and /nj/, are marginal in modern Norwegian.[24] The cluster /nj/ only occurs in a few personal names and place names, but /mj/ is more common. It occurs in quite a few names, but there are only four lexical items containing this cluster that are in common use: [¹mjæʈk] 'milk', [¹mjæːʈ] 'flour', [¹mjʉːk] 'soft' and [²mjæw.wə] 'to miaow'. The three first have alternative pronunciations without /j/, [¹mɛlk], [¹meːl] and [¹myːk], which have considerably higher sociolinguistic prestige. Among other lexical entries beginning in /mj/ we find [¹mjøːd] 'mead', and a few extremely rare, archaic words probably not known to the average Norwegian speaker, but listed in comprehensive dictionaries.

The other type of permissible two-place initial clusters in Norwegian are the three obstruent + obstruent sequences /sp/, /st/ and /sk/. We can delimit this type by the constraint stated in (13).

(13)   *Obstruent + obstruent constraint*
        If: # Obs₁ Obs₂ (Son) V
        Then: Obs₁ = /s/, and Obs₂ = [−cont]

These obstruent + obstruent sequences are included in the set of permissible three-place clusters, and three-place clusters may therefore be seen as a combination of

---

[23] The significance of these data is somewhat weakened by the fact that dictionaries state their pronunciation with a palatalized /n/, but I consider this as learned pronunciation which is not evident from the spelling.

[24] Both clusters reflect Old Norse phonotactic structure, which allowed all possible sequences of nasals (/m/ and /n/) or liquids (/r/ and /l/) plus /j/, most of which have disappeared today. These sequences could also be combined with preceding /s/, e.g. *snjór* 'snow' and *strjúka* 'to stroke'. Such clusters are very rare in contemporary dialects, in the majority /j/ has been eliminated, giving e.g. [¹snoː]. There are *some* vestiges, but as far as I know, a thorough investigation of the degree of survival of these clusters in modern dialects has not been undertaken.

the two permissible two-place cluster types, where the stop is the shared segment. But there are two permissible (voiceless) stop + sonorant sequences where the addition of an initial /s/ is blocked: /kn/ and /tv/. It does not seem possible to subsume these under one statement. We must therefore posit two constraints that will block sequences of /sknV/ and /stvV/ respectively. These are given in (14) and (15). I know of no arguments in favour of these being accidental gaps.

(14) /skn/-constraint
      * # s k n

(15) /stv/-constraint
      * # s t v

In this connection a proposal by Vogt (1942) should be mentioned. In order to account for the fact that the /s/ + stop clusters may occur in non-reversed order after the vowel, Vogt suggests that we might regard the /s/ + stop as what we today would call contour segments, see for example McCarthy and Prince (1986: 87ff.). Similar proposals concerning English can be found in Selkirk (1982: 346f.) and Durand (1990: 217). Contour segments are segments with linearly ordered internal structure, in this case minimally [+cont][–cont] in the case of /st/, and an additional difference in place features in /sp/ and /sk/. Such an account would simplify the description, because the upper bound on prevocalic consonants would be reduced to two, obstruent + sonorant.

But even if this is a desirable simplification, there are counter-arguments that lead me to reject the proposal. First of all, if such clusters are monosegmental, we would expect them to occur after long vowels on par with other single segments. In fact a few examples exist, [²poːskə], *påske* 'Easter', [¹pruːst], *prost* (clerical rank) and [¹beːst], *best* 'beast'. Only the first has obligatory long vowel, and here we could assume an open syllable, even if the normal pattern is short vowel in this environment. Except for these examples, a vowel is obligatorily short preceding clusters of /s/ + stop.[25] Second, one usual condition on contour segments is that there should be no internal shift in place features, only in manner features (McCarthy and Prince 1986: 89). The clusters /sp/ and /sk/ violate this condition.

I therefore conclude that such sequences should be seen as true clusters, and that we accordingly must maintain three segments as the upper bound on initial consonant clusters.

3.2.3 Single postvocalic consonants in monovocalic roots

3.2.3.1 Consonants after long vowels

Most consonants (i.e. segments that are [–voc]) may occur alone after a long vowel, but the following restrictions hold: /ŋ/ can only occur after a short vowel, there is a word [¹saŋ] 'song' in Norwegian, but *[¹saːŋ] is outside the class of possible

---

[25] See Chapter 8.2.2 for further discussion of the distribution of long vowels before clusters.

words. (The same holds for /ŋ/ inter-vocalically.) I know of no loan word that constitutes an argument for this being an accidental gap.

The obstruent /f/ is also marked in this environment. The only examples known to me with /f/ after a long vowel are loan words like [ˈʂeːf], 'chief', *autograf, seraf, filosof*, the final three with main stress on the final syllable. The latter must therefore be an accidental (semi-) gap. Other labial segments are also rare after long vowels. [b] is almost excluded, the only clear examples in Norsk Termbank (1986) are the loan words [ˈstaːb], 'staff' and [çeˈrʉːb], 'cherub'. Also excluded from the C-slot following a long vowel are the glides [j] and [w], with a few exceptions. The name of the Constitution Day, the 17th of May, is often pronounced [ˌsœt.tn̩.nə.ˈmaːj], *syttende mai*, along with [ˌsœt.tn̩.nə.ˈmɑj], and the name of the former Chinese leader is pronounced [ˈmɑːw], *Mao*.[26]

3.2.3.2 Single consonants after short vowels

As after long vowels, there are few constraints on which consonants can occur alone after a short vowel. Single [ʋ] is blocked after a short vowel, however, as is [ɽ]. There are in other words very few constraints on what kind of non-vocalic segment may immediately follow a short vowel.[27]

3.2.4 Postvocalic sequencing of two consonants in monovocalic roots

As stated in (16) postvocalic consonant clusters consisting of two members come in all four possible types as defined by the major class distinction between sonorants and obstruents.

(16)   *Postvocalic sequences consisting of two consonants*

      sonorant + obstruent: /salt/ [ˈsɑlt] *salt* (id.)
      obstruent + obstruent: /kraft/ [ˈkrɑft] *kraft* 'power'
      obstruent + sonorant: /pepr/ [ˈpɛp.pr̩] *pepper* (id.)
      sonorant + sonorant: /kʋalm/ [ˈkʋɑlm] *kvalm* 'nauseated'

3.2.4.1 Sonorant + obstruent clusters

(17) shows the possible combinations. Looking at the columns, we note that /b/ is practically absent. This absence becomes even more marked when we take into consideration that the loan word [ˈʋærb] is the only member of the /rb/ group. /b/ is therefore a marginal final member of two-place codas, but this is clearly an accidental gap.[28]

---

[26] An alternative interpretation of these clusters might be as bisyllabic, that is, [ˈmɑː.i] and [ˈmɑː.u].

[27] /ʋ/ occurs after short vowel in the onomatopoetic *vov-vov*, 'bow-wow', and the English loan word *Love*, pronounced [ˈlɔʋ], which was the title of a popular magazine some decades ago. The retroflex flap occurs after short vowels in the Grenland region around the town of Skien, some 150 km. south-west of Oslo.

[28] Vogt (1942: 15) gives [ˈdærb] 'compact, speaking of ore', but this must be considered obsolete today, or at least not part of the lexicon of the majority of speakers. Vogt's only example of /lb/, the loan word [ˈbœlb] 'bulb' is also not a word in use today.

The rows representing /m, n, ŋ/ in (17) show that the very common pattern of place of articulation harmony between nasals and following stops also holds in Norwegian. The only class of obstruents that allows preceding nasals with a different point of articulation is coronals. If the obstruent is a labial or a velar, a preceding nasal must agree in place of articulation. At this point, I will not formulate this as co-occurrence restriction, but suspend further discussion until the question of nasal place assimilation is taken up in Chapter 11.4.

(17)   *Co-occurrence pattern within two-place postvocalic*
       sonorant + obstruent clusters[29]

	p	b	f	ʋ	t
j	[ˈslæjp]		[ˈstræjf]	[ˈlæjʋ]	[ˈfæjt]
w	[ˈstæwp]			[ˈklæwʋ]	[ˈstæwt]
ʋ					
r	[ˈskɑrp]	[ˈʋærb]	[ˈʂærf]	[ˈʂærʋ]	
l	[ˈjɛlp]		[ˈgɔlf]	[ˈkɑlʋ]	[ˈsalt]
m	[ˈgɑmp]		[ˈtrumf]		[ˈɑmt]
n					[ˈfɑnt]
ŋ					[ˈpuŋt]

	d	s	ʂ	k	g
j	[ˈslœjd]	[ˈsʋæjs]		[ˈrœjk]	[ˈtæjg]
w	[ˈlæwd]	[ˈtæws]		[ˈgæwk]	
ʋ	([ˈhɛʋd])				
r	[ˈsʋærd]			[ˈkɔrk]	[ˈsɔrg]
l		[ˈhals]		[ˈkɑlk]	[ˈʋɑlg]
m	[ˈnɛmd]	[ˈbrɛms]			
n		[ˈdɑns]	[ˈlœnʂ]		
ŋ		[ˈʂɑŋs]		[ˈtɑŋk]	

Another regularity that can be extracted from (17) is the absence of word-final sonorant + voiced obstruent (b, d, g) with shared place features. Again we see that /r/ is not included in the constraint, but /w, l, m, n, ŋ/ cannot be combined with a homorganic voiced stop. This constraint can be stated as in (18).[30]

This constraint is limited to word-final position. Intervocalically such sequences

[29] Glosses: [ˈʂlæjp] 'slippery', [ˈstræjf] 'gleam', [ˈlæjʋ] 'piece of bread', [ˈfœjt] 'fat', [ˈʂlœjd] 'woodwork', [ˈsʋæjs] 'hair-style', [ˈrœjk] 'smoke', [ˈtæjg] 'piece of land', [ˈstæwp] 'beaker', [ˈklæwʋ] 'hoof', [ˈstæwt] 'healthy', [ˈlæwd] 'university grade level', [ˈtæws] 'silent', [ˈgæwk] 'illegal liquor dealer', [ˈhɛʋd] 'established right', [ˈskɑrp] 'sharp', [ˈʋærb] 'verb', [ˈʂærf] 'scarf', [ˈʂærʋ] 'contribution', [ˈsʋærd] 'sword', [ˈkɔrk] 'cork', [ˈsɔrg] 'sorrow', [ˈjɛlp] 'help', [ˈgɔlf] 'golf', [ˈkɑlʋ] 'calf', [ˈsalt] 'salt', [ˈhals] 'neck', [ˈkɑlk] 'chalk', [ˈʋɑlg] 'election', [ˈgɑmp] 'horse', [ˈtrumf] 'trump', [ˈɑmt] 'county', [ˈnɛmd] 'committee', [ˈbrɛms] 'brake', [ˈfɑnt] 'vagabond', [ˈdɑns] 'dance', [ˈlœnʂ] 'lunch', [ˈpuŋt] 'point', [ˈʂɑŋs] 'chance', [ˈtɑŋk] 'tank'.

[30] Spellings like *land* 'land' and *sang* 'song' reflect an older stage. Only a few, rural dialects of western Norway have retained the stops in these words (Chapman 1962). In all other dialects the pronunciation of these words must be [ˈlɑn] and [ˈsɑŋ].

(18)   *Postvocalic *Shared Place Constraint*

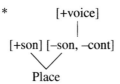

occur, as seen in examples like [²ɾum.bə], *rombe* 'rhombus', [²kʉn.də], *kunde* 'customer', [²vɑn.dl̩], *vandel* 'conduct' and [¹taŋ.gu], *tango* (id.). It therefore appears
to be a coda constraint.

The apical segments /r/ and /ɽ/ do not occur before another coronal consonant.
This holds whether the second coronal is an obstruent (/t, s/) or a sonorant (/n, l/).
The only exception is /rd/-clusters, cf. *sverd* in (17). Other clusters of this type have
been changed into corresponding apicals by the Retroflex Rule, but for reasons that
will become clear in Chapter 4.3, I shall assume that this rule applies in derived
environments only in the synchronic grammar.

One additional property of (17) remains to be commented upon. The [ʋ]
row, which has been shaded, has only one cell that is filled, viz. /ʋd/. I argued in
Chapter 2.3.2.3 that [ʋ] is ambiguous between a glide interpretation and an obstruent interpretation. Here we find another instance of that ambiguity. Given that both
sonorant + obstruent and obstruent + obstruent sequences are possible
postvocalically, the /ʋd/ sequence in [¹hɛʋd] in (17) can be interpreted as either a
sonorant + obstruent cluster or an obstruent + obstruent cluster. However, its distribution suggests that it is an obstruent in this environment. While it is completely
isolated in (17), it fits well into the distributional patterns found in postvocalic
obstruent + obstruent clusters, to which we shall turn below.

3.2.4.2   Obstruent + obstruent clusters

(19) gives the possible combinations of postvocalic obstruent + obstruent clusters.

(19)   *Co-occurrence restrictions within two-place postvocalic*
       obstruent + obstruent clusters[31]

	p	t	d	s	k
p		[¹krypt]		[¹slips]	
f		[¹krɑft]		[¹tʉfs]	
v			[¹hɛʋd]		
t				[¹sats]	
k		[¹ɑkt]		[¹sɑks]	
g			[¹bygd]		
s	[¹jisp]	[¹rʉst]			[¹rɑsk]

[31] Glosses: [¹krypt] 'crypt', [¹slips] 'tie', [¹krɑft] 'power', [¹tʉfs] 'insignificant person', [¹hɛʋd]
'established right', [¹sats] 'movement' (mus), [¹ɑkt] 'act', [¹sɑks] 'scissors', [¹bygd] 'rural community',
[¹jisp] 'gasp', [¹rʉst] 'rust', [¹rɑsk] 'quick'.

There are two principles governing the phonotactics of this cluster type. On the bottom line, we find the s + stop clusters that are also found prevocalically and after sonorants postvocalically.

In addition to these we find that two obstruents may be combined if the second member of the cluster is coronal, and both members agree in voicing. The only expected cluster not found given this constraint, is /bd/. We now see why /ʊ/ should be classified as an obstruent in this position. While /ʊd/ emerges as an isolated cell horizontally in (17), it groups with /gd/ in (19).

The voicing constraint can be expressed as in (20). In Chapter 4.2, we shall see that this constraint to a considerable extent is imposed when combinations of obstruents with different specifications for laryngeal features are created by the morphology.

(20) *Voicing constraint in postvocalic + obstruent clusters*

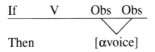

The constraint that the final obstruent must be a coronal, given that the preceding segment is not an /s/, can be expressed by the constraint under (21), which says that in a final, postvocalic sequence of two obstruents, the final one must be a coronal, given that the first one is a non-strident.

(21) *Final coronal constraint*

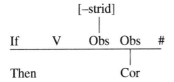

3.2.4.3 Obstruent + sonorant clusters

We now turn to the type which in underlying forms contains one vowel but where the sonority cline in the postvocalic consonants is such that they are realized as disyllabic.

A possible alternative would be to see these structures as underlyingly bivocalic, with an /e/ intervening between the final sonorant and the penultimate obstruent. On the first account the obstruent and sonorant are adjacent in the underlying root; on the second they are not.

To decide between these, different types of evidence can be drawn upon. First, the phonetic reflex of the assumed underlying vowel under the second alternative is very slight. Only in very emphatic speech is a clear vowel audible. In other environments the vocalic element between the two consonantal sounds is minimal and can therefore be interpreted as the result of a minimal phonetic transition. This in itself is not a very strong argument for a vowel not being present in underlying structure, but in the absence of further evidence supporting such a vowel, the analysis without it would be the simpler alternative. It also represents a simpler analysis because the vowel would have to be deleted in many instances when another vowel is inserted after the sonorant, as for instance the adjective [²ɛŋ.klə], from underlying /enkl-e/, where /-e/ is an agreement suffix. The fact that this minimal vowel is present only when needed for syllabification speaks in favour of it not being underlying.

Another piece of evidence can be drawn from the pronunciation of the acronym *Acem*, which is pronounced with a full vowel: [¹ɑː.kɛm]. On the assumption that only coronal sonorants may be syllabic, we can explain why a full vowel is heard in this environment, but not for example in the geographical name *Aker*, [¹ɑː.kɾ].

A third argument for there not being an underlying vowel is that if it is assumed to be an underlying /e/, we would expect it to lower to [æ] before /r/. This generally does not happen, except in one environment. Before the sequences /rn/ and /ln/, as in def. sg. /sykl-n/, a full vowel is realized: [¹syk.kæn̩]. We can account for this if we assume that an /e/ is epenthesized in just this environment. But if the /e/ is assumed to be generally present in the environment, the manifestation of a full vowel in just this environment becomes harder to account for.[32] Held together, the evidence strongly suggests that there is no vowel present underlyingly between the obstruent and the sonorant.

The possible sequences of obstruent + sonorant clusters are given in (22). Both underlying forms (roots) and surface forms are given. To enhance readability, information necessary to derive vowel length has been omitted from the root forms.

(22)   *Sequences of postvocalic obstruent + sonorant*[33]

	r U.l. form	Surface	l U. l. form	Surface	n U. l. form	Surface
p	/pepr/	[¹pɛp.pɾ]	/popl/	[¹pɔp.pl̩]	/ʋopn/	[¹ʋoː.pn̩]
b	/febr/	[¹feː.bɾ]	/bibl/	[¹biː.bl̩]	/lʉbn/	[²lʉb.bn̩]
f	/ofr/	[¹ɔf.fɾ]	/gafl/	[¹gaf.fl̩]	/gʉfn/	[²gʉf.fn̩]
ʋ	/beʋr/	[¹bɛʋ. ʋɾ]	/drøvl/	[¹drœʋ.ʋl̩]	/leʋn/	[¹leː.ʋn̩]
t	/etr/	[¹eː.tɾ]	/spatl/	[¹spɑː.tl̩]	/utn/	[²ʉː.tn̩]
d	/hedr/	[¹heː.dɾ]	/sedl/	[¹sɛd.dl̩]	/sidn/	[²siː.dn̩]
s	/lasr/	[¹lɑː.sɾ]	/gisl/	[¹gis.sl̩]	/asn/	[¹ɑː.sn̩]
k	/okr/	[¹oː.kɾ]	/pukl/	[¹puk.kl̩]	/çøkn/	[¹çœk.kn̩]
g	/magr/	[¹mɑː.gɾ]	/regl/	[¹reː.gl̩]	/egn/	[²eː.gn̩]

---

[32] See Chapters 4.3.7 and 8.4.2 for more detailed discussions.

[33] Glosses: [¹pɛp.pɾ] 'pepper', [¹pɔp.pl̩] 'poplar', [¹ʋoː.pn̩] 'weapon', [¹feː.bɾ] 'fever', [¹biː.bl̩] 'bible', [²lʉb.bn̩] 'chubby', [¹ɔf.fɾ] 'victim', [¹gaf.fl̩] 'fork', [²gʉf.fn̩] 'unpleasant', [¹bɛʋ. ʋɾ] 'beaver', [¹drœʋ.ʋl̩] 'uvula', [¹leː.ʋn̩] 'noise', [¹eː.tɾ] 'ether', [¹spɑː.tl̩] 'spatula', [²ʉː.tn̩] 'without', [¹heː.dɾ] 'honour', [¹sɛd.dl̩] 'slip of paper', [²siː.dn̩] 'later on, since', [¹lɑː.sɾ] 'laser', [¹gis.sl̩] 'hostage', [¹ɑː.sn̩] 'donkey', [¹oː.kɾ] 'field', [¹puk.kl̩] 'hump', [¹çœk.kn̩] 'kitchen', [¹mɑː.gɾ] 'thin', [¹reː.gl̩] 'rule', [²eː.gn̩] 'peculiar'.

We see that all obstruents are possible in the first slot. /f/ after long vowel is rare, however; the only example I know is the loan word [ˈʂeː.fr̩] 'Alsatian' (dog). /ʋ/ on the other hand, which in CVC-words only can occur after long vowels, has a much freer distribution in this type.

The second slot can only be filled with a coronal sonorant. (23) formalizes the constraint, incorporating the fact that it also holds if the first segment is a sonorant; see the following section.

(23)   *Place constraint on word-final obstruent + sonorant sequences*

We see that the distributional requirement we found in obstruent + obstruent sequences discussed above, namely that the final segment must be a coronal, can be generalized to obstruent + sonorant sequences. But while this pattern did not obtain when the first of the two obstruents was a strident, it is without exceptions in obstruent + sonorant sequences.[34]

3.2.4.4 Sonorant + sonorant clusters

Two sonorants may also co-occur in two-member clusters postvocalically. Here the sonority relationships become more unclear. For that reason it will be necessary to take syllabification and sonority differences into account in this section, thus anticipating the full discussion of syllabification in Chapter 5.

In final obstruent + sonorant sequences it is to be expected that the sonorant will be realized in a separate syllable, given the clear increase in sonority between the two consonants. When both segments are sonorants, however, the sonority distance is much smaller. Still, sonority differences are assumed to exist between sonorants, see for example Kenstowicz (1994: 254f.) and Clements (1990). If sonority differences govern syllabification, we would predict that different order between sonorants of different sonority will give an opposite syllabification pattern. If the first sonorant is less sonorous, we expect the final one to surface as syllabic; if the inverse relationship obtains, we will expect a monosyllabic surface form. The prediction is in other words that this will be a mixed class with respect to syllabification of the final sonorant.

The possible combinations of sonorants in codas with their respective syllabification patterns are given in (24). The sonorants have been ranked by sonority from left to right and from top to bottom with glides as the most sonorant segments and nasals as the least.[35] Note that there is no column for /ʋ/, because /ʋ/ is interpreted

---

[34] In terms of syllabic licencing (Itô 1988, Goldsmith 1989) we might say that at most one non-coronal consonant is licensed in codas.

[35] I assume the following sonority ranking: Glides > Liquids > Nasals, see Chapter 5.1.4 for further discussion.

as an obstruent in second position. There is not a column for /w/ and /ŋ/ either, because these sounds can only occur immediately after a short vowel, and not after another consonant.

(24) *Co-occurrence restrictions within two-place postvocalic sonorant +*
      sonorant clusters[36]

	j	r	l	m	n
j		/lejr/ [ˈlæjɾ]	/sejl/ [ˈsæjl]	/rejm/ [ˈræjm]	/løjn/ [ˈlœjn]
		/sejr/ [ˈsæj.jɾ]	/fløjl/ [ˈflœj.jl̩]		
w		/mewr/ [ˈmœwɾ]	/gewl/ [ˈgæwɽ]	/gawm/ [ˈgæwm]	/fewn/ [ˈfæwn]
		/bewr/ [ˈbæw.wɾ]			
υ		/mewr/ [ˈmæυ.υɾ]	/gaυl/ [ˈgɑυl]		/saυn/ [ˈsɑυn]
r	/berj/ [ˈbæɾj]			/orm/ [ˈɔrm]	
l	/helj/ [ˈhœɽj]			/kυalm/ [ˈkυɑlm]	/køln/ [ˈkœln][37]
	/çelr/ [²çel.lɾ]				/poln/ [ˈpɔl.l̩n]
m		/kamr/ [ˈkɑm.mɾ]	/skuml/ [ˈskʉm.ml̩]		/emn/ [²ɛm.mn̩]
n		/banr/ [ˈbɑn.nɾ]	/kenl/ [ˈkɛn.nl̩]		
ŋ		/fiŋr/ [ˈfiŋ.ŋɾ]	/raŋl/ [ˈrɑŋ.ŋl̩]		/saŋn/ [ˈsɑŋn]
					/lyŋn/ [ˈlyŋ.ŋn̩]

---

[36] Glosses: [ˈlæjɾ] 'camp', [ˈsæj·jɾ] 'victory, [ˈsæjl] 'sail', [ˈflœj·jl̩] 'velvet', [ˈræjm] 'strap', [ˈlœjn] 'lie', [ˈmæwɾ] 'ant', [ˈgæwl] 'howl', [ˈgæwm] 'attention', [ˈfæwn] 'faun', [ˈmæυ·υɾ] 'ant', [ˈbæw.wɾ] 'family name', [ˈgɑυl] 'gable', [ˈsɑυn] 'loss', [ˈbæɾj] 'hill', [ˈɔrm] 'snake', [ˈhæɽj] 'week-end', [ˈkυɑlm] 'nauseated', [ˈkœln] 'Cologne', [²çel.lɾ] 'cellar', [ˈpɔl.l̩n] 'pollen', [ˈkɑm.mɾ] 'small room', [ˈskʉm.ml̩] 'creepy', [²ɛm.mn̩] 'numb, [ˈbɑn.nɾ] 'banner', [ˈkɛn.nl̩] 'kennel', [ˈfiŋ.ŋɾ] 'finger', [ˈrɑŋ.ŋl̩] 'drinking spree', [ˈsɑŋn] 'legend', [ˈlyŋ·ŋn̩] 'Lyngen' (place name). Note that [υ] has been excluded from the second position, because the examples containing this structure have been classified as sonorant + obstruent above.

[37] This place name (= Cologne) is the only example of a final /ln/ cluster in a monosyllabic word.

There are two aspects of these data that are worth discussing. First there are the gaps in the distribution, and second we must consider the variability with respect to the syllabic status of the final sonorant.

The most conspicuous gap in the pattern shown in (24) is the lack of j-final clusters other than those consisting of liquids + /j/. But in view of the analysis offered below that /j/ may in fact be an obstruent in these clusters, we can explain the lack of the other clusters as well as the seemingly inverted sonority sequencing in these clusters. Another gap that may be explained in a similar manner is the absence of /ʋm/ clusters. It was argued in Chapter 2.3.2.3 that /ʋ/ may appear as an obstruent in some environments. Above we argued that postvocalic clusters of /ʋ/ plus another obstruent should be interpreted as consisting of two obstruents. Given the fact that we find monosyllabic /gaʋl/ and /saʋn/, where /ʋ/ precedes sonorants within the same syllable, we cannot straightforwardly extend this analysis to /ʋ/ + sonorant clusters. I know of no data that may shed light on whether this is an accidental gap or not.

Clusters of /r/ + /l, n/ are lacking because these clusters historically have been changed into apical segments by the Retroflex Rule; see Chapter 4.3.6. Since this rule is still a productive rule of the language, this gap can be seen as due to a true phonotactic constraint.

The absence of clusters consisting of two nasals with /m/ as the final one appears as another instantiation of the pattern that we saw in clusters of two obstruents, where the final had to be coronal, as in (21) above, and the parallel pattern found in obstruent + sonorant clusters, where the final member also has to be a coronal, as in (23). But we do find /m/ as a second member in sonorant + sonorant clusters, the constraint is limited to sequences of nasals, where the final must be coronal.

We now turn to the syllabification pattern in (24). Cells where the surface form is disyllabic have been shaded. The pattern predicted is that the monosyllabic forms will be found in the upper right part as defined by a diagonal, where the combinations with decreasing sonority are found, and that the disyllabic forms will occur in the lower left part where sonority between the two segments is increasing. To a considerable extent we see this pattern materialize in (24). But we also see that for several of the combinations, we find that the final sonorant is realized as syllabic in some forms, and as non-syllabic in others. How to encode this variation in lexical representations will be discussed in Chapter 5.3.2.

One aspect of the table must be treated here, namely the occurrence of final [j]. If [j] underlyingly has the same feature specifications as the high front vowels, we would expect that an underlying glide in this position would surface as a vowel, rendering a disyllabic structure. This in fact has taken place in some dialects in Trøndelag and Nordland in the north, where a process of apocope truncated final unstressed vowels in open syllables, so that an infinitive like *kasta* 'to throw' became *kast*. In verbs with intervocalic /Cj/, such as *sørja* 'to mourn', apocope will result in a final underlying /j/. On the assumption that this is identical with underlying /i/, we would expect it to surface as a (syllabic) vowel after the following vowel had been truncated. This result has apparently been seen as marked, because in some dialects, apocope is blocked in this environment (Larsen 1897: 86). But in others, such as the dialects of Skogn in Trøndelag (Dalen 1985: 135) and Salten in Nordland (Skånlund 1933: 81, Hanssen 1985: 25f.), the apocope also hit the final vowel in this type, and the result was as would be expected if the underlying segment is a vowel, *sørri*.[38]

In the light of these developments in other dialects, the exceptional forms with final /j/ in the leftmost column are difficult to explain. The best explanation is probably that as with /v/, we are dealing with a segment that has the same surface realization, but which can underlyingly be either a sonorant or an obstruent. In the forms in (24), /j/ derives historically from /g/, and even if it has been changed into an approximant-like articulation, the fact that it occurs after a liquid in a coda suggests that phonologically it is non-vocalic in this environment. Its relationship with /g/ might suggest that it is still an obstruent, but since it may occur after obstruents prevocalically, as for example in [²djeː.ʋl], djevel 'devil', it is better analysed as a sonorant. Further arguments in favour of this, having to do with syllabification, will be discussed in Chapter 5.2.2 and 5.3.2.

3.2.5 Clusters of three or more postvocalic consonants

Monosyllabic roots ending in sequences of three or more consonants can be seen as extensions of the basic two-member types discussed above.[39] Possible types of three-member clusters with examples are listed in (25).

(25) *Possible postvocalic sequences consisting of three consonants*

    Frequent combinations

sonorant + obstruent + obstruent:	/blomst/ [¹blɔmst] *blomst* 'flower'
sonorant + obstruent + sonorant:	/mandl/ [¹mɑn.dl̩] *mandel* 'almond'
obstruent + obstruent + obstruent:	/tekst/ [¹tɛkst] *tekst* 'text'
obstruent + obstruent + sonorant:	/kapsl/ [¹kɑp.sl̩] *kapsel* 'capsule'

    Rare combinations

obstruent + sonorant + sonorant:	[¹blik.nɾ̩] *Blichner* (family name)
obstruent + sonorant + obstruent:	Non-existent as root
sonorant + sonorant + sonorant:	/forml/ [¹fɔr.ml̩] *formel* 'formula'
sonorant + sonorant + obstruent:	/bernt/ [¹bærnt] (UEN [¹bæ ɳ ̩t])
	Bernt (man's name)

---

[38] These forms are obsolete today, and have been either changed into forms ending in a schwa, such as *sørje*, or modified in other ways.

[39] Consonant groups following a *short* vowel may consist of up to five members. Nearly all forms with five and four postvocalic consonants are morphologically complex. The only example of the five-member type that I know of is the neuter form of the rarely used adjective *skjelmsk*, 'roguish' [¹ʂelmskt]. This form is morphologically complex, and can be given the analysis /ʂelm-sk-t/, where the root is nominal, the /sk/ is a suffix deriving adjectives from nouns, and /t/ is the neuter concord marker, or an adverbial derivational suffix.

3.2.5.1 Sonorant + obstruent + obstruent or sonorant

The possible clusters of sonorant + obstruent extended by another obstruent are given in (26). We see that the possibilities are heavily restricted. Only groups of sonorant + /s/ can be further extended, and the only two obstruents that can be added are /t/ and /k/.[40]

(26)   *Co-occurrence restrictions within three-place postvocalic sonorant + obstruent + obstruent clusters*[41]

	t		*k*	
js	/bejst/	[¹bæjst]	/bejsk/	[¹bæjsk]
ws	/newst/	[¹næwst]		
ls	/svʉlst/	[¹svʉlst]	/falsk/	[¹fɑlsk]
ms	/blomst/	[¹blɔmst]	/lumsk/	[¹lumsk]
ns	/kʉnst/	[¹kʉnst]	/vrinsk/	[¹ʋrinsk]
ŋs	/aŋst/	[¹ɑŋst]		

Historically, many of the roots belonging to this type can be seen as morphologically complex, deriving from the addition of the suffix /st/, a nominalizing suffix added to verbs, or /sk/, an adjectivizing suffix added to nouns. But many of these derivations, especially of the /-st/ type, are opaque in the synchronic lexicon. Even if nouns like [¹bɑkst] and [¹faŋst] can be transparently related to the verbs [²bɑːkə] 'to bake' and [²fɑŋ.ŋə] 'to catch', having a resultative meaning with respect to the verbs, there are numerous examples where such a relationship is not evident. Examples are [¹kʉnst] 'art' and [¹blɔmst] 'flower'. These forms must therefore be analysed as lexical items with no internal structure. The /-sk/ suffix is more transparent, but word forms like [¹fɑlsk] 'false' cannot be morphologically parsed, and show that at least for some members of this set, the three consonants must be part of a root.

As noted, the first member of these three-place clusters must be sonorants, the second /s/ and the final member either /t/ or /k/. /p/ is in other words excluded. All sonorant types can appear, including glides. Words like [¹bæjsk], *beisk* 'bitter', [næwst], *naust* 'boat-house' and [¹bæjst], *beist* 'beast' are often seen as exceptions to the constraint that long vowels cannot precede consonant clusters in roots, on the assumption that diphthongs should be classed with long vowels. If we analyse diphthongs as sequences of short vowel plus glide, these examples fit neatly in with other examples of monosyllabic words with three-place clusters following a short vowel. In fact, these words complete the pattern, by allowing for the whole range of non-syllabic sonorants to appear before the obstruent sequences in question.[42]

---

[40] [¹mʉlkt], *mulkt* 'fine' is a possible exception, even if it is given as [¹mʉlt] in the pronouncing dictionaries, it may occasionally be heard with the /k/ pronounced.

[41] Glosses: [¹bæjst] 'beast', [¹næwst] 'boat-house', [¹svʉlst] 'tumour', [¹blɔmst] 'flower', [¹kʉnst] 'art', [¹ɑŋst] 'anxiety', [¹bæjsk] 'bitter', [¹fɑlsk] 'false', [¹lumsk] 'sly', [¹ʋrinsk] 'neigh'.

[42] It should be noted, however, that these diphthongs have been monophthongized in many dialects: small variations in vowel quality set aside we find forms like [¹bɛsk], [¹nœst] and [¹bɛst].

A sonorant + obstruent group may also be extended by a sonorant, resulting in the final sonorant being syllabified. There do not seem to be any additional restrictions on combinations here, except that I have not found any examples where /l/ occurs in both sonorant slots. Examples of this type are [ˈɑm.pf̩], *amper* 'short-tempered'; [ˈmɑn.dl̩], *mandel* 'almond'; [ˈhil.sn̩], *hilsen* 'greeting' and [ˈœr.kn̩], *ørken* 'desert'.

3.2.5.2 *Obstruent + obstruent + obstruent or sonorant*

A group of two obstruents may also be extended by either an obstruent or a sonorant. The type with three obstruents is rare and severely constrained, in that (almost) only /ks/ clusters can be extended, and the only possible extension is /t/. The only clearly non-derived examples that I know of are [ˈtɑkst], *takst* 'value estimate' and [ˈtɛkst], *tekst* 'text', but other combinations of obstruent + /st/ or /sk/ are derived in the morphology.[43]

With respect to the type with two obstruents plus a sonorant, the constraints on the two obstruents, given in (19) above, are respected, but there do not seem to be further, principled restrictions on the further combination with a following coronal sonorant. But this is not a common type, so all possible combinations are not actually attested. Recall that the possible obstruent clusters are either of the /s/ + stop type or clusters of obstruent which agree in voicing and where the final one must be a coronal. Examples of the first type combined with a sonorant are [ˈtis.tl̩], *tistel* 'thistle' and [ˈvɛs.pf̩], *vesper* (id.). Examples of the second type are [ˈɑg.df̩], *Agder* 'name of region'; [ˈkɑp.s̩l], *kapsel* 'capsule' and [ˈsɛp.tf̩], *septer* 'sceptre'.

3.2.5.3 *Other combinations*

The types discussed above all consist of an obstruent-final cluster extended by either a sonorant or an obstruent. All other types are rare. Examples of a cluster of two sonorants + another sonorant are [ˈfɔr.ml̩], *formel* 'formula' and the man's name [ˈhɛl.mf̩], *Helmer*.

The complementary combination of two sonorants plus an obstruent is non-existent in UEN, but occurs in other dialects. Examples are the man's names [ˈbærnt], *Bernt* and [ˈɑrnt], *Arnt*. In all dialects that have the Retroflex Rule, the pronunciation will be [ˈbæɳ̍ʈ] and [ˈɑɳ̍ʈ]; see Chapter 4.3.4, which makes them instantiations of the common sonorant + obstruent type. As far as I can see, the only combination possible is /rnt/. But others can be derived in the morphology, e.g. [ˈvɑrmt], *varmt* 'hot' (neuter).

Another possible, but close to non-existent, group is an obstruent + sonorant cluster extended by another sonorant. The only examples I know of are family names. A prominent example of foreign origin is [ˈhit.lf̩], *Hitler*. Others are [ˈblik.nf̩], *Blichner* and [ˈhɑt.ln̩], *Hatlen*. I do not know the origin of the two latter

---

[43] [ˈnɛʊnd], 'committee' is an exception of native origin. An alternative form is /nemnd/, which is usually pronounced (and frequently written) [ˈnɛmd].

names, but the fact that they exist clearly shows that the type is within the constraints of the phonology.

The remaining type, obstruent + sonorant + obstruent, is not represented in any lexical root as far as I know, but it can be found in derived structures, such as the neuter form of adjectives like *enkel*, where a suffixal /-t/ is added, giving the surface form [¹ɛŋ.kɫt].

Before we close this section, we must take a short look at the maximal postvocalic consonant group, which may consist of four members. This pattern is also severely constrained. The initial pair of segments consists of a sonorant + /s/. The two final members must belong to the obstruent + sonorant type, so that the surface form will be disyllabic. The first consonant can be any sonorant, at least if we include loan words such as *gangster*. The obstruents must be /st/, and except for the man's name *Karsten*, the final sonorant must be /r/.[44] Examples are few, but they include [¹hyl.stɽ], *hylster* 'cover'; [¹hɑm.stɽ], hamster (id.) and [¹mœn.stɽ], *mønster* 'pattern'.

3.2.5.4 Conclusion

The postvocalic patterning that we have discussed in this section has been broken down into many different subtypes. Founded on a basic division of the consonants into sonorants and obstruents, we have seen that almost all possible subtypes up to a limit of three consecutive segments have been attested. Some of these subtypes are rare, and others again have been further constrained by conditions on what segments can occur in the different slots. One governing generalization that can be stated is that following the vowel, there can only be one segment whose place of articulation is not coronal. As already noted, this seems to be consistent with a pattern found in other Germanic languages; see Booij (1995: 44) and Yip (1991). Within the different subtypes, we have also identified a number of gaps pertaining to combinations of specific segment types. Some of these gaps were argued to be accidental, while others were argued to be true constraints. For some of the missing combinations we had to leave open the question whether we had to do with an accidental gap or a true phonotactic constraint.

3.2.6 Bivocalic roots

This type can be divided into two subtypes, those ending in a vowel and those which end in a full vowel plus at least one consonant. The latter type is rare, except in personal names such as *Arild, Erik, Olaf, Gunnar*, etc. The first type can be further subdivided into two types, those ending in full vowels, most of them of foreign origin, such as *tango, kobra, taxi* and brand names such as *Omo, Blenda* and *Milo*, (all detergents), and those ending in a schwa, such as [²bɑk.kə], *bakke* 'hill'; [²kɑː.kə], *kake* 'cake' and [²rɑk.lə], *rakle* 'catkin' etc. Most of the latter

---

[44] Again we may be dealing with accidental gaps. The Dutch place name and beer brand *Amstel*, where we find /l/ instead of /r/ as the final sonorant, causes no difficulties whatsoever for Norwegians.

belong to the native vocabulary, but loan words also occur such as *kaffe* 'coffee' and *ordre*, 'order'.

As in monovocalic roots, at most one consonant may normally occur after a long vowel. The set of consonants that may occur is the same as in monovocalic roots, that is, all except the glides /j, w/, the velar nasal /ŋ/, plus /h, ç/. Some examples are [²skɑː.də], *skade* 'damage'; [²struː.fə], *strofe* 'stanza'; [²hɑː.kə], *hake* 'chin'; and [²dɑː.mə], *dame* 'woman'. We also find roots where there is no consonant between the vowels. In this type, the first vowel is always long. Some examples are [²kløː.ə], *kløe* 'itch'; [²boː.ə], *båe* 'skerry' and [²kʋɑː.ə], *kvae* 'resin'.[45]

One consonant can also appear intervocalically after a *short* vowel. As with preceding long vowels, the restrictions are in principle the same as after a short vowel in a monovocalic root. The only difference is that /ç/ occurs in one word, [²biç.çə], *bikkje* 'dog', while it is completely blocked postvocalically in monovocalic roots. Other examples of this type are [²pɑd.də], *padde* 'toad'; [²fɑŋ.ŋə], *fange* 'prisoner'; [²ʂlɛg.gə], *slegge* 'sledge' and [²pil.lə], *pille* 'pill'. Note that the consonant will be geminated in this environment due to syllabification constraints; see Chapter 5.1.3.

Intervocalic consonant groups seem to obey the following principles in roots:[46]

(27) *Constraints on intervocalic clusters*

    (a) The maximum number of consonants intervocalically is three, thus defining a maximum structure corresponding to a $C^0VC_1C_2C_3V$ string.

    (b) The set of consonants that may occur in the first position (C_1) is the same as those that can occur alone after a short vowel in monovocalic roots. In addition, /ʋ/ can occur in this position when followed by another consonant.

    (c) Consonants filling the second and third slot ($C_2 + C_3$) obey the same restriction as prevocalic clusters. Both s + stop clusters and obstruent + sonorant clusters may occur. The actual clusters found are limited to /st/, /sk/, /sl/, /kl/ and /dr/, however; see Kristoffersen (1991: 93).

Principles (b) and (c) come very close to a statement governing syllabification over the $C^0VC_1C_2C_3V$ string, with C_1 defining a heavy syllable with the preceding vowel by principle (b), and C_2C_3 a subsequent onset built by the same phonotactic principle as we have identified word-initially by principle (c).

But if it is the case that the structure of such strings is governed by a syllabification constraint, and not a morpheme structure constraint, a natural deduction from this would be that no additional constraints hold across the boundary, that is, between C_1 and C_2, as long as internal syllabification constraints are respected. With no co-occurrence restrictions between C_1 and C_2 we would in other words expect

---

[45] Glide Formation (Chapters 2.3.1.2 and 5.4.2) will apply after high vowels, and in emphatic speech after mid vowels as well. In colloquial style, the final schwa may be filled by spreading of the stem vowel after mid and low vowels, giving e.g. [²kʋɑː.ɑ].

[46] I use 'consonant' as a cover term for referring to true consonants and non-syllabic glides.

all combinations of well-formed postvocalic (monosegmental) and prevocalic monosegmental and bisegmental sequences to appear. But there are in fact several restrictions that can be shown to hold over the syllabic boundary, and which therefore must be identified as morpheme structure conditions holding over bivocalic roots.[47] That these must indeed be sequential constraints can also be deduced from the fact that they to a large extent are the same as those restrictions holding over postvocalic clusters in monovocalic roots which we stated in the preceding section. This suggests that we are dealing with a set of sequential constraints holding over both monovocalic and bivocalic roots, and not syllable constraints.

If syllable constraints cannot be called on to delimit the possible intervocalic clusters defined over the $C_1C_2(C_3)$-string, a set of alternative hypotheses can be construed as to how these strings are organized, can be construed. The simplest one would be that only all or a subset of the combinations allowed postvocalically in a monovocalic root are allowed intervocalically in a bivocalic root. If this is the case, the constraint that only one consonant may be non-coronal must hold on intervocalic clusters as well. But it is also possible that other cluster types are allowed *in addition to* those found in monovocalic roots.

Let us first turn to the question whether all or only a subset of the postvocalic clusters are allowed. In roots at least, there are several of the types, specially those with clusters of three or four consonants, that are unattested intervocalically. For instance, the four-member string is not attested in roots, although derived examples are easily found, such as the infinitive [²mœn.strə] which can be derived from [¹mœn.stɽ]. In general, the types with a final sonorant found postvocalically in monovocalic roots can be accommodated intervocalically by the sonorant being syllabified as the onset to the final vowel. The only types that must be excluded systematically are those ending in obstruent + two sonorants. To construe a verb *hitlre* from *Hitler* is impossible.[48]

In addition, there are two types of attested intervocalic strings that do not occur postvocalically. The first is actually a more general type of a marginal string we found postvocalically, namely strings ending in /j/. While forms like [¹bærj] and [¹hæɽj] could be found postvocalically, we find in addition sequences of nasal plus /j/ ([²lin.jə], *linje* 'line') and obstruents plus /j/ ([²mid.jə], *midje* 'waist') intervocalically.

The second type is one consisting of two consonants, an obstruent + /m/. Thus we find [²ryt.mə], *rytme* 'rhythm'; [²fɛd.mə], *fedme* 'fatness'; [²brɔs.mə], *brosme* 'kind of fish' and [²dɔg.mə], *dogme* 'dogma'. This discrepancy between mono-vocalic and bivocalic roots *can* be ascribed to a syllabification constraint. While for example English and German allow syllabic non-coronal sonorants, as in English [¹riθm̩] *rhythm* (see for example Mohanan 1985) and German [¹geːbm̩] *geben*

---

[47] For example, *ap.skle, *pif.sve and *ram.kne are all excluded, even if each of the syllables making up the forms is well-formed.
[48] Whether the same actually is true for the three-sonorant type, I am not sure. There are no attested infinitives with this structure, but a form like ?*formle* is clearly pronounceable without an epenthetic vowel. A family name listed in the Oslo directory which would seem to belong to this category is *Amble*.

(Wiese 1996: 222), Norwegian only allows coronal sonorants as syllabic heads.[49] This constraint will block syllabification of /m/ as syllabic into *[¹ryt.tm̩], for example. The sonority difference between the obstruent and the /m/ will on the other hand preclude syllabification into a coda of a monosyllabic word *[¹rytm]. Inserted into a bivocalic root, however, such sequences can be syllabified because the sonorant will adjoin to the second vowel as an onset.

Note also that *dogme* represents a rare example of a cluster with more than one non-coronal consonant. Two further examples are *drakme* 'drachma' and *afganer* 'afghan'. All examples of this type are loan words.

---

[49] Except when derived by Nasal Place Assimilation. Thus underlying /opn-bar/ *åpenbar* 'evident', may be pronounced [²oː.pm̩.ˌbɑːr]. See Chapter 11.4.1 for further discussion.

4

WORD PHONOLOGY

In this chapter phonological rules which interact with morphology, but which are not triggered nor in a substantial way constrained by prosodic features, will be discussed. Rules conditioned by prosodic structure are mainly discussed in the chapters on prosody. Examples of such rules are Glide Formation (Chapters 2.3.1.2 and 5.7.2) and Mora Insertion and Mora Linking (Chapters 6.4.8 and 8.2). In Section 4.2 rules usually referred to as voice assimilations will be discussed. The subject of Section 4.3 is rules operating within the coronal node. Section 4.5 deals with a rule of consonant cluster simplification. It is preceded by a discussion of the relationship between [e] and [æ] (Section 4.4). Some minor vowel alternation patterns will be discussed in Section 4.6.

4.1 LEXICAL PHONOLOGY

Lexical Phonology (Kiparsky 1982, 1985; Kaisse and Shaw 1985; Mohanan 1986; Booij and Rubach 1987; Hargus and Kaisse 1993a and b; and Booij 1981, 1994) is a theory that seeks to derive a set of phonological generalizations from the interaction between phonology and morphology. The basic premise of the theory is that morphological rules and phonological rules interact, in the sense that morphological structure may influence the application of phonological rules and phonological structure may constrain the application of morphological rules. This means that when a given underived word has been subjected to syllabification and other applicable phonological rules, a morphological rule can apply to it. This creates a new domain to which phonological rules may apply. The result can then undergo another morphological rule, to which the same set of phonological rules may apply once more, and so on. Phonology and morphology in other words apply 'in tandem', as shown in (1), with the phonological rules applying in a cyclic fashion. A classic example of this interaction is stress assignment in many languages. While simplex words will be stress domains in their own right, the addition of an affix will often create a new domain to which the stress rule may reapply, either deleting the former stress or demoting it to a secondary stress.

Phonology not only interacts with morphology in the lexicon, where word structure is accounted for, but also with syntax on the postlexical level, where the phonological rules apply that take syntactic structure as input. So in a wider sense Lexical Phonology is a theory of how phonology interacts with other components of grammar. Lexical Phonology thus defines two main levels on which phonologi-

(1) *The structure of the lexicon*

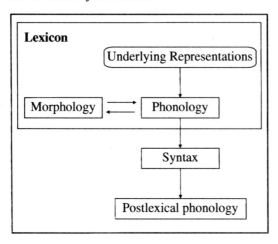

cal rules may apply—the lexicon, where it interacts with morphology, and the postlexical level, where it interacts with syntax. An important part of the theory is that both the rules and the conditions under which they apply may be different on the two levels.

   Rules that apply in the lexicon are usually seen as having special properties which postlexical rules will lack. (2) lists a set of properties that have commonly been seen as distinguishing between the two types of rules. As Hargus and Kaisse (1993b: 16) note, most of these assumptions have been contested in some way or other (see also Booij 1994 and Cole 1995), but I shall nevertheless use them as a starting point for the discussions that follow in the remaining sections of this chapter, in Chapter 7 on cyclic stress assignment, in Chapter 8 on cyclic syllabification, and in Chapter 11, where the postlexical, segmental phonology is treated.

(2) *Difference between lexical and postlexical rules*

Lexical rules	*Postlexical rules*
• apply within words	• apply across word and phrase boundaries
• may be cyclic	• apply once
• may have exceptions	• are exceptionless
• are structure preserving (neutralizing)	• are not structure preserving (allophonic)
• apply categorically	• may have gradient outputs

The basic difference is that lexical rules apply within words, while postlexical rules may apply across word boundaries. The property that links morphology and phonology in the lexicon is cyclicity. Phonological rules are cyclic when they take the output of morphological rules as their input, and therefore may (re)apply whenever a morphological rule has applied. They are then usually assumed to be subject to the Strict Cycle Condition (SCC), which requires that the sequence created by the morphological rule must figure in the environment for the phonological rule. Rules that can apply before morphology, such as syllabification and stress, must therefore be exempted from this requirement in some way. The solution usually appealed to is that only structure-changing rules are subject to the SCC.[1]

But not all lexical, phonological rules are cyclic in this sense. As pointed out in Booij and Rubach (1987), some lexical rules seem to apply at the end of the lexical derivation only, in a non-cyclic, across-the-board fashion. These are the so-called word-level rules, which then define yet another level within the lexicon in addition to the cyclic level.[2] Lexical Phonology thereby defines a minimum of three ordered levels of rule application, as shown in (3).

(3)   *Three levels of rule application*

   Cyclic level[3]
   Word level (postcyclic level)
   Postlexical level

Another property often connected with lexical rules is that they may have exceptions, while postlexical rules are assumed to be automatic, and therefore exceptionless. Structure Preservation means that lexical rules cannot produce segment types that are not already present in underlying structure. This means that the effect of lexical rules may be neutralizing, since the output will be present as a type already. Conversely, they may not be allophonic, since predictable allophones are not part of underlying structure. Allophones are therefore supposed to be derived postcyclically.

Finally, the output of lexical rules is assumed always to be discrete in the sense that a feature is either present or absent, or in the case of binary features, represented either by '+' or '−'. This will also be the case at the postlexical level, but here outputs may also be gradient in the sense that a specification may be multivalued. However, the importance of this point is unclear, since it presupposes that the dividing line between phonology and systematic phonetics can be drawn on independent grounds such that some gradient specifications still must be assigned to the phonology.

---

[1] See Cole (1995) for a critical discussion of the SCC.

[2] Booij (1994: 531f.) cites several examples of word-level rules, of which Final Devoicing in Dutch is one example. If this rule were cyclic, it would devoice the final stop in /held/ 'hero' on the first cycle. The result of adding the feminine suffix /-in/ is resyllabification of the final stop, which would then give *[heltin] instead of [heldin]. Only if Final Devoicing is applied after all cyclically-triggered syllabification rules have applied will the right surface form emerge. This is obtained if the rule is assumed to be a word-level rule, applying after all morphological rules have applied.

[3] The cyclic level is often assumed to be subdivided into strata (or sublevels). We shall return to the question whether such a subdivision is needed in Chapter 7.1.

4.2 CO-OCCURRENCE CONSTRAINTS ON
LARYNGEAL FEATURES

4.2.1 Theory

In current literature, two views are opposed with respect to the feature [voice]. The traditional view, dating back to the SPE-tradition, holds that it is a binary feature. This implies that both values may be active phonologically. Within under-specification theory, radical underspecification predicts that only one of them will be active in the early stages of the phonology of a given language, while contrastive underspecification would hold that both are necessary in underlying structure in languages where the feature is contrastive. Since the assimilation rules with respect to voice imply devoicing in Norwegian, [–voice] would seem to be the active value that must be specified in underlying structure.

However, a more recent view, see for example Mester and Itô (1989) and Lombardi (1994, 1995) holds that voicing should be captured phonologically by means of a privative feature [voice]. Only presence of voicing can be active phono-logically; in other words, only [voice] can spread. This means that devoicing, i.e. processes whereby an obstruent which is voiced in other environments is realized as voiceless when adjacent to another voiceless obstruent, cannot be interpreted as assimilation in terms of spreading. One must instead take recourse to licensing or markedness conditions on [voice], which will bar it from environments where the 'devoicing' effects can be observed.

In Lombardi's theory only obstruents may be specified for voice in underlying structure. Voicing in vowels and sonorants is redundant and introduced at a late level. Voiceless obstruents lack laryngeal features, and therefore a Laryngeal node altogether (Lombardi 1994: 28ff.). Languages where we find syllable or word final neutralization of voice have the following, positive licensing constraint, the Voice Constraint: [*voice*] *is only licensed in an obstruent if it stands before a* [*+son*] *segment in the same syllable*. This means that in the languages that have this constraint, [voice] cannot appear in codas, except when the feature is also linked to a following onset. As a result, [voice] is neutralized into absence of voice in environments where the feature is not licensed. Final devoicing, as found in German, Dutch and Polish, is seen to follow from this assumption.

Another feature of the theory is that languages may have a specific rule, Spread [voice], which spreads a Laryngeal node onto segments that lack it. This rule ac-counts for voicing assimilation. Since only [voice] is available for spreading, devoicing effects are interpreted as consequences of delinking due to the Voice Constraint. The third parametric option in the theory is Final Exceptionality: the Voice Constraint may be suspended with respect to word-final segments, but imple-mented elsewhere.

Lombardi's theory includes three laryngeal features, [voice], [asp(irated)] and [gl(ottalized)] (Lombardi 1995: 19), which are sisters under the Laryngeal node. In later sections of her 1994 book, the Voice Constraint is generalized into a Laryn-geal Constraint, that is, a constraint that restricts the appearance of laryngeal contrasts to presonorant positions. The constraint may be fully or partially active in some languages, while others will lack it.

In most Germanic languages aspiration occurs as a salient property of the voiceless series of stops. In analyses where [voice] is posited as contrastive, aspiration in the voiceless series must be introduced by an allophonic rule; see for example Kiparsky (1979). But the fact that aspiration plays a fundamental part in the phonetic realization of the 'voicing' contrast in these languages has led some analysts to propose that the underlying contrast should be captured by means of a feature that encodes this directly. Within this approach voicing would be an allophonic feature that would enhance the aspiration contrast by fully or partially voicing non-aspirated stops.[4] Iverson and Salmons (1995) propose that the basic laryngeal contrast in most Germanic languages should be captured by means of the privative feature [spread glottis]. This directly mirrors the glottal configuration that is supposed to cause aspiration, since moving the vocal cords together from a maximally spread position may require more time than the occluded phase of the stop articulation. A short period of silence will therefore occur after the release, before the vocal folds are sufficiently adduced for voicing to be possible.

The feature [spr. gl.] will block simultaneous voicing. Only segments not specified for [spr. gl.] may be phonetically voiced. But the feature does not cause phonetic aspiration in all environments where it is present. Since its non-compatibility with voicing depends on timing, a consonant cluster will give enough time to move the vocal cords together before the vowel articulation starts.[5] This explains why no aspiration is heard in /s/ + stop clusters, even if both members of the cluster are specified for [spr. gl.]. The lack of aspiration in stops after /s/ is in other words not connected with some specific property of /s/, but with the fact that the feature is linked to a cluster of obstruents. The prediction that follows from this is that segments that are singly linked to [spr. gl.] will be realized with the period of voicelessness characteristic of phonetic aspiration, while obstruent clusters where both members share the feature will lack it.

Iverson and Salmons (1995) point to another distributional property connected with the phonetic realization of [spr. gl.]. It is more prevalent in stressed onsets and in word initial position. This is captured by the principle that '[v]ocal fold abduction in syllable onsets is enhanced in relation to metrical prominence' (p. 378).

It follows that there is no one-to-one relationship between the presence of [spr. gl.] in phonological representations and phonetic aspiration. The latter will only occur when other requirements are met as well. When these are not met, [spr. gl.] will be realized as unaspirated or minimally aspirated voicelessness. Since segments which are not specified for [spr. gl.] in underlying structure will not be obligatorily voiced in surface structure, neutralizations are therefore predicted to occur.

---

[4] In some languages, such as Icelandic, voicing is phonetically absent in stops. Here the contrast rests solely on aspiration.
[5] This depends on the assumption that only one abduction of the vocal folds is involved also with respect to clusters.

4.2.2 Surface distribution of aspiration and voice in simplex words

In what follows I shall test the theories of Lombardi (1994, 1995) and Iverson and Salmons (1995) against the UEN data. It should be noted that there is no incompatibility between the two theories, since Lombardi also includes [asp] in her feature inventory. Her analysis of Klamath (Lombardi 1994: 83) assumes [asp] as the basic, contrastive feature in this language. The difference between the two theories is that Iverson and Salmons (1995) give the feature a clearer articulatory definition than Lombardi, who specifically states that features are abstracts that may be realized phonetically in different ways depending on language and environment (Lombardi 1994: 2ff.)

As shown in Chapter 2.1.2, UEN, as well as all other varieties of Norwegian, contrasts two series of stops, a voiceless, aspirated series [pʰ, tʰ, kʰ] with a (partially) voiced, unaspirated series [b, d, g].[6] The two series may contrast both in simple onsets and in clusters consisting of stop + sonorant. In codas the contrast is found in simple codas as well as in clusters of /r/ plus stop. When a stop immediately follows /s/, the contrast is neutralized in a voiceless, unaspirated stop. Norwegian therefore appears as prototypically 'Germanic' in terms of the theory of Iverson and Salmons.

The phonetic realization of aspiration and voicing is as follows: aspiration in the voiceless series is most prominent in single onset stops in stressed syllables. But aspiration is also audibly present in single intervocalic stops and single stops at word ends. Voice cannot co-occur with aspiration. Single, unaspirated stops are usually fully voiced intervocalically, and partially or fully voiced in onsets and codas. The unaspirated stop occurring after /s/ is always voiceless. In clusters consisting of two stops, such as /gd/ and /kt/, both stops are normally released.[7]

Examples are given in (4), where minimal pairs are shown on the same line. Note that either voicing or aspiration is redundant in the environments where the two series contrast.[8] One of them therefore seems to suffice in order to express the phonological contrast. Note also that the perceptual contrast seems to be based mainly on aspiration. If aspiration disappears, the result is indistinguishable from the unaspirated member of the contrast. Thus the underlying sequences /han##spil-r/ 'he plays' and /hans##bil-r/ 'his beetles' are homophonous, (= [hɑn.²spil.lɾ]), as mentioned in footnote 19 in Chapter 2.

Postvocalic obstruent clusters must be either voiced or voiceless; see Chapter 3.2.4.2. Thus we find [¹bygd], bygd 'rural community' and [¹frykt], frykt 'fear', but neither *[¹bygt] nor *[¹frykd]. Likewise, /f/ can only be combined with /t/, as in

---

[6] Fricatives are voiceless only, with the possible exception that some instances of /v/ and /j/ should be interpreted as [–son], cf. Chapters 2.3.2.3 and 3.2.4.4. There are no other contrasts involving laryngeal features, such as glottalization, in Norwegian.

[7] Non-released stops may occur in clusters, but not systematically; cf. Vanvik (1958).

[8] For simplicity reasons the phonological contrast will in most cases be encoded by means of symbols denoting voiced and voiceless segments. After /s/ the voiceless stop symbols are used. Lack of overtly marked aspiration on a voiceless stop or fricative should therefore not be taken to imply absence of aspiration in the pronunciation.

(4)   *Distribution of aspiration and voicing in stops*

['piːl] *pil* 'arrow'	['biːl] *bil* 'car'
['tɑm] *tam* 'domesticated'	['dɑm] *dam* 'dam'
['kʉt] *kutt* 'cut'	['gʉt] *gutt* 'boy'
['plɑs] *plass* 'place'	['blɑs] *blass* 'pale'
['trik] *trikk* 'tram'	['drik] *drikk* 'drink'
['krum] *krum* 'curved'	['grum] *grom* 'excellent'
['lɑp] *lapp* 'patch'	['lɑb] *labb* 'paw'
['mit] *mitt* 'my' (poss.)	['mid] *midd* 'mite'
['tryk] *trykk* 'print'	['tryg] *trygg* 'safe' (adj.)
['værp] *verp!* 'lay (an) egg!'	['værb] *verb* 'verb'
[²lʉn.tə] *lunte* 'fuse'	[²lʉn.də] *Lunde* (name)
['mɑrk] *mark* 'field'	[mɑrg] *marg* 'marrow'
['spoː] *spå* 'to predict'	
['stoː] *stå* 'to stand'	
['skuː] *sko* 'shoe'	
['jɛsp] *gjesp* 'yawn'	
['jɛst] *gjest* 'guest'	
['fisk] *fisk* 'fish'	
['rips] *rips* 'red currant'	*['ribs][9]
['ʋits] *vits* 'joke'	*['ʋids]
['lɑks] *laks* 'salmon'	*['lɑgs]

['sɑft], *saft* 'juice', while /ʋ/ combines with /d/ only, as in ['hɛʋd], *hevd* 'acquired right'.

There is one cluster type where this constraint is violated. Two words contain clusters of voiced plus voiceless stop. These are the name *Vidkun* ['ʋid.kʉn] and ['ʋɔd.kɑ], *vodka* (id.).[10] The fact that these may also be pronounced with voiceless coronal, ['ʋit.kʉn] and ['ʋɔt.kɑ], shows that the exception is marginal.[11]

Another distributional pattern connected with laryngeal features is found in sequences where a non-nasal sonorant (including [ʋ]) follows a voiceless stop or /f/. The sonorant is then fully or partially devoiced. The rule governing this distri-

---

[9]   But see footnote 31 below.

[10]   Due to the fact that *Vidkun* was the first name of prime minister Quisling of the German-controlled government during the occupation 1940–1945, it is hardly used today. It is an Old Norse name revived in the late nineteenth century. According to Lind (1905–1915) it is found with assimilated cluster [kk] in manuscripts from the fourteenth century on. The modern pronunciation is therefore directly based on Old Norse spelling. There are in addition two words listed in dictionaries, *idke* and *blidke*, both old derivations with a non-productive causative suffix /-k/. The first means 'anxiety' as a noun, and 'to be industrious, energetic' as a verb. *Blidke* means 'to make content'. These words are hardly in use, and most Norwegians are probably unaware of their existence. Due to this fact, they are likely to pronounce them by the letter when confronted with them, that is, as [²id.kə] and [²blid.kə]. As with *Vidkun*, the spellings are etymological, however, and it is significant that all pronunciations given in old dialect dictionaries such as Aasen (1873) and Ross (1895) have fully assimilated clusters, such as [²ik.kə] and [²blik.kə] or [²blig.gə].

[11]   Sigurd (1965: 113) lists the sequence as non-marginal in Swedish. His examples are *vodka, idka* and *blidka*, the latter two being the Swedish cognates of *idke* and *blidke* referred to in the previous footnote.

bution is constrained by the PWd, and I shall argue below that it must be post-lexical. But since an exhaustive analysis of the laryngeal phonology of Norwegian must include this pattern, it will be treated in this chapter. (A parallel process in English is used in Iverson and Salmons (1995) in support of their analysis of laryngeal contrasts in Germanic.)[12] Examples of this process are given in (5), where the effects of devoicing are shown in the left-hand column, and the environments where no devoicing takes place are exemplified in the right-hand column. Note that this devoicing will not be marked in transcriptions unless relevant for the problem under discussion.

(5)   *Progressive devoicing of non-nasal sonorants*[13]

/pris/ [¹pr̥iːs] 'price'	/bris/ [¹briːs] 'breeze'
/trakt/ [¹tr̥akt] 'funnel'	/drakt/ [¹drakt] 'attire'
/krev-e/ [²kr̥eː.və] 'to demand'	/greve/ [²greː.və] 'count'
/plas/ [¹pl̥as] 'place'	/blas/ [¹blas] 'pale'
/klu/ [¹kl̥uː] 'claw'	/glo/ [¹gluː] 'to stare'
/pjok/ [¹pço̥k] 'boy'	/bjørk/ [¹bjœrk] 'birch'
/tjen-r/ [²tçeː.n̥r̥] 'servant'	/djevl/ [²djeʋ.l̩] 'devil'
/tvil-e/ [²tf̥iː.lə] 'to doubt'	/dvel-e/ [²dʋeː.lə] 'to linger'
/kvan/ [¹kf̥an] 'angelica' (bot.)	/gvarv/ [¹gʋarʋ] (place name)
	/sprek/ [¹sprɛk] 'crack'
	/stro/ [¹stroː] 'straw'
	/skrut/ [¹skruːt] 'junk'
	/splejs/ [¹splæjs] 'splice'
	/spjer-e/ [²spjæː.rə] 'to rip'
	/stjene/ [²stjæː.ŋə] 'star'
	/skvis-e/ [²skʋiː.sə] 'to squeeze'
/fri/ [¹fr̥iː] 'free'	/vri/ [¹ʋriː] 'to wring'
/fly/ [¹fl̥yː] 'to fly'	/vladimir/ [¹ʋla.di.mir] (name loanwd.)
/fjen/ [¹fçæːn̥] 'far'	—
	/slo/ [¹sl̥oː] 'to beat'
	/svi/ [¹sʋiː] 'to scorch'

4.2.3 Alternations

4.2.3.1 Regressive devoicing[14]

The constraint against obstruent clusters with different laryngeal specifications is implemented in the morphology as well. Across word boundaries, in compounds

---

[12] Progressive devoicing in Norwegian is mentioned in passing, but not discussed in a systematic manner in the introductory chapter of Alnæs (1925). Kristoffersen (1982) represents an SPE-based analysis. Devoicing in Danish is briefly mentioned in Sweet (1873–74: 106f.).

[13] Most of the examples are taken from Kristoffersen (1982).

[14] Pending the analysis that follows below, I shall informally refer to the alternations involved as 'devoicing'.

as well as in the syntax, where any combination is possible, there are no assimilatory effects.

The adjectival agreement suffix /-t/ causes devoicing when added to a stem ending in /g/ or /ʋ/, such as /tryg/, *trygg* 'safe', /groʋ/, *grov* 'coarse' and /stiʋ/, *stiv* 'stiff'. Uninflected, these adjectives are pronounced ['tryg], ['groːʋ] and ['stiːʋ]. The suffix induces the surface forms ['trykt], ['grɔft] and ['stiːft]. Even if the suffix cannot be combined with all stems, the devoicing pattern is quite regular. There is at least one exception: the stem /gløg/, *gløgg* 'intelligent', which uninflected is pronounced ['glœg], surfaces without devoiced /g/, as ['glœgt], not *['glœkt].[15]

A much more complicated pattern emerges when we look at cohering suffixes, including clitics, beginning in /s/. The only productive element is the clitic /-s/, which denotes possession, and which attaches to the right edge of NPs.[16] The fact that this generally does not cause devoicing shows that it is not constrained by a prosodic constituent such as the PWd, it is in fact lexical.[17] (6) shows two examples of noun phrases where devoicing does not take place, even if the clitic is clearly part of the PWd defined by the stress on the host.[18]

(6) [ɛt. ˈlaŋt. ˈliːʋ.s æ.ˈfaː.riŋ]
     et langt livs erfaring
     a long life's experience

     [ɛn. ˈskuːg.s ˈaʋ.kast.niŋ]
     en skogs   avkastning
     a forest's yield

When the /-s/ suffix on the other hand represents the old genitive case marker /-s/ in idiomatic prepositional phrases headed by *til*, for example *til vanns* 'on water' and *til fjells* 'to the mountains', cf. *vann* 'water' and *fjell* 'mountain', we find devoicing and vowel shortening in stems ending in a voiced obstruent preceded by a long vowel. This is also the case when /s/ is used as linking phoneme in compounds where stems of this type appear as first member. Examples are given in (7).

(7) *Shortening and devoicing before lexicalized case marking /-s/*

     /liv/   [ˈliːʋ] *liv* 'life'
             [ˌsɛt.tə.ti.ˈlifs] *sette til livs* 'to eat'
             [ˈlif.sæ.ˌfaː.riŋ] *livserfaring* 'experience in life'

---

[15] I owe this example to Ove Lorentz (p.c.). Other examples, where devoicing may possibly be optional (Arne Torp p.c.), are /treg-t/, *tregt* 'slow' and /sløv-t/, *sløvt* 'blunt'.

[16] The clitic is mostly used in UEN and in dialects of the southern part of Southern Norway. Alternative constructions for expressing possession are available in all Norwegian dialects, see for example the relevant passages in Faarlund *et al.* (1997).

[17] The only exception that I am aware of is the proprium /gud/ 'God', which is pronounced [ˈguːd] in isolation. In phrases where it modifies another noun, such as *Guds bud* 'God's commandments', *Guds sønn* 'God's son', etc. we find vowel shortening and devoicing [ˈguts]. According to my own intuition, any combination involving attributive use gives shortening and devoicing, but if used alone as a predicative, as in *Denne er Guds* 'This is God's (= belongs to God), the pronunciation is [ˈguːds].

[18] The PWd is discussed in Chapter 7.3.2.

/skug/ ['skuːg] *skog* 'wood'
[ˌdrɑː.til.'skuks] *dra til skogs* 'go to the woods'
['skuk.sɑr.ˌbæj] *skogsarbeid* 'lumbering'

/lag/ ['lɑːg] 'team'
[ˌjøː.rə.ti.'lɑks] / [ˌjøː.rə.ti.'lɑːgs] *gjøre til lags* 'to satisfy somebody'
['lɑːg.sɑr.ˌbæj] *lagsarbeid* 'team work'

/ʋeg/ ['ʋɛg] 'wall'
[ˌsɛt.tə.til.'ʋɛgs] (*[til.'ʋɛks]) *sette til veggs* 'drive into a corner'

/fut/ ['fuːt] 'foot'
[til.futs] *til fots* 'on foot'

Note the stem /ʋeg/, with short vowel. Here devoicing does not take place. It therefore seems as if devoicing is dependent on shortening. Shortening can on the other hand take place independently of devoicing, as shown by the stem /fut/, where the necessary condition for devoicing is not present.

Another idiom where the stem vowel is short and where devoicing does not apply is the adverb [²fɔ.ˌlɔds] *forlodds*, 'in advance', which consists of the noun [²fɔ.ˌlɔd], *forlodd* 'advance' and the genitive marker. However, these are the only short voweled stems I have been able to find which may combine /s/ in idioms or compounds, so this generalization is not founded on a solid amount of data.

A non-productive derivational suffix which induces devoicing is the nominalising /-sl/ which attaches to verbal and adjectival stems. (8) contains the four relevant examples that I have found. Note especially that the short-voweled stem /red/ here in fact induces devoicing. There are no exceptions in this environment, that is, stems ending in a voiced obstruent where devoicing has not applied.

(8)   *Examples of /-sl/ derivations with devoicing*

/fød/   [²føː.də] *føde* 'to give birth'   ['fœt.sl̩] *fødsel* 'birth'
/triʋ/   [²triː.ʋəs] *trives* 'to thrive'   ['trif.sl̩] *trivsel* 'well-being'
/blyg/   ['blyːg] *blyg* 'shy'   ['blyk.sl̩] *blygsel* 'shyness'
/red/   ['rɛd] *redd* 'afraid'   ['rɛt.sl̩] *redsel* 'fear'

Yet another suffix which at least historically has induced devoicing is the superlative marker /-st/ when added to stems ending in the derivational suffix written -*lig*. This suffix should be listed with two allomorphs, /-lik/ and /-li/, where the first appears when followed by the superlative suffix. Thus *vanlig*, 'common' is pronounced [²ʋɑːn.li] in all environments except when the superlative /-st/ suffix is added. In that case the pronunciation is ['ʋɑːn.likst]. Since there is no robust alternation involving a voiced stop in any variety of UEN, there seems to be no reason to assume an underlying /g/, even if this complies with the historical form.[19] But if independent evidence for an underlying /g/ were found, the /k/ that appears in the

---

[19] We shall return to the analysis of this suffix in Chapter 7.3.8.

surface before the superlative marker could be analysed as the result of devoicing. In this environment devoicing would also be exceptionless.

A final environment where devoicing can be found is in patronymics, which as a type is very common in Norway. Patronymics are created by means of the suffix [-sn̩], spelled *-sen*. When the syllable to which the suffix attaches is unstressed, devoicing seems to be the rule. Thus we find [²dɑː.ʋit.sn̩], *Davidsen* and [¹kɔn. rɑt.sn̩], *Konradsen*, built on the stems [²dɑː.ʋid] *David* and [¹kɔn.rad] *Konrad*. I have, however, been unable to find clear examples of devoicing and/or shortening in monosyllabic, and hence stressed, stems. For some reason, monosyllabic names ending in a voiced obstruent are rare so we may be dealing with an accidental gap.[20]

Summing up, we see that regressive devoicing before /s/, but not before /t/, shows a rather irregular pattern. This irregularity represents additional support for the claim made above that regressive devoicing is lexical.

A related process, which is quite regular, but not neutralizing since it applies to sonorants, is the (full or partial) devoicing of /r/ that takes place when a voiceless, non-coronal obstruent follows. Thus the adjective /skarp/ 'sharp' and the nouns /kork/ 'cork' and /ʂerf/ 'scarf' are pronounced [¹skɑɾ̥p], [¹kɔɾ̥k] and [¹ʂæɾ̥f] respectively. Nasals and /l/ are not affected by this rule, and neither are the glides /j/ and /w/. Nor is the latter devoiced when hardened into [ʋ] in the diphthong /ew/. Thus /newt/, *naut* 'cow' may be pronounced [¹næwt] or [¹næʋt], but not *[¹næft].[21]

4.2.3.2 Alternations in verb inflection

Another morphological pattern which shows alternations with respect to laryngeal features is the pronunciation of the preterite suffix /-Te/ and the past participle /-t/, which are used with one of the two major classes of weak verbs. (The capital letter signifies that the segment may be realized as voiced or voiceless depending on the final segment of the stem.)[22] When the stem ends in an obstruent, including /ʋ/, the resulting cluster will agree in voicing. In stems ending in [+son] segments the following pattern appears: after stems ending in vowels and glides we find [d], after stems ending in sonorants we find [t]. Examples are given in (9).

[20] The name *Knudsen* is invariably pronounced [¹knʉt.sn̩], but despite the spelling, the stem is always pronounced [¹knʉːt], never *[¹knʉːd].

[21] Due to the facts that the rule does not apply to /l/, that the duration of /r/ in UEN is very short and that the Retroflex Rule will have changed sequences of /rt/ and /rs/ into retroflexes in all environments, the rule is less conspicuous in UEN than in other Norwegian dialects. In southern and western dialects with uvular /r/ and no Retroflex Rule, its output is a very audible voiceless velar or uvular fricative. Northern dialects, from Trondheim and northwards, have palatalized or palatal /l/ after short vowels, which is turned into a voiceless lateral fricative before a voiceless stop, and /r/, which phonetically tends to be a voiced retroflex fricative in these dialects, is turned into voiceless [ʂ] before /p/ and /k/. Devoicing of non-palatal /l/ is found in the rural dialects spoken in the northernmost regions of Central Southern Norway (Arne Torp, p.c.).

[22] See the sketch of the verb inflectional system in Chapter 3.1.4.

(9)   *Voicing alternations in the preterite /-Te/ and participle /-T/ suffixes*

Stem	Gloss	Preterite	Past Participle
/sy-/	'sew'	[²syd.də]	[¹syd]
/kna-/	'knead'	[²knɑd.də]	[¹knɑd]
/bøj-/	'bend'	[²bœj.də]	[¹bœjd]
/føl-/	'feel'	[²føːl.tə]	[¹føːlt]
/hør-/	'hear'	[²hœt̪.tə]	[¹hœt̪]
/pin-/	'torture'	[²piːn.tə]	[¹piːnt]
/døm-/	'judge'	[²dœm.tə]	[¹dœmt]
/sleŋ-/	'throw'	[²ʂl̪ɛŋ.tə]	[¹ʂl̪ɛŋt]
/prøʋ-/²³	'try'	[²prœʋ.də]	[¹prœʋd]
/byg-/	'build'	[²byg.də]	[¹bygd]
/brʉk-/	'use'	[²brʉk.tə]	[¹brʉkt]
/slip-/	'hone'	[²ʂl̪iːp.tə]	[¹ʂl̪iːpt]
/ʋis-/	'show'	[²ʋiː.stə]	[¹ʋiːst]

4.2.4 Analysis

Regressive devoicing of obstruents and the alternation found with respect to the preterite /-Te/ and the participle /-T/ suffixes have clear lexical properties. They are triggered by morphology, and the output conforms with constraints that hold for simplex words, but not across word boundaries. Two other properties, the facts that they are neutralising and have exceptions support the analysis that they are lexical. Progressive devoicing, and regressive devoicing when it applies to sonorants, are less clear with respect to their status as lexical or postlexical. Their outputs are allophonic, since there is no underlying laryngeal contrast in sonorants, they are exceptionless, and possibly gradient in that only part of the sonorant may surface as voiceless. Progressive devoicing is apparently not constrained by the prosodic word.²⁴ No devoicing takes place across PWd boundaries in regressive devoicing of sonorants, however. This holds not only for UEN, but for all the varieties of the rule that I am aware of in any Norwegian dialect.

   Given that all the alternations and distributional patterns seem to involve the same type of laryngeal alternation which I informally have referred to as devoicing, we must now ask what kind of featural specification of the laryngeal node will allow for a maximally coherent analysis of the data. As mentioned above, only one feature seems to be called for, since there is only one laryngeal contrast to be captured. Ideally, the feature selected to represent this contrast should also allow us to account

---

²³ [²ɔf.tə] from /lov-/ 'promise' is exceptional. Due to the distribution of verbs over the two main inflectional classes described in Chapter 3.1.4, stems ending in voiced obstruents that select /-Te/ are rather rare.

²⁴ Cf. the phrase *Et langt liv* 'a long life', which may be pronounced [ɛ.¹t̪l̥ɑɳt.¹liːʋ], and possibly also [ɛ.¹t̪l̥ɑɳt.¹l̥iːʋ]. This point needs further investigation.

coherently for all the distributional patterns presented in the previous section.

Two privative candidates will be considered: [voice] and [asp]. I shall use the latter as a cover term for the phonological property that manifests itself as aspiration in prevocalic, voiceless stops, and that is claimed by Iverson and Salmons (1995) to underlie the laryngeal contrast found in obstruents in most Germanic languages. The reason why I want to avoid the term 'spread glottis' is that this may well be a necessary physiological condition for the phonetic realization of the feature, but since timing of the glottal abduction with respect to the supralaryngeal articulatory movements must also be controlled, spread glottis cannot be seen as a sufficient condition. The distinction is not a trivial one: below, I shall argue that /s/ lacks [asp], even if it is articulated with spread glottis.

One argument that the underlying feature in Norwegian should be [asp] and not [voice] is the clear parallel between the distribution of aspiration in prevocalic stops and progressive devoicing of sonorants. If we assume that [asp] at the stage where the rule applies is present in all stops before vowels and sonorants, the devoicing of the latter can be accounted for by spreading this feature onto the sonorants.[25] But the fact that progressive devoicing seems to be postlexical does not force us to assume that [asp] is the underlying feature. We might also assume that the spreading takes place after the redundant [asp] feature has been inserted on obstruents not being specified for [voice].

A more radical solution, which eliminates the need for [asp] in the analysis, would be to assume that absence of [voice] on a preceding obstruent will block insertion of voice on the sonorant. But besides the fact that this will categorically 'devoice' sonorants in this environment, it will give the wrong result in connection with /s/.[26] As can be seen from (5), devoicing does not take place after /s/. This means that /s/ is special in some way. Within an [asp]-based analysis, this property can be assumed to be absence of [asp]. Hence there will be nothing to spread. In a [voice]-based analysis, a parallel solution is not available. Since /s/ clearly is voiceless in Norwegian, it would be completely ad hoc to specify it with [voice] in order to block devoicing of following sonorants. I therefore conclude that [asp] is necessary in order to account for the progressive devoicing pattern in (5). At the stage

---

[25] This raises the question of how 'aspirated' sonorants should be interpreted phonetically. They are certainly not characterized by a moment of silence before the following segment, as in obstruents. But this problem may be a superficial effect of how aspiration is conceptualized. Phonetically, aspiration can be seen as a property that is realized at the boundary between an obstruent and a [+son] segment. When the latter is a vowel, aspiration is by convention interpreted as a property of the obstruent. When it is a sonorant, as in the present case, co-articulation facts force us to interpret it as part of the sonorant. But the same interpretation is surely available also in the case of vowels, since from an articulatory point of view, prevocalic aspiration is a moment of voicelessness otherwise characterized by the same vocal tract configuration as the following vowel. Aspiration can therefore be given a more general, phonetic interpretation if it is seen as a period of voicelessness during the initial phase of the [+son] segment that follows the triggering obstruent. This means that even if, phonologically, aspiration can be seen as a property of the obstruent, its phonetic interpretation is not so clear.

[26] /s/ and /f/ are the only fricatives that can appear in obstruent + sonorant clusters. /s/ is pronounced [ʂ] before /l/; see Section 4.3.8 below.

where devoicing takes place, voiceless obstruents and /f/ are specified as aspirated, while /s/ will lack this feature.

Note that these data do not accord with the English data given in Iverson and Salmons (1995), where /s/ *does* devoice a following sonorant. The fact that /s/ does not induce aspiration when combined with a sonorant in Norwegian makes English and Norwegian different on this point. It is perhaps significant that /s/ has a voiced counterpart in English, but not in Norwegian. Laryngeal setting is therefore fully predictable with respect to /s/ in Norwegian, it surfaces as phonetically voiceless in all environments. Hence it may be assumed to be unspecified with respect to laryngeal features in underlying structure as well as in surface structure. It will lack [voice] because it is never realized as voiced, and it will lack [asp] because it does not devoice a following sonorant. This provides us with an alternative explanation of the lack of aspiration in s + stop clusters. Since obstruent clusters must agree in their specification of laryngeal features, an unviolable constraint against [asp] on /s/, whether singly or doubly linked, will block its appearance in clusters with /s/ as well.

While this solution will derive the progressive devoicing facts in a simple manner, it will complicate the analysis of *regressive devoicing*. If /s/ is unspecified with respect to laryngeal features, the fact that it *does* seemingly induce regressive devoicing becomes harder to explain. Since regressive devoicing has characteristics which clearly identify it as a lexical rule, we may assume that only the contrastive feature is present when the rule applies.

Let us for the moment revert to the hypothesis that this feature is [voice]. The devoicing effect of /t/ and /s/ must then be analysed as delinking of [voice] in a stem-final obstruent when the suffix-initial obstruent lacks [voice]. This will make the output meet the co-occurrence constraint against different specifications of laryngeal features in clusters found in simplex words, but it does not explain why we do not get spreading of voice from the stem instead. In other words, we lack an explanation why the input /tryg-t/ is turned into ['trykt] and not *['trygd], which is well-formed and in fact an attested word.

Devoicing of /r/ also seems hard to account for under this approach, since /r/ as a sonorant is unspecified for [voice] at this level. But if we assume that this part of the rule is postlexical, constrained by the PWd, we may conceive this as a constraint on the insertion of [voice] on /r/ if followed by a voiceless obstruent. Note that the assumption that /s/ is different from /t/ in not being specified for [asp] does not create any problems under this analysis, since it is absence of [voice] in the suffix that triggers delinking in the stem.

Under the alternative analysis, assuming underlying [asp], this is harder to account for. The derivation from /tryg-t/ into ['trykt] would now follow from the assumption that [asp] spreads onto the unspecified, stem-final obstruent. Since /s/ is not specified for [asp], spreading cannot be generalized to obstruent + s clusters, however. But due to the much greater degree of lexicalization in connection with /s/, this may not be totally unjustified. As shown above, devoicing of a preceding obstruent only occurs in connection with non-productive suffixes. The idiomatic phrasal frame constituted by the preposition *til* and the old genitive marker is used with a limited set of nouns. The same holds for the use of /s/ as a linking phoneme in compounds, and as shown in (7), not all obstruent-final nouns will undergo devoicing in these environments. The alternations involved can therefore clearly be accounted for by listing the alternative forms in the lexicon.

/r/ also represents a problem for the hypothesis that regressive devoicing before /s/ is lexicalized. While obstruents are devoiced in the irregular fashion shown above, /s/ seems to cause a preceding /r/ to devoice in those dialects where this is a possible surface cluster. (Due to the Retroflex Rule, it is merged into [ʂ] in all East and North Norwegian dialects.) In West Norwegian devoicing is regular, how-ever, and there seems to be no difference between /f/ and /s/ in this respect. This poses a serious problem for any analysis that tries to deduct the different behaviour of /s/ and /f/ in progressive devoicing from the assumption that /s/ is unspecified for laryngeal features even at the postlexical level, where progressive devoicing seems to apply.

Returning now to the main question, it can be concluded that regressive devoicing does not provide crucial data that allow us to choose between [asp] and [voice] as the underlying contrastive features. Analyses of regressive devoicing can be built on both assumptions, given the additional assumption that devoicing before /s/ is a result of lexical marking instead of a rule. Let us therefore now turn to the variation found in the realization of the preterite and past participle markers /-Te/ and /-T/ as given in (9).

If the underlying feature is [voice], the suffix may have the feature or lack it. If it is underlyingly voiced, the forms with stems ending in vowels and voiced obstru-ent follow directly. I shall argue in a moment that the voicelessness in the sonorant final stems is due to the co-occurrence restriction given as (18) in Chapter 3, the *Postvocalic *Shared Place Constraint*. This leaves us for now with the stems end-ing in voiceless obstruent. Since the suffix surfaces with its voiceless allomorph, these forms must be analysed as the result of delinking after obstruents lacking [voice].

The alternative, that the suffix is unspecified for [voice], is not viable on the assumption that sonorants are unspecified for [voice], since the fact that the suffix appears as voiced after vowels cannot then be accounted for. The forms with obstruent-final stems can be accounted for by spreading from the stem when the stem ends in a voiced obstruent, however.

If we instead assume that [asp] is underlying, the correct distribution is most straightforwardly obtained if the suffix lacks the feature. In that case the voicing after vowels follows directly, the voiceless allomorph after sonorants will fall out from the co-occurrence constraint that we shall discuss in a moment, the voicing after voiced (= non-aspirated) obstruents will follow automatically and the voice-lessness after stems ending in voiceless (= aspirated) can be accounted for by spreading of [asp] from the stem. The converse assumption, that the suffix stop is underlyingly [asp], presupposes delinking after vowel-final stems.

As just mentioned, the fact that the suffix is voiceless after stems ending in

sonorants may be connected with the phonotactic well-formedness constraint
*Postvocalic *Shared Place Constraint* stated as (18) in Chapter 3.2.4.1. This constraint, which forbids sequences of /l, m, n, ŋ/ plus a voiced stop in word-final
position, would effectively rule out participle forms with voiced suffix after
sonorant-final stems.[27] Historically, this constraint also applied to intervocalic clusters, but as noted in Chapter 3, a considerable number of loan words with intervocalic clusters of this type violate the constraint in present day Norwegian. However,
it seems that the constraint still holds for intervocalic clusters in verbs and adjectives. While there are many nouns with intervocalic clusters of this type, such as
[²bil.də], *bilde* 'picture' and [²rʉn.də], *runde* 'round', there are only a few infinitives with such clusters.[28] For example, the verb corresponding to the noun *runde*
has the same spelling, but is pronounced [²rʉn.nə], 'to make round'. Since the same
holds for the definite agreement form *runde* of the adjective [¹rʉn], *rund* 'round',
we may infer that the constraint that holds on the verbal and adjectival roots such
as /rʉn/ continues to hold in derived forms and therefore blocks preterite forms
such as *[²piːn.də] and *[²føːl.də].[29]

Summing up, we see that technically it is possible to develop analyses based on
underlying [asp] as well as [voice]. But there is an important difference between
the two approaches. While the analyses based on [asp] in most cases imply that the
alternations are accounted for by feature spreading, the analyses based on [voice]
imply a considerable degree of delinking in order to obtain the correct surface distribution. A common requirement of an underlying phonological feature, both in
underspecification analyses and in analyses involving privative features, is that it
is phonologically active. If degree of 'activity' is measured in a feature's ability to
cause changes in a given structure, either by forcing incompatible features to delink
or by spreading, there can be no doubt that [asp] in the above analyses comes out
as the more active compared with [voice].

Example (10) shows the consequences of the two solutions with respect to
spreading vs. delinking. For progressive and regressive devoicing the underlying
specification follows from the choice of feature, while the suffix may be specified
as either having the feature or being unspecified for it. This gives four possible
solutions with respect to the suffix. An inspection of the table shows that if [voice]
is chosen as underlying, [asp] is still needed in order to account for progressive
devoicing. Regressive devoicing must be accounted for by delinking, while the
preterite and past participle pattern require delinking if [voice] is present in the
suffix, and insertion in one environment and spreading in another if it is absent.

---

[27] /r/ again represents an exception; cf. (17) in Chapter 3.

[28] I have found four infinitives in fairly common use with such clusters in Norsk Termbank (1986).
These are *synde*, 'to sin', *avhende* and *innynde*, both particle compounds meaning 'to sell' and 'to
ingratiate' respectively, and *ånde*, 'to breathe'. All except *innynde* are listed as varying between [n] and
[nd] in Berulfsen (1969).

[29] The suffix may be voiced after sonorants in some West Norwegian dialects. The fact that word-
final clusters of sonorant + voiced stop are preserved in these dialects supports my analysis, but a systematic investigation of co-occurrence patterns between voiced suffix and preserved clusters in these
dialects is lacking.

(10)   *Consequences of assuming either [voice] or [asp] as contrastive feature*

	/-T/	Progressive devoicing	Regressive devoicing
[voice] is the underlying feature		Requires additional specification of [asp]	Suffix is *unspecified*: delinking in stem-final voiced obstruent
[voice] present in suffix	Delinking after voiceless obstruent		
[voice] absent in suffix	Insertion after vowel. Spreading from stem-final voiced obstruent		
[asp] is the underlying feature		Spreading from aspirated obstruents onto sonorants	Suffix is *specified*: spreading from suffix onto stem final, unaspirated obstruent
[asp] present in suffix	Delinking after vowel and after voiced obstruent in stem		
[asp] absent in suffix	Spreading from stem-final [asp] obstruent		

If [asp] is posited as underlying, both progressive and regressive devoicing can be analysed as spreading. On the assumption that the T-suffix is unspecified for the feature, we can further capture also this alternation pattern as spreading. I therefore conclude that the optimal analysis, i.e. the analysis that is able to give substance to the assumption that underlying features are phonologically active, is the one where [asp] is considered as the relevant feature for capturing the phonological structure behind laryngeal activity.

The rules involved can now be provisionally stated as in (11) and (12).[30] The restriction that (11) applies only within prosodic words is necessary in order to block it from applying across compound boundaries.

Two sets of data cannot be accounted for by these rules, however, namely regressive devoicing of sonorants and lexicalized devoicing caused by /s/.

Regressive devoicing of sonorants can be accounted for by a postlexical, regres-

---

[30] The fact that devoicing in many cases will not be total can perhaps be accounted for by assuming that redundant [voice] has been inserted in sonorants prior to the application of (12). Their mutual incompatibility, combined with the fact that [asp] is linked to the previous segment as well, will secure that the two features are realized sequentially. Note also that nasals are not targets, but on the assumption that Nasal is privative, this restriction cannot be expressed directly by the rule.

(11)   [asp]-*spreading* (*mirror image*)

Domain: lexical, postcyclic, PWd

(12)   *Progressive devoicing*

Domain: postlexical

sive only version of (11) where the target is specified as [+son, −nas] and, depending on dialect, [−lat]. However, this will not account for the fact that /s/ may also induce this type of postlexical devoicing. In UEN, where only /r/ is subject to the rule, this is no problem, since sequences of /rs/ are merged into [ʂ] by the Retroflex Rule, bleeding devoicing. But in other dialects postlexical devoicing of sonorants caused by /s/ cannot be accounted for if we assume that /s/ is unspecified for laryngeal features altogether.

The analysis can also not account for devoicing of obstruents caused by /s/ in the lexicon. As noted above, we might perhaps analyse this type of devoicing as lexicalized, since it is found in idioms and lexicalized compounds only and since it has exceptions even in this restricted class of environments. But it is still a fact that the ban against voiced obstruent + /s/ is unviolated in simplex words. A recently introduced name of a food store chain, *Obs*, is invariably pronounced [¹ups] (or [¹ɔps]), never *[¹ubs], despite the spelling.

With respect to derived environments within PWds, we lack a real test, because there is no really productive inflectional suffix /-s/. But English loan words sometimes retain a plural /-s/. In many cases, this is obviously interpreted as part of the root, as in *en caps*, 'a cap' (headwear). But in others it signifies 'plural', a few words, such as scone, in fact take /-s/ as plural marker in the official norm. Words of the latter type where the stem ends in a voiced obstruent might be used as data. But the fact that these words for most people are clearly English, may very well induce an English pronunciation, given the fact that the majority of Norwegian speakers today have at least a rudimentary knowledge of English. So when (*spare*) *ribs* is pronounced [¹ribs],[31] it is unclear whether this is loan word pronunciation or expected Norwegian pronunciation because the principle that postvocal obstruent

---

[31] The Norwegian word is [²rib.bə], *ribbe*, so speakers should clearly be able to identify the /-s/ as a plural marker in *ribs*.

clusters must share laryngeal features is no longer an active constraint in Norwegian. The fact that a form such as [til.¹vɛgs] already exists makes it impossible to exclude this interpretation.

The picture that emerges is therefore rather unclear. But even if an analysis based on monovalent laryngeal features and lexical prespecification of exceptions can be worked out for UEN, we should look for alternatives that do not exclude these data as exceptions and which at the same time are able to encompass other dialects. One alternative would be to return to the assumption that [voice] is binary.[32] Assuming underspecification, voiceless stops and fricatives could then be posited as [–voice] underlyingly. By substituting [–voice] for [asp] in (11), as shown in (13), the lexical alternations are then accounted for.

(13)   [–voice]-spreading (mirror imag

Given underspecification of [+voice], this rule is structure-filling in that it inserts the feature on roots which are previously not specified for the feature. If insertion of [+voice] takes place at the end of the lexical level, we derive the fact that the clitic /-s/ never causes desonorization. Lack of desonorization before /s/ in the lexicon might likewise be accounted for by assuming that stem-final obstruents that do not undergo regressive devoicing are exceptionally specified as [+voice] in the lexical representation of the exceptional items, which would block spreading (see Inkelas and Cho, 1993).

Progressive devoicing is not spreading of [–voice], but [asp], as stated in (12) above. On the assumption that [asp] is a redundant feature that is inserted on voiceless stops which are not part of clusters and non-strident fricatives, progressive devoicing can be conceived of as postlexical spreading of [asp] onto following non-nasal sonorants, whose ability to mask the [+voice] specification is gradient.

4.3 THE PHONOLOGY OF CORONALS

We now turn to the complex pattern of alternations found in coronal consonants.[33] The coronal segments, repeated from Chapter 2.3.2.2, are given in (14), with the

---

[32] Another solution, which would save [voice] as a privative feature, would be to exclude /s/ from the class of triggers in (12) by invoking an additional feature, [–strident]. /s/ could then be specified as [asp], and the feature would be able to spread by (11). In (12) however, the class of triggers would have to be specified as [–strident]. But this seems arbitrary; there is no apparent reason why stridency should be relevant for laryngeal activity.

[33] In addition to the rules discussed in this section, a minor rule assimilating /n/ to a following /ʂ/ will be briefly discussed in Chapter 11.4.2.

palatals /ç, j/ omitted since they do not participate in the alternations that we shall analyse in this section. The distribution is to a considerable extent predictable, and in this section I shall show that much of it can be accounted for by assuming a rule complex that I shall refer to as the Retroflex Rule, which merges clusters of /r/ or /ɽ/ plus unmarked coronals into corresponding apicals. I shall argue that the Retroflex Rule does not apply in non-derived environments. Instead, lexical items which formerly contained such clusters are assumed have underlying apicals in the synchronic grammar.

(14)   *Coronal segments*

	Laminal (denti-alveolar)					Apical (retroflex)						
	t	d	s	n	l	ṭ	ḍ	ṣ	ṇ	ḷ	ɽ	r
Posterior											✓	
Apical						✓	✓	✓	✓	✓	✓	✓

4.3.1 Distribution

The laminal series /t, d, s, n l/ represents the unmarked series of coronals, that is, the series with the widest distribution. However, the tables (18) and (25) in Chapter 3 show that surface combinations of /r/ and /t, s, n, l/ are non-occurring in simplex words, while combinations of /r/ and /d/ do occur. A form such as [¹svæɾd], *sverd* 'sword' is in other words well-formed, while the pronunciations *[¹svɑɾt], *[¹væɾs], *[¹bɑrn] and *[¹jɑrl] for orthographic *svart* 'black', *vers* 'verse', *barn* 'child' and *jarl* 'earl' do not occur in normal UEN speech. These words are instead pronounced [¹svɑṭ], [¹væṣ], [¹bɑːṇ] and [¹jɑːḷ].[34] With only a few marginal exceptions concerning *rl* and *rn*, orthographic sequences of /r/ + /t, s, n, l/ are pronounced in this way in underived contexts.[35]

Across morphological and syntactic boundaries all sequences of /r, ɽ/ plus unmarked coronals, including /d/, are merged into apical [ṭ, ḍ, ṣ, ṇ, ḷ]. The apical series is therefore found in non-derived environments where we historically find /rt, rs, rn, rl/, and in derived environments where /r/ or /ɽ/ is combined with /t, d, s, n, l/.[36]

---

[34] 'Split' pronunciation of these sequences is regarded as part of the stage language, but few actors manage to suppress the merged cluster consistently, and such suppression is mostly found, as far as I have been able to observe, in non-derived environments and in some derivations.

[35] The retroflex flap cannot occur before unmarked coronals in non-derived contexts. Its historical origin is either /l/ or /rð/. With respect to /rð/, no three-consonant cluster of the form /rðC/ was ever possible in non-derived contexts, and with respect to the lateral, only the lateral realization occurs adjacent to an unmarked coronal. Thus /salt/, *salt* (id.) can only be realized as [¹salt].

[36] The exceptional behaviour of /d/ in non-derived environments is restricted to the central parts of East Norway. Outside this area, but within the geographical domain of the Retroflex Rule, which extends over the eastern part of South Norway all the way north to the Russian border, historic /d/ is targeted also in non-derived environments. Here, the pronunciation of *sverd* is therefore [¹svæḍ].

4.3.2 The Retroflex Rule: postlexical or cyclic?

Since the apical segments are present in simplex words as well as in derived environments, the normal strategy would be to assume underlying clusters in roots also, and then assume the Retroflex Rule to be a postlexical rule applying to all relevant clusters irrespective of their status as derived or non-derived. But this maximally simple analysis is problematic, because the rule is not exceptionless in non-derived contexts. First of all there are the numerous /rd/ clusters, as in *sverd*. Exceptions involving other coronals are the man's name [²stʉr.lɑ], *Sturla* and [²nɔr.nə], *norne* 'norn', which may also occur with assimilated pronunciations, [²stʉː.ɭɑ] and [²nuː.ɳə]. Also foreign names, such as those of the Swedish painter *Anders Zorn* and the former Indonesian president *Soeharto*, may be pronounced with unassimilated clusters. If the Retroflex Rule were a postlexical rule, exceptions like this would not be expected, since only lexical rules are expected to have exceptions.

Complicating matters further is the fact that even the /rd/-exception is not exceptionless, since the male name *Bård* is pronounced [¹boːɖ], or [¹boːr]. More interesting is the fact that split pronuciation of /rd/ is governed by stress. After a stressed vowel we almost always find only [rd] and rarely [ɖ], while in unstressed vowels the opposite holds. Here we invariably find [ɖ], while [rd] is not possible. Thus we find obligatory [fɔ.¹ɖiː], *fordi* 'because', and [gɑ.¹ɖiːn], *gardin* 'curtain'. This pattern is also reflected in alternations. The word *garde*, 'guard' is pronounced [²gɑr.də], while the derived *gardist*, 'guardsman', where stress is moved to the suffix, is pronounced [gɑ.¹ɖist]. An example where stress is moved to the vowel preceding the /rd/ sequence is the male name *Edvard* and the corresponding female name *Edvarda*. The former is pronounced [¹ɛd.ʋɑɖ] (or [¹ɛd.ʋɑʈ]), and the latter [ɛd.¹ʋɑr.dɑ].

While a postlexical rule cannot deal with patterns such as these, they can be accounted for if we assume that the Retroflex Rule applies in derived environments only. Apicals in non-derived environments would then have to be underlying, so that for example the adjective [¹sʋɑʈ], *svart* would have the underlying form /sʋɑʈ/. *Sverd* would on the other hand be underlyingly /sverd/. On this assumption, the non-application of the rule in tautomorphemic sequences of /rd/ follows without stipulation. Exceptions concerning other clusters such as in *Sturla*, where apical is not obligatory, can be handled by assuming alternative underlying forms, /stʉrla/ and /stʉɭa/. At the same time, exceptions such as [¹boːɖ], *Bård*, can be handled by assuming that the apical is underlying.

This solution entails that the Retroflex Rule must apply cyclically in the lexicon, since the erasure of morphological brackets at the end of the cyclic level would make non-derived and derived clusters indistinguishable. The only problematic cases which cannot be accounted for directly are those where [rd] alternates with [ɖ] governed by stress. The cases where the root is pronounced with a cluster, such as in [²gɑr.də]/[gɑ.¹ɖist] would require an extended definition of 'derived environment' in order to make the rule apply in the latter, while the [¹ɛd.ʋɑɖ]/[ɛd.¹ʋɑr.dɑ] case cannot be handled at all on the assumption that the Retroflex Rule is cyclic. A solution to this problem will be proposed in Section 4.3.6 below.

4.3.3 The distribution of the retroflex flap

As pointed out in Chapter 2.1.2.4, the status of the retroflex flap as a phoneme in the language is precarious. In a few words only the flap is obligatory. In the great majority of roots where it may surface, it stands in a free variation relationship with the lateral [l̪] or [l]. In a much smaller set, it may alternate with [r]. These alternations are governed by sociolinguistic constraints against the flap, rather weak in the cases where the alternant is a lateral, very strong in the much fewer cases where the alternant is [r]. The examples in (15) show the distribution of the flap compared with that of the lateral.[37] Lexical exceptions, where the flap is idiosyncratically either blocked or obligatory, are not included. In the Lateral column, the laminal variant is used in the transcription only in the cases where it is obligatory. 'Retroflex environments', indicated in spelling by *rl*, where the apical lateral is obligatory and the flap therefore predictably blocked, are not included in the table.

(15)   *Distribution of ɽ*

	Flap	*Lateral*	
Word-initially	*	[¹l̪oːt]	*låt* 'sound'
	*	[¹l̪iː]	*li* 'hillside'
Initial clusters	[¹bɽoː]	[¹bl̪oː]	*blå* 'blue'
	[¹fɽyː]	[¹fl̪yː]	*fly* 'air plane'
	[¹skɽiː]	[¹skl̪iː]	*skli* 'to glide'
	*	[¹ʂl̪oː]	*slå* 'to beat'
Medial clusters	[²rɑk.ɽə]	[²rɑk.l̪ə]	*rakle* 'catkin'
	[²çɛʋ.ɽə]	[²çɛʋ.l̪ə]	*kjevle* 'rolling pin'
	[²bɔb.ɽə]	[²bɔb.l̪ə]	*boble* 'bubble'
	*	[²ɑt.lə]	*Atle* 'man's name'
	*	[²rʉʂ.l̪ə]	*rusle* 'to saunter'
After long vowels	(see the table in (16) in Chapter 2)		
After short vowels	*	[¹ʋil̪]	*vill* 'wild'
	*	[¹tɑl̪]	*tall* 'number'
Final clusters[38]	[¹fɔɽk]	[¹fɔlk]	*folk* 'people'
	[ʋɑɽp]	[¹ʋɑlp]	*valp* 'puppy'

---

[37] The table is a somewhat simplified summary of the accounts given in Endresen (1974b), Papazian (1977) and Jahr (1981).

[38] The distribution given is the same in medial clusters of sonorant + obstruent. Also here, the flap is blocked after /i, y, e/. In final obstruent + sonorant clusters, as in *høvel*, where the sonorant will surface as syllabic, the flap is possible in simplex forms of some lexemes but blocked in others; see further footnotes 53 and 56 below.

[ˈkaʈʊ]	[ˈkalʊ]	*kalv* 'calf'
*	[ˈstiʟk]	*stilk* 'stalk'
*	[ˈhals]	*hals* 'neck'
*	[ˈstɔlt]	*stolt* 'proud'
[ˈhœʊ.ʊç]	[ˈhœʊ.ʊʟ]	*høvel* 'hone'

4.3.4 Assumptions about underlying representations

An adequate analysis of the coronal phonology of UEN must be able to account for the free variation between retroflex flaps and laterals in postvocalic position as well as the Retroflex Rule. The lexical representation of the items where we find this variation interacting with the Retroflex Rule should therefore be construed in such a way that it allows for a maximally simple analysis of both phenomena. I shall argue that the following assumptions will meet this requirement.

1. The unmarked coronal series, phonetically realized as anterior and laminal, can be analysed in two ways. They can either be considered as lacking a Place-node altogether, or they can be considered as Coronals, but with no dependent features. The question whether (unmarked) coronals are universally lacking a Place node, has been much debated in the literature (see for example the articles collected in Paradis and Prunet (1991), Booij (1993) and McCarthy and Taub (1992). I shall assume the more conservative view that unmarked coronals have a Coronal node. Their unmarked status among the coronals is expressed in their lack of dependent features.

2. Instead of [±anterior] and [±distributed], two monovalent features are assumed: apical [ap] and posterior [post]. The defining characteristic of apicals is that the constriction is made by means of the tongue tip. The defining characteristic of posterior coronals is that the constriction is located behind the alveolar ridge. Hence the unmarked status of laminal, anterior articulation follows from the absence of these features.[39]

3. As argued for above, non-alternating surface apicals are assumed to be specified as such in underlying representations of morphemes. I shall in other words assume that the Retroflex Rule is cyclic in that it applies in derived environments only.[40]

4. In the next section I shall argue that in the underlying representations of lexical items where a lateral may alternate freely with a retroflex flap, the features [+lat] and [post] are both present, but floating. The basic segment underlying this alternation can therefore be seen as the unmarked, coronal sonorant, speci-

---

[39] Universally, this is perhaps not self-evident, but note that the claim is only made with respect to systems where apicals and laminals are contrasted phonologically. In systems where this contrast is not phonologically relevant, the choice between laminal and apical articulation may be seen as one pertaining to phonetic realization.

[40] This is essentially the analysis argued for in Rinnan (1969). Later SPE-analyses, such as Hovdhaugen (1971: 146f.) and Endresen (1974b) do not explicitly distinguish between non-alternating and alternating forms in the same way as Rinnan does.

fied as [–voc, +son] and Coronal only. A similar assumption will be made for
the few morphemes where [r] may alternate with [ʈ].

4.3.5 The underlying representation of the retroflex flap

The most important phonological property of the retroflex flap is that in most lexical items where it occurs, it may alternate with another segment. This segment is
in most cases /l/, but in a few morphemes the alternant is /r/. This strongly suggests
that the flap should be derived from the same underlying source as /l/ or /r/ in these
cases.

We shall start the discussion by addressing the relationship between the more
complicated pair, that between *l* and *ɽ*, where the symbol *l* denotes any (coronal)
lateral. (16) shows simplified feature trees for the two segment types. Note that [ap]
in *ɽ* is predictable from the presence of [post], but it is included here because it is
crucial for the application of the Retroflex Rule.

(16) *Feature specification of l and ɽ*

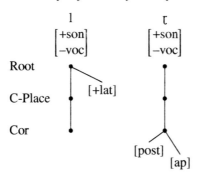

The basic problem with respect to this alternation is that the contrast rests on the
presence vs. absence of two mutually exclusive features. The presence of [+lat]
excludes the presence of [post] and vice versa, since [post] is not contrastive for
laterals at any point of the derivation, and since the flap is not lateral, at least not
in the usual sense of that term.[41] The alternation between the two sounds nevertheless suggests that they form a natural phonological class. But as first pointed out
in Fretheim (1974a), a specific feature or a feature combination that uniquely specifies this combination is difficult to identify. This holds with respect to the SPE-
framework, within which Fretheim (1974a) was written, as well as within Feature
Geometry.

This means that if one of the segments is taken as underlying, one cannot derive
the other by means of simple modification such as adding or deleting a feature. The
rule by which the other is derived will instead consist of two separate operations:

---

[41] In Foldvik (1974) it is suggested that at least some degree of lateral air flow may be present during
the articulation of [ʈ], but it does not follow that this is of phonological relevance.

delinking of one feature and subsequent insertion of another. Since these operations are in principle independent events, a rule-based analysis that takes either of the structures under (16) to be underlying will not be able to capture the close relationship between the two segment types.

Another problem with an analysis based on a rule which derives one of the alternants from the other is the large amount of exceptions, that is, lexical items where the retroflex flap is blocked even if the structural description of the rule is satisfied, and the (rarer) cases where the flap is obligatory.[42] This pattern, which is especially conspicuous in the urban varieties discussed in this book, has led some analysts, such as Faarlund (1974) and Hovdhaugen (1974) to propose that we are dealing with a system that comprises two different varieties, one where the flap is part of the inventory, and one where it is banned. The variation can then be seen as due to code, or dialect, mixing. But even if the variation can be ascribed to dialect mixing constrained by sociolinguistic factors such as style, social background of the speaker etc., it is still a fact that the alternation between l and r is part of most UEN speakers' competence. A formal analysis that accounts for this part of their competence is therefore called for.

Given the problems connected with a rule-based account, we may instead try to encode the alternations into the lexical representations themselves. In order for this approach to succeed, the representations must meet two requirements. First, they must be able to distinguish between the three relevant groups of lexical items in question where the structural description of the alternation is satisfied. The first and most important consists of those words where the sounds may actually alternate. The next comprises the words where the flap is blocked, and the third those where it is obligatory. The second requirement is that the representations must allow for a maximally simple and coherent rule accounting for the alternations in the first type, where only one elementary operation, linking or delinking, is involved.

Both requirements can be met if we assume with Archangeli and Pulleyblank (1994) that features in underlying representations may be floating and associate by rule in the course of the derivation. Archangeli and Pulleyblank refer to the featural specification of lexical formatives as *Combinatorial Specification* (p. 47), which comprises the set of F-elements (= 'positive or negative feature specifications ([+F], [−F], etc.) and the class nodes that group them into larger sets') and their association status. The latter refers to 'whether a particular F-element is *free* (unassociated) or *linked* (associated), familiar concepts from the autosegmental literature'. Further, there is '. . . a large class of co-occurrence restrictions [which] prohibit or require particular combinations of F-elements *on paths with each other*' (p. 49, emphasis in original).[43]

---

[42] Note that this lack of predictability cannot be ascribed to the rule no longer being productive. Endresen (1974a) offers several examples of recent loan words where the flap may be used.

[43] A path is formally defined as follows (p. 50): 'There is a *path* between α and β iff (a) α and β belong to a linked set Σ of nodes or features or prosodic categories, and (b) in the set Σ, there is no more than one instance of each node or feature or prosodic category.'

The three groups of lexical items can then be distinguished by means of the structures shown under (17).

(17)   *Underlying representations of l and ɽ*

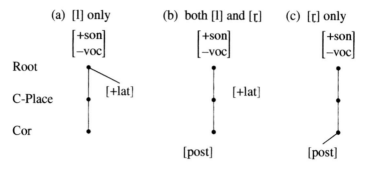

Since [+lat] and [post] are floating in the b-type, they must associate during the course of the phonological derivation. But as noted above, there are co-occurrence restrictions that will bar *both* from being linked in the same path, since a phonologically posterior lateral is not well-formed, at least not at the lexical level. The first two restrictions in (18) state this relationship formally. (Note that the first can be simplified if we assume that there is a separate condition barring [+lat] from associating in obstruents (and vowels)). The first will block [+lat] from being associated once [post] has been linked, and the other will block association of [post] in paths where [+lat] is already linked. The third condition states the implicational relationship between [post] and [ap]: any non-vocalic, coronal sonorant that is posterior is also apical.[44]

(18)   *Coronal co-occurrence restrictions (lexical)*

Domain: Lexicon

(a) [post]/[+lat] condition: if [+son, –voc, post], then not [+lat]
(b) [+lat]/[post] condition: if [+lat], then not [post]
(c) [post]/[ap] condition: if [–voc, +son, post], then [ap]

How are the floating features in (17b) associated? I propose that this is accounted for by means of the optional rule stated as (19). Once this rule has applied, the floating [+lat] cannot link, since this will violate (17a). It will consequently be erased at some point in the derivation. The output of (19) will be the phonological

---

[44] This does not hold for all dialects which have the Retroflex Rule. Northern dialects spoken mainly in parts of Trøndelag and Northern Norway have two additional series of coronals, a posterior laminal (=alveo-palatal) series as well as a distinction between a non-posterior and a posterior apical series (Sandøy 1996: 160f. and 166, Skjekkeland 1997: 92ff. and 105) developed from /r/ + coronal and /ɽ/ + coronal respectively. In these dialects, all the combinatorial possibilities under the coronal node are exploited.

representation of the retroflex flap. If (19) fails to apply, however, [+lat] will associate by default, and the result will be a lateral, that is, the structure shown as (18a).
The lateral being the alternant that is realized whenever (19) does not apply, it
represents the unmarked member of the pair. This accords well with the fact that
this is the segment that has the widest phonotactic distribution and from a universal
point of view the segment type that is by far the more widespread of the two. For
reasons that will become clear below, (19) must be cyclic, while [lat]-linking will
apply at the word-level in cases where (19) did not apply.

Since the flap is needed as input for the Retroflex Rule, (19) must apply before
it. And since the principal element of the latter is spreading of [ap], this feature
must be inserted as soon as [post]-linking has applied, in accordance with restriction (18c).

(19)   *[post]-linking (optional)*

Finally, let us briefly see how the alternation between the flap and [r] can be accounted for in the same way as the alternation between [l] and [ɭ] has been accounted for, that is, by means of floating features in the underlying representation
of those morphemes where the alternation is found. These are few, and the alternation is restricted to words where the segment follows a long vowel. Some examples
of alternating and non-alternating roots are given in (20).

(20)   *Alternations between r and ɽ*

With r	With ɽ		
[ˈhɑːr]	[ˈhɑːɽ]	*hard*	'hard'
[ˈgoːr]	[ˈgoːɽ]	*gård*	'farm'
[ˈfɑːr]	–	*far*	'father'
[ˈʋoːr]	–	*vår*	'spring'
[ˈmurd]	–	*mord*	'murder'

The alternation can be encoded by means of a floating [post] feature, but now combined with the underlying representation for /r/, as shown in (21).

(21) *Underlying representation of r*

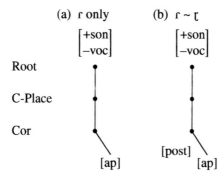

Again, the flap alternant can be accounted for by optional linking of the floating [post] feature. In the following I shall refer to /r/ and /ɽ/ as rhotics.

4.3.6 The Retroflex Rule

Essentially, the Retroflex Rule (henceforth RR) applies to heteromorphemic sequences of the rhotics /r/ or /ɽ/ plus a member of the unmarked coronal series, /t, d, s, l, n/. The output is one segment, which corresponds to the unmarked coronal, except that it is apical. The rule is therefore a rule whereby two adjacent segments are fused into one by combining features from both. Examples are given in (22).

(22)   *The Retroflex Rule*

Input	Surface of stem in isolation	Output of RR	
Inflection			
/sʉr-t/	[¹sʉːr]	[¹sʉːʈ]	*surt* 'sour' + agr.
/tør-t/	[¹tœr]	[¹tœʈ]	*tørt* 'dry' + agr.
/gʉl-t/	[¹gʉːɽ]	[¹gʉːʈ]	*gult* 'yellow' + agr.
	(or [gʉːl̩])	(or [gʉːlt])	
/bar-n/[45]	[¹baːr]	[¹baːɳ]	*baren* 'bar' + def. sg.
/nar-n/	[¹nar]	[¹nar.r̩ɳ]	*narren* 'fool' + def. sg.
/dal-n/	[¹daːɽ]	[¹daːɳ]	*dalen* 'valley' + def. sg.
	(or [daːl])	(or [daː.ln̩])	
Derivation			
/vor-li/	[¹voːr]	[²voː.l̩i]	*vårlig* 'spring+like'
/çør-sl/	[çøːr]	[¹çœʂ.ʂl̩]	*kjørsel* 'drive'(v) + nominalizer

---

[45] Def. sg. of this type may also be pronounced as disyllabic [¹baː.aɳ]: cf. Chapter 8.4.1.

Input	Surface of stem in isolation	Output of RR	
Clitics			
/brur-s/	[ˈbruːɾ]	[ˈbruːʂ]	*brors* 'brother' + poss.
/bær-n/	[ˈbæːɾ]	[ˈbæːɳ]	*bær han* 'carry him!'
/spør-n/	[ˈspœɾ]	[ˈspœɳ]	*spør han* 'ask him!'
/stjel-n/	[ˈstjæːɽ]	[ˈstjæːɳ]	*stjel han* 'steal him!'
Compounds			
/vor-tejn/	[ˈʋoːɾ]	[²ʋoː.ˌʈœjn]	*vårtegn* 'spring sign'
/vor-dag/		[²ʋoː.ˌɖɑːg]	*vårdag* 'spring day'
/vor-sul/		[²ʋoː.ˌʂuːɭ]	*vårsol* 'spring sun'
/vor-luft/		[²ʋoː.ˌɭʉft]	*vårluft* 'spring air'
/vor-nat/		[²ʋoː.ˌɳɑt]	*vårnatt* 'spring night'
/sul-dag/	[ˈsuːɽ]	[²suːl.ˌdɑːg]	*soldag* 'sun(ny) day'
		[²suːɽ.ˌdɑːg]	
		[²suː.ˌɖɑːg]	
/sul-ṣin/		[²suːl.ˌʂin]	*solskinn* 'sunshine'
		[²suːɽ.ˌʂin]	
		[²suː.ˌʂin]	

The RR can be factored into two separate sub-rules. The first is the spreading of [ap] from an apical coronal onto a following unmarked coronal. This will account for the fact that the resulting segment is apical instead of the unmarked laminal. Second, the other features of the triggering rhotic, including its root node, are delinked and subsequently deleted. The alternative would be to state spreading and deletion as one process. This has been the most common way to conceive of the rule, but combining both into one rule makes for a more cumbersome formal statement. For simplicity I shall all the same continue to refer to both rules as the Retroflex Rule (RR) where no misunderstanding can arise.[46]

The spreading rule is stated formally in (23), and the delinking rule in (24).[47] Both are subject to the Strict Cycle Condition. In cases where the rhotic is dominated by a moraic position, the following coronal will take its place, as in the [ˈtœr] ~ [ˈtœʈ] alternation in (22). Otherwise, the syllable structure of the stem will remain intact.

---

[46] [ap]-spreading is stated such that any apical segment will spread. There exist data that suggest that this is correct which at the same time represent evidence that the two sub-rules are indeed independent of each other. Spreading of [ap] may take place from other segment types than /r/ and /ʈ/, as in e.g. the def. sg. of /bat/, *bart* 'moustache', which is [ˈbɑʈ.ʈɳ], where the apicality of the final stem consonant has spread onto the nasal suffix, which underlyingly is non-apical. But the segment from which [ap] spreads is not deleted in this case, this happens only to /r/ and /ʈ/. Some aspects of this process suggest that this is better seen as a phonetic interpretation rule, however, in which case (23) must be constrained to non-nasal sonorants. We shall discuss this in more detail in Chapter 11.3.4.

[47] If [ap] is translated into [–distributed], the origin of the proposal embodied in (23) can be traced back to the SPE-based analysis of Endresen (1974b).

(23)   *The Retroflex Rule a: [ap]-spreading*

Cor   Cor

|........⁼
[ap]

(24)   *The Retroflex Rule b: Rhotic Delinking*

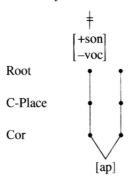

Finally, I assume a rule that inserts [post] on all apical coronals derived by (23) and
(24). This must not apply to underlying /r/, however, which is anterior. This can be
obtained if the rule is assumed to be subject to the Strict Cycle Condition; only
derived apicals will be subject to (25).[48]

(25)   *The Retroflex Rule c: [post]-insertion*

$$[\ \ ] \rightarrow [\text{post}] / \left[\underline{\quad}\atop \text{ap}\right]$$

As noted above, the assumption that the RR applies in derived contexts only also
allows us to account for the fact that there are mono-morphemic exceptions to the
rule, such as *sverd*, but no morphologically complex ones. But the derived environment constraint does not hold in the lexicon only. The RR also applies postlexically, and here as well it applies in derived environments only; the underived
clusters are still protected. The RR in other words appears to apply at the cyclic
level in the lexicon and at the postlexical level.

The Strong Domain Hypothesis of Kiparsky (1985) predicts that in this case the
rule should apply at the non-cyclic word level as well. But if allowed to apply
freely at the word level, the result would be that all sequences of underlying /rd/
would be targeted by the rule, thereby wrongly changing /sverd/ into *[ˡsʋæɖ], for
example.

---

[48]   As noted in Chapter 2.1.2.2, there appears to be some variation with respect to the actual phonetic
anteriority of the retroflex series. One might therefore argue that it should be left unspecified for [post]
also in surface structure.

However, if constrained properly, we can by allowing the RR to apply at the word level as well, obtain the desirable result that the stress-induced alternation with respect to /rd/ clusters can be accounted for at this level. Since stress assignment is cyclic, all forms at the word-level will have their stress pattern in place. If the RR is allowed to apply at this level, but only when /r/ belongs to an unstressed syllable, we can derive the alternation between *garde* ([²gɑr.də]) and *gardist* ([gɑ.¹ɖist]) and that between *Edvard* ([¹ɛd.ʋɑɖ]) and *Edvarda* ([ɛd.¹ʋɑr.dɑ]) discussed above in a simple and straightforward way. At the same time, the prediction made by the Strong Domain Hypothesis is met.

The analysis in other words assumes that the RR applies throughout the phonological derivation, but in different fashions at the three different levels. It is summarized in (26).

(26)   *Stratal application of the Retroflex Rule*

Stratum	*Mode of application*
Cyclic level	Subject to the Strict Cycle Condition
Word level	Applies to underlying rd-clusters when /r/ belongs to an unstressed syllable[49]
Postlexical level	Applies in derived environments only[50]

If the RR applies in the lexicon as well as at the postlexical level, we would expect it to be structure-preserving in its lexical application, that is, its output should comply with the distribution of apicals in underlying structure. One of the more peculiar details of the distribution shown in (22), viz. that the RR does not apply to /rn/ after a short vowel, can be given a simple explanation on this assumption. In simplex words, retroflex nasals only occur after long vowels in a stressed syllable. A word like [¹bɑːɳ], *barn* 'child' is in other words well-formed, while *[¹baɳ] is not.[51] If this distribution is seen as following from a basic phonotactic constraint on underlying forms, then the difference between [[nar]n], where the rule is blocked, and [[baːr]n], where it applies, follows from Structure Preservation, because the former would result in a structure not allowed for in non-derived environments. Note that this is another argument in favour of not deriving non-alternating apicals in UEN by rule, since this would entail a rule that lengthens vowels in front of apical sonorants, deriving [¹bɑːɳ] from underlying /barn/. Given this rule, it would be very difficult to explain why it could not apply in [[nar]n] as well, giving *[¹nɑːɳ] instead of [¹nɑr.rɳ].[52]

---

[49] A problem that arises here is that the application of (25) must be limited to the output of (24) also at this level. Since the Strict Cycle Condition cannot be assumed to hold at the word level, this must be stipulated.

[50] We shall return to the postlexical properties of the RR in Chapter 11.3.3.

[51] One exception known to me is the casual greeting used by most speakers of UEN, [¹mɔɳ], 'hello', usually written *mor'n*, which etymologically is a shortened form of [¹moː.ɔɳ], *morgen* 'morning' (but which now may be used at all times of the day). Another possible exception is *fornem*, 'noble', which may be pronounced [²fɔɳ.ɳɛm] as well as [fɔ.¹ɳɛm].

[52] According to Lie (1984), [¹nɑːɳ] seems to be possible only in dialects where the sg. form has long vowel.

Since Structure Preservation is a property of the lexicon, it is not supposed to hold at the postlexical level. If the non-application of the RR to /rn/ after short vowels is due to Structure Preservation, we would therefore expect it to hold only with respect to words derived in the lexicon proper. This prediction is borne out, as can be seen from the forms in (22) with the clitic pronoun /n/ added to short-voweled stems ending in /r/, such as [[spør]n]. Here the input is structurally identical to [[nar]n]. But the RR applies in this case, giving the output ['spœɳ].

4.3.7 The interaction between the Retroflex Rule and [post]-linking

Consider the data in the a-section of (27). Putting the def. sg. aside for the moment, we see that the lateral appears in the indef. sg. forms, where the underlying liquid surfaces as syllabic, while it may appear as flap in the indef. pl. form, where it forms an onset.[53] A similar distribution is found in adjectives: /gaml/ 'old' has the simplex form [²gɑm.ml̩], where a flap is blocked, but with the agreement marker /-e/ added, it may surface in [²gɑm.ɽə].

(27)   Alternations between [l] and [ɽ] in nominal paradigms

	Underlying form	Gloss	Indef. sg.	Def. sg.[54]	Indef. pl.
(a)	/nøkl/	'key'	[²nœk.kl̩]	[²nœk.kæɳ]	[²nœk.ɽɽ]
	/bibl/	'bible'	['biː.bl̩]	['biː.bæɳ]	['biː.bɽɽ]
	/skavl/[55]	'snow drift'	['skɑʊ.ʊl̩]	['skɑʊ.ʊæɳ]	[²skɑʊ.ɽɽ]
(b)	/titl/	'title'	['tit.tl̩]	['tit.tæɳ]	['tit.lɽ]
	/mandl/	'almond'	['mɑn.dl̩]	['mɑn.dæɳ]	['mɑn.dlɽ]

These data suggest that the underlying form of at least the three lexical items in (27a) should be as in (17b). In order to derive the correct surface forms, [post]-linking must now be further specified with a condition saying that linking is blocked if the liquid is syllabic.[56] This condition cannot take effect until the syllabic affiliation of the flap has been decided. [post]-linking must therefore follow syllabification.

Let us now turn to the def. sg. forms in (27), where we see that the Retroflex Rule has applied.[57] For the forms in section (a), the plural forms show that [post]

---

[53] The liquid *may* surface as syllabic [ɽ̩] in the indef. sg., but except for a very restricted class, whose members were monosyllabic in Old Norse and to which /skavl/ belongs, a syllabic flap seems to be a rather recent development and to be still quite marked (Vanvik 1975, Papazian 1984). When occurring in onset position in the same paradigm, the flap is quite common, however.

[54] Alternative forms are given in Chapter 8.4.2.

[55] In the indef. sg., this word may also be pronounced as a monosyllable; cf. Chapter 2.3.2.3.

[56] For those speakers for whom syllabic flaps are possible, the relevant lexical items must be listed in two versions, one with a pre-specified flap (= linked [post]) and one with [lat] and [post] floating. If the former is chosen, the flap will surface in the indefinite forms, while it will trigger the Retroflex Rule in the definite forms. If the latter is chosen, it will be subject to the regular analysis that follows below.

[57] The quality of the vowel preceding the retroflex nasal will be discussed in Chapter 8.4.2.

must be part of the underlying representations anyway. But the forms in section (b) are problematic, and raise the question whether all underlying segments which can surface as laterals should be specified with a floating [post] feature. There would seem to be no reason to do so with respect to laterals that occur in environments where the flap is not possible, for instance word-initially and after a short vowel when no obstruent follows, since the feature cannot link in these environments in the first place. Also from a learnability viewpoint this seems implausible. This means that representations with floating [post] and [+lat] should only be assumed in lexical items where the flap may surface.

It is with respect to this point that the forms in the (b)-section of (27) are problematic. As shown in (15), one of the environments where the flap is blocked is when the underlying liquid is adjacent to another coronal consonant. This is why the indef. sg. and the plural forms in this section obligatorily surface with a lateral. But assuming that there is no floating [post] underlyingly makes the def. sg. forms hard to account for. The fact that the Retroflex Rule has applied shows that [post]-linking must have applied as well, since this is necessary to trigger the Retroflex Rule. And if [post]-linking has applied, it follows that the underlying representations of these nominal roots must contain a floating [post] feature. In this environment at least, it therefore seems necessary to assume underlying forms with this feature, even if a flap never surfaces directly. This means that [post]-linking with respect to these paradigms must be blocked in all environments except where a subsequent rule saves it from being realized as a flap. Within a rule-based analysis it seems to follow that [post]-linking must be given the power to look ahead in the derivation, a property that violates the principle that conditions on rule application are strictly local.

But an alternative solution is available. Let us first return to the data in (27a), using underlying /bibl/ as the principal example. It will be argued in Chapter 8.3 that sonorants in nouns, but not in adjectives and verbs, may be made syllabic cyclically, as can be seen from the minimally reduced form of the def. sg. [ˈbiː.bl̩.ln̩]. The constraint against syllabic flaps will block derivation of *[ˈbiː.br̩.ɽn̩]. The flap can surface in the indef. pl. [ˈbiː.br̩ɽ], however, because it is non-syllabic. The def. sg. [ˈbiː.bœɳ] can be accounted for in the same way if we assume optional resyllabification at the cyclic level of intermediate [ˈbiː.bl̩.ln̩] into [ˈbiː.bln̩]. On the assumption that [lat]-linking is a word-level rule, [post] and [+lat] are still floating at this stage, and since the liquid is no longer syllabic, [post] may now link. The following segment is a coronal, and linking therefore creates an environment where the RR may apply, giving [ˈbiː.bɳ̩]. From here on the analysis follows the derivational track argued for in Chapter 8.4.2, giving [ˈbi.bæɳ]. If [post]-linking, being optional, does not apply, [lat]-linking will apply at the word level, giving [ˈbiː.bln̩].

If we add another assumption the analysis may also be made to account for the look-ahead problem connected with the data in (27b). The assumption is that [post]-linking applies persistently in the sense of Myers (1991), and that a filter will rule out flaps which are illicit because they follow a coronal at the word level. This will work in the following way with respect to underlying /mandl/ in (27b). After resyllabification has given indef. pl. [ˈmɑn.dlɽ] from [ˈmɑn.dl̩.lɽ], [post]-linking may apply, giving [ˈmɑn.dɽɽ]. The filter, which can be stated as in (28), will eliminate this form, because the segment preceding the flap is a coronal.

(28)   *Coronal + flap filter*

Domain: word level

*Root   Root
  | |
[Cor]   [Cor]
          /\
       [post] \
             [ap]

If [post]-linking applies in the resyllabified def. sg. [ˈmɑn.dln̩], however, giving [ˈmɑn.dɽn̩], the cyclic RR will forestall (28), since the resulting surface form [ˈmɑn.dæn̩] does not violate the filter.[58]

Finally, a small detail concerning adjectives should be mentioned. When added to a stem ending in /r/ or /ɽ/, the neuter agreement suffix /-t/ triggers the RR. Thus the input /gul-t/, *gult* 'yellow' is realized as [ˈgʉːʈ] (or [ˈgʉːlt]). But if the stem ends in an obstruent plus sonorant cluster, /-t/ does not trigger the RR. Thus underlying /gaml-t/ can only surface as [²gɑm.ml̩t], not as *[²gɑm.məʈ]. Since [post]-linking may apply in similar opaque contexts in nouns, such as [ˈbiː.bæɳ], we need to explain why it is blocked here.

A solution can be derived from the difference mentioned a moment ago between nouns and adjectives with respect to the stage at which sonorants may be made syllabic. In Chapter 8.3 I shall argue that in adjectives, sonorants cannot be made syllabic until the word level. This means that in forms such as /gaml/ and /gaml-t/ the liquid cannot be accessed by [post]-linking at the cyclic level, since the liquid has not been syllabified yet. But it may apply in [²gɑm.lə], because the liquid here is an onset and therefore syllabified at the cyclic level. When the liquid is syllabified at the word level, [post]-linking is no longer applicable, however, since it is a cyclic rule. The only alternative is therefore default linking of [+lat]. The difference between nouns and adjectives with respect to opaque application of [post]-linking can therefore be derived from a difference with respect to syllabification for which independent motivation is given in Chapter 8.3. At the same time, this is an argument in support of [lat]-linking being a word-level rule, while [post]-linking is cyclic.

4.3.8   /sl/-sequences

In vernacular varieties of UEN there has for a long time been a complementary

---

[58] This seems to be a case where Optimality Theory would render a more simple and perspicuous analysis, however. At stake here seems to be constraints that ban syllabic retroflex flaps (violable) as well as retroflex flaps next to another coronal (unviolated). None of these will be violated in the def. sg. forms.

distribution between [s] and [ʂ], such that the latter occurs before a lateral (Larsen 1907: 74, Broch 1927, Haugen 1942b). One may therefore write a rule that turns underlying /s/ into [ʂ] before a lateral, turning underlying /slo/, *slå* 'hit' into [¹ʂ|oː], while for example /snø/, *snø* 'snow' is pronounced [¹snɵː].[59] Even if Larsen (1907: 74) writes that [ʂ] before laterals is almost exceptionless in the vernacular, both word-initially and word-medially, there exists as far as I know no systematic survey of its distribution. In addition to the word-initial and word-medial positions, one must with respect to the latter distinguish between the environment where the lateral is in the onset of the second syllable, as in [²rʉʂ.|ə], *rusle* 'to saunter', and the environment where it represents the head of the second syllable, as in [¹ʉs.s|], *ussel* 'despicable'. As we shall see, [ʂ] seems to be less common in the latter environment than in the former; hence the transcription with [s]. There is also nothing concise in the sources on the vernacular on the importance of morphological boundaries, such as that before the derivational suffix /-li/ and in compounds. Examples with [ʂ] are given of both types in Broch (1927). [ʂ] before a lateral across a word boundary is excluded, however (Broch 1927), so the distribution is clearly lexical.

The norms in upper- and middle-class speech have on the other hand until recently been to pronounce sequences of /sl/ as [sl], the [ʂ] pronunciation being considered vulgar. But the sources do not agree. While other descriptions of so-called *dannet dagligtale* (= 'educated everyday speech'), such as Brekke (1881), Western (1889) and Alnæs (1925) do not mention [ʂ] before laterals as an option, Broch (1927) writes that [ʂ] + lateral in word-initial position is near obligatory, while in word-medial position the apical is '. . . not equally consistent in my social circles'.[60]

In the course of this century, the vernacular usage appears to have become more established in word-medial position also in the prestige varieties of UEN. But there is still a fair amount of variation, and due to the fact that the cluster appears word-medially in the name of *Oslo*, its pronunciation has acquired even greater sociolinguistic significance. In linguistically conservative circles, [²us.lu] is still regarded as the only acceptable option, [²uʂ.|u] being regarded as substandard, even if it probably is the more common of the two.

The unmarked environment is onset clusters as in *slå*, and intervocalic clusters which belong to the same root, such as in *Oslo*, *rusle* etc. Here, the [ʂ] pronunciation seems to be limited by sociolinguistic factors alone. When the lateral is syllabic, the restrictions against [ʂ] may be structural; pronunciations such as [¹ʉʂ.ʂ|], *ussel* 'despicable' do not seem to be the norm in any variety.[61] We may therefore find alternations such as [¹ʉs.s|] vs. [²ʉʂ.|ə] in individual grammars. Also morphological boundaries seem to play a role. Jahr (1981: 333n) refers to a discussion that

---

[59] [ʂ] may also turn up as a free variant of [s] in other preconsonantal positions, where it is used as an expressive, intensifying marker (Broch 1927, see also Haugen 1942b:884ff.). Thus the adjective /svær/, *svær* 'big', may be pronounced both as [¹svæːr] and [¹ʂvæːr], the latter normally being considered as signifying size to a greater, or more intensive, degree; compare the difference between *big* and *really big* in English.

[60] Norwegian: '. . . ikke så gjennomført i mine kredse' (p. 6). (Olaf Broch (1867–1961) was professor of Slavonic languages at the University of Oslo.)

[61] The only exception seems to be [¹fɛŋ.ʂ|], *fengsel* 'prison', which is rarely heard with [s].

took place in one of the major Oslo newspapers in 1978, where the participants all acknowledged [ʂl̩] in word-initial position, but rejected it in compounds such as *husleie*, '(house) rent' and *Island*, 'Iceland'. Once in a while nevertheless one hears it in such words. Additional examples are *huslig*, (derivation) 'domestic' and *Russland*, (compound) 'Russia'. (As to the expressive adjective *koselig*, 'cozy', the pronunciation [²kuː.ʂl̩i] seems to be the norm.)

An appropriate analysis would therefore be that we are dealing with a lexical rule which turns an /s/ immediately preceding a lateral into an apical [ʂ]. The rule is inhibited by structural properties of the environment (syllabic status and morphology) as well as sociolinguistic constraints.

The question of how this rule is best formulated has already been subject to some debate in the international literature. Foley (1973, 1977: 37f.), who assumes that the lateral is dental, claims that the rule cannot be interpreted as phonetically motivated assimilation, given the fact that the sibilant changes from dental to 'palatal' (*sic*) adjacent to another dental. Instead he claims that the assimilation is phonological, motivated by /l/ being 'phonologically stronger' than the sibilant. On the assumption that the output of the rule is stronger than the input, the sibilant therefore has been made stronger by the lateral. Apart from the fact that Foley got the phonetic facts wrong, since the result is apical, the main weakness of this analysis is that the concept of phonological strength remains undefined.

This was pointed out in Ohala (1974), who offers an alternative explanation based on auditory confusion between [ʂ] and a voiceless, initial phase of the lateral which may be caused by its adjacency to the voiceless sibilant. Ohala's proposal is criticized as unmotivated by Lass (1980: 39ff.), but since Old Norse /sl/ sequences in many dialects have in fact developed into a voiceless lateral, this cannot be refuted as an impossible development, or unlikely for that matter. Ohala's explanation is purely diachronic, however; it cannot be stated as a synchronic rule. It is therefore not possible to base the formulation of the optional rule operating in UEN today on his hypothesis. Ohala's analysis also goes counter to the claim made in Section 4.2.3 above that sonorants generally do not devoice after /s/ in present day UEN.

(29)   */s/-assimilation*

Domain: lexical, postcyclic

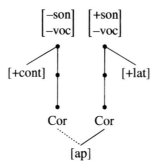

The explanation of the synchronic rule must therefore be sought elsewhere. I shall base myself on the analysis given in Jahr (1985).[62] Here the rule is seen as a consequence of the change that the lateral phoneme has undergone during this century, described in Chapter 2.1.2.4 above, whereby an apical articulation is taking over in most environments from an older laminal one (Jahr 1988). The change from [s] into [ʂ] can then be interpreted as an assimilation rule which spreads [ap] from the lateral onto the preceding sibilant. This is formally stated in (29). The rule must be lexical, since it cannot apply across word boundaries.[63] Since it applies in non-derived environments, it cannot be cyclic. It must therefore be a word-level rule.

Support for this can be found in the fact that apical laterals do not trigger the Retroflex Rule. Above I argued that (23), [ap]-spreading, which is one of the two sub-rules under the RR, must be cyclic. Recall also that the underlying representation of laterals contains floating [+lat] and [post] features. If the [post] feature associates, we derive the retroflex flap which along with /r/ will trigger [ap]-spreading. If [post] does not associate, [+lat] will associate by default at the word level. The apical lateral must then be the result of a rule that inserts [ap] in lateral segments. This must in other words follow [lat]-linking, and at the same time it must not precede the RR, since this would create yet another environment for [ap]-spreading under the RR-complex. [ap]-insertion in laterals must therefore be postcyclic in order to produce the correct counter-feeding order. Hence (29), which is crucially fed by [ap]-insertion, must also be postcyclic.[64]

4.4 E-LOWERING

As noted in Chapter 2.1.1.2, there is a near-complementary distribution between [eː, ɛ] and [æː, æ], in that the latter tend to occur before apical consonants and the glides /j, w/ only, while the non-low vowels occur in other environments. In this section we shall discuss whether this distribution should be accounted for by rule, or whether the mid and low front unrounded vowels should be seen as derived from different underlying segments.

---

[62] A Norwegian version of the article is published in Fossestøl et al. (1984: 184–95).

[63] Since there is no clitic beginning in /l/, it is not possible to test whether the domain is in fact purely lexical or bounded by the PWd.

[64] I have not tried to state [ap]-insertion in laterals formally. An SPE-style rule where the environmental constraints are stated can be found in Jahr (1988). As stated in Chapter 2.1.2.4, the environments blocking insertion are preceding back, non-high stressed vowels and preceding non-apical coronal obstruent. The latter should probably be simplified to adjacent non-apical coronal, thus including such words as *stolt*, 'proud'. This seems to be a natural environment, given the possibility of interpreting the lateral as sharing its Cor-node with the adjacent obstruent. It is more difficult to explain the former environment, non-high, back vowels, however. But if Jahr (1988) is right, the reason that the insertion rule is blocked in this environment is sociolinguistic: low-prestige dialects of the Østfold region southeast of Oslo have generalized apical /l/ irrespective of the quality of the preceding vowel. Non-apical *l* after non-high back vowels has thereby come to function as a shibboleth that distinguishes Oslo-speech from less prestigious neighbouring varieties.

The basic pattern has been noted in most analyses of East Norwegian phonology, at least in its most rudimentary form as a remark saying that [æ] occurs only before *r*. Other analyses include the retroflex flap and the apicals in the environment where the low vowel may occur.[65] Generative analyses are found in Hovdhaugen (1971: 144f.) and Weinstock (1970, 1972). The most interesting of these is Weinstock (1972), which is based on marking conventions in the style of Chomsky and Halle (1968), and thereby anticipates later analyses based on underspecification combined with prespecification of exceptions, such as Inkelas and Cho (1993). Here [±low] specifications in underlying /e/ (= [+syl, –back, –high, –round, +stress]) are supplied by means of a rule that rewrites unmarked low ([u low]) into [+low] before [r], and [–low] elsewhere. In lexical items where it does not apply, the rule is blocked by the vowel being underlyingly specified as [–low].

Turning now to the data, examples that show the distributional pattern are given in (30).

(30)   *e-lowering: distributional pattern*

(a)   *Short vowels in stressed syllables*

[ˈʋæj] *vei* 'road'   [ˈʋɛg] *vegg* 'wall'

[ˈhæwk] *hauk* 'hawk'   [ˈhɛk] *hekk* 'hedge'

[ˈhæʈj] *helg* 'weekend'   [ˈhɛlg] (id., more formal pronunciation)

[ˈmæɾ] *merr* 'mare'   [ˈmɛn] *menn* 'men'

[ˈʋæt̪] *vert* 'host'   [ˈʋɛt] *vett* 'intelligence'

[²hæʂ.ʂə] *herse* 'to bully'   [²hɛʂ.ʂə] *hesje* 'haydrying rack'

(b)   *Short vowels in closed, unstressed syllables*

[sæɾ.ʋi.ˈjɛt] *serviett* 'napkin'   [sɛn.ti.mɛn.ˈtɑːl] *sentimental* (id.)

[ɑ.læɾ.ˈgiː] *allergi* 'allergy,   [ɑ.nɛk.²duː.tə] *anekdote* 'anecdote'

(c)   *Long vowels in closed, stressed syllables*

[ˈhæːɾ] *hær* 'army'   [ˈheːs] *hes* 'hoarse'

[ˈhæːʈ] *hæl* 'heel'   [ˈheːl] (id., more formal pronunciation)

[ˈpeːɾ] *Per* (man's name)

[ˈmeːɾ] *mer* 'more'

(d)   *Open, stressed syllables*

[²ʋæː.rə] *være* 'to be'   [ˈʋeː.tə] *hvete* 'wheat'

[²stjæː.ʈə] *stjele* 'to steal'   [²stjeː.lə] (id., more formal pronuncia-
                                             tion)

[ki.²mæː.rə] *kimære* 'chimera'   [²sæː.bœ.,neːs] or [²seː.bœ.,neːs],
                                             Sæbønes (family name)

[ɑ.ˈfæː.rə] *affære* 'affair'

[ˈstjæː.ɳə] *stjerne* 'star'

[ʋʉ.ˈdeː.rə] *vurdere* 'to appraise'

---

[65] See e.g. Brekke (1881: 21f.), Western (1889: 264), Alnæs (1925: 35), Borgstrøm (1938: 252).

(e) *Open, unstressed syllables*
   [gɛ.ˈril.jɑ] *gerilja* 'guerrilla'   [gɛ.ˈsims] *gesims* 'cornice'
   [tɛ.ˈrɑs.sə]/[tæ.ˈrɑs.sə]   [ʂɛ.lɑ.ˈtiːn] *gelatin* (id.)
    terrasse 'terrace'
   [ʋæ.ˈrɑn.dɑ] *veranda* 'balcony'
   [pæ.ˈʂuːn] *person* (id.)   [sɛ.ˈʂuːn] *sesjon* 'session'

The first point that can be made is that the environments where [æ] occurs, which are before apical consonants and glides, cannot be collapsed into one natural class; there is no single feature or set of features that characterize these segments uniquely. In addition, the rule is almost exceptionless before the glides, while the picture is much more complex with respect to the apicals. I shall therefore assume that a separate rule accounts for the occurrence of [æ] before glides.

Since glides are [+high], insertion of [+low] on a preceding vowel cannot be the result of assimilation. Neither can it be a case of delinking as OCP-driven dissimilation, because the underlying /e/ is unspecified with respect to [high] in underlying structure, and [–high] after feature insertion. The specification of the vowel as [+low] must therefore be the result of an arbitrary insertion rule without a clear phonological or phonetic motivation. It is stated as (31). The loan words which among younger speakers are exceptions to the rule—see footnote 13 in Chapter 2 —must be prespecified as [–low] in their underlying representation.

(31) [+*low*]*-insertion before glides*

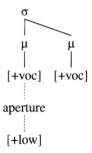

We now turn to the distribution before apicals. A rule inserting [+low] will be surface-true with respect to a following [ɽ] irrespective of syllable structure; see (30). It will also be surface true before all moraic apicals except [ʂ]; see (30b). With respect to [ʂ], we find variation, such as the minimal pair [²hɛʂ.ʂə]/[²hæʂ.ʂə] in (30a), but in most cases we find [æ] also here.[66] New words entering the language

___
[66] A possible account of this contrast would be to posit /herse/ as the underlying form of *herse*, and let e-lowering apply before the Retroflex Rule. However, this would mean that we would have to reconsider the status of the Retroflex Rule as limited to derived environments, cf. Section 4.3.4 above, since the /rs/-cluster in /herse/ would be a non-derived environment. As mentioned in Section 4.3.1 above, an unfortunate consequence of letting the RR apply in non-derived environments would be that the lexical exceptions can no longer be accounted for directly. We would instead have to revert to

comply with this distribution: the name of a Dutch skating champion from the 1960s, [fær.¹kærk], *Verkerk*, is a case in point.

But when /r/ follows a long vowel in the same syllable, or forms the onset of a following syllable, we find a great deal of variation: see (30c–e). (30c and d) show that in stressed syllables [æː] as well as [eː] can occur before [r], both in final, closed syllables and in non-final, open ones. In open, unstressed syllables, we likewise find variation, as in (30e). These exceptions would have to be excluded from the scope of a rule of general e-lowering before apicals. Note that they are not systematic, they must be stated in the form of a list of arbitrary lexemes and suffixes, the latter comprising the latinate, stressed suffix /-er/ which derives verbal stems, and the non-syllabic present tense marker /-r/, as in [nɑ.ʂu.nɑ.li.¹seː.rə], *nasjonalisere* 'to nationalize' and the present tense form of *å be*, 'to pray', which is [¹beːr].

There are a few alternations that would seem to speak in favour of a rule. First, while the non-syllabic present tense marker does not trigger e-lowering, the non-syllabic plural marker /-r/ does, as in [¹treː], *tre* 'tree' and [¹kneː], *kne* 'knee', whose indefinite plural forms are [¹træːr] and [¹knæːr]. But these are the only stems taking a non-syllabic suffix. All other nouns ending in /e/ select the syllabic variant, which does *not* trigger lowering.[67] Thus the indefinite plural of [¹breː], *bre* 'glacier' is [²breː.ər], not *[bræːr]. Since this is a non-productive, lexicalized pattern, it may be accounted for by stem allomorphy in the absence of a rule.

The other pattern cannot be accounted for by allomorphy or prespecification, however. In Chapter 8.4.2 (see also discussion in Section 4.3.7 above) I shall argue that the [æ] in the final syllable of def. sg. forms such as [¹biː.bæn̩], *bibelen* 'the bible' and [¹fɛt.tæn̩], *fetteren* 'the male cousin', which derives from underlying [[bibl]n] and [[fetr]n] respectively, is the result of an epenthesis rule. On the assumption that the epenthetic vowel is the empty vowel, the [+low] specification of the vowel in this environment can only be explained by the final apical.

Summing up, we have seen that only in syllables closed by a moraic apical, the pattern is surface true, (or near surface true with respect to a following [ʂ]). For this environment, the following rule (32) can therefore be stated.[68]

---

prespecification of rd-clusters in order to block the rule from this environment. But this cannot be done without reverting to binary dependent features under the Coronal node: the /d/ would have to be specified as [+distributed] in order to block spreading of [–distributed] from the preceding /r/. Besides the fact that the representational constraints become less restrictive by such a move, the fact that the rule *may* apply to /rd/-clusters when the preceding vowel does not head a stressed syllable now becomes inexplicable, because it would no longer be possible to distinguish between cyclic and word-level application of the RR. The costs incurred by having the RR plus e-lowering account for the low vowel in *herse* therefore seem to be too high.

[67] See Chapter 8.3.3 for a discussion of the distinction between syllabic and non-syllabic suffixes.
[68] A rule can also be stated that inserts [+low] before all retroflex flaps irrespective of syllable structure.

(32) [+*low*]-*insertion before apicals*

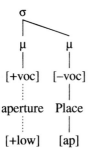

The rule is fed by the Retroflex Rule, which is cyclic, but there is no evidence that it must itself be cyclic. I therefore assume that it is a word-level rule. Again, lexical items which surface with a non-low vowel in front of [ʂ], such as [²hɛʂ.ʂə], must have the vowel prespecified as [–low]. In all other cases surface [æ] should be analysed as derived from underlying /æ/.

4.5 SIMPLIFICATION OF THREE-CONSONANT CLUSTERS

In a cluster of three consonants, which e.g. may arise when an obstruent-initial suffix such as the adjectival agreement marker /-t/ or the tense suffix /-Te/ is added to a stem ending in two consonants, the final consonant of the stem in many cases optionally deletes. Some relevant examples are given in (33).

(33) *Simplification of three-consonant clusters*
    (a) /tenk-e/ [²teŋ.kə] *tenke* 'to think'   /tenk-te/ [²teŋk.tə] or [²tɛŋ.tə]
    (b) /velg-e/ [²vɛl.gə] *velge* 'to choose' /valg-te/ [²vɑlk.tə] or [²vɑl.tə][69]
    (c) /skarp/ [¹skɑrp] *skarp* 'sharp'   /skarp-t/ [¹skɑrpt] or [¹skɑʈ]
    (d) /sterk/ [¹stærk] *sterk* 'strong'   /sterk-t/ [¹stærkt] or [¹stæʈ]
    (e) /ordn/ [¹ɔr.dn̩], *orden* 'order'   /ordn-e/ [²ɔr.dnə] or [²oː.n̩ə],
                                          'to arrange'

In Chapter 3.2.5.1 it was noted that only /s/ may occur as the first obstruent in an underlying sonorant + obstruent + obstruent cluster. Intervocalic sonorant + obstruent + sonorant clusters, such as /rdn/, are not found in roots at all. The derived clusters in the right-hand column in (33) are therefore not allowed by the phonotactic principles governing roots. Simplification can accordingly be seen as a means to bring the derived clusters in agreement with constraints on root structure.

---

[69] Note that the form with retained /g/ is an exception to the rule that verbal stems ending in a voiced obstruent surface with voiced coronal stop in the affix, cf. the discussion in Section 4.2.3.2 above. Deletion of the obstruent results in a sonorant-final stem, where the suffix allomorph with voiceless stop is according to rule.

(33c–e) show that the rule feeds the Retroflex Rule. Since the Retroflex Rule is cyclic, cluster simplification must be cyclic as well. The rule can be stated as delinking of the Place node of oral stops when preceded by a [–voc] sonorant and followed by another stop. Delinking will make the Place nodes of the flanking segments adjacent, and the Retroflex Rule ((23) and (24) above) can therefore apply when the sonorant is a rhotic and the final segment a coronal, giving [ˈstæʈ] and [ˈskɑʈ]. None of the consonants that the cluster consists of can be syllabic; see [ˈɔr.dn̩], where a corresponding *[ˈoː.ɔn̩] is impossible.

The rule, Stop Delinking, is given in (34). As it stands, nasal stops are not excluded, either as the penultimate or the final segment. Example (e) shows that the final segment may indeed be nasal. As to the possibility that the penultimate stop may be nasal, there is in fact one example: the neuter form of /ʋarm/, *varm* 'warm', pronounced [ˈʋɑrm], may surface as [ˈʋɑrmt] or [ˈʋɑn̩ʈ], the latter showing dele-tion of the medial nasal.[70] Other adjectives with the same cluster, such as *harm*, 'angry' and *enorm*, 'enormous', apparently cannot be simplified. But even if it is isolated, it shows that simplification is indeed possible also in clusters of this type.

(34) *Stop Delinking in three-consonant clusters*

   Domain: Cyclic

In (33e) we see another example of the constraint that an apical nasal cannot follow a short vowel at the lexical level; see remarks in Section 4.3.6 above concerning the failure of the Retroflex Rule to apply in /nar-n/, 'the fool'. In view of the blocking involved with respect to /nar-n/, we would have expected obligatorily [²ɔr.nə], which *is* indeed a possible surface form. But in the present case, the Retroflex Rule *may* apply. If it applies, the constraint against short vowel plus apical nasal is still enforced, however, in that the mora which dominated /r/ in the input shows up in surface structure as lengthening of the preceding vowel. I have no explanation for why *[ˈnɑː.ɑn̩] apparently is not a possible output of underlying /nar-n/. The only difference seems to be that while morphology alone creates the derived environ-ment in the latter, the input for the Retroflex Rule is created by another rule, Stop Delinking, with respect to underlying /ordn-e/.

---

[70] The rule cannot account for the fact that nasality is retained in this example. This might perhaps be remedied by assuming Place delinking instead of Root delinking, but since the example is isolated in that no other adjective with the same structure undergoes the rule, I prefer the more simple statement given in (34).

4.6 SOME MINOR ALTERNATION PATTERNS

4.6.1 Umlaut

As in the other West- and North-Germanic languages, Old Norse lexical phonology was characterized by i-umlaut, an alternation found mainly in stressed vowels, whereby an /i/ or /j/ in a following unstressed syllable caused back underlying vowels in the stressed syllable to front.[71] As in English, and unlike German and Icelandic, there are only a few traces of this rule left in the Norwegian lexicon. Even if two almost regular patterns can be identified, viz. that almost all masc. and fem. nouns whose roots end in /ut/ or /an/ have umlauted plurals, it is difficult to see what unites these two environments. In addition, there are exceptions to both, and also several nouns with different root structure which nevertheless have umlauted plurals.[72]

(35) offers some examples of nouns with umlauted plurals.

(35)   *Umlaut in noun-inflection*

	Underlying root	*Indef. sg.*	*Indef. pl.*	
	/kʉ/[73]	[ˈkʉː]	[ˈçyːɾ]	*ku/kyr* 'cow'
	/buk/	[ˈbuːk]	[ˈbœː.kɾ]	*bok/bøker* 'book'
	/gos/	[ˈgoːs]	[ˈjɛs]	*gås/gjess* 'goose'
	/but/	[ˈbuːt]	[ˈbøː.tɾ]	*bot/bøter* 'fine'
	/man/	[ˈmɑn]	[ˈmɛn]	*mann/menn* 'man'
	/stran/	[ˈstrɑn]	[ˈstrɛn.nɾ]	*strand/strender* 'beach'

Note that the changes in some cases involve vowel height ([u] > [ɵ], [ɑ] > [ɛ]) as well as backness. This is due to two changes in the vowel system that took place in the late medieval period: raising and fronting of back, round vowels,[74] and neutralization of /æ/ and /e/. In addition, we see that the umlaut trigger, /i/ or /j/ in the unstressed syllable, has been lost. A rule account of umlaut would have to take all these complicating factors into consideration, easily leading to analyses where the underlying vowel system posited corresponds to Old Norse. SPE-analyses along these lines, including on a vowel shift rule, can be found in Fretheim (1969), Weinstock (1970) and Hovdhaugen (1971: 157).

Given the lack of productivity, combined with the difficulties involved in stating a simple, general rule, the umlaut alternations should therefore be treated as the result of lexical marking rather than as the outcome of a rule. This means that each individual morpheme that undergoes umlaut must be marked idiosyncratically,

---

[71] A similar type of alternation, u-umlaut, caused underlying /a/ to round when followed by a /u/. Unlike modern Icelandic (see e.g. Kiparsky 1984), there are few vestiges of this rule in modern Norwegian, and none in UEN.

[72] Outside UEN, mostly in western and northern dialects, umlaut may also be used to mark present tense of irregular (ablaut) verbs.

[73] The most commonly used indef. pl. form of this noun in UEN is the regular [ˈkʉː.wɾ], but the umlauted form is still well known.

[74] The original quality is still reflected in the orthography, cf. Chapter 12.3.

either by means of suppletive root allomorphs or as subcategorized for a specific umlauting plural allomorph. Since the latter solution would imply two different umlauting allomorphs, zero and /-r/; as in (35), it seems to me that the simpler analysis would be to posit suppletive stem allomorphs in the lexicon.

4.6.2 Palatalization of dorsal stops

In all Norwegian dialects the dorsal stops /k, g/ were changed into palatal continuants [ç, j] before front vowels and /j/ by a sound change that started as early as the thirteenth century (Skjekkeland 1997: 97). When an /s/ preceded the dorsal, the two fricatives fused into [ʃ], which later probably changed into [ʂ]; see discussion in Chapter 2.1.2.3. The result was a complementary distribution that led earlier analysts such as Hovdhaugen (1971: 152), Fretheim (1969: 325f.) and Weinstock (1970: 589) to posit a rule that changes /k, g/ into [ç, j] before velar stops, and a subsequent rule that fuses the result of the first with a preceding /s/ into [ʂ].

The constraint against velar stops in this environment is no longer enforced, however. New words entering the language tend to maintain stop pronunciation before front vowels, a development that perhaps started in the nineteenth century with spelling pronunciation of revived Old Norse names such as *Gerd*, *Gyrid* as well as imported names such as *Gina* and *Gitte*, all female names. Corresponding male names are *Geir* of Old Norse origin, and for example *Gerhard* imported from German. Other examples of words where the constraint against dorsal stops before coronal vowels is no longer respected are *genser* 'sweater', *kimono* (id.), *gitar* (id.).

The fact that both velar stops and palatal continuants may occur in this environment suggests that continuants preceding front vowels should be analysed as underlying. There are, however, a few morpho-phonological alternations that arise in connection with umlaut- and ablaut-induced alternations between coronal and dorsal vowels, that might suggest that a rule is still called for. Examples of such alternations are given in (36).

(36) *Morpho-phonological alternations caused by palatalization of velars*

[¹gʉl] *gull* 'gold'	[²jyl.ln̩] *gylden* 'golden'
[¹kʉː] *ku* 'cow'	[¹çyːr] *kyr* 'cows'
[¹skʉt] *skutt* 'shot' (past pts)	[²ʂyːtə] *skyte* 'to shoot'
[¹skʉt] *skutt* 'shot' (past pts)	[¹ʂøːt] *skjøt* 'shot' (past)
[¹goːs] *gås* 'goose'	[¹jɛs] *gjess* 'geese'
[¹gɑː] *gav* 'gave' (past)	[¹jiː] *gi* 'give'

These alternations are regular in the sense that in all paradigms where ablaut or umlaut induces alternations between coronal and non-coronal vowels following dorsal consonants, we find concomitant alternations between velar stops and palatal continuants. But if umlaut (and ablaut) is suppletive, as suggested in the preceding section, it follows that palatalization must be suppletive as well, since there will be no unique underlying form from which the alternants can be derived.

SYLLABLE STRUCTURE

In this chapter the principles by which segments are grouped into the basic prosodic constituent type, syllables, will be discussed. Section 5.1 will be devoted to syllable structure in general. In Section 5.1.1, the prosodic hierarchy and its relationship with morphological structure will be discussed. Approaches to syllable structure will be taken up in Section 5.1.2, while the topic of Section 5.1.3 is the representation of quantity and syllable weight. Section 5.1.4 deals with the Sonority Hierarchy and how sonority determines intrasyllabic phonotactics. The structure of surface syllables is the topic of Section 5.2. In Sections 5.3 and 5.4 the rules that are needed to account for syllabification in UEN are discussed. Core syllabification rules in the sense of Clements (1990), which are needed to derive the structure that is necessary for stress assignment, are discussed in Section 5.3. In Section 5.4 the language-specific syllabification rules will be stated which must be assumed in order to account for exhaustive syllabification of any morphologically well-formed string. Prosodic structure above the syllable will be discussed in Chapters 6.3 and 7.3.

5.1 INTRODUCTION

5.1.1 The Prosodic Hierarchy

A string consisting of one or more words is not only defined by morphological and syntactic constituency. The *phonological constituency* of a string is defined by the way segments are gathered into a multi-leveled hierarchy of prosodic constituents called the Prosodic Hierarchy. The model of the prosodic hierarchy, shown in (1), is adapted from McCarthy and Prince (1986: 7). The basic constituents of this hierarchy are the syllable, the foot and the prosodic word. The latter represents the highest level assigned in the lexicon. Note that I do not interpret moras as prosodic constituents on a par with syllables and feet. Moras represent the segmental positions that contribute to the weight of a given syllable, and which therefore must be obligatorily filled for a syllable to be well-formed; see Section 5.1.3 below. Segments filling non-obligatory positions are non-moraic. This means that a syllable does not exhaustively consist of moras in the same way that a foot exhaustively consists of syllables.

With Booij and Lieber (1993) I shall assume that phonological rules may make direct reference to morphological as well as prosodic constituency. In line with this assumption, the initial domain of syllabification rules can be seen as defined morphologically, while the result of syllabification and foot formation within this

(1)   *The Prosodic Hierarchy*

PWd   Prosodic Word (or Phonological Word)
F   Foot
σ   Syllable
(μ   Mora)

domain is the prosodic word, which will often, but not by necessity, be co-extensive
with the morphological domain on the basis of which it is built.

If syllabification rules take a morphologically defined string as their domain, we
must ask what this domain is. Two kinds of domains are possible, roots or words.[1]
If roots constitute the initial domain of syllabification, prosodic structure is built
prior to any morphological operation. If words are the proper domain, however, the
input of syllabification will be a structure that has been turned into a word by one
or more morphological rules. I shall assume that prosodic structure is initially assigned to roots prior to any morphological operation, and that further syllabification
may take place following each morphological operation that adds structure in the
shape of affixes. Syllabification is in other words assumed to be cyclic.

This means that for all word-classes initial syllabification may result in structures that will form minimal prosodic words that are co-extensive with lexical
roots. These constitute the class of simplex words, which may form prosodic stems
with respect to any additional affixation. When cohering affixes are added, a natural hypothesis would be that constraints on syllabification that can be identified
across simplex words will be respected. But as we shall see, inflectional rules may
in some cases result in syllable patterns that do not conform with the prosodic constraints identified over simplex words.

The syllabic pattern that can be defined over the set of simplex words can be
regarded as the unmarked prosodic pattern from which the more marked patterns
can be derived. In the present chapter the unmarked constraints on syllable structure found in simplex words will be discussed. The marked structures that violate
these constraints will be presented briefly at the end of the chapter. They will be
extensively discussed in Chapter 8.

5.1.2 Syllabic constituents

Basically, syllabification implies a grouping of the members of a given segmental
string around segments that represent sonority peaks, that is, segments which are
preceded and followed by less sonorous ones or a boundary, including word-
internal edges that block continuous syllabification.[2] Each such peak represents a
syllable. The order of tautosyllabic melodic units on each side of the peak is in the
unmarked cases characterized by falling sonority. Two units preceding the peak
must constitute a rising sonority profile, while a pair of tautosyllabic melodic units

---

[1] See Chapter 3.1 for a discussion of word structure.
[2] Sonority can be defined as the inherent relative loudness of speech sounds produced with the same
input energy related to human perception of sound (Blevins 1995: 207). It will be further discussed
below.

following the peak must constitute a decreasing sonority profile. Vowels, being the most sonorous sound type, will normally constitute syllable peaks, but sonorants may also be syllabic in some languages. UEN belongs to this type.

Syllables are often analysed into sub-constituents; see for example Selkirk (1982). The two main constituents are the onset and the rhyme, where the onset consists of the melodic units up to, but not including, the peak, while the rhyme consists of the peak and any following segments. The rhyme can be further divided into a nucleus (= peak) and coda, which comprises those units that follow the peak. (2) is a representation of the syllabic structure of the string /slaŋk/, 'slim', constructed in accordance with these principles.

(2)   *Syllabic structure of the string /slaŋk/*

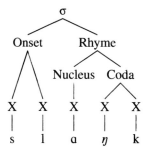

Any syllabification algorithm must be able to perform two basic tasks, the identification of the syllabic peaks and the identification of the boundary between a given pair of syllables. In the literature, two approaches to the construction of syllables that meet these criteria can be distinguished: the structure building approach and the structure matching approach.

In this book, a version of the structure building approach will be assumed (Levin 1985; see also Kenstowicz 1994: 253f.).[3] This assumes that syllables are constructed on a string of melodic units, often mediated through a so-called skeleton, also called CV- or X-tier, but where the feature specification of at least the root node is available to the rules. In its maximally simple version, the algorithm can be seen as consisting of three general rules. The first will seek out vowels on the basis of root specifications and assign a nucleus to each of these. The next, which is often called the onset rule, attaches one or more consonants to the left of each nucleus as syllable onsets, normally respecting the principle that sonority must increase towards the nucleus. In its most unconstrained form, this rule will result in onsets being maximized. Finally, the coda rule will associate any left-over consonants to the left, creating codas, again respecting the principle that sonority must be decreasing towards the edge.

---

[3] In the structure matching approach a given string of melodic units is mapped to a predefined syllable template (Itô 1988, 1989). Such a (language-specific) template expresses the well-formedness conditions on syllables in a given language, and is conceived of as an 'empty' syllable consisting of the maximal number of positions that a syllable can encompass in that language. The string of melodic units is directionally mapped onto these positions, respecting sonority sequencing. A template is most often construed as a sequence of Cs around a V, which represents the syllabic peak.

In the string /slaŋk/, the vowel will be associated to a nucleus. Then the onset rule may associate both the prevocalic consonants, which are ordered by increasing sonority (obstruent + sonorant). Finally, the two final consonants may be incorporated in the syllable as a coda because they are ordered by decreasing sonority (sonorant + obstruent).

If we take a slightly more complicated example, the same root as in (2), but with the agreement marker /-e/ added, so that the input form is /slaŋke/, the nucleus rule will associate both vowels to nuclei. The onset rule will associate the /sl/-sequence as onset to the first vowel as before, and because it takes precedence over coda formation, the /k/ as onset to the second vowel. But due to its greater sonority with respect to /k/, the nasal cannot be associated to the second syllable, and the coda rule will therefore associate it as coda of the first syllable.

This is a brief outline of the syllabification principles that will be assumed in this book. In more detail, they will be stated as a set of core syllabification rules in the vein of Clements (1990). But before we can proceed to a discussion of how these should be stated and how they interact with each other, we must establish the data, that is the actual form of the set of surface syllables in Norwegian. This implies a discussion of how syllable weight, or quantity, is best represented, which will be dealt with in Section 5.1.3.

5.1.3 Moraic structure and the representation of quantity

Norwegian is a language where syllable weight plays an important role in stress realization. An exceptionless surface generalization is that a stressed syllable must be heavy.[4] This is implemented by the requirement that the rhyme of a stressed syllable must minimally consist of a long vowel, or a short vowel plus at least one consonant. Translated into the representation shown in (2), this means that a stressed syllable must either have a branching nucleus or a branching rhyme.

In order to capture this generalization in a more unified way I shall assume that syllable weight is represented by means of moras (Hyman 1985, McCarthy and Prince 1986, Hayes 1989, Perlmutter 1995), such that a heavy syllable contains two moras, while a light syllable contains only one. A stressed syllable is thereby obligatorily bimoraic. In what follows, syllable weight will be directly encoded in syllable representations by means of moras as shown in (3) below. In accordance with the assumptions laid out in McCarthy and Prince (1986), I shall further assume that prosodic structure is built on root nodes directly, that is, unmediated by a skeleton in the form of CV-slots (Clements and Keyser 1983) or X-slots (Levin 1985). Only segments on which quantity is expressed are linked to moras, hence onset consonants are assumed to be directly linked to the syllable node.[5]

---

[4] A few dialects in Norway and Sweden, the so-called 'level-stress dialects', allow light, stressed syllables; see for example Riad (1992: Chapter 6), Kristoffersen (1990) and Bye (1996). This is an archaic feature inherited from Old Norse, which in most dialects has been eliminated through the so-called quantity shift that took place in late medieval times; see footnote 25 of Chapter 6.

[5] Some researchers, see e.g. Perlmutter (1995), have proposed that in order to avoid violations of

The quantity contrasts of Norwegian can now be represented by different association patterns between the root tier and the moras of heavy and light syllables. A vocalic root linked to both moras in a heavy syllable is realized as long, while a vocalic root linked to only one mora is short. In the latter case, the following consonant will be linked to the second mora in a heavy syllable. Monosyllabic and disyllabic examples of such structures are given in (3).[6]

(3) *Moraic representation of vowel length and consonant ambisyllabicity*

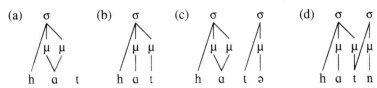

In all the examples in (3) the segmental make-up of the stressed syllable is assumed to be the sequence /hat/. There must therefore be some additional information available in the lexical entries or a subset of them that allows us to account for the distribution of vowel length and consonant gemination. Two general points must be taken into consideration. First, long vowels occur in stressed syllables only.[7] Second, in simplex words they are restricted to open syllables, and to syllables where at most one consonant follows *word-finally*. Long vowels are therefore found in two environments only: in open stressed syllables, and in final, stressed syllables closed by at most one postvocalic consonant. Translated into a linear constraint, the common feature of these environments is that there may be at most one consonant available for syllabification after the vowel. *In non-final syllables* this consonant will syllabify as onset for the following syllable, due to the principle that syllables have onsets wherever possible. Vowel length in this environment can consequently be seen as arising from the requirement that the stressed syllable be heavy, as seen in (3c).

But it is not the case that all underlying vowels found in VCV environments are realized as long. An alternative strategy to secure that stressed syllables are heavy is also available, namely gemination of the consonant, as shown in (3d). Whether a given root will show vowel lengthening or gemination is not predictable, this must be encoded on each relevant root in the lexicon. The correct way to do this is

---

the Strict Layer Hypothesis (Selkirk 1984), all segments should be subsumed under moras. This is based on the assumption that moras are prosodic constituents on a par with syllables and feet. If moras are seen as prosodic place holders and not prosodic constituents on a par with syllables and feet, as assumed here, this problem does not arise.

⁶ The words used in the examples are [¹hɑːt] *hat*, 'hate'; [¹hɑt] *hatt*, 'hat'; [²hɑː.tə] *hate*, 'to hate' and [¹hɑt.tn̩] *hatten*, 'the hat'.

⁷ In addition, it is possibly the case that unstressed vowels are long before another vowel, as in *kreol* [kre.¹uːl] 'Creole', and *kreosot* [kre.u.¹suːt] 'creosote', but no durational data that can shed light on this exist as far as I know. Vowels have the tense quality of long vowels in this environment, but my own intuition is that they should be grouped with the short vowels with respect to duration. If this should prove to be the case, insertion of a segmental feature, e.g. [+ATR] on non-low vowels, would probably be a better solution than analysing them as long.

one of the most debated subjects within the phonology of Norwegian and Swedish; see Elert (1970: 54ff.) for a survey of the different proposals that have been made, and Fretheim (1969), Jahr and Lorentz (1983b) and Lass (1984: 157). Some authors, working within a structuralist framework, have interpreted the vowel + consonant as one unit, a prosodeme, which can be realized as either long vowel plus short consonant or short vowel plus long consonant (Borgstrøm 1938, Vogt 1942). Apart from this one can distinguish between two main approaches. One holds that vowel length is phonemic, and therefore underlying. The other encodes the quantity distinction on the consonant, and holds that vowel length, having the most restricted and regular distribution, should be seen as derived.

An obvious alternative, perhaps most closely related to the prosodeme analysis, is to assume that it is the requirement that stressed syllables be heavy that is basic, and that vowel length and gemination represent different ways of meeting this requirement in cases where the segmental level does not supply enough intervocalic consonants for both coda and onset to be built on separate segments. In Kristoffersen (1991: 134ff.) I took this line, and proposed that quantity in Norwegian should be encoded in the lexicon as in (4a–b).[8] Vowel length can then be derived by the simple rule that is informally stated as (4c).

(4)   *Constraints on Norwegian quantity*

   (a) Some postvocalic single consonants are underlyingly moraic.
   (b) Final postvocalic consonants are made extraprosodic if not underlyingly moraic.[9]
   (c) Vowels lengthen in open, stressed syllables.

Quantity in underlying structure is phonologically coded on consonants in the form of a minimal amount of prosodic structure, a mora. Moraic consonants will be realized as prosodic geminates when another vowel follows, since they in these cases must fill the coda position of the heavy syllable as well as the following onset position. Being prosodically prespecified, this will exempt them from being subject to extraprosodicity. Extraprosodicity will on the other hand ensure that long vowels are restricted to open syllables, which means that in a given string that has been syllabified, and where stress has been assigned, vowel length can be predicted by the rule stated in (4c).

This analysis is close in spirit to the one argued for in Fretheim (1969) and by Stig Eliasson in several articles, for example Eliasson and La Pelle (1973) and Eliasson (1978) and (1985). Under their analyses, which are couched within the SPE framework, long consonants are interpreted as geminates, that is, as a string of two identical segments. Vowel length is then derived by a rule that lengthens a vowel in open, stressed syllables and before a single consonant. From a conceptual

---

[8] A precursor of this view can be found in Haugen (1955: 73), where it is pointed out that the obligatory nucleus of a Norwegian stressed syllable must consist of a long vowel or a short vowel plus a consonant.

[9] By 'extraprosodicity' (or 'extrametricality') is meant that a constituent that is situated at the edge of an immediately superior constituent is made invisible to rules of prosodification that target the superior constituent. See Kenstowicz (1994: 274) for a recent discussion with reference to syllabification.

point of view, it may be argued that my 1991 analysis is a translation of Fretheim's and Eliasson's analyses into a more recent framework, moraic phonology, since in McCarthy and Prince (1986) and Hayes (1989) it is claimed that a consonantal geminate should be interpreted as an underlyingly moraic consonant. But as pointed out by Hayes (1989: 258) we must distinguish between a segment's underlying representation and its surface realization. A moraic consonant is not a structural geminate per se, but it will be *realized* as such when syllabified as part of a rhyme in order to preserve its moraic status, and at the same time as an onset of a following syllable. It is therefore not obvious that a PWd-final moraic consonant should be analysed as a geminate, at least in structural terms. There is no double linking to prosodic structure involved since a following onset position is absent. A moraic consonant should therefore be interpreted not as the structural equivalent of a geminate, but as a segment that in certain environments, but not all, will be prosodified as a geminate due to general constraints on syllable structure.

What unites single consonants following short vowels both in mono- and polysyllabic forms under my (1991) analysis is their moraicity, from which both the preceding lack of vowel length and the ambisyllabicity of the consonant can be derived in a simple way. Positing underlying geminates seems to me to be an indirect and therefore less illuminating way of capturing the distribution of long and short vowels in a situation where gemination and vowel length clearly are prosodically conditioned.

Another objection against the geminate analysis is that a minimal word constraint (McCarthy and Prince 1986) cannot be expressed in a unified way under this analysis. If the consonant following a short vowel in a monosyllabic word is interpreted as a geminate, the two minimal rhyme types, long vowel and short vowel plus geminate consonant, cannot be subsumed under one structural type. In the present proposal the minimal word emerges as a bimoraic, heavy syllable, where the two moras can be instantiated segmentally as either a long vowel, C^0V, or a short vowel plus moraic consonant, C^0VC.

This analysis has one major weakness, however, which it shares with all analyses that assume that quantity is wholly or partly encoded in the lexicon as a segmental feature. As has been pointed out in the works by Stig Eliasson referred to above, it is primarily the bimoraic constraint (or length in Eliasson's terms), and not vowel length *per se*, that is dependent on stress. This means also that gemination is a function of stress, as can be seen from the alternations given in (5).[10]

(5) *Stress-dependent quantity alternations*
    [ˈdrɑː.mɑ] *drama* (id.)   [drɑ.ˈmɑː.tisk] *dramatisk* 'dramatic'
    [dɛ.ˈspuː.t] *despot* (id.)   [dɛ.spu.ˈtis.mə] *despotisme* 'despotism'
    [grɑ.mɑ.ˈtik.kn̩] *grammatikken*   [grɑ.mɑ.ti.kɑ.li.ˈteː.t] *grammatikalitet*
      'the grammar'   'grammaticality'
    [tæ.ˈrɑs.sə] *terrasse* 'terrace'   [tæ.rɑ.ˈseː.rə] *terrassere* 'to turn into a
                                         terrace'

---

[10] That gemination is dependent on stress was pointed out in Brekke (1881: 66ff.).

To the extent that stress is assigned by rule, encoding of vowel length or consonant gemination directly on lexical items is problematic because it represents a sort of covert prespecification of stress in the input forms. The data in (5) clearly show that we are not dealing with segmental properties of vowels or consonants, but with properties of the stress system. This requires that stressed syllables must meet a bimoraic minimum, and in cases where the input string does not supply enough material for all syllabic positions to be associated with different segments on a one-to-one basis, the requirement must be met by double linking between segments and syllabic constituents. The choice of segment for double association, vowel or postvocalic consonant, is idiosyncratic, however, and must therefore be marked for each lexical item.

Marking some roots as having underlyingly moraic consonants partially masks this relationship and represents a prespecification of stress. As shown by the data in (5), it will also force us to assume a degemination rule that will apply to syllables that contain an underlying moraic consonant, but which have not been assigned stress. This rule will be without independent motivation since the moraic status seems to be a function of stress in the first place. In the analysis that follows in this and the following chapter on stress assignment, I shall therefore as a hypothesis assume that vowel length as well as gemination are properties that are assigned to *stressed* syllables. This means that they are dependent on stress, and will be assigned *after* stress assignment has taken place. Since stress assignment is dependent on a syllabified input, this further entails that neither vowel lengthening nor gemination can be accounted for as part of the prestress syllabification algorithm. And to the extent that stress can be assigned without reference to weight instantiated as vowel length or consonant gemination, these properties should not be encoded directly as prespecified, prosodic properties.

This leaves us with the problem of how the choice between vowel length and consonant gemination is encoded in the lexicon. These problems will be addressed in Chapter 6.4.8 as part of the discussion of stress, and in Chapter 8.2. In the present chapter, we shall therefore concentrate on the syllabification that is necessary in order for proper foot building to be possible.

5.1.4 The Sonority Hierarchy, Sonority Sequencing and the Core Syllabification Principle[11]

As mentioned above, syllables in many cases will meet the condition that sonority must decrease from the peak towards the edges. For such a characterization of the prototypical syllable to make sense, a definition of the term sonority is needed. In footnote 2 above, I briefly mentioned one approach, based on auditory phonetics, where sonority is defined as the inherent relative loudness of speech sounds pro-

---

[11] Analyses of syllable structure based on sonority go back to the latter part of the 19th century, and have played an important role since that time. Clements (1990: 284ff.) offers a succinct historical overview beginning with Sievers (1885). See also the work of Hans Basbøll, e.g. Basbøll (1991), for a related approach to syllabification, with special reference to Danish.

duced with the same input energy, related to human perception of sound (Blevins 1995: 207). This is perhaps the most common way of defining sonority, but because it is phonetically based, it must be translated into phonological terms in order to make part of a phonological analysis. The usual way this is done is by translating it into a ranked list of phonological segment types, often ranked by degree of stricture (obstruents, sonorants, vowels), supplemented by other features such as voice (among obstruents), nasality, etc. The underlying assumption is presumably that these features contribute to the loudness of a given sound, so that a given combination of the relevant feature specifications constitutes some kind of bio-physiological programming that will render the correct degree of relative loudness in the phonetic output.

Obviously, this assumption is difficult to test. In Clements (1990), it is proposed that the attempt to base sonority on phonetics should be given up. Like other elements of a phonological theory, it should be defined in purely phonological terms, and its justification should be sought in 'its ability to account for cross-linguistic generalizations involving phoneme patterning . . .' (1990: 291). Clements then defines sonority by means of an implicational scale constituted by the major class features [vocoid], [approximant], and [sonorant], the features that in Chapter 2.2.2 we assigned to the root node. This scale renders four sonority levels or classes among the non-syllabic segment types, obstruents (O), nasals (N), liquids (L) and glides (G), as shown in (6).[12]

(6)   *The Sonority Hierarchy as defined by major class features*

O <   N <   L <   G <

–	–	–	–	'syllabic'
–	–	–	+	vocoid
–	–	+	+	approximant
–	+	+	+	sonorant

The feature 'syllabic', as used by Clements, denotes the syllabic status of the segments in question. Syllabic heads have (+) for this feature, which does not refer to sonority *per se*, but to a given segment's status as peak vs. non-peak. If the minus in the syllabic row is turned into plus, the glide class would automatically turn into full vowels, while the other columns will denote syllabic consonants. We shall return to how this feature is assigned in Section 5.2.2.

The Sonority Sequencing Principle (henceforth SSP) which is expressed by Clements (1990: 285) as in (7), now predicts that the most unmarked order of segments within a syllable is one where sonority decreases towards the syllable edges.

(7)   *The Sonority Sequencing Principle*

Between any member of a syllable and the syllable peak, only sounds of higher sonority rank are permitted.

---

[12] The table is cited from Clements (1990: 292).

A prediction that falls out from this principle is that segments that occur in an order that violates the SSP with respect to a given peak, or that are of equal sonority, normally cannot be encompassed within the same syllable, they will be split by a syllable boundary.

As Clements points out, many violations of this principle have been documented in the literature. But while such violations should be seen as language-specific, unmarked syllable structure as defined by the SSP is hypothesized to be part of the lexical phonology of every language. The algorithm that builds these unmarked syllables is referred to by Clements as the *Core Syllabification Principle* (henceforth the CSP). Segments that are not syllabified by this algorithm are either syllabified by language-specific rules at a later stage, or deleted. More specifically, the CSP is assumed to govern syllabification in the lexicon, but its output is not necessarily a fully syllabified string (Clements 1990: 298).

I end this section by citing the algorithmic formulation of the principle, as stated in Clements (1990: 299, footnotes added).[13]

(8)   *The Core Syllabification Principle (CSP)*

    (a)   Associate each [+syllabic] segment to a syllable node.

    (b)   Given P (an unsyllabified segment) preceding Q (a syllabified segment), adjoin P to the syllable containing Q iff P has a lower sonority rank than Q (iterative).[14]

    (c)   Given Q (a syllabified segment) followed by R (an unsyllabified segment), adjoin R to the syllable containing Q iff R has a lower sonority rank than Q (iterative).[15]

5.2 STRUCTURAL PROPERTIES OF UEN SYLLABLES

5.2.1 Boundaries

Criteria that identify the boundaries between syllables within a domain are often hard to come by. While speakers in the majority of cases can determine how many syllables a given string consists of, they will more often hesitate when it comes to determining the exact cut-off point between two given syllables.

Unlike other Germanic languages such as German, Dutch and English, there are few pervasive structural properties of Norwegian that clearly signal syllable or foot boundaries, comparable to syllable final devoicing in German (Wiese 1996: 200ff.) and Dutch (Booij 1995: 22), foot-initial insertion of glottal stops in German (Wiese

---

[13] Note that the concept 'core syllabification' in the following will be used in the wider sense implied by the algorithm given in (8), and not in the more narrow sense which is the creation of 'core' CV-syllables.

[14] It is stated explicitly (p. 300) that '(t)he first iteration of [. . .] b, which creates CV syllables, is not restricted by the sonority condition, since languages allowing syllabic sonorants may permit segments of equal or higher sonority to be syllabified to their left'.

[15] Given that coda-less syllables are defined as maximally simple (Clements (1990: 306), it follows that the optimal grammar does not include clause (c).

1996: 58ff, Féry 1995: 88) and Dutch (Booij 1995: 65) and foot- or syllable-initial aspiration in English, see for example Kiparsky (1979) and Selkirk (1982). In Norwegian, [voice] is distinctive also in syllable-final obstruents, as in Chapter 3.2.3. Insertion of glottal stops is morphologically and not prosodically bounded in Norwegian, it can be inserted word-initially if the lexical item begins with a vowel, but normally not word-internally before a stressed, onsetless syllable; see Chapter 2.1.2.2. Unlike English, aspiration in Norwegian seems pervasive in voiceless stops, except following /s/. It is not limited to foot- or syllable-initial position. There is for example audible aspiration after the final stop in ['tɑk], *takk* 'thank', and unlike English, both postvocalic stops are fully released in words like ['tɑkt], *takt* 'beat, measure'. If we assume that the first one is also aspirated, the obligatory full release can be seen to follow from that property.

In the absence of such properties, identification of syllable boundaries must be based on other cues, mostly phonotactic, which will be reviewed shortly below. One should, however, also bear in mind the following observation made in Clements (1990: 291):

Thus, no adequate phonetic definition has ever been given of the phoneme, or the syllable —and yet these constructs play a central and well-understood role in modern phonology. Similarly, the notion of sonority is justified in terms of its ability to account for cross-linguistic generalizations involving phoneme patterning, and need not have a direct, invariant expression at the level of physical phonetics.

Even if this passage is primarily concerned with sonority, it makes the general point that abstract constructs which are part of linguistic theory cannot always be tied to a constant and easily observable phonetic feature. They are as often constructs that we use to parse and interpret linguistic data, and should as such be justified by their 'ability to account for cross-linguistic generalizations'. As Clements observes, the syllable is such a construct. This means that the algorithms that we construct for parsing a string into syllables must be able to render important generalizations about the language we investigate. At the same time, the construct cannot be totally dissociated from the phonetic output, it must in some form be reflected in the way we perceive an utterance as a string of syllables. But where the phonetic output does not render clear-cut distinctions, we must be allowed to choose the solution that renders a maximally coherent analysis.

In section 5.1.3 the weight of a stressed syllable was structurally interpreted as a minimal rhyme size of two moras, while an unstressed syllable only needs one mora in the rhyme to be well-formed. For stressed syllables this means that the boundary cannot fall within a long vowel, or before the consonant immediately following a short vowel. At least a part of the latter must be part of the rhyme of the stressed syllable. We have thereby established a point in stressed syllables to the left of which a syllable boundary cannot be inserted. But it does not follow from this that the boundary must fall exactly at this point. Indeed, many monosyllabic words, such as ['ɑŋst], *angst* 'anxiety' and ['fɑlsk], *falsk* 'false' have additional segments following the moraic part of the rhyme. But when further morphological material is added to these words, rendering for example [ˈaŋstn̩], *angsten* 'the anxiety' and the adjectival form agreeing in number or definiteness [ˈfalskə], *falske*, it is not self-evident that the postmoraic material from the stem should be mapped to the stressed syllable also in this case.

There are in fact well-known arguments against such an analysis in its pure form, that is, that all segmental material that is syllabified as coda in monosyllabic forms should without exception remain in the coda when another syllabic head is added to its right. It is commonly assumed that syllables with an onset are better than onsetless syllables. Both the suffixes added in the examples just given consist of a bare syllabic head. In order to supply this head with an onset, and thereby to create a more optimal syllable, at least the final consonant of the stem should be assigned as onset to the final syllable.

But what about the penultimate stem consonant of the two examples? It is not needed in the initial, stressed syllable to fulfil the moraic requirements. Neither is it needed in the final syllable to supply it with an onset. A principle that is often invoked in order to solve indeterminacies like this is the principle of Onset Maximization, which says that onsets should be made to comprise as many segments as possible within an intervocalic string, to the detriment of codas (Steriade 1992, Blevins 1995: 230). The sequence of segments that is incorporated into onsets by this principle must respect the sequencing principles that are valid for onsets in that language.

Without further justification this principle may seem stipulative. While adding the indeterminate segments to the onset in both cases would give sequences that are attested word-initially, adding them to the coda of the first syllable results in a well-formed sonority cline as well, consisting of a sonorant plus an obstruent. But at least for Norwegian, there are additional arguments for choosing onset maximization in these cases. If we parse the segments in monosyllabic and mono-morphemic words from left to right until the moraic minimum is satisfied, the remaining, unparsed string, whether it consists of one, two or three consonants, will nearly always be identical to a string found in word-initial position (Kristoffersen 1991: 85ff.).[16] This means that whenever a vowel-initial syllable is added to a stem, postmoraic consonants can always create well-formed onsets to the new syllable. From this we can tentatively conclude that the final mora represents a kind of abstract right edge, after which any remaining segments may be parsed as onsets. This position may therefore serve as a general cut-off point between any two syllables.

But if the set of postmoraic strings represents well-formed onsets, so will any subset of that set. We must therefore examine the possibility that the general cut-off point should be moved one position to the right, so that the first postmoraic consonant also, if there is any, is parsed as part of an obligatory syllable coda. In the examples discussed so far, [ˈaŋ.stn̩] and [ˈfal.skə], this is clearly possible without the SSP being violated in the codas so created. But by means of disyllabic exam-

---

[16] The only mono-morphemic exceptions are to my knowledge the nouns *skjebne*, 'destiny', which is pronounced [²ʂeːbnə], *verft*, 'shipyard', and *korps*, 'corps', both pronounced in accordance with spelling.

ples where the number of intervocalic consonants is smaller, it is easy to show that such an approach would lead to untenable results if posited as a general principle. One such example is /eple/, *eple* 'apple', where parsing of one postmoraic position, as in /epl.e/, would render two violations of the well-formedness principles assumed above. First the coda /pl/ would violate the SSP, and second, the final syllable would be left without an onset. If the boundary is inserted after the moraic /p/, no violations occur. I therefore conclude that the optimal syllable in Norwegian corresponds to a structure where the final moraic segment of a syllable represents the right edge. Only this definition renders a consistent structural description that can be generalized over all syllables found in any simplex word of Norwegian.

This means that onset maximization plays an important role, but seems to be overridden by the moraic minimum requirement in stressed syllables. In a word like /eple/, *eple* 'apple', where the entire intervocalic consonant sequence meets the onset requirements, the first consonant is all the same affiliated with the rhyme of the initial syllable in surface structure: [²ɛp.lə]. Since the first vowel is short, this is necessary in order to meet the bimoraic requirement of the initial, stressed syllable.[17] The interaction between the bimoraic minimum constraint in stressed syllables and onset maximization also renders a bimoraic maximum constraint. At least in simplex words syllables cannot include more than two moras.

From the above discussion a set of well-formedness constraints emerges that can be ranked with respect to each other. First, syllables must have a head. Second, the rhyme must meet certain minimality constraints, that are different for stressed and unstressed syllables. In stressed syllables, this principle seems to take precedence over the Onset Maximization principle. But note that this precedence relation is derived from the fact that the syllable in question is stressed. Since stress is assigned after syllabification, and since there is a possibility that the bimoraic minimality constraint is induced by stress, we cannot assume that this precedence holds at the level of core syllabification.

Note that removal of the bimoraic minimality constraint from core syllabification does not entail that bimoraic syllables cannot be derived at this level. Heavy syllables can still arise, such as in [¹ɑŋ.stn̩] and [¹fɑl.skə], where the postvocalic consonant cannot be included in the onset of the following syllable because of the SSP. It can be syllabified only as a coda of the initial syllable, which would thereby emerge as a closed syllable, and therefore possibly metrically heavy. In fact, the generalization stated above, that moraic segments represent right edges of syllables, will only hold if they are analysed as bimoraic.

In /eple/ on the other hand, the initial syllable will emerge as light if onset maximization takes precedence over coda formation. Here, the bimoraicity of the initial syllable must therefore be made to follow from it being subsequently stressed.

---

[17] A possible alternative analysis is that all moraic consonants that can be grouped with the following consonants in a possible onset, such as in *eple* and *kiste*, should be seen as ambisyllabic. This would imply that both Onset Maximization and the moraic minimum could be satisfied. As far as I can see, no independent arguments in favour of this position are available.

Finally, core syllabification of /çiste/ will depend on what status /s/ plus stop sequences are given with respect to onset formation. Since /st/ does not describe a rising sonority cline as defined above, it cannot be encompassed by the CSP, and application of the coda rule will therefore give [²çis.tə].

The exclusion of /s/ + stop clusters from onsets of core syllables has consequences for the applicability of the coda rule. This can be shown by means of the root /ønske/, *ønske* 'wish'. Onset formation will associate the /k/, but not the /s/, with the final syllable. If applied without further constraints, the coda rule will now incorporate the /n/ as well as the /s/ into the initial syllable, so that the result is *[²œns.kə]. Given the fact that /s/ invariably syllabifies with a following stop intervocalically when not needed to meet the bimoraic minimum constraint in stressed syllables, this is an undesirable result. I therefore assume that the coda rule is non-iterative with respect to Norwegian. This will leave the /s/ in /ønske/ unsyllabified at this level. It can subsequently be incorporated into the following onset by a later, language-specific rule.

5.2.2 Nuclei

Vowels and coronal sonorants may constitute syllabic nuclei in Norwegian. A nucleus is in general a sonority peak as defined by the sonority hierarchy, but there are some exceptions to this principle.[18] In Chapter 3.2.4.4 we saw that when a sequence of two sonorants follows the vowel in a monovocalic root, it is not always predictable whether the second sonorant will be realized as syllabic. Thus we find for example [¹læjr], *leir* 'camp' vs. [¹sæj.jf], *seier* 'victory', where a glide in some cases, but not all, may be an onset to a syllabic liquid. Similarly, both glides and liquids (the former only in derived contexts) may be onsets before syllabic nasals.[19] These are all cases where the syllabicity of the final sonorant cannot be predicted from the sonority difference between the two segments, and where the syllabic status of the sonorant in question therefore must be part of the underlying representation of the segments in question.

We also find examples of sonority plateaux where nucleus projection cannot be derived from the sonority hierarchy. Some examples of liquid + liquid and nasal + nasal sequences are also discussed in Chapter 3.2.4.4. A related set of examples arises in the inflectional morphology. The difference between *bønne* 'bean' and *bønnene* 'the beans' is that the former is pronounced [²bœn.nə], the latter [²bœn.n̩.nə], at least in careful speech. Forms like these will be further discussed in Chapter 8.4.2.

We find another example of a possibly underlying sonority plateau in words

---

[18] See Clements (1990: 287f.) and Steriade (1992) for references to other languages where such exceptions are found. According to Steriade such examples suggest that the SSP holds within onsets and rhymes, but not between them. This, however, would seem to undermine the fundamental insight that a syllabic segment in the vast majority of cases constitutes a sonority peak. It therefore seems better to regard them as marked exceptions to the SSP.

[19] See (24) in Chapter 3 for more examples.

pronounced with initial [ji] and [jy] such as [¹jiː], *gi* 'to give' and [²jyː.sə], *gyse* 'to shudder'. If the first segment is phonologically a high front glide, the two initial segments should have identical underlying feature specifications in cases where the following vowel is /i/ or /y/, since the only difference between a glide and a vowel is their different affiliation with syllabic positions. One possible analysis would be to assume a kind of lexical geminate along the lines of the two-root structures proposed in Selkirk (1991). Given that syllables with onsets seem to be preferred over onsetless syllables, the optimal way of syllabifying the two root nodes would be as an onset + nucleus sequence.[20]

However, a diachronic process that has changed /s/ into /ʂ/ before the high, front glide but not before the corresponding high, front vowel in most Norwegian dialects constitutes an argument against specifying the initial glide by means of the same feature set as the following high vowel. A word that formerly had the underlying structure /sjel/, and a corresponding surface structure, is today pronounced [¹ʂeːl] in all but a few south-western dialects, where the change seems to be taking place now (Papazian 1994). If the glide and the vowel are the same segment, we would expect them to influence a preceding /s/ in the same way. But an /s/ is never changed in front of the vowel /i/.

It is difficult to see how this difference can be derived from differences in syllabic affiliation in a plausible way if [i] and [j] are phonologically the same segment with respect to featural composition. An alternative interpretation of the [ji] sequences might therefore be one similar to the one I assumed for /ʋ/ in Chapter 2.3.2.3, namely that we must distinguish between two versions of this segment, a vocalic and a non-vocalic one, see also Chapter 3.2.4.4. If a specification of prevocalic /j/ as [–voc] can be justified, there is no longer a sonority plateau to be accounted for.[21] This will also render a simple account for the difference between [²fær.jə] *ferge* 'ferry' and [¹feː.ri.jə] *ferie* 'holiday', whose underlying forms then can be assumed to be /ferje/ and /ferie/ respectively.

5.2.3 Onsets

Sequencing constraints that can be identified word-initially do not necessarily deliver the full set of possible onsets. The set of constraints identified word-initially may be isomorphic with the set of possible onsets in the language, but the possibility cannot be excluded that some of the gaps found, when all possible sequences respecting sonority sequencing are evaluated, may be accidental. What *can* be asserted is that the set of well-formed surface onsets must at least encompass the prevocalic sequences identified in Chapter 3.2.2.

---

[20] Note that the simpler alternative, automatic onset formation on morpheme initial /i/, so that the same segment is syllabified as nucleus as well as onset, is not tenable, given the numerous words that begin with /i/ in Norwegian.

[21] This proposal is also supported by, and at the same time supports, the tentative analysis of postsonorant /j/ as consonantal in sonorant + sonorant final roots like /berj/, as proposed in Chapter 3.2.4.4.

As such they may also be expected to occur as onsets word-initially. In this section we shall therefore take a closer look at non-initial onsets. Let us as a starting point assume the following two hypotheses on the basis of what we have found word-initially:

(a) The onset types established word-initially represent the set of possible onsets in the language.

(b) All onset types found word-initially also occur non-initially.

Two types of deviations are possible from the expectations stated in these hypotheses. First, some onsets that occur word-initially may be absent word-medially, and second, there may be onsets word-medially that are not encountered word-initially. As we shall see, both types of deviation occur.

Let us begin by examining the first type. If a long vowel represents the final segment in the initial syllable, the zero-hypothesis would be that all the onset types found word-initially can also be found after a long vowel word-medially. But this is not the case. As has been pointed out already, only one consonant can normally follow a long vowel intervocalically in simplex words. This means that for example the type consisting of /s/ + stop is not found word medially after long vowels in morphologically simple words.[22] Thus, while words such as [²tis.pə], *tispe* 'bitch', [²tɑs.kə], *taske* 'bag' and [²çis.tə], *kiste* 'coffin' are common, the forms *[²tiː.spə] and *[²tɑː.skə] are impossible, while (*)[²çiː.stə] is unacceptable as a simplex word, but acceptable as a possible preterite for the non-existent, but well-formed infinitive (*)[²çiː.sə].[23] The /s/ + stop onset is therefore not fully legitimate word-medially after long vowels, it can only be derived morphologically in this environment.

This ban against complex onsets after long vowels generalizes to all possible consonant groups intervocalically except one, which is obstruent + liquid.[24] Clusters of this type can be found after long vowels, but they also occur after short vowels, as shown by the examples in (9).

(9)   *Simplex words with intervocalic obstruent + liquid sequences*

Long vowel	*Short vowel*
[¹ɑː.fri.kɑ] *Afrika* 'Africa'	[²ɛp.lə] *eple* 'apple'
[¹leː.prɑ] *lepra* 'leprosy'	[²bɔb.lə] *boble* 'bubble'
[¹hʉː.brʉ] *hubro* 'kind of owl'	[²mɛk.rə] *mekre* 'to bleat'
[¹dʉː.plu] *Duplo* brand name	
[²sɑː.blɑ] *sabla* intensifying adverb	

The difference between long and short vowel seems to be correlated with the quality of the final vowel. If the latter is /e/, here realized as schwa, the stressed vowel

---

[22] The word *påske* 'Easter', cited in Chapter 3.2.2.2, is the only disyllabic exception I am aware of.

[23] This pattern will be further discussed in Chapter 8.2.2.

[24] I know of no examples of long vowels before /sl/-clusters, however. A likely candidate would be *musli* (or *mysli*), a mixture of cereals and dried fruit, from German *müsli*, but as far as I know this is generally pronounced with short vowel.

is short. Before other short, final vowels, the stressed vowel seems to be realized as long. This pattern does not hold up completely, however. There is at least one exception of each type. First there is the word *eskadre* 'squadron', pronounced [ɛ.ˈskɑː.drə], showing that a long vowel may occur before a schwa. Second, the word *gabbro* (id.), pronounced [ˈgɑb.ru], shows that a short stressed vowel may occur in this environment also when the final vowel is not schwa.

Looked at from a strictly distributional point of view, this ban on complex onsets after long vowels is perhaps surprising, but it is explained by the assumption already made above that open syllable lengthening of stressed vowels is a last resort strategy when no following consonant is available as a bearer of the second mora.

Let us now turn to the other possible mismatch between word-initial and word-internal onsets: the possibility that onsets may be derived intervocalically that are not found word-initially. The occurrence of such onsets will constitute arguments that their absence in initial position is due to accidental gaps, lest we want to posit different syllabification principles in the two environments. If we confine ourselves to simplex words, the match seems indeed to be very good. As noted in footnote 16, the only disyllabic, mono-morphemic word of Germanic origin where these criteria conflict is [²ʂeː.bnə], *skjebne* 'destiny'. Another possible example is [ˈbeː.tlɛm], *Betlehem* 'Bethlehem'. On the assumption that long vowels invariably occur in open syllables in simplex words, the onsets /bn/ and /tl/ result. Both can be seen as marginal, but it does not necessarily follow that we should instead opt for a syllabification of these words where the postvocalic consonant is syllabified as a coda. In Chapter 3.2.2.2 we noted that sequences of labial stop + n are practically unattested word-initially, but there is at least one example, viz. *pneumatisk*. Lacking clear independent evidence with respect to where the syllable boundary in clusters of this type falls, I leave the question open.

5.2.4 Codas

In the course of the discussion in the preceding sections, we have established that a stressed syllable will incorporate the first postvocalic consonant, if there is more than one, as carrier of the second mora. There are few restrictions on what segments can be mapped to the second mora to meet this requirement. In monovocalic roots, the retroflex flap /ɽ/ and /ʋ/ cannot occur as the only consonant. Other consonants are obligatorily syllabified as moras; they can never occur after long vowels. The relevant co-occurrence constraints are stated in Chapter 3.2.

But if core syllabification precedes stress assignment, this stress-dependent coda formation cannot be part of the CSP.[25] The only available segments for coda formation at the core syllabification level are postvocalic consonants that are left unsyllabified after onset formation. In this respect coda formation will apply blindly, and heavy syllables will be built in all environments where coda formation

---

[25] This problem, which involves rule ordering, is discussed from an Optimality Theoretic viewpoint in Kristoffersen (1999).

can apply, irrespective of stress. The result is that a given word may contain more than one heavy syllable in surface structure, as for example in [ṣɑm.pin.ˈjɔŋ], *sjampinjong* 'kind of mushroom' from underlying /ṣampinjoŋ/.

5.2.5 Appendices

For reasons that were given above, I assume that the coda rule does not apply iteratively in Norwegian. When a root ends in more than one consonant, a string of consonants may therefore be left at the right edges of prosodic words that cannot be syllabified by the principles established above. Such strings have been named appendices (to prosodic words), for example by Halle and Vergnaud (1980) and Booij (1995: 29), and extrasyllabic by Wiese (1996: 47). In both cases the extra segments are interpreted as being outside the syllable structure proper.

Booij (1995: 26) defines the Dutch rhyme by means of a minimality constraint that says that it must contain at least two skeletal positions. Its maximum size is set to three positions (p. 24). Appendices in Dutch, which arise when rhymes exceed this maximum, can consist of coronal obstruents only. This coronality condition takes precedence when the final syllable boundary is identified, so that any string of coronal obstruents following a minimal rhyme will be interpreted as an appendix, even if the first one could have been accommodated within the maximum rhyme size. This 'active' interpretation of appendix formation is motivated by a rule of schwa-insertion that can only apply properly if appendices are maximally interpreted in this way (Booij 1995: 127f.).

In Norwegian, however, the boundary between the rhyme and the appendix must be identified by a different principle than the coronality constraint. In the preceding sections the claim was made that syllable boundaries should be inserted after the final mora of any syllable. From this it follows that all consonants found between the syllable boundary established by the only application possible of the coda rule and a PWd-boundary must be analysed as belonging to an appendix, irrespective of segmental content. (10) gives some examples of appendices derived by this principle.

(10)   *Appendices at the right end of prosodic words*

    Word   *Syllabification*

    /kʉnst/, 'art'   kʉn.(st)

    /falsk/, 'false'   fal.(sk)

    /skarp/, 'sharp'   skar.(p)

The examples show that no coronality constraint can be stated with respect to UEN. By rejecting the coronality condition, the appendix is seemingly reduced to a residual category that is negatively defined with respect to the preceding syllable. Nothing is said about its internal structure. But in Section 5.2.1 above it was shown that the postmoraic sequences that are left unsyllabified in all cases correspond to well-formed onsets. An alternative definition of appendices can therefore be built on the concept 'potential onset', which is used in Kristoffersen (1991: 183). The approach there is based on the *Contiguity Constraint* of McCarthy and Prince (1990: 15), which says that 'Syllabic well-formedness is enforced over contiguous strings of subsyllabic elements'. This means that edge segments which cannot be accommodated within complete syllables, are nevertheless affiliated with syllabic positions. Hence, consonants that cannot be accommodated within the maximum template defined for rhymes are syllabified as an onset of a final, defective syllable lacking a nucleus.

Given the fact that the model of syllabic representation that is assumed here does not include a separate onset node, and nor does it assume internal structure of the onset beyond the general constraints defined by the SSP, it seems difficult to express this insight in formal terms. But the necessity of such a separate statement can be questioned. If potential onsets can be shown to follow from more general principles governing the interaction between morpheme structure and syllable structure, there is no need to establish the constraints defining appendices separately.

Such a general principle can be formulated, I believe. If we assume that the relationship between morpheme structure and syllabification is the simplest possible, that is, that in the unmarked case any morpheme string constituting a domain of syllabification may be syllabified without recourse to epenthesis or truncation, the fact that UEN contains vowel-initial cohering suffixes will lead to the expectation that any unsyllabified, stem-final string can be construed as a well-formed onset. This can be seen as a necessary condition for continuous syllabification to be carried out successfully without epenthesis or truncation. The appendix under this view is therefore simply what is left of postvocalic stem consonants at the right end of a domain when no syllabic head is supplied that they can attach to. Its form conforms in other words to the well-formedness constraints on syllable structure in general.

This leaves us with the problem of how to represent this defective syllable as part of the higher prosodic structure. This will be dealt with in section 5.4.1.

5.3 CORE SYLLABIFICATION

5.3.1 The lexical input

Before the rules of unmarked syllabification are stated, I shall briefly present the assumptions that I make with respect to the input for these rules. I assume that the lexicon provides forms where only the prosodic information necessary to derive the correct output structure in all forms is encoded. In Chapter 6.4 it will be shown that stress placement is quantity-sensitive in that closed syllables at the right word edge attract stress. The pattern emerges independently of vowel length and consonant gemination. If vowel length or gemination are marked in underlying structure, this pattern will be obscured. This implies that the underlying forms can be simplified so that the underlying representations of [²hɑk.kə], *hakke* 'pickaxe' and [²hɑː.kə], *hake* 'chin', and [¹hɑt], *hatt* 'hat' and [¹hɑːt], *hat* 'hate' respectively will be identical with respect to segmental content. The first pair will therefore be represented as /hake/, the other as /hat/. Prestress syllabification will produce identical syllable structures as input to the stress algorithm. The difference with respect to moraic expansion of light, stressed syllables, lengthening of the vowel, or gemination of the postvocalic consonant, must then be marked in some other way than by underlying moraicity.

The only type where lexical marking of prosodic structure will be assumed consists of monovocalic roots that end in a sonorant + sonorant sequence. It was shown in Chapter 3 that the syllabification patterns of such sequences to a large degree are unpredictable when the two members belong to the same major class, that is, nasals or liquids, and there are also examples where the final sonorant emerges as syllabic even if it is less sonorous than the preceding one, see (24) in Chapter 3.2.4.4 for examples. In roots with a final group of sonorants belonging to the same sonority class, the items which turn out with a final, syllabic sonorant in surface structure will therefore be assumed to have the feature [syllabic] in the lexicon. An example of a pair where this makes a difference is given in (11). Here, the root underlying ['saŋn], *sagn* 'legend' will lack [syllabic] in its lexical representation, while in that underlying ['lyŋ.ņņ], *Lyngen* (place name), the final nasal is marked as syllabic. This will secure that a syllable is built over the two nasals.

(11)   *Underlying specification of final sonorant + (syllabic) sonorant sequences*

    (a)   (b)

    /s ɑ ŋ n/   /l y ŋ n /$_{[syllabic]}$

5.3.2 Nuclei

Clements and Hume (1995: 269) assume that the core syllabification rules have access to root nodes only, that is, to the nodes that for each melodic unit are linked to prosodic structure. The major class features of each melodic unit are specified on its root node, as shown in Chapter 2.2.2. The sonority relationship between two given segments as defined in (6) above can therefore be read off their respective root nodes.

The CSP as stated in (8) presupposes that the syllabic segments have been identified and marked as [syllabic] before the algorithm applies. This raises the question whether this feature can be assigned by rule, or whether segments must be marked as [syllabic] in the lexicon. Clements (1990: 299) suggests that this may vary, and we must therefore ask whether assignment of [syllabic] can be seen as grammar-driven in UEN. I shall argue that this is the case to a considerable degree.

Sonorants will predictably surface as syllabic at word ends when they are preceded by a segment that is less sonorous. If the preceding segment is of equal or greater sonority, syllabic status must be marked in the lexicon, as assumed in Section 5.3.1 above. This can be formalized by means of an SPE-type rule as in (12), where R stands for root node. It will be argued in Chapter 8.3 that this rule applies at different stages of the derivation depending on word class.

(12) *Assignment of [syllabic] to non-vocalic sonorants*

$$R_i \rightarrow [\text{syllabic}] \ / \ R_{i-1} \ \underline{\quad} \ \#$$
$$\begin{bmatrix} -\text{voc} \\ +\text{son} \end{bmatrix} \qquad\qquad [-\text{voc}]$$

Condition: Sonority R_i > Sonority R_{i-1}

We now turn to segments that are [+voc] in underlying structure. The basic principle with respect to this type is that they surface as nuclei. This suggests a rule that assigns [syllabic] to all segments that are underlyingly [+voc].

But unsyllabified strings may contain sequences of two [+vocalic] segments which surface as falling diphthongs. Hence, only the first segment in such sequences surfaces as a nucleus, and the second is syllabified as a coda. The first member of diphthongs must be non-high, either /e/, /ø/, /o/ or /a/.[26] The glide that follows is either [j] or [w], whose corresponding vowels are [i] and [ʉ]: see Chapter 2.1.2.5.[27] These diphthongs can be accounted for by assuming that only the first segment is assigned [syllabic], while the second does not receive this feature. But this is only applicable when the second segment in fact *can* be realized as a glide. It must in other words be either /i/ or /ʉ/. Other sequences of [+voc] segments are realized as disyllabic. This holds for vowels that have the same height, such as /triu/, *trio* (id.) and /dʉu/ *duo* (id.), pronounced ['triː.ju] and ['dʉː.wu] respectively, as well as for vowels that are of different height, such as /piano/ *piano* (id.), pronounced [pi.'jɑː.nu].

But there are simplex exceptions where a high, coronal vowel is realized as syllabic following another vowel. Examples mostly include propria such as *Louis* and *Zaire*, pronounced ['lʉː.is] and [sɑ.²iː.rə] and *Moum* and *Veum*, pronounced [²muː.ʉm] and [²veː.ʉm]. Given the fact that examples such as these are fairly marginal, I assume that high, coronal [+voc] segments which following another [+voc] segment are realized as separate nuclei must be marked underlyingly as [syllabic]. Those that are not marked will not be assigned the feature by the algorithm.

We also find sequences of /j/ + vowel, such as /ja/ and /ji/. Word-initial instances were discussed in section above, where it was argued that the initial glide should be analysed as underlyingly non-vocalic, that is, as a sonorant. This analysis can now be extended to non-initial, prevocalic glides, as in the noun /djevl/, *djevel* 'devil', pronounced [²djeː.ʋl̩]. If we assume that all prevocalic [j] are underlying

---

[26] I am aware of two marginal exceptions to this, the onomatopoetic [²hʉj.jə], *huie* 'to shout', and the semantically empty ['hʉj] used as an exclamation of pleasure and in the lexicalized expression *i hui og hast*, meaning 'very fast' (lit. 'in 'h.' and haste').

[27] It is unclear whether /y/ should be included in this set. The round, front glide [ɥ] can be seen as a contextually determined realization of /i/, occurring when adjacent to round vowels. /i/ and /y/ can on the other hand contrast when realized as syllabic in this environment, as shown by the following examples: [si.jɑ.'meː.sɽ], *siameser* '(a) Siamese' and [sy.ɥɑ.'niːd], *cyanid* 'cyanide'.

sonorants, the correct syllabification pattern will follow on the assumption that, modulo (12) above, only [+voc] segments will be assigned [syllabic]. Since the other glide, [w], does not occur prevocalically, this assumption takes care of the potential cases of prevocalic glides. All instances of underlying, prevocalic /ʉ/ will be realized according to the basic principle stated above, and assigned [syllabic]. This will account for forms such as /gʉanu/ *guano* (id.) and /dʉu/ *duo* (id.), pronounced [gʉˈwɑː.nu] and [ˈdʉː.wu].

The rule can now be stated as in (13). After [syllabic] has been assigned, the input strings for syllabification will contain the necessary information for rule (a) of the CSP (see (8) above) to apply, which says that each [syllabic] segment is associated to a syllable node. I assume that this takes place by an intermediate mora, so that all syllabic segments will be moraic.

(13)   *Assignment of* [*syllabic*] *to* [+*voc*]

Assign [syllabic] to all [+voc], except to [+high] when immediately following a segment that is [+voc, –high].

Using the inputs /kumplimaŋ/, *kompliment* 'compliment' and /investa/, *Investa* (name of investment firm) as examples, (13) will assign [syllabic] to the vowels, and rule (a) of the CSP will then associate them with a syllable node. The result is shown in (14).

(14)   *Association of syllabic segments to syllable nodes*

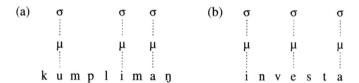

5.3.3 Onsets

Rule (b) of the CSP is repeated in (15), with a proviso added in Clements (1990: 300) following in parentheses.

(15)   *Onset Formation*

Given P (an unsyllabified segment) preceding Q (a syllabified segment), adjoin P to the syllable containing Q iff P has a lower sonority rank than Q (iterative) ('The first iteration of (13b) [= (15)], which creates CV syllables, is not restricted by the sonority condition, . . .')

This rule is ordered before the one building codas. (15) will scan the string from right to left starting from every Q, and adjoin any segment that is lower on the sonority scale than its neighbour to the right to the following syllable.

I assume that Onset Formation applies maximally. On its first iteration it applies blindly, that is, to any preceding segment. On subsequent iterations, resulting in complex onsets, the constraints imposed by the Sonority hierarchy are respected. This means that for example sequences of obstruent + sonorant can be subject to Onset Formation, while obstruent + obstruent sequences cannot. More specifically, the rule is applicable to a sequence such as /pl/, but not for example to /st/. The results of Onset Formation on the examples used in (14) are shown in (16). A complex onset is formed over the sequence /pl/, but the preceding /m/ cannot be incorporated in the same onset since its sonority is greater than /p/. Likewise, the /s/ preceding the /t/ in /investa/ cannot be incorporated, since it has the same sonority value as /t/.

(16) *Onset Formation—examples of results*

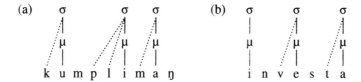

5.3.4 Codas

Coda Formation was stated as (8c) above. It is repeated here as (17). As it stands, this will incorporate any unsyllabified segment into a preceding syllable if it is less sonorous than a preceding, syllabified segment. The result of applying Coda Formation to the examples used above is shown in (18).

(17) *Coda Formation*

Given Q (a syllabified segment) followed by R (an unsyllabified segment), adjoin R to the syllable containing Q iff R has a lower sonority rank than Q (iterative).

Without further qualifications, Coda Formation cannot be reconciled with the definition of the UEN syllable that was given above. Recall that the final moraic segment of a syllable was identified as constituting the final segment of core syllables. This suggests that a coda rule should not only syllabify segments, it should also make them moraic for the result to be well-formed. This in turn raises the question whether Coda Formation should be seen as iterative in UEN. In final syllables where more than one consonant follow the vowel, such as /slaŋk/, syllabification

(18) *Coda Formation—examples*

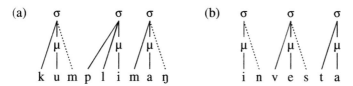

and moraification of all coda consonants will result in trimoraic and even tetra-
moraic syllables word-finally. There is no independent evidence for syllables being
superheavy in UEN, so this would come as an undesirable result.

A coda formation rule that at the same time assigns weight is the Weight by
Position rule (WbP) of Hayes (1989), which assigns a mora to coda consonants.
WbP, cited from Hayes (1989: 258), is given in (19).

(19)   *Weight by Position (WbP)*

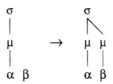

While syllables with long vowels are regarded as universally heavy, and open syllables with short vowels as universally light, closed syllables will vary over languages with respect to weight.

In the next chapter we shall see that closed syllables do attract stress. This suggests that closed syllables are heavy and must be assigned a mora before the stress
algorithm applies. In order to simplify the analysis, I shall therefore combine coda
formation as defined by the CSP and WbP. The latter will thereby function as the
coda rule of UEN. WbP cum Coda Formation will apply once, and will thereby
make coda building non-iterative. A welcome result of this assumption is that
word-final appendices emerge as the residual segments left at the right edge when
WbP has applied. Thus only the nasal in /slaŋk/ will be subject to Coda Formation,
while the /k/ is left unsyllabified and will therefore represent an appendix.

(20) shows the result of applying WbP to our examples [kum.pli.¹maŋ] and
[in.¹ʋɛs.tɑ].

(20)   *Weight by Position as Coda Formation*

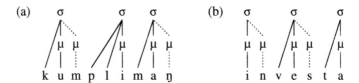

5.3.5 Summary

In this section I have proposed a set of core syllabification rules that will assign
basic syllable structure to strings of unsyllabified segments. This set consists of the
three rules of the CSP cited in (8), where the third, Coda Formation, has been combined with Weight by Position, a rule that assigns weight in the form of a mora to
a coda consonant. The resulting string will function as input for stress assignment.

While the CSP will syllabify most segments in a given string, there will in some cases remain unsyllabified segments after the CSP has applied. Syllabification of such segments will be discussed in the next section, along with some other residual phenomena.

5.4 LANGUAGE-SPECIFIC SYLLABIFICATION RULES

Two types of language-specific rules can be distinguished. The first, which I shall refer to as *patch-up rules*, consists of those rules that syllabify segments left over by the CSP. The second consists of one rule, Glide Formation, which has already been discussed in Chapter 2.3.1.2. In addition, we shall take a short look at syllable types that are not directly derivable by either the CSP or the language-specific rules discussed in the following sections, but which result from morphologically governed constraints on derived structures. These deviant syllable types will be discussed in detail in Chapter 8.

5.4.1 Patch-up rules

5.4.1.1 Appendix Formation

The rule of Appendix Formation can be stated as in (21). In words such as /laks/, *laks* 'salmon', /slank/, *slank* 'slim' and /falsk/, *falsk* 'false', (21) will create an Ap-node over the final consonant. Assuming that the CSP has already applied, the result will be as shown in (22).

(21)　*Appendix Formation*

Given Q (an unsyllabified segment) at a right edge of PWd, build an Ap(pendix) node over Q.

(22)　*Appendix Formation*

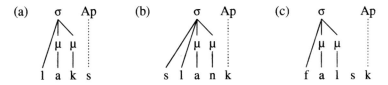

The only segment that now remains unsyllabified is the /s/ in /falsk/. This will be taken care of by the second and final patch-up rule, /s/-*incorporation*.

5.4.1.2 /s/-incorporation

Since only complex onsets with a rising sonority profile can be derived by Onset Formation, sequences of /s/ preceding stops will be left unsyllabified if not subsequently syllabified by Coda Formation. Examples are word-initial sequences, such as that in /stal/, *stall* 'stable', and word-medial sequences where /s/ does not occur immediately after a vowel, as in /hanske/, *hanske* 'glove' and /falsk/. The structure after the CSP and Appendix Formation have applied in these strings is shown in (23). The unsyllabified /s/ can now be incorporated into the following syllable or appendix by the rule stated in (24).

(23)   *After CSP and Appendix Formation*

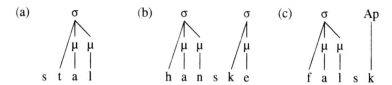

(24)   */s/-incorporation*
       Given an unsyllabified segment /s/ preceding P (a syllabified segment) or an appendix, adjoin /s/ to the syllable containing P or to the appendix.

Application of /s/-incorporation to the forms shown in (23) will result in the structures shown in (25).

(25)   */s/-incorporation–application*

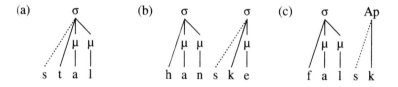

5.4.2 Glide Formation

Glide Formation, discussed in Chapter 2.3.1.2, is a rule that spreads the root node of the first vowel in a vowel sequence onto the following syllable node, provided that it is non-low. The result is that the vowel whose root note spreads comes to function as an onset for the following syllable. This rule can now be seen as a language-specific extension of Onset Formation in that it targets segments that have already been syllabified. The phonetic result is an onset glide which is homorganic with the preceding vowel.[28]

   Relevant data were presented in (17) in Chapter 2.3.1.2. They are repeated here as (26) for convenience.

---

[28] See footnote 36 in Chapter 2 for a short discussion of the possibility that the rule may be one of phonetic implementation.

(26) *Glide Formation*

Underlying form	Surface form	Gloss
/dialyse/	[di.jɑ.²lyː.sə]	'dialysis'
/syanid/	[sy.ɥɑ.¹niːd]	'cyanide'
/dʉalisme/	[dʉ. w̥ɑ.¹lis.mə]	'dualism'
/koala/	[ku.¹waː.lɑ]	'koala'
/real/	[²reː.ʲɑl]	'straightforward'
/røa/	[¹rɵː.w̥ɑ]	place name

Glide Formation can be stated formally as in (27). Given the fact that it will apply across word boundaries, as in [¹siː².jɑn.nə], *si Anne* 'say Ann', Glide Formation must be postlexical.

(27) *Glide Formation—formula*

5.4.3 Deviant syllable types conditioned by morphology

In morphologically derived environments only we find two syllable types that are not found in simplex words. Both types will be discussed in more detail in Chapter 8.

The first type is the result of length preservation in cases where a consonant initial, cohering suffix is added to a stem ending in long vowel plus one consonant, or when a vowel initial suffix is added to a stem ending in long vowel + obstruent + syllabic sonorant. An example of the first subtype is the verbal stem [hyːl], *hyl-* 'scream'. When the preterite suffix /-Te/ is added, the vowel remains long, so that the derived surface form is [²hyːl.tə].[29] An example of the other subtype is the adjectival stem [²ʋɑː.ln̩], *valen* 'numb'. Adding the agreement marker /-e/ gives the surface form [²ʋɑːl.nə]. In both cases, the result is a non-final syllable not encountered in simplex words in that the coda includes a postmoraic consonant.

The other type consists of imperatives of verbs whose root ends in obstruent + sonorant. In this type, the sonorant is realized as non-syllabic in violation of the SSP. Examples are [¹sykl̥] and [¹dɔbl], cf. the corresponding infinitives [²syk.lə] *sykle*, 'to cycle' and [²dɔb.lə] *doble*, 'to double'.

---

[29] The capital T in the suffix is an archi-phoneme covering voiced and voiceless variants: cf. Chapter 4.2.

STRESS ASSIGNMENT IN SIMPLEX WORDS

Like all other Germanic languages, Norwegian has culminative word stress.[1] The topic of this chapter is the constraints governing placement of stress in simplex words, that is, in cases where morphology has no influence.[2] Section 6.1 will serve as a general introduction to the problems that will be discussed in the sections to follow. In Section 6.2 earlier accounts of Norwegian stress will be surveyed, and in Section 6.3 the theoretical underpinnings of the analysis to follow will be presented. Section 6.4, which contains the analysis of UEN main stress assignment, can be seen as the central section of the chapter. In the following Section 6.5, noncyclic secondary stress will be discussed.

6.1 INTRODUCTION

6.1.1 Foot structure and foot assignment

Foot structure, which forms the basis of stress assignment, is assumed to be built on the output of the Core Syllabification Rules discussed in the previous chapter. Two questions arise in connection with how a syllabified string is footed. The first is the shape of the foot, and the other is the question whether a given string of syllables is exhaustively or only partially footed.

The shape of the foot will be discussed in section 6.3.3 below, where I shall argue that a maximally consistent analysis can be built on the assumption that the main stress foot in UEN is a moraic trochee built on the right edge of the word. There is, however, little evidence that the domain is exhaustively footed by iterative assignment of moraic trochees in the sense that rhythm as well is based on this foot type.

6.1.2 How many stress levels?

In most analyses of Norwegian stress, three levels are assumed: primary stress, secondary stress and no stress. All words will contain a primary stressed syllable

---

[1] I shall refer to the stresses that result from the application of the cyclic Main Stress Rule, which applies within prosodic words, as *main stress*, and the result of the Compound Stress Rule (Chapter 7.3), which relates the stresses assigned by the Main Stress Rule to each other within compounds, as *primary stress*. When a full transcription of a given example does not seem to be called for, I shall use accents placed over vowels to signal stress. In accordance with common use, acute accent signifies primary stress and grave accent secondary stress.

[2] The relationship between morphological structure and stress will be analysed in Chapter 7. Rhythm will be analyzed in Chapter 10.6.

when pronounced in isolation, where the property of being stressed is identified by the phonetic criteria discussed in the next section. Secondary stresses can originate from main stress demotion in compounds. In addition I shall argue that a stress foot in the shape of a moraic trochee is built on the left edge

This renders two types of secondary stress, initial secondary stress and demoted primary stress. Because these types have different phonetic correlates, they should probably be assigned to different stress levels. This means that we must assume two levels of secondary stress, and therefore four stress levels all in all: primary stress, demoted primary stress, initial secondary stress and no stress. For reasons given below, I shall refer to demoted primary stress as *strong secondary stress* and to initial secondary stress as *weak secondary stress*.

6.1.3 Phonetic correlates of stress

Syllables carrying primary stress in Norwegian are different from other syllables in that they are the only possible locus of two phonological properties in conjunction, weight and tonal accent. In Chapter 5.1.3, I argued that vowel length and consonant gemination should be seen as properties induced in order to meet the weight requirement of stressed syllables. Phonetically, syllable weight is normally implemented as relative duration.

In many languages, stress can also be signalled by certain pitch movements associated with stressed syllables, pitch accents.[3] In Norwegian, pitch movements associated with primary stressed syllables may be phonemic, in that there are two distinct melodies, accent 1 and accent 2.[4] As the contrast can only be realized on syllables carrying primary stress, it is reasonable to interpret them as phonologically dependent on stress and at least partially part of the stress realization system.

Strong secondary stress is characterized by the same weight requirements as primary stress syllables. Weight encoded as vowel length or consonant gemination is therefore preserved when a syllable is demoted from primary to secondary stress under compounding. But the tonal accents are neutralized into a contour that is neither accent 1 nor accent 2. The difference between primary stress and strong secondary stress can therefore be phonetically detected by the presence of syllable weight, but absence of contrastive pitch movement. This means that tonal contrasts will be neutralized when a given minimal pair is inserted as the second member of a compound. The most commonly cited example is the word [tu.ˈmɑːt.ˌbœn.nr̩], which can mean either *tomatbønner* 'beans in tomato sauce' or *tomatbønder* 'to-mato growers'. With primary stress, *bønner* and *bønder* are realized with accent 2 and 1 respectively, that is, as [²bœn.nr̩] and [¹bœn.nr̩].

There are also no specific tonal properties associated with the weak secondary stress on initial syllables. As we shall see in Section 6.5.1, some analysts claim that single postvocalic consonants are somewhat lengthened in this position, but no pho-

---

[3] See van der Hulst (in press a: 62ff.) for a discussion of how stress and tone may interact.
[4] Tonal accent will be discussed in detail in Chapter 9.

netic data exist in support of this claim, which may be phonologically interpreted as
a weight requirement. Phonetic cues are therefore at best elusive. There are, however, some arguments connected with the realization of the empty vowel /e/ for there
being a foot at the left edge, which we shall return to in Section 6.5.1 below.

6.2 EARLIER ACCOUNTS OF NORWEGIAN WORD STRESS[5]

6.2.1 The traditional view

What I will here call the traditional view builds on the assumptions that the Germanic languages at a certain stage developed initial stress which supplanted the
Indo–European accent system, and further that this state of affairs still obtains in
Norwegian.[6] In the chapters on phonology in descriptive grammars of Norwegian
only a few paragraphs are devoted to stress placement. Some version of the above
analysis is usually assumed. Primary stress is said to occur on the initial syllable,
or the root syllable. The latter is primarily a diachronic term referring to the part
of a root in Old Norse that remained stable when suffixes were added, at least with
respect to number of segments, and therefore could be seen as the part that carried
the meaning associated with the root. There are two types of exceptions: morphological structure may disturb the pattern because some suffixes cause the main
stress to move away from the root syllable, and loan words are generally said to be
stressed as in the language from which they are borrowed, or, for the numerous
words of Latin or Greek origin, as in the language through which they have been
borrowed, in most cases German, French or English. As there is generally no discussion in the sources of any language-internal principles constraining the distribution of main stress in this group, it can be inferred that its location is regarded as
an idiosyncratic property of each individual word, and therefore lexicalized.

6.2.2 SPE-based analyses

The first generative analysis of Norwegian where stress assignment is discussed is
Fretheim (1969). Two rules are offered, the Main Stress Rule and the Graeco–
Romance Rule. They apply to separate sections of the lexicon, identified by means
of the diacritic feature [±native].[7] As suggested by this initial partition of the lexicon, Fretheim's analysis can be seen as a translation of the traditional analysis into
a generative framework. The Main Stress Rule (p. 89) assigns [1 stress] to the
leftmost vowel in a domain, while the Graeco–Romance Rule (p. 90) assigns
[1 stress] to the rightmost vowel in a domain. Both are cyclic, and therefore also
purport to account for secondary stresses due to stress demotion. But as the author

---

[5] Jahr and Lorentz (1983b: 13–15) give a condensed overview of the issues that have been raised in
the literature on Norwegian stress.

[6] See Halle (1997) for a recent overview and analysis of stress and accent in Indo–European.

[7] The [–native] part of the lexicon is further divided into [+Graeco–Romance] and [+English], but
a stress rule pertaining to the latter group is neither mentioned nor stated.

himself admits, the analysis is 'much too simple' (p. 89). An inspection of the relevant data in Alnæs (1925), for example, will reveal that the rules will generate a host of forms where stress is not located according to fact. So even as a replication of the traditional analysis, the analysis is not adequate.

Weinstock (1970) assumes underlying consonant geminates, and like Fretheim (1969) he divides the lexicon into a native and non-native part. The overall generalization is that 'in the large majority of cases, stress can be predicted, viz., on the vowel occurring before the consonant length' (p. 575). The term 'consonant length' refers to geminates as well as clusters of non-identical consonants. Two rules are assumed: The 'Foreign Stress Rule' assigns stress to the penultimate syllable when the final one is light, that is, CV or CVC, otherwise to the final, and the 'Main Stress Rule' assigns stress to the initial vowel (p. 578f.). Exceptions to the rules are dealt with by means of lexical listing and use of boundary symbols, but many exceptions remain, for example words that have stress on the antepenultimate syllable. It is also unclear how the Foreign Stress Rule would deal with words like *maskín*, 'machine', with final stress on a long vowel, since lack of underlying vowel length would make the final syllable light and therefore unstressable.

Hovdhaugen (1971: 166ff.) also bases his stress rule on the disjunction between non-native and native lexical formatives, where the former group receives stress on the final vowel or penultimate vowel, while the first has stress assigned to the initial vowel. Penultimate stress is derived when the final vowel is short, non-low and non-high, possibly followed by /r/.[8] The rule will fail to generate a considerable part of the words with penultimate stress, also among the examples given by Hovdhaugen in the text. Words which end up with more than one lexical formative, and therefore more than one stress, such as compounds, are subject to a cyclic stress demotion rule. A minor stress rule, where the relevant suffixes are listed in the rule environment, accounts for the stress pattern in words with prestressing, native suffixes.

Standwell (1972) is the first published work to my knowledge where a unified analysis is attempted without reference to the [± native] division. A fundamental assumption is that both long vowels and geminates may be present in underlying representations when necessary for the stress rule to work. Based on this, Standwell states a main stress rule that seeks out and assigns stress to the final ' "long" syllable' in a domain (p. 182). The rule is cyclic, and will work for native words as well as non-native, because these as a rule only consist of one heavy syllable when morphologically simple. If no heavy syllable is present, as in /ananas/ 'pineapple', a default rule places stress on the first syllable (p. 183). The influence of morphology is expressed by means of boundary symbols, or directly by listing suffixes in rule environments.

While the above authors use segmental length or syllable structure to predict stress, *Endresen* (1977) chooses the tonal accents as the starting points, and assigns

---

[8] There is no value provided for the feature [høy] (= [high]) in the rule on p. 168. I assume that the missing value is meant to be '–', since the vowel in question is schwa.

stress to the syllables that carry the accents.[9] Given the fact that these are only real-ized on (main) stressed syllables, stress can be located by rule once the accents are in place. The relationship between tone and stress is stated in the following way:

If a syllable S of a word W has a tone movement which deviates from the tone movement of the other syllables of W in such a way that S is thrown into relief in relation to the other syllables of W, then we shall say that S is stressed (p. 24).

Underlying representations are assumed to be marked for stress in the shape of underlying, autosegmental tones, where different lexical association lines between the phoneme string and the same basic melody represent the two accents (p. 39). Stressed syllables are therefore identified on the basis of specific tonal configura-tions in these representations, which means that stress indirectly is seen as non-predictable.

No analyses of Norwegian stress based on Metrical theory have emerged until Rice (1999), which I shall come back to in connection with my own analysis pre-sented in Section 6.4 below.

6.3 THEORETICAL ASSUMPTIONS

6.3.1 Metrical Theory

Metrical Theory is a formal theory which seeks to account for stress and rhythmic structure in language by means of constructing a set of abstract, hierarchically layered, headed constituents over a given domain.[10] The lowest constituent in the metrical hierarchy is the syllable or the mora, depending on language type. These are grouped into feet, the heads of which define the potentially stressed syllables in the domain. One of these heads is then identified as the one where the primary stress is expected to fall, and is consequently promoted to head of the domain. Within a phonological word, this will be the syllable carrying the main stress. The other heads within the domain will then either represent weaker, rhythmically re-curring stresses, or they may ultimately be realized as stressless.

Metrical structure is built by means of a formal algorithm that specifies the size and headedness of a foot, how a given domain is parsed into feet, and how the constituents above the feet are constructed. Two basic ways of representing this structure have been proposed in the literature, trees and grids: see the references cited in footnote for further explication. In this book, I will assume the so-called bracketed grid. This is a two-dimensional grid consisting of abstract marks. Over each syllable in a domain a column of marks represents the relative degree of prominence of that syllable. The lines in the grid represent the levels in the metrical

---

    [9] Note that this is not an example of the type of analysis where stress is attracted to syllables carrying high tone, where this is interpreted as a kind of prominence on a par with syllable weight (Hayes, 1995: 271). It is the tonal melodies themselves, and not a specific component tone, that are relevant.
    [10] For recent overviews and introductions to metrical theory, see Hayes (1995), Kenstowicz (1994: Chapter 10), van der Hulst (1995b, 1999a) and Kager (1995).

hierarchy. Each syllable or mora has a mark on level 0. These marks are grouped into feet by means of brackets, and each foot head is assigned a mark on line 1. The marks on line 1 are then grouped into constituents, in the unmarked case one, which is then supplied with a head on line 2. Further structure is needed when words, each with a main stress mark on line 2, are grouped into compounds. Then the line 2 marks are bracketed as a constituent, and one of them is promoted to head of this constituent on line 3. The structure in (1) is an example of a bracketed grid constructed by means of these principles over a domain consisting of six syllables. Three left-headed, disyllabic feet are constructed over these, defining an alternating rhythmic pattern. On line 2, the rightmost of these feet is promoted to head with respect to the complete domain, ensuring penultimate main stress.

(1) *Example of a bracketed grid*

```
Line 2                      x
Line 1   (x      x      x)
Line 0   (x   x) (x   x) (x   x)
          σ    σ   σ   σ   σ    σ
```

Following van der Hulst (1999a: 27), formal algorithms which build metrical structure can be stated parametrically as in (2).

(2) *Metrical structure: parameters*

Foot structure:
  i. left-headed (LH) / right-headed (RH)
  ii. assigned from left to right (LR) / right to left (RL)

Word structure:
  i. left-headed (LH) / right-headed (RH)

This basic theory must be enriched with further components, such as *weight sensitivity* , the influence that syllable weight may have on stress placement, and *extraprosodicity*, the fact that peripheral constituents such as segments, syllables and feet often seem to be invisible to stress rules. Syllable weight will be discussed in the following section, while extraprosodicity will be discussed in Section 6.3.5.

6.3.2 *Syllable weight*

An unviolated requirement on all surface syllables in UEN carrying primary or strong secondary stress, which has been mentioned several times already, is that they must be heavy, i.e. bimoraic. Weight is in the unmarked case implemented by a VC-rhyme. When no free C is available for the final mora, gemination of the following onset consonant or vowel lengthening may take place. As noted in Chapter 5.1.3, both vowel length and gemination are dependent on stress and must therefore be assigned after stress assignment. They should accordingly be absent from underlying representations.

This observation does not necessarily go counter to that made on the basis of other languages, that '[h]eavy syllables characteristically attract stress', to take one representative formulation from Hayes 1995: 50. This could also be an operative principle in UEN, but with the proviso that only CVC-syllables can have this effect, given the absence of long vowels and geminates in underlying structure.

6.3.3 Foot structure

I assume that the foot in Norwegian, as in other Germanic languages, is left-headed, that is trochaic, and I will therefore limit the discussion to trochaic foot types. Hayes (1995) assumes two types of binary trochaic feet, both of which are even in the sense that there is no requirement that one of the parts be heavier than the other. One is the *Moraic Trochee*, where each foot consists of two moras, either distributed over two light syllables, or contained in one heavy syllable. If we let L represent a light syllable and H a heavy, a moraic trochee accordingly comes in two shapes: LL and H. LH and HL are illicit forms for a moraic trochee.

The alternative trochaic foot form allowed by Hayes' theory is the *Syllabic Trochee*. This is a weight-insensitive foot whose unmarked version consists of two syllables of any size corresponding to the left-headed setting of the foot structure parameter in (2). Hayes (1995: 104f.) also includes a bimoraic version of this foot type as its minimal realization type, but the principle that prosodic structure is created maximally will ensure that a disyllabic foot is created whenever possible.

Since CVC-syllables are the only heavy syllable type that can be constructed by the syllabification rules discussed in Chapter 5.3, they represent the only syllable type in the input that may support a full foot on their own within a mora-based analysis.

6.3.4 Foot parsing

We now turn to the second parameter of the foot structure algorithm in (2), which assumes that feet are built iteratively from either the right or the left edge. Both the foot types introduced in the last section presuppose that parsing into feet implies a grouping of elements in pairs. This means that strings that contain an odd number of syllables under a syllabic parse will render the initial or final one unparsed, depending on the direction of the parse.

In cases where foot structure is computed over moras, the question arises whether a foot may split a syllable, for example when an LH sequence is parsed from left to right. I follow Hayes (1995: 49f.) in assuming that a foot cannot split a syllable. Instead of splitting the H in an LH sequence the L may be skipped by the parse, and a foot will consequently be built on the H. Single Ls may therefore be left unparsed, or 'trapped', either at the edges or between feet inside the word.

The alternative to skipping is to build a *degenerate* foot over a single L. Whether and under what conditions such feet should be allowed is still under debate (Kager 1995: 399f, van der Hulst 1999a: 34ff, Hayes 1995: 87). The latter proposes that they should be allowed only if they occupy strong positions with respect to word stress, that is, if they are assigned a grid mark on the next level, but languages will differ with respect to whether they allow this option or not. This difference is referred to as *strong* vs. *weak* prohibition on degenerate feet.

Another question relating to foot construction is whether the whole string of syllables is parsed into feet before main stress is assigned. The algorithm under (2) implies as the unmarked case that the full string is exhaustively footed, and that main stress is dependent on this footing. When a string contains more than one foot, the feet whose heads are not promoted to main stress will therefore represent evenly distributed secondary stresses. In many languages this seems to be the case, but in others there seems to exist no evidence for such secondary stresses (Hayes 1995: 119).

In yet other cases main stress can be assigned independently of secondary stress because it consistently appears on the first foot built from an edge. For such systems van der Hulst (1984: 170ff.) proposes that main stress should be assigned first at the relevant edge of the word; see also van der Hulst (1999a: 72). Rhythmic secondary stresses, if present, can according to van der Hulst be assigned after the main stress has been assigned either by a foot parse starting from the main stress foot (echo rhythm) or by a parse starting from the opposite edge (polar rhythm). These ideas are further elaborated in van der Hulst (1996), where the hypothesis is explored that primary word stress is non-metrical and therefore independent of a rhythmic foot parse. Within this approach, primary word stress is assigned before secondary stresses. The former is assigned in the course of the lexical derivation, while the latter may be exponents of phrasal, that is, postlexical rhythm. Below, we shall see that this fits well with the Norwegian data to be discussed.

6.3.5 Extraprosodicity

Extraprosodicity can make a given constituent type invisible with respect to assignment of metrical structure when it occurs at the edge of the domain over which structure is assigned at a given stage in the derivation (Kager 1995: 379 ff., Hayes 1995: Chapters 3.11 and 5.2, and van der Hulst 1999a: 33 ff.).

Extraprosodic constituents may be segments, syllables or feet, and the unmarked edge for extraprosodicity is the right edge. They will be invisible to stress rules. In systems where final syllables in general are extraprosodic, right edge stress will therefore be assigned to the penultimate syllable. For Norwegian, I shall argue that extraprosodicity is an unpredictable property of a subset of all lexical items.

6.4 MAIN STRESS ASSIGNMENT

In this section we shall review the data that must be accounted for in a comprehensive analysis of UEN stress. *Ex hypothesi* both phonological and morphological structure can influence stress placement, and we must therefore try to establish whether this in fact is the case. In order to reveal phonologically-governed constraints, we shall start with reviewing morphologically simplex words. I have divided these into three classes, native words except names, names and loan words.

With a few exceptions, such as [²leː.gə.mə], *legeme* 'body' and [²hɛl.ʊə.tə], *helvete* 'hell', native simplex words are maximally two syllables long, with the final syllable always being open with either a vowel or a sonorant as head.[11] Names without internal morphological structure are usually bounded by a trisyllabic maximum, but unlike the native non-names the second syllable in disyllabic words may be closed. This is also the case for loan words, which in addition may consist of more than three syllables. Examples of the different types will be given below.

6.4.1 To what degree is stress assignment rule-governed in UEN?

The essence of the traditional analysis of Norwegian stress is that the lexicon must be divided into two disparate domains with respect to stress assignment. In the native part of the vocabulary, stress can be predicted from morphological structure ('Stress the leftmost syllable of the root'), while no rule, or a different rule, is stated for loan words, whose stress pattern is regarded as part of the loan, and therefore lexicalized.

This analysis gives rise to two questions. First, is stress placement in loan words amenable to a principled analysis, or is it really unpredictable and therefore part of the lexical information of each item of this class? If the answer should prove to be that principles *can* be established, the next question is whether the analysis established for loan words can be extended to the native part of the vocabulary, including names, so that a unified analysis of the whole language can be established. This is the line of attack taken in Standwell (1972) and which we shall pursue in greater detail and within another theoretical framework, Metrical theory, in this section.

6.4.2 Native simplex words

Examples of native simplex words are given as types 1 and 2 in (1) in Chapter 3. When syllabified, these are realized as either monosyllabic and disyllabic, cf. [¹tɑːk], *tak* 'roof', [¹syk.kl], *sykkel* 'bicycle' and [²kɑː.kə], *kake* 'cake'. Stress always falls on the initial syllable, that is, the root syllable. But note that in trisyllabic items, such as [²hɛl.və.tə], *hélvete* 'hell', it may be difficult to decide which is the root syllable independently of the stress pattern, since none of the syllables is more semantically prominent than the others.

6.4.3 Names

Only personal first names are used as examples in this subsection.[12] While quite a few of these will comply with the other types discussed in this section, some of

---

[11] A third exception is [²bil.lə.də], *billede* 'picture'. This is archaic, however: the modern form is [²bil.də], *bilde*. The longer form is still commonly used as a compound stem, however, as in *billedspråk*, 'metaphorical language'.

[12] One will find the same structural type in place names and in family names.

them define a separate type in that they may end in a full vowel or a full vowel plus one or more consonants. This they have in common with loan words, but unlike loan words, they may take a set of native, derivational suffixes that influence the stress pattern. Etymologically, they may be of native as well as foreign origin, and foreign names may have a more or less nativized form.[13]

Examples are given in (3). All have stress on the initial syllable, just like native simplex words.[14] But notice that it is not possible to identify any root syllable in these words. To the extent that names have a semantic content at all, no claim can be motivated that the main semantic load is associated with one of the syllables in these words. A generalization with respect to stress placement would have to be based on phonological structure alone, saying that stress falls on the initial or the penultimate syllable.

(3) *Disyllabic personal names*

['uː.lɑf] *Olaf* man's name
[²hɑr.rɑl] *Harald* man's name
[²hoː.kɔn] *Håkon* man's name
['ɛd.ʋɑɖ] *Edvard* man's name
['hɛn.rik] *Henrik* man's name
[²mɑː.rit] *Marit* woman's name
[²kris.tin] *Kristin* woman's name
[²gʉː.ri] *Guri* woman's name

If we now turn to trisyllabic names, we find that it is the last alternative that carries over into this group: most trisyllabic names have stress on the penultimate, and not the first, syllable. Examples are given in (4).[15] What emerges here is therefore the contours of a rule that assigns stress *not* to the initial syllable, but to the penultimate.

(4) *Trisyllabic personal names*

[ɑn.'dreː.ɑs] *Andreas* man's name
[kri.'stɔf.fɽ] *Kristoffer* man's name
[ɛ.'liː.sə] *Elise* woman's name
[ɛl.'ʋiː.rɑ] *Elvira* woman's name
[ɑŋ.'neː.tə] *Agnete* woman's name

6.4.4 *Simplex loan words*

We now turn to the most complex, and therefore also the most interesting type of data from the class of simplex words, the large group of loan words of two sylla-

---

[13] For example, the Hebrew name *Jochanan*, borrowed through Greek *Ioannes*, can be found as *Johánnes, Hans, Johán, Johs, Jan, Jon, Jo*.
[14] There are also examples of disyllabic names with non-initial stress, such as *Johán*, with stress on the final syllable.
[15] We also find examples of antepenultimate stress, such as *Téodor, Elísabeth, Súnniva*.

bles or more. The data underlying the generalizations reached in this section are taken from a database consisting of 678 mono-morphemic loan words, the bulk of which I have built by a search through the first half (A through K) of a loan word dictionary, Selmer (1966). About half of these are disyllabic words, and the rest consist of three syllables or more.[16] The database consists of nouns (632) and adjectives (46) only. Verbs have not been included, since only imperatives represent simplex structures.

Even if only simplex words have been entered into the base, it should be noted that the concept 'morphologically simplex' is difficult to apply in a non-arbitrary fashion in this context. Loan words may be morphologically complex in terms of the lending language, but it is not always evident that speakers of the borrowing language will recognize this structure in terms of their own competence. The search therefore rendered a sizeable number of words where some part of each may be analysed as a cranberry morpheme in Norwegian (Aronoff 1976).[17] This has surely led to some degree of arbitrariness in the selection of items to be entered, but I do not think that this will undermine the validity of the patterns that can be extracted from the base.

(5) shows the number of words consisting of two syllables or more, with the stress patterns found for each category. The first thing to notice here is that stress is confined to a three-syllable window on the right edge, as in most other Germanic languages (van der Hulst, Hendriks and van de Weijer 1999: 426). Within this window, we find a substantial amount of variation, which shows that stress cannot be predicted solely by counting syllables from an edge. We must therefore ask to what degree the internal structure of the syllables in the window might influence the distribution.

The zero hypothesis would be that syllable structure has no influence, and that stress placement accordingly is idiosyncratic within the window. This is in fact the solution suggested by Borgstrøm (1938: 262), who writes that '[d]ie Stellung des Gipfels innerhalb des Wortes ist prinzipiell frei, und kann zur Bedeutungs-differentiation dienen'. There are indeed some minimal pairs, even if this possibility, as Borgstrøm remarks, is not widely exploited, and some of them can be

---

[16] As the aim of creating the base has not been to investigate lexical frequency, but to provide a set of representative examples of the different patterns that are found, the number of disyllabic words ending in an open syllable has been limited. This is a very common type, whose members in most cases are stressed on the initial syllable. All disyllabic words with closed second syllable that I have come across have, on the other hand, been entered in the base, as well as all tokens with three syllables or more.

[17] One example is that while the noun *estetikk* 'aesthetics' can be parsed into two units, a stem *estet-* 'aesthete' and a derivational ending *-ikk*, the same is not obviously the case with the noun *fysikk* 'physics', where the stem *fys-* cannot be associated with some semantic content that reappears in other contexts. But just as one can establish a formal relationship between *estetikk* and the adjective *estetisk*, one can relate *fysikk* and *fysisk*. Based on that relationship, one can argue that *fysikk* should be analysed as morphologically complex, and that *fys-* is a cranberry morpheme. Neither of them have been entered in the database for that reason. Other cases are even less clear. Of the following nouns ending in stressed *-ør*, *kulør* 'colour', *dusør* 'reward', *honnør* 'honour' and *frisør* 'hairdresser', only the last one can be related to another word where the stem reappears, the verb *frisere*. For this reason, the three former have been entered, but not the latter.

(5)   *Stress patterns in loan words*

	σσ	σσσ	≥ σσσσ
Stress pattern	(N = 354): %	(N = 267): %	(N = 57): %
Final	76.6 (271)	40.8 (109)	5.3 (3)
Penultimate	23.4 (83)	44.2 (118)	75.4 (43)
Antepenultimate		15.0 (40)	19.3 (11)
Preantepenultimate			0 (0)

analysed as deriving their stress pattern from different morphological structure.[18]

The alternative hypothesis is that there *are* constraints that govern the location of stress within the three-syllable window. We shall therefore discuss some predictions that follow from the assumption that heavy syllables attract stress. In its simplest form, it predicts that a heavy final syllable attracts stress. If the final is light, the penultimate will be stressed irrespective of weight.

If closed syllables attract stress, the relevant stress foot can be assumed to be computed on moras. If they on the other hand do not attract stress, we may assume that it is built on syllables. In both cases the foot is binary and trochaic, a moraic trochee in the first case, and a syllabic trochee in the second. If we further assume that main stress is accounted for by assigning the word layer head to the rightmost foot, we must for both moraic and syllabic trochees assume that final syllables can be extraprosodic in order to derive antepenultimate stress.

But in other respects the two types of stress feet make different predictions. (6) shows the different patterns predicted by the two foot types over a three-syllable window on the assumption that final syllables may be lexically marked as extraprosodic. The left hand column shows the different syllabic combinations that are possible, and in the columns representing the two foot types the predicted pattern will be indicated. The types where the two foot types predict different stress patterns are shaded.

The cases where we derive different predictions are those where there is a final heavy syllable. In that case, a moraic trochee will be built on that syllable, deriving final stress, while a syllabic trochee will result in penultimate stress. In the case of extraprosodicity, the pattern is moved one syllable leftwards, so that a heavy penult will be assigned stress by the moraic trochee, while the antepenult irrespective of weight will get the stress if syllabic trochees are assumed. This means that under a moraic system, antepenultimate stress can only be derived when the penult is light. Stress will in other words never be able to reach beyond a heavy penult.

---

[18] One such example is the singular noun *tékniker* 'technician' vs. the plural noun *tekníkker* 'techniques' (Jahr and Lorentz 1983b). The common stem is *teknikk*. The suffix /ikr/, which is further analysed in Chapter 7.2.4, moves stress to the antepenultimate syllable, giving *tékniker*, while the homophonous plural marker as an inflectional suffix has no influence on the stress pattern, giving *tekníkker*. A minimal pair where morphology cannot account for the difference is *allé* 'alley' vs. *álle* 'all'. In both cases, the difference in stress is accompanied by weight differences in the stressed syllable in accordance with the principles stated in Chapter 5.1.3.

(6)   *Stress patterns predicted by moraic and syllabic trochees*[19]

	Syllabic composition of input	Moraic trochee	Syllabic trochee
(a)	CV.CV.CV	Penultimate	Penultimate
(b)	CV.CV.CVC	Final	Penultimate
(c)	CV.CV. ⟨CV⟩	Antepenultimate	Antepenultimate
(d)	CV.CVC.CV	Penultimate	Penultimate
(e)	CV.CVC.CVC	Final	Penultimate
(f)	CV.CVC.⟨CV⟩	Penultimate	Antepenultimate
(g)	CVC.CV.CV	Penultimate	Penultimate
(h)	CVC.CV.CVC	Final	Penultimate
(i)	CVC.CV.⟨CV⟩	Antepenultimate	Antepenultimate
(j)	CVC.CVC.CV	Penultimate	Penultimate
(k)	CVC.CVC.CVC	Final	Penultimate
(l)	CVC.CVC.⟨CV⟩	Penultimate	Antepenultimate

A system based on syllabic trochees will on the other hand predict non-final stress, and antepenultimate stress irrespective of syllable structure in cases where the final syllable is extraprosodic.

Let us now compare these predictions with the actual data from the database. The distribution of stress in words of three syllables or more sorted by syllable structure is given in (7). In the database, stressed syllables that surface with either long vowel or geminate coda consonant have been coded as light, that is as CV, in accordance with the conclusion reached in Chapter 5.1.3 that these properties are the effect of stress and not its cause. The data have been sorted into three groups defined by the size of the final syllable: light, heavy and superheavy. The distinction between the latter two has been made in order to detect any evidence of final consonant extraprosodicity. This would render CVC-syllables light within an analysis based on moraic trochees, but CVCC would still be heavy, and therefore potentially stress-attracting.

When we compare the results with the predictions in (6), we see that the best match is obtained by using the moraic trochee. If we first look at words with an open final syllable (lines 1–4), we see that the majority pattern with penultimate stress, such as *aróma* (id.) and *barrikáde* 'barricade', can be derived both by a syllabic and moraic trochee. The exceptional cases where stress falls on the final syllable, as for instance in *orkidé* 'orchid', and in disyllabic words such as *allé* 'alley', must under both approaches be accounted for by marking the final syllable as stressed in the lexicon. Antepenultimate stress can be accounted for by both foot types by assuming that the final syllable of the words in question is extraprosodic.

---

[19] ⟨CV⟩ stands for extraprosodic syllable of any shape.

(7) *Attested stress pattern in simplex words of three syllables or more*[20]

Syllabic structure of the final three syllables	N	Antepenultimate stress		Penultimate stress		Final stress	
		%	N	%	N	%	N
1 CV.CV.CV	114	25.4	29	71.9	82	2.7	3
2 CVC.CV.CV	30	20.0	6	76.7	23	3.3	1
3 CV.CVC.CV	41		0	100.0	41		0
4 CVC.CVC.CV	3		0	100.0	3		0
5 CV.CV.CVC	70	12.9	9	10.0	7	77.1	54
6 CVC.CV.CVC	32	18.7	6		0	81.3	26
7 CV.CVC.CVC	11		0	27.3	3	72.7	8
8 CVC.CVC.CVC	2		0	50.0	1	50.0	1
9 CV.CV.CVCC	17		0		0	100.0	17
10 CVC.CV.CVCC	3	33.3	1		0	66.7	2
11 CV.CVC.CVCC	1		0	100.0	1		0
12 CVC.CVC.CVCC	0						
	324	15.7	51	49.7	161	34.6	112

The pattern that establishes the moraic trochee as superior is the absence of antepenultimate stress in forms with a heavy penult, such as *canásta* (id.) and *balánse* 'balance'. Forms such as **bálanse* would have been expected under an analysis based on syllabic trochees, since in forms with extraprosodic final syllable, a syllabic trochee would have assigned stress to the antepenult in all cases. A moraic trochee will stress the penult if that is heavy, and the antepenult if the penult is light, thus excluding **bálanse* as a possible form.

Going on to the next group, words with final heavy syllable (lines 5–8), we note that the hypothesis that the applicable foot type is the moraic trochee is further supported. Moraic trochees predict final stress in these forms, while syllabic trochees predict penultimate stress. Within the group as a whole, 77.4% out of 89 tokens have final stress.

The majority of the remaining examples can again be accounted for by assuming that the final syllable is extraprosodic. Stress is then assigned to the penultimate syllable if that is heavy (lines 7–8), and to the antepenultimate if the penultimate is light (lines 5–6). We would in other words expect no antepenultimate stress if the penult is heavy, and only antepenultimate stress if the penult is light. The first of these predictions is borne out, but the seven examples of penultimate stress in line 5 show that the second is not. If the final syllable is extraprosodic, we would expect

[20] The cells containing exceptions to the rule stated below are shaded, while the cells whose pattern depends on extraprosodicity are framed.

antepenultimate stress when the penult is light, as in *ánanas* 'pineapple' and *génesis* (id.). Among the seven counterexamples are *amaryllis* 'kind of flower' and *adónis* (id.). In order to account for these, a possible solution would be to follow van der Hulst (1999a: 65), who assumes that the equivalent word *Messías* in Dutch should be analysed as having both final-syllable extraprosodicity and diacritic stress on the penult. Another possibility would be to assume final consonant extraprosodicity in these examples. Rendering the final syllable light, a foot could be built on the two final syllables. A prediction that follows from this analysis is that penultimate stress should not arise in a CV.CV.CVCC word. Final consonant extraprosodicity would not influence the weight of this syllable, so also in this case final stress would be derived. Final syllable extraprosodicity would lead to antepenultimate stress. Unfortunately all of the 17 tokens in the base with this structure have final stress, so data that could decide the issue is lacking. I therefore tentatively assume van der Hulst's analysis, extraprosodic final syllable and stress marked on the penult.[21]

The conclusion that follows from the pattern in (7) is that stress placement *is* quantity sensitive in Norwegian, *but independent of vowel length and consonant gemination*. The pattern in lines 5–8 shows that CVC-syllables clearly constrain stress placement in a significant way, and syllable weight must therefore be available for the rule that determines stress placement. This constitutes strong evidence in favour of the conclusion reached in Chapter 5.3.4 that the coda rule should be instantiated by Weight by Position.

The conclusion that CVC-syllables attract stress is corroborated if we now look at the disyllabic examples in the database with final CVC. There are 254 examples with this structure. 201 of these, that is 79.1%, have final stress, which is basically the same proportion as in longer words with final CVC (77.4%). The structure of the first syllable may have a slight influence on the pattern. If the initial syllable is CV, as in *trafíkk* 'traffic' and *hállik* 'pimp', the proportion of final stress is 83.0% out of 176 tokens, while in words with initial CVC, such as *altán* 'balcony' and *fósfor* 'phosphorus', the proportion of final stress is 70.5% out of 78 tokens.

Let us now return to the pattern in (7). The types in lines 9–12 are only supported by 21 tokens, with one pattern not represented at all (line 12) and one by only one token (line 11). But we see that the conclusions above are supported. Final stress is dominant, but extraprosodicity seems possible also here, in which case stress is assigned to the penult, as in *appéndiks* 'appendix' or the antepenult, as in *ásterisk* 'asterisk'. Unfortunately, examples of non-final stress are lacking for CV.CV.CVCC and in CVC.CVC.CVCC, where no heavy syllable, or more than one, precedes the final syllable. Here we would expect antepenultimate stress in the first case, and penultimate stress in the second. The percentage of final stress across lines 9–12 is 90.5 %. In disyllabic words with final CVCC the percentage is slightly

---

[21] One might ask why the penult cannot be marked diacritically for stress without at the same time assuming extraprosodicity. The motivation is presumably that by assuming extraprosodicity, diacritically marked stress can be limited to one environment, final, open syllables.

lower; out of 71 tokens, 80.3% have final stress. The weight of the initial syllable does not seem to influence the proportion in disyllabic words.

The above analysis has been worked out based on loan words. If we now turn to words of native origin, we see that the analysis can accomodate this type as well without further modifications. The vast majority of native roots are either mono- or disyllabic, the latter ending in an open syllable. The 'initial' stress pattern of the latter type is therefore automatically derived, since a moraic trochee cannot be built on the final syllable alone. The lexical representations of the very few trisyllabic roots such as *hélvete*, 'hell', must be marked for extraprosodicity. The initial stress pattern of native roots is in other words epiphenomenal, it is due to the fact that the members of this class are so short that final stress in monosyllables and penultimate stress in disyllabic words will at the same time be initial.

6.4.5 Vowel length in closed, final syllables

In Kristoffersen (1991) I explained vowel length as the effect of open syllable lengthening under stress. In closed, final syllables such as [ˈtɑːk], *tak* 'roof' and [kɑ.ˈmeːl], *kamel* 'camel', I then had to invoke final consonant extraprosodicity in order to be able to generalize the account to this environment. The pattern in (7) now confronts this analysis with a serious problem. If single final consonants are posited as extraprosodic in order to account for the fact that word finally, at most one consonant may follow a long vowel, a prediction that follows is that words of the structure CVC.CV:C with final stress should not occur, or at least should be severely marked, because a final CV⟨C⟩ will count as light and therefore not be stressable on its own.

Note that monosyllabic words with this input structure will cause no problems in this respect. Stress must be assigned to the only syllable available, which conse- quently must undergo lengthening because it is light. But if the same syllable type, CV⟨C⟩, is final in a polysyllabic word, the penultimate syllable is available for stress assignment. If this is light, a foot can be built over the final and penultimate syllable, and if it is heavy, the final, light syllable will be left unfooted, and the stress foot will be built over the two moras of the penultimate syllable. The predic- tion is therefore that long vowels before a word-final consonant should only appear in monosyllabic words.

A consultation of the relevant, polysyllabic forms with final stress in the database reveals that this hypothesis is falsified. 290 words have stress on a final CVC-syllable. Out of these 167, that is 57.6%, are realized with long vowel. Compared with the very small minority of words which are truly vowel final and that are stressed on the final syllable, this number cannot be attributed to some exception feature. We are therefore forced to admit that the final consonant in cases where the stressed syllable is realized as V:C cannot be invisible to syllabification, and thereby to the stress rule. The paradox can be stated in the following way: consonants that follow long vowels at word ends must be syllabified in order for the syllable to have sufficient weight to attract stress, but for vowel length to be derived as the effect of open syllable lengthening, they cannot be syllabified.

In order to 'derive' vowel length once stress is assigned, it would be necessary to delink final consonants from their moras in just those cases where the vowel surfaces as long. If the distribution of long vowels could be predicted from the segmental properties of the following consonant, we might attribute such delinking to an inability of certain consonants to be licensed as moraic codas. But (8) shows that no general pattern can be established.[22] The percentages of words ending in a CVC-syllable with non-final stress have also been included, to detect any possible pattern with respect to stress-attracting properties in the consonants themselves.

(8)   *Distribution of long vowels with respect to following consonant in final, stressed CVC-syllables*

Segment type	N	Non-final stress: %	Final stress Short vowel: %	Long vowel: %
p	5	40.0	40.0	20.0
t	58	3.4	63.8	32.8
k	27	22.2	74.1	3.7
f	6		83.3	16.7
s	52	65.4	19.2	15.4
m	16	31.2		68.8
n	64	15.6		84.4
ŋ	22		100.0	
l	56	5.4	37.5	57.1
r	42	21.4	4.8	73.8

We see that consistent behaviour with respect to choice of vowel length is almost absent. The nasals represent the only group which consistently selects short or long vowel, /m/ and /n/ long vowel and /ŋ/ short. These are the only discrete patterns in the data, the rest can at best be stated as statistical tendencies on which no grammatical principles can be based.[23]

Does this mean that we have reached a point where we have to revert to an analysis where underlying long vowels are assumed, either in general or limited to the problematic environment just discussed? In my opinion this would create as many problems as it solves. First, the dependency of vowel length and gemination on stress remains a fact that must be accounted for. Positing underlying long vowels and geminates would beg the question, and therefore would not render an adequate analysis. Assuming underlying long vowels and geminated consonants would also force us to posit shortening rules limited to unstressed syllables, that are otherwise completely unmotivated. Second, the fact that long vowels only occur in open syllables, except at word ends, and that geminates must be adjacent to vowels on both sides, would appear as a coincidence. Third, positing an underlying long vowel in

---

[22] Only segment types with more than five tokens in the database have been included in the table.

[23] The five voiced, non-nasal stops show the same pattern as /m/ and /n/, but the tokens in the database are too few to venture a generalization.

a substantial proportion of final CVC-syllables immediately raises the question why long vowels are so scarce in final CV-syllables, as can be inferred from lines 1–4 in (7). A plausible explanation, fully in accordance with the weight-sensitive analysis that has been outlined above, would be that the difference between these syllable types does not reside in vowel length, but in the presence of the final consonant in CVC-syllables, which in all cases contributes weight and thereby makes the CVC-syllable stressable. Assuming long vowels in some of these syllables would block such a generalization and render their absence in final, open syllables in polysyllabic words completely mysterious. Only within an analysis where vowel length and consonant gemination are analysed as properties derivable from stress can these generalizations be accounted for.

6.4.6 How is poststress quantity assigned?

The data discussed in the previous section have revealed that an analysis of UEN stress placement is fully feasible without recourse to underlying geminated consonants or underlying long vowels. Given lexical syllable extraprosodicity, and the possibility to mark some words for exceptional final stress, the location of stress can be predicted almost solely by means of a moraic trochee placed at the right word edge. The only type of heavy syllables that needs to be available in the input consists of the closed syllables derived by the CSP outlined in Chapter 5.3.4.

But the effect of not marking quantity directly in the lexicon will be that [²haː.kə], 'chin' and [²hɑk.kə], 'pickaxe' will have identical underlying representations in terms of segmental structure: /hake/. How can we then derive their different surface structure? The result of syllabification will be two light syllables, /ha.ke/, on which the stress rule in both cases will build a moraic trochee so that stress will be assigned to the initial syllable. This is light, and therefore does not meet the requirement that a stressed syllable must be bimoraic. It must therefore be expanded. Two modes of expansion are available, vowel lengthening and consonant gemination.

This expansion can be accomplished by means of two rules, *Mora Insertion* in light stressed syllables followed by *Mora Linking*. The latter can be instantiated in two ways, vowel lengthening and consonant gemination. The choice between these seems completely arbitrary from a synchronic point of view: there is nothing in the non-predictable features of a given lexeme, semantic, morphological or phonological, that lets us predict it. The language user must in other words just know which expansion type is appropriate for a given lexical item, just as he or she has to know which gender a given noun belongs to. Just as gender in most cases has to be included in the non-predictable properties of a given noun, expansion type can be seen as a property that must be assigned to each lexical item as a kind of class-membership index.[24] And just as gender applies to a subset of the lexical items defined on morphological and syntactic features, the quantity index will apply to

---

[24] The vague term 'lexical item' is used on purpose. We shall return to the question of how expansion type is encoded in the lexicon in Chapter 8.2, where it will be argued that expansion type is primarily a property of roots and non-cohering affixes.

a subset of the lexemes defined on a phonological property, those that have at most one consonant following the vowel that will receive stress.

A similar analysis must be assumed for final CVC-syllables. Vowel lengthening seems completely arbitrary in this environment, and the lack of a possible synchronic explanation becomes even more evident. The fact that it is arbitrary and without base in any observable phonological property is expressed directly if it is accounted for with a lexical index rather than an abstract, pseudo-phonological, but in essence diacritic feature such as underlying moraicity.

The impact of this analysis is therefore a rejection of a synchronic, *phonological* analysis when it comes to predicting the choice between geminates or long vowels as a means to expand a subminimal, stressed syllable. The impossibility of such an analysis is supported by the indeterminacy in choosing vowels or consonants on which to mark underlying quantity, which has ridden the discussion of Norwegian and Swedish quantity as long as linguists have occupied themselves with the problem. The explanation must instead be sought in diachrony, and like many other traces of diachronic, fossilized processes, the results must be seen as idiosyncratic from a synchronic point of view and therefore be marked as unpredictable in the lexicon.[25]

What must be accounted for in the phonology however, is the fact that Mora Insertion only occurs in stressed syllables. This is taken care of by the assumption that expansion is dependent on stress. Any underlying, direct encoding of quantity will miss this generalization, which is perhaps the only phonological one worth making within a synchronic analysis.

6.4.7 The Main Stress Rule

In this section I shall try to state the generalizations arrived at in the preceding section in a more formalized way. In the format of Hayes (1995), an algorithm which assigns main stress to a Norwegian simplex word can be stated as in (9). In the following, I shall refer to the algorithm embodied in (9) as the Main Stress Rule (MSR).

(9) *Cyclic main stress assignment in simplex words (MSR)*

Syllable Weight:	CVC = heavy
Extraprosodicity:	$\sigma \rightarrow \langle \sigma \rangle / \_\_]_{Root}$ (Subject to lexical marking)
Foot Construction:	Form a moraic trochee at the right end
Word Layer Construction:	End rule right

---

[25] The diachronic explanation is as follows: Old Norse had *phonemic* quantity in that long vowels and consonants could contrast independently of each other in stressed syllables and thus had to be encoded as such in the lexicon. The same segmental VC-string could therefore be realized in four different ways with respect to length: VC, V:C, VC: and V:C:. In the late medieval period, the so-called quantity shift took place (Riad 1992, 1995, Kristoffersen 1995), reducing the prosodic structure possible in a stressed syllable to a heavy syllable. After this change, vowels and consonants could no longer contrast independently, and the contrast was now transferred to different realizations of the heavy syllable requirement, which cannot be directly coded as segmental length, because the segments in question are no longer contrastively long or short *qua* segments.

In (10) some sample derivations are given of words that are not exceptionally marked in any way, either for extraprosodicity or exceptional final stress. I have only shown the derivation up to the foot level. Word layer construction will add another mark on top of the foot head, but will not change the location of the prominence assigned by foot construction. In (10e) the final syllable is skipped, because a foot cannot be built on the mora of the final syllable plus the last mora of the penultimate. In all the other cases the foot is built at the right edge. After stress assignment, the light, stressed syllables in (b), (c) and (d) must be expanded according to the expansion type they belong to.

(10)   *Examples of main stress assignment*

Input:	(a)	(b)	(c)	(d)	(e)
	hat	ha.ke	tra.fik	a.ro.ma	ca.nas.ta
	'hat/hate'	'chin/axe'	'traffic'	(id.)	(id.)
Line 0 assignment:	xx	x x	x x x	x x x	x xx x
	hat	ha.ke	tra.fi k	a.ro.ma	ca.nas.ta
Foot assignment:	x	x	x	x	x
	(xx)	(x x)	x(x x)	x (x x)	x (xx)x
	hat	ha.ke	tra.fi k	a.ro.ma	ca.nas.ta

In (11) examples are given of stress assignment in words that either have final stress assigned in the lexicon, that are lexically marked for final syllable extraprosodicity, or both. This raises the question how exceptional stress should be marked in the lexicon. I propose that this be done by prosodic prespecification in the form of two moras assigned to vowels realized as long, and a mora assigned to the vowel as well as one to the following consonant in cases where the weight requirement is met by consonant gemination. Syllabification will yield heavy syllables in these cases, and the MSR will locate stress correctly, to the rightmost heavy syllable. Note that this will not give the right result if there is a heavy syllable fol-

(11)   *Stress assignment in exceptionally stressed words*

Input:	(a)	(b)	(c)	(d)	(e)
				$\mu \quad \mu$	$\mu \quad \mu$
				$\vee$	$\vee$
	ha.⟨lik⟩	ko.le.⟨ra⟩	in.di.⟨go⟩	ar.me	me.si.as
	'pimp'	'cholera'	(id.)	'army'	'Messiah'
Line 0 assignment:	x	x x	xx x	xx xx	x xx
	ha.⟨lik⟩	ko.le.⟨ra⟩	in.di.⟨go⟩	ar.me	me.sí.⟨as⟩
Foot assignment:	x	x	x	x	x
	(xx)	(x x)	(xx) x	xx (xx)	x (xx)
	ha.⟨lik⟩	ko.le.⟨ra⟩	in.di.⟨go⟩	ar.mé	me.sí.⟨as⟩

lowing the prespecified one in words with antepenultimate stress. As can be seen from (7), no such examples exist.

Note also that in example (a) the Unstressable Word Syndrome of Hayes (1995) becomes relevant. I assume that a degenerate foot is built on the only available syllable, which is then expanded into a bimoraic foot by Mora Insertion and subsequent linking.

The analysis presented in this section does not rely on exhaustive footing of a given word. Main stress is assigned at the right edge of any lexical word by the algorithm given in (9) in the form of a moraic trochee. Any preceding syllables are left unfooted by the algorithm. As mentioned in Section 6.3.4 above, this is fully in accordance with the hypothesis defended in van der Hulst (1984, 1996) that word stress assignment is independent of a full foot parse.

In Section 6.5 below I shall argue that a foot should also be assigned to the initial syllable of the word, defining an initial secondary stress. Both the right edge primary stress and the initial secondary stress must be analysed as lexical. The intervening, alternating rhythm defined over syllables which manifests itself in longer words and phrases, should on the other hand be interpreted as postlexical. Rhythm will therefore be treated in Chapter 10.6.

6.4.8 Mora Insertion and Mora Linking

The analysis of stress placement in simplex words developed in this chapter assumes that the grammar contains what can be called a 'stress-to-weight' principle that insures that light, stressed syllables that head a disyllabic foot will be expanded to bimoraic size after stress has been assigned. This principle can be seen as formally instantiated by two rules, Mora Insertion, which inserts a mora in light, stressed syllables, followed by Mora Linking, which links either the vowel or the postvocalic consonant to the inserted mora.

Mora Insertion is stated formally as (12), and Mora Linking as (13a and b). Mora Insertion seems to go against an important hypothesis, at least within some versions of Metrical theory, that prosodically induced lengthening of syllables that are heads of feet is only expected in iambic systems, while in trochaic systems, shortening is the expected mode of prosodic adjustment. Hayes (1995) derives this from what he calls the Iambic/Trochaic Law, which on the basis of perception tests predicts that rhythmically paired elements in a string of sounds that contrast in

(12) *Mora Insertion*

(13) *Mora Linking*

    (a) Consonant Gemination   (b) Vowel Lengthening

duration will be perceived as having final, i.e. iambic, prominence, while an equivalent string of elements that contrast in intensity will be perceived as having initial, i.e. trochaic, prominence. Lengthening will therefore enhance an iambic system, while it will have the opposite effect on a moraic system.

Kager (1993: 384ff.) derives the same asymmetry from a rhythmic drive towards an alternating sequencing of strong and weak moras with respect to foot structure. If the final syllable in a right-prominent, even foot is lengthened, the prominent mora, which is the head of the final syllable, will end up having one weak mora on each side. If the same type of lengthening takes place in the head syllable of a left-prominent foot, however, the result is a stretch of two weak positions following the strong. This lapse will break up an even alternation between strong and weak moras, and render the output less eurhythmic than the input. Kager therefore posits an anti-lapse filter that will block moraic lengthening.

In light of these insights, which are substantiated with a considerable body of data in both the sources referred to, moraic insertion posited for Norwegian may seem somewhat surprising, and even a potential counterexample to this difference between iambic and trochaic systems which Hayes and Kager analyse. Note, however, that both the Iambic/Trochaic law and Kager's alternative refer to *rhythmic* systems where prominent and non-prominent elements alternate in an iterative fashion, see the following statement from Kager (1993: 395): 'To the extent that the Anti-Lapse Filter is language-specific, it seems to characterize precisely the set of systems with iterative foot assignment.'

In our analysis we have established that main stress can be assigned without exhaustive, iterative footing that at the same time defines a rhythmic pattern of secondary stresses. To the extent that Hayes' and Kager's generalization is a significant one, moraic insertion in UEN indirectly supports the hypothesis that no iterative rhythm is assigned *as part of* main stress assignment in Norwegian. Mora Insertion can be seen as a rhythm-independent enhancement of the main stressed syllable within a system where this syllable is not the anchor of an exhaustive, rhythmic grid defined by iterative feet. This of course does not preclude that a rhythmic pattern can be assigned at a later stage on strings of unfooted syllables. The point is that a rhythmic grid is not a prerequisite for main stress assignment.

6.4.9 A short comparison with Rice (1999)

The only other published metrical analysis of Norwegian stress is Rice (1999), which is 'an analysis of a select portion of the Norwegian data', analysed by means of Optimality Theory. Rice also argues that a moraic trochee is the appropriate stress foot, and that stress 'tends to be towards the right edge of the word' (p. 549). The difference between the two analyses becomes clear when we look at how final syllables are represented in the input. With reference to the orthographic conventions of Norwegian, where a short vowel is signalled by means of consonant gemination, Rice gives this convention a substantial interpretation when he writes:

It should be emphasized that writing C_aC_a word-finally in Norwegian is not simply a convention for indicating that the vowel is short but rather indicates a real phonological geminate. (p. 549)

No further evidence for this conclusion is given, however. Underlying vowel length is assumed without comment in the same environment, but as far as I can see, not non-finally, where it is not necessary in order for the constraints to select the correct candidate. Syllables are assumed to be maximally bimoraic. This means that the final part of a final geminate, and any consonant following a long vowel, will find itself outside the final full syllable. Instead they are analysed as onsets of a following, defective syllable.

Stress itself is assumed to be non-final in the normal case. The syllables followed by a defective syllable in the form of a single onset consonant are therefore candidates for primary stress, because they are non-final. This is not the case with respect to final VC-syllables where the final C is non-geminate, however, because this will be in absolute final position. The difference between *hállik* and *trafíkk* is therefore that the latter has a final, defective syllable realized by the final half of a phonological geminate that the former lacks. The stress pattern in both is therefore penultimate.

Rice's analysis does without extraprosodicity by assuming that the stressed syllable itself cannot be domain-final. The defective syllables ensure that the right pattern is selected when the final syllable is closed, but it is difficult to see how the analysis can generate exceptional, final stress on an open syllable without some kind of exception marking. The same holds for roughly 20% of the words with a final consonant cluster that do not have final stress, as in lines 9–12 in (7).

6.5 INITIAL PROMINENCE

6.5.1 Weak secondary stress in simplex words

As mentioned in Section 6.1.3 we can distinguish between two sources of secondary stress in Norwegian. The first type arises from demoted primary stresses, and will be further discussed in Chapter 7.3. We shall now discuss the evidence for a secondary stress due to another once-only assignment of a foot, this time at the initial edge of the domain. Consider the following citation from van der Hulst (1984: 175):

It has been observed many times that in languages having final stress, the initial syllable of a word, if separated by at least one syllable from the main stressed syllable, bears a strong secondary stress. [. . .] I will use the term *antipole stress foot* for this second foot, which, I emphasize, does not result from iterative application of the stress rule, but by means of a separate convention.

Such an initial, secondary stress seems to be present also in UEN in words where the main stress does not fall on the initial syllable. The first to point this out, at least to my knowledge, is Brekke (1881: 65).[26] Alnæs (1925: 23) also cites initial stress as typical of loan words consisting of more than two syllables. Some examples given in these sources are *àllegorí* 'allegory', *dèlikát* 'appetizing' and *pròtestantísme* 'Protestantism'. Brekke also claims that no secondary stress can be heard when there is no intervening syllable between the initial syllable and the main stress syllable, by comparing *protést* (id.), without a secondary stress, with *pròtestantísme*, where a secondary stress can be heard.

Later sources do not mention such secondary stresses as part of the prosodic system of Norwegian. We must therefore ask what evidence can be found that might support or cast doubt on the existence of initial, secondary stress. Alnæs claims that the phonetic reflex of this initial stress is a slight lengthening of the following onset consonant in cases where the initial syllable is open, such as in *dèlikát* and *pròtestére* 'to protest'. This lengthening is difficult to hear, and the claim has not been investigated instrumentally. But if a small but significant difference in duration can be found, it may be interpreted as a weight requirement realized by consonant gemination.

Additional evidence, also indirect, is supplied by the realization pattern of the empty vowel /e/. In Chapter 2.1.1.5 it was stated that /e/ is realized as [ɛ] in closed syllables, and in open syllables when heading a foot not carrying main stress. We can now formulate these rules more precisely by invoking the principle of van Oostendorp (1995, 1998) that schwa cannot appear in metrically strong positions due to its lack of features. These positions include 'head of a foot' as well as closed syllables.[27] When underlying /e/ ends up as head of a closed syllable by the rules discussed in Chapter 5.3, or when a syllable headed by /e/ is made head of a foot, it will therefore need vocalic features in order to be licenced in these

---

[26] According to Brekke, the principle can be overridden in cases where the stress on a previous cycle is non-initial, as in *inténs* 'intense'. In the derivation *intensitét* 'intensity', the secondary stress may fall on the second syllable. The reason for this is according to Brekke the fact that the previous stress can survive. My own judgement is that the secondary stress also in these cases falls on the first syllable.

[27] The same holds if the syllable headed by /e/ lacks a preceding (underlying) consonant that may serve as onset. The constraint is in fact even narrower: the consonant must have Place features of its own. Thus /e/ cannot be realized as schwa if the onset consonant is /h/. This is revealed by the fact that an initial /he-/ apparently cannot be optionally realized as schwa when the following syllable carries main stress. Thus while *betóng*, 'concrete', may be realized as [bɛˈtɔŋ] or [bə.tɔŋ] (see below), only [hɛˈtit] seems possible for *hetítt*, 'hittite'.

positions. We can therefore state a rule saying that if /e/ heads a prosodic structure that is right-branching on the syllable or foot level, the features [Coronal: –high, –low] are inserted.[28]

This rule can now account for the fact that the first syllable of words such as *tèlefón* 'telephone' and *èlefánt* 'elephant' cannot be pronounced as schwa, while the second vowel can. By assuming that a moraic trochee is built on the initial syllable only, we derive the consonant lengthening invoked by Alnæs (1925).

Assuming a *monosyllabic* moraic trochee will also solve another problem. A light initial syllable immediately followed by the main stressed syllable will fall victim to the 'Unstressable Word Syndrome' of Hayes (1995: 110ff.), because no bimoraic foot can be built over the two first syllables in this case. If a foot is assigned to the first syllable only, this problem does not arise. It means that in cases where an initial light syllable is followed by a primary stress, a degenerate foot can all the same be built on the initial syllable which is then expanded to legitimate size by gemination of the postvocalic consonant. Only if no consonant is available, as for example in *diagrám* (id.), the vowel is lengthened instead, giving [ˈdiː.jɑ.ˈɡrɑm].

Evidence for such an initial foot can be found in words where the initial syllable is headed by /e/, as in *betóng* 'concrete' and *metríkk* 'metrics'. If a foot is built on these syllables, with subsequent gemination of the following consonant, we would expect it to be realized with a full vowel, being both the head of a foot and the head of a closed syllable. If no foot is built, we would expect schwa. In fact, the syllables in question may be pronounced with both schwa and [ɛ]. The fact that [ɛ] is possible, but not obligatory, suggests that the initial foot is built also in these cases. The pronunciation with schwa can then be seen as due to facultative destressing in clash, because the following syllable carries main stress.

If the variability between [ɛ] and [ə] in the first syllable of words like *betóng* is indeed due to destressing in clash, we will expect [ɛ] to be obligatory also in cases where the second syllable is heavy, but does not bear main stress. This seems to be the case in a word like *sèleksjón*, only [ɛ] seems to be possible in the initial syllable. This means that in cases where the 'Unstressable Word Syndrome' arises, but no stress clash results from building a foot on the initial, subminimal syllable, the initial foot is obligatory.

This analysis implies that a stress foot is also built on the first syllable in words of identical structure whose first vowel is not /e/, such as *protést*. Here its presence is harder to detect, however, because there is no vowel alternation by means of which it can be diagnosed. Note that it goes counter both to the general observation made by van der Hulst (1984), cited above, that an unstressed syllable must intervene between the initial secondary stress and the final primary stress, and the observation made by Brekke (1881) and Alnæs (1925) that this also holds for Norwe-

---

[28] The rule is only stated informally, given the formal complexity involved in giving a unified statement of the environment, which must also include the requirement that the syllable must have a 'substantial' onset for insertion to be blocked.

gian. We should therefore look for further evidence in support of the analysis offered here. Such evidence will be discussed in the following section.

6.5.2 Initial primary stress

The other phenomenon that supports the presence of a stress foot on the initial syllable is a rule found in vernacular East Norwegian by which primary stress may be moved to the initial syllable in simplex words. Instead of *pròtestére* we get *prótestère* (phonetically [²pruːt.tə.ˌsteː.rə]), and instead of *sèleksjón* we get séleksjòn (phonetically [²sɛl.lɛk.ˌʂuːn]).[29] If there is a secondary stress present in the first place, initial stress can be accounted for by a rule that moves the line 2 mark from the final foot to the initial foot.

The rule is lexical, even if it has a closely related phrasal counterpart, which will be discussed in Chapter 10.4.2. It may apply in simplex words as well as in morphologically complex words, but the presence of an unstressed prefix such as /be-/ and /for-/ blocks the rule. This suggests that the initial stress foot itself cannot be constructed over a cohering prefix. The fact that the prefix /be-/, as in *be-svíme* 'to faint', is obligatorily pronounced with schwa, supports this. Thus stress can be moved to the initial syllable in *bèkkasín* 'kind of bird' and *bètóng* 'concrete', but not in *be-tóne* 'to accentuate' and *be-kláge-lig* 'regrettable'.

The main stress may be moved to the initial syllable also in words where the post-initial syllable normally bears the main stress. *Pròtést* may therefore be pronounced [²pruːt.ˌtɛst] and *bètóng* as [²bɛ.ˌtɔŋ]. This supports an analysis where an initial stress foot is assigned blindly as long as there is at least one unfooted syllable available at the left edge.

When stress is moved to an initial, open syllable, we very rarely find vowel lengthening, only consonant gemination.[30] The expansion type is therefore predictable in this case. If initial secondary stress, as Alnæs (1925) suggests, is realized by means of consonant gemination, then this explains why initial main stress, being parasitic on the initial secondary stress foot, is realized almost exclusively by gemination, which of course will be phonetically enhanced when stress is moved to this syllable.

The syllable assigned stress by the MSR is realized with secondary stress and with quantity preserved. This suggests that initial stress is the result of a movement rule which applies after the MSR has applied and the appropriate expansion type has been assigned. If this results in a long vowel, as in *sèleksjón*, the length will

---

[29] The rule is subject to strong sociolinguistic prejudice, and at least in towns there is probably no one who applies it consistently irrespective of style (Larsen 1907: 34). Its low prestige may be the reason why it has not received much attention in the literature. It is usually only mentioned in passing, with a few examples, and in prescriptive grammars such as Popperwell (1963) is referred to as an incorrect or vulgar pronunciation of loan words.

[30] The only exceptions to this rule that I know of are *ápril* 'April' and *ávis* 'newspaper', where a long vowel is possible, but not obligatory. Larsen (1907: 34) provides another two, *fábrikk* 'factory' and *gésell* 'apprentice'. The former I have only heard with short vowel, the second is hardly in use today.

prevail even if the word is pronounced with initial primary stress.[31] This seems to exclude an alternative analysis where main stress is accounted for by a set of disjunctively ordered rules, End Rule Left and End Rule Right. If main stress is not first assigned near the right edge by the MSR discussed in Section 6.4.7 above, and then moved, long vowels and consonant geminates at the original stress site cannot be accounted for. The rule that assigns initial stress is therefore not an alternative stress rule which can apply instead of the right edge MSR of Section 6.4.7; it is a rule that takes the result of the latter as input. Since the MSR will be shown to apply cyclically in Chapter 7.2, this suggests that the rule is postcyclic. The rule is formalized in (14). Since the demoted main stress retains the characteristics of a strong secondary stress, I shall refer to the resulting stress as primary stress.

(14)   *Initial Primary Stress Rule (IPSR) (preliminary version)*

$$
\begin{array}{ccc}
\quad\quad\quad\text{x} & \quad\quad\quad\text{x} & \\
(\;\text{x} \quad\quad \text{x}\;) & \rightarrow & (\;\text{x} \quad\quad \text{x}\;) \\
_{\omega}[(\;\text{x}\;\text{x}\;)\ldots\;\;(\text{x}\;\text{x}\;) & & _{\omega}[(\;\text{x}\;\text{x}\;)\ldots\;\;(\text{x}\;\text{x}\;)
\end{array}
$$

Note that the result is always accent 2 when stress is moved. If the main stress in its original site is realized with accent 2, however, the IPSR is blocked in UEN. Thus, in *rutíne* 'routine' and *sjokoláde* 'chocolate', which are pronounced with accent 2, initial primary stress is not possible, while it is perfectly all right in *bagásje* 'luggage', which is pronounced with accent 1 when stress is on the penultimate syllable. We shall return to this restriction of the rule in Chapter 9.6.2, where the final version of the rule will be stated.

6.6 CONCLUSION

In this chapter I have argued that two foot-building rules are necessary to account for syllable prominence in simplex words. Left Edge Foot Assignment builds a monosyllabic foot at the left edge of a word, while the MSR (9) builds a foot at the right edge and then assigns word level prominence to the right edge foot. In addition, we have stated a rule that optionally moves the the word-level prominence from the right edge foot onto the left edge foot (14).

Before we conclude the chapter, we must relate these rules to each other. The apparent absence of a left edge foot on cohering prefixes, which will be further discussed in Chapter 7.2.6, can be accounted for if we assume that the left edge foot is built at the root level only. But the MSR must take precedence, since in a disyllabic CV.CV input, the right edge MSR, Mora Insertion and vowel lengthening when applicable will be blocked by there being a moraic trochee instantiated by gemination on the initial syllable in the input. Left Edge Foot Assignment must therefore be interleaved between the foot-level and the word-prominence part

---

[31] In stress clashes, as in *bagásje*, the retention of length seems to be optional. Here we find both [²bɑɡ.,ɡɑː.ʂə] and [²bɑɡ.ɡɑ.ʂə].

of (9). This can be done by partitioning (9) into a foot building rule and a word prominence rule. The foot building rule, which we may call Right Edge Prominence, is given in (15).

(15) *Right Edge Foot Assignment (cyclic)*

Syllable Weight: CVC = heavy
Extraprosodicity: $\sigma \rightarrow \langle \sigma \rangle / \_\_]_{Root}$ (Subject to lexical marking)
Foot Construction: Form a moraic trochee at the right end

Left Edge Foot Assignment, which applies after (15), can be formally stated as (16).

(16) *Left Edge Foot Assignment (root level only)*

Syllable Weight: Weight insensitive
Foot Construction: Build a moraic trochee on the leftmost syllable by associating the rightmost mora to the postvocalic consonant, or by default, to the head vowel.

Word stress can now be accounted for by the statement in (17). Note that I assume that this part of main stress assignment is also cyclic. Mora Insertion and Mora Linking, which are cyclic as well, will apply to the output of (17). The motivation for the claim that these rules are cyclic will be given in Chapter 8.2.

(17) *Word Prominence (cyclic)*

End rule right.

(18) shows how the prominence pattern in *anakónda* is derived by these rules.

(18) *Derivation of word stress*

Right Edge Prominence

```
                    x
                  (x   x)
[ a  .  n  a  .  k  o  n  .  d  a ]
```

Left Edge Prominence

```
  x                      x
(x   x)                (x   x)
[ a  n  .  n  a  .  k  o  n  .  d  a ]
```

Word Prominence

```
                       x
  x                   x)
(x   x)              (x   x)
[ a  n  .  n  a  .  k  o  n  .  d  a ]
```

CYCLIC STRESS ASSIGNMENT

This chapter is divided into two main sections where different aspects of the interaction between morphology and stress assignment are discussed. Section 7.2 is concerned with cyclic application of the Main Stress Rule (MSR), while the subject of Section 7.3 will be stress demotion in compounds.

7.1 LEVEL ORDERING IN LEXICAL PHONOLOGY

An important assumption in many versions of Lexical Phonology has been that the lexicon can be divided into even more sublevels than the two assumed in Chapter 4.1, the cyclic and the postcyclic (or word) level. These levels are usually morphologically defined, such as the difference often assumed in analyses of English between two levels which are defined by the set of *non-native*, stress-affecting derivational suffixes, and the set of *native*, stress-neutral derivational suffixes respectively.[1] A corollary of this difference in behaviour with respect to stress is the pattern that native suffixes are attached outside of non-native affixes. This suggests the existence of two ordered lexical levels. First there is a cyclic level where the morphological rules involving non-native suffixes apply, and where the stress rule can be argued to be applicable after each morphological rule. Following this level one can assume a non-cyclic derivational level where native suffixes are attached, and where the stress rule is inapplicable.

This way of reasoning can be applied to other morphologically defined 'domains' within the lexicon, leading to the positing of additional lexical levels. Thus Halle and Mohanan (1985) argue that in addition to the two derivational levels characterized by different stress assignment principles, one needs to assume for English a third level defined by compounding and a fourth level where inflection is accounted for, giving a total of four ordered levels in the lexicon. This hypothesis, which assumes two derivational plus a compound level, is often referred to as the Extended Level Ordering Hypothesis; see for example Scalise (1984: 93ff. and 116ff.). The approach rests on the assumption that the order of the levels should be mirrored in the order affixes are combined with stems within a word, so that all affixes belonging to level$_n$ are attached outside all affixes attached at level$_{n-1}$.

---

[1] I shall use the term 'stress-affecting' to denote affixes that change the stress pattern of the resulting word, either by attracting the main stress or by causing it to shift to another syllable than the one where it is located in the stem with which the suffix combines. 'Stress-neutral' affixes lack this property.

Booij (1994: 540ff.) discusses the evidence that supports level-ordering. He points out that the level ordering hypothesis does not follow from the theory of Lexical Phonology, because a theory where phonology and morphology interact in the lexical derivation of words is clearly possible without the assumption that the lexicon is partitioned into ordered levels. While the assumption of levels may account for the fact that different morphological categories trigger different rules or different ways of application of the same rules, and conversely, that a given phonological rule does not seem to be applicable throughout the lexical derivation but only with respect to certain classes of morphological rules, it also leads to problems. The most important one derives from the so-called bracketing paradoxes, of which the English word *ungrammaticality* is an often cited example. Here, the level 1, stress-affecting suffix /-ity/ is combined with the stem *ungrammatical*, where we already find a level 2 prefix, /un-/. Within a level-ordering approach, the presence of /un-/ suggests that the derivation has reached level 2, while the suffix suggests that it is still on level 1. In order to account for such examples, loops were introduced which are able to take a form back to a previous level. But loops are powerful devices that in principle make the level order hypothesis impossible to falsify. They therefore seriously undermine the very hypothesis.

We shall see below, in Sections 7.3.7 and 7.3.8, that no level ordering seems possible between derivation and compounding in UEN because derivational suffixes may combine with compound bases, taking prosodic scope over the complete base. Any analysis that assumes level ordering between two derivational levels, or between one derivational level and a compounding level, will run into problems on account of this. I shall therefore base the analysis on the following principle, discussed in Booij (1994: 526, 1995: 54).[2]

(1) *Rule application*
Apply a phonological rule whenever its structural description is met.

This can be seen as the unmarked mode of rule application. The only additional information that must be supplied with respect to level ordering is whether a rule is postlexical or lexical, and for the latter type, whether it applies at the word level or at the cyclic level.

But by itself (1) does not give us the distinction between the stress-affecting and stress-neutral affixes in English, for instance, referred to above. In order to account for this difference without recourse to levels, two research strategies are possible. One is to appeal to structure, and let the two classes of suffixes combine with two different types of stems; see discussion in Booij (1994: 544ff.), where it is suggested that stress-affecting suffixes combine with stems, while stress-neutral suffixes combine with prosodic words. Ideally one would need independent evidence for the different stem types assumed. Clear evidence seems hard to come by with respect to Norwegian, so I shall opt for the second strategy and assume that

---

[2] The actual formulation is taken from Booij (1995).

cyclicity is marked on affixes.[3] Stress-affecting suffixes can thus be marked as cyclic. When combined with a stem, they will cause existing metrical structure above the syllable to be erased, and trigger reapplication of the main stress rule. Stress-neutral affixes, on the other hand, are non-cyclic, and will therefore not have this effect.

Note that this view on the organization of grammar implies that the cyclic level cannot be seen as a level where only the cyclic affixes are added. Instead, it must be seen as the level where all morphology and the phonological effects of the morphological rules are accounted for. In other words, non-cyclic affixes are also added on the 'cyclic' level, but being non-cyclic, no cyclic rules are triggered.

7.2 CYCLIC APPLICATION OF THE MAIN STRESS RULE

7.2.1 Classification of affixes

As stated in Chapter 3.1, affixes may be cohering or non-cohering. Cohering affixes are prosodically dependent on their stems, and are therefore incorporated as part of the prosodic word that the stem belongs to. Non-cohering affixes are affixes that are morphologically dependent in the sense that they must combine with a stem, but phonologically independent in the sense that they form a prosodic word of their own, and therefore a separate domain of stress-assignment. All non-cohering affixes are derivational, while cohering affixes can be subdivided into derivational and inflectional. All inflectional affixes are in other words cohering.[4]

Like all Germanic languages, Norwegian has a set of affixes that have been borrowed from Romance languages. They have originally been borrowed as part of loan words, but after a number of words with the same affix have been borrowed, speakers will start to recognize the affixes as separate, recurring entities. But even if the affixes themselves are recognizable, the stems to which these affixes belong are often idiosyncratic and difficult to establish as separate and independent lexical items. Thus while the suffix /-sjon/ occurs in a great number of words,[5] the stems that it is combined with are often units that cannot function as independent words. This underscores the assumption made in Chapter 3.1 that all complex words that are outcomes of non-productive word formation, are listed in the lexicon with their internal structure represented by means of labelled brackets. The more or less idiosyncratic stem allomorphy in Romance loan words is thereby accounted for directly. Thus the word *nasjon* 'nation' and derivations built on it by means of other non-native suffixes are assumed to be listed as separate entries as

---

[3] I here follow the approach taken in Halle and Vergnaud (1987: Chapter 3), Halle and Kenstowicz (1991) and Booij (1995).

[4] They are also suffixes; there are no inflectional prefixes in Norwegian.

[5] Norsk Termbank (1986) lists more than 400 words ending in this suffix.

shown in (2). The root then is simply what is left when all the recognizable suffixes have been peeled off, even if this is a meaningless morpheme, as in *na-sjón*.[6]

(2) *Structure of Romance loan words*

[[na]sjon]$_N$ 'nation'
[[[na]sjon]$_N$al]$_{Adj}$ 'national'
[[[[na]sjon]$_N$al]$_{Adj}$itet]$_N$ 'nationality'
[[[[na]sjon]$_N$al]$_{Adj}$isme]$_N$ 'nationalism'
[[[[na]sjon]$_N$al]$_{Adj}$ist]$_N$ 'nationalist'
[[[[[na]sjon]$_N$al]$_{Adj}$iser]$_V$e]$_{Inf}$ 'to nationalize'

As noted above, non-native affixes will normally appear inside native affixes, such as inflectional suffixes and native derivational affixes. In (3), three examples, *nasjonalisérbàr*, *nasjonalisérbàrhèt* and *nasjonalisérbàrhèten* are given where the native non-cohering derivational suffixes /-bar/ and /-het/ and the inflectional def. sg. /-n/ appear outside the cohering non-native suffixes /-sjon/, /-al/ and /-(is)er/.

(3) *Native suffixes added outside Romance suffixes*

[[[[[na]sjon]$_N$al]$_{Adj}$iser]$_V$ bar]$_{Adj}$ 'being possible to nationalize'
[[[[[na]sjon]$_N$al]$_{Adj}$iser]$_V$ bar]$_{Adj}$het]$_N$ 'state of being possible to
                                       nationalize'
[[[[[na]sjon]$_N$al]$_{Adj}$iser]$_V$ bar]$_{Adj}$het]$_N$en   'the state of being possible to
                                       nationalize'

7.2.2 Cyclic stress assignment

Cyclic affixes will cause formerly assigned stresses to be erased, and the MSR to reapply within the greater domain created by the affix. Since the MSR builds metrical structure at the right edge of the domain, only suffixes can be shown to have a cyclic effect. Only cohering suffixes may be cyclic, at least with respect to rules that affect prosodic structure. This follows from the fact that non-cohering suffixes are separate prosodic domains. We can therefore say that the primary division among affixes is that between cohering and non-cohering, with cohering suffixes being further subdivided into cyclic and non-cyclic.

While most of the generative analyses of Norwegian stress referred to in Chapter 6.2 provide a cyclic Compound Stress Rule, they have not much to say about the relationship between derivational suffixes and stress assignment. The reason for this may be oversight, but it may also stem from the fact that it may be questioned whether cyclicity is crucially involved here. In Chapter 6.4 we established a main stress rule that builds a moraic trochee at the right edge of a simplex word domain without exhaustive footing of the domain. We also noted that when a stressed suffix

---

[6] In the unmarked case, nouns ending /-sjon/ can be seen as nominalizations of verbs ending in /-er/ (Faarlund *et al.* (1997: 102), as in *emigrére* 'to emigrate' and *emigrasjón* 'emigration'. *Nasjón* is an exception in this respect.

is added to a stem, no traces of the former stress on the stem show up, as shown by absence of vowel length and gemination on any syllable other than the stressed one. This suggests that the MSR, instead of being a rule that applies at the cyclic level, can be stated as a non-cyclic rule that applies once after all the stress-affecting suffixes have been added. Since no trace of former cyclical stresses is present in the output, this would give the right result as well. The assumption that the stress rule applies cyclically after each stress-affecting suffix will on the other hand force us to assume a stress-erasure convention along the lines of Halle and Vergnaud (1987: 83) in order to account for the absence of secondary stresses on syllables presumably stressed on earlier cycles.

The former alternative would therefore at the outset appear to be a simpler solution, and therefore preferable. But as we shall see in Chapter 8.2.1, Mora Insertion provides us with indirect evidence that the MSR is cyclic. I therefore assume that stress is assigned cyclically, and erased on every new cycle introduced by another cyclic affix.

The suffixes that are cyclic with respect to stress are all derivational. I shall distinguish between stress-attracting suffixes, that is, suffixes that surface as stressed if no other cyclic suffix follows them, and prestressing suffixes, that is, suffixes which assign stress to the preceding syllable.

7.2.3 Stressed cyclic suffixes

(4) contains examples of suffixes that attract main stress when combined with a given stem. Only elements with a clear affix status have been included; see the discussion in Chapter 6.4.4 on the problems of parsing loan words morphologically. But since the MSR assigns final stress irrespective of the final syllable being part of a suffix or a root, this indeterminacy does not compromise the analysis in any way.

(4)   *Stress-attracting, cyclic suffixes*[7]

	Orthography	Underlying form	
	-abel	-abl]$_{Adj}$	komfortábel 'comfortable'
	-al	-al]$_{Adj}$	sentimentál (id.)
	-(i)aner	-(i)anr]$_N$	meksikáner 'inhabitant of Mexico'
	-ant	-ant]$_N$	emigránt (id.)
	-asje	-aşe]$_N$	spionásje 'espionage'
	-ast	-ast]$_N$	gymnasiást 'secondary school pupil'
	-ener	-enr]$_N$	italiéner 'inhabitant of Italy'
	-er-	-er]$_V$	konkurrére 'to compete'
	-esse	-ese]$_N$	baronésse 'baroness'

---

[7] The list, which is not exhaustive, is based on Popperwell (1963: Chapter 8). Although not in every detail in accordance with current pronunciation, this source is probably the best systematic overview of Norwegian stress patterns available.

Orthography	Underlying form	
-ine	-ine]$_{Pr}$	Jensíne (woman's name)
-isme	-isme]$_N$	kommunísme 'communism'
-ist	-ist]$_N$	kommuníst 'communist'
-itet	-itet]$_N$	universitét 'university'
-itt	-it]$_N$	konvertítt 'convert'
-iv[8]	-iv]$_N$	objektív 'camera lens'
-sjon	-şun]$_N$	invasjón 'invasion'

Building a moraic trochee on the suffix after Stress Erasure will in each case give the correct stress pattern. The stress pattern can therefore be accounted for by assuming that any previous stress on the stem is erased when the suffix is added, whereupon the MSR is reapplied to the new domain constituted by the stem plus suffix. Note that in the present case, only the right edge stress assigned by an earlier application of the MSR may be deleted. Given the assumption that the left edge moraic trochee accounting for the initial weak secondary stress is assigned at the root level only, full erasure of previously assigned metrical structure would obliterate any trace of initial stress. That Stress Erasure only deletes the right edge stress makes sense under the commonly held assumption that a cyclic rule only applies in derived environments. Strictly speaking, the derived environment is confined to the right edge, that is, to the edge where the cyclic suffix is added. Only here will previously assigned structure be deleted, while at the opposite edge, where no changes have occurred, metrical structure will be left unchanged.

When the suffix is monosyllabic and consonant-final, this will result in final stress, and when it is disyllabic and vowel-final, we correctly derive penultimate stress. Cyclic application of the MSR can be illustrated by means of the word [[[[na]sjon]$_N$al]$_A$isme]$_N$ 'nationalism', repeated from (2). In (5) we see how the MSR is reapplied after the inclusion into the domain of each successive suffix with subsequent erasure of the former stress. Given the fact that the stem /na/ does not exist as a free form, I have skipped the root cycle. I assume that brackets are erased at the end of the cyclic level (Kaisse and Shaw 1985: 11).

(5)   *Cyclic main stress assignment*

	1. cycle	2. cycle	3. cycle
Stress erasure:		[[[na]sjon]$_N$al]$_{Adj}$	[[[[na]sjon]al]$_{Adj}$isme]$_N$
MSR:	[[na]sjón]$_N$	[[[na]sjon]$_N$ál]$_{Adj}$	[[[[na]sjon]al]$_{Adj}$ísme]$_N$

We see that cyclic stress erasure and reapplication of the MSR will give the correct stress pattern directly in words derived by means of one or more cyclic suffixes. No

---

[8] The only consonants that may precede the vowel in /-iv/ are /s/ and /t/, of which /t/ is by far the most common. It might therefore be argued that the suffix is consonant-initial /-tiv/, with a lexically governed allomorph /-siv/. Note that two homophonous suffixes, one deriving adjectives and the other used in nouns mainly denoting philosophical and grammatical terms, will be argued to be non-cohering in Section 7.3.4 because of non-final main stress and secondary stress on the suffix.

postcyclic readjustment is necessary in these cases, and the domain of the MSR can therefore be limited to the cyclic level.

7.2.4 Prestressing cyclic suffixes

Prestressing suffixes can be defined as cyclic suffixes where stress ends up on a syllable preceding the suffix itself. The most important prestressing suffixes are listed under (6).

(6)   *Prestressing suffixes*

Orthography	Underlying form	Cohering?	
-e	-e]$_{Pr}$	Yes	*Fredríkke* (woman's name)
-a	-a]$_{Pr}$	Yes	*Edvárda* (woman's name)
-or	-ur]$_{N}$	Yes	*administrátor* (id.)
-isk	-isk]$_{Adj}$	Yes	*dramátisk* 'dramatic'

Note that the term prestressing does not necessarily mean exceptional. When a suffix consists of a V or a CV sequence only, it will be syllabified as a light, final syllable, and the prestressing property therefore follows directly from the phonological make-up of the suffix itself. Since a final vowel cannot accommodate a moraic trochee on its own, the head of the foot will be placed on the immediately preceding syllable, which is the final syllable of the stem. This class is therefore perfectly normal with respect to stress. The first two suffixes in (6), which are used to derive female first names from male ones, can be accounted for in this way. Since both /-e/ and /-a/ add a light syllable to the stress domain, the suffix itself is not stressable. But building a moraic trochee as near as possible to the right edge will derive penultimate stress irrespective of the weight of the penultimate syllable. In (7) some examples are listed.

(7)   *Derivation of female first names*

Base	Suffix	Output	Orthography
[éd.ʋard]$_{Pr}$[9]	-a]$_{Pr}$	[ed.ʋár.da]$_{Pr}$	*Edvard, Edvarda*
[ú.le]$_{Pr}$	-a]$_{Pr}$	[u.lé.a]$_{Pr}$	*Ole, Olea*
[ú.lav]$_{Pr}$	-a]$_{Pr}$	[u.lá.va]$_{Pr}$	*Olav, Olava*
[té.u.⟨dur⟩]$_{Pr}$	-a]$_{Pr}$	[te.u.dú.ra]$_{Pr}$	*Teodor, Teodora*
[hén.rik]$_{Pr}$	-e]$_{Pr}$	[hen.rík.ke]$_{Pr}$	*Henrik, Henrikke*
[krís.ti.⟨an⟩]$_{Pr}$	-e]$_{Pr}$	[kri.sti.áne]$_{Pr}$	*Kristian, Kristiane*

We turn next to the two final suffixes listed in (6), /-ur/ and /-isk/. Here the stress pattern cannot be directly accounted for by the MSR because they constitute heavy syllables in themselves and should therefore be stressable. We shall see that if both

---

[9] The Retroflex Rule will merge the /rd/ sequence at the word level when not in a stressed syllable; cf. Chapter 4.3.6. The surface form of the stem alone is therefore [ˈɛd.ʋɑɖ] or [ˈɛd.ʋɑʈ]. Only the former can be directly related to the female name.

suffixes are to be subsumed under the same analysis, stress assignment by building a moraic trochee at the right edge will not work in this case. Instead, I shall argue that for these suffixes, we need to assume a syllabic trochee as the basic constituent.

Let us first take a look at /-ur/, cf. *administrátor* in (6). As in Dutch (Booij 1995: 103) and German (Wiese 1996: 293), this suffix normally assigns stress to the preceding syllable, but there are three words, *débitor* 'debtor', *kréditor* 'creditor' and *mónitor* (id.) that have stress one syllable removed to the left from the suffix. The stressed syllable may be underlyingly closed, as in *detéktor* 'detector', or open. If open, Mora Linking can be realized by gemination, as in *proféssor*, or by vowel lengthening, as in *konservátor* 'curator'.

An important property of the /-ur/ suffix is that stress, with the three exceptions mentioned above, falls on the presuffixal syllable. A possible analysis would be to assume the suffix to be extraprosodic, and therefore unstressable on its own cycle. Stress would then have to be placed to the left of the suffix. By the MSR we would then expect penultimate stress if the presuffixal syllable is heavy and antepenultimate stress if the presuffixal syllable is open, and therefore underlyingly light. As in simplex words like *Messías*, stress on an open penult would be marked and therefore expected to be rare on this analysis. But contrary to what we found for simplex words, the 'Messias-pattern' does not seem marked in this context, at least if judged by frequency. Out of 71 relevant entries in Norsk termbank (1986), 61 have an open syllable preceding the syllable that contains /-ur/. Of these, 53 have the sequence /at/ preceding /-ur/, however, and one might therefore argue that this sequence should be seen as part of the suffix, defining an allomorph /-atur/ used when the stem can also take the verb-deriving suffix /-er/, as in *konservátor ~ konservére*, 'curator ~ to preserve'.[10] Seeing this as one unit would reduce the number of exceptions considerably. But the pattern is still so prevalent that to define it simply as a marked and lexicalized pattern should only be decided upon if a more principled analysis seems unavailable.

In Chapter 6.4.4 I followed van der Hulst (1999a) in assuming that the stress in words like *Messías* is derived by combining the two properties that account for exceptional stress placement, final prespecification of stress and extraprosodicity. It was also noted that an alternative analysis would be to assume consonant extraprosodicity, so that the final syllable is rendered metrically light.[11] A moraic trochee built at the right edge would then automatically give penultimate stress irrespective of its being light or heavy. While the rarity of this pattern in simplex words seemed to lend support to the use of lexical prespecification, its prevalence in the present case lends support to the alternative analysis. If it can be shown that consonant extraprosodicity is needed for independent reasons, the analysis of penultimate stress in words ending in /-ur/ irrespective of weight by means of this analytical device would be preferable.

---

[10] *alligátor, gladiátor, senátor* and *orátor* are exceptions to this generalization.

[11] This is the solution proposed for Dutch in Booij (1995: 103).

Positive independent evidence of this sort does not seem available, however, but the very fact that we are dealing with a derived environment makes an extension of the simplex word analysis problematic. Lexical prespecification would on its most reasonable interpretation mean that a non-derivable property is assigned to a given lexical entry as a general property of that entry. Prespecification of final stress in the case at hand, however, implies that we prespecify the entry for a property that it will have only in a specific morphological environment, viz. when combined with the suffix /-ur/. In that case, it would seem more natural to assign that property to the morpheme that creates the environment, and not the stem. Prespecification of the stem will in addition make stress placement on light syllables before /-ur/ a coincidence with no principled relation to the fact that this suffix induces penultimate stress in general. We would in other words miss a generalization. If we on the other hand assume consonant extraprosodicity as a prespecified property of /-ur/, the pattern can be derived by the general MSR without problems. Only the three examples of antepenultimate stress would be exceptional. But before we conclude that the final consonant of /-ur/ should be analysed as extraprosodic, we must see whether this analysis can be extended to the final case listed in (6), that of /-isk/. As we shall see, this is not possible. The final consonant extraprosodicity hypothesis is thereby seriously weakened.

Before we leave /-ur/, however, we must discuss the fact that stress can be assigned to the suffix itself when a plural suffix is added to stems ending in /-ur/. Note that plural suffixes are stress neutral, and therefore non-cyclic. This is especially clear for the disyllabic def. pl. /-ene/, which would attract stress on the first syllable of the suffix itself if the MSR is applied.[12] Unlike German, where the plural allomorph used in this environment can be argued to be cyclic (see Wiese 1996: 293), we therefore cannot account for the stress pattern in def. pl. *professórene* by assuming that the MSR applies after the plural suffixes have been added. An important fact here is that the pattern is no longer obligatory: one will often hear *proféssorene* instead of *professórene*. The deviant pattern seems in other words to be in the process of regularization. This suggests that the forms with stress on the suffix /-ur/ should be seen as lexicalized exceptions, where we must assume a set of stem allomorphs that contains the /-ur/ suffix and where stress is marked on the suffix. These allomorphs must then be subcategorized for inflectional suffixes signalling plural.

A possible objection to this solution might be its resemblance to the analysis with respect to the fixed, penultimate stress on the /-ur/ cycle that I just rejected. But there is a crucial difference between the two cases because the stress pattern induced by /-ur/ is obligatory, while the pattern discussed here is variable, suggesting that the marked option is in the process of being eliminated. In addition, it is not

---

[12] Note that the suffix itself cannot be parsed into a sequence of a plural plus a definite morph without at the same time assuming an abstract analysis based on rules that would be applicable in this environment only. The indef. marker of plurality is /-r/, and if def. pl. is analysed as /-r-ne/, the rule deleting /r/ would be completely *ad hoc* since the sequence /rn/ in all other environments triggers the Retroflex Rule.

amenable to an alternative analysis by the general principles underlying main stress assignment in the language. The marginality and the variability of the pattern could be captured in a more accurate way by assuming an analysis based on allomorphy if it is the case that for a given speaker, some lexical entries will show stress shift in plural forms while others may be variable or lack stress shift altogether. Such variation between lexical items across individual grammars would be expected under an analysis based on allomorphy, since allomorphy can be listed as an idio-syncratic property of a given lexical entry. An alternative approach based on a minor rule triggered by the affix cannot capture the pattern in the same way, since we would expect a rule to apply uniformly over its domain. Whether the pattern *is* in fact lexicalized in this way is an open question, however, and I must therefore set it aside for future research.

We now return to the question whether consonant extraprosodicity can be gener-alized to account for other patterns as well. In Chapter 6.4.4 we noted that conso-nant extraprosodicity might possibly be appealed to with respect to simplex words that unexpectedly receive stress on an open penult preceding a heavy final syllable, as for example in *Messías*. We noted that this could only be the case if words end-ing in a superheavy syllable did not show the same pattern, since in this case the final syllable would still be heavy even if the final consonant is extraprosodic. We would in other words not expect penultimate stress on an open syllable preceding a superheavy final, as in the constructed and non-existent word *?messíast*. Since the database does not contain many examples of this type, the absence of the pattern in simplex words cannot be taken as clear evidence in favour of the extra-prosodicity hypothesis. But the prestressing suffix /-isk/, which is the next one on the list in (6), provides us with a test case since it ends in two consonants and there-fore is superheavy. By this test the hypothesis that the pattern at hand can be de-rived by means of any kind of extraprosodicity is falsified. As can be seen from the examples in (8), we find several examples of stress on an open syllable preceding this suffix.[13] This excludes syllable extraprosodicity. An analysis by means of con-sonant extraprosodicity is likewise excluded, because the suffix would still repre-sent a heavy, and therefore stressable, syllable if the final consonant is made extraprosodic.

(8) *Stress shifts in words ending in /-isk/*

	Base	Suffix	Result
	dráma(t)	-isk]$_{Adj}$	[drɑ.ˈmɑː.tisk] 'dramatic'
	sálomo(n)	-isk]$_{Adj}$	[sɑ.lu.ˈmuː.nisk] 'Solomonic'
	prósa	-isk]$_{Adj}$	[pru.ˈsɑː.isk] 'prosaic'
	kánon	-isk]$_{Adj}$	[kɑ.ˈnuː.nisk] 'canonical'

This means that at least the /-isk/ cases must be accounted for by some kind of

---

[13] In most of the cases, Mora Linking is realized through vowel lengthening. This is the case in the examples given in (8).

exceptionality feature other than prespecification of stress and extraprosodicity.

Since the suffix itself consists of a heavy syllable, and stress is assigned to the preceding syllable irrespective of weight, one possible alternative would be to assume a *syllabic* trochee built on the right edge to account for at least this prestressing suffix. This would have the undesirable consequence that two foot types are called for in a comprehensive analysis of Norwegian main stress assignment, the moraic trochee as the unmarked default pattern, and a syllabic trochee for at least the /-isk/ suffix. This is incompatible with the metrical coherence hypothesis of Dresher and Lahiri (1991) which predicts that only one metrical foot will be involved in the metrical system of a given language. But it seems to be the only analysis that can account for the facts in this case. I am not aware of decisive additional evidence in support of the syllabic trochee as an additional foot type for stress assignment. But since no viable alternative analysis seems available, I tentatively propose that a syllabic trochee is needed in this case. In addition, we shall see that the syllabic trochee seems to constitute a prosodic template with respect to other phenomena; see Chapter 10.6.4 for a summary.

A suffix that also appears to be prestressing is the noun-deriving suffix /-ikr/. On the surface this seems to be composed of two suffixes, the cyclic, nominal suffix /-ik/ and the agentive suffix /r/, which can also combine with native stems, as in *lærer* 'teacher' from *lære* 'to teach'. If we assume that /-ikr/ consists of two morphemes that are added on two subsequent cycles, /-r/ must be cyclic, extraprosodic and inducing a syllabic trochee in this particular context, since it would change a stem such as [tɛk.ˈnik] into [ˈtɛk.ni.kr̩]. But the fact that we find some words ending in /-ikr/ which do not have any corresponding nouns ending in /-ik/ allows us to disregard this hypothesis. Since we find *alkohóliker* 'alcoholic', *diabétiker* 'diabetic' and *pykniker* 'pyknic', but not **alkoholíkk*, **diabetíkk* nor **pykníkk*, I conclude that /-ikr/ should be analysed as one suffix.

But also on this interpretation, /-ikr/ is problematic. After syllabification it will consist of two syllables, and a moraic trochee built on the edge would assign stress to the first syllable of the suffix and not to the final one of the stem. But if the final syllable of the suffix is made extraprosodic, we can derive the antepenultimate pattern by means of a moraic as well as a syllabic trochee.[14]

7.2.5 Prestressing, non-cohering suffixes

A set of suffixes that at first blush might seem to be prestressing in the same way as those discussed in the preceding subsection, are exemplified in (9). The stems

---

[14] Another possible solution would be to interpret /-ikr/ as stress neutral, and assume that the final stress is accounted for on the previous cycle. But the form *prosáiker*, 'prose writer' speaks against this, as the stem here has initial stress, *prósa*. An alternative analysis could be worked out based on Correspondence Theory (McCarthy 1995), taking advantage of the fact that almost all the words ending in /-ikr/ have a corresponding adjective in /-isk/. We could then assume that stress is determined on the /-isk/ cycle and require that stems combining with /-ikr/ correspond prosodically to stems prosodified before /-isk/.

are *hóvmod* 'arrogance', *álvor* 'seriousness' and *árbeid* 'work', and we see that the suffixes cause the stress to move to the syllable preceding the suffix.

(9) *Orthography*   *Underlying form*
  -ig   -i]$_A$/ -ik]$_{Adj}$ *hovmódig* 'arrogant'
  -lig   -li]$_A$/ -lik]$_{Aadj}$ *alvórlig* 'serious'
  -som   -som]$_{Adj}$ *arbéidsom* 'hard-working'

There is one important difference, however. The stems used in the examples in (9) can all be analysed as compounds. When we add these suffixes to simplex stems, a different pattern emerges, as can be seen from the examples given in (10). Given the scarcity of relevant data, the crucial examples all involve the suffix /-li/, but I shall argue in Section 7.3.8 that the others, plus the clearly non-cohering suffix /-bar/, must belong to the same type.

(10) *Stem*   *Derivation*
  [^{2}yn.də] 'beauty'   [^{2}yn.di] 'beautiful'
  [^{1}frykt] 'fear'   [^{2}fryk.tli] / [^{2}fryk.tl̩.li] 'terrible'
  [^{1}lɑt.tʃ] 'laugh'   [^{2}lɑt.tə.l̩i] 'ridiculous'
  [^{2}bil.lə.də] 'picture' (archaic)   [^{2}bil.lə.dli] 'metaphorical'
  [leː.gə.mə] 'body'   [^{2}leː.gɛm.li] 'bodily'

Since these suffixes only combine with native stems, long simplex stems are hard to come by. The data in (10) nevertheless show beyond doubt that with respect to simplex stems, the stress remains on the same syllable as when the stem is realized as an independent word. This suggests that these suffixes are basically stress neutral, and that the pattern shown in (9) cannot be due to cyclic stress assignment by the algorithm defined in Section 7.2.3 above.

Lack of cyclic effects can be ascribed to two sources. Either the suffixes in question are cohering, but non-cyclic; or they are non-cohering. In the latter case, the lack of cyclicity follows from the fact that the suffixes constitute separate PWds, and therefore separate stress domains.

As will become clear in Section 7.3.8 below, the most coherent analysis can be built on the assumption that these suffixes are in fact non-cohering. An apparent problem with this analysis is that the shorter allomorphs of the /-li ~ -lik/ and the /-i ~ -ik/ suffixes do not seem to meet the minimal word requirement, which must be met in order for an element to constitute a separate stress domain. The reason is that they end in short vowels. But on closer inspection, this is not so clear. Even if words ending in these suffixes are normally pronounced with a short vowel, a pronunciation with long, or at least tense vowel, is also well-formed. If we compare their pronunciation with that of clear compounds whose last member ends in a secondary stressed /i/, we discover that the same alternation between long and short vowel is found here. Thus the compound family name *Grønnli*, which means 'green hillside', and whose second member *li*, 'hillside' is pronounced [^{1}liː] in isolation, may be pronounced [^{2}grœn.liː] or [^{2}grœn.li]. The derived adjective *grønnlig*, 'greenish' is in principle homophonous, even if pronunciation with a clearly long vowel may be rare. Another, more indirect argument in favour of this analysis is that in (non-UEN) dialects where the final /g/ is retained, the pronunciation of the suffix is [-leːg], that is, with long vowel.

The well-formedness of the variants with long vowel follows if we assume that -*lig* and -*ig* represent non-cohering suffixes. The neutrality with respect to stress when added to simplex stems, which they share with /-som/ (and /-bar/), follows from this assumption as well. Their influence on compound stems must then be ascribed to something else than cyclicity. An analysis will be proposed in Section 7.3.8 below.

7.2.6 Prefixes

Most of the prefixes in Norwegian are non-cohering, and will therefore constitute separate domains to which the MSR will apply. The Compound Stress Rule, to be discussed below, which in its unmarked version assigns stress to the leftmost constituent, will then in most cases assign primary stress to the prefix. But there is a small set of prefixes that are unstressed and which therefore must be given a different analysis. These are /be-/, /er-/ and /for-/, all of Germanic origin. The two first are used exclusively with verbal stems and are always unstressed. The latter is unstressed when attached to a verbal stem, but usually stressed when attached to a bare nominal stem, see Popperwell (1963: 119) and Faarlund *et al.* (1997: 94f.). Examples are given in (11).

(11)   *Unstressed prefixes in verbs*

be-tone	[bə.ˈtuː.nə]	'to accentuate'
be-ordre	[be.ˈɔr.drə]	'to order'
er-klære	[æ(r).ˈklæː.rə]	'to declare'
er-obre	[æ.ˈruː.brə]	'to conquer'
for-banne	[fɔ(r).ˈbɑn.nə]	'to curse'
for-akte	[fɔ.ˈrɑk.tə]	'to despise'

The prefixes are cohering with respect to syllabification. Being vowel-final, /be-/ can always combine syllabically with a following stem. In the case of the two others, the final /r/ will be phonetically realized before a vowel-initial stem, where it will syllabify as an onset. Before a consonant-initial stem it will usually delete in informal speech (Rykkvin 1946, Haugen 1948), except before anterior coronals, where it will be merged with the coronal by the Retroflex Rule. The result is in all three cases that the prefix is realized as a light syllable.[15]

A peculiar property of these prefixes is that they can never be the head of a stress foot, which means that they never carry the initial, weak secondary stress described in Chapter 6.5.1.[16] This can be shown directly only for /be-/, because the

---

[15] These alternations are further analysed in Chapter 11.3.

[16] The only exception is to my knowledge *béarbèide* 'to process', where the primary stress on the initial syllable is realized by a long /e/.

vowel is invariably realized as schwa, not as [ɛ]. Recall from Chapter 6.5.1 that the same vowel in a light, initial syllable belonging to a root can be variably realized as schwa or [ɛ] when immediately preceding the main stress, and always as [ɛ] when more than one syllable removed from the main stress. This was ascribed to a rule of optional, initial destressing in clash. Thus the /e/ in *betóng* 'concrete' can be variable, while in the first syllable of *betóne* 'to accentuate' it can only be realized with a schwa. I interpret this difference as due to its being impossible to build a foot on the prefix.

If this is also the case with the two other prefixes, it follows that the optional initial primary stress described in Chapter 6.5.2 should be impossible in words beginning with these prefixes, because of the lack of an initial foot. As pointed out there, the prediction is borne out. While *bétong* with initial primary stress is all right, **bétone*, **érklære* and **fórbanne* are impossible.

This difference between initial syllables which are part of the root, and initial syllables provided by cohering prefixes, follows from the assumption made in Chapter 6.6 that left edge foot assignment takes place on the root level only. When the cohering prefixes are added, the rule is no longer applicable, and the prefixes will therefore be left unfooted. The Initial Primary Stress Rule will be blocked in these words, because the foot assigned at the root level is no longer word-initial after the prefixes have been added.

There is an interesting exception, however. If the prefix is added to a stem that already has an initial, unstressed syllable, the result seems to be initial primary stress. The stem *árbeid*, 'work', is a German loan word with no clear root syllable. When subjected to infinitive formation, the infinitive suffix /-e/ may cause the main stress to shift to the final syllable of the stem. Both *árbeide* and *arbéide* are well-formed.[17] Adding /be-/ to the infinitive obligatorily gives *béarbeide*, 'to work on (something)', with initial primary stress. This suggests that when an unmetrified disyllabic domain is cyclically created at the left edge, a stress foot may be built that will attract primary stress by the Compound Stress Rule discussed below. No other clear examples of such structures seem to exist, so it is difficult to say whether this reflects a general constraint or a lexicalized exception.[18]

7.3 COMPOUND STRESS

In this section we shall discuss how stresses are distributed in compounds. At the outset, the rule that accounts for this distribution may be cyclic or postcyclic. We shall see in what follows that there are arguments in favour of both analyses. After having discussed the implications of both, I shall conclude in Section 7.3.7 that the

---

[17] When the agentive suffix /-r/ is added, stress shift is obligatory, cf. *arbéider*.

[18] Two other words may be examples of the same type, *fór-arbeide*, 'to prepare', and *for-be-holde* 'to reserve'. However, both may be derivations based on the nouns *fór-arbeid* 'preparatory work' and *fór-be-hold*, 'proviso'. In nouns, /for-/ carries primary stress, and in these cases the stress pattern in the verbs may have been carried over from the stems.

Compound Stress Rule is best conceived of as cyclic. The final version of the rule is stated in (28) below.

7.3.1 Non-cohering affixes

Non-cohering derivational affixes are those that constitute separate prosodic words.[19] I assume that the property of being a separate prosodic word can be derived from their being marked as non-cohering in the lexicon. These affixes are therefore morphologically dependent in that they cannot occur as free forms, but they are phonologically independent in that they are not integrated prosodically into the stems that they combine with. This means that they will constitute stress domains on their own, and that the MSR therefore will apply to these suffixes in the same way as it applies to morphologically independent words.

A prediction that follows from this is that the stress pattern in a word that results from combining a stem with a non-cohering affix will be the same as that found in compounds. Compounds are words created by the combination of two morphologically and phonologically independent units. Since the difference between non-cohering affixes and roots is a morphological one, and the output in both compounds and derivations involving non-cohering affixes is two independent stress domains, we expect that the stress pattern will be the same in both types. The rule responsible for relating the two stresses into one stress contour is the Compound Stress Rule, henceforth the CSR. The final version of the CSR is stated formally under (28) in Section 7.3.7 below.

7.3.2 The prosodic word

Before we proceed, I shall make clear my assumptions about the structure and derivation of the prosodic word in Norwegian. The term itself indicates that its defining properties are prosodic. At the same time, its status as a word relates it in some way to morphological structure.

In Chapter 3.1 I divided the lexicon into two basic categories, roots and affixes. Roots are those morphemes that belong to the lexical categories Noun, Adjective, Verb, Adverb and Preposition, that is, morphemes that can be realized as free forms. That means that they constitute separate domains for the building of prosodic structure, i.e. syllabification and stress assignment. This building of prosodic structure can be seen as a function that takes a morphological unit, at the outset a root, as input and returns a prosodified domain which is *the prosodic word*.

Non-cohering affixes behave in the same way, since they are morphemes where morphological dependency is not coupled with phonological dependency in the sense just mentioned. Even if they must morphologically attach to a stem, they are prosodified as separate units in the same way as roots. This means that they are assigned stress by the MSR, and therefore constitute separate prosodic words.

---

[19] Examples of this type are provided in (2) in Chapter 3.

When a cohering affix is added to a stem, however, its coheringness entails that it must be prosodically integrated with its stem. The prosodic output that results from affixation of this type is in principle of the same type as the input stem, i.e. a prosodic word. This is a unit which is characterized by uninterrupted syllabification, i.e. with no internal appendices, and which must contain a stressed syllable near its right edge. The affix itself must be syllabified, and at the edge between stem and suffix syllabic adjustments may take place in order to secure consecutive syllabification. If the affix is cyclic, Stress Erasure and reapplication of the MSR will take place; if it is non-cyclic, the stress pattern of the input stem will survive unchanged.

Consecutive syllabification and stress are therefore both possible defining properties of a prosodic word. Of these, the stress assignment algorithm, Stress Erasure and the MSR, should be seen as the basic defining property of a prosodic word in Norwegian. A prosodic word thereby corresponds to a morphological domain defined by a right edge stress foot built by the MSR.

If syllabification were to be used as the defining property instead of stress, the syllable constraints defined over prosodic words must not hold across the boundary between two compound members for the criterion to be decisive. In other words, consecutive syllabification must be interrupted at compound boundaries. This is the case in the sense that appendices are tolerated at the boundaries between compound members, as in [¹ɑŋgst.ˌskriːk], *angstskrik* 'cry of anxiety'. But there is on the other hand no *necessary*, syllabic divide in this environment. In cases where the second compound member is vowel-initial, a final consonant which is part of the initial member will resyllabify into onset position with respect to the following vowel, across the word boundary. When an initial compound member ends with a /r/, such as [¹ʋæːr], *vær* 'weather', we get the same effect as that described for the prefix /for-/ in Section 7.2.6 above: if the second compound member begins with a non-coronal consonant, the /r/ may delete, as in [²ʋæːˌmɛl.liŋ], *værmelding* 'weather forecast'.[20] The crucial evidence appears when the second member starts with a vowel. Then the /r/ is realized as an onset for that vowel, as in [²ʋæːˌrɔm.ʂlɑːg], *væromslag* 'change of weather'. *[²ʋæːˌɔm.ʂlɑːg] is impossible.

This shows that syllable boundaries in themselves cannot be used as a diagnostic for identifying a prosodic word, and the domain for stress assignment is therefore the only possible defining criterion that can be appealed to. If a given domain in Norwegian contains more than one stress assigned by the MSR, we are dealing with the same number of prosodic words as with main stresses even if we find that the domain is consecutively syllabified so that the boundary between the morphological constituents does not coincide with a syllable boundary, and therefore not with a PWd boundary.

This definition diverges from those implied for English in Booij and Rubach (1984: 14) and for Dutch in Booij (1995: 50), where the MSR is seen as bounded by the prosodic word and not as its defining property. In the latter source, a

---

[20] This rule is subject to a set of intricate constraints that will be discussed in detail in Chapter 11.3.2.

prosodic word is explicitly defined as a sequence of well-formed syllables, of which at least one must contain a full vowel (i.e. not a schwa), since only full vowels can receive stress (p. 47).[21]

In summary, the boundaries and the prosodic structure of prosodic words can be derived from the distinction between cohering and non-cohering lexical items, plus the interaction between morphological rules, syllabification and stress assignment.

7.3.3 Primary stress in compounds

From the above it is clear that a compound in prosodic terms minimally is a conjunction of two prosodic words with their own stress pattern. The stress of the input of one of the members, usually the second, is demoted to secondary stress, while that of the other surfaces as primary. This is in essence the rule accounting for the stress pattern in simple compounds in UEN. Phonetically, demotion to secondary stress is manifested in deletion of the tonal accents associated with primary stress, but retention of quantity. Vowel length and consonant gemination are therefore preserved in demoted secondary stress in compounds, and can be seen as a diagnostic for the presence of such stresses.

(12) contains sample derivations of two simple compounds, *hvítvìn* 'white wine' and *sákspapìr* 'document pertaining to a specific subject'. Both consist of two simplex constituents, *hvit* 'white' and *vin* 'wine' in the first, and *sak* 'case' and *papír* 'paper' in the other. The simplex constituents involved are separate stress domains, where the MSR will have applied before compounding.[22]

(12)	Input	[hvit] [vin]	[[sak]s] [papir]
	MSR	[hvít] [vín]	[sáks] [papír]
	Compounding	[[hvít] [vín]]	[[sáks] [papír]]
	CSR	[[hvít] [vìn]]	[[sáks] [papìr]]
	Bracket erasure	[hvítvìn]	[sákspapìr]

Let us, before we proceed to more complicated examples, try to state a preliminary version of the rule, based on the data that we have reviewed till now.

(13)   *Compound Stress Rule: preliminary, cyclic version*[23]

In a word formed by two non-cohering constituents, form a left-headed constituent on the highest grid level.

---

[21] Since no underlying difference between schwa and full vowels is assumed in the present analysis, this requirement is trivially met, and can therefore not be used as a defining criterion.

[22] The /-s/ added to [sak] is a semantically empty linking phoneme that is a former genitive marker. Another common linking phoneme is /-e/. The occurrence of linking phonemes is lexically governed, as is the choice between /-s/ and /-e/, except in cases where an initial compound member is complex itself. We shall return briefly to the distribution of linking phonemes in footnote 30. A fuller account will be given in Chapter 9.5.

[23] Since one or both input constituents can consist of a compound, the rule cannot be stated over prosodic words.

This rule is general across word classes. There is a small set of exceptions, however, with stress on the second compound member instead of the first, such as [ˌlɑŋ.ˈfreː.ˌdɑːg], *langfredag* 'Good Friday', [ˌʂæː.ˈtoːʂ.ˌdɑːg], *skjærtorsdag* 'Maundy Thursday', [ˌkɔʂ.ˈfɛs.tə], *korsfeste* 'to crucify', [ˌsmoː.ˈpiː.kə], *småpíke* 'small girl', [ˌskuː.ˈmɑː.kʄ], *skomaker* 'shoemaker'.[24] In most place names where the first constituent is a Danish or Norwegian king's name, such as *Fredrik*, *Kristian*, *Håkon* and *Olav*, stress falls on the second member. Apart from the place names most of these examples can also be pronounced with main stress on the first compound member in accordance with (13).

For these instances we may state a marked version of the Compound Stress Rule that is the mirror image of the rule stated in (13), and which I shall refer to as the CSR^{RIGHT}. It will apply to a limited set of lexicalized compounds, which consequently must have some information included in their lexical representation to the effect that this marked version of the CSR is applicable. Application will bleed the unmarked CSR, which we may refer to as the CSR^{LEFT}.

For ordinary compounds such as *hvítvìn* and *sákspapìr* the CSR^{LEFT} will result in derivations as those shown in (14), where I assume that the MSR has applied within each constituent.[25]

(14) Input   x   x   x   x
                    (x x) (x x)   (x x) (x x)
                    [[h v i t] [v i n]]   [[s a k s] [p a p i r]]

      CSR^{LEFT} x   x
                    (x   x)   (x   x)
                    (x x) (x x)   (x x) (x x)
                    [h v i t v i n]   [s a k s p a p i r]

(13) will also derive the right result when one of the non-cohering constituents is an affix, a type that can be referred to as a *prosodic compound* (Booij (1995: 59)). Non-cohering prefixes will receive primary stress, while non-cohering suffixes will be assigned secondary stress. The derivation of the word *mìstànke* 'suspicion', with the prefix /mis-/, and *vítenskàp* 'science', with the non-cohering suffix /-skap/, are shown in (15).

---

[24] Note also [ˈsmoː.ˌgʉt], *smågutt* 'small boy', with main stress on the leftmost constituent in sg. but with possible right hand stress in the plural: [ˌsmoː.ˈgʉt.tʄ] *smågutter*.

[25] To avoid unnecessary detail, I do not take the initial secondary stresses discussed in Chapter 6.5.1 into account at this stage. We shall return to them at the end of Section 7.3.6.

(15) Input   x   x   x   x
                    (x x)   (x x)   (x x)   (x x)
                    [[m i s] [b r u k e]]   [[v i t e n] [s k a p]]

      CSR^{LEFT} x   x
                    (x   x)   (x   x)
                    (x x)   (x x)   (x x)   (x x)
                    [[m i s] [b r u k e]]   [[v i t e n] [s k a p]]

7.3.4 Non-native prosodic compounds

The suffix /-iv/ is a non-native suffix that behaves as if it is non-cohering and therefore non-cyclic.[26] The stress pattern of words derived by /-iv/ can be predicted if
it is assumed that the suffix is non-cohering, and therefore represents an independent domain for the MSR with respect to the stem. The evidence that supports this
interpretation comes from the fact that even if the primary stress is on another syllable, the suffix is realized with long vowel, which shows that there is a strong
secondary stress on the suffix. The pattern is found in adjectives, and in some
nouns, most of them denoting grammatical and philosophical terms.[27] Relevant data
are given in (16).

(16)   *Word form*   *Word class*   *Gloss*
      (a) óbjektìv   Adj.   'impartial'
      (b) pósitìv   Adj.   'positive'
      (c) súbstantìv   N   'noun'
      (d) intúitìv   Adj.   'intuitive'
      (e) kvántitatìv   Adj.   'quantitative'

The secondary stress on the suffix will follow from the CSR^{LEFT} if it is assumed that
/-iv/ is a non-cohering suffix and therefore an independent domain for the MSR.
The fact that primary stress falls on the left-hand constituent also follows from the
CSR^{LEFT}, but its location within this constituent is less straightforward to account
for.

   If the domain preceding the suffix is a separate stress domain, we would expect
the MSR to assign stress to a final, heavy syllable, as in *objéktiv, and if the final
is light, to the penultimate syllable. Extraprosodicity of the final syllable is expected to move this pattern one syllable leftwards. These predictions are not in
accordance with the observed facts, however. The primary stress never docks on
the final syllable of the stem, cf. *objéktiv, so the weight of the final syllable is

---

[26] This suffix must not be confused with the stressed cyclic suffix /-iv/ listed in (4); cf. footnote 8
above.

[27] All other nouns ending in this suffix are regular in the sense that they have one stress, on the final
syllable as predicted by the MSR. With respect to these stems it is therefore cyclic.

clearly irrelevant. As with the prestressing suffixes, we seem to be dealing with a system that counts syllables instead of moras. It therefore seems that the relevant foot type also in this case is the syllabic trochee. On this assumption extra-prosodicity can be called on to account for the difference between (d) and (e), by marking the final stem syllable in the former as extraprosodic.

7.3.5 Formal compounds

We have defined the prosodic word as the domain for stress assignment by the MSR. Due to cyclic Stress Erasure before reapplication of the MSR, there will only be one stress foot present at the right edge of any prosodic word. In compounds, on the other hand, several stresses may be present, one primary stress and one or more secondary stresses. Given this, it follows that simplex words will leave the cyclic level with only one stress assigned by the MSR. Since vowel length is dependent on main stress, it further follows that long vowels can only occur in the main stressed syllable in simplex words.

In general this is the case, but there are some exceptions to this prediction which we shall address in this section. Consider the two words [²noː.ˌɾeːg] *Noreg*, 'name of Norway in Nynorsk' and [²eː.ʋn̩.ˌtyːɾ] *eventyr*, 'fairy tale'. In both examples the final syllable contains a long vowel, even if it does not carry primary stress. Since long vowels may occur in syllables carrying secondary stress, but not in unstressed syllables, I interpret the vowel length in these cases as realizations of secondary stress. The forms therefore appear as if they are derived by the CSR^{LEFT}. But since it is not possible to parse them into two morphological constituents, the CSR^{LEFT} cannot derive them directly. What is problematic with these words is that they have the prosodic structure of a compound, but lack the morphological structure that would justify an analysis of them as compounds.

One of the assumptions underlying the theory assumed in this book is that mor-phological and prosodic structure are not isomorphic. Prosodic structure is built on inputs provided by the morphology, but the hierarchical structure that results from syllabification, footing and prosodic word formation of a given string may differ from the morphological structure of the same string. In most cases the prosodic structure can be derived from morphological structure by general rules. But we have seen cases where aspects of prosodic structure such as unpredictable syllabifi-cation patterns (see the difference between [¹saŋn] vs. [¹lyŋ.ŋn̩] in Chapter 5.3.2) and final stress on open syllables (Chapter 6.4.4), had to be prespecified in the lexicon. The present case can be solved in a similar way if we assume that prosodic word structure can also be prespecified as shown in (17). I shall refer to this type as *formal compounds*.[28] The members of this type are different from both real com-pounds and the prosodic compounds that consist of a free stem plus a non-cohering affix, in that it is not possible to identify internal constituents by means of morpho-logical criteria.

---

[28] The same term is used for Dutch in Booij (1995: 116).

(17)   *Formal compounds*

   $[(no)_\omega (reg)_\omega]_{PR.}$ $[(eʊn)_\omega (tyr)_\omega]_N$

This representation will secure that the MSR applies twice within these words, once within each bracketed subdomain. On the word level, the CSR^{LEFT} will project the first stress as primary, giving the correct surface forms.

7.3.6   *Is compound stress assignment cyclic or non-cyclic?*

We must now address the question on which level in the lexicon compound stress is assigned. Let us assume for the moment that both versions of the CSR will apply cyclically in accordance with (1), which says that a rule is applied whenever its structural description is met. This means that any time a constituent that consists of at least one prosodic word is concatenated morphologically with another constituent of the same type, either the CSR^{RIGHT} or the CSR^{LEFT} will apply. Since compounding in Norwegian is recursive and apparently without any upper grammatical bound, cyclic assignment predicts, like the corresponding rule of Chomsky and Halle (1968), an infinite number of stress levels, depending on the depth of embedding. The question therefore arises to what extent this formal prediction is reflected in the phonetics: do we find several, discernible stress levels corresponding to the different levels of embedding in complex compounds constructed by cyclic recursion of compound stress assignment?

   Before we proceed, we must deal with a technical detail. Under recursive application, structures may arise where the stresses to be related to each other, i.e. the highest grid mark in each constituent, are not on the same grid level because the two input constituents are of different complexity. In addition to the stress assignment algorithm itself, we therefore need a convention that assures that the stresses that are related to each other are formally equal with respect to grid level. This can be achieved by assuming the Stress Equalization Convention of Hayes (1995: 378).[29]

(18)   *Stress Equalization Convention*

When two metrical constituents are concatenated, and their tallest grid columns are unequal, then grid marks are assigned to the shorter column if necessary to avoid violating the Continuous Column Constraint.

   One way to test whether compound stress assignment is cyclic or not is to construct examples where minimally contrasting branching predicts minimal differences in stress which will correspond to differences in meaning. The well-known example of Chomsky and Halle (1968: 20ff.) is *black board eraser*. A corresponding Norwegian example is *høstmakrellfiske* 'autumn-mackerel-fishing' which can mean (a) 'fishing of autumn mackerel' or (b) 'mackerel fishing in the autumn'. (19)

---

[29]   The Continuous Column Constraint referred to in the convention requires that a given column is continuous in the sense that a grid mark on a given line presupposes grid marks on all lines beneath it in the column.

shows the derivation of the stress pattern in the two different structures by two passes of the CSR[LEFT]. The first derives from a left-branching structure where the inner cycle consists of *høstmakrell*, (19a), while the other is right-branching with the inner cycle constituted by *makrellfiske*, (19b).

(19) *Input*   (a)   x   x   x   (b)   x   x   x
                          (xx)   (xx)   (xx)   (xx)   (xx)   (xx)
                          [[[høst][makrell]][fiske]]   [[høst][[makrell][fiske]]]

      1st cycle   x   x
      CSR[LEFT]   (x   x)   x   x   (x   x)
                          (xx)   (xx)   (xx)   (xx)   (xx)   (xx)
                          [[[høst][makrell]][fiske]]   [[høst][[makrell][fiske]]]

      2nd cycle   x   x   x   x
      Stress   (x   x)   x   x   (x   x)
      Equalization   (xx)   (xx)   (xx)   (xx)   (xx)   (xx)
                          [[[høst][makrell]][fiske]]   [[høst][[makrell][fiske]]]

      CSR[LEFT]   x   x
                          (x   x)   (x   x)
                          (x   x)   x   x   (x   x)
                          (xx)   (xx)   (xx)   (xx)   (xx)   (xx)
                          [[[høst][makrell]][fiske]]   [[høst][[makrell][fiske]]]

The output forms in (19) predict that there should be a discernible difference between the two non-primary stresses and that their distribution is different in the two forms. But this difference in structure is not mirrored in pronunciation: to my ears the two meanings are homophonous.[30]

Before we discuss what consequences this should have on the analysis, we must briefly go into another phenomenon that has been ascribed to scaling of secondary stresses in Norwegian. In words with more than one secondary stress, the final one is usually perceived as slightly more prominent than the non-final (Jahr and Lorentz 1983b: 14). This raises the question how secondary stresses are realized phoneti-

---

[30] Interestingly, Norwegian allows an alternative way to mark internal structure in compounds, viz. by means of linking phonemes. As mentioned in footnote 22 there are two common linking phonemes in Norwegian, /s/ and /e/. Their occurrence at the right edge of simplex words as initial constituents of compounds is lexically marked. Thus *sild* 'herring', like most other monosyllabic names of fishes, takes an /e/, cf. *síldefiske* 'fishing of herring'. When the initial compound member is complex, however, this may be signalled in two possible ways. One can either add the linking phoneme /s/, cf. *vínglàss* 'wine glass' vs. *hvítvìnsglàss* 'glass for white wine', or, in cases where the final member of the initial constituent takes an /e/ in its simplex form, the /e/ is left out in the complex form, cf. *sildefiske* vs. *vårsildfiske* 'fishing of spring herring'. This contrasts minimally with *vårsildefiske*, which is right branching and means 'fishing of herring in the spring'. Since s-insertion is only a fairly strong tendency, and e-truncation is dependent on its presence after the simplex form, this pattern is not predictable, but prevalent enough to be cited as a tendency in most grammars, cf. Faarlund *et al.* (1997: 68ff.).

cally. Recall that vowel length and consonant gemination seem to be the only observable, phonetic cues of secondary stress. The most easily observed of these is vowel length. Consonant geminates are much more unstable cues, given the much smaller durational differences involved, and the lack of distinctions in tenseness, a distinction which in addition to durational differences is found between long and short non-low vowels. The lack of clear phonetic cues with regard to geminates in syllables with demoted primary stress in compounds has led at least one analyst to doubt the very existence of phonetically realized secondary compound stress in Norwegian (Endresen 1977, see also Sandøy 1996: 34f.). But as pointed out by Jahr and Lorentz (1983b: 13f.), the fact that it is possible to distinguish between ['film.ˌtɛk.ni.kf], *filmtèkniker* 'film technician' and ['film.tɛ.ˌknik.kf], *filmteknìkker* 'film techniques' is a strong argument in favour of the presence of secondary stresses also when vowel length is absent.

The fact that syllable weight is an elusive criterion for secondary stress in itself makes it even more problematic as a means to distinguish between *degrees* of secondary stresses. That a final secondary stress is often heard as more prominent than any preceding non-primary stress is therefore somewhat mysterious. As noted by Alnæs (1925: 23), the constraint also seems to induce stress shifts in cases where a non-final stress is the stronger one in the input. In structures similar to (19b), that is, in right-branching structures where the first member of the branching constituent is a monosyllabic word, this member will be realized with weaker stress than the immediately following final foot, even if it is the stronger of the two in the input. Examples from Alnæs (1925: loc. cit.) are *óppgjør* 'settlement' vs. *årsoppgjør* 'annual settlement', and *pålègg* 'increase' vs. *lønnspålègg* 'wage increase'. A rule that shifts the prominence pattern of the two final syllables in words like *årsoppgjør* would account for Alnæs' data, and also for the neutralization of the forms in (19). But the pattern is not limited to environments where a stress clash can be postulated, and this might suggest that instead of a stress shift rule there is a more general rule that reduces all secondary stresses but the final, as proposed by Jahr and Lorentz (1983b: 14).

There is, however, evidence that this relative strengthening of the final foot is not due to a lexical rule at all, but is instead the effect of a postlexical rule of boundary tone insertion. As will become clear from the discussion in Chapter 9, a tonally defined constituent can be identified above the prosodic word which I shall refer to as a postlexical *Accent Phrase* (AP). An AP starts with a primary stress as realized by one of the two tonal accents, and extends to the following primary stress. The end of the phrase is signalled by a very high boundary tone if the phrase is focused. Any word pronounced in isolation is focused in this sense, and will therefore have a high tone at the right edge. It may well be that the prominence that is heard on the final foot may be caused by this tone. This conclusion is supported by the effect of insertion of a word such as *årsoppgjør* 'annual settlement' into an Accent Phrase that extends into the following word because the latter has non-initial primary stress. In the utterance *De avslutter [årsoppgjør på kon]tóret* 'They finish annual settlements in office-the', brackets enclose the relevant AP. The phrase-final high tone will associate with the first syllable of *kontoret*, and there is no longer any prominence heard on the last syllable in *årsoppgjør*. Since the final prominence seems to be associated with a tone insertion rule that must be postlexical, this leads to the conclusion that final prominence heard in complex compounds when pronounced in isolation is not assigned in the lexicon. This implies that neither CSR^{LEFT} nor CSR^{RIGHT} can be responsible for the final prominence perceived in APs. The only difference in stress levels which can be ascribed to compound stress assignment is the difference between primary and secondary stress. Substantial evidence for any further differences between non-primary stresses is lacking. The phonetic data therefore do not support the hypothesis that compound stress assignment is cyclic.

We therefore arrive at an analysis where the prominence patterns derived by cyclic assignment of compound stress may diverge considerably from those that can actually be observed. In order to show this more clearly, we shall take a closer look at how cyclic application of the CSR^{LEFT} will deal with a very complex compound, viz. *únderekstremitètsprotèsemàker*, which can be glossed as 'lower-extremity-prosthesis-maker', that is, 'maker of artificial legs'.[31] Again, I assume

(20) *Input*
```
          x           x          x       x
        (xx)        (xx)       (xx)    (xx)
   [[[[under][ekstremitets]][protese]][maker]]
```

1st cycle
CSR^{LEFT}
```
          x
        (x          x)        x       x
        (xx)        (xx)      (xx)    (xx)
   [[[underekstremitets][protese]][maker]]
```

2nd cycle
Stress Equalization
+ CSR^{LEFT}
```
          x
        (x                     x)
        (x          x)        x       x
        (xx)        (xx)      (xx)    (xx)
   [[underekstremitetsprotese][maker]]
```

3rd cycle
Stress Equalization
+ CSR^{LEFT}
```
          x
        (x                              x)
        (x                     x)     x
        (x          x)        x       x
        (xx)        (xx)      (xx)   (xx)
   [underekstremitetsprotesemaker]
```

---

[31] The word was observed in an advertisement in an Oslo newspaper posting a vacant position some years ago.

that the MSR has assigned stress to all the constituents that form the input to the CSR-cycles.[32]

This result differs radically from a representation of the observable stress pattern, shown in (21), where the postlexically assigned AP-final prominence on the last foot has not been included. We see that the derivation in (20) is far off the mark with respect to the perceived pattern, and will therefore need considerable adjustment in the form of tier conflations to eliminate non-attested differences between secondary stresses.

The much simpler structure in (21) would suggest that the cyclic analysis is flawed, and that assignment of compound stress perhaps should not be conceived of as cyclic after all. If it is not cyclic, it must instead be a word-level rule.

(21)   x
        (x   x   x   x
        (xx)   (xx) (xx) (xx)
        [underekstremitetsprotesemaker]

Even if at the end we shall arrive at an analysis where compound stress assignment is cyclic, we shall explore the consequences of this hypothesis in some more detail. If the compound stress assignment is assumed to take place at the word level, nothing will happen to the stress feet of the two constituents when a compound is formed. This means that a compound will leave the cyclic level with as many main stress feet as there are compound constituents. For *hvitvin* and *underekstremitetsprotesemaker* the inputs to the word level would therefore be those represented in (22).

(22)   x   x   x   x   x   x
        (xx)(xx)   (xx)   (xx) (xx) (xx)
        [hvitvin] [underekstremitetsprotesemaker]

The only rule that is now needed on the word level, is the one stated in (23). It is given in its default, left-oriented version.

(23)   *Compound Stress Rule: preliminary, word-level version*

On the highest grid level, build an unbounded, right-headed constituent, subject to lexical marking (=CSR^{RIGHT}). Otherwise, build an unbounded, left-headed constituent (=CSR^{LEFT}).

The output of this rule will be a string of prosodic words, each characterized by a separate stress. The leftmost (or rightmost) stress will be stronger than the others, heading a prosodic domain that on this level will be isomorphic with the morphological word. At the postlexical level, heads of this type are characterized by having tonal accent, and we may therefore refer to them as *lexical* Accent Phrases. This

---

[32] For ease of exposition, I have removed brackets cyclically, even if bracket erasure is not assumed to take place before the end of the cyclic level.

means that the hierarchy relating lexical, prosodic constituents will be dominated by the lexical AP, which in its turn will dominate one or more PWds.[33]

There is one detail lacking in this picture. The demoted main stresses resulting from compound stress assignment were referred to as strong secondary stresses in Chapter 6.1.2, and distinguished from the weak secondary stresses that can be detected on initial syllables. In the derivations given above, these weak secondary stresses have not been included, but to complete the picture, they must now be taken into account.

The only constituent in the long example analysed in (20) through (22) where a weak secondary stress will be assigned at the root level, is *èkstremitét*. (I disregard the initial syllable in *protese*, since this is a site where destressing in clash is possible.) The input for the CSR^LEFT would accordingly be as in (24).

(24)   x
        x   (x   x)   x   x
      (xx) (xx   x x)(xx)   (xx) (xx)
      [underekstremitetsprotesemaker]

The surface structure can now be derived by assuming that the Stress Equalization Convention projects the other stresses one level up before the CSR^LEFT applies. The resulting surface structure is shown in (25). Since there does not seem to be a perceptible difference between the two secondary stress levels beyond the fact that a heavy syllable is obligatory with respect to the strong secondary stresses only, it may be that the representation should be further flattened, so that the result will be like the representation in (21). Another complicating factor is the fact that the alternating stresses in (25) will be derived by the algorithm assigning rhythm, which will be discussed in Chapter 10.6.

(25)   x
       (x   x   x   x
       (x) (x   x)   (x) (x)
       (xx) (xx) x x)(xx)   (xx) (xx)
       [underekstremitetsprotesemaker]

The above suggests that a simpler account of the unmarked, left-headed compound stress pattern can be obtained if we assume that the rule is a non-cyclic word-level rule. But in the following sections we shall see that when we include data that appear to be derived by the CSR^RIGHT, the non-cyclic analysis developed above fails to account for the interaction between the two rules. The rule given as (23) is therefore not adequate.

---

[33] See Chapter 9.6.1 for a discussion of Compound H-Delinking, a rule that delinks any H that is not associated to the head of a lexical AP.

7.3.7 Compound stress assignment is cyclic:
the case of the derivational suffix -inne

The traditional assumption regarding the relationship between derivation and compounding, dating back to early versions of Lexical Phonology and embodied in the Extended Level Ordering Hypothesis, is that they belong to different levels, where the level where compounding applies is ordered after all derivation. The hypothesis predicts that derivations may form constituents in compounding, but not the other way round.

The suffix /-²ine/, which is used to derive female counterparts of nouns denoting male individuals, is a counterexample to this claim. It can combine with compounds, and in this capacity it has some interesting properties that we shall take a closer look at in this section. Consider the data in (26), where we find examples of -*inne* combined with different types of stems.

(26) *Derivation with the suffix* -inne

Stem	Derivation
(a) [¹ʋɛn] *venn* 'friend'	[ʋɛ.²nin.nə] *venninne* 'female friend'
(b) [¹ʋæt] *vert* 'host'	[ʋæ.²tin.nə] *vertinne* 'hostess'
(c) [²tjeː.nɽ] *tjener* 'servant'	[ˌtjeː.nɽ.²rin.nə] *tjenerinne* 'female servant'
(d) [¹flyː.ˌʋæt] *flyvert* 'male cabin attendant'	[¹flyː.ˌʋæt.ˌtin.nə] *flyvertinne* 'female cabin attendant'
(e) [²skʉː.wə.ˌspil.lɽ] *skuespiller* 'actor'	[skʉ.spil.lɽ.²rin.nə] *skuespillerinne* 'actress'

Looking at examples (a) and (b) only, one might be led to believe that the suffix is cyclic. But once we take (c) into consideration, we see that this cannot be the case, since the vowel length of the stem is retained. If the suffix were cyclic, the result should have been vowel-shortening in the stem, as in the analysis given in Section 7.2.5 above. The retained vowel length of the stem instead suggests that we are dealing with a non-cohering suffix which induces the marked CSR^{RIGHT}. Another argument in favour of -*inne* not being a cyclic suffix, is the fact that when the stem ends in a syllabic sonorant, as in e.g. [ˌsʋiː.gɽ.²rin.nə], *svigerinne* 'sister-in-law', the sonorant does not resyllabify as onset. This takes place when the cyclic suffix -*esse* is added to a stem of this type, cf. [nɛ.²grɛs.sə], *negresse* 'Negress', derived from [¹nɛː.gɽ], *neger*.[34]

On this analysis there is no cyclic Stress Erasure in the stem, the stress on the suffix is the result of there having been built a right-dominant metrical constituent over the two prosodic words of the input, the stem and the suffix.

This assumption also derives the different stress patterns in the (d) and (e) examples directly. In (d), we can assume that the internal structure is [[fly][[vert][inne]]], where *fly-* and *vertinne* are the primary constituents. Since

---

[34] See also Chapter 8.3.4.1.

-inne is not one of the primary constituents, it will not determine primary stress placement, which is therefore derived by the default CSR^{LEFT}. In *skuespillerinne* on the other hand, the primary constituents must be the compound *skuespiller* and *-inne*, since there is no word **spillerinne* in the language. *-inne* will trigger the CSR^{RIGHT}, giving the correct output.[35]

But this result can only be obtained on the assumption that the CSR in either version applies cyclically. Examples (d) and (e) both have the suffix *-inne* at the right edge, but only in (e) does the primary stress surface on the suffix. The reason is, as just noted, that *-inne* in (e) influences stress placement on an earlier cycle, while the CSR^{LEFT} applies on the last cycle. In (f) the order is the opposite. The derivations are shown in (27).[36]

(27)	*Input*	(a)	x	x	x	(b)	x	x	x
			(xx)	(xx)	(xx)		(xx)	(xx)	(xx)
			[[fly] [vert][inne]]				[[[[skue][spil]r]][inne]]		

1st cycle

CSR^{RIGHT} (a)		x			x		
CSR^{LEFT} (b)	x	(x	x)	(x	x)	x	
	(xx)	(xx)	(xx)	(xx)	(xx)	(xx)	
	[[fly] [vertinne]]			[[skuespilr][inne]]			

2nd cycle

Stress Equalization	x			x		
CSR^{LEFT} (a)	(x	x)	(x	x)		
CSR^{RIGHT} (b)	x	(x	x)	(x	x)	x
	(xx)	(xx)	(xx)	(xx)	(xx)	(xx)
	[[fly] [vertinne]]			[[[skuespilr]] inne]		

Morphologically, the above process is a case of derivation which may take compounds as stems. In this respect it is difficult to reconcile with the level ordering hypothesis. But phonologically it is a case of compounding, where the second member is a non-cohering suffix which triggers the CSR^{RIGHT}. In all other respects it accords with other cases of derivation by means of non-cohering suffixes. The prosodic output will in all cases be a compound, i.e. a concatenation of two or more PWds dominated by one primary stress.

The discussion in this section shows that we must revert to the cyclic version of the CSR stated as (13) above. The final version of the Compound Stress Rule is stated in (28), and subsumes the CSR^{RIGHT} as well as the CSR^{LEFT}.

---

[35] The fact that the first syllable is often pronounced as given in (26), with a shortened vowel, does not accord with this analysis, since as in example (c), *tjenerinne*, we would have expected retention of vowel length. But the pronunciation [ˌskuː .spil.lr̩.²rin.nə] is possible as well. This suggests that vowel shortening in this case must be seen as a separate low-level, optional and probably speech tempo-dependent process that applies after compounding and the CSR.

[36] The cycle where the non-cyclic agentive suffix /-r/ is added to *skuespill* is skipped.

(28) *Compound Stress Rule: final, cyclic version*

In a word formed by two non-cohering constituents, form a right-headed constituent on the highest grid level, subject to lexical marking (=CSR^{RIGHT}). In unmarked cases, form a left-headed constituent on the highest grid level (=CSR^{LEFT}).

7.3.8 Extraprosodic, non-cohering suffixes

In Section 7.2.5 above we discussed a class of suffixes whose members are stress-affecting when the stem is a compound, but not when the stem is a simplex word. The lack of influence on simplex stems was argued to derive from their being non-cohering. We now turn to the fact that they attract primary stress to the immediately preceding PWd when they are combined with stems consisting of more than one PWd. The above analysis of derivations made by *-inne* now puts us in a position where we can give an analysis of these suffixes as well. Let us first look in some more detail at the relevant data. (29) shows how the suffixes *-lig*, *-ig*, *-som* and *-bar* interact with the non-cohering negative prefix *u-*. In all cases where these suffixes are not present at the right edge, *u-* attracts primary stress, which is the expected outcome on the assumption that it is non-cohering.

(29) *Derivations with the non-cohering prefix /u-/*

	Base	Derivation
(a)	[¹klɑːr] *klar* 'clear'	[²uː.ˌklɑːr] *uklar* 'unclear'
	[¹sik.kr̩] *sikker* 'sure'	[²uː.ˌsik.kr̩] *usikker* 'unsure'
	[sy.stə.¹maː.tisk] *systematisk* 'systematic'	[²uː.sy.stə.ˌmaː.tisk] *usystematisk* 'unsystematic'
	[¹ʂyl] *skyld* 'guilt'	[²uː.ʂyl] *uskyld* 'innocence'
	[bɑ.laŋ.¹seːt̩] *balansert* 'balanced'	[²uː.bɑ.laŋ.ˌseːt̩] *ubalansert* 'unbalanced'
(b)	[²riːm.ˌli] *rimelig* 'reasonable'	[ˌu.¹riːm.ˌli] *urimelig* 'unreasonable'
	[²loːʋ.ˌli] *lovlig* 'legal'	[ˌu.¹loːʋ.ˌli] *ulovlig* 'illegal'
	[ˌsɑn.¹syːn.ˌli] *sannsynlig* 'probable'	[ˌu.ˌsɑn.¹syːn.ˌli] *usannsynlig* 'improbable'
	[ˌtil.¹roːd.ˌli] *tilrådelig*³⁷ 'advisable'	[ˌu.ˌtil.¹roːd.ˌli] *utilrådelig* 'inadvisable'
	[²ʂyl.di] *skyldig* 'guilty'	[ˌu.¹ʂyl.di] *uskyldig* 'innocent'
	[²føːl.ˌsɔm] *følsom* 'sensitive'	[ˌu.¹føːl.ˌsɔm] *ufølsom* 'insensitive'
	[²bruːk.ˌbɑːr] *brukbar* 'useful'	[ˌu.¹bruːk.ˌbɑːr] *ubrukbar* 'useless'

In cases where the suffixes appear at the right edge of the word, however, primary

---

[37] Note that in this example, *-lig* has been combined with a compound verb *tílr`åde* 'to advise', so that we have a conversion of a compound into one prosodic word caused by *-lig*.

stress is on the PWd preceding the suffix. The suffixes in other words cancel the effect of the prefix. A possible analysis of this pattern is that these suffixes trigger the marked, right-oriented option in (28), the CSR^{RIGHT}, but are themselves extra-prosodic.

A problem with this analysis, however, is that the prefix is incorporated after the suffixes. In most cases there are no words *úrìm, *úlòv, *úsànnsyn etc. that can constitute stems that they can attach to. The semantic structure also demands the prefix-last order, it is the content of the suffixed words that is negated by the prefix. Given this order, we would expect that the prefix would determine the stress pattern, that the output in other words would be parallel to *flyvertinne* in (27a) above, and not to *skuespillerinne* in (27b), which is the attested output. The suffixes must therefore be able to extend their influence on the stress pattern beyond the cycle on which they are added.

Before we proceed, we must take account of the fact that the pattern is variable.[38] According to Faarlund *et al.* (1997: 92) stress placement will vary according to dialect in words with bases consisting of three syllables or more, with speakers of East Norwegian preferring initial stress, that is, [²ʉː.san.syːn.li] instead of [ʉ.san.¹syːn.li], more often than speakers from other parts of the country. In words with a base consisting of two syllables, the authors note variation without mentioning any dialectal or social constraints. Another possible constraint is noted by Hovdhaugen (1970), in that non-initial stress seems less acceptable in words ending in *-ig* than *-lig*. Alnæs (1925: 26) and Popperwell (1963: 122) note that we find obligatory non-initial stress in words with no unprefixed counterpart, as for example in *umistelig*, 'indispensable', where *mistelig* is not a word in the language.

Because of the variability, non-initial stress might perhaps be treated as exceptional, and marked on each lexical item. But the pattern is still strong enough to deserve mentioning, and to the extent that it reflects an earlier, rule-governed system, we might also ask how it might be analysed. Recall that the problem involved is that the suffixes seem to extend their influence on compound stress beyond the cycle on which they are attached. An account of this can be derived from the assumption that the suffixes are extraprosodic. As long as they remain extraprosodic, they will constitute separate units outside the prosodic structure of their stems. If we assume that they remain extraprosodic throughout the cyclic level as long as no other suffix is added to the word, their transcyclic power might be derived from this property. In other words, I propose that as long as they have not been prosodically incorporated into the words to which they are suffixed, they may influence stress placement.

On this analysis the suffixes are neutral with respect to the Main Stress Rule, as argued in Section 7.2.5 above, and extraprosodic triggers with respect to the

---

[38] Hovdhaugen (1970) claims that the variability is due to a change in progress towards regularization with initial stress, but the fact that the description that appears in Alnæs (1925: 25f.) accords very well with those that are found in later works such as Popperwell (1963: 121ff.), Hovdhaugen (1972) and Faarlund *et al.* (1997: 92) suggests that the variability is a relatively stable feature. But no systematic investigation has been conducted, so the reliability may be questioned of the sources as descriptions that generalize beyond the authors' intuitions about their own or their informants' speech.

CSR^{RIGHT}. When another prosodic word, be it a non-cohering suffix or a word, is added at the left edge, it will remain extraprosodic and be able to trigger the CSR^{RIGHT} once again. Let us see how this might work in [ʉ.til.ˈroːd.ˌli] in (29b). The derivation is shown in (30).

(30) *Input*

```
                    x   x   x   x
                   (xx) (xx) (xx) (xx)
                   [[ʉ] [[[til] [råd]] [lig]]]
```

1st cycle   x
CSR^{LEFT}

```
                    x   (x   x)   x
                   (xx) (xx) (xx) (xx)        cf. [ˈtil.ˌroːdə]
                   [[ʉ] [[t i l r å d] [lig]]]   tilråde 'to advise'
```

2nd cycle   x
Stress Equalization   (x   x)
+ CSR^{RIGHT}

```
                    x   (x   x)   x
                   (xx) (xx) (xx) (xx)        cf. [ˌtil.ˈroːd.ˌli]
                   [[ʉ] [t i l r å d l i g]]   tilrådelig 'advisable'
```

3rd cycle   x
Stress Equalization   (x   x)
+ CSR^{RIGHT}

```
                    x   (x   x)
                    x   (x   x)   x
                   (xx) (xx)(xx)(xx)
                   [ʉ   t i l r å d l i]
```

The alternative pattern, primary stress on the prefix, can be derived by applying CSR^{LEFT} on the final cycle.

Let us now look at an example where two of these suffixes are involved, followed by another non-cohering suffix that does not trigger CSR^{RIGHT}. The word is [ˌspɑː.ˈşɔm.ˌli.ˌheːt], *sparsommelighet* 'thrift'. The morphological structure of the input and the derivation are shown in (31). /spar/ is a verbal root meaning 'to save'.

We see that when another suffix is added to -*som*, its extraprosodicity is cancelled, and it may receive primary stress by the application of the CSR^{RIGHT} triggered by the next suffix -*lig*. The final suffix -*het* is also non-cohering, but since it does not belong to the class that triggers the CSR^{RIGHT}, the result is a final application of the unmarked CSR^{LEFT}, which will leave the stress where it was in the input, on the suffix -*som*.

In the forms beginning with *ʉ-* which have non-initial stress, I have transcribed the vowel as short. This is the same phenomenon as we saw in *skuespillerinne* in the preceding section. The vowel may be pronounced with long or short vowel, probably at least partly dependent on speech rate. The important thing is that vowel

(31) *Input*   x   x   x   x
                                      (xx) (xx) (xx)(xx)
                                      [[[[spar] [som]] [li]] [het]]

1st cycle   x
CSR^RIGHT   (x   x   x)   x
                                      (xx) (xx) (xx) (xx)   cf. [²spɑ:.ʂɔm],
                                      [[[spar som] [li]] [het]]   *sparsom*, 'thrifty'

2nd cycle   x
Stress Equalization   (x   x)
+ CSR^RIGHT   (x)   x   x   x
                                      (xx)(xx)(xx)(xx)   cf. [ˌspɑ:.ˈsɔm.ˌli],
                                      [[spar som li] [het]]   *sparsommelig*, 'thrifty'

3rd cycle   x
Stress Equalization   x (x   x)
+ CSR^LEFT   (x   x)   x
                                      (x)   x   x   x
                                      (xx)(xx) (xx) (xx)
                                      [spar som li het]

length *may* be retained, since this shows that we are not dealing with cyclic application of the MSR. The shortening must therefore be ascribed to a later, low-level
rule, as conjectured in footnote 35 above.

7.3.9 Tier conflation

The conclusion that compound stress assignment takes place at the cyclic level,
combined with the fact that there is no formal upper bound on the size of Norwegian compounds, implies that upon leaving the cyclic level, a compound will have
as many structural stress levels as the number of PWds that it contains. As noted
above, however, the phonetic realization of compounds does not support more than
two stress levels, main stress characterized by tonal accent and a weight requirement, and secondary stress which is characterized by the weight requirement only.
I shall not propose a tier conflation algorithm which may turn representations such
as the output in (20) into the representation shown in (21) above, for the following
reason: the means that languages have at their disposal for distinguishing stress
levels in the phonetic output are limited. In Norwegian it seems that only two features are of primary relevance, tonal accent and duration as a function of syllable
weight. This allows for the phonetic expression of two levels, and the conflation of
the different levels of secondary stress in the phonological surface representations
may therefore be interpreted not as a result of a categorical operation performed on
the phonological representation, but as a result of the latter being turned into a

physical object, subject to severe limitations with respect to the number of reliably perceptible differences that can be produced.

7.4 SUMMARY

In this chapter we have analysed stress placement in morphologically complex words. The Main Stress Rule, which was stated in the preceding chapter, has been shown to apply cyclically, triggered by suffixes of mostly foreign origin. In addition, we have seen that in compounds, stresses are demoted by the Compound Stress Rules. This has been argued to have two versions, one marked version which demotes the leftmost of two juxtaposed stresses and an unmarked version which demotes the stress on the rightmost compound member. The marked CSR^{RIGHT} is triggered in a few lexicalized compounds, and by a limited set of non-cohering suffixes.

Although there is no phonetic motivation for positing cyclic stress demotion, the interaction between the marked CSR^{RIGHT} and the unmarked CSR^{LEFT} can only be accounted for if the CSR applies on the cyclic level.

CYCLIC SYLLABIFICATION

This chapter consists of three main sections. In Section 8.2 the relationship between Mora Insertion, the rule responsible for expanding light, stressed syllables, and the cyclic derivation of complex words, will be discussed. I shall argue that Mora Insertion is a cyclic rule, and that long vowels and geminated consonants are retained through the cyclic level in cases where Stress Erasure and reapplication of the MSR move the stress to another syllable. Closed Syllable Shortening will also be discussed in this section. The topic of Section 8.3 is the distribution of syllabic sonorants. It will be argued that sonorants are syllabified at the cyclic level in nouns, at the word level in adjectives, and that syllabic sonorants are blocked at both levels (as well as postlexically) in verbs. In Section 8.4 variable syllabification patterns in inflected nouns will be analysed as triggered by differences in sonority between adjacent, syllabic nuclei juxtaposed by the morphology.

8.1 INTRODUCTION

8.1.1 Continuous syllabification

In Itô (1988) syllabification is claimed to be continuous in the sense that any unsyllabified string that arises in the course of a derivation is syllabified as soon as the structure is created, be it due to a morphological rule or to phonological rules that alter the syllabic make-up of a string, for instance through vowel deletion. This point is also made in Rubach and Booij (1990: 139), who argue that syllable structure assignment (in Polish) cannot be seen as a set of ordinary, phonological rules that must be ordered with respect to other phonological rules in the language.

Unsyllabified strings form the input on the root cycle, and, on the assumption that affixes, like roots, in the unmarked case are represented in the lexicon without syllable structure, syllabification is applicable each time an affix is added to a stem. This means that every time a morphological rule has added an affix to a syllabified stem, the syllabification algorithm defined in Chapter 5.3 will have to syllabify the affix. If the affix is cohering, it must also be prosodically integrated into the stem. Syllabification triggered by affixation therefore must accomplish two tasks if the affix is cohering, syllabification of the segment string that the affix consists of, and prosodic integration into the stem.

8.1.2 Cyclic resyllabification

The most common view of syllabification as part of Lexical Phonology has been that as a structure building process, it is not blocked by Strict Cyclicity and Structure Preservation when it applies to unsyllabified material. It can therefore apply to a root before any morphological rule has applied, and in consequence, I assume that any stem will have been syllabified before an affix is added to it.

In order to integrate a cohering affix into its stem, resyllabification of some of the already syllabified material of the stem may seem necessary in some cases. It is not clear to what extent rules of resyllabification can alter an already syllabified structure in this way, in the course of the cyclic derivation as well as on later levels. With respect to the cyclic level, Structure Preservation, which says that no structure not already present in the lexical input, can be derived, seems irrelevant, since the basic syllabification patterns are not encoded in underlying forms in the first place.[1] The role of Strict Cyclicity also seems unclear, since it is difficult to decide exactly how much of the derived string comes within the scope of the derived environment by the addition of an affix, and since syllabification itself in general does not seem to be subject to Strict Cyclicity.[2]

A restrictive approach to cyclic resyllabification would be that only the stem syllable closest to the affix can be subject to cyclic restructuring. This is the approach taken by Rubach and Booij (1990) on Polish syllabification and in Rubach (1990) and Hall (1992) on German syllabification. In these works it is contended that syllabification is continuous, and that only elements belonging to the final coda of the stem can resyllabify as a result of adding a suffix. In Polish a rule of Coda Erasure is assumed to apply as the first rule belonging to the Polish syllable structure assignment, which 'prepares the ground for syllabification' (Rubach and Booij 1990: 146). For German it is assumed that the universal CV-rule will have the same effect by resyllabifying the final stem consonant only.

A more radical approach to cyclic resyllabification, which we shall explore and ultimately reject below, would be that it is total in the sense that it takes scope over the whole domain created by the morphological rule. This presupposes that the cyclic affix triggers deletion of all previously assigned syllable structure on the stem. *Prosodic Erasure* in this sense would return a domain without any prosodic structure at all, which would then have to be reprosodified, that is, syllabified and subjected to the MSR anew. This predicts that the affixes that trigger prosodic erasure also trigger reapplication of the MSR, since erasure of all prosodic structure implies stress erasure.

In most cases the effects of such resyllabification would be invisible, because

---

[1] Borowsky (1989) claims that structural constraints such as syllable templates also induce Structure Preservation. Since structural templates interpreted as inviolable constraints literally define the limits of well-formedness, it follows trivially that they preserve it on the levels at which they hold. In this sense, templates are different from rules changing segmental content, since their output will either comply or not comply with the set of underlying segments assumed in the analysis.

[2] See Cole (1995) for a recent discussion of the relationship between Strict Cyclicity and Syllabification.

the segmental make-up of the stem will be the same as on the previous cycle. Only at the boundary between stem and affix would we expect adjustments. The resyllabification of the rest of the stem will render the same pattern as in the input stem if the same algorithm applies on each cycle. Full resyllabification is therefore difficult to establish as part of the phonology, since decisive evidence seems hard to come by. But the fact that certain aspects of Norwegian syllabification are dependent on stress makes it a possible test case. Stress Erasure and reapplication of the MSR will remove the conditions under which Mora Insertion has taken place on a former cycle, if Mora Insertion is indeed cyclic, and the question therefore arises how vowel length and consonant gemination are undone once stress has been erased. If this can be argued to take place on the following cycle as part of the restructuring induced by Stress Erasure and reapplication of the MSR, this constitutes an argument in favour of resyllabification beyond the syllable adjacent to the affix. This will be the topic of the following section.

8.2   MORA INSERTION AND CYCLIC SYLLABIFICATION

8.2.1   At what point in the derivation does Mora Insertion apply?

In Chapter 5.1.3 I argued that gemination and vowel lengthening should be seen as effects of stress assignment. This means that stressed syllables must be expanded at some point after stress has been assigned to them. This was formally accounted for by two rules: Mora Insertion, which applies in light, stressed syllables, and Mora Linking, which can manifest itself in two ways, and is therefore a cover term for two disjunctively ordered rules: Vowel Lengthening and Consonant Gemination.[3] In final, open syllables, or before another vowel, Vowel Lengthening is predictable. When a consonant follows as onset in a following syllable, the choice is unpredictable, and must be encoded in some way in the lexicon. In addition, Vowel Lengthening may apply in word-final VC-syllables. This pattern must also be encoded in the lexicon.[4]

The question to be addressed now is whether the syllabic expansion that is expressed by means of Mora Insertion should be seen as part of the cyclic derivation, or as a process that applies at the word level after the final application of the MSR. In order to arrive at an understanding of this issue, we must at the same time take a closer look at how the choice between vowel lengthening and gemination is encoded in the lexicon. If this can be shown to be encoded on the minimal, lexical units, roots and perhaps affixes, the surface pattern is most easily accounted for if Mora Insertion applies at the same time as when the unit where this is encoded is inserted into word structure.

---

[3]   When no misunderstanding seems possible, I shall for simplicity refer to Mora Insertion and subsequent linking simply as Mora Insertion.

[4]   In order to simplify the discussion, I shall also refer to the resyllabification in final VC-syllables, by which the vowel is lengthened, as Mora Insertion, even if this strictly speaking is a delinking rule followed by Mora Linking.

Recall from Chapter 5.1.3 that vowel length and gemination only surface in syllables carrying surface stress. Syllables where Stress Erasure has removed a former stress therefore bear no trace of Mora Insertion in surface structure. If Mora Insertion is cyclic, then a heavy syllable dominating a long vowel or a geminate has to shorten at some point if its stress has been erased and moved to another syllable further to the right by reapplication of the MSR on a later cycle.[5] Thus we find [tæ.ˈrɑs.sə], 'terrace', but [tæ.rɑ.ˈseː.rə], 'to make a terrace', and [bɑ.ˈruːn], 'baron', but [bɑ.ru.ˈniː], 'barony'. If it can be shown that Mora Insertion is cyclic, that is, that it has to follow each application of the MSR, then the question also arises whether the subsequent demoraification, or Mora Delinking, is cyclic.

If Mora Delinking were cyclic, a very simple way to account for it would be to assume the radical resyllabification hypothesis sketched in the previous section. This would imply that Stress Erasure is part of a more comprehensive erasure process which eliminates not only stress feet, but also all syllable structure assigned on the previous cycle. The syllabification algorithm defined in Chapter 5.3 could then reapply, and since Mora Insertion is not part of this algorithm, the input for the MSR would not contain any syllables containing long vowels or consonant gemination. Another advantage of this hypothesis is that Stress Erasure would follow from Prosodic Erasure; the resyllabification of formerly stressed syllables and Stress Erasure would in other words follow from the same assumption.

But this is not the only possible hypothesis. An analysis where Mora Insertion is postcyclic is also conceivable. On this hypothesis, the information necessary to make the correct choice with respect to Mora Linking must be available postcyclically, but since Mora Insertion applies only once on the postcyclic level, there will be no need for a rule that erases moras inserted on earlier cycles, be it in the shape of full prosodic erasure on each cycle, or as a more local rule that constrains the occurrence of geminates in heavy syllables and long vowels to syllables that carry main stress in the surface. A constraint of the latter type can itself be postcyclic, also in the event that Mora Insertion is cyclic.

This leaves us with several possible ways that the relationship between Mora Insertion and cyclicity can be accounted for. Assuming that the algorithm accounting for word stress at least consists of the following rules: Stress Erasure (or possibly Prosodic Erasure), the MSR, the CSR, Mora Insertion, Mora Linking, and possibly Mora Delinking in unstressed, heavy syllables dominating a doubly linked segment, at least the following possible subgrammars accounting for the relationship between cyclic stress and syllable structure can be conceived of.[6]

---

[5] It is necessary to qualify the syllables where the shortening takes place as heavy, in order to exclude the geminates that arise when a syllabic sonorant provides an onset for a following syllable, cf. the ambisyllabic geminate spanning the boundary between the second and third syllable in [ˀboː.tn̩.nə], *båtene* 'the boats'. In this case the syllable dominating the first part of the geminate is light.

[6] Since syllabification is assumed to be continuous, I have not included syllabification of affixes in (1b–d).

(1) (a) Prosodic Erasure   (b) Postcyclic Mora Insertion
         Cyclic: *Cyclic*:
         Prosodic Erasure   Stress Erasure
         Syllabification   MSR
         MSR   CSR
         Mora Insertion + Mora Linking
         CSR
         Postcyclic (word level):   *Postcyclic (word level)*:
         –   Mora Insertion + Mora Linking

     (c) Cyclic Mora Delinking   (d) Postcyclic Mora Delinking
         Cyclic: *Cyclic*:
         Stress Erasure   Stress Erasure
         Mora Delinking   MSR
         MSR   Mora Insertion + Mora Linking
         Mora Insertion + Mora Linking   CSR
         CSR
         Postcyclic (word level):   *Postcyclic (word level)*:
         –   Mora Delinking

The algorithm under (1a) includes full, prosodic erasure, followed by resyllabification on each cycle. Since stress-induced vowel length and gemination from the
previous cycle will be erased as part of the general erasure triggered by cyclic suffix, there is no need for a specific Mora Delinking rule. This is also the case for the
grammar under (1b), since Mora Insertion is assumed to be postcyclic.[7] In that
capacity it will only apply once, and therefore Mora Delinking is not called for. In
(1c, d), only Stress Erasure is assumed, and Mora Insertion is in both cases assumed to be cyclic. The difference between them is that Mora Delinking in (1c)
must be seen as an extension of the Stress Erasure Convention in that it erases the
changes in syllable structure induced by stress assignment on the previous cycle,
thereby clearing the way for reapplication of the MSR, while Mora Delinking in
(1d) is seen as a word-level rule that applies to the output of the cyclic derivation.
   One prediction that follows from (1b) is that the information ensuring that the
correct choice with respect to Mora Linking must be available at the word-level.
If the information is encoded on roots and affixes, it must in other words be able
to percolate up to the highest node in the word tree. Since vowel lengthening and
gemination under this solution are made available only at the word level, it also
presupposes that vowel length and gemination are not needed as input information
for a morphological or phonological rule on the cyclic level. A similar prediction
follows from (1a, c), where vowel length and gemination will only be available on
the cycle where they are assigned, but not on the following.
   It now follows that if it can be shown that a morphological or cyclic phonologi-

---

[7] It may also be postcyclic in (1a), but this would remove much of the motivation for assuming full
prosodic erasure in the first place.

cal rule needs to refer to vowel length and gemination assigned on a previous cycle, this will simultaneously falsify the hypotheses embodied in (1a, b, c). (1a) will be falsified because the effects of Mora Linking must not be erased on the following cycle by full prosodic erasure, since it must be available on this cycle. (1b) will be falsified because Mora Linking, and therefore Mora Insertion, on the same evidence must be cyclic, and (1c) because Mora Delinking will have the same (local) effect as Prosodic Erasure in that it will eliminate vowel length and gemination from the representation before the MSR reapplies. This type of data would in other words leave us with d) as the only alternative.

Evidence of this type is indeed available. In order to show this, we must assume that expansion type (i.e. Mora Linking instantiated either as vowel lengthening or consonant gemination) is marked on roots, stressed cyclic affixes and non-cohering affixes in the lexicon. (We return to the prestressing, cyclic suffixes in a moment.) The simplest way to do this is to mark the roots where it is applicable for vowel lengthening, and then derive gemination by default. Thus, roots like /hat/ 'hate' and /hake/ 'chin' must be specifically marked for vowel lengthening in order to derive the correct surface forms [¹haːt] and [²haː.kə]. Roots which surface with short vowel and geminate, such as /hat/ 'hat' and /hake/ 'pickaxe', realized as [¹hat] and [²hak.kə] respectively, can then be left unmarked. /hat/ will be syllabified as heavy without Mora Insertion, while /hake/ will be subject to Mora Insertion, and subsequent consonant gemination by default.

Mora Insertion and Mora Linking can now be thought of as applying cyclically. On the root cycle, the expansion type marked on the root is triggered. If a cyclic, *stressed* suffix is added, stress will be removed from the stem, and the expansion type marked on the suffix itself will apply instead. Prestressing suffixes represent a possible problem, however. Since these assign stress to the final syllable of the stem, we may ask where expansion type is encoded in this case, on the stem or on the suffix. If it is encoded on the root underlying the stem, we must also take into account that stress may fall on another syllable of the stem in unsuffixed forms. If the expansion type therefore is encoded on the stem, this entails that it is expected to be uniform irrespective of the location of surface stress. One example of such a root with variable stress is /drama/ 'drama'. Here the first syllable will receive stress if it is realized as a simplex word, and the second syllable will receive stress if the prestressing suffix /-isk/ is added. In both cases we find a long vowel, as shown in [¹draː.ma] and [dra.¹maː.tisk], so this example meets the expectation. But this is not the case in /kanada/ 'Canada'. If realized as a simplex word, stress falls on the first syllable, and the inserted mora is linked to the following consonant so that the result is gemination: [¹kan.na.da]. If realized with /-isk/, however, the stress falls on the second syllable, but here the vowel is realized as long: [ka.¹naː.disk]. Uniform coding of expansion type on the root therefore does not render the right result. This leaves us with the suffix itself. Since we find a long vowel before /-isk/ in both cases, a natural hypothesis would be that the suffix induces vowel length on the syllable to which it assigns stress when there is only one consonant between the vowel and the suffix.

There is one exception where lengthening induced by the suffix is overridden, however. If it is the case that the syllable that receives stress by /-isk/ had stress on the same syllable in the input stem, the expansion type associated with the stem overrides the influence from the suffix.

The most straightforward analysis of this pattern is that /-isk/ in the unmarked case induces vowel lengthening when only one consonant occurs between the vowel of the final stem syllable and the initial /i/ of the suffix. However, if the final syllable of the stem is stressed in the input, and therefore already has been expanded by Mora Insertion, then the expansion type already assigned is carried over into the new word. Vowel lengthening on the /-isk/-cycle will therefore only take place if Mora Insertion takes place on the same cycle and thereby creates an input for Mora Linking.

This analysis rests crucially on the assumption that Mora Insertion and subsequent linking are cyclic, and that syllable structure is maximally preserved at the cyclic level. This is in other words an argument against full Prosodic Erasure. If syllable structure is cyclically erased, the expansion type of the formerly stressed syllable will not be available any more, and the outcome of Mora Linking should in principle be unpredictable, or predictable from information encoded on the suffix. The latter seems, as just noted, to be the case with respect to /-isk/, but only if the syllable that is stressed has not received stress by the MSR on the previous cycle.

If on the other hand only stress feet are erased, and Mora Delinking in heavy, unstressed syllables is postponed until the word level, then Mora Insertion will not be applicable, since the syllable stressed by /-isk/ has already been expanded. Examples in the form of partial derivations are provided in (2), where the syllabification after /-isk/-suffixation of *balsá:misk* 'fragrant', *voká:lisk* 'vocalic' and *metállisk* 'metallic' is shown, derived from *bálsam* 'balm', *voka:l* 'vowel' and *metáll* 'metal' respectively.

In *bálsam*, the final syllable is extraprosodic, but as soon as /-isk/ is added, it becomes subject to syllabification along with the suffix itself. The resulting stressed syllable is light, and since the suffix induces vowel lengthening, the result is [bɑl.ˈsɑː.misk]. In the two others, the final syllable is stressed in the input, and on the assumption that syllable structure is preserved, the heavy syllable is therefore carried over into the new cycle. The long vowel in *vokal* is accordingly still long on the /-isk/ cycle, and the final, moraic consonant in *metall* will cause gemination to take place when the onset rule applies to the initial vowel of the suffix.

Suffixation with /-isk/ thereby provides evidence that Mora Insertion and Mora Linking are cyclic processes that take place every time the MSR has applied. Of the four alternatives listed under (1) above, (1d) is the only one that can account for the data. This means that the type of Mora Linking can be marked on both roots and affixes. Stressed, light syllables will be expanded by means of Mora Insertion and Mora Linking on each cycle, and the resulting syllable structure will be preserved through the cyclic level. Only when the prestressing suffix /-isk/ assigns stress to a syllable not previously stressed, Mora Insertion and Mora Linking can apply and induce vowel lengthening.

(2)   Input

Syllabification

Mora Insertion + Vowel lengthening

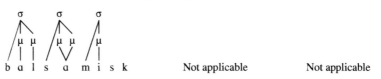

Not applicable   Not applicable

The pattern induced by /-isk/ represents evidence in favour of the hypothesis that resyllabification plays a very limited role at the cyclic level. Once syllable structure has been assigned, it is in other words respected. If *full* preservation of previous syllable structure is hypothesized to hold in general, however, it seems to represent a too strong prediction, since it will not allow for the adjustments in Polish analysed by Rubach and Booij (1990) and Rubach (1990). It also seems to exclude the quite common rule of closed syllable shortening, to which we now turn.

8.2.2 *Closed syllable shortening in VC-final stems*

When a consonant-initial suffix is added to a stem ending in long vowel plus a consonant, the resulting consonant cluster will in many languages cause the vowel to shorten. This process is often referred to as Closed Syllable Shortening, cf. Myers (1987), Borowsky (1989) and Rubach (1996) and a commonly cited example is the alternation in English between the infinitive *weep* and the past tense *wept*. In all dialects belonging to UEN, Closed Syllable Shortening occurs only in *some* of the stems where the structural conditions for its application are met.[8] In the following, I shall show why this cannot be a rule in UEN, but a property that must be encoded as an idiosyncratic property associated with some lexical items. Next

---

[8] Closed Syllable Shortening occurs as a synchronic and exceptionless cyclic rule in some western Norwegian dialects (Odd Monsson, p.c.).

I shall discuss the implications of this pattern for the analysis developed in the preceding and the present chapter.

For English, Myers (1987) and Borowsky (1989) assume that closed syllable shortening is a rule that applies on level 1, where it manifests itself in various environments such as irregular inflection. On level 2, on the other hand, where regular inflectional affixes are added, the bipositional rhyme constraint that conditions vowel shortening is assumed no longer to hold. This accounts for the difference between the irregular, level 1 *weep ~ wept*, and the regular, level 2 *reap ~ reaped*.

A similar morphological distinction between the stems where vowel shortening applies and where it does not, cannot be invoked for UEN. As the data presented below will show, the UEN pattern is found in regular inflection, where some members show shortening while others do not within the same category. The most important morphological environment where shortening may take place consists of verbs belonging to the class which selects /-Te/ in the past tense and /-T/ in the past participle.[9] Examples are given in (3). We see that examples (a–c) show vowel shortening, and thereby adjustment to the pattern found in simplex words. But in the three remaining examples the vowel remains long, despite the fact that a consonant cluster follows.

(3) *Vowel length preservation in inflected verb forms*

	Root	Infinitive	Past tense	Participle
(a)	/hør/ 'hear'	[²høː.ɾə]	[²hœt̠.t̠ə]	[¹hœt̠]
(b)	/bak/ 'bake'	[²bɑː.kə]	[²bak.tə]	[¹bakt]
(c)	/spis/ 'eat'	[²spiː.sə]	[²spis.tə]	[¹spist]
(d)	/ʊrak/ 'discard'	[²ʊrɑː.kə]	[²ʊrɑːk.tə]	[¹ʊrɑːkt]
(e)	/hyl/ 'scream'	[²hyː.lə]	[²hyːl.tə]	[¹hyːlt]
(f)	/ʋis/ 'show'	[²ʋiː.sə]	[²ʋiː.stə]	[¹ʋiːst]

Statistically, length preservation is by far the most common.[10] Norsk Termbank (1986) contains 313 past tense forms of the relevant class with long vowel and one postvocalic consonant in the infinitive. Of these, as many as 87.2% retain their length in the past tense.[11] As (4) shows, the final stem consonant has a marked influence on the degree of length preservation.

---

[9] See also Chapter 4.2.3.2.

[10] The numbers are based on counting of dictionary entries. Statistics performed on running text occurrence based on casual speech corpora might give different results, since most of the verbs showing vowel shortening are verbs that commonly occur in everyday speech.

[11] The figure must be seen as an estimate only. Many of the verbs included in the data have double membership with respect to inflectional class, and the preferred suffix (/-Te/, /-a/ or /-et/) may vary with speaker, geographical background, social background and style. The choice of suffix is based on my own intuitions, which should be more or less identical in this respect with that of most UEN speakers, except for verbs with /ʋ/ and /g/ stem-finally, where UEN speakers, depending on the specific verb, will vary between /-Te/ with shortening or /-et/ or /-a/ without shortening, while speakers with my southern background more often, but probably not quite consistently, will use /-Te/, with or without shortening. The figures in (4) are based on the number of verbs where shortening seems possible.

(4)   *Frequency of vowel length preservation
       in verbs, ranked by final stem consonant*

Stem-final consonant	Number of examples	% with length preservation
t	8	0.0
d	2	0.0
g	5	0.0
v	27	63.0
p	23	65.2
k	39	87.2
s	49	98.0
r	57	98.2
l	59	100.0
n	36	100.0
m	8	100.0
Total	313	87.2

The consistent shortening pattern in stems ending in coronal stops will be treated separately in Section 8.2.4 below. The only other discrete patterns that emerge are that /g/ induces shortening, and that sonorants (excluding /v/), in all but one single case, block shortening.[12]

Variation is also found among adjectives containing the neuter agreement suffix /-t/. As with the corresponding verbs, the pattern in stems ending in a coronal stop will be treated in Section 8.2.4 below. In stems that end in other consonants length is retained in the majority, but in some the vowel may shorten. Examples are given in (5). The degree of length preservation, classified by final stem consonant, is shown in (6). Again, the data underlying the latter table have been culled from Norsk Termbank (1986).

(5) shows a pattern very similar to the one shown for verbs in (6). The segment types that are most prone to induce shortening are voiceless stops, plus /v/, while sonorant final stems consistently preserve the vowel length. But for no category among the verbs and adjectives, except after stem final /g/ in verbs, is vowel shortening fully predictable. Vowel shortening is optional in some of these, such as /lage/ 'to make', so we are dealing with non-predictability also in this case.

Because closed syllable shortening only applies to *some* stems within a given morphological category, it cannot be analysed as a general cyclic effect triggered by a lexical stratum or a specific set of suffixes, as in English. It must instead be encoded on the lexical items in which it applies. Since vowel length is preserved in the majority of cases, it also seems clear that lack of shortening should be interpreted as the regular pattern, at least with respect to inflection.

This means that the well-formedness constraints on syllable structure that can

---

[12] The r-final stem where shortening is possible, but not obligatory, is /hør/, 'to hear', whose past tense may be either [²hœt̪.t̪ə] or [²høː.t̪ə].

(5) *Vowel length preservation in adjectival neuter agreement*

	Root	Simplex	Neuter /-t/
(a)	/grov/ 'coarse'	['groːʋ]	['grɔft]
(b)	/dyp/ 'deep'	['dyːp]	['dypt]
(c)	/syk/ 'sick'	['syːk]	['syːkt]
(d)	/stiv/ 'stiff'	['stiːʋ]	['stiːft]

(6) *Frequency of vowel length preservation in neuter adjectives, ranked by final stem consonant*

Stem-final C	Number of examples	% with length preservation
t[13]	10	40.0
p	3	66.7
v	8	87.5
k	15	93.3
g	6	100.0
s	11	100.0
r	26	100.0
l	15	100.0
n	13	100.0
m	6	100.0
Total	113	92.0

be identified for simplex words are relaxed when certain suffixes are added. The effect of this is that syllabic well-formedness is not uniform across the lexicon, since the syllable canon defined over simplex words may be violated in morphologically complex words. In the latter a long vowel can occur in a closed non-final syllable, as in [²hyːl.tə] 'screamed', or in a final syllable followed by more than one consonant, as in [¹stiːft] 'stiff (neuter)'. As has been noted by some authors, such as Torp (1982: 38) and Sandøy (1994: 238), prosody thereby seems to play an active role in the form–meaning relationship, since overlong syllables of this type signal that a given word is a derived or inflected form.

Note that the UEN pattern is consistent with the proposal made above that Mora Insertion and Mora Linking take place on the cyclic level, not on the word level. If the long vowel is derived on the cycle where Mora Insertion is applicable, this structure will be preserved on later cycles so that no adjustment is possible when the non-cyclic, consonant-initial cohering suffix is added. This will account directly for the long vowel in the suffixed form.

---

[13] The absence of /d/ from the table is due to the fact that stem final /d/ occurs after a long vowel in only one example, /ʋred/, which is hardly used with the suffix.

8.2.3 Vowel shortening in vowel-final stems

We now turn to a case of closed syllable shortening where the alternation between long and short vowel in word forms derived from the same root is predictable, and where the analysis developed above seems to run into problems. Regular verbs whose root ends in a vowel, and which lack a suffix in the infinitive, always take the consonant-initial suffix /-Te/ in past tense and participle formation. Some examples are given in (7).[14] The same effect can be observed in the neuter agreement form of adjectives where the root ends in a vowel. Examples are given in (8).[15]

(7) *Vowel shortening in vowel-final verbs*

	Root	*Infinitive /-Ø/*	*Past tense /-de/*	*Participle /-d/*
(a)	/ru/ 'to row'	[ˈruː]	[ˈrud.də]	[ˈrud]
(b)	/spa/ 'to spade'	[ˈspɑː]	[ˈspɑd.də]	[ˈspɑd]
(c)	/flo/ 'to skin'	[ˈfloː]	[ˈflɔd.də]	[ˈflɔd]
(d)	/sy/ 'to sew'	[ˈsyː]	[ˈsyd.də]	[ˈsyd]

(8) *Vowel shortening in vowel-final adjectives*

	Root	*Simplex*	*Neuter /-t/*
(a)	/gro/ 'grey'	[ˈgroː]	[ˈgrɔt]
(b)	/rø/ 'red'	[ˈrøː]	[ˈrœt]
(c)	/fri/ 'free'	[ˈfriː]	[ˈfrit]
(d)	/bre/ 'broad'	[ˈbreː]	[ˈbrɛt]

After the MSR and Mora Insertion have applied on the root cycle, the only available segment that the inserted mora can be linked to is the vowel. When the consonant-initial suffix is added on the following cycle, our analysis so far predicts that the vowel length will be preserved, since length preservation seems to be the prevailing pattern. This prediction is not borne out, however; we see that the vowel is consistently realized as short in all forms where a suffix has been added. We must therefore ask how these data can be reconciled with the assumptions that Mora Insertion applies on each cyclic level where the MSR applies, and that the results of Mora Insertion and Mora Linking are preserved throughout the cyclic level.

Note that the suffixes in question are non-cyclic. Neither the MSR, Mora Insertion nor Mora Linking are therefore expected to apply again. But the shortening shows that the suffix nevertheless triggers delinking of the final mora of the stressed syllable in this environment, while in the unmarked case it leaves it untouched when the stem is consonant-final.

---

[14] A few verbs whose root end in a vowel take the infinitive suffix /-e/. These invariably select the /-a/ ~ /-et/ past tense and participle allomorph, cf. (4) in Chapter 3.

[15] Some adjectives of this type resist the adding of the agreement suffix, however, cf. Faarlund *et al.* (1997: 369f.). In these we do not find shortening. Examples are /bra/ 'good', /sta/ 'stubborn', /slʉ/ 'sly'. These tend not be used in environments where the t-suffix is called for.

The most general formulation of the rule, which I shall refer to as Vowel Shortening, is that it applies in derived environments where the input, a sequence of stressed long vowel + obstruent, is created by any word formation rule that adds an obstruent-initial suffix. Its application is subject to Strict Cyclicity in the sense that the V:C-environment must have been created on the cycle where it applies. This will limit the rule to V:]C-environments, that is, to environments where the morpheme boundary is situated between the vowel and the consonant.

The rule must be constrained in two ways. First, it only applies when the suffix begins with an obstruent. In addition to the suffixes involved in the examples above, we find vowel shortening before the cohering, deverbal suffix /-sl/, as for example in [¹tɾʉs.sl̩], *trussel* 'threat', which can be compared with the infinitive [²tɾʉː.wə], *true* 'to threaten'. We also find it in some idiomatic prepositional phrases where the old genitive case ending /-s/ is still present, as in [təˈʂœs], *til sjøs* 'to sea', cf. [ʂøː], *sjø* 'sea'. No shortening takes place, however, when the present tense marker /r/ is added. The present tense forms of the examples in (7) are [¹rʉːr], [¹spɑːr], [¹floːr] and [¹syːr], respectively.

The rule is stated in (9). After the vowel has been shortened, the free mora will associate to the following suffix consonant.

(9)   *Vowel shortening*
       Domain: Cyclic level, within prosodic words

Shortening does not apply across a prosodic word boundary. It is in other words triggered by cohering suffixes only.[16] It therefore does not apply before a non-cohering suffix like /-bar/, as can be seen from [²smiː.bɑːr], *smibar* 'malleable', cf. [¹smiː], *smi* 'to forge'. Nor does it apply to /-som/, as can be seen from [²bryː.sɔm], *brysom* 'troublesome', related to [¹bryː], *bry* 'to bother'.

The analysis so far suggests that morphological properties of the suffixes that trigger vowel shortening are not relevant. The passive suffix /-s/, however, represents counter-evidence to this. The suffix can be added to verbal stems, and depending on a set of morphological, syntactic and semantic constraints it may alternate with the periphrastic passive constructed by means of the copula verbs *være* or *bli* plus a past participle. When this suffix is added to a vowel-final stem, no shortening takes place. This can be seen from the examples in (10). These data suggest that the shortening is triggered by specific morphemes in addition to the requirement that the suffix must be cohering and begin with an obstruent. In Chapter 11.6.4 we shall see that shortening is triggered by the negative clitic /-ke/ as well.

---

[16] In a number of cases shortening may occur across a compound boundary in UEN, such as in [²blɔb.bæɾ], *blåbær* 'blueberry', cf. [¹bloː], *blå* 'blue', and [²smɔt.tiŋ], *småting* 'trifles' (lit. 'small things'). In both cases the pattern is variable. See Alnæs (1925: 41f.) and Fretheim (1988) for more examples, all of which can be considered as lexicalized.

(10)   *Inflectional passive*

	Root	Infinitive	Passive
/ru/ 'to row'		[¹ruː]	[¹ruːs]
/spa/ 'to spade'		[¹spɑː]	[¹spɑːs]

8.2.4 Shortening in stems ending in a coronal stop

As can be seen from (4) and (6), shortening is obligatory when the stem ends in
either /t/ or /d/. Some additional examples are given in (11). Since this is a case
where the addition of the suffix will create a segmental geminate, it has been used
in earlier analyses as evidence for positing consonantal geminates as part of the
phonological inventory of Norwegian and Swedish (Lass (1984: 255ff, Lorentz
1996). The vowel shortening is then derived from the assumption that a geminate
is only licensed after a short vowel in mono-morphemic environments. Under the
present analysis, a similar account is excluded because consonant geminates can
only be licensed by ambisyllabicity, and therefore are not licit word-finally. The
shortening found in these verbs and adjectives must therefore be accounted for
differently.

(11)   *Vowel shortening in stems ending in a coronal stop*

Simplex word	Inflected word
[²leː.tə] *lete* 'to search'	[²lɛt] *lett* 'searched'
[²møː.tə] *møte* 'to meet'	[²mœt] *møtt* 'met'
[¹ʋiːt] *hvit* 'white'	[¹ʋit] *hvitt* 'white' (neuter)
[¹flɑːt] *flat* 'flat'	[¹flɑt] *flatt* 'flat' (neuter)

Within a moraic framework where no skeleton is assumed, consonant geminates
are, as just mentioned, single segments in environments where the first half is
linked to a mora and the second to an onset. This means that if a sequence of two
identical segments is created by the morphology, it must be simplified, irrespective
of the manner in which it is linked to syllabic constituents. Consider now the input
structure of the neuter form of the adjective /ʋit/, *hvit* 'white', which is shown
in (12a).

(12)   (a)   σ   (b)   σ

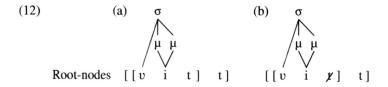

Root-nodes [[ʋ   i   t]   t]   [[ʋ   i   ɣ]   t]

The derived sequence of two identical coronals must now be changed into one. This
can be accomplished by deletion, as shown in (b). The rule, which must be cyclic,
is stated under (13). This will create the proper environment for (9), Vowel Shortening, which will then shorten the vowel.

(13) *Degemination*
      Domain: Cyclic level, within prosodic words
      [Coronal: –cont] → Ø / __] [Coronal: –cont]

8.2.5 Summary

In this section the relationship between stress-dependent syllable quantity and morphology has been discussed. I have argued that the expansion of light, stressed syllables, embodied in the rules Mora Insertion and Mora Linking, must be rules that apply after each application of the cyclic Main Stress Rule. The structure built by Mora Insertion and Mora Linking is with some lexically marked exceptions respected throughout the cyclic level. Vowel length and consonant gemination that occur in unstressed vowels, due to reapplication of the MSR, must then be undone at the word level.

Unpredictable cases of closed syllable shortening due to attachment of a consonant-initial suffix to a consonant-final stem with a preceding long vowel are best seen as vestiges of a rule that is no longer part of the phonological rule system of UEN. Preserved vowel length in this environment can then be seen as the unmarked option which follows from the assumption that the effects of Mora Insertion and Mora Linking are preserved throughout the cyclic level.

Vowel shortening in vowel-final stems, when an obstruent-initial cohering suffix is added, was analysed as the effect of Vowel Shortening, a delinking rule subject to Strict Cyclicity. On the assumption that a sequence of identical coronal stops across a morpheme boundary is simplified through deletion, this rule also accounts for the shortening found when a suffix beginning with a coronal stop is added to a stem ending in another coronal stop.

8.3 SYLLABIFICATION OF SONORANTS

In this section we shall discuss in more detail the constraints that govern the distribution of syllabic sonorants. In Chapters 3 and 5 we saw how syllabic sonorants may arise in environments where they occur between an obstruent or another sonorant to its left and a word boundary to its right. Thus an underlying form such as /sykl/, *sykkel* 'bicycle' will surface with the syllable structure [ˈsyk.kl̩].

Syllabic sonorants will often alternate with non-syllabic ones in different realizations of the same root. The basic principle governing their distribution is that when the sonorants constitute local sonority maxima, they will surface as syllabic.[17] (14) shows some examples of alternations in adjective inflection, where the addition of the agreement marker /-e/ causes the stem-final sonorant to surface as an onset, while in the non-inflected simplex forms it is syllabified as head due to the fact that it constitutes a local sonority maximum.

---

[17] Syllabic sonorants can never bear stress, but since in most cases they constitute light syllables at word ends, no special stipulation seems necessary in order to block the MSR from assigning stress to them.

(14) *Alternation between syllabic and non-syllabic sonorants in adjectives*

Simplex	Inflected
[¹bit.tr̩] *bitter* 'bitter'	[²bit.rə] *bitre*
[²nɑː.kn̩] *naken* 'naked'	[²nɑː.knə] *nakne*
[¹ɛŋ.kl̩] *enkel* 'simple'	[²ɛŋ.klə] *enkle*

8.3.1 Which sonorants may be syllabic?

As shown in Chapter 3.2.4.3, only coronal sonorants can be syllabic in Norwegian. Of these, only the non-posterior /r, l, n/ can be syllabic when singly linked to syllable structure. The apical, posterior sonorants /ɭ, ɳ/ can only be syllabic when they share and have received their [ap]-specification from a preceding segment, while a syllabic retroflex flap is very marked; see Chapter 4.3.7. Thus in /ʋaʂl/, *varsel* 'warning', the [ap]-specification of /ʂ/ is spread onto the final /l/. The surface result is [¹ʋɑʂ.ʂɭ]. The same effect can be observed in /baʈ-n/, *barten* 'the moustache', where the suffix is retroflexed by spreading, giving [¹bɑʈ.ʈɳ]. If the environment for retroflection is created by the morphology so that the result would be a singly linked non-anterior syllabic sonorant, as in /fetr-n/, *fettern* 'the cousin', a vowel is epenthesized instead so that the result is [fɛt.tæɳ].

We therefore seem to need a filter that will block singly linked coronal, apical and posterior syllabic sonorants. The filter, which forbids surface forms such as *[¹fɛt.tɳ] (from underlying /fetr-n/), is stated in (15).

(15) *Filter blocking singly linked apical, posterior sonorants*

Assuming the Linking Constraint of Hayes (1986), which says that association lines in a representation must be interpreted exhaustively, this filter will block singly linked syllabic retroflexes, but not multiply linked. The filter will also exclude syllabic retroflex flaps. Due to the fact that flaps cannot follow another coronal, doubly linked structures will not arise.

8.3.2 Late syllabification or resyllabification?

In Chapter 5.3.2 the rule which assigns [syllabic] to sonorants was given. It is repeated as (16) here.

(16) *Assignment of [+syllabic] to non-vocalic sonorants*

$$R_i \rightarrow \text{[syllabic]} \ / \ R_{i-1} \ \underline{\quad} \ \#$$

$$\begin{bmatrix} -\text{voc} \\ +\text{son} \end{bmatrix} \qquad\qquad\qquad [-\text{voc}]$$

Condition: Sonority R_i > Sonority R_{i-1}

This rule makes root-final sonorants syllabic when they occur after another consonant which is lower in sonority. In this environment the sonorant represents a local sonority peak, and therefore cannot be syllabified as a coda with respect to the preceding vowel in the root.

In Chapter 5 it was simply assumed that (16) applies at the same time as the other syllabification rules. When the effect of morphology is taken into consideration, however, it is clear that the local sonority maximum present on the root cycle can be suspended by the addition of a suffix that begins with a more or equally sonorous segment, that is, a vowel or another sonorant. If final sonorants therefore are made syllabic on the root cycle, the analysis must allow for resyllabification into onsets when such suffixes are added. If their syllabification is suspended until suffixation has taken place, no resyllabification will be necessary.

The latter assumption accords with the analyses of lexical syllabification of Rubach and Booij (1990), Rubach (1990), and Hall (1992). Based on data from Polish and German, these authors claim that only codas can be subject to resyllabification. This assumption implies that sonorants cannot be made syllabic on the root cycle, but must be left unsyllabified until a later stage of the derivation. When cohering, vowel- or sonorant-initial suffixes before which syllabic sonorants do not occur are added, the non-syllabified sonorant is syllabified as onset across the morpheme boundary. When a suffix is added which begins with a consonant less sonorous than the stem-final sonorant, the latter will constitute a local sonority peak and will therefore be syllabified as a head. The fundamental principle implied is that sonorants are syllabified as heads only in environments where they may surface as syllabic: once they have been made syllabic, they remain so during the rest of the lexical derivation.

This approach seems to be the prevalent one in the existing analyses of syllabic sonorants in English and German, two languages closely related to Norwegian. The central claim of the analysis of German in Wiese (1986) is the same as that set forth for English in Mohanan (1986) and Borowsky (1993): syllabification of sonorants as heads is suspended until all suffixes have been added to a given stem. There is therefore no cyclic resyllabification of sonorants in the lexicon once they have been made syllabic. This conforms with the claim of Rubach and Booij (1990), Rubach (1990), and Hall (1992) that only codas can be resyllabified cyclically. In the subsections to follow we shall test this hypothesis against UEN data.

8.3.3 Syllabic and non-syllabic sonorant suffixes

Of the three coronal sonorants /r, l, n/, /r/ and /n/, but not /l/, are used as inflectional suffixes. /r/ is used to signify present tense in verbs and indefinite plurals of nouns, while /n/ is most widely used as the def. sg. marker on masculine nouns. It seems that these suffixes can be underlyingly syllabic or non-syllabic. Underlying syllabicity will reveal itself when the sonorant is added to a vowel-final stem. Since the syllable canon allows a single coda consonant after a long vowel word finally, we would expect a non-syllabic suffix to syllabify as a coda when added to a vowel-final stem. If another syllable is generated, this may be explained as being a reflection of underlying syllabicity.

The data in (17a–c) reveal that not all suffixes of the relevant type surface as syllabic. While the indef. pl. marker /-r/ on nouns always surfaces as syllabic, the present tense marker surfaces as non-syllabic when added to a vowel-final stem.

(17)   *Syllabicity in suffixes*

Verb inflection	Present tense	Infinitive	Gloss
(a)	[¹byːr] *byr*	[¹byː] *by*	'offer'
(b)	[¹breːr] *brer*	[¹breː] *bre*	'cover'
(c)	[¹sviːr] *svir*	[¹sviː] *svi*	'burn'
(d)	[²ruː.wɽ] *roer*	[²ruː.wə] *roe*	'calm
(e)	[²læj.jɽ] *leier*	[²læj.jə] *leie*	'rent'
(f)	[¹biː.tɽ] *biter*	[²biː.tə] *bite*	'bite'

Noun inflection	Indef. pl.	Indef. sg.	Gloss
(a)	[²byː.jɽ] *byer*	[¹byː] *by*	'town'
(b)	[²breː.ɽ] *breer*	[¹breː] *bre*	'glacier'
(c)	[²stiː.jɽ] *stier*	[²stiː] *sti*	'path'

The data given as (d–f) seem to contradict this principle, however, at least on the assumption that the stem to which the present tense marker attaches is the verbal root. But the difference between (a–c) and (d–f) can be made to follow from properties of the stem if we assume that the stem for present tense formation instead is the infinitival stem. The syllabic status of the present tense ending in (d–f) therefore can be seen as a result of a coalescence of the empty vowel which represents the infinitive marker, and the non-syllabic sonorant suffix marking the present tense.

But there is at least one problem with this analysis. When a suffix is added to a foot that in itself consists of more than one syllable, underlying syllabicity is cancelled (Fiva 1983). Thus when the def. sg. suffix /n/ is added to the bivocalic masculine stems /bake/, *bakke* 'hillside' and /sufa/, *sofa* (id.) the results are [²bɑk.kn̩] and [¹suf.fɑn] respectively. A telling example is the masculine stem /mutur/, *motor* (id.), which as a simplex word may be pronounced either [mu.¹tuːr] or [¹mut.tur]. In the former, the foot to which a suffix is added, is monosyllabic, and the def. sg. form is accordingly [mu.¹tuː.un̩].[18] In the latter the output is [¹mut.tun̩], since the

---

[18] The form of the final syllable will be accounted for in Section 8.4.1 below.

stem foot already consists of two syllables. This suggests that the syllabicity of the suffix is governed by prosody: the suffix will only surface as syllabic if the result is a disyllabic foot headed by the stressed syllable.

In Chapter 7.2.4 we found that a disyllabic foot seems to be called for in the analysis of cyclic stress induced by some of the prestressing suffixes. Here we see another instance where a disyllabic foot seems to be needed. To formalize this constraint is not an easy task, however. Since not all suffixes are realized as syllabic when added to a monosyllabic foot, the suffixes that are must be marked in some way. The best analysis therefore seems to be to maintain that suffixes may be underlyingly marked as syllabic, and to assume a rule that pares down trisyllabic feet resulting from adding a syllabic suffix consonant to a stem that ends in a disyllabic foot. As will become clear in Section 8.2.4 below, however, this is not always obligatory when the stem itself ends in a syllabic sonorant. Given the complexity of the data discussed there, I therefore shall not venture to formalize the rule.

8.3.4 The distribution of syllabic sonorants

In the following four subsections, the distribution of syllabic sonorants in derivation and inflection will be presented. It must be emphasized at this point that the data are rather difficult to establish with a reasonable degree of accuracy. The difference between a syllabic and non-syllabic sonorant immediately preceding a vowel can be difficult to hear in normal speech. No systematic investigation exists of alternations in syllabicity in this environment, and the question whether the facts can be established by means of objective procedures, such as acoustic measurements, is an open one. It may well be that we are dealing with grammatical distinctions which are present in the speakers' competence, but not realized consistently in the phonetics. As a basic principle of analysis I shall assume that in all forms where a syllabic sonorant is at all possible in the surface in slow speech, this is present in the output of the cyclic derivation. Desyllabification in such forms will be seen as postcyclic, either at the word level or postlexically. But in forms where syllabic sonorants seem impossible even in slow speech, no syllabic sonorant will be assumed in the form leaving the cyclic level.

8.3.4.1 Derivation

As can be seen from the examples in (18a), syllabic sonorants are not found before cohering vowel-initial derivational suffixes. This holds for cyclic, i.e. stress-affecting, as well as stress neutral suffixes.[19]

---

[19] The fact that a syllabic sonorant is obligatory in front of the suffix -inne when the stem ends in a syllabic sonorant, as in e.g. [ˌsʋiː.gr̩.²rin.nə], and not *[sʋi.²grin.nə], *svigereinne* 'sister-in-law', supports the analysis of this suffix as non-cohering, as noted in Chapter 7.3.7. Note that syllabification between the two PWds all the same is continuous; the final /r/ of the stem also links up as an onset with respect to the initial vowel of the suffix.

(18)   *Syllabic sonorants in derivation*

    (a) *Cohering, stress-affecting suffixes*

/-er/$_V$	/filtr/	[fil.¹treː.rə] *filtrere* 'to filter'
	/møbl/	[mœ¹bleː.rə] *møblere* 'to furnish'
/-at/$_N$	/filtr/	[fil.¹trɑːt] *filtrat* 'filtrate'
/-isk/$_{Adj}$	/sentr/	[¹sɛn.trisk] *sentrisk* 'centric'
/-al/$_{Adj}$	/sentr/	[sɛn.¹trɑːl] *sentral* 'central'
/-²ese/$_N$	/negr/	[nɛ.²grɛs.sə] *negresse* 'Negress'

    (b) *Cohering, stress-neutral suffixes*

/-ing/$_N$	/megl/	[²mɛg.liŋ] *megling* 'arbitration'
/-r/$_N$	/megl/	[²mɛg.l̩r] *megler* 'arbitrator'

    (c) *Non-cohering suffixes*

/-aktig/$_{Adj}$	/filtr/	[¹fil.tr̩.rɑk.ti] *filteraktig* 'filterlike'
/-²ine/	/svigr/	[ˌsʋiː.gr̩.²rin.nə] *svigerinne* 'sister-in-law'

8.3.4.2 Verb inflection

When a vowel-initial suffix such as the infinitive /-e/ or the past tense /-a/ is added
to a verb stem ending in an obstruent plus sonorant, the sonorant is predictably
always syllabified as onset. Examples of relevant verb forms are given in (19). In
addition to roots, examples of infinitives, present tense forms and two alternative
realizations of imperatives are given.

Syllabic sonorants are in fact lacking in verbs, except in present tense forms
where the suffix /-r/ will surface as syllabic when added to stems ending in the
infinitival marker /-e/, the empty vowel. As mentioned above, the syllabicity of the
sonorant can here be derived from the adjacent vowel representing the infinitive
suffix, and can therefore be seen as the result of a late adjustment rule.

(19)   *Syllabic sonorants in verb inflection*

Root	Infinitive /-e/	Present tense /-r/	Imperative 1 /-Ø/	Imperative 2 /-e/
/bit/ 'bite'	[²biː.tə]	[¹biː.tr̩]	[¹biːt]	
/ru/ 'row'	[¹ruː]	[¹ruːr]	[¹ruː]	
/ru/ 'calm'	[²ruː.wə]	[²ruː.wr̩]	[¹ruː]	
/megl/ 'arbitrate'	[²mɛg.lə]	[²mɛg.l̩r]	?[¹megl]	?[²mɛg.lə]
/klatr/ 'climb'	[²klɑt.rə]	[²klɑt.rər]	?[¹klɑtr]	?[²klɑt.rə]
/opn/ 'open'	[²oː.pnə]	[²oː.pnr̩]	?[¹oːpn]	?[²oː.pnə]

The evidence for the claim that syllabic sonorants are banned in verbs is found in
the imperative forms. Imperatives lack a specific affix, and their segmental composition corresponds to that of the root. In roots ending in a sequence that meets the
structural description of the sonorant syllabification rule (16), we would therefore
expect the final sonorant to be syllabified as a head. But as can be seen from (19),
this is blocked in UEN. When an imperative of this type is pronounced in isolation,

or preceding a consonant-initial word, it is in fact unclear what form is used. Hence the two alternative forms, both with a question mark. When asked to pronounce imperatives of this type, speakers of UEN will often produce examples where a vowel-initial word follows, or they will claim that they avoid these forms, that they are in fact unpronounceable in isolation or before a consonant. These speakers will readily produce [²oː.pnɔp], *åpn opp!* 'open up', but [¹oːpn], *åpn!* and [¹oːpn.dn̩], *åpn den!* 'open it' are difficult to elicit. A third option is to insert an /e/ at the end, as in the Imperative 2 alternative in (19).[20] This is the recommended way of writing these imperatives, but it is unclear to what extent such forms are used in spoken language. Note that the vowel-final imperatives are only possible with respect to verbs ending in sonorants preceded by a less sonorous consonant.

In more western dialects the first alternative with a monosyllabic form is obligatory and unmarked, however. The result is that the rhyme violates the SSC. Such forms are limited to verbs, however, in adjectives and nouns they are impossible. Here, sonorants in the same environments are invariably made syllabic.

8.3.4.3 Adjective inflection

The relevant data are presented in (20). The generalization that emerges from the table is that sonorants are never syllabic in front of a vowel, only at word ends and before an obstruent. A syllabic pronunciation of the sonorants in Agreement 2, comparative and superlative is in other words unacceptable irrespective of speech rate and style.

(20) *Syllabic sonorants in adjective inflection*

Root	Simplex form	Agr. 1 /-t/	Agr. 2 /-e/	Comp. /-ere/	Sup. /-est/
/enkl/ 'simple'	[¹ɛŋ.kl̩]	[¹ɛŋ.kl̩t]	[²ɛŋ.klə]	[²ɛŋ.klə.rə]	[¹ɛŋ.kləst]
/bitr/ 'bitter'	[¹bit.tr̩]	[¹bit.tət̩]	[²bit.rə]	[²bit.rə.rə]	[¹bit.rəst]
/nakn/ 'naked'	[²naː.kn̩]	[²naː.kn̩t]	[²naː.knə]	[²naː.knə.rə]	[¹naː.knəst]

8.3.4.4 Noun inflection

As shown in Chapter 3.1.4, nouns in UEN are inflected for number and definiteness by means of suffixes. This renders four possible combinations, indef. sg., def. sg., indef. pl. and def. pl. Within all four categories, different allomorphs are in use, whose selection to a considerable extent can be predicted from grammatical gender. Single sonorants as well as vowels are used as suffixes. The most common suffixes are given in (5) in Chapter 3. An allomorph for indef. pl. not given there, but which is of crucial relevance within the present context, is /-e/, which is selected by stems ending in syllabic /r/.

---

[20] Diderichsen (1953) contains a short discussion of the same phenomenon in Danish.

The data are given in (21), sorted by gender. Feminines with this structure are rare, so only masculines and neuters are given. The sonorant suffixes /r/ and /n/ are assumed to be underlyingly syllabic.

(21) *Syllabic sonorants in noun inflection*

Root	Indef. sg. (simplex)	Def. sg. /-n ~ -e/	Indef. pl. /-r ~ -e/
Masculine			
/bibl/ 'bible'	[¹biː.bl̩]	[¹biː.bl̩.l̩n̩]	[¹biː.bl̩.l̩ɾ]
/fetr/ 'male cousin'	[¹fɛt.tɾ̩]	[¹fɛt.tɾ̩.r̩n̩]	[¹fɛt.tɾ̩.rə]
/ordn/ 'order'	[¹ɔr.dn̩]	[¹or.dn̩.n̩]	[¹ɔr.dn̩.n̩ɾ]
Neuter			
/stempl/ 'stamp'	[¹stɛm.pl̩]	[¹stɛm.pl̩.lə]	[¹stɛm.pl̩.l̩ɾ]
/ankr/ 'anchor'	[²aŋ.kɾ̩]	[²aŋ.kɾ̩.rə]	[²aŋ.kɾ̩.rə]
/bekn/ 'bedpan'	[¹bɛk.kn̩]	[¹bɛk.kn̩.nə]	[¹bɛk.kn̩.n̩ɾ]

The crucial property of noun inflection is that syllabic sonorants *can* occur before vowels and another syllabic sonorant at morphological boundaries. This can only be accounted for if stem-final sonorants are continuously syllabified at the cyclic level, so that a final sonorant is already syllabic when a suffix is added. If syllabic sonorants were blocked at the cyclic level, they would have been syllabified as onsets as soon as an onsetless suffix were added.

The forms given in (21) represent the structures that can be derived directly by application of the syllabification rules given in Chapter 5.3. They are all forms that I consider possible in slow careful speech, even if sonorants will often appear as non-syllabic in normal and rapid speech. The difference between nouns and adjectives is therefore not consistently produced at the phonetic level: see Section 8.4.2 below.

8.3.5 Analysis

We have seen that the distribution of syllabic sonorants differs markedly in verbal, adjectival and nominal paradigms. In verbal roots, syllabic sonorants are not allowed at all, in adjectives, they only occur when the structural description of (9) is satisfied at the word level, that is, never before a vowel. In nouns, syllabic sonorants can occur before vowels when a morphological boundary occurs between the two segments.

I shall account for this difference by positing the filter stated under (22), which rules out syllabification of sonorants.

(22) *Filter blocking syllabic sonorants*

$$*\begin{bmatrix} +syll \\ -voc \end{bmatrix}$$

This filter can now be seen as holding for verbal roots at all levels. For adjectives it holds on the cyclic level, and for nouns it does not hold at all. This means that sonorants cannot be made syllabic in verbal roots at any level, in adjectives only at the word level, and on both the cyclic and the word level in nouns. On this assumption, final sonorants preceded by obstruents or sonorants of lower sonority remain unsyllabified in verbs and adjectives at the cyclic level. On the word level, sonorants are made syllabic in adjectives by (16), while in verbs, where (22) is still active at the word level, a final sonorant will be linked to the preceding syllable as a coda. Since (22) is not active with respect to nouns, (16) will apply as soon as it gets a chance at the cyclic level, that is, on the root cycle. In this case, the stem for the inflected forms in (21) will contain a final, syllabic sonorant.

In addition to the distributional facts themselves, there are at least two types of independent evidence which support the assumption that sonorants are syllabic already on the root cycle in nouns. First, the indef. pl. suffix /-r/ induces accent 2 on monosyllabic stems (see Chapter 9.4.1), while it has no accentual influence on other stem types. If the final sonorant in, for example, /ordn/ is not syllabified on the root cycle, it will be monosyllabic, and we would therefore expect accent 2 on the result. This is not the case, and it can be explained on the assumption that the stem is disyllabic with initial stress because the sonorant has been made syllabic on the root cycle.

The other type of evidence comes from the allomorphy between /-r/ and /-e/ in indef. pl.: /-e/ is selected by stems which end in a syllabic /r/. Thus the monosyllabic /leir/ 'camp' takes the /-r/, *leirer*, while the disyllabic /sejr/, spelled *seier*, 'victory' selects /-e/, *seiere*. The rule accounting for this distribution must refer to the syllabic status of the stem-final /r/, and from that it follows that this must be syllabified before the indef. pl. suffix is added.

(23) shows the derivation of the indef. pl. of /ordn/ [[ordn]r] and the def. sg. of /stempl/ [[stempl]e]. These are both trisyllabic in careful speech, and differ minimally on that account from the disyllabic present tense *ordner* 'arranges' and the infinitive *stemple* 'to stamp'.

(23) *Cyclic syllabification of sonorants in nouns*

    (a) Syllabification, root cycle

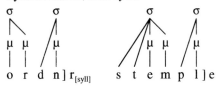

    (b) Syllabification, suffix cycle

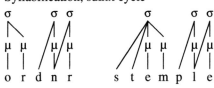

Up till this point, our findings are consistent with the conclusions of Rubach and Booij (1990), Rubach (1990), and Hall (1992) that syllable structure established on a previous cycle can be altered only to a very limited extent. Since sonorants syllabified on the cyclic level in nouns are preserved, and sonorants in adjectives are made syllabic only at the word level, there is no need to assume a rule of resyllabification with respect to inflection. But an inspection of (18) shows that this is not the case with respect to derivation. If final sonorants in nominal stems have been syllabified on the root cycle, this is undone when other cyclic suffixes are added. In some cases this may be ascribed to the fact that the result is an adjective or verb. In that case one might assume that the filter (22) will take effect and revoke the syllabicity of the sonorant. This is nevertheless a case of cyclically induced resyllabification of a syllabic head, a change that is not predicted in the sources cited above. That such resyllabification cannot only be ascribed to a well-formedness constraint such as (22) can be seen from the form with the cyclic suffix /-²ese/.[21] The crucial form is *negrésse*. Here the stem is nominal and therefore must be assumed to end in a syllabic sonorant, and the suffix derives another noun, so (22) is not applicable with respect to the output. We nevertheless find that the sonorant is resyllabified into an onset. The pronunciation *[nɛ.gɽ.²rɛs.sə] is not possible in any style of speech.

From this it follows that some affixes may cause resyllabification of syllabic sonorants, and must be marked for this in the lexicon. This implies that not only codas can be resyllabified during the lexical derivation, as claimed by Rubach and Booij (1990), Rubach (1990), and Hall (1992), but also syllabic heads. There is all the same a strong parallelism between the analyses found in these sources and the one proposed here. In all the cases discussed it is the CV-rule, the rule that builds the minimal, obligatory onsets wherever possible, that is responsible for resyllabification. In Norwegian, this rule may link a syllabic stem sonorant as onset for a following vowel across a morphological boundary. This creates a disyllabic structure consisting of two adjacent segments which constitute a rising sonority cline. In unmarked cases such sequences are syllabified as onset plus nucleus. At least one cyclic suffix, /-²ese/, induces resyllabification so that the unmarked structure is restored, as in *negrésse*, while others leave the marked structure unchanged.

8.4 SONORITY-DRIVEN RESYLLABIFICATION

8.4.1 Nucleus adjustment in sequences of vowel plus syllabic sonorant

Consider the examples in (24) of masculine noun inflection in stems ending in a vowel or a nonsyllabic /r/ or /l/. We see that the vowel spreads onto the syllable head provided by the suffix, except when the vowel is high, where vowel spreading instead creates an onset. At the same time, the sonorant realizing the suffix is

---

[21] This suffix is used on a few stems only: Norsk Termbank (1986) lists only five. It is also found in a few deadjectival derivations, such as *delikatésse* 'delicacy', *noblésse*, 'nobility' and *finésse* (id.).

delinked from the mora.[22] In /r/- and /l/ final roots, this spreading is fed by the Retroflex Rule, and takes place irrespective of vowel height. This difference can be seen as due to the ban against syllabic posterior sonorants stated at (15) above.

(24) *Nucleus spreading in sequences of vowel + syllabic sonorant*

Root	Indef. sg. (simplex)	Def. sg. /-n̩/	Indef. pl. /-r̩/
/sti/ 'path'	['stiː]	['stiː.jn̩]	[²stiː.jɾ]
/bru/ 'bridge'	['bruː]	['bruː.wn̩]	[²bruː.wɾ]
		['bruː.un̩]	['bruː.uɾ]
/tro/ 'thread'	['troː]	['troː.ɔn̩]	[²troː.ɔɾ]
/bar/ 'bar'	['baːɾ]	['baː.ɑn̩]	[²baː.ɾəɾ]
/fyr/ 'fire'	['fyːɾ]	['fyː.yn̩]	[²fyː.ɾəɾ]
/ol/ 'eel'	['oːɭ]	['oː.ɔn̩]	['oː.əɾ]

Let us now see how these surface forms can be derived. The prosodic structure resulting from the syllabic integration of the def. sg. suffix /-n̩/ into the stems /tro/ and /bar/ is shown in (25).

(25) *Resyllabification in sequences of vowel + syllabic sonorant 1*

(a) *Input, suffix cycle*

(b) *Syllabification of suffix*

After the Retroflex Rule has applied to (25b) and merged /r/ and /n/ into a retroflex nasal, the resulting structures consist of a long vowel immediately preceding an onsetless syllabic sonorant, as in (26a). Such sequences can be seen as marked with respect to the Sonority Sequencing Constraint, since the syllabic nasal does not constitute a sonority peak with respect to the preceding segment. In addition, the output of the Retroflex Rule cannot be syllabic by (17), and is therefore doubly infelicitous. The marked structures are repaired by delinking of the head of the least

---

[22] With /u/ there is variation, with spreading more easily taking place before /n/ than before /r/. This makes it difficult to state the rule in a precise fashion.

sonorous syllable, the sonorant, upon which the stressed vowel will spread its features onto the evacuated mora, as shown in (26a–b). As can be seen from (24), the same happens when the indef. pl. /-r/ is added to a vowel-final stem.

(26)   *Resyllabification in sequences of vowel + syllabic sonorant 2*

    (a)   *The Retroflex Rule*

Not applicable

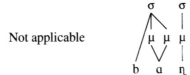

    (b)   *Delinking and spreading of vowel*

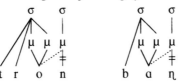

The rules that account for this adjustment, are stated in (27). I assume that the delinked sonorant will finally be linked to the preceding syllable as a coda. (27) as it stands only accounts for sequences with falling sonority. The overriding principle that emerges when sequences of stem final syllabic sonorant + suffix-initial vowel, discussed in the preceding section are taken into consideration, is that when two adjacent syllabic heads are juxtaposed, the less sonorous segment may lose its syllabic status.[23]

(27)   *Sonority-Driven Delinking and Nucleus Spreading*

    (a)   *Delinking (SDD)*   (b)   *Spreading (NS)*

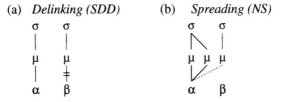

Conditions: α is a nucleus and [−high]
sonority α > sonority β

In words of this type with accent 1, such as the def. sg. forms in (24), the syllable

---

[23] There is of course also the possibility that stress may be of influence, since it is the unstressed syllable that succumbs. But the fact that the rule can be generalized to sequences of light syllables when both are headed by syllabic sonorants, cf. Section 8.4.2, speaks in favour of stress not being of decisive importance here.

itself may also be deleted, giving for example [ˈtroːn] instead of [ˈtroː.ɔn]. In accent 2, such reduction is blocked because a disyllabic foot is the minimal span
across which this accent can be realized, see Chapter 9.3.4. Conceivably this could
be an optional rule dependent on speech rate and style. There may also be dialectal
or sociolectal differences involved, as assumed in Sandøy (1996) between vernacular and middle-class Oslo speech, where a rule of desyllabification is stated only
for the vernacular. The rule can be stated as (28). Since it can apply to inputs where
the final syllable stems from the clitic pronoun /n̩/, as in Chapter 11.6.3, it must be
postlexical, bounded by the PWd.

(28) *Syllable Pruning*

Condition: the leftmost syllable must not be tonally specified as H

8.4.2 *Cyclic desyllabification of sonorants*

The analysis proposed for nouns in Section 8.3.5 above, where syllabic sonorants
are assumed to remain syllabic also in cases where a vowel-initial suffix is added,
does not account directly for all the surface forms that are possible. In many cases
we find alternative forms where a sonorant that has been made syllabic on an earlier cycle is nevertheless realized as non-syllabic. A case in point is the two possible surface forms of the indef. pl. form of the neuter noun /ankr/, 'anchor'. The
input form is /ankr-e/. On the assumption that sonorants are syllabified cyclically,
with no resyllabification, the expected surface form is [²ɑŋ.kr̩.rə]. This is in fact
a possible pronunciation, but a surface string [²ɑŋ.krə], where the /r/ is realized
as part of the onset of the suffix vowel, is equally well-formed. Likewise, the
indef. pl. form of /bibl/, 'bible' may be trisyllabic [ˈbiː.bl̩.lr̩], but it may also be
[ˈbiː.blr̩].[24] We therefore need rules that optionally induce desyllabification of
sonorants when adjacent to another syllabic head. Two principles, which may conflict, seem to be involved: sonority sequencing and a need to eliminate syllabic
sonorants that are not word-final.

We first turn to sonority sequencing. We have already seen that this plays a role
when the def. sg. /n̩/ is added to a vowel-final stem, as in the preceding section. If
we assume that sonority is the driving force behind the reduction from [²ɑŋ.kr̩.rə]

---

[24] There is a minimal schwa present in the phonetics between the two sonorants, so a phonetic transcription might as well be [ˈɔr.dnər]. But as argued in Chapter 3.2.4.3, this can be interpreted as an
effect of universal phonetic principles without phonological relevance. The important phonological
point is that the first sonorant is resyllabified as an onset.

to [²ɑŋ.krə], we derive the mirror image of the resyllabification of disyllabic [¹troː.n̩] to [¹troːɔn]: In a sequence of two syllable heads, the syllable headed by the least sonorous segment is eliminated.

When one of the syllables in such a sequence is headed by a vowel and the other by a sonorant, the difference in sonority is clear. When both are sonorants, the picture gets more complicated. In Chapter 5.1.4 we established that liquids as [+appr, + son] are one level higher in the Sonority Hierarchy than nasals, which are [–appr, +son]. A sonority difference between liquids was not assumed. This means that when two syllabic heads, one dominating a nasal and the other a liquid, are juxtaposed, the latter will be the more sonorous. When two syllabic liquids or two syllabic nasals are combined, they will define a sonority plateau. Since syllabic sonorants must be coronals, there are two underlying liquids, /l/ and /r/, and one nasal, /n/, that may be combined. In all cases to be considered, the first one will be stem-final, while the second will belong to or constitute the suffix. Examples of the different possible combinations are given in (29), sorted into three categories: rising sonority, falling sonority and equal sonority. The suffixes used in the examples are the def. sg. /-n̩/ and the indef. pl. /-ɽ/. As can be seen, a number of alternative surface forms are possible.

In (29a), where the sonority relation between the two sonorants is rising, we would expect the first syllabic head, being the less sonorous, to resyllabify as onset. This is indeed what seems to have taken place in the alternative pronunciation shown in the table. The derivation can be conceived as one where the syllable dominating /n/ is delinked. The nasal will then resyllabify as onset, giving [¹ɔr.dn̩ɽ].

(29) *Adjustments in sequences of syllabic sonorants*

	Segment combination	Input examples	Cyclic output	Alternative pronunciation
(a)	*Rising sonority*			
	n̩] ɽ]	[[ordn] r] 'order'	[¹ɔr.dn̩.n̩ɽ]	[¹ɔr.dn̩ɽ]
(b)	*Falling sonority*			
	ɽ] n̩]	[[fetr] n] 'male cousin'	[¹fɛt.tɽ.rn̩]	[¹fɛt.tæn̩]
	l̩] n̩]	[[bibl] n] 'bible'	[¹biː.bl̩.ln̩]	[¹biː.bl̩n]
				[¹biː.bl̩n̩]
				[¹biː.bæn̩]
(c)	*Equal sonority*			
	n̩] n̩]	[[ordn] n] 'order'	[¹ɔr.dn̩.n̩]	[¹ɔr.dn̩.nən]
				[¹ɔr.dnən]
	l̩] ɽ]	[[stempl] r] 'stamp'	[¹stɛm.pl̩.lɽ]	[¹stɛm.pl̩ɽ]
				[¹stɛm.pɽɽ]
				*[stɛm.pl̩r]
	ɽ] ɽ]	Impossible due to the fact that the plural allomorph is /-e/ in this environment		

Let us now turn to the cases of *falling* sonority in (29b).[25] The prediction based on sonority differences is that the first syllable is preserved, while the second is made non-syllabic. From the inputs [ˈfɛt.tɽ.r̩n] and [ˈbiː.bl̩.l̩n] we would therefore expect [ˈfɛt.tr̩n] and [ˈbiː.bl̩n]. While the latter is clearly possible, the former is not. The reason is that the Retroflex Rule applies to the /rn/ sequence. The result is a structure that violates the filter stated as (15) above, which blocks syllabic, retroflex sonorants. This will therefore delink, and the surface form [ˈfɛt.tæɳ] is derived by the unlinked mora subsequently being filled by the epenthesis rule stated as (30), followed by [+low]-insertion, as in Chapter 4.4.[26]

(30) *Epenthesis*

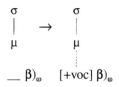

$$\_\_ \; \beta)_\omega \qquad [+voc] \; \beta)_\omega$$

Turning now to the other possible surface forms that can be derived from the cyclic output [ˈbiː.bl̩.l̩n], we also find the surface form [ˈbiːbl̩n], where the most sonorous of the syllabic heads has been desyllabified. As mentioned above, I assume another principle to be active in the derivation of these forms as well, viz. a need to limit the occurrence of syllabic sonorants to the end of a prosodic word. The principle can be stated as one that resyllabifies a sequence of two syllables, both headed by a sonorant, into one by changing the first head into an onset, irrespective of sonority. This is stated as (31). In cases where the head of the first syllable is more sonorous than the second, the latter may alternatively be made into a coda, as in [ˈbiː.bl̩n].

(31) *Sonorant resyllabification*

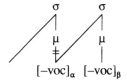

Condition: $\alpha \neq \beta$

---

[25] An analysis of similar data in an SPE-framework is found in Lie (1983). Fiva (1983) is an early autosegmental analysis of the same phenomena in a North Norwegian dialect.
[26] A surface form that might be transcribed as [ˈfɛt.trən] is also possible. This might suggest that the Retroflex Rule is optional in this environment. But if the /r/ is indeed non-syllabic, we would expect it to be subject to progressive devoicing, cf. Chapter 4.2.2. Devoicing does not seem possible, however, and I therefore interpret this as a fast speech variant of [ˈfɛt.tɽ.r̩n]. The only possible output with respect to desyllabification is therefore [ˈfɛt.tæɳ].

This rule will account directly for [ˈbiːblŋ̩].[27] Since the liquid has been transferred to onset position, [post]-linking can now apply and derive a retroflex flap. The flap will trigger the Retroflex Rule. The resulting apical nasal will subsequently delink due to the filter stated in (15), and Epenthesis and [+low]-insertion will give [ˈbiː.bæɳ].[28]

Let us now sum up the analysis so far by showing step by step how the two words [[bibl]n] and [[fetr]n] are derived, the former in two versions.

(32)   [[bibl]n]   [[bibl]n]   [[fetr]n]

Input

$$
\begin{array}{ccc}
\sigma\ \sigma & \sigma\ \sigma & \sigma\ \sigma \\
\mu/\mu\ \ | & \mu/\mu\ \ | & \mu/\mu\ \ | \\
b\ i\ b\ l\,]n & b\ i\ b\ l\,]n & f\ e\ t\ r\,]n
\end{array}
$$

Sonorant Resyllabification

$$
\begin{array}{ccc}
\sigma & \sigma & \sigma \\
\mu & \mu & \mu \\
b\ i\ b\ l\ n & b\ i\ b\ l\ n & f\ e\ t\ r\ n
\end{array}
$$

[post]-linking

Does not apply

$$
\begin{array}{c}
\sigma \\
\mu \\
b\ i\ b\ \textrm{ɾ}\ n \\
[post]
\end{array}
$$

Not applicable

The Retroflex Rule

Not applicable

$$
\begin{array}{cc}
\sigma & \sigma \\
\mu & \mu \\
b\ i\ b\ \textrm{ɳ} & f\ e\ t\ \textrm{ɳ}
\end{array}
$$

---

[27] A possible alternative would be to assume this form to be a fast speech variant of the full form, in parallel with the account given of [ˈfet.tɾ̩.rŋ̩] in the preceding footnote. But /l/ is different from /r/ in that it may in fact be subject to progressive devoicing. Thus the def. sg. of /upl/, *Opel* (car brand) may at least in my own speech be realized as phonetic [ˈuː.p̥o̩ən].

[28] In view of the analysis developed so far, the surface form that results from adding the neuter agreement suffix /-t/ to adjectival stems ending in syllabic /r/ is perhaps unexpected. As can be seen from the example given in (20), [[bitr] t], the surface form is [ˈbit.tət], not *[bit.tæt]. This means that epenthesis cannot have applied here, since this would have triggered [+low]-insertion. This result in fact follows from the analysis, since only sonorants are subject to delinking due to (15). But it entails that when the Retroflex Rule applying to a syllabic /r/ followed by an unmarked coronal derives a retroflex obstruent, its status as syllabic is not revoked. Instead it remains syllabic until the surface level, where a schwa will be inserted for phonetic reasons. The analysis in other words has the rather strange consequence that retroflex syllabic obstruents are allowed in the phonology, while retroflex syllabic *sonorants* are banned.

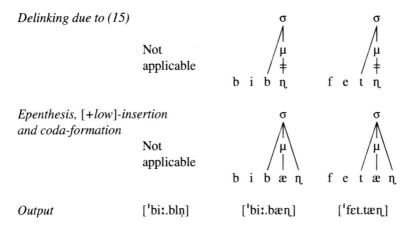

Delinking due to (15)

Not applicable

b i b n̩

f e t n̩

Epenthesis, [+low]-insertion and coda-formation

Not applicable

b i b æ n̩

f e t æ n̩

Output   ['biː.bln̩]   ['biː.bæn̩]   ['fɛt.tæn̩]

We now turn to the data under (29c), which illustrate structures where the two syllabic sonorants are of equal sonority. Only two combinations are found, [. . . n]n] and [. . . l]r]. These two types describe rather different patterns, and we shall therefore discuss them separately. In the case of the two nasals, we are dealing with identical segments. What we find here is a vowel inserted between the two segments, so the cyclic output as listed in (29) is an intermediate form. But since they are identical, a possible alternative scenario would have been merger. Consider now the data given in (33), where masculine nouns whose root ends in non-syllabic /n/ are given in def. sg. and def. pl.

(33)   *Cyclic syllabification of identical nasals*

	Root	Indef. sg. (simplex)	Def. sg. /-n̩/	Def. pl. /-n̩e/
(a)	/man/ 'mane'[29]	['maːn]	['maː.n̩]	[²maː.n̩.nə]
(b)	/man/ 'man'	['man]	['man.n̩]	['mɛn.n̩.nə]

Here we see that merger actually takes place. There is therefore a difference between stems that end in syllabic /n/ and stems ending in non-syllabic /n/. In the latter type the two adjacent nasals will merge, and in the former a vowel is epenthesized. Both alternatives can be seen as OCP-driven. We can account for the data in (29c) if we assume that the rightmost of two adjacent nasals, both of which are syllabic nuclei, is delinked. In order to fill the vacated syllable, (30) will apply. ([+low]-insertion before apicals, stated as (32) in Chapter 4.4, is inapplicable, since the following segment is not a retroflex.) Delinking is shown in (34a), while the effect of epenthesis and coda-formation appears as (34b).

---

[29] In line with the transcription conventions used elsewhere in the book, the definite forms should perhaps be transcribed with an onset nasal as well, as e.g. ['maː.nn̩]. I know of no empirical evidence in favour of this, and therefore opt for the simpler forms.

(34) (a)

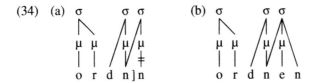

Only the second type in (29c), viz. /lr/-sequences, now remains to be discussed. Since the two segment-types by the Sonority Hierarchy given in Chapter 5.1.4 are equal in sonority, we would expect epenthesis between them as well. A minimal vocalic transition between the two segments is normally present, but the fact that we do not find the vowel realized as [æ], which we would expect before /r/, is an argument against epenthesis having taken place.

An alternative approach would be to reconsider the relationship between /l/ and /r/ with respect to sonority. An inspection of the table in (24) in Chapter 3 reveals that there are no /rl/ sequences in simplex words, since the Retroflex Rule historically has merged such sequences into /ɭ/. In dialects lacking the Retroflex Rule, postvocalic sequences of /rl/, as in /jarl/, *jarl* 'earl' are pronounced as a monosyllable, i.e. [ˈjɑrl]. One never finds a syllabic lateral in this environment. The inverse order, /lr/, is on the other hand always realized with a syllabic /r/ in simplex words, see again (24) in Chapter 3. These facts suggest that there is in fact a rising sonority relationship between the two, and the sequence therefore belongs to the type under (29a). We would accordingly expect variation between forms with syllabic and non-syllabic /l/, and that is indeed the case, as shown in (29c). The assumption that /l/ and /r/ differ in sonority therefore can account both for the syllabification pattern found in simplex words and for the variable surface patterns found in sequences of syllabic /l/ and /r/.

9

TONAL ACCENTS

Contrastive use of pitch characterizes most Norwegian dialects. Two distinctive melodies are found, usually called *accent 1* and *2*, or within structuralist analyses more often *toneme 1* and *2*. Their realization is dependent on primary stress, and accent 2 normally requires at least one unstressed or secondary stressed syllable following the syllable carrying primary stress. The normal case is therefore that no accentual contrast is possible between monosyllabic words.[1]

In the present chapter, we shall concentrate mainly on the lexical aspects of the tonal accents and their relationship with word stress. Their relationship and interaction with intonation will also be taken up to the extent that is deemed necessary, but this aspect will be discussed in more detail in Chapter 10.

9.1 INTRODUCTION

9.1.1 A terminological note

I have chosen to refer to the contrastive use of pitch found in Norwegian and Swedish as 'tonal accent'.[2] This is not a fully satisfactory term, however, since the term 'accent' may seem to imply that we are dealing with some kind of prominence independent of stress, that is phonetically realized by means of pitch. But since the tonal differences that we are dealing with here are dependent on *primary* stress, the term accent is not equivalent with stress within the present analysis. Rather, it is a phenomenon that is part of the stress *realization* system, serving as one of the phonetic parameters through which primary stress is signalled. What sets Norwegian off from most other languages that use pitch as a phonetic means for signalling stress is that we find not one, but two lexically contrastive melodies that may have this function.

'Pitch accent' has been used by some authors to refer to the distinction, for example Monrad-Krohn (1947) and Haugen (1963). Hayes (1995: 49), defines a 'pitch accent language' as one where the tonal realization of stressed syllables is an invariant, lexical property, and not a more variable property determined by the

---

[1] In some dialects we find the contrast on monosyllabic words as well; see Section 9.1.3 below for a short discussion.

[2] The most common Norwegian term for designating the tonal accents is *tonelag*, a noun that can be roughly glossed as 'tone setting'. The two melodies are then referred to as *tonelag 1* and *tonelag 2*. Another common term is *enstavings* ('monosyllabic') vs. *tostavings* ('disyllabic') *tonelag*, which points to the historical origin of the contrast; see Section 9.1.3 below.

postlexical intonational rules. For Norwegian we could therefore employ the term 'contrastive pitch accent' in order to capture that we are dealing with two contrastive and lexically determined patterns.[3] But given the common use of 'pitch accent' as a term that can also refer to the *intonational* tunes that link to stressed syllables (Hayes 1995: 259; see also Ladd 1996: 45f.), the term has become ambiguous and should therefore be avoided, even if epithets like 'contrastive' or 'phonemic' would disambiguate it.

At the same time, the term *accent* clearly points to the fact that the tonal contrast is part of the accentual pattern of the language, since it is part of the stress realization system. Accent is therefore preferable to the more neutral terms *tone* (for instance Fretheim 1969, Standwell 1972, Halvorsen 1983) or *word tone* (for example Haugen and Joos 1952, Jasanoff 1966, Haugen 1967), since the close connection with stress is not apparent from these terms. Neither does the term *toneme* (Jensen 1961, Vanvik 1969, Endresen 1977, Elstad 1980) seem appropriate, since the functional load of the contrast has been shown to be very low (Haugen 1967: 185), and since its principal phonological function lies elsewhere, viz. as part of the stress (and intonational) system.

With the proviso stated above that we are not dealing with an independent prominence system based on tone, I shall therefore refer to the tonal contrast as 'tonal accent', and to the two contrastive melodies as accent 1 and accent 2.

9.1.2 Geographical overview

As just mentioned, most Norwegian dialects have distinct tonal accents. But they are lacking in an area around Bergen on the western coast,[4] in the Brønnøy area north of Trondheim and in many dialects of the two northernmost counties, Troms and Finnmark. Their absence in the latter area may perhaps be ascribed to substratal influences from the Finno–Ugric Sami language, also spoken in this area.

Corresponding tonal contrasts are found in Danish and Swedish, and it should therefore be seen as a common Scandinavian feature rather than a specific feature of Norwegian.[5] Tonal accents are used in standardized speech in Norway as well as Sweden. Since they are lacking in most of the Swedish varieties spoken in Finland, they are on the other hand not part of standard spoken Finland Swedish (Wessén 1970: 47).

The majority of Swedish dialects spoken in Sweden have tonal accents, but they are lacking in the northernmost communities, perhaps due to substratal influence from Sami or Finnish, and in a part of Uppland county north-east of Stockholm.

Most Danish dialects lack tonal accents in the sense implied above, but tonal accents are, or perhaps were, part of dialects spoken in the very south of Jutland and some neighbouring islands (Ringgaard 1973: 21, and see the map in Bjerrum

---

[3] Haugen (1963) in fact uses 'phonemic pitch accent'.
[4] Note, however, that the town dialect of Bergen itself has tonal accents.
[5] See Gårding (1977) for an overview.

1948: 8). However, the so-called 'stød', which is found in the majority of Danish dialects, and which is also part of standard spoken Danish, sems to be closely related to the tonal accent systems found in Norwegian and Swedish.[6] It does not seem to occur in the Danish dialects with tonal accents.[7] Moreover, its distribution corresponds in many respects to the distribution of accent 1 in Norwegian and Swedish. Since we find dialects with tonal accents in the south of Denmark, it is conceivable that stød is an innovation in Danish developed from an earlier system characterized by tonal accents.

The other North-Germanic languages, Icelandic and Faroese, lack tonal accents and stød altogether.

9.1.3 Historical background

The origin of the tonal accents is not quite clear.[8] The most common explanation relates it to a supposed tonal difference between mono- and polysyllabic words in Old Norse. Since the two melodies pertained to two different domains defined by number of syllables, they were predictable and non-contrastive. Two developments that took place in the late Medieval Age altered this. First, Old Norse monosyllables ending in the sequence obstruent + sonorant, such as *akr* 'field' and *vápn* 'weapon' developed into disyllabic structures by the insertion of an epenthetic vowel between the obstruent and the sonorant (or in the eastern dialect group perhaps by direct syllabification of the final sonorant). This change was not accompanied by a change into the disyllabic tonal pattern, and the result was that two different tonal patterns could now be found in disyllabic words.[9] The UEN pronunciation of the word stemming from the Old Norse disyllabic word *opinn* (adj.) 'open' is therefore [²oː.pn̩], with accent 2, while the modern cognate of the Old Norse monosyllable *vápn* is [¹ʋoː.pn̩], with accent 1. The melody associated with Old Norse disyllabic words is accordingly today's accent 2, while the melody associated with former monosyllables is accent 1.

A parallel development, which introduced disyllabic accent 1 on a massive scale, took place in connection with the development of suffixed, definite articles. These developed from syntactically independent clitics showing full agreement with the head noun in case and number in Old Norse. Perhaps due to the breakdown of the case system in the late Medieval Age, which drastically reduced the array of suf-

---

[6] Stød is a glottal constriction which accompanies the articulation of long vowels and sonorants following a short vowel in stressed syllables. There is a considerable body of literature on the phonology of the Danish stød. The interested reader may consult Basbøll (1985) and the references cited there for a more comprehensive account.

[7] The map given in Bjerrum (1948: 8) shows a few dialects marked for both stød and tonal accents, but since they are all situated on the border between the pure stød area and the pure tonal accent area, and since stød has been an expanding feature in Danish, these dialects were probably undergoing a change from tonal accents to stød when the data underlying the map were collected.

[8] See e.g. Oftedal (1952), Elstad (1980) and Riad (1998) for discussion and further references.

[9] As Tomas Riad (p.c.) has pointed out to me, this is not an explanation in itself, since it derives the pattern from an assumed property of Old Scandinavian which in itself is in need of explanation.

fixes that could intervene between the nominal stem and the clitics, the latter developed into suffixes in their own right, resulting in merged exponence of definiteness and number in def. pl., as in (5) in Chapter 3. Again, the new disyllabic words that resulted did not adjust tonally, but maintained the melody formerly associated with monosyllables only. Therefore, when the syllabic suffix expressing def. sg. is added to a monosyllabic stem, no change in melody takes place. On the other hand the addition of a suffix expressing plural, which represents a much older morphological category, induces a change from accent 1 to accent 2. Thus the def. sg. of the masc. noun *lek* 'play', from Old Norse *leikr*, is [¹leː.kn̩] *leken*, derived from the Old Norse clitic-phrase *leikr-inn*. The indef. pl. is pronounced with accent 2, [²leː.kɾ]; compare the Old Norse cognate *leikar*. Note also that the def. sg. [¹leː.kn̩] contrasts minimally with the derived adjective *leken* 'playful', whose Old Norse cognate was *leikinn*, and which accordingly is pronounced with accent 2 today, [²leː.kn̩].

The origin of the tonal contrast can therefore be traced back to the monosyllabic melody expanding into disyllabic domains due to historic change. The opposite development, the disyllabic melody encroaching upon monosyllabic domains, causing the contrast to arise also with respect to monosyllabic words, has taken place in some dialects (parts of Trøndelag and North Norway) due to truncation of final vowels in disyllabic words. Accent 2 in monosyllabic words is traditionally referred to as *circumflex accent*, see Kristoffersen (1992a) for further discussion and references.

9.1.4 Phonetic realization: the basic patterns

Norwegian dialects are by most dialectologists divided into two main groups, East and West Norwegian, where East Norwegian includes the dialects of the eastern and central parts of Southern Norway, while West Norwegian includes the western and southern part of Southern Norway plus North-Norway, that is, the three northernmost counties, Nordland, Troms and Finnmark. One of the features that correlates quite well with this division is the phonetic realization of the tonal accents.

The relationship between stress and tone appears in its most simple form in accent 1. In East Norwegian accent 1 is realized by means of a low tone on the stressed syllable, while in most West Norwegian dialects, accent 1 is realized by means of a high tone on the stressed syllable. The two groups are accordingly often referred to as 'low tone' dialects (East Norwegian) and 'high tone' dialects (West Norwegian). UEN, belonging to East Norwegian, is therefore a group of 'low tone' dialects.

(1) shows typical F0 trajectories for accent 1 across a two-syllable span in low tone and high tone dialects respectively.[10] (a) represents my own low tone pronun-

---

[10] I have used recordings of my own speech as illustrations of the different patterns involved. Since the basic patterns of East Norwegian tonal accents are fairly well known, the examples given here, at least of the basic patterns, can be checked against previously published literature, e.g. Fintoft (1970). In order to provide a fairly representative set of examples, I have prepared a database of 20 short sentences. Each token was recorded 5 times, and processed by means of a KAY Computerized Speech Lab 4300B for extraction of F0 contours and measurement of segment duration. All examples taken from

ciation of the noun [¹moː.lə], *målet* 'the goal'. The contour represents the averaged pitch values of 30 tokens of the word, all pronounced before a pause, that is, as phrase- and utterance-final. (b) shows accent 1 as pronounced in the high tone dialect of Bergen. The example used shows the F0 contour of one realization of the word [¹num.maʁ], *nummer* 'number', pronounced by a male speaker born in 1949.

(1) *Tonal contours of accent 1 in Arendal (East Norwegian) and in Bergen (West Norwegian)*

(a) East Norwegian: [¹moː.lə]   (b) West Norwegian: [¹num.maʁ]

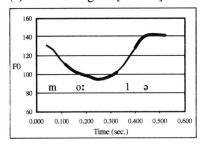
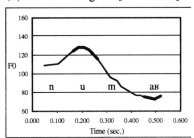

Abstracting away from the initial fall, to which we shall return in a moment, a reasonable phonological interpretation of the F0-trajectories in (1) is that the full melody in the East Norwegian low tone variety is LH, where L represents 'low tone', and H 'high tone'.[11] The L is anchored to the stressed syllable, with the minimum falling late in the vowel, while the H is anchored to the unstressed, poststress syllable. The melody of the Bergen high tone variety can likewise be analysed as HL.

We now proceed to accent 2 realizations. A typical East Norwegian accent 2 F0 contour is given as (2a), representing my own pronunciation of [²maː.lə], *male* 'to paint', averaged across 30 tokens. (2b) represents the corresponding Bergen accent 2 contour of the word [²nɔn.nɛ], *nonne* 'nun', based on one token as pronounced by the same speaker as (1b). Again both words were pronounced phrase-finally before a pause.

The accent 2 contours have in common that their final parts are identical to the accent 1 contour. They differ from accent 1 in having an initial tone of the opposite value, an H in the low-tone East Norwegian type and an L in the high-tone Bergen

my own speech therefore represent means over at least five tokens. The mean contours were obtained by aligning each token at the CV-boundary of the stressed syllable. The F0 readings of each token at each preceding and following measuring point were then averaged, and the average duration for each segment was then superimposed on the resulting F0 contour. I have used the conventions used in Bruce (1977) and Bruce and Gårding (1978) in marking the vocalic part of the contours with a thicker line. Note that the database is intended for illustrative purposes only. Due to the casual way in which it has been compiled, it does not allow for any statistical inferences, nor secure generalizations in cases where it diverges from earlier findings or where previous research is lacking.

[11] I interpret minima, that is, falling pitch followed by a rising pitch, as realizations of a phonologically low tone, and maxima, that is, rising pitch followed by falling pitch, as realizing a phonological high tone.

type. The full accent 2 melodies thus seem to be HLH in East Norwegian, and LHL in Bergen.[12]

(2)   *Tonal contours of accent 2 in Arendal (East Norwegian) and in Bergen (West Norwegian)*

(a) East Norwegian: [²mɑːlə]   (b) West Norwegian: [²nɔn.nɛ]

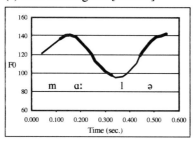
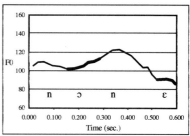

Finally, let us take a brief look at a dialect which lacks contrastive tonal accents. (3) shows the realization of ['num.mɛʁ] and ['nɔn.nɛ] of a man, born in 1949, who speaks the dialect of a small village about 20 km. east of Bergen, Trengereid. (a) represents the cognate of the accent 1 words in the preceding figures, while (b) represents the cognate of the accent 2 words. We see that in this dialect there appears to be a high tone on the stressed vowel in both words, followed by a low tone on the following syllable.

(3)   *Tonal contours of words corresponding to accent 1 and accent 2 in a dialect lacking the tonal accent contrast*

(a) ['num.mɛʁ]   (b) ['nɔn.nɛ]

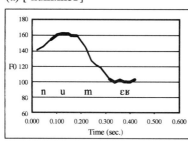
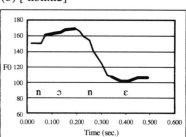

---

[12] While the East Norwegian example given can probably be generalized to all dialects belonging to this dialect group, the Bergen example does not represent all West Norwegian dialects. The Haugesund, area south of Bergen seems to have a system that in some respects resembles the East Norwegian one, while the Stavanger area, south of Haugesund seems to have an HL for accent 1, but an HLHL for accent 2, cf. the tracings published in Fintoft (1970: 226). Even further south, in Egersund, we find the Bergen pattern, but somewhat differently aligned with respect to the tone-bearing units (Hognestad 1997). In many North Norwegian dialects, the initial L of accent 2 seems to be absent, so that the difference between the two accents is not one of tonal composition, but of timing, cf. the tracings published in Elstad (1980) and Kristoffersen (1992a).

9.1.5 Earlier literature

The literature concerning the Scandinavian tonal accents is considerable.[13] It goes back to the middle of the nineteenth century and the tonal accents have attracted a constant interest from Scandinavian linguists since that time. Phonetic studies of Norwegian dialects are reported in Storm (1884), Selmer (1920, 1921 and 1927), Haugen and Joos (1952), Fintoft (1970), Fintoft et al. (1978), Fintoft and Mjaavatn (1980), Kristoffersen (1990) and Hognestad (1997).

The first structuralist analysis of East Norwegian appeared in 1938 (Borgstrøm 1938). Haugen (1967) can be considered as one of the most important, not only within the structuralist tradition, but with respect to the whole research tradition concerning the Scandinavian tonal accents. Other often cited works are Rischel (1960, 1963), Vanvik (1957, 1962) and Jasanoff (1966).

There are several SPE-inspired analyses from the 1970s: Standwell (1972), Hovdhaugen (1971), Weinstock (1970) and Endresen (1976). The three first of these are mainly directed at predicting the distribution of the accents. The fourth, Endresen (1976) also tries to develop a formal tonal analysis where the actual tonal patterns of the East Norwegian dialect under investigation are generated.

The first autosegmental analysis of East Norwegian was published as early as 1977, viz. Endresen (1977). Lorentz (1981, 1984) also represent analyses of tonal accents from an autosegmental point of view, while different aspects of the tonal accents are discussed in a series of articles by Meg Withgott and Per Kristian Halvorsen (Withgott and Halvorsen 1984, 1988, Halvorsen 1983). Typological analyses are Fintoft (1970), Fintoft et al. (1978), Fintoft and Mjaavatn (1980) and Gårding (1977), the latter discussing Scandinavia as a whole.[14]

The relationship between the tonal accents and intonational structure has been discussed in a series of articles by Thorstein Fretheim and Randi Alice Nilsen, see Nilsen (1989, 1992) for an introduction to their model and for further references.[15] The roots of the analysis that will be presented in the sections to follow can be found in Lorentz (1990, 1995) and Kristoffersen (1990, 1993a and b).

9.1.6 The Accent Phrase

As mentioned in Section 9.1 above, the Norwegian and Swedish tonal accents are often referred to as 'word tones', which seems to imply that the domain of the melodies involved is the morphological word, and that the domain of the melodies is constrained by lexical structure.[16] At least for East Norwegian this is not correct,

---

[13] A useful survey of the literature up to the mid seventies concerning tonal accents as well as stød can be found in Gårding (1977: Chapter 1).

[14] For literature on the historical development, see references cited in footnote 8.

[15] See also Chapter 10.3, where their model, which will be referred to as the Trondheim Model, will be applied to UEN intonation.

[16] See e.g. the analysis of Norwegian and Swedish in Laver (1994: 462ff.), where the contour patterns are claimed to be associated with 'the entire word', and Hognestad (1997: 34-35) for a critique of Laver's position.

however, since the final H of both melodies can only associate with the syllable immediately preceding the next primary stress. (If there is no following primary stress within the utterance, the H will associate with the utterance-final syllable, or with a syllable preceding some syntactic boundary between the last primary stress and the utterance-final syllable.) This means that more than one syntactic constituent, that is, any word not carrying primary stress that intervenes between two syllables with primary stress, will be included in the domain of the full melodies. This also means that in cases where the primary stressed syllable of a word is non-initial, the prestress part of the word will be included in the tonal melody starting from the preceding primary stress, while the rest of the word, the stressed syllable and any poststress syllables, will be included in the following tonal melody.

The rules of association of the final H as well as its actual height are pragmatically conditioned, and will be further discussed in Chapter 10. Within the present context it is important to point out that since it may be linked to a syntactic constituent other than the one that carries the initial part of the melody, the full melody cannot be accounted for within the lexicon. This has already been shown in another context, in Chapter 7.3.6, where it was noted that while the initial accent 1 L falls on the primary stress on the initial syllable of the compound *årsoppgjør*, the final H may fall on the initial syllable of *kontoret* in the phrase [ˈoː.ʂɔp.jøːr.pɔ.- kun.ˈtuː.ɾə], [*årsoppgjør på kon*]*toret* 'annual settlements in the office', where the phrase spanned by the accent 1 melody is marked by brackets in the italicized orthography.

The prosodic domains defined by the full tonal melodies LH and HLH will be referred to as the postlexical 'Accent Phrase' (AP). Its left edge is delimited by a primary stressed syllable. The right edge is defined by the next primary stress or by the utterance final syllable. The AP accordingly comprises the part of a given word beginning with the primary stressed syllable, plus any syntactic constituents that intervene between the L and the next tonal accent. Since it will split words that have non-initial primary stress and also straddle word boundaries, the Accent Phrase must be seen as a postlexical prosodic constituent whose domain is not co-extensive with one or more of the highest prosodic constituents created in the lexicon, the Prosodic Word. There is in other words no Strict Layering relationship (Selkirk 1984: 26) between the Prosodic Word and the AP.[17] Instead, the tonal accents seem to enforce a restructuring of the prosodic constituent structure that will not only incorporate clitics and unstressed words into the prosodic constituent headed by the nearest primary stress to the left, but also break up prosodic words created in the lexicon by assigning any unstressed prestress syllable belonging to a word with non-initial stress to the constituent defined and headed by the preceding primary stress. We shall return to this point in greater detail in Chapter 10.2.

---

[17] See also Nilsen (1992: 70ff.) for a discussion of the Strict Layer Hypothesis with respect to Norwegian intonational structure.

9.2 PHONOLOGICAL AND PHONETIC REPRESENTATION

From this section on, the focus will be narrowed down to East Norwegian tonal accents, in accordance with the principal focus of the book. As mentioned above, the manifestation of the tonal accents seems to be relatively uniform across the East Norwegian area. The analysis that follows will therefore cover all dialects belonging to the East Norwegian area, not only UEN.[18]

The analysis to be presented in this chapter will be based on Autosegmental Theory.[19] Tonal phenomena have been central to the development of this theory (Goldsmith 1976, Williams 1976), due to the fact that tonal patterns are often preserved or changed independently of the segmental string over which the tones are realized. An analysis based on Autosegmental Theory presupposes that the melodies can be decomposed into sequences of single tones. That this is indeed the case for the Scandinavian tonal accents has been shown by Lorentz (1981).

Two questions have been central in autosegmental analyses of tone: (1) What are the tone bearing units (henceforth TBUs), and (2) how are TBUs and tones linked in the course of the phonological derivation? In what follows, I shall try to answer both these questions with respect to East Norwegian. The answers will provide us with phonological representations of the tonal accent contrast.

9.2.1   The tone bearing units of East Norwegian: moras or syllables?

With respect to the first question, it has been assumed that the TBUs of a language are one of the prosodic constituents: the mora, the syllable or perhaps the foot. The simplest assumption is that only one type of TBU is relevant in a given language, but that the choice of TBU can vary from language to language.[20] We must therefore ask what is the relevant TBU in East Norwegian, the mora or the syllable?[21]

This choice can only be made by inspecting the distribution of tone within the stressed, bimoraic syllable. In the poststress monomoraic syllable, where mora and syllable are coextensive, no evidence bearing on the choice is likely to be found. We must in other words take a closer look at how tones are linked to the stressed syllable in order to establish an answer to the second question raised above, concerning the association patterns between tones and the segmental string.

---

[18] Studies of different aspects of West Norwegian tonal accents can be found in Selmer (1921, 1927), Christiansen (1933), Jensen (1961), Fintoft (1970), Elstad (1979, 1980, 1982), Kristoffersen (1992a) and Hognestad (1997).

[19] I assume that the reader is familiar with the basic tenets of Autosegmental Theory, as presented in e.g. Roca (1994: Chapter 1) or Kenstowicz (1994: Chapter 7).

[20] This claim has recently been challenged in Lorentz (1995): see footnote 23 below.

[21] Bruce (1987) proposes that the foot is the TBU in Stockholm Swedish. His proposal is based on the observation that the fixed point of alignment of the tonal melodies is the stressed syllable, and that their subsequent extension in time can be fixed independently of the segmental tier. This is an interesting proposal that deserves further consideration, but as Bruce himself observes, his data do not preclude an analysis where the syllable acts as TBU. Lacking decisive evidence, I leave this point for further research.

Within Autosegmental Theory it was originally assumed that there is a linear correspondence between tones and TBUs in the sense that a sequence of tones is linked to TBUs from one of the edges of a domain in a one-to-one fashion. In cases where there are more tones than TBUs, contour tones will arise at the opposite edge of the domain, and if there are more TBUs than tones in the melody to be associated, the final tone will spread over the remaining TBUs after each tone has been assigned to a TBU. In more recent developments of the theory, for example by Pierrehumbert and Beckman (1988), it has been claimed that the tonal level may be underspecified in the sense that not all the units that *may* function as a TBU *must* be linked to a phonological tone. This view allows for phonological representations where only some potential TBUs are actually tone-bearing at a given stage of the phonological derivation.

This allows for three types of autosegmental relationship between phonological tones and TBUs. A TBU may be linked to no tone, one tone or more than one tone. Conversely, a given tone may be floating, linked to one TBU or to more than one TBU. I shall assume that the unmarked situation in the latter case is that a given tone is linked to one TBU only. Spreading is in other words assumed to be rule-governed, and not automatic—see Pulleyblank (1986).

Let us as a starting point for the analysis adopt the more conservative auto-segmental hypothesis that the tones that make up a tonal melody are associated with TBUs in a one-to-one fashion from the left or the right edge. In (4) the two melodies of East Norwegian are juxtaposed. In addition to the segment boundaries, the position of the boundary between the stressed and the poststress syllable has been indicated by a vertical bar.

In order to infer an underlying phonological representation from phonetic signals like this, a number of non-trivial assumptions have to be made. First it must be established that the phonetic signals that the construction is based on, are representative, not only with respect to the speaker, but with respect to the dialect(s) under analysis. In the present case, we may with a reasonable degree of confidence assume that last requirement is met, since the signals illustrated in (4) in all relevant aspects are identical with East Norwegian data from other dialects that have been published in other sources, for instance Haugen and Joos (1952), Fintoft (1970) and Kristoffersen (1990, 1993 a,b).

(4)   *East Norwegian accentual melodies juxtaposed*

    (a) [¹moː.lə]   (b) [²maː.lə]

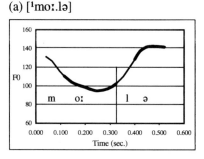
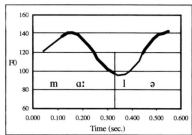

Another important assumption is connected with how phonological tones can be 'extracted' from F0 trajectories. As mentioned in footnote 11 I assume that phonological tones are abstract reference points that guide the F0 trajectory across a phonological domain. The F0 will thus fall towards a low tone and rise towards a high tone. But simple falls or rises are in themselves not sufficient for the establishment of tonal LH or HL sequences. Falls and rises can also be created by aberrations from a neutral pitch level towards a high or a low tone, but the neutral level in these cases represents neither a high nor a low tone in itself. Only *tonal turning points* can be safely assumed to represent phonological (or intonational) tones.

Such turning points are not always well defined with respect to location, in the sense that a rising F0 at a given point always turns into a falling trajectory immediately after it has reached its maximum or minimum level. Often we find that the trajectory levels out for a certain span of time before it turns into the opposite direction. The simplest hypothesis would be to assume that a given stretch of level tone corresponds to one or more TBUs that are associated with the same tone.

Studies of East Norwegian where individual contours are published, such as Selmer (1920), Haugen and Joos (1952), Fintoft (1970) and Kristoffersen (1990, 1993a,b) show that there is frequently, but not consistently, a short fall at the beginning of an accent 1 melody, and that it is in the final part of the stressed syllable, provided both moras are linked to voiced segments, that we consistently find the tonal minimum. I interpret this as a realization of a phonological structure where there is an L linked to the final part of the stressed syllable. This suggests that the mora should be interpreted as the TBU in East Norwegian, since the pattern can be straightforwardly accounted for by assuming that the L is linked to the second mora of the stressed syllable in accent 1.[22]

Note that this implies that the initial mora must be tonally unspecified, and that the edge-anchored association pattern that was assumed in early, autosegmental analysis of tone is not supported by this analysis. The final high tone in the accent 1 melody can now be accounted for by assuming that there is an H linked to the mora of the final, unstressed syllable. The resulting representation of an accent 1 melody realized over a disyllabic span is shown in (5a).

If we now turn to accent 2, we observe from (4b) that there seems to be a high tone associated with the initial phase of the stressed syllable rhyme. From this H the F0 falls through the rest of the stressed syllable towards a minimum that is located in the initial phase of the poststress syllable. From this minimum the tone rises towards another maximum. This means that the final part of the melodies is identical for the two accents. The difference between them manifests itself in the stressed syllable only. For accent 2, the stressed syllable can now be represented

---

[22] Some provisos are in order here. First, the data coverage is not overwhelming, so more fine-grained investigations may reveal dialectal differences. Second, when the second mora dominates a voiceless segment, the L is realized on the initial mora. This is also the case in monosyllabic words: in order to accommodate the LH melody within the only syllable available, the L is realized early. This difference has in fact made some researchers distinguish between monosyllabic and disyllabic accent 1; see Kristoffersen (1992a) for discussion and some references.

as in (5b), by having an H linked to the initial mora, with the second mora left unspecified.

(5) *Phonological representations of accents 1 and 2 with the mora as TBU*

    (a) [¹moː.lə]   (b) [²maː.lə]

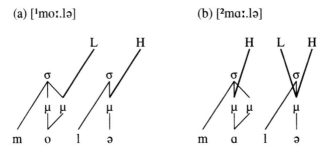

While the location of tones in the stressed syllable, late L in accent 1 and early H in accent 2 suggests that the mora functions as TBU, other aspects of the representations in (5) cast doubts on this. First, in none of the accents are both moras of a stressed syllable used as TBUs simultaneously. Second, on the assumption that tones are associated from the left edge in a one-to-one manner, the gaps in the shape of apparently skipped TBUs are difficult to account for. In accent 1 it must be explained why the initial mora is skipped. Although one might assume that this can be attributed to extraprosodicity, the skipped second mora in accent 2 cannot be accounted for in the same way. Under the standard linking conventions of Autosegmental Theory, an assumption that the mora is the relevant TBU makes it completely mysterious why the L in accent 2 is not associated with the second mora of the stressed syllable instead of with the poststress mora along with the final H.

If we instead assume that the syllable is the TBU in East Norwegian, these problems are solved directly by left to right association. The first tone of each melody will then link with the first syllable, the second tone then links with the second syllable, and finally the final tone of accent 2 must also link with the final syllable. What is left unexplained under this assumption is the location of tones within the stressed syllable. This must therefore be accounted for by means of a later rule. In order to state this rule in a maximally simple way, we seem to need the mora as a secondary TBU at a later stage in the derivation.[23]

The assumption that the syllable is the primary TBU gives the alternative representations shown in (6).

---

[23] An analysis along similar lines, where both the syllable and the mora are exploited as possible TBUs in both East and West Norwegian, is proposed in Lorentz (1995). Lorentz argues the syllable is the optimal TBU. But in cases where there are not enough syllables for each tone, as in cases where the HLH melody of accent 2 is realized over two syllables, the distribution will default on the mora as TBU instead. The result will be one tone per mora. Note, however, that this analysis will not work for East Norwegian, since the L of accent 2 will link with the poststress syllable also in cases where the domain consists of only two syllables—cf. (4b).

(6) *Phonological representations of accents 1 and 2 with the syllable as TBU*

(a) [¹moː.lə]   (b) [²mɑː.lə]

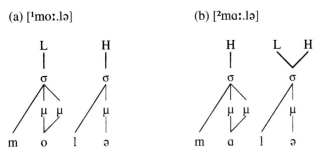

The one-to-one relationship betweeen tones and TBUs becomes clearer if we expand the domain from two to three syllables in order to see what happens to the distribution of the tones of the more complex HLH melody of accent 2. The result of such an expansion is shown in (7), which shows the averaged curves of five tokens of the def. plurals [¹mɔː.lə.nə], *målene* 'the targets', and [²mɑː.lə.nə], *malene* 'the templates'.[24] We see that the pattern is basically the same as over two syllables for both accents. In the more complicated accent 2 contour, we find the initial maximum in the stressed vowel, that is, early in the stressed syllable rhyme. The following minimum comes in the second syllable, while the final maximum is on the final vowel. In other words, we see that the three tones of accent 2 seem to be linked to syllables in a one-to-one fashion.[25]

But note that in accent 1, where there are now two tones to be linked to a domain consisting of three syllables, the second, high tone is not associated to the second syllable, but to the final, contrary to the expectations derived from the association convention. We shall return to this question in the next section.

(7) *Accents 1 and 2 realized over three syllables*

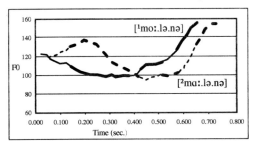

Summing up this section, I claim that the syllable should be interpreted as the primary TBU in East Norwegian. This conclusion is based on the fact that no syllable

---

[24] The examples may also be pronounced with syllabic sonorants: [¹moː.l̩.nə] and [²mɑː.l̩.nə].

[25] The durational differences in the stressed vowel may be coincidental. A corresponding difference does not emerge in the disyllabic examples, cf. (4). A study of four informants from the Nord-Gudbrandsdal region did not reveal such differences in disyllabic words either (Kristoffersen 1990: 77ff.). To my knowledge, systematic studies of phonetic realization over longer domains are lacking.

within an Accent Phrase, except the rightmost, may be linked to more than one tone. The rightmost syllable may only be linked to more than one tone when there are fewer syllables than tones to be accommodated within the AP. Within the bimoraic, stressed syllable, the L of accent 1 seems to prefer the last part of the rhyme, while the H of accent 2 is aligned with the first part.

9.2.2 Functional decomposition of the accentual melodies

The discussion in the preceding section was founded on the basic assumption within Autosegmental Theory that the tones of a melody are associated with the relevant TBUs on a one-to-one basis from the left or right edge of the tonal domain. In most of the examples discussed above, the facts were consistent with the assumption that the tones making up the two melodies are associated to syllables from left to right, with left-over tones associated to the rightmost syllable when there are not enough syllables to accommodate each tone separately. However, one of the tracings suggested that this conclusion may be a spurious result of the fact that only short domains were investigated. The only example given in the preceding section where there are more syllables than tones, is (7), where the accent 1 melody LH is realized over three syllables. Here we see that the L is realized on the stressed syllable, as expected. The following H does not occur on the second syllable, however, but on the last.

What (7) in fact reveals is that the tones of the two accentual melodies cannot be seen as one cohering melody in the sense implied by the association convention that links tones one by one from an edge. The Scandinavian tonal accents should instead be analysed as consisting of single tones which serve independent functions and which are assigned at different levels of the grammar. The linking site of the final H is therefore independent of the linking sites of the preceding tones.

Although it was stated informally in Haugen (1955: 74), the first to establish this based on systematic tests was Bruce (1977). In his study of the interaction between tonal accents, called 'word accents', and sentence intonation in Stockholm Swedish, it was shown that the complete melodies only occurred when the domain carried sentence accent. The complete Stockholm melodies are claimed by Bruce to be HLHL for both accents, with the difference between them constituted by different timing of the first HL sequence with respect to the stressed syllable. In accent 1, the L is linked to the syllable carrying primary stress, with the H docking on the preceding syllable, if present, while accent 2 has the H linked to the stressed syllable. This melody occurred in all syllables carrying primary stress. The penultimate H occurred only when the tonal domain was marked for sentence accent, that is as a constituent carrying a high degree of pragmatic prominence, while the final L was limited to cases when the sentence accent in addition was sentence final. This tone was accordingly interpreted as a boundary tone, termed 'terminal juncture' (Bruce 1977: 12).

An important aspect of the analysis is that the independence of the sentence accent H manifests itself in the fact that it does not associate to the syllable immediately following the one that carries the final tone of the word accent. Long enough (lexical) domains for this to be shown can only be constructed by means of compounds. While the word accent melody is realized on the primary stressed syllable of the first compound member, the sentence accent H invariably manifests itself near the syllable carrying secondary stress in the second member.

The East Norwegian system bears strong resemblance to the Stockholm system as analysed by Bruce. In this system also the final high tone, which is common to both accents, can be analysed as a tone which is part of the intonational system in the same sense as the sentence accent H of Stockholm Swedish. In the extensive research on the relationship between pragmatics and intonation in East Norwegian carried out by Thorstein Fretheim and Randi A. Nilsen, this tone is referred to as a *focus tone*.[26] It differs from the Stockholm counterpart in that it does not seem to be attracted to the syllable carrying secondary stress in compounds. Instead it seems to seek out the very last syllable of the accentual domain. In the next section this property of the focus tone will be investigated more closely by looking at how the tonal accents are realized in long compounds.

9.2.3 Poststress tonal structure

(8) shows the tonal contour of the semantically somewhat contrived compound [ˈmɑn.nɑ.lɑ.nu.ḷiː.n̩], *mannalanolinen* 'the manna lanolin', with five syllables following the one carrying primary stress, and with the secondary stress on the penultimate syllable. The word was pronounced phrase-finally with sentence accent in the sentence *Manne måler mannalanolinen*, 'Manne measures the manna lanolin', and the curve represents an average across five tokens. We see that there is a slight rise from the stressed syllable to the first poststress syllable, where the curve settles into a stable pitch level running up to the final syllable, which is then characterized by a steep rise. This shows that the boundary H is linked to the final syllable only.

(8)   *Accent 1 realized across the compound* [ˈman.na.la.nu.ḷiːn̩]

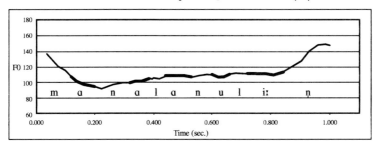

---

[26] See e.g. Fretheim (1992a,b), Fretheim and Nilsen (1989, 1991), Nilsen (1989, 1992). Their model will be discussed in detail in Chapter 10.3, where the motivation for associating the final rise with focus, instead of the preceding low tone, will be given.

A corresponding accent 2 compound realization, viz. [²mɑn.nə.lɑ.nu.ḷiːṇ], *manne-lanolinen* 'the lanolin for men', is shown in (9). This also represents the average across five tokens pronounced in the same environment as the preceding example. Here as well we see that the final rise manifests itself on the final syllable only.

(9) *Accent 2 realized across the compound [²man.nə.la.nu.ḷiːṇ]*

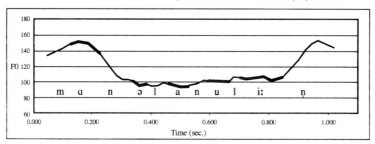

Some comments on the tonal specification of the intervening syllables are called for. They are clearly not associated with an H, so on the assumption that we are dealing with a binary opposition between H and L, they must either be linked to L or be tonally unspecified. On the latter interpretation we would not expect the even pitch level which is evidenced by the curves, but rather an even rise from the L to the final H. This leaves us with the interpretation that the level pitch manifests low tone. But the marked rise from the minimum on the stressed syllable in accent 1, which is also visible in (7) and in (10), makes it somewhat unclear whether this is indeed the case with respect to both accents. Since no independent evidence seems to exist for a third intermediate tone level of phonological relevance, I tentatively choose to interpret the poststress level tone as the result of rightwards spreading of the L in both accents.[27] The rise in accent 1 may then be due to an intonational adjustment.

What is the scope of this spreading rule? Conceivably it may either encompass all syllables up to the final one, or, since we are dealing with compounds, up to the syllable carrying secondary stress. A system similar to the latter has been argued to exist in the North Norwegian Narvik dialect (Lorentz 1984: 174), albeit in accent 2 only, and such a constraint would also make it resemble the Stockholm system,

---

[27] Endresen (1977) claims that pitch rises evenly across poststress syllables toward the final H. This suggests an analysis where intermediate syllables are unspecified for tone. However, no data are presented in support of the claim. Alnæs (1916: 63, 78), on the other hand, supports the view taken here in claiming that pronunciations with even [low] tone on syllables intervening between the stressed syllable and the final H represent ' . . . en meget almindelig uttale' (i.e. 'a very common pronunciation') (p. 63). However, examples given by Alnæs (p. 78 vs. 94) suggest that there is a difference between words and syntactic phrases, in that L-spreading is confined to words, while in accent phrases consisting of several words, the tone will rise evenly. If this is the case, L-spreading must be lexical, and so must L-insertion, contrary to the view argued in Chapter 10 that L-insertion is postlexical. Thorstein Fretheim (p.c.) rejects the possibility that the tonal trajectory between the L and the final H is rule-governed. It should accordingly be left tonally unspecified. This point is therefore clearly in need of further investigation.

where the sentence accent seeks out the syllable carrying secondary stress in compounds (Bruce 1977: 65). The data in (8) and (10) do not provide decisive evidence on this question, since the syllable carrying secondary stress is penultimate.

In order to test whether L-spreading is constrained by secondary stress or may include all the syllables between the L and the final syllable, irrespective of the position of the secondary stress, we must compare these examples with examples where the secondary stress of the second member is antepenultimate. I have therefore paired the two first compound members used above, *manna* and *Manne*, with [li.ˈnuː.li.jʉ.mən], *linoleumen* 'the linoleum' in order to create a suitable test pair.[28] The tonal accents realized over these two words, [ˈmɑn.nɑ.li.ˌnuː.li.jʉ.mən] and [²mɑn.nə.li.ˌnuː.li.jʉ.mən], are given in (10) and (11).

(10)   *Accent 1 realized across the compound* [ˈman.na.li.ˌnuː.li.jʉ.mən]

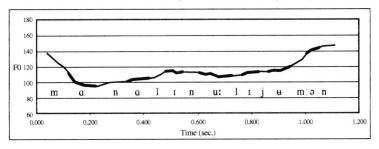

(11)   *Accent 2 realized across the compound* [²man.nə.li.ˌnuː.li.jʉ.mən]

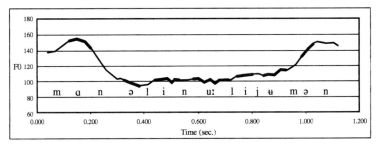

As can be seen from these curves, secondary stress does not seem to constrain the L-spreading. I conclude that the spreading therefore takes the complete AP as its domain, except the final syllable, which is linked to the boundary H. If L-spreading is ordered after the final H-insertion, this result is derived directly.[29]

---

[28] Contrary to the transcription conventions adopted elsewhere in this book, I have transcribed the final syllable with a schwa instead of a syllabic nasal, in order to make it correspond to the F0 curve, where a short, transitional schwa, which I have argued to be phonetically conditioned, occurs between the two nasals.

[29] Note that the curves shown in (8) through (11) show that secondary stresses do not seem to be marked by specific pitch contours. The neutralization of the tonal accents under secondary stress can therefore be made more precise: secondary stresses are not signalled by means of pitch. This means that

We are now in a position where we can sort out the contributions from a lexical, tonal system that is independent from the contribution made by sentence intonation to the two melodies. We have seen that the final phase of the two melodies, the rise from L to H, is common to both accents, and it has also been pointed out that the final H is used to signal that a given constituent carries sentence accent, or is focused. This final H is therefore a tone that is added by sentence intonation, independently of the nature of the preceding melody.

9.2.4 The 'word tones'

It follows from the discussion in the last section that it is the difference between the L of accent 1 and the HL of accent 2 that constitutes the accentual opposition that may serve as phonologically contrastive. But since both melodies contain an L, the difference can be further decomposed into one where it is the presence versus absence of an initial H that constitutes the basic opposition. On the assumption that this tone is inserted first, and that tones are inserted from left to right starting from the stressed syllable, this will cause the L, which is common to both melodies, to be realized later in accent 2 than in accent 1. Both the H and the following L are confined by the morphological word.

(12) shows the two melodies of (4) superimposed, where the final intonational rise has been excluded. We see clearly that the L of accent 1 is reached late in the stressed syllable, while the L of accent 2 is reached in the poststress syllable.

(12) *Idealized realizations of the accentual contrast*

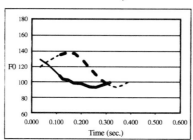

Note that there is a clear fall towards the initial L of accent 1. This might lead one to suspect that there is an initial H also in this melody, which falls outside the realm of the stressed syllable. This has indeed been proposed in earlier literature, for example Haugen and Joos (1952), Endresen (1977), Hoel (1981) and Lorentz (1984).[30] In these works it is claimed that the melodies of accents 1 and 2 can be seen as identical, and it is timing only that differentiates them. If this were the case, the melody would in both cases be HL. The timing difference can be captured by

the phonetic corollaries of syllable weight must bear the burden alone.

[30] See Lorentz (1984) for a more detailed discussion. The same basic structure has, as mentioned above, been proposed for Stockholm Swedish by Gösta Bruce (1977 and subsequent work).

means of Goldsmith's model for describing tonal prominence systems (see for example Goldsmith 1982), where both the tone to be aligned with the accented syllable and the accented syllable itself are marked with an asterisk.[31] Accent is then assigned by aligning the marked tone with the marked syllable. For East Norwegian, the accentual melodies might be represented as in (13).

(13)   *Accentual contrast expressed by means of tone marking*

Accent 1   Accent 2

   *   *

HL   HL

The effect of linking the L of accent 1 to the marked syllable would be that the preceding H must link up with the immediately preceding syllable. If no such syllable is available, it may either delete or associate with the stressed syllable as well.

For UEN, at least, this is not a tenable analysis, however. (14) shows the F0 curves of two utterances, each consisting of two APs. The first AP in both utterances is accent 2, while accent 1 and 2 are contrasted in the last one.[32] We see indeed that there is a maximum immediately preceding the accent 1. Abstracting away from the AP-boundary, one might therefore infer that the two accentual melodies are identical, but differently aligned with respect to the stressed syllable. But once we realize that the preceding APs contain a final boundary H, the similarity finds a different explanation. The H preceding accent 1 is not part of that melody, but the right edge boundary H of the initial AP.

(14)   *Chains of two APs*

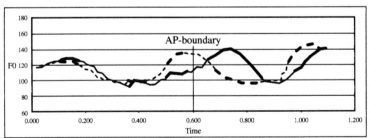

This does not constitute a proof that there is no initial H in the accent 1 melody, however, since it could have been masked by the final H of the preceding AP.[33] Conclusive evidence must be sought in environments where there is no preceding

---

[31]   An analysis of East Norwegian tonal accents based on Goldsmith's proposal is given in Endresen (1977).

[32]   The two utterances are [²mɑn.nə.nɔ.¹moː.lə] (*Manne når*) (*målet*) 'Manne reaches the goal' (final AP accent 1) and [²mɑn.nə.mɔ.²mɑː.lə], (*Manne må*) (*male*) 'Manne must paint'. Each curve represents an average across five tokens.

[33]   More difficult to explain is the absence of a final H in the initial AP preceding the one realized with accent 2. An H in this position seems in fact to be difficult to produce. This may perhaps be interpreted as an OCP-related phenomenon, but lacking more systematic data, I have no further comments to offer.

AP that can supply an H, but where there is at least one syllable present with which the putative prestress H can associate. Words with non-initial stress pronounced in utterance-initial position provide us with an environment of this type. The syllables preceding the stress will be unstressed, and since there is no preceding AP, no phrase-final H will be able to mask the possible presence of the high tone. (15) shows the superimposed, averaged F0 curves of the two utterances [kɑ.ru.²liː.nə. mɔ.²mɑː.lə], *Karoline må male* 'K. must paint' and [kɑ.ru.¹liː.nɑ.nɔ.¹moː.lə], *Karolina når målet* 'K. reaches the goal'. If there is an initial H in the accent 1 melody, we will expect it to show up on the prestress syllable of the first AP of the latter, but not on the former, where we find accent 2 in this position.

(15) *Pitch in unstressed, utterance-initial syllables*

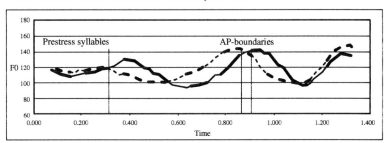

We see that this prediction is not borne out. There seems to be no crucial difference with respect to F0 movement between the prestress syllables depending on the following accent type.

We can therefore follow Lorentz (1995) and Kristoffersen (1993a,b) in assuming that the contrast which constitutes East Norwegian tonal accents resides in the presence vs. absence of the initial H of accent 2.[34] The L is common to both accents, and its location is predictable once we know the distribution of the accent 2 H. In other words, once we know the distribution of accent 2, the tonal representations are predictable. In accent 2, a high tone is inserted on the initial, or leftmost, TBU. Then the L common to both accents can be assigned to the first available TBU from the left, i.e. on the second syllable when the initial one is occupied by an H, and on the first when no H is present.

As will be shown in Section 9.3 below, the H must partly be assumed to be part of lexical representations. But its presence is in some cases predictable from the morphological composition of a word, since certain suffixes induce accent 2 if the stem meets certain prosodic conditions. This means that the H is inserted in the lexicon. Since it is only realized on syllables carrying primary, as opposed to secondary, stress in compounds and some derivational suffixes, we must assume that the H is deleted in cases where its TBU has not been assigned primary stress at the end of the cyclic level, that is, after the Compound Stress Rule (CSR) has applied.

---

[34] Challenging the analysis of Bruce (1977 and subsequent work), Engstrand (1995) reaches the same conclusion for Stockholm Swedish by means of a similar testing procedure.

In order to underline the fact that it is the presence vs. absence of this lexical H that constitutes the accentual contrast, I shall refer to it as a *lexical tone*.

The L on the other hand can now be interpreted as a tone whose contribution is purely prosodic, in that its presence signals primary stress. I shall therefore refer to it as a *prominence tone*.[35] Since primary stress can be assigned independently of this tone, as in the analysis presented in Chapter 6.4, it can be seen as part of the phonological stress realization system of East Norwegian.[36] From this it follows that the L should be assigned after primary stress has been assigned, that is, after the CSR. This means that the L should be assigned not earlier than at the postcyclic level, that is, after all morphology. For reasons that will become clear in Chapter 10, I shall assume that the L is inserted even later, that is, at the postlexical level.

We have now decomposed the accentual melodies in a way that leads to the conclusion that the accents are not assigned as cohering melodies by means of an association convention in the traditional sense. The tones that make up the melodies serve different functions, and are assigned at different levels of the grammar. Since the contrast involved is clearly privative, with accent 2 having an initial tone that is absent in accent 1, one way to state the contrast would be to say that only accent 2 represents tonal accent proper, while accent 1 is characterized by tonal prominence only.[37] Tonal accent would then be directly interpretable as the presence of a high tone on a syllable carrying main stress. But due to the fact that *both* melodies function as accents linked to stressed syllables, I shall continue to refer to them as accent 1 and 2 respectively.

9.3 DISTRIBUTION IN UNDERLYING FORMS

In this section we shall discuss to what extent the distribution of the tonal accents in simplex words is predictable, that is, to what extent it can be inferred from structural properties of the underlying forms.[38] The discussion will be based on the same division that was made in Chapter 3.1.2: monovocalic roots, bivocalic roots and longer roots. Since the first group contains members such as /sykl/, that due to the Sonority Sequencing Principle are realized as disyllabic ['syk.kl̩], the accent contrast is potentially present in all three groups. Only monovocalic roots that are realized as monosyllabic words are at the outset predictably accent 1.

To the extent that it is necessary to mark a given underlying form for accent, I assume that this is done by supplying the relevant forms with an H. Forms that

---

[35] The terms *lexical tone* and *prominence tone* have been taken from Lorentz (1995).

[36] A slightly different way of interpreting the role of the two melodies, HL as well as L, would be to interpret them as pitch accents in the sense for example of Ladd (1996: 50), that is, primarily parts of the intonational system that align with syllables carrying a specific degree of stress, and which thereby contribute cues to the location of stresses in a given utterance without themselves being part of the phonological domain of stress. We shall return to this question in Chapter 10.2.3.

[37] This insight is originally due to Einar Haugen: see Haugen and Joos (1952: 51), Haugen (1963) and Haugen (1967).

[38] Morphologically-induced accent 2 will be discussed in Section 9.4.

surface without accent do not need to be explicitly marked, since the tonal characteristics of this type will be an automatic effect of inserting the prominence tone L
on tonally unspecified syllables carrying primary stress. At the outset an underlying
H can be conceived as floating, and therefore subject to a general association convention. Since the alternative, prelinking, at the same time will represent a covert
prespecification of stress placement, this is not an attractive option. I shall therefore
assume that underlying Hs are floating, and linked as part of the phonological
derivation.

9.3.1 Accent distribution in monovocalic roots

Since accent 2 demands a minimal domain of two syllables, where the first must
carry primary stress, an accentual contrast is only possible in monovocalic roots
that are realized as disyllabic. These are roots that end in a sequence of obstruent
or sonorant plus a coronal sonorant, where the final sonorant in both cases is realized as syllabic; see the discussion in Chapter 3.2.4. The majority of these words
are nouns or adjectives, but we also find some adverbs and prepositions with this
structure. It turns out that the patterning is different in the three classes, with adjectives as the deviant group, since the distribution here seems fully predictable. In
nouns we find examples of both types, although accent 1 is by far the most common. In the third group, named *Other* in (16) below, the distribution is more even.

   The data in (16) are based on a database which includes 459 *disyllabic* simplex
words ending in syllabic sonorant. Proper names are not included. The database
also contains words consisting of more than two syllables with penultimate stress

(16)   *Distribution of tonal accent in disyllabic simplex words ending in*
       syllabic sonorants

			Accent 1		Accent 2	
	N	%	N	%	N	%
Nouns	357	77.8	322	90.2	35	9.8
/l/	151		142	94.0	9	6.0
/n̩/	28		23	82.1	5	17.9
/r̩/	178		157	88.2	21	11.8
Adjectives	77	16.8	40	51.9	37	48.1
/l/	16		15	93.8	1	6.2
/n̩/	36		0	0.0	36	100.0
/r̩/	25		25	100.0	0	0.0
Other	25	5.4	15	60.0	10	40.0
/l/	0					
/n̩/	11		4	36.4	7	63.6
/r̩/	14		11	78.6	3	21.4
Total	459	100.0	377	82.1	82	17.9

(92 tokens), such as [mɑ.ˈgis.tɾ], *magister* (id.) and [lɑ.ˈvɛn.dl̩], *lavendel* 'lavender'. Here we invariably find accent 1, and this group is therefore not included in the table.

In adjectives the distribution is predictable.[39] The pattern can be captured by means of a redundancy rule which will assign underlying accent 2 in the shape of a floating H to all adjectives ending in syllabic /n/. Accent 2 is rare in nouns, and I assume that in the few words where it occurs, it is marked in underlying structure by means of a floating H. The same may be assumed for the relevant members the group named *Other*.

The assumption that accent may be underlying in this type leads to an apparent paradox having to do with sonorants not being marked as syllabic in underlying structure. Since accent 2 is dependent on a disyllabic domain, underlying marking of it seems in fact to represent a kind of prespecification of disyllabicity. The assumption that the syllabicity of the sonorant is a predictable result of the Sonority Sequencing Principle is thereby preempted to a certain degree.

It also becomes mysterious why only this type of monovocalic roots may be marked for accent 2, and not others, for example those that end in a consonant group with rising sonority, such as [ˈmalm], *malm* 'ore'. One might speculate that such lexical marking is indeed possible, and that the reason we do not find accent 2 in simplex surface forms is precisely the disyllabic minimum constraint which is not met when these forms are realized as simplex words. This solution predicts that the underlying accent in such cases will surface when a syllabic and accentually neutral inflectional suffix such as def. sg. is added. There are in fact a few such examples. The kinship terms *far*, *mor* and *bror*, 'father', 'mother' and 'brother' respectively, were all disyllabic in Old Norse. This is the historical reason why they have exceptional accent 2 in their def. sg. forms. Synchronically, this can be accounted for if we also assume for these an underlying H, which in this case surfaces only if the disyllabic minimum constraint is met through suffixation. The existence of such forms therefore supports an analysis where also monovocalic roots may be marked for underlying accent.

9.3.2 Bivocalic roots with penultimate stress

Within this type we must distinguish between those that end in a vowel and those that end in vowel plus consonant. The distribution within the first group is almost predictable, and is constrained by the quality of the final vowel. If this is /e/, which due to the fact that it occurs in an unstressed, open syllable is realized as schwa, we get accent 2 . I know of only a few exceptions to this generalization, the direction-

---

[39] There is one exception, [²gɑm.ml̩], *gammel* 'old', which as stated in footnote 5 in Chapter 3 in fact has an alternative pronunciation with full vowel in the unstressed syllable, [²gɑm.mɑl]. The accent 2 in the form with reduced vowel is the result of exceptional vowel reduction with the original accent maintained, since other adjectives ending in -*al* do not show reduction. Due to this exceptionality, I assume that both forms are listed in the lexicon, and that the form with reduced vowel contains an H in its underlying representation.

als [¹hœj.rə], *høyre* 'right' and [¹vɛn.strə], *venstre* 'left', and the nouns [¹ak.ʂə], *aksje* 'share', [¹ɔr.drə], *ordre* 'order, command' and [¹kaf.fə], *kaffe* 'coffee'.[40] Most words ending in any other vowel than /e/ have accent 1, except names ending in a full vowel, which often have accent 2. The female names *Eva*, *Hanna*, *Mona*, *Lisa*, etc. are all pronounced with accent 2, and so is the male name *Ola*.

But the productive default patterns seem to be accent 2 when a word ends in /e/, and accent 1 when a word ends in any other vowel. However, a redundancy rule that assigns accent 2 to all underlying items ending in /e/ is difficult to block with respect to the four exceptions mentioned above. We can instead account for the productive pattern by assuming that the grammar contains a phonological rule similar to the 'once-only' word formation rules of Aronoff (1976: 22) that will assign accent 2 to the underlying form of all words of this type at the moment when they enter the language.

No such rule can be assumed with respect to disyllabic words ending in (full) vowel plus consonant. Native words with this structure are rare, again we have to appeal to proper names. These mostly have accent 2; examples are *Erik* and *Håkon*, both male names, and the female names *Bodil* and *Gudrun*.[41] The great majority of words of this type outside the realm of names, all loan words such as *krokus* 'crocus' and *faktor* 'factor', have accent 1. The only exception with accent 2 that I know of is *harpiks* 'resin'. For this type we therefore have to include a floating H in the lexical representations whose surface forms are realized with accent 2.

9.3.3 Longer roots with penultimate or antepenultimate stress

In words with penultimate stress that end in a vowel, we find the same near-complementary distribution as in disyllabic words. Words ending in /e/ usually have accent 2. But exceptions are more common here: words with /ns/, /j/ or /ʂ/ preceding the final /e/ seem to have accent 1 in most cases. Examples are [fɑ.¹jɑn.sə], *fajanse* 'faience', [bɑ.¹tɑl.jə] *batalje* 'fight' (but [vɑ.²nil.jə], *vanilje* 'vanilla') and [kɑ.¹lɔʂ.ʂə], *kalosje* 'galosh'. Haugen (1967: 192) offers the following generalization: accent 1 usually occurs when a ('present or former') consonant group intervenes between the stressed vowel and the schwa. This is definitely not correct with respect to current pronunciation, however. Contrary to Haugen's claim, words that end in *-asme*, *-ense*, *-erne* are now commonly pronounced with accent 2.[42] This all

---

[40] *Kaffe* can also be pronounced with a full vowel finally, [¹kaf.fi]. In addition, foreign names such as *Halle*, *Celle*, *Heine*, etc., all German, may be pronounced with accent 1, but are very often heard with accent 2. In fact, the established pronunciation of *Goethe* is with accent 2; cf. the pronunciation given in Berulfsen (1969). The pattern is also productive. When the name of the Dutch soccer team Twente, which until that time probably was unknown to most Norwegians, was read on the national news several times for some days in September 1997, it was consistently pronounced [²tvɛn.tə].

[41] An exception is Olaf (or Olav), which, despite being a variant of the name Ola, has accent 1.

[42] Since many words of this type show variation, and since I have no reason to doubt the correctness of Haugen's observations, which in general are most reliable, this difference suggests that there has been a change going on during the past 30 years aligning former exceptions with the majority pattern.

the same shows that accent 2 at least to a considerable degree can be predicted solely on the basis of a final schwa and preceding consonant(s), and that the once-only rule assumed for bivocalic roots is applicable here also.

With respect to words ending in other vowels than schwa, I know of only one instance of accent 2, the (definitely marginal) interjection [hɑ.lə.²lʉː.jɑ], *halleluja* 'hallelujah', which may also be pronounced with antepenultimate stress and with accent 1, [hɑ.¹leː.lʉ.jɑ]. Words that end in vowel plus consonant, such as *alligátor* (id.) never have accent 2. More interestingly, the same holds for all loan words with antepenultimate stress. This suggests that the disyllabic minimum in fact also constitutes a maximum in this class of roots, in the sense that accent 2 can only occur in domains that consist of a stressed syllable plus exactly one unstressed syllable.

But this holds only in loan words. There are a few native simplex words which consist of three syllables, and which have initial stress and accent 2. Examples are [²hɛl.ʋə.tə], *helvete* 'hell', [²mɛn.nə.skə], (or [²mɛn.skə]) *menneske* 'human being' and [²leː.gə.mə], *legeme* 'body'.

9.3.4 H-linking

I have argued that underlying forms may come with a floating H as part of the representation, which will result in accent 2 in the surface. We must now ask what the principles are that govern the association of this H with the rest of the prosodic structure. Since the H is floating, we need a rule that will link a floating H with a primary stressed syllable.

Since linking cannot take place with respect to *any* stressed syllable, the rule must be further constrained. We have seen that the distribution of accent 2 in roots to a considerable extent depends on underlying specification, and since there is no reason to assume that there are underlying Hs in the lexicon that never surface, the constraints on H-linking will function as statements that express under what conditions accent 2 may occur as part of an underlying form.

The essential constraint involved is that accent 2 may only occur when the stressed syllable occurs in one of two positions in the phonological word: either as the initial syllable or as the penultimate. This constraint can be simply captured if we assume that the H heads a special kind of foot that I shall refer to as a Tonal Foot (TF), and which must be distinguished from a metrical foot. The TF can be identified as a syllabic trochee. The distribution of accent 2 can now be captured by stating that the TF can only occur at the edge of a phonological word. The distributional restriction to initial or penultimate syllable follows from this. Placed at the left edge, the TF will be headed by the initial syllable, and at the right edge the head of the TF will be the penultimate syllable. H-linking can now be captured formally by the statement in (17).

(17) *H-linking*

(x
[X (x x) Y]$_\omega$
σ σ
⋮
H

Condition: Either X or Y must be empty

H-linking will also apply whenever a floating tone is introduced by a suffix, and it will apply after the rule that inserts accent 2 in adjectives ending in syllabic /n/. Since sonorants in adjectives cannot be made syllabic until the word level, the domain of H-linking must include the cyclic as well as the word level.

9.4 ACCENT ASSIGNMENT GOVERNED BY MORPHOLOGY[43]

9.4.1 *Tonally specified and tonally neutral suffixes*

Examples of how suffixes may influence tonal accent are shown in (18). We see that while the indef. pl. suffix induces accent 2, the def. sg. appears to be neutral. We can account for this by assuming that the former has a floating H as part of its representation.[44] Suffixes of this type can be referred to as *accented*. They are marked with an H as part of their representation. Note that the underlying tone will not always surface; see the discussion that follows.

An important restriction with respect to the indef. pl. suffix is that the underlying H can only link when the stem is monosyllabic. If the stem consists of more than one syllable, the tonal properties of the stem take precedence. Thus if the stem has accent 2, the accent prevails; note the bivocalic root /^{H}lake/ in (18), where both the indef. pl. and def. sg. surface with accent 2. Similarly, if a stem ending in a syllabic sonorant has accent 1, such as /sykl/, we see that both the indef. pl. and the def. sg. surface with accent 1.

The constraint that seems to be involved is that the association of the H must be local in the sense that it can only associate with the final syllable of the stem. I shall refer to this as a *locality constraint*. In Chapter 8.3 I argued that sonorants in nouns may be made syllabic on the root cycle. Since /sykl/ is a noun, this means that the H can only associate with the final, syllabic sonorant. Being unstressed, this results in an illicit structure, since H can associate with stressed syllables only in order to surface. The constraint is stated as an association rule in (19).

---

[43] The basic assumption of the analysis to be presented in this section, that accent to a considerable degree is governed by properties of suffixes, was first explored in a systematic way in Rischel (1960, 1963), and Haugen (1967), but the relationship is mentioned as early as in Knudsen (1856: 408).

[44] Prefixes may also be specified underlyingly with an H. Examples are /^{H}mis-/, *mis-*, which has roughly the same meaning as in English, and the negative prefix /^{H}u-/, *u-*.

(18)   *Tonal effect of indef. pl. /ɽ/, def. sg. /n̩/ and infinitival /-e/ on accent*[45]

	Stem	Suffix	Surface form
Monosyllabic	/bil/ 'car'	/-ɽ, H/ (indef. pl.)	[²biː.lɽ]
stems		/-n̩/ (def. sg.)	[¹biː.ln̩]
	/kant/ 'edge'	/-ɽ, H/ (indef. pl.)	[²kɑn.tɽ]
		/-n̩/ (def. sg.)	[¹kɑn.tn̩]
	/svar/ 'answer'	/-e, H/ (infinitive)	[²svɑː.ɾə]
Polysyllabic	/ᴴlake/ 'brine'	/-ɽ, H/ (indef. pl.)	[²lɑː.kɽ]
stems		/-n̩/ (def. sg.)	[²lɑː.kn̩]
	/sykl/ 'bicycle'	/-ɽ, H/ (indef. pl.)	[¹syk.lɽ]
		/-n̩/ (def. sg.)	[¹syk.ln̩]
	/sykl/ 'cycle' (verb)	/-e, H/ (infinitive)	[²syk.lə]
	/ekl/ 'disgusting'	(sg.)	[¹ɛk.kl̩]
		/-ere, H/ (comp.)	[²ɛk.lə.ɾə]
	/pilut/ 'pilot'	/-ɽ, H/ (indef. pl.)	[pi.¹luː.tɽ]
		/-n̩/ (def. sg.)	[pi.¹luː.tn̩]
	/besvar/ 'answer' (trans.)	/-e, H/ (infinitive)	[bə.¹svɑː.ɾə]
	/balans-er/ 'balance'	/-e, H/ (infinitive)	[bɑ.lɑŋ.¹seː.ɾə]

(19)   *Locality Constraint*

Recall further from Chapter 8.3 that the constraints on syllabic sonorants in adjectives and verbs were assumed to be different from those on nouns. Stem-final sonorants in adjectives can be made syllabic only at the postcyclic level, while in verbs, syllabic sonorants are blocked altogether. Since H-linking is cyclic, this predicts that the H of tonally specified suffixes will be able to link to the stressed syllable in adjectival and verbal roots which end in an obstruent + sonorant sequence. This prediction is borne out. The infinitive marker /-e/ induces accent 2, and as can be seen from the example [²syk.lə] in (18), it takes effect also in stems of this type. On the assumption that the /l/ is unsyllabified at this stage, given the constraint blocking syllabic sonorants in verbs, the nearest syllable for the H to link to is the stressed one. Hence we get accent 2 also in these cases. The same effect can be seen in adjectives. The adjectival root /ekl/ is itself without an underlying H. When the accented comparative suffix /-ere/ is added, the result is accent 2.

---

[45] Underlying Hs in stems are represented as superscripted at the left edge.

Again, on the assumption that the syllabification of final sonorants in adjectives takes place at the postcyclic level, this result follows without the locality constraint governing cyclic H-linking being violated.

In the cases just reviewed, we have seen that H-linking fails in cases where the stressed syllable is not stem-final. Let us now consider another case, where the stem is polysyllabic, but where the stressed syllable is stem-final, so that the locality constraint is met. Here we would expect linking to take place when a tonal suffix is added, giving accent 2 in such forms. But as can be seen from the three final examples of (18), this is not the case. The reason for this is apparently that the constraints on the distribution of the Tonal Foot are further narrowed when morphology comes into play. At the root cycle the TF could occur both at the right and left edge of the PWd. A tonal foot built by a morphological rule can on the other hand only occur at the left edge. This accounts for the lack of accent 2 in the indef. pl. of *pilót* as well as in the two infinitives. After the root level, the condition on H-linking must be further restricted to the effect that X *must* be empty. This means that TFs created in the morphology never violate the constraint that they must be PWd-initial.

Note that the locality principle derives the other part of the condition on H-linking, viz. that Y must be empty. This secures that the TF is placed at the right edge in all cases where the suffix involved is monosyllabic. On the root cycle, we saw that the relationship between the two distributional possibilities of the TF holds as an either/or relationship: the TF occurs either at the left or at the right edge. In the morphology, we now see that in most cases they stand in a both/and relationship: in order for the H to link, the resulting TF must be *both* initial and final, as in e.g. [²biː.lɾ]. There are exceptions, however, which emerge when the suffix itself consists of more than one syllable, such as the comparative suffix /-ere/. Then linking takes place, but the final syllable of the suffix will not be part of the TF, which therefore will be PWd-initial, but not final. The result is words that structurally correspond to the *légeme* type among the simplex roots.

In the examples examined so far, we have seen that Hs introduced as part of suffixes always associate locally, that is to the final syllable of the stem, iff that syllable at the same time is stressed and PWd-initial. If we now proceed to the data given in (20), we see that some accented suffixes seem to induce violations of this locality constraint in the sense that their H may associate with an initial, stressed syllable that is *not* stem-final. There are two suffixes of this type: the derivational suffix /-li/~/-lik/,[46] and the adjectival agreement suffix /-e/. When added to a given stem, both may induce accent 2 across unstressed syllables that intervene between the stressed syllable and the suffix, provided that the stressed syllable is initial. Thus we see that when -*lig* attaches to the accent 1 noun /hedr/, which is disyllabic, the result is accent 2. When the superlative suffix, which we shall return to in a moment, is added, the stem accent is deleted, giving an accent 1 output. Finally,

---

[46] Recall from Chapter 4.2.3 that this suffix has two allomorphs, of which /-lik/ occurs in the superlative only. In the following I shall refer to it by means of its written form -*lig*.

when the agreement marker /-e/, which is accented, is added to a superlative stem, the surface output is again accent 2.

(20) *Derivation of* [²heː.də.[ik.stə]

Stem	*Suffix*	*Surface form*
/hedr/ (noun)	(Root cycle)	[¹heː.dɾ] 'honour'
/hedr/ (noun)	/-li/~/-lik/ (adj.)	[²heː.də.[i] 'honest'
/hedrlik/ (adj.)	/-st/ (sup.)	[¹heː.də.[ikst] 'most honest'
/hedrlikst/ (sup.)	/-e/ (agr.)	[²heː.də.[ik.stə] 'most honest'

One possible analysis is to regard these two suffixes as exceptions, in that the floating H that is part of these suffixes will be able to link to a stressed initial syllable even if other syllables intervene between it and the suffix. But the evidence is not as clear as it may look from the examples given in the table. Recall that *-lig* is atypical with respect to stress placement as well, as in Chapter 7.3.8. When added to a stem, stress is always assigned to the stem-final syllable, unless this is a syllabic sonorant or a schwa. This means that in most cases, the locality constraint is met by way of the stress-inducing properties of the suffix. When added to a monosyllabic stem, it consistently gives accent 2. Since stems ending in schwa invariably have accent 2 themselves, they cannot be used to test the accent-inducing properties of the suffix. Stems ending in syllabic sonorants can have accent 1, however. Here we find that when the suffix is added to a stem ending in syllabic /r/ without an underlying H, the result is accent 2; see the example given in (20). Other examples are *vínterlig* 'wintry', *rídderlig* 'chivalrous' and *únderlig* 'strange'.[47] The force of these data is weakened by the fact that stems ending in syllabic sonorants which as simplex words have accent 1 often induce accent 2 in compounds where they occur as the initial member; see the discussion of the data in (25) in Section 9.5.2 below. It could therefore be an exceptional property of the stem that is responsible for the accent 2 in *héderlig*, and not the suffix. This is corroborated by the fact that two words where the stem ends in syllabic /n/ followed by /t/, *égentlig* 'actual' and *vésentlig* 'considerable', have accent 1. These are both German loan words, but with relatively transparent semantic relationship to the roots *egen* and *vesen*. If indeed the suffix is able to violate the locality constraint, these exceptions cannot be explained. The alternative analysis is therefore that *-lig does* obey the locality principle, and that the accent in *héderlig* is due to properties of the stem, and not of the suffix.[48]

The second suffix that is apparently able to override the locality principle is the agreement marker /-e/. As can be seen from the fourth line in the table, accent 2 reappears when the suffix is added to the accent 1 superlative form. But as with

---

[47] I know of no clear examples of stems ending in syllabic /n/ or /l/.

[48] This analysis has one serious weakness. If the accent-changing property of the stem is the same phenomenon as that found in compounding, we would expect each individual root to behave in identical fashion in compounds and when combined with *-lig*. This is not the case, however. /hedr/ for instance takes the linking phoneme /s/ in compounds, but not, as can be seen from (20), when combined with *-lig*. /ridr/, *ridder* 'knight' belongs to the roots of this type that do *not* change accent in compounds, but it does so when combined with the suffix.

-*lig*, this behaviour is not consistent. For accent 2 to appear as a result of suffixation of /-e/, there seems to be a condition involved that accent 2 must have been present on the cycle *before* the superlative suffix is added. Thus the two accent 1 examples with -*lig* discussed above, *égentlig* and *vésentlig*, do not surface with accent 2 when /-e/ is added to the superlative form. A related fact is that accent 1 disyllabic roots with initial stress neither seem to surface with accent 2 when /-e/ is added. But this type is rare, I know of only two, *pássiv* 'passive' and *mássiv* 'massive', of which the latter more commonly has final stress.[49] Neither of them is pronounced with accent 2 when the agreement marker is added. This means that the 'long distance' effect of this suffix is a phenomenon tied up with superlatives. But since accent 2 only turns up when the stem to which the superlative marker was added on the previous cycle had accent 2, this cannot be a property of the morphological environment in itself. It seems rather that this is a case of an accent that is 'masked' by the superlative marker, and which reappears when the agreement marker is added.

(20) reveals another suffix type, represented by the superlative /-st/, which seems to obliterate tonal specification of the stem without being tonally specified itself. The output is therefore accent 1, also in cases where the stem itself has accent 2. To my knowledge there are two suffixes which exhibit this property, the superlative suffix /-st/ and the derivational suffix /-isk/.[50] Neither of them seems exceptionless. /-isk/ appears with accent 2 in some words with initial stress, such as [²nuɖ.ɖisk], *nordisk* 'Nordic' [²juɖ.ɖisk], *jordisk* 'earthly' and variably in [¹/²sɑː.misk], *samisk* 'Sami'. In longer stems with non-initial stress the result is invariably a change from accent 2 to accent 1, however; see the alternation in [ɑ.pu.kɑ.²lyp.sə], *apokalypse* 'apocalypse' vs. [ɑ.pu.kɑ.¹lyp.tisk], *apokalyptisk* 'apocalyptic'. But since there are other changes in the stem as well, the data cannot be said to be as clear as might be wished. The superlative suffix is also somewhat dubious as cyclic, since accent 2 reappears when the agreement suffix is added, and since it shows tendencies of being regularized into a neutral non-cyclic affix in current speech.[51]

The accent-deleting suffixes may be interpreted as cyclic in the same sense as suffixes can be cyclic with respect to stress, in that they delink tonal information that may be present on the stem. But since they are not accented themselves, they do not supply another H.

Conceivably, cyclic suffixes with a floating H may exist that delete tonal information on the stem so that the tone supplied by the suffix may link to the stressed syllable. But these would be difficult to detect. The normal type of accented suffix, which can only supply the resulting word with accent 2 if the stem-final syllable is stressed, will have no visible cyclic effect, since any tone on the stressed syllable will be replaced by the suffix tone. The conclusion that ensues is that there is a

---

[49] A third one is *grátis* 'free of charge', but this does not take the agreement suffix.

[50] The derivational suffix /-sl/ also induces accent 1, but I know of no clear example where it combines with a stem that has accent 2. It is therefore clearly neutral, but not necessarily cyclic.

[51] Although my own intuitions seem fairly secure, and accord with those of Haugen (1967: 194), many younger speakers claim that they use accent 2 in superlatives when the stem itself has accent 2, as in *hederlig*.

minimal amount of cyclic restructuring involved in the tonal system, in that only the two H-deleting suffixes just discussed are cyclic in the sense that they change structural properties of the stem instead of merely adding information.

9.4.2 Exceptions

Most of the generalizations made above have exceptions. A descriptively adequate analysis therefore requires a fair amount of lexical marking. In the following, I shall mention some of these exceptions that seem difficult to capture by means of rules.

The indef. pl. suffix /-r/ in general induces accent 2 if the stressed syllable is stem-final.[52] But a few words, such as ['blɔmst], *blomst* 'flower' and ['æt], *ert* 'pea', have accent 1 plurals, ['blɔm.stɽ] and ['æt.tɽ]. The class where indef. pl. is marked by umlaut, in addition to suffixing, represents a more principled exception to the main pattern. Thus the indef. pl. of ['ɑn], *and* 'duck' is ['ɛn.nɽ], *ender*, not *['ɛn.nɽ]. But this pattern also has exceptions: the indef. pl. of ['krɑft], *kraft* 'force' is ['krɛf.tɽ], *krefter*, not *['krɛf.tɽ]. Another unexpected and isolated change in accent takes place from the accent 2, disyllabic indef. sg. ['bun.nə], *bonde* 'farmer' to indef. pl. accent 1 ['bœn.nɽ]. Exceptional is also the fact that the names of some weekdays, such as the names for Saturday and Sunday, change from sg. accent 1 ['løː.ˌdɑːg], *lørdag* and ['sœn.ˌdɑːg], *søndag*, into pl. accent 2 ['løː.ˌdɑː.gɽ] and ['sœn.ˌdɑː.gɽ]. These data suggest that we need two allomorphs of the indef. pl. marker /-r/, one with a floating H and one without. Nouns must then be marked for which of these they may combine with.

Another inflectional suffix is the present tense marker /-r/. Some present tense forms have accent 2, others have accent 1. Historically, accent 1 is tied to the strong ablaut verbs and one class of weak verbs, which all had monosyllabic present tense forms in Old Norse. But there are several exceptions in the synchronic grammar, so morphological class cannot be used as a rule feature. Again it seems necessary to assume two present tense allomorphs, one with a floating H and one without.

9.5 ACCENT DISTRIBUTION IN COMPOUNDS

9.5.1 Data

Compounds whose first member is polysyllabic, show in most cases the same accent as the first member has as an independent form.[53] This suggests that the accent is controlled by properties of the first compound member; see the data in (21a). Accent in this type can be straightforwardly derived from the accentual properties

---

[52] Indef. pl. may also be signalled by means of a zero allomorphs, mostly used with neuters, and with /-e/, used with stems ending in syllabic /r/.

[53] The analysis presented in this and the following section represents a summary of Kristoffersen (1992b).

of its first member, since the rule Compound H-Delinking, stated as (28) below, will give the correct form directly.

Section (b) shows that accent is not controlled in the same way when the initial compound member is monosyllabic. Here we see that the result in some cases is accent 2, and in others not. But despite this fact, one can say that also in these cases, the accentual pattern *is* controlled by the first member, since a given morpheme normally induces the same accent irrespective of what follows. Most roots exhibit this kind of consistent behaviour when used as compound stems.[54] In the database on which my earlier work on compound accent is built (Kristoffersen 1992b), 82.5% of the 617 roots that made up the database were consistent in this way.

(21)　*Tonal accent in compounds*

(a)　*Polysyllabic initial member*

[¹feː.bɾ] [¹nɑt]	[¹feː.bə.ˌn̩ɑt] *febernatt* 'fever night'
[¹feː.bɾ] [²ɑn.fɑl]	[¹feː.bɾ.rɑn.fɑl] *feberanfall* 'attack of fever'
[²sɔm.mɾ] [¹nɑt]	[²sɔm.mə.ˌn̩ɑt] *sommernatt* 'summer night'
[²sɔm.mɾ] [²ʋɑr.mə]	[²sɔm.mɾ.ˌʋɑr.mə] *sommervarme* 'summer heat'

(b)　*Monosyllabic initial member*

[¹ʋɔks] [¹lyːs]	[¹ʋɔks.ˌlyːs] *vokslys* 'wax candle'
[¹ʋɔks] [²tɑʋ.lə]	[¹ʋɔks.ˌtɑʋ.lə] *vokstavle* 'wax tablet'
[¹tɑlg] [¹lyːs]	[²tɑlg.ˌlyːs] *talglys* 'tallow candle'
[¹tɑlg] [¹çæt.t̩l]	[²tɑlg.ˌçæt.t̩l] *talgkjertel* 'sebaceous gland'
[¹bɑl] [¹sɑl]	[¹bɑl.ˌsɑːl] *ballsal* 'ballroom'
[¹bɑl] [²çuː.lə]]	[¹bɑl.ˌçuː.lə]] *ballkjole* 'ball gown'
[¹bɑl] [¹spil]	[²bɑl.ˌspil] *ballspill* 'ball game'
[¹bɑl] [²trɛː.niŋ]	[²bɑl.ˌtrɛː.niŋ] *balltrening* 'ball exercise'

What kind of property of the first member is responsible for the choice of accent? Both phonological and morphological properties are possible candidates. But the contrast between *ball*₁ 'dance' and *ball*₂ 'round object' shows that it cannot be the segmental make-up of the stem itself that is decisive.[55] In the analysis of Halvorsen (1983) and Withgott and Halvorsen (1984, 1988) the property is assumed to be another and more abstract phonological one, viz. a floating H as part of the lexical representation of those roots that induce accent 2. As shown in Kristoffersen (1992b), convincing evidence in favour of this solution is hard to come by, and since the only environment where the underlying H turns up is com-

---

[54] For reasons that will become clear below, I shall in the following refer to the first member of a compound as a *compound stem*.

[55] But in a statistical sense, it can be shown to influence the choice quite heavily. In Kristoffersen (1992b) I show that the more voicing is present in the rhyme of the compound stem, the higher is the probability that it will induce accent 2. Thus a rhyme consisting of a long vowel plus a voiced consonant renders the highest probability of accent 2, while a short vowel plus voiceless consonant(s) render the lowest probability.

pounds, it requires a rather complicated classification of suffixes as H-inducing, L-inducing and neutral on the one hand, and a cross-classification of them as dominant vs. recessive on the other, in order to block this floating H to show up in all other environments.

Since this property is restricted to compounds, it makes at the outset more sense to assume that it springs from a morphological property of these roots. This will be the starting point of the analysis to be presented in the next section. But in order to lay the ground for it, some more data are necessary. A specific behaviour with respect to tonal accent is not the only morphological property that can be attributed to monosyllabic (and polysyllabic) stems when used as first members of compounds. A number of noun roots require, as in other Germanic languages, the insertion of a semantically empty linking phoneme between the compound members. There are two main types, /-s/ and /-e/. Examples are provided in (22).

(22)   *Compounds concatenated by means of linking phonemes*

   (a) */s/ as linking phoneme*
       [²gleːdə] [¹hyːl]   [²gleː.dəs.ˌhyːl] *gledeshyl* 'cry of joy'
       [¹ʋɛr.dn̩] [¹mɛs.tʃ]   [¹ʋɛr.dn̩s.ˌmɛs.tʃ] *verdensmester* 'world
                                                   champion'
       [¹doːp] [²hɑn.dliŋ]   [¹doːps.ˌhɑn.dliŋ] *dåpshandling* 'act of baptizing'
       [¹buːt] [²øːʋl̩.sə]   [¹buːt.ˌsøː.ʋl̩.sə] *botsøvelse* 'penance'

   (b) */e/ as linking phoneme*
       [¹fisk] [²sʉp.pə]   [²fis.kə.ˌsʉp.pə] *fiskesuppe* 'fish soup'
       [¹sɑns] [bə.ˈdrɑːg]   [²sɑn.sə.bə.ˌdrɑːg] *sansebedrag* 'illusion'

The data given in the table also illustrate the tonal properties of the linking phonemes. With a few exceptions, /s/ induces accent 1 when the initial member is monosyllabic, and /-e/ induces accent 2.

9.5.2 Analysis

The linking phonemes can be interpreted as cohering suffixes that take the first compound member as stem. They thus become part of the first phonological word of the compound. The existence of linking phonemes in compounds shows that some roots must be morphologically converted into a specific shape in order to function as an initial compound member. I interpret this as the result of a set of derivational rules that take as input a subset of the nominal and adjectival lexemes, and return what I have already named a *compound stem* as output. The roots belonging to this subset must be marked for either /-s/-suffixation or /-e/-suffixation. This marking can be done by means of statements of the following type, which must be part of the underlying representations of the relevant stems.[56]

---

[56] The exact way these rules are stated is orthogonal to the question discussed. The main point is that certain lexemes require morphological and phonological adjustments before they can function as initial members of compounds.

(23)   (a) e-suffixation   (b) s-suffixation

                   H

        $[[X]_{N, A} e]_{\text{Compound stem}}$ $[[X]_{N} s]_{\text{Compound stem}}$

In e-suffixation, the floating H will link to the stressed syllable by H-linking, as in (17) above.

The assumption that we need statements of the kind exemplified in (23) in the grammar paves the way for a morphologically based analysis of the accent distribution in compounds. Given the autosegmental relationship between the tonal tier and the segmental tier, the representation under (a) suggests that it may be decomposed into two independent statements, suffixation of the segmental suffix /-e/ only, and suffixation of a tonal morpheme that consists of an H only. The suffix consisting of an H only will under this analysis account for the cases where a monosyllabic stem induces accent 2. It can be represented as in (24), and it can be assumed to be part of the underlying representations of all stems that induce accent 2 without further formal modification of the stem.

(24)   H

        $[[X]_{N, A}]_{\text{Compound stem}}$

A considerable number of roots require this statement as part of their underlying specification. In the database underlying the research reported in Kristoffersen (1992b), 179 out of 326 tokens induce accent 2 when compounded. The other possible combinations of tone and segmental content that are predicted by this decomposition are rare, however. But the fact that at least one of them occurs supports the analysis. Tonally marked /-s/ occurs in three stems, *loft*, 'loft', *ovn* 'oven' and *kveld* 'evening', out of the 22 entries of this type in the database. These lexemes can be represented with the suffix under (23b) combined with a floating H.

Tonally unmarked /-e/ seems to be non-occurring, on the other hand. There are a few examples of disyllabic compound stems ending in schwa without accent 2, such as ['tril.lə.ˌboːr], *trillebår* 'wheelbarrow', but the most plausible morphological analysis of these is that their first members are infinitives, and that the final schwa therefore represents the infinitival marker. Still this leaves the lack of accent 2 unexplained, since infinitives with initial stress invariably have accent 2 as independent words.

Another problem that is easily accounted for within the present analysis, and which an approach based on phonological marking of the root itself would have difficulties in accounting for, is the pattern exhibited by some roots that surface with syllabic sonorant as simplex words. The pattern is variable, and may vary between speakers, but is still quite widespread. The relevant words have accent 1 as independent words, but show accent 2 in compounds. Some examples are given in (25).

(25) *Accent shift*

['fiŋ.ŋf] ['riŋ]   [²fiŋ.ŋf.,riŋ] *fingerring* 'finger ring'
['sœp.pl̩] [²kas.sə]   [²sœp.pl̩.,kas.sə] *søppelkasse* 'garbage can'
['has.sl̩] ['nœt]   [²has.sl̩.,nœt] *hasselnøtt* 'hazelnut'
['ʋin.tf] ['haː.gə]   [²ʋin.tf.,haː.gə] *vinterhage* 'winter garden'

These forms can be accounted for by assuming that the roots themselves are without an underlying H, but that the statement under (24) is part of their lexical representation.

9.5.3 Particle compounds

The data given in (26) show that the pattern identified above cannot be generalized to compounds where the first member is an adverb or preposition. I shall refer to this type as 'particle compounds'.[57] They follow the normal pattern with respect to stress, which is on the initial adverb, as predicted by the unmarked version of the Compound Stress Rule (CSR), as in Chapter 7.3. But they exhibit a property that is fundamentally different from other compounds, in that it is the word class of the second compound member, and thereby of the compound itself, that determines the accent. Verbs have accent 1, nouns accent 2.

(26) Accent in particle compounds

['om] (prep.) [²taː.lə] (n.)   [²ɔm.,taː.lə] *omtale* (n.) 'mention, report'
['om] (prep.) [²taː.lə] (v.)   ['ɔm.,taː.lə] *omtale* (v.) 'to discuss, refer to'
['poː] (prep.) ['bʉːd] (n.)   [²poː.,bʉːd] *påbud* (n.) 'command'
['poː] (prep.) ['byː] (v.)   ['poː.,byː] *påby* (v.) 'to command'
['an] (prefix) [²klaː.gə] (n.)   [²aŋ.,klaː.gə] *anklage* (n.) 'accusation'
['an] (prefix) [²klaː.gə] (v.)   ['aŋ.,klaː.gə] *anklage* (v.) 'to accuse'

The distribution of accent in nominalizations of particle verbs complicates the pattern further. Consider the data in (27). The first section contains nominalizations by means of suffixes that induce accent 2, while the second section shows the apparently neutral effect of two other suffixes.

---

[57] Withgott and Halvorsen (1984, 1988) interpret the particles as prefixes. The fact that they may occur as free forms speaks against this. Their meaning in some cases may be somewhat idiosyncratic when they occur in compounds, but this cannot count as an argument in favour of this analysis, since compounds as well as derivations in general may take on idiosyncratic meanings. One argument in favour of a prefix analysis might be the fact that the stressed prefix /an-/ behaves in the same fashion as prepositions and adverbs, as can be seen from (26). This element has no clear meaning of its own, but interestingly it may all the same serve as an independent particle in some cases, as in *føre an*, 'to lead', which nominalized has the form *anfører* with accent 2, and as a verb, *anføre*, with accent 1.

(27)   *Accent in particle compounds with nominalized second member*

    (a) *With accent 2*[58]

       /før-sl/   [²im̩.fœʂ.ʂl̩] *innførsel* 'import'

       /byt-r/ (agentive) [²im.byt.tɽ] *innbytter* 'substitute'

       /grip-n/   [²iŋ.gɾiː.pn̩] *inngripen* 'interference'

       /skriʋ-t/   [²in.skɾift] *innskrift* 'innskrift'

    (b) *With accent 1*

       /før-iŋ/   [¹im̩.føː.ɾiŋ] *innføring* 'introduction'

       /leʋ-lse/   [¹in.leː.ʋl̩.sə] *innlevelse* 'empathy'

We see that while some suffixes seem to induce accent 2, others apparently do not. One possible analysis is that the suffixes in question are cyclic, and that the locality condition is suspended, so that their domain extends over the whole compound, not just the stem-final syllable. This hypothesis would imply that the suffixes in section (a) contain a floating H that will attach to the initial syllable, while those in section (b) will induce delinking of any H that might be present on the first member of the base. This cannot be correct however, because for at least some of them, their effect in this context cannot be reconciled with their effect on tonal accent when added to non-compound stems. The suffix /-sl/ for instance, which gives accent 2 here, consistently induces the opposite pattern, i.e. accent 1, when added to non-compound stems. It must therefore be tonally neutral. The suffixes /-lse/ and /-ing/ on the other hand, which here appear as neutral, consistently induce accent 2 when added to non-compound stems. They must therefore be accented. But these data show that their effect does not extend to compounds. I therefore conclude that the distribution shown in (27) cannot be due to underlying, accentual properties of the suffixes involved.

The origin and only explanation of this pattern is to be found in older stress patterns that are almost obsolete today, but which still determine the deviant distribution of tonal accent in particle compounds. Given the paucity of sources with respect to spoken Norwegian before 1800, we have to extrapolate from Danish.[59] According to Fischer-Jørgensen (1993), particle compounds in the seventeenth- and eighteenth-century Danish had different stress patterns according to the word class membership of the final member, and therefore of the compound itself. Nouns had primary stress on the first syllable, that is, on the particle, while verbs had primary stress on the penultimate syllable, that is, on the stressed syllable of the verb. In present-day Norwegian, this pattern is only found consistently with the prefix /for-/. Here we can still find alternating pairs such as [²fɔr.bɾʉːk], *forbruk* 'consumption' vs. [fɔr.¹bɾʉː.kə], *forbruke* 'to consume' and [²fɔr.fal], *forfall* 'decay' vs. [fɔr.¹fal.lə], *forfalle* 'to decay'. There is also at least one example where /for/ argu-

---

[58] The first constituent is the adverb /in/. The nasal undergoes place assimilation triggered by the following consonant; cf. Chapter 11.4.

[59] Knudsen (1856: 404f.) mentions the same pattern for Norwegian, but no conclusions can be drawn with respect to how widespread the pattern was in Norwegian around 1850.

ably functions as a particle, viz. in *spenne for*, 'to hitch up (horses)'. Here we find the related noun [²fɔ.ʂpɑn], *forspann* 'team of horses drawing a carriage' and the participle adjective [fɔ.¹ʂpɛnt], *forspent*, which followed by the preposition *med* means 'drawn (by), equipped with'.

From this earlier stress pattern the current distribution of accents can be deduced. If we assume that the normal pattern is that particles induce accent 2 in compounds, this general rule is of the same type as the one we have identified for other compounds. In verbs with non-initial stress, the rule cannot apply since the constraints that the H must link to stress and at the same time be initial cannot be met simultaneously. This means that the H that comes with the particle cannot link properly, and instead must delete.

The different behaviour of the suffixes in (27) can be explained in the same way. Fischer-Jørgensen (1993: 46) mentions that the two deviant suffixes, written -*else* and -*ing*, induced penultimate stress in compounds, but that this property was already on the decrease in the period which she examined. These were in other words prestressing in the sense defined in Chapter 7.3.8, and again we derive the right result on the assumption that the particles induce accent 2, but only when the stressed syllable is initial.

In current Norwegian (and Danish) the stress pattern of most of these words has been regularized so that they fall in under the domain of the CSR, which assigns them initial stress. But the accent has not been regularized, hence the deviant pattern of particle verbs and nominalizations of such verbs by means of the two suffixes /-lse/ and /-iŋ/. An analysis that reconstructs this diachronic development by assigning penultimate stress on the cyclic stage of the derivation, where tone is assigned, followed by the CSR, that will regularize the stress, is difficult to motivate on independent grounds, however. In current Norwegian the language learner must therefore learn that particle compound verbs have accent 1, as opposed to the corresponding nouns, but that some derived nouns, viz. those derived by the two suffixes /-lse/ and /-iŋ/, nevertheless have accent 1.[60]

9.5.4 *Some minor patterns and exceptions*

As mentioned above, not all monosyllabic stems consistently induce the same accentual pattern when compounded. In some cases we may be dealing with singular exceptions, as for example with respect to /dyr/, 'animal', which as a rule will combine with the linking phoneme /e/, except in [¹dyː.ˌleː.gə], *dyrlege*, 'veterinarian'. In other cases, we seem to be dealing with more regular sub-patterns. When the monosyllable is a verb, the compound has nearly always accent 1. Examples are

---

[60] For at least some dialects, including my own, there are still traces of the prestressing pattern with respect to these suffixes. I find for instance the pronunciations [¹im.bil.niŋ] and [im.¹bil.niŋ] equally acceptable for *innbilning*, cf. (27), and while I would prefer [¹in.leː.ʋ].sə] with initial stress as stated in (27), I feel [ɔp.¹leː.ʋ|sə], *opplevelse* 'experience' to be more acceptable than its correspondent with initial stress. The distribution is clearly lexicalized, and data are lacking that can shed light on how common penultimate stress is in these environments.

['syː.,dɑː.mə], *sydame* 'seamstress' (lit. 'sew lady') and ['ʂ\o̞ː.mɑ.,ʂiːn], *slåmaskin* 'mowing machine'.

When the first member is a colour adjective, we find the rather curious semantic criterion that if the meaning of the compound is something edible or drinkable, the result is normally accent 1. Other compounds headed by the same adjectives have accent 2. Thus we find ['ʋiːt.,ʋiːn], *hvitvin* 'white wine' vs. [²ʋiːt.,mɑː.liŋ], *hvitmaling* 'white paint', ['rø̞ː.,koːl], *rødkål* 'red cabbage' vs. [²rø̞ː.,strʉː.pə], *rødstrupe* '(European) robin'.

Finally, compound street names have accent 1 where the first member represents the name of a person after whom the street has been named, also in cases where the same word induces accent 2 in other compound types. The accent 2 [²strɑn.,ʋæj.jn̩], *Strandveien*, 'the beach road' is therefore a road or street that follows the waterfront, while ['strɑn.,ʋæj.jn̩] is a road that has been named after a person whose family name derives from a place name *Strand* with the same original meaning, i.e. 'beach, seashore'.[61]

9.6 OTHER RULES

9.6.1 *Delinking rules*

Recall that accent can only be assigned to syllables carrying primary stress, and that secondary stresses induced by the CSR seem to have no constant tonal characteristics that help identifying them; see the contours shown in (8) through (11). This means that any H that finds itself linked to a syllable whose stress has been demoted by the CSR must delink. The CSR being cyclic, H-delinking may apply either at the cyclic level to the output of each application of the CSR or at the word level as a once-only rule deleting all Hs not linked to a primary stress. There is no reason to assume that it applies later, the constraint that there can only be one accent per word is clearly part of word prosody, and not intonation.

The rule will delink any H that is not linked to the syllable carrying the highest grid mark. Thus the H that is linked to the second member of *julestjerne*, 'Christmas star', whose constituents are the compound stem [²jʉː.lə], from *jul*, 'Christmas' and [²stjæː.ŋ̍ə], *stjerne* 'star', is deleted, giving [²jʉː.lə.,stjæː.ŋ̍ə]. The rule is formally stated in (28). Due to the fact that we have defined two versions of the CSR in Chapter 7.3, the rule must be a mirror image rule.

(28) *Compound H-delinking (mirror image)*

```
     x
    (x         x)
    (xx)  ...  (xx)
     σ         σ
               ǂ
               H
```

---

[61] I owe this observation to Arne Torp.

Consider now the derivation of *urimelig*, 'unreasonable', whose morphological structure is [[u][[rim][lig]]]. The suffix *-lig* will assign accent 2 to its stem; note the surface form [²riːm.li], *rimelig* 'reasonable'. The non-cohering prefix *u-* has an underlying H as well, which will surface when it carries primary stress—see for example the forms given in table 7.29. After the prefix has been added to the stem, both elements will therefore be linked to an H. Recall now from Chapter 7.3.8 that primary stress in words beginning with *u-* and ending in *-lig* is placed on the PWd immediately preceding the suffix, so that the output will be [ˌʉ.¹riːm.li]. Here we see that both Hs have been eliminated. As is shown by the derivation in (29), (28) alone will not give the correct result here.

(29)   *Input*

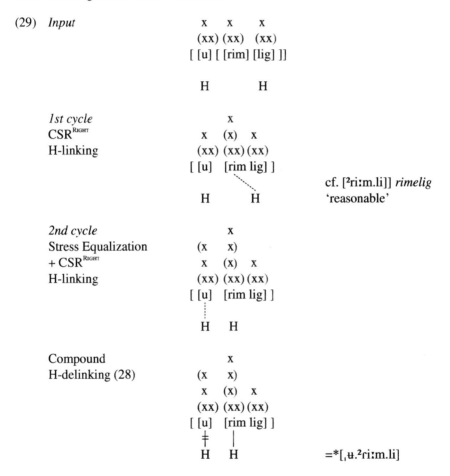

cf. [²riːm.li]] *rimelig* 'reasonable'

=*[ˌʉ.²riːm.li]

We see that (28) gives the wrong result because the H that was assigned to the root on the first cycle must be deleted as well. This is a consistent pattern: when a cyclically-assigned H ends up on non-initial syllable, it is delinked. Since we have seen that non-initial accent 2 is possible in simplex words, as in Section 9.3.4

above, this must be a cyclic rule. Indeed, this is a rule that makes representations meet the more strict constraint on accent distribution in derived words discussed in Section 9.4.1, where it was shown that H-linking can only take place at the left edge of a given constituent. The rule needed to derive the correct output in (29) repairs representations where an earlier rule has resulted in this constraint being violated. The rule is stated as (30).

(30)   *Cyclic H-delinking*

$$\begin{array}{c} \text{H} \\ \vdots\kern-0.5em\neq \\ {}_\omega(\sigma \ \ldots \ \sigma \end{array}$$

Note that (30) and (28) do not have to be ordered with respect to each other in order for the right result to obtain. Whether the latter should be analysed as cyclic or a word-level rule is therefore unclear when we limit the discussion to the data at hand. Data taken from the Trøndelag dialect to be discussed towards the end of the next subsection suggest that it should be conceived of as a word-level rule.

9.6.2   *Tone in simplex words with vernacular initial primary stress*

In Chapter 6.5.2 we discussed a word-level rule of primary stress movement, the Initial Primary Stress Rule (IPSR), which is part of vernacular varieties of UEN, whereby primary stress is moved to the initial syllable of the PWd from a non-initial syllable stressed by the cyclic Main Stress Rule (MSR).

We shall now address the fact that the output of the IPSR always has accent 2. In order to account for this, the IPSR must be supplemented by a rule that inserts an H on its output. The rule will seek out and apply to the foot at the left edge. It will in other words respect the condition that the H must link to an initial syllable. Since it seems to be dependent on the IPSR, one possible solution would be to order it after stress movement. But it is not only fed by the IPSR, it is in fact dependent on the prior application of the IPSR. It must be blocked from applying in words with initial stress assigned at the cyclic level by the MSR. Thus [¹pɑs.siʋ], *passiv* 'passive' cannot undergo the rule, *[²pɑs.siʋ] is not a possible form.

The simplest way to obtain this would be to make H-insertion part of the IPSR. This captures the dependency between primary stress movement and tone insertion in the most direct manner possible. The revised IPSR, with tone insertion added, is stated in (31).

(31)   *Initial Primary Stress Rule (IPSR) (final version)*

$$\begin{array}{ccc} \text{x} & & \text{x} \\ (\text{x}\quad \text{x}) & \rightarrow & (\text{x}\quad \text{x}) \\ {}_\omega[(\text{xx}\,.\,.)(\text{xx}) & & {}_\omega[(\text{xx}\,.\,.)(\text{xx}) \\ & & \vdots \\ & & \text{H} \end{array}$$

Finally, let us turn to a dialect difference with respect to the IPSR which concerns its applicability in cases where the input has accent 2, as for instance in *sjokoláde*. The output created by (31) will in these cases contain two syllables with tone. Since only accents linked to primary stress can surface, we will expect the H to delink that is linked to the syllable from which the primary stress is moved by the IPSR.

This is what seems to happen in the Trøndelag region around Trondheim. Here all words with non-initial stress are subject to the IPSR. Thus the accent 2 input [ʂu.ku.²lɑː.də] as well as the accent 1 [kuŋ.ku.¹rɑŋ.sə] (or in the vernacular often [kuŋ.ku.¹rɑŋ.ʂə]), *konkurranse* 'competition', where penultimate stress in both cases has been assigned by the MSR, are turned into [²ʂuk.ku.ḷɑː.də] and [²kuŋ.ku.ˌrɑŋ.ʂə] by H-insertion and the IPSR.

In the Østlandet area further south, that is, the region in the south-east dominated by Oslo, within which UEN is spoken, the IPSR seems to be blocked when the input has accent 2. Thus initial stress is not possible in [ʂu.ku.²lɑː.də], and the same holds for example for [ru.²tiː.nə], *rutine* 'routine'. But initial stress is perfectly all right in [kuŋ.ku.¹rɑŋ.sə] and [bɑ.¹gɑː.ʂə], *bagasje* 'luggage'. We therefore find [²kuŋ.ku.ˌrɑŋ.sə] and [²bɑg.ˌgɑː.ʂə], but neither *[²rut.tiː.nə] nor [²ʂuk.ku.ḷɑː.də] in UEN.

This means that in the Trøndelag variety, the IPSR can be seen as a persistent rule in the sense of Myers (1991). It will apply blindly, even when it creates a structure that is not well-formed in that it contains two accented syllables. Rule (28), Compound H-delinking, must therefore be called upon to restore the output by delinking the H that is linked to the stress that is subordinate after application of the IPSR. Since I have argued in Chapter 6.5.2 that the IPSR is a word-level rule, Compound H-delinking must be postcyclic as well, at least in the Trøndelag dialects, since it applies to the output of the IPSR.

In the Østlandet variety on the other hand, the constraint against more than one accent 2 seems to block application of the IPSR in cases where the syllable carrying primary stress in the input already has accent 2. This suggests that the extent to which a rule can apply persistently may be a parametric option on which dialects may differ.

INTONATION AND RHYTHM

The major part of the present chapter will be devoted to a presentation of the phonological aspects of the so-called Trondheim model of East Norwegian intonation. The topic of Section 10.2 will be the (postlexical) Accent Phrase (AP). briefly introduced in Chapter 7.3.6 and 9.1.6. The way APs are strung together and organized into higher intonational units will be discussed in Section 10.3, while other aspects of intonation, including postlexical adjustments of the distribution of tonal accents, will be discussed in Sections 10.4 and 10.5. Finally, rhythm will be treated in Section 10.6.

10.1 THE RELATIONSHIP BETWEEN TONAL ACCENT AND INTONATION

Anyone who wants to get a grasp on East Norwegian intonation must take into account the fundamental role played by the tonal accents. The phrase defined by the accentual melodies, the Accent Phrase, can in fact be seen as the basic building block from which the range of possible intonational patterns can be constructed.

Since the tonal accents may occur on syllables carrying primary stress only, it might seem natural to interpret them as pitch accents in the sense for example of Ladd (1996), that is, different tunes that may associate to stressed syllables and that convey different, intonational meaning. English, which is probably the best-known language with such a system, has been subject to a long line of investigation which is reported in Ladd (1996), for instance. But even if English and Norwegian are closely related, we shall see that there are fundamental differences with respect to intonation between the two. Apparently due to a need to maintain the tonal accent contrast, the freedom to assign pitch accents to stressed syllables which differentiate intonational meaning is virtually non-existent in Norwegian.

East Norwegian intonation has recently been analysed in a number of publications by Thorstein Fretheim and Randi Alice Nilsen, who have developed the so-called Trondheim model for analysing East Norwegian intonation.[1] Their main focus is on the pragmatic functions of intonation, that is, on how intonation makes it possible to identify which parts of the information conveyed are given and which

---

[1] The model originated in work published by Fretheim in the first part of the 1980s. Their predecessors are few; the most important earlier works on Norwegian intonation are Alnæs (1916) and Haugen and Joos (1952).

are new in an utterance. Speakers' use of intonation to disambiguate syntax, to convey attitudes, modality, etc., has not been treated in the same systematic manner, although one may find some discussion of these topics. See for example Fretheim (1981a, 1990b, 1992b), Fretheim and Nilsen (1989) and Nilsen and Fretheim (1992). Our present knowledge of East Norwegian intonation is therefore somewhat imbalanced. We know a great deal of how intonation is put to pragmatic use, but less of how other aspects, linguistic or metalinguistic, of a given utterance may be conveyed through intonation.

10.2 THE ACCENT PHRASE

In Chapter 9.1.6 the postlexical Accent Phrase was defined as the domain bounded by the stressed syllable associated with one of the the tonal accents at the left edge. and a final H boundary tone at the right. Rules and constraints were discussed that account for the distribution of the H of accent 2 in the lexical output. Every word inserted into the syntax will therefore contain a stressed syllable, some of which will be associated with an H representing accent 2. Depending on different factors. some of these stresses will be reduced or deleted, in the unmarked cases often on pronouns, prepositions and verbs. The resulting sentence will consist of a string of syllables, some of which will be marked as stressed. Any H that is linked to a stress that is deleted, will automatically be deleted as well, since the tone can only be linked to a stressed syllable (see Chapter 9.3). In this section we shall give an account of how the two other tones of the complete melodies, the prominence L and the right-edge boundary H, are inserted.

10.2.1 Accent Phrase formation

As noted on several occasions, APs are constituents that are bounded by syllables carrying *primary* stress. The AP can now be built by assuming an algorithm that starts from any primary stressed syllable and scans the string rightwards until it encounters the next syllable that is the head within the morphological word that it is part of. Each AP has a primary stressed syllable at its left edge. AP formation will therefore cut across the division of the lexical string of prosodic words, since lexical stress placement is right-edge oriented, as shown in Chapter 6.4.

The result is a prosodic constituency that is organized in a totally different way from the one inferrable from morphological structure in the lexicon; see Chapter 5.1.1. Whether this represents a drastic restructuring of the prosodic hierarchy at the postlexical level, or evidence that we must assume two prosodically defined hierarchies at this level, one consisting of intonational constituents and another built on the string of prosodic words supplied from the lexicon, is difficult to decide. The simpler analysis would be to assume the former solution, since this entails only one postlexical prosodic hierarchy. But it would at the same time represent a solution where the lexical and postlexical prosodic hierarchies cannot be directly related within the same hierarchy, since the basic constituent type of the postlexical hierarchy, the postlexical AP, will no longer be isomorphic with the maximal prosodic category in the lexicon, the *lexical* AP, which is derived from morphological constituency. The two types will have in common that they are headed by stress. But while stress in the the lexical PWd is oriented towards the right edge (see the discussion of the Main Stress Rule in Chapter 6.4) all primary stressed syllables are situated at the left edge in postlexical PWds and APs.

Turning to an example of how an utterance may be divided into a string of APs, consider the sentence *Jeg tror jeg finner et sted å sove*, 'I think I find a place to sleep', taken from Fretheim and Nilsen (1991). It consists of six lexical words, the first person singular pronoun *jeg* and the present tense verb *tror* 'think', plus a subordinate clause whose subject is another instance of the first person singular, the present tense *finner* 'find', the object NP *et sted å sove* 'a place to sleep'. A perfectly normal pronunciation will be [jæ.**truːr**.jæ.**fin**.nə.rɛt.**steː**.dɔ.**soː**.ʋə], where the four syllables carrying primary stress are printed in boldface.

Since there are four primary stressed syllables in the sentence, it will consist of four APs, each of them consisting of only one PWd, since there are no compounds involved. In accordance with the principles defined above, the left edge of each AP is identified with the left edge of each syllable carrying primary stress. Right edges can now be inserted immediately to the left of these boundaries, and at the end of the sentence. The result is as shown in (1).[2]

(1)   jeg (**tror**-jeg)$_{AP}$ (**fin**ner-et)$_{AP}$ (**sted**-å)$_{AP}$ (**so**ve)$_{AP}$

Note that the initial, unstressed pronoun is not included in any AP, since it does not carry primary stress itself and is not preceded by any primary stressed syllable in the string.

10.2.2 L-insertion

In Chapter 9.2.4 it was stated that L-insertion should be seen as a postlexical process rather than a postcyclic, lexical one. Anticipating the arguments for this, which will be presented in Section 10.4 below, we can now state the rule that inserts the L. Taking the sentence in (1) as example, the input string can be represented as in (2), where only the infinitive *sove* has a lexical H.

(2)   H
                                            |
       jeg (**tror**-jeg)$_{AP}$ (**fin**ner-et)$_{AP}$ (**sted**-å)$_{AP}$ (**so**ve)$_{AP}$

A low tone L must now be associated with each AP, more specifically with the head syllable if there is no H already associated with this syllable, and with the following syllable if the head is linked to an H. The rule can be stated as in (3).

---

[2] To avoid unnecessary detail, orthography will be used instead of phonetic transcriptions. Hyphens are used to connect different lexical items belonging to the same AP.

(3) *L-insertion*

Starting from the left edge of each AP, insert an L on the first free TBU.

The output of (3) will be the representation shown under (4).

(4)   L   L   L   H L
        | | | | |
    jeg (**tror**-jeg)$_{AP}$ (**fin**ner-et)$_{AP}$ (**sted**-å)$_{AP}$ (**so**ve)$_{AP}$

10.2.3 Are the accentual melodies pitch accents?

After L-insertion has applied, the contrastive parts of the tonal accent melodies are in place. As pointed out in Chapter 9, the contrast is manifested on stressed syllables only; a low toned stress signals accent 1, while a falling tone towards an L on the poststress syllable signals accent 2. Their close association with stress suggests that they should be analysed as pitch accents in the sense given the term in the metrical, intonational framework represented by Pierrehumbert and Beckman (1988) and Ladd (1996), for example. The latter defines pitch accents as follows:

> A pitch accent may be defined as a local feature of a pitch contour—usually but not invariably a *pitch change*, and often involving a local maximum or minimum—which signals that the syllable with which it is associated is *prominent* in the utterance.   (1996: 45f., emphasis in original)

Pitch accents in this view are part of intonational melodies that associate with stressed syllables. In this respect they may act as phonetic cues for the local phonological prominence assigned to stressed syllables. It is not difficult to see that this definition captures important aspects of the tonal accents as we have analysed them in Chapter 9 and in the present section. They represent a tonal maximum (accent 2) and a tonal minimum (accent 1) respectively, associated with the stressed syllable. By their close association with primary stressed syllables, they can be said to cue stress, along with syllable weight.

In the words of Ladd (1996: 157) the difference between a language like Norwegian and for example English is that '. . . the choice of pitch accent type seems to be influenced by lexical considerations as well as postlexical ones'.[3] This statement correctly captures the fact that lexical properties play an important role. But at least with respect to East Norwegian, it does not go far enough. The two melodies, or tunes, illustrated in (4) are in fact the only possible melodies that can be associated with a stressed syllable. Excepting the marginal patterns discussed in Section 10.5 below, no other melodies are possible; all pitch contours associated with stressed syllables in a given utterance will be modulations of one or the other of the two tonal accents. Indeed, it will be argued in Section 10.4 that rules that change intonation are to a large degree constrained by the accentual melodies, so that that any

---

[3] Note that Ladd here implies that the tonal accents in fact *are* pitch accents.

categorical change in the pitch contour associated with a stressed syllable implies a change from one accentual melody to the other.

This state of affairs differs strikingly from that in English, for example, where there is a whole range of different tunes that may associate with stressed syllables, and thereby function as pitch accents with different intonational meanings; the list given in Ladd (1996: 82) gives examples. Since the choice between the two melodies in Norwegian is lexically determined, the contrast itself cannot be used for intonational purposes. Any contrast in intonational meaning must therefore be expressed at other places in the pitch contour, or by modulations within the structural confines of each of the accentual melodies.

10.2.4 The right-edge H%

In addition to stressed syllables, there is evidence for one other location within the AP which is tonally specified. This is the final syllable, where we find a boundary H. This H, whose phonetic reflex in many cases is quite weak, will be masked by the focal H inserted on the same syllable in focused APs; see Section 10.3 for further explication.

(5)   *Boundary tones*

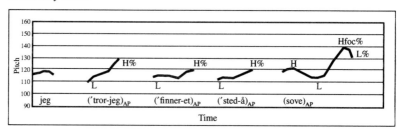

Consider now the pitch contour in (5), which is one of several possible versions of (1), adapted from Fretheim and Nilsen (1991). The first three APs are non-focal and precede the only focal phrase, which can be recognized by the marked rise at the end. In the non-focal phrases there is a weak rise, and the tone level is reset at the beginning of AP. This pattern is difficult to account for if a boundary H% is not assumed, since a series of L tones would trace a level or falling contour. We can therefore assume a rule that will insert an H% on the final syllable of any AP. Applied to the representation in (4), it will insert H% on the final syllable of each AP. The output is shown in (6).

(6)   L   H%   L   H%   L   H%   H L H%
             | | | | | | | | ⟋
          jeg (**tror**-jeg)$_{AP}$ (**fin**ner-et)$_{AP}$ (**sted**-å)$_{AP}$ (**sove**)$_{AP}$

This string of tones can also be represented in the way used in earlier chapters, by means of superscripted numbers at the beginning of each stressed syllable denoting accent 1 or 2. A simpler representation of the string in (6) is therefore the one found in (7).

(7)   jeg (¹tror-jeg)$_{AP}$ (¹finner-et)$_{AP}$ (¹sted-å)$_{AP}$ (²sove)$_{AP}$

10.3 HIGHER ORDER CONSTITUENTS:
THE TRONDHEIM MODEL

In the preceding section we have seen that a given utterance can be divided into minimal intonational phrases headed by stressed syllables and bounded by the accentual melodies associated with the stressed syllable plus a right-edge boundary tone. We shall now see how APs are grouped into higher order intonational constituents in the Trondheim Model (henceforth the TM), viz. Intonational Phrases (IPs) and Intonational Utterances (IUs).[4]

10.3.1 Two degrees of phrasal prominence: focal and non-focal APs

A basic concept in the TM is focus. Focus can be defined as a syntactic or intonational means to foreground a discourse constituent. The constituent that is subject to intonational focus marking in East Norwegian is the Accent Phrase, and the means by which this is done is the insertion of an H tone at the right edge of the phrase. This tone differs from the right-edge boundary tone H% which we have already identified in this environment, in that it reaches a much higher pitch level. This is clearly shown in (5), where the final AP is focal, the others non-focal.

APs can accordingly be divided into two subtypes by means of the feature [±focal] (Fretheim and Nilsen 1991). APs that are [+focal] have an Hfoc associated at the right edge. Since this will also assume the function of the boundary tone, the result can be interpreted as two merged Hs with different functions, an H% and an Hfoc, so that the full specification of a focal H becomes Hfoc%. The final AP of (5) should accordingly receive a Hfoc% specification at the right edge, as shown in (8).

(8)   L H% L   H%   L H% H L Hfoc%
          │ │   │   │   │ │   │ ∨
     jeg (**tror**-jeg)$_{AP}$ (**fin**ner-et)$_{AP}$ (**sted**-å)$_{AP}$ (**so**ve)$_{AP}$

In the TM the Hfoc% is assumed to delimit a higher order intonational constituent:

---

[4] The Accent Phrase is referred to as a Tonal Foot and tonal accents as word tones in the Trondheim Model. These differences are terminological only. My analysis differs from the Trondheim Model at one point, however, in that I assume that the accent tones are linked to syllables, and not to the 'phonological word'', ω, which in the TM is intermediate between the AP and the syllable. It dominates all syllables beginning with the stressed syllable up to the next word boundary. It is therefore a hybrid constituent, its left edge being defined by phonology and its right edge by morphology, and accordingly, it is not a purely phonological constituent, as implied by its name.

the Intonational Phrase (IP). The defining characteristic of an IP is that it ends in a focal AP, and includes all preceding, non-focal APs. Since the utterance in (8) contains one focal AP, it therefore contains one IP. (9) shows its hierarchical structure, where the highest order constituent, the Intonation Utterance (IU), has been included as well. (10) shows the corresponding linear representation, where the hierarchical structure is shown by means of labeled parentheses.

(9) *The intonational hierarchy*

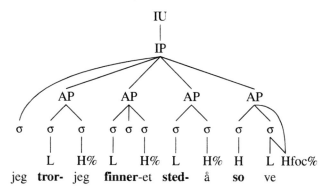

(10) ((jeg (^{1}tror-jeg)$_{AP}$ (^{1}finner-et)$_{AP}$ (^{1}sted-å)$_{AP}$ (^{2}sove)$_{AP}$)$_{IP}$)$_{IU}$

(9) shows how the difference between the two types of boundary H can be accounted for structurally. By assuming that the Hfoc% is associated with the AP itself as well as with the phrase-final syllable, while an H% is associated with the final syllable only, we derive a structural difference that allows us to predict the different scaling of the two tone types.

An IU may contain at most two IPs (Nilsen 1992: 107). This means that a given IU may contain at most two focal APs. (11), which is another version of the sentence discussed above, also adapted from Fretheim and Nilsen (1991), shows an IU with two focal APs.[5]

(11) *IU consisting of two IPs*

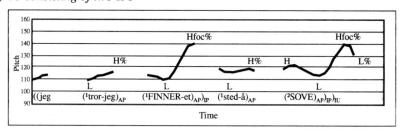

---

[5] Note that the morphological unit in focal APs which contains the stressed syllable from now on is marked by means of capital letters in transcriptions, in accordance with the transcription conventions of the model.

The hierarchical structure of the utterance shown in (11) is given in (12). An utterance-final boundary L has also been included; see Section 10.3.5 below.

(12) *Hierarchical structure of the utterance in (11)*

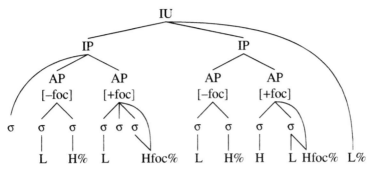

As implied by the term [focal], the function of the Hfoc% is to impart intonational prominence to the phrase to which it belongs. This is exactly the function assigned to pitch accents in the quote from Ladd (1996: 45f.) given above, where it is said that a pitch accent '. . . signals that the syllable with which it is associated is prominent in the utterance.' The fact that this function is signalled by means of a boundary tone in East Norwegian strengthens the argument given above that the tonal accents are not pitch accents in the sense laid down by Ladd, since the main function assigned to pitch accents in languages like English is associated with tones that are not part of the tunes assigned to stressed syllables in East Norwegian. *Intonational* prominence is in other words primarily signalled by scaling of the right boundary tone and not by endowing stressed syllables with certain tonal contours.[6]

Thorstein Fretheim (1992a: 124, 1992b: 225) cites the hypothesis that focus tones, or phrase accents, are universally realized as prominent pitch peaks, that is, as high tones. This suggests the interesting hypothesis that in languages where pitch accents are commonly realized by means of high tones linked to stressed syllables, the marking of focus can be accomplished by means of the tonal contour associated with stressed syllables. In languages such as East Norwegian, however, where

---

[6] An interesting claim with respect to East Norwegian intonation, which is made in Gårding and Stenberg (1990), should perhaps be mentioned here. These authors found, both in their own comparative research on East Norwegian and West Swedish intonation and in an earlier comparative study on East Norwegian and American English intonation (Wiig 1967), that the pitch range in East Norwegian intonation is unusually wide. The East Norwegian speaker in their own sample used a range of almost two octaves, compared to one octave used by their West Swedish speaker. If this proves to be a general feature of East Norwegian, the feature responsible for this property is apparently the steep rise at the end of focal APs. A popular way to parody East Norwegian intonation, among foreigners as well as among speakers of West Norwegian dialects, is indeed to raise the pitch rapidly to the very top of one's range at the end of a given phrase.

stressed syllables are generally associated with a low tone, a conflict arises, since the low prominence tone in accent 1 will make insertion of a high focus tone on the same syllable non-optimal with respect to the commonly observed pattern that tones are associated with TBUs in a one-to-one fashion when possible. The association of focus marking with a boundary tone in East Norwegian can therefore be seen as a way of avoiding this type of conflict.[7]

Note finally that in cases where there are nonfocal APs after the last Hfoc%, these cannot be assigned to any IP, since an IP is always terminated by an Hfoc%. Postfocal APs of this type will be associated directly to the IU node, and their AP node will be marked as [–focal].[8]

10.3.2 Stress levels

Based on the discussion above and in previous chapters, three levels of postlexical prominence can now be identified: focal primary stress marked by syllable weight, tonal accent and phrase-final Hfoc%, non-focal primary stress marked by syllable weight and tonal accent, and secondary stress marked by syllable weight alone. The latter type, which is not explicitly recognized within the TM, consists of syllables assigned secondary stress in the lexicon by the Compound Stress Rule given in Chapter 7.3, and of primary stresses that are deaccented in the syntax, but not turned into completely destressed, cliticized elements. The different levels are all present in the example given in (13), as prosodically transcribed in (d).

(13) (a) Har du ikke skrevet boka ennå?
      (b) 'Have you not written the book yet?'
      (c) [ˌhɑː.rʉ.kə.ˌskreː.vət.ˈbuː.kɑ.²ɛn.nɔ]
      (d) ((har-u-kke)$_{PWd}$ (skrevet)$_{PWd}$ ((('boka)$_{Pwd}$)$_{AP}$ ((²ENNÅ)$_{Pwd}$)$_{AP}$)$_{IP}$)$_{IU}$

The material preceding the accented *boka* would in the TM be treated as unstressed, since the lexical items that make up the string all lack accent. But the long vowels in the two verbs show that these items still carry a certain degree of prominence, and since retention of length is the diagnostic used for secondary stresses in lexical compounds, it follows that they may be analysed as carrying secondary stress. The pronoun and the negation marker have on the other hand both been reduced to clitics adjoined to the first verb. The example therefore consists of four PWds, each headed by a stressed syllable. The heads of the two first carry secondary stress, and the two final primary stress, signalled by tonal accent.

From this it follows that an important function of the tonal accents is to differentiate between primary and secondary stress also at the postlexical level. Only phrases headed by a primary stress may be accented, and only accented phrases

---

[7] In West Norwegian dialects, where the prominence tone is an H, focus seems to be marked by this H being boosted.

[8] In earlier work within the TM, postfocal feet were analysed as constituting a separate IP, but this has later been abandoned: see discussion in Nilsen (1992: 105ff.).

may be focal. Therefore only phrases headed by a primary stressed syllable may be made intonationally prominent through assignment of focal accent.

10.3.3 The relationship between intonation, syntax and information structure

In the TM, intonation is regarded as a separate module of grammar whose *linguistic* function is primarily pragmatic. This function can only be served if intonation can be related to syntactic structure, where the sense units of a given sentence are represented. Intonation serves to highlight some of these units, marking them as more important than others. But as mentioned above, the basic constituents of the intonational hierarchy are in many cases not isomorphic with the syntactic constituents, since the AP is bounded by stress and not morpho-syntactic boundaries. The relevant information must therefore be transferred from intonation to syntax.

According to Nilsen (1989: 28, 1992: 37f.) for example, and Fretheim and Nilsen (1991), focus is mapped into the syntax from any accented *wordform* heading a focal AP. This is one of the motivations for the ω-constituent as part of the model. [±focal], which in the intonational representation is associated with the AP-node, is transferred to the next level down, the ω, from which it is transferred onto the corresponding syntactic terminal symbol, that is, the word which contains the ω. But the crucial linking point can just as well be conceived of as the accented syllable. The rule will look for the leftmost syllable in the AP and transfer [±focal] to this. (The result will be a representation that will correspond to the one that is derived directly in languages where focus is signalled by tones associated to the stressed syllable.) From this, the feature can be transferred to the terminal symbol in the morpho-syntactic representation which contains this syllable. In other words, the hybrid phonological word as conceived within the TM is not strictly needed in order for focus to be transferred from the phonologically conditioned intonational structure to the morpho-syntactic structure.

From the terminal symbol, focus domains will be assigned to the syntactic representation according to the following rule, translated from Nilsen (1992: 37):[9]

Mark as FOCUS the highest syntactic node **n** up in the tree from a given instance of [+focal] assigned to a terminal symbol **x**, such that **n**
  (i)dominates no other instances of [+focal], and
  (ii)dominates no instance of [–focal] assigned to a symbol located to the right of **x**.

The rule implies that a syntactic node assigned FOCUS cannot dominate another node assigned FOCUS on its left, and no node dominating a word assigned [–focal] on its right. The result of applying the rule will be sense units that are derived from the IP-structure of the intonational representation. IPs can therefore be said to constrain focus domains in the syntactic representations.

Focus domains may be assigned thematic or rhematic function by a set of rules

---

[9] See also Nilsen (1989: 29) and and Fretheim (1991) for earlier versions, where the Focus feature is conceived as binary.

that take into consideration the number of IPs in the IU (one or two), their syntactic position and their order. A detailed discussion of these interpretation rules would take us too far away from the phonological aspects of intonation, and the interested reader should therefore consult, for example, Nilsen (1989: 30ff.) or Fretheim (1992a: 127ff.).

10.3.4 Declination: Prefocal and postfocal APs

As will have become clear from the previous section, East Norwegian intonation can be analysed as consisting of a string of Accent Phrases, some of which are focal in that they have a high boundary tone at the right edge. Within the confines of the IU, these strings can be subsumed under a more global pattern, defined by the general direction of the mean frequency, as measured for instance in the low tones on the stressed syllable in accent 1 and on the poststress syllable in accent 2. Before the first focal AP, the baseline defined by these Ls as well as the topline defined by the H of accent 2 will be level, while after the first focal AP, both will decline (Fretheim 1992a: 117). A final, postfocal AP will very often lack a final rise altogether.

The lack of declination in prefocal APs can be seen from (5) and (11). (14) shows an example of postfocal declination. The utterance is the same as in the examples given above, but with only one focal AP, headed by the verb *finner*.[10] Note that evidence for an H% on the prefinal AP is hardly present, and totally absent with respect to the final AP.

(14) *Decination in postfocal APs*

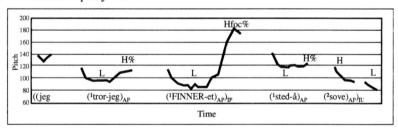

10.3.5 AP-external syllables

Utterance-initial syllables that are not preceded by an accented syllable will by definition not be part of any AP; see (1) and (13) for examples. Utterance-final syllables that are not accented and follow the H% delimiting the last AP of the

---

[10] This intonation pattern gives constrastive, or polarity focus on the verb, with the following APs conveying given information. While (5) and (11) are adapted from Fretheim and Nilsen (1991), (14) shows my own rendering of the utterance, since this realization type is not given in the source. The pattern is fully consistent with postfocal intonation given in other articles by Fretheim and Nilsen, however; see e.g. Fretheim (1992a).

utterance will likewise fall outside the string of APs. Such utterance-final syllables will often represent syntactic tag particles. In addition we may find utterance-internal but AP-external syllables, because the Hfoc% may in some instances be linked to a syllable that is *not* the one immediately preceding the following accented syllable. The syllables intervening between this Hfoc% and the next accented syllable will accordingly not be part of any AP. Since all the tones discussed in the previous section, and which make up the basic intonational pattern of East Norwegian, are tones constituting APs, we may ask to what extent AP-external syllables are tonally specified, and what the source of these specifications may be.

The unmarked pattern with respect to utterance-initial, preaccent syllables seems to be a more or less even, mid tone. A plausible analysis would be that such syllables are tonally unspecified, and that this is mirrored phonetically in a neutral tone level, neither high nor low. From this level, pitch will rise towards the initial H if the first AP has accent 2, and fall towards the initial low of an accent 1; see (15) in Chapter 9 for a clear example.

The second case, right-detached tag particles, is discussed for example in Fretheim (1990a), Fretheim and Nilsen (1989) and Van Dommelen, Fretheim and Nilsen (1998). According to the latter, such particles may be specified for either H% or L%, that is, for a specific utterance-final boundary tone which may convey different intonational meanings. They may be produced as part of the final AP, or as AP-external. In both cases, however, they should be seen as tones originating outside the AP, as being directly governed by the utterance level. They seem to represent one of the few cases where specific phonological tones in the intonational melodies associated with utterances are not part of the basic AP-constrained set of tones: the lexical H, the prominence-driven L and the focal or non-focal right-edge H%.

The third type of AP-external syllables, syllables occurring between but outside APs, is also discussed in Fretheim (1990a). Such syllables arise in strings where the accented word is followed by one or more unaccented words, when the Hfoc% is associated with the final syllable of the accented word instead of with the syllable immediately preceding the next accented syllable. It is argued that the syllables following the Hfoc% in such cases can be interpreted either as part of the preceding or of the following IP. Consider the examples under (15), (16) and (17) which are adapted from Fretheim (1990a).[11] In (16) and (17), the two syllables in boldface are AP-external, but included in the IP to the left or right, respectively. According to Fretheim, the difference between the two will be that in (16), the pitch of the two syllables will be determined by the preceding Hfoc%, while in (17), it will be determined by the following, lower lexical H of the next foot. Phonetically, these patterns are manifested by the AP-external syllables describing a plateau determined by the Hfoc% in (16), and a lower plateau determined by the following H in (17); see the pitch tracings presented in Fretheim (1990a).

---

[11] The sentences can be glossed as 'It seems as if this is solution-the'. In the source they are described as phonologically distinct, but 'information-structurally equivalent'.

(15)   H   L   Hfoc%   H   L Hfoc% H L
            | | | | | | | |
     ((det (VIRKER-som-om)_AP)_IP ((DETTE-er)_AP)_IP (løsningen)_AP)_IU

(16)   H   L Hfoc%   H   L Hfoc% H L
            | \/ | | | | |
     ((det (VIRKER)_AP som-om)_IP ((DETTE-er)_AP)_IP (løsningen)_AP)_IU

(17)   H   L Hfoc%   H   L Hfoc% H L
            | \/ | | | | |
     ((det (VIRKER)_AP)_IP (som-om (DETTE-er)_AP)_IP (løsningen)_AP)_IU

We can therefore account for the pitch on these syllables by assuming that it results
from spreading from adjacent tones. On the additional assumption, also made in
Fretheim (1990a), that spreading is blocked by an IP-boundary, we derive the right
result. If the stray syllables are adjoined to the IP on their left, spreading takes place
from the final tone of the preceding AP. If they are adjoined to the following IP,
spreading takes place from the initial tone of the following AP.

Summing up, we see that AP-external syllables can get their tone from different
sources, depending on where in the structure they occur. Utterance-initial syllables
are tonally neutral, and will be realised as such. Medial syllables are also tonally
neutral, but will be tonally specified by spreading from adjacent tones belonging
to the same IP. Finally, utterance-final, AP-external syllables may have their own
tonal specification, supplying the utterance with different intonational meaning.

10.4 POSTLEXICAL ACCENT SHIFT

Since the distribution of the tonal accents is determined in the lexicon, a natural
hypothesis with respect to the postlexical level would be that no further changes
take place here, except for the effect of sentence stress distribution on accent. This
hypothesis would in other words imply that if a given word retains primary stress
at the postlexical level, nothing happens to the tonal accent it has been assigned in
the lexicon.

A weaker hypothesis would be that changes may occur, but no tonal information
may be added to stressed syllables at this level. This would imply that the high tone
of accent 2 may be deleted, so that changes from accent 2 to accent 1 may occur,
but accent 1 may not turn into accent 2 since this would mean that a high tone is
added to the representation, blurring the distinction between the accent 2 H as lexical and the other tones as postlexical.

The weakest hypothesis would be that tone insertion is also possible at
the postlexical level, so that lexical accent 1 may change into postlexical
accent 2. In that case the source of the high tone underlying accent 2 would no
longer be the lexicon only, since postlexical rules as well may produce accent 2.

As will be shown in a moment, it is the latter situation that seems to hold.

The conclusion that some cases of accentual H must be inserted postlexically motivates the claim that L-insertion as well should take place postlexically. If L-insertion were ordered before the rules of H-insertion discussed in Sections 10.4.2 and 10.4.3 below, we would need a rule of L-delinking and relinking to the following syllable. If all Hs are in place before L-insertion applies, no such extra apparatus is needed.

10.4.1 H-delinking after for

The adverb *for*, used in front of adjectives and meaning 'too', causes any adjective that in citation form is pronounced with accent 2 to shift to accent 1. Some examples are given in (18).

(18) *Accent shift in adjectives after* for
[fɔ.¹[iː.tn̩] < [²liː.tn̩] *liten* 'small'
[fɔ.¹gɑm.ml̩] < [²gɑm.ml̩] *gammel* 'old'
[fɔ.¹çeː.dl̩.li] < [²çeː.dl̩.li] *kjedelig* 'boring'
[fɔ.¹dum.mə] < [²dum.mə] *dumme* 'stupid' (pl.)

Since *for* generally occurs without stress, and since there is no possibility for any other syntactic or morphological element to intervene between *for* and the adjective, one might claim that *for* in this case is a prefix. Prefixation of *for* would in that case be fully productive, to my knowledge there is no adjective that cannot be combined with *for*, even if the result for semantic reasons is rather odd with adjectives whose meaning is non-gradeable, such as *død*, 'dead'. But the status of the morphological process involved would be rather unclear. The fact that it is fully productive would suggest inflection. But this would be the only inflectional process in the language which is realized as prefixation, all other inflection is by means of suffixation or vowel modification. The alternative is that *for* represents a cohering, derivational affix. Since a homophonous derivational prefix already exists, used with verbs as well as nouns, this cannot be rejected on formal grounds.

But there is an additional fact that weakens the hypothesis that we are dealing with word formation. The same shift takes place after the synonymous adverb *altfor*, where *for* occurs as the second member of a compound. This word, however, is always pronounced with stress and accent 1. If a sequence of *altfor* plus adjective were to be interpreted as a word, it would therefore have to be a compound. But this interpretation is not possible, since compounding invariably results in *elimination* of tonal accent on the second member. If *altfor* plus adjective were a compound, we would therefore expect the latter to lack any trace of accent, that is, the accent 2 H as well as the L occurring in both accents. But this is not the case: the adjective is clearly pronounced with accent 1, that is, as a separate AP, and therefore not as part of the phrase headed by *altfor*. We must therefore be dealing with two separate syntactic words. Hence, the accent shift caused by *altfor* is determined by syntax and not by morphology. The difference between *altfor* and *for* is minimized if *for* is analysed as a proclitic, as proposed in Fretheim (1974b).

The rule can be stated as one delinking an H from the head of an Adjective Phrase when *for* or *altfor* occurs in the SPEC position. The rule is given in (19).

(19) *H-delinking after* for

$$
\begin{array}{c}
H \\
\ddagger \\
[[Y]_{AdvP} \, [X]_A]_{AP}
\end{array}
$$

Condition: Y=*for* or *altfor*

10.4.2 Stress shift and H-insertion in particle groups

The shift after *for* and *altfor* is obligatory; accent 2 in this environment is not grammatical. We now turn to a pattern that is variable, viz. the alternation in phrases consisting of verb plus an adverbial particle (henceforth *particle groups*) between primary stress on the particle and primary stress on the verb.[12] If stress is placed on the verb, accent 2 is obligatory. Hence verb forms which have not been assigned accent 2 in the lexicon will aquire accent 2 by this rule. Some examples are given in (20).

(20) *Stress alternation in particle groups*

No accent shift in accent 2 words

[²kɔm.mə]	*komme*	[¹frɑm]	*fram*	[kɔ.mə.¹frɑm] ~ [²kɔm.mə.ˌfrɑm]
	'come'		'ahead'	'to arrive'
[²fin.nə]	*finne*	[¹ʉːt]	*ut*	[fi.¹nʉːt] ~ [²fin.ˌnʉːt]
	'find'		'out'	'to find out'
[²kɔm.mə]	*komme*	[¹ɔː.ʋf]	*over* (id.)	[kɔ.¹moː.ʋf] ~ [²kɔm.ˌmoː.ʋf]
				'to come across'
[²kɔm.mə]	*komme*	[²ɛt.tʃ]	*etter*	[kɔ.²mɛt.tʃ] ~ [²kɔm.ˌmɛt.tʃ]
			'after'	'to come later'

Accent shift in accent 1 words

[¹kɔm.mʃ]	*kommer*	[¹frɑm]	[kɔ.mə.¹frɑm] ~ [²kɔm.mə.ˌfrɑm] 'arrives'
	'comes'		
[¹fin.nʃ]	*finner*	[¹ʉːt]	[fin.nə.¹rʉːt] ~ [²fin.nə.ˌrʉːt] 'finds out'
	'finds'		
[¹kɔm.mʃ]	*kommer*	[¹ɔː.ʋf]	[kɔm.mə.¹roː.ʋf] ~ [²kɔm.mə.ˌroː.ʋf]
			'comes across'
[¹kɔm.mʃ]	*kommer*	[²ɛt.tʃ]	[kɔm.mə.²rɛt.tʃ] ~ ?[²kɔm.mə.ˌrɛt.tʃ]
			'comes later'

---

[12] Earlier discussions of this rule can be found in Fretheim (1974b) and Fretheim and Halvorsen (1975). These particles, which must be distinguished from the modal particles discussed in the next section, are most often prepositions or adverbs with locative or temporal meaning. Adjectives and even nouns occur as well; however, see Fretheim (1974b) for an extensive discussion.

We see that lexically determined accent 1 changes to accent 2 in particle groups when primary stress is placed on the verb. This is therefore a case where an H must be supplied at the postlexical level. This alternation bears a strong resemblance to the Initial Primary Stress pattern that was discussed in Chapters 6.5.2 and 9.6.2. In both cases primary stress is moved from a non-initial syllable to the initial one, and the result invariably is accent 2. Another parallel is that when the particle itself has accent 2 when pronounced with primary stress, stress shift seems less felicitous. This ties in with the observation made in Chapter 6.5.2 that initial stress is blocked in UEN when the non-initial stress is realized with accent 2, as for example in [ṣu.ku.²lɑː.də], *sjokolade* 'chocolate'. Another partial parallel is the fact that if the initial syllable represents a cohering prefix, e.g. /be-/ or /for-/, stress shift, but no accent shift, may take place. *Betale inn*, 'to make a down payment' and *forsøke ut*, 'to try out' can only be pronounced [bə.ˌtɑː.¹lin] or [bə.¹tɑː.lin] and [fɔ.ˌṣøː.¹kʉːt] or [fɔ.¹ṣøː.kʉt], respectively.

This suggests that we are dealing with the same rule in a lexical and a postlexical version, where the latter applies to syntactic phrases where the head is unstressed and the complement consisting of one word only, bears primary stress.[13] This accent shift should therefore be stated as a syntactically constrained version of the IPSR given in Chapter 9.6.2.

To state the relevant postlexical environment for the IPSR based on intonational structure is complicated, since the structural description would straddle, but not necessarily exhaust two consecutive APs. When primary stress is on the particle, the verb will belong to the tail of the preceding AP, while primary stress on the verb gathers verb and particle into the same AP. A much more straightforward formulation follows if the rule is seen as constrained directly by syntax. The postlexical version of the IPSR is stated as (21).

(21) *Initial primary stress in particle groups*

$$
\begin{array}{ccc}
x & & x \\
x \quad x & \rightarrow & (x \quad x) \\
(xx \, . \, .)(xx) & & (xx \, . \, .)(xx) \\
[[X]_V \;\; [Y]_{Part.}]_{VP} & & [[X]_V \;\; [Y]_{Part.}]_{VP} \\
& & \qquad \vdots \\
& & \qquad H
\end{array}
$$

Finally, it should be noted that there are very different sociolinguistic constraints on the two versions of the rule. Initial primary stress in lexical items where stress also may be non-initial, is heavily constrained and confined to vernacular varieties of UEN. In particle groups initial stress is on the other hand acceptable, and seems to have been so at least since the beginning of this century; see Alnæs (1916: 98) who describes it as rapidly becoming part of educated East Norwegian speech.

---

[13] As far as I know, this type of stress pattern is found in particle groups only.

10.4.3 Accent shift as marker of emotional involvement

Accent shift is not accompanied by a shift in intonational meaning either after *for* or in particle groups. There is another rule that shifts the accent from 1 to 2, how-ever, where the shift adds intonational or pragmatic meaning. The structural envi-ronment corresponds to that of particle groups, but the particles in this case are modal particles that in most cases cannot bear stress. The contrast is therefore be-tween accents 1 and 2, with stress on the verb in both cases. This is different from the particle group type, where stress on the verb and accent 1 is ungrammatical.

It is difficult to pinpoint exactly what this added meaning of accent 2 is, but the shift seems to be used in order to signal greater emotional involvement on the part of the speaker. Since no shift can be added to APs which already have accent 2, the rule is only applicable in accent 1 environments. As just mentioned, it is restricted syntactically in that it only takes place in *verbs* immediately followed by a small set of unaccented modal particles or the negator *ikke* (Fretheim 1974b, 1984).[14]

According to Fretheim (1984), two constraints hold on the rule. First, an AP must follow; the verb + negator phrase cannot be utterance-final or followed by postfocal APs only. Second, if more than one modal particle co-occur with *ikke*, the latter cannot be accented for accent shift to take place.[15] Some examples are given in (22).

(22)   *Accent 2 as involvement marker*

[²dæː.ɖɑ.¹sɑnt] < [¹dæː.ɖɑ.¹sɑnt], *Det er da sant!* 'It is indeed true'
[hɑ̃.²fɔk.kə.²loːnənu] < [hɑ̃.¹fɔk.kə.²loːnənu], *Han får ikke låne noe* 'He is not allowed to borrow anything'
[di.²fin.nə.ri.kə.¹biː.lɳ] < [di.¹fin.nə.ri.kə.¹biː.lɳ], *De finner ikke bilen* 'They cannot find the car'

Compared to the modal particles, *ikke* is special in that it may also occur with stress (and accent) following a deaccented verb. In cases where the speaker needs to fo-cus on the negation itself, the negator may be pronounced with (emphatic) stress and with no accent on the preceding verb. But in order for accent shift to take place, the negator cannot bear stress and must therefore be a clitic; see Chapter 11.6.4.[16]

---

[14] See also Haslev (1987), where the shift is argued not to be an accent shift *per se*, but an intonational pattern whose phonetic result coincides with the accent 2 contour.

[15] This co-occurrence restriction does not hold between the set of modal particles and the adverbial particles discussed in the preceding section. Nor does it hold between *ikke* and adverbial particles. We can therefore find accent shift triggered by a modal particle, even if a stressed adverbial particle follows, as in the following example taken from Fretheim (1984): ((de (²sa-da)_F (¹FRA-om)_F)_IP (¹det)_F)_IU, *de sa da fra om det* 'But they spoke up about it, didn't they'. The particle group is *si fra*, 'speak up', and the modal particle *da* signals that the speaker is convinced that the propositional content of what he says is true. We see that both verb and particle are accented. The normal accent on the verb is accent 1. Accent 2 is clearly triggered by the modal particle, underlining the speaker's commitment to what he says.

[16] Other clitics may intervene between the verb and the negator, as in [di.²fin.næ.ɳi.ki.¹jɛn], *De finner den ikke igjen* 'They cannot find it [again]'. Note that if the direct object is changed into a clitic pronoun in the third example in (22), the accent shift becomes ungrammatical, because the AP headed by the verb then will be utterance-final. Thus [di.¹fin.næ.ɳi.kə] is good, while *[di.²fin.næ.ɳi.kə] is ungram-matical. As noted above, the ungrammaticality persists also when a non-focal AP follows.

From a structural point of view, an alternation pattern involving *ikke* can therefore be established that corresponds to the alternation found in particle groups which was discussed in the preceding section: accent on the negator and no accent on the preceding verb, or accent on the verb and no accent on the negator. Since there is no pragmatic difference between these alternants with respect to particle groups, the question arises whether this also might be the case with verb + negator, in the sense that accent 2 on the verb has the same pragmatic meaning as accent on the negator, both being different in pragmatic meaning from accent 1 on the verb and no accent on the negator.[17] If it could be established that the difference between the neutral and the more involved pronunciations in (22) involves the same pragmatic difference as that between the neutral pronunciation and one with deaccented verb and accent on the negator, we would have an alternation that is not only formally parallel to accent shift in particle groups, but also pragmatically, since no pragmatic meaning is added when accent is shifted from the negator to the verb.

While it seems possible to interpret *some* utterances with accent shift involving *ikke* in this way, it is difficult to generalize and claim that shift from accent 1 to 2 in verbs followed by cliticized *ikke* in all cases implies greater pragmatic weight on the negation and only that. Even if the structural constraints on the two rules seem identical, accent shift involving *ikke* seems to have taken on a more general, pragmatic meaning that is no longer contained in the meaning expressed by having (emphatic) accent on the negator instead of the verb.

In a synchronic analysis it is therefore difficult to conflate accent shift in particle groups and accent shift in verb + *ikke*, even if there are strong formal resemblances. The fact that there are different intonational constraints on the two, viz. that only shift in particle groups can take place when no focal AP follows, can be seen as supporting evidence for analysing the two as different.[18]

These differences notwithstanding, accent shift triggered by *ikke* and accent shift in particle groups can formally be seen as having overlapping structural constraints in that both shift primary stress from a non-initial position within a given domain to the left edge, a shift that always gives accent 2 on the stressed syllable. Vernacular Initial Primary Stress, stress shift in particle groups and accent shift in verb + *ikke* constructions can therefore all be analysed as H-insertion on an initial stress foot accompanied by shift of the primary stress to that foot.

But accent shift triggered by *ikke* also interacts with the shift triggered by the set of modal particles. As mentioned, modal particles cannot trigger accent shift if followed by an accented *ikke*, while adverbial particles have no such inhibiting effect on accent shift in verb + modal particle; see footnote 15. Since modal particles rarely occur accented, it is not possible to set up an alternation corre-

---

[17] Recall that the latter pattern is not grammatical in particle groups.
[18] Another difference is that *ikke* has accent 2 when pronounced in isolation. Since disyllabic particles with accent 2 seem to inhibit accent shift in particle groups, accent shift in verb + negator should be inhibited as well if the two patterns were the same. This lack of parallelism may be due to the fact that *ikke* has a separate, monosyllabic clitic form /-ke/, however, even if this for phonological reasons is not usable in all contexts. Cf. Fretheim (1988) and Chapter 11.6.4.

sponding to the one that can be set up with respect to particle groups and verb + *ikke* between accented verb and accented particle. This type therefore defies the formal analysis proposed for the latter types. A formal analysis of this type must include accent on the verb in the structural description and H-insertion triggered by the presence of of a modal particle belonging to the AP headed by the verb. Note that the rule must have direct access to morpho-syntactic information, i.e. the information necessary to delimit the class of triggering particles. This is therefore another case where a postlexical phonological rule is constrained by non-phonological information, that is, information that is not encoded in postlexical *phonological* constituency.

10.4.4 Summary

The picture that emerges from the discussion above is that East Norwegian intonation can basically be seen as a string of Accent Phrases, whose melodies are characterized by accentual tones associated with stressed syllables and right peripheral edge tones. Variation in this pattern is introduced along two binary dimensions. The accented head syllable can vary with respect to tonal accent, it may be either accent 1 or accent 2. The high tone on the right-edge syllable can vary systematically in scaling in that a very high tone signals that the phrase is focal, while a moderately high tone (or none at all utterance-finally) signals that the phrase is non-focal. The latter distinction is fundamental for the understanding of how intonation in East Norwegian contributes to the pragmatic meaning of a given utterance.

These two parameters, accent type and focal vs. non-focal edge tone, constitute the rigid intonational framework that most East Norwegian utterances must adapt to. Only the 'calling contour' discussed in the following section entails a complete cancelling of the tonal pattern associated with APs.

10.5 OTHER INTONATIONAL PATTERNS

One of the main claims embodied in the TM is that East Norwegian intonational structure can be seen as generated by concatenation of instances of the same simple building block, the Accentual Phrase, governed by the further constraint that at least one of these must end in a focal high tone. We now turn to some minor patterns where this pattern is incompletely realized or downright cancelled.

10.5.1 The 'No big deal' intonation

This can be characterized as an incomplete pattern that according to Nilsen and Fretheim (1992: 459) is used in order to give '. . . the hearer(s) an impression of being casual and carefree, and of having full control of the situation'. The characteristic property of the pattern is that it lacks a focal AP. The intonation instead describes a falling contour from an initial H, where APs can be distinguished, but where none of them has the final high tone that would mark it as focal. The melody therefore has the same formal properties as a series of postfocal APs in an utterance following the normal pattern, where the initial high tone corresponds to the focal high preceding postfocal APs. But the initial H of the 'No big deal' pattern cannot be an Hfoc%, since no accented syllable precedes it.

Since the pattern consists of a series of one or more non-focal APs, the deviation incurred by this pattern is that no IP can be identified. Actually, in Nilsen and Fretheim (1992) it is assumed, in accordance with earlier versions of the TM, that postfocal APs make up a separate IP. Therefore 'No big deal' contours are analysed as IPs as well in the article, but in the current version of the model, only APs that are [+focal] may head IPs; see footnote 8 above. It follows that 'No big deal' contours do not contain any IPs, and they must be analysed as one or more APs directly dominated by an IU node.

10.5.2 The 'calling contour'

The only intonational pattern that I am aware of where neutralization into a third tune actually takes place, is the so-called 'calling contour'. As noted by Ladd (1996: 136ff.), this contour, used for vocative purposes, is found in many European languages, with minor variations from one language to another. The basic pattern seems to consist of two tones, the first one high and the following somewhat lower, analysed by Ladd as an accentual H* followed by a downstepped ¹H.

In East Norwegian, where the contour is mostly used with names, the H* goes on the stressed syllable, while the ¹H links up with the following syllable. Monosyllabic names are pronounced with the two tones clearly distinct, creating the impression that the word is pronounced with two syllables. If more than one syllable follow the stressed syllable, the ¹H will spread rightwards.

The contour is the same in all contexts, and therefore cancels the distinction between the tonal accents. There is therefore no tonal difference between *Ola*, which has accent 2, and its variant form *Olav*, which has accent 1. When pronounced with the calling contour, both have the accentual H* on the initial stressed syllable, and the downstepped ¹H on the second.

10.6 RHYTHM

10.6.1 The representation of linguistic rhythm

Rhythm can informally be characterized as a tendency to distribute stressed syllables as evenly as possible in a given string. A perfect rhythm is obtained when every stressed syllable is preceded and followed by an unstressed syllable and every unstressed syllable is preceded and followed by a stressed one. Such an alternation is often referred to as a 'perfect grid' (Prince 1983), due to the fact that it can be represented formally by means of a layered grid where every second mark on line 0, the syllable layer, is dominated by a mark on line 1. In a language where every syllable in a given domain is footed by means of a syllabic trochee or iamb, such a grid will result automatically.

A grid can be disrupted in two ways. Two adjacent stresses represent a *clash*, and two adjacent unstressed syllables represent a *lapse*. Clashes may arise when stress is cyclically assigned, and when independent rules assign primary stress and secondary stress at opposite edges, as in Norwegian. Clashes can also arise on the phrasal level when two stresses are juxtaposed across a word boundary. Lapses can arise when a language lacks iterative footing, or when stressing of a syllable trapped between an unstressed and a stressed syllable would create a clash.[19]

One important diagnostic of rhythm in much recent literature has been the existence of rules that shift a stress away from an adjacent stronger stress to avoid a stress clash. One well-known example from English is the shift from *thirtéen* to *thìrteen* in the phrase *thìrteen mén*, called 'The Rhythm Rule' or 'Move X' (Hayes 1995: 370f.). The important generalization underlying such shifts is that stress does not move to the next syllable away from the primary stress, but to the nearest stressed syllable. Thus *Tennessée* becomes *Tènnessee*, not **Tennèssee* in *Tènnessee Érnie* (Hayes, loc. cit.). This presupposes a representation where only some syllables are marked as stressed and therefore possible sites for the moved prominence. Other mechanisms that may improve the rhythm of a given string, and therefore presuppose a rhythmic organization, are destressing in clash and beat addition onto a lapse.

10.6.2 Evidence for rhythmic structure

Rhythmically spaced secondary stresses are not a salient and easily observable feature of Norwegian. There seem to be no general phonetic correlates of such stresses such as specific tone movements, quantity and intensity, for example. Any evidence must therefore be of an indirect nature.

Nor is there much evidence for secondary stresses caused by cyclic stress assignment. When stress is moved rightwards as the result of suffixation, no trace is left of the former stress in the form of long vowel, geminated consonant or tonal accent, as in [ˈdrɑː.mɑ], *drama* (id.), [drɑ.ˈmɑː.tisk], *dramatisk* 'dramatic' and [drɑ.mɑ.ˈtik], *dramatikk* 'dramatic events'. Secondary stress originating in stress assignment at an earlier stage is only found in compounds and in words that have undergone the Initial Primary Stress Rule discussed in Chapters 6.5.2 and 9.6.2.

In long simplex words and long words where stress falls on, or is conditioned by, suffixes, there may be a stretch of several syllables where a rhythmic pattern might be imposed between the initial secondary stress and the final primary stress. An example would be *universitét*, 'university'. Also in compounds one can look for secondary stresses in cases where there are several syllables between the primary

---

[19] Weight sensitivity introduces a complication with respect to a syllabic grid, because footing is defined on moras. In such systems, every heavy syllable will represent a foot, and therefore a stress, while every second light syllable in a string of more than two will represent a stress.

stress on first the compound member and the secondary stress on the others; see Chapter 7.3.

Since we have established on independent grounds that stress feet are built at each edge of a word, the question that we must address here is whether there is evidence for exhaustive footing in UEN, that is, for footing of any intermediate stretch of syllables not metrified by the initial and final foot. All foot heads between the initial and the final one will then represent abstract stress marks that may be heard as rhythmic beats that together with the initial and final stress can constitute a rhythmic grid over the domain.

Exhaustive footing can in principle be diagnosed in different ways. One of these is perceived rhythm which corresponds to the abstract foot structure. But even if such rhythm should be absent, or difficult to observe, one can also appeal to different reduction patterns connected with alternating syllables as evidence for exhaustive footing. This was used to establish the initial foot in Chapter 6.5.1, because /e/ is realized as full vowel in initial syllables, and as schwa or syllabic sonorant in the second.

Let us now briefly review how rhythm has been analysed in earlier literature on Norwegian. Alnæs (1925: 23) claims that in longer words there will be a rhythmic alternation between stronger and weaker stress, with a somewhat stronger stress on every odd syllable, as in *nèapòlitànerínnene* 'the women from Naples'. In simplex words, the count starts from the first syllable. Morphologically complex words may contain unstressed prefixes, however, as in the other example given by Alnæs, the compound *forfátterhònoràrer* 'author's royalties', where the initial syllable represents an unstressed suffix. The two examples suggest that the computation of rhythm excludes cohering prefixes, but includes all suffixes, and that it is left-to-right-directional, starting from the leftmost foot.[20] Alnæs himself suggests that rhythm is computed on syllables. Since the rhythm is trochaic, the appropriate foot would seem to be a syllabic trochee. Alnæs's proposal is taken up in Jahr and Lorentz (1983b: 14), who use the words *ùnivèrsitét* 'university' and *kàtamarán* 'catamaran' as examples.

The most thorough discussion of Norwegian rhythm to date is Broch (1935). The bulk of his discussion deals with how rhythmic principles cause a drastic reduction of phrases in rapid speech. The template that these reductions seem to be striving towards is a syllabic trochee, where the first syllable is heavy and carries stress, while the final is light. One of his examples is the sentence *Je[g] har ikke snakket me[d] andre a[v] dem* 'I have not spoken with others of them', where the brackets enclose letters that are not pronounced even in careful pronunciation. In its maximally reduced form, it is rendered by Broch as a sequence of three trochees: *²jakke ²snaktme ²andram*. Longer *words*, 'content words' in Broch's terminology, can be also divided into trochaic stress groups, but unfortunately he is much less specific on this type. The conclusion is quite clear, however. Translated into contemporary terminology, he claims that phrases in rapid speech are organized into syllabic,

---

[20] Recall from Chapter 7.2.6 that cohering prefixes can never head a foot.

quantity-sensitive trochees, so that there will be ideally one, and at most two, un-stressed syllables between each stressed syllable carrying a tonal accent. However, the fact that his conclusions are reached on the basis of rapid speech makes it diffi-cult to apply them directly to the question of rhythm as part of a phonological rep-resentation where the effects of speech style are disregarded.

One plausible hypothesis would be that these reductions hit unstressed syllables, and not stressed. Applied to a perfect grid, with the initial syllable stressed, we would expect the second and fourth syllable to be more susceptible to reduction than the first and third. This might seem to be supported by a word like *universitét*, which in rapid speech can be rendered as [ʉn.ʋæʂ.ˈteːt]. But upon closer examina-tion, this effect seems to depend on vowel sonority, and not position in the syllable string. The syllables that are reduced in *universitét* have high vowels, and this seems to be the cause of reduction.[21] We see this if we compare with a word with high vowel in the first syllable and low in the second, such as *tyranní* 'tyranny', where rapid speech reduction renders [trɑ.ˈniː].[22]

To control for this effect, we must therefore examine words with identical vow-els in the first and second syllable, such as *prosodí*, 'prosody', *kalamitét* 'calamity' and *generére* 'to generate'. In rapid speech it is the second vowel that will tend to disappear. In fact, forms like *generére*, with two consecutive /e/'s, show this ten-dency also in careful speech because /e/ is realized as schwa or syllabic sonorant in open, unstressed syllables. As mentioned above, this reduction is blocked in initial syllables, except when the primary stress syllable immediately follows, where re-duction is optional. In unstressed syllables in post-initial position, we find schwas or syllabic sonorants also in reasonably careful speech. Other examples are *elefánt* 'elephant', *referére* 'to report' and *generasjón* 'generation'. Reduction seems to be independent of the weight of the initial syllable. Also in *kompresjón* 'compression' and *konferére* 'to confer', the /e/ in the post-initial syllable may be realized as schwa. This supports the hypothesis that the relevant foot type is syllabic.

Having established the initial syllable as strong, and the second as weak, the crucial question with respect to rhythm is of course what happens with a third and fourth unstressed syllable counting from left. We need examples with at least four syllables before the primary stress and with /e/ as head in the third, fourth or both. Two examples where /e/ heads the third syllable are *parallellitét* 'parallelism' and *suverenitét* 'sovereignty'. With /e/ in the third syllable, a possibly strong position, we would not expect it to reduce to a syllabic /l/ or /n/, which is possible when the same configuration is found in a second syllable, as for example in *elefánt*. This expectation seems to be borne out; the most natural pronunciation in both cases is with a clearly audible vowel: [pɑ.rɑ.lɛ.li.ˈteːt] and [sʉ.ʋə.rɛ.ni.ˈteːt].

As to an /e/ in a fourth syllable, a possible example is *analfabetísme* 'illiter-

---

[21] It also seems to be the opposite of the pattern found in Dutch (Booij 1995: 134), where high vowels are shown to resist reduction. But it should be noted that the Dutch phenomenon concerns reductions to schwa, while the present reduction is a kind of truncation. They are therefore not completely parallel.

[22] Note that we are not dealing with a reduction to schwa in these cases, but a syncopation process that will delete the vowels in question totally, or leave a trace in the form of slightly syllabified consonant.

acy'.[23] The stem *alfabét* 'alphabet', pronounced with long, stressed /e/, shows that there must be an underlying /e/ in the fourth syllable. In *analfabetísme* it may reduce to a very short schwa. We find a similar reduction with respect to the /i/ in the fourth syllable of *parallellitét*. It will easily disappear or manifest itself as syllabification of the preceding /l/.

The evidence presented cannot be considered as conclusive, but it suggests that rhythm in Norwegian can be represented by means of syllabic trochees, assigned from left to right after primary stress and initial, secondary stress have been assigned. Since rhythm seems to be syllable-based, we have arrived at an analysis where culminative stress is assigned by means of edge-anchored moraic trochees in the lexicon, and rhythm by an exhaustive parse of syllabic trochees across the relevant domain, but which respects already assigned stresses.[24] This supports the proposal made in Bruce (1984: 33) for Swedish, who in line with an original proposal of Liberman and Prince (1977) argues that rhythm is based on metrical structure, but can itself be organized as a simple alternation of strong and weak beats.

The resulting double metrical representation of *pàrallèllitét*, as pronounced in isolation, and therefore as an IP, is shown in (23).

(23)   *Biplanar representation of culminative stress and rhythm*

Line 2					x	
Line 1	(x				x)	
Line 0	(x x	x	x	x	(x x)	Culminative stress plane
	p a r	r a	l e	l i	te: t	
Line 0	(x	x)	(x	x)	(x)	Rhythmic plane
Line 1	(x		x		x	

Being anchored to the initial stress foot, rhythm in UEN is in other words dependent on, and not a prerequisite for, the assignment of main stress. We can account for this formally by assuming that the stresses assigned by moraic trochees in the lexicon are copied onto another plane as line 0 and line 1 marks at the postlexical level. With the line 1 marks as anchoring points, syllabic trochees are then built from left to right, resulting in lapses where there is an uneven number of syllables between the stresses.

10.6.3 A Norwegian Rhythm Rule

A rhythm rule similar to the one in English briefly described in Section 10.6.1 above is found in UEN, although it seems restricted to phrases consisting of a title or a first name followed by a family name. It was first described in Knudsen (1856),

---

[23] This word may also be pronounced with initial main stress, although Berulfsen (1969) lists it with final main stress only.

[24] Lacking relevant data, I can only speculate that this domain will be the Intonational Phrase; cf. Section 10.3 above.

and a short discussion can also be found in Jahr and Lorentz (1983b). In isolation *kaptéin*, 'captain' and the first name *André* have final stress. When combined with a family name, such as *Dahl*, the results are *káptein Dahl* and *Ándre Dahl*. A un-equivocally unstressed syllable intervening between the two words will block stress retraction, as in *kaptéinen Dahl*, 'the captain Dahl.' However, also when the family name has main stress on a non-initial syllable, retraction takes place, as for example in *káptein Rosén* and *káptein Rocambóle*. This suggests that the initial syllables in *Rosén* and *Rocambóle* are stressed, supporting the analysis that words with non-initial main stress have an initial stress-foot as well; see Chapter 6.5.1.

Likewise, stress may be retracted to the initial syllable of the title or first name even if this is a light, open syllable. Thus *majór* (id.) is pronounced with retracted stress when followed by a family name, as in *májor Dahl*. Finally, in order to show that this is not a question of moving the stress mechanically one syllable leftwards, we can include *generál* (id.) in the data. Also here stress retracts to the initial syl-lable, cf. *géneral Dahl*. **Genéral* is clearly ill-formed. These data also support the hypothesis that there is invariably an initial foot present in all words with non-initial stress.

10.6.4 The syllabic trochee as a prosodic template

We have seen that two types of feet, the moraic trochee and the syllabic trochee, seem to play a role in the phonology of UEN. The moraic trochee is edge-based, and serves as the structural basis for identification of main stress at the right edge of words, and also for the initial prominence that is present at the left edge of words.

The syllabic trochee on the other hand defines rhythm. It is anchored to the ini-tial syllable of the relevant domain, and respects main stress in the sense that this cannot occur in a weak syllable in the rhythmic alternation. In the preceding chap-ters we have seen that the syllabic trochee seems to define a prosodic template for other purposes. Most salient is that it serves as the minimal unit for assignment of accent 2 (Chapter 9.3.4), and the alternation between a syllabic and non-syllabic realization of the masc. def. sg. suffix /n/ also seems to be governed by the syllabic trochee as the optimal realization form (Chapter 8.3.3). It also seems to serve as a template for the drastic, speech rate-governed reductions discussed in Broch (1935). Finally, given the fact that only the syllabic foot is exhaustively assigned to a given string, this must form the building block from which the next constituent in the prosodic hierarchy, the (postlexical) prosodic word, is formed.

In a sense, this template can also be seen as defining a maximum size on words belonging to the native vocabulary, but with the proviso that an extra syllable is allowed. This gives a maximum size of three syllables, which seems to be respected in simplex words (hélvete), as well as in inflection and cohering derivation, such as the trisyllabic def. pl. of masc /bil/, *bil* 'car', which is [²biː.lɳ.nə]. When the stem is disyllabic, as in masc. /nøkl/, *nøkkel* 'key' and /sufa/, *sofa* (id.), the def. pl. is still trisyllabic: [²nœk.lə.nə] and [¹suf.fɑ.nə]. Four syllables are rare, if existent at all, in this group.

POSTLEXICAL SEGMENTAL PHONOLOGY

In this chapter the postlexical phonology of UEN will be discussed. Section 11.1 contains a discussion of the most important characteristics of postlexical phonology. In Section 11.2 postlexical prosodic constituency will be discussed, based on the analysis of intonational structure given in Chapter 10. Postlexical r-phonology will be discussed in Section 11.3 below, while Nasal Place Assimilation will be discussed in section 11.4. In Section 11.5 the constraints governing the distribution of schwa will be discussed in more depth. Finally the topic of Section 11.6 will be clitics.

One topic that would have found its natural place in the present chapter is fast speech phenomena. These have not been systematically investigated in UEN, however, the only source that can be referred to is Broch (1935), which was discussed briefly in Chapter 10.6.2.

11.1 THE POSTLEXICAL LEVEL

There are different, and in many respects opposing, theoretical approaches to postlexical phonology. The main theoretical divide is perhaps that between those adhering to the hypothesis that postlexical phonology may be directly conditioned by syntax, e.g. Selkirk (1984, 1986) and Kaisse (1990), and those who argue that the relationship is indirect and mediated through a prosodic constituency mapped from syntactic structure (Nespor and Vogel 1986). When examined more closely, however, these alternative approaches do not seem to exclude each other. Nespor and Vogel (1986: 24) refer to rules that may be conditioned by morphological and syntactic properties, but which lie outside the scope of their theory. Likewise, given the fact that the categories that constitute the prosodic hierarchy of Nespor and Vogel are mapped from syntactic structure, it may be difficult in all cases to decide whether a given rule is constrained by the constituent resulting from the mapping or the syntactic one that lies behind it. Thus Kaisse (1990: 132) notes that '[A] characteristic mark of a P1 rule, *or of a rule occurring within phonological phrases*, is the failure to apply across syntactically not very distant but nonetheless recognizable structural junctures.' (emphasis added). Since a P1 rule (see below) is defined as a (postlexical) rule sensitive primarily to syntactic information, the statement explicitly allows both syntactic and prosodic constituency to play a role.

Complicating this picture is the hypothesis that some rules, i.e. those whose output is not categorical, but rather statable in gradient, phonetic parameters, belong to a separate module of grammar, Phonetic Implementation, which is ordered after the postlexical phonology proper (Keating 1996).

11.1.1   The lexical/postlexical divide and the prosodic hierarchy

In Chapter 4.1, the properties given under (1) were listed as typical of rules applying at the postlexical level. The first of course holds per definition: postlexical rules are rules that apply across word and phrase-boundaries.

(1) *Typical properties of postlexical rules*
  1. apply across word and phrase boundaries
  2. apply once (non-cyclic)
  3. are exceptionless
  4. are not structure-preserving (allophonic)
  5. may have gradient outputs.

The second property, that postlexical rules apply only once, implies that postlexical rules are not interleaved with syntactic rules in the same way as lexical rules are interleaved with morphological rules. This follows from the assumption that lexical insertion takes place into complete phrase markers. In its strong version, it implies that postlexical rules are expected to apply across the board, constrained by neither syntactic nor prosodic constituency. Much subsequent work has proved this hypothesis to be too strong, see for example Nespor and Vogel (1986) and the articles published in Inkelas and Zec (1990), where the ways in which postlexical rules are constrained by prosodic and perhaps syntactic constituency are explored. The prosodic hierarchy assumed in these works implies a division of postlexical phonology into levels. It follows that rules may apply at some levels but not others, a prediction we shall discuss at several points below. Thus a given rule may be constrained by a given constituent level in the sense that it applies across the board within this level, or across boundaries defined by a given level. However, postlexical rules may exhibit so-called strict cycle effects, in the sense that they will apply across boundaries only (Kaisse 1990).

That postlexical rules are exceptionless follows from the assumption that exceptions are encoded in the lexicon. Rules with lexical exceptions should therefore be lexical. However, we shall see examples of rules that apply across word boundaries, but which nevertheless must refer to specific lexical items, especially modal verbs.

That all lexical rules are structure-preserving is one of the more contested aspects of the theory. See for example Hall (1989) and Borowsky (1993) for arguments that allophonic distinctions may be derived in the lexicon. Much less controversial is the claim that postlexical rules are not structure-preserving. But Nasal Place Assimilation, discussed in 11.4, has properties that suggests that structure preservation may play a role postlexically as well.

The final property of (1), that postlexical rules are gradient, has in later work been ascribed to phonetic implementation in the sense that rules whose output may be gradient are not part of phonology proper, but rules converting phonological surface structure into a phonetic representation.

11.1.2 Syntactic and lexical constraints: P1 versus P2 rules

In the preceding section, it was suggested that the division between lexical and postlexical rules does not seem as clear-cut as originally assumed in classical Lexical Phonology. An alternative classification of postlexical rules is proposed in Kaisse (1990). She divides the postlexical module into two strata, characterized by different rule types called P1 and P2 rules. Some important properties that characterize P1 rules are listed in (2).

(2)   *Some properties of P1 rules*
  1. sensitive primarily to syntactic information, insensitive to intonational phrasing
  2. possibly requiring syntactic and lexical information beyond category-neutral, X-bar statements
  3. neutralizing (structure-preserving)
  4. ingradient (categorical)
  5. style sensitive
  6. rate insensitive
  7. possibly having lexical exceptions
  8. having a lexicalizable output
  9. possibly showing strict cycle effects.

As can be seen from the list, Kaisse's hypothesis is that P1 rules will resemble lexical rules. Given their hypothesized sensitivity to syntactic environments, they are different from the rules discussed in Nespor and Vogel (1986), for example, which are all sensitive to prosodic categories. P2 rules are on the other hand rules that correlate with postlexical rules in the classical sense, that is, rules that have the characteristics listed in (1). P2 domains are recognized '. . . by their variable size and by the fact that they do not necessarily resemble any syntactic constituent' (Kaisse 1990: 132). Whether they can be equated with the prosodically bounded rules of Nespor and Vogel (1986) is not clear, however.

11.1.3 Phonetic implementation rules

One of the characteristic features of P2 rules in Kaisse's framework is that their output may be gradient. In Keating (1996) the same property is ascribed to phonetic implementation rules, expressed by the following statement: '[P]honology deals in discrete symbolic elements, while phonetics deals in numbers (on continuous dimensions).' (emphasis in original omitted). Phonetic implementation is thus assumed to be a separate module of grammar that is ordered after the postlexical phonological module. While this distinction may seem straightforward enough as a theoretical tool, it may be difficult to establish whether the output of a given rule is gradient or not. The distinction should all the same be kept in mind when a given rule is discussed.

11.2 PROSODIC CONSTITUENCY BEYOND THE LEXICON

While the syntactic coupling of words into higher order syntactic constituents creates sequences of phonological units that will form the input to the set of postlexical phonological rules in a given language, it has been claimed that postlexical phonology only to a very limited degree is constrained directly by syntactic structure. The relationship between syntax and phonology is rather seen as mediated by a separate type of constituency, the Prosodic Hierarchy. This constituency must in some way be related to the syntactic constituency, and the relationship is usually seen as the result of mapping from syntactic structure onto prosodic structure.[1]

In Chapter 10.3 we saw that the intonational structure of Norwegian utterances is constrained by a prosodic constituency that can be derived from prominence relationships and focus assignment. This is in other words a constituency that is derived *independently* of syntax: the governing forces are phonological and pragmatic. The question therefore arises whether we need two types of postlexical phonological constituencies, one governing prominence and intonation and the other mapped from syntactic structure in accordance with the principles outlined in the works referred to in footnote 1, which governs postlexical segmental phonology.

This question will be the topic of the present section. We shall start by reviewing some of the relevant literature on postlexical phrasing derived from syntax.

11.2.1 A prosodic hierarchy derived from morpho-syntactic structure

The simplest hypothesis with respect to how syntax and phonology interact would be that once internal word structure is deleted, phonological rules apply independently of boundaries, that is, whenever their structural description is met, whether this is found within a word or across a word boundary. This seems to be the hypothesis embodied in earlier versions of Lexical Phonology: see for instance Kaisse and Shaw (1985).

However, many of the authors referred to in footnote 1 argue that at least a major group of postlexical rules is constrained by a hierarchy of prosodic domains derived from syntactic structure. The prosodic hierarchy invoked by Nespor and Vogel (1986), which we shall use as representative of this approach, includes the lexical categories discussed in previous chapters, the syllable, the foot and the PWd. At the postlexical level, the Clitic Group, the Phonological Phrase, the Intonational Phrase and the Phonological Utterance are added.

---

[1] See e.g. Selkirk (1984, 1986), Nespor and Vogel (1986) and the different articles published in Inkelas and Zec (1990).

Syntactic structure plays an important role in the delimitation of all of them. The Clitic Group consists of a host PWd and zero or more clitics, which are interpreted as prosodically weak PWds. The Phonological Phrase consists of one or more Clitic Groups. It is derived by taking any lexical head A as its strong member, and including all other constituents on its non-recursive side, which is the left side in Norwegian, up to the next lexical head B that is not dominated by the maximal projection of A. The Intonational Phrase is more loosely defined. The basic type corresponds to the syntactic structure dominated by a simple S-node, but in cases where a separate Intonational Phrase, such as a non-restrictive relative clause, breaks up the S-structure, the parts that are broken apart by the intervening IP will define separate IPs. The Phonological Utterance is in most cases co-extensive with the highest maximal projection of the syntactic phrase marker, but it may also consist of more than one sentence if these are closely connected semantically. For all levels above the Clitic Group certain types of restructuring may take place. Note that since the constituents are mapped directly from syntactic constituents, prosodic boundaries will at all levels coincide with word boundaries.

These levels are nested domains to which postlexical phonological rules can be related in three different ways, as (a) *domain span rules*, which may apply anywhere within a given domain, (b) *domain juncture rules*, which apply across the boundary between two domains of a given type, and (c) *domain limit rules*, which apply at the edge of a given domain. For example, a domain juncture rule relating to the Phonological Phrase will apply between phonological phrases, but not between intonational phrases. Nespor and Vogel give numerous examples, especially from English, Romance languages and Greek, of rules relating to the different domains of the prosodic hierarchy which they propose. On the assumption that the categories of the hierarchy are universal, we would expect that corresponding domains, derived from syntactic structure, play a similar role in UEN.

11.2.2 A prosodic hierarchy based on prominence relations and pragmatics

In Chapter 7.3.2 I argued that stress assignment can be seen as a function that takes a morphological domain as input, and returns a prosodic word. A lexically derived PWd is hence a string of syllables whose boundaries coincide with morphological boundaries, and which contains only one stress as assigned by the Main Stress Rule (MSR). Lexical stress is oriented towards the right edge of the word, and a lexical PWd can therefore consist of several unstressed syllables preceding the stressed one.

The lowest constituent in the postlexical *intonational* hierarchy, the postlexical AP, is on the other hand left-headed. This means that all syllables preceding a primary stressed one within a *lexical* PWd will be included in the AP on their left. In the absence of a preceding stress, they will end up outside any AP. This analysis implies that the boundaries of the postlexical constituents cut across morphological structure so that there will be no necessary coincidence between a postlexical AP boundary and a word boundary.

The lexical and postlexical levels are nevertheless related. Since stressed syllables are heads of lexical PWds as well as of APs, the postlexical hierarchy can be seen as being based on stress as well. We must therefore take a closer look at how many different levels of prominence can be defined, in order to establish a more coherent picture of the hierarchy and the properties that define each category.

In the lexicon, three levels of prominence were established in Chapters 6 and 7, primary and two degrees of secondary stress, strong and weak. Syllables with primary stress must meet two necessary conditions: they must have tonal accent and be heavy. Only the latter condition applies to syllables with strong secondary stress, and possibly to syllables with weak secondary stress, which is positionally defined as a prominence that occurs on the initial syllable of words with non-initial primary stress. In the lexicon, primary and strong secondary stress are juxtaposed in compounds, where the first member will have primary stress, while the stressed syllable of the second member will retain its weight, but lose its eligibility as bearer of tonal accent.[2] This means that a (simple) compound can be characterized in prosodic terms as a concatenation of two PWds, where the stress of the leftmost assumes the role of primary with respect to the second. In Chapter 7.3.6 I termed the output of the Compound Stress Rule a *lexical* AP, which in parallel with PWds is not necessarily co-extensive with a postlexical AP, since the stress on the first compound member in a lexical AP does not have to be initial.

Strings of syllables preceding a primary stress, as in *telefón* 'telephone', will have a weak secondary stress on the first syllable. We can therefore at least assume that there is a foot at the left edge of such words. A word such as *telefónkatalògene* 'the telephone directories' can therefore be parsed into two PWds, each consisting of two rhythmic feet, an initial foot headed by a weak secondary stress followed by the foot headed by the primary stressed syllable. The structure is therefore as shown in (3), where the vertical bar shows the boundary between the two PWds.

```
(3)                          x    |
     Line 2                 (x    |              x)
     Line 1      (x         x)    | (x           x)
     Line 0      (x    x)   (x    | (x    x)  (x    x    x)
                 t e   l e  f on  | ka    t a  l o   ge   n e
```

The prosodic input for postlexical AP-formation is a string of lexical APs supplied by the lexicon with prosodic structures such as that shown in (3). Postlexical AP-formation will split them in cases where PWds precede the head foot. These will be subsumed under APs to their left. The example in (3) will accordingly be re-structured into te.le.((fón.ka.ta.)$_{PWd}$ (ló.ge.ne)$_{PWd}$)$_{AP}$. The initial foot (te.le) will, if utterance-initial, be incorporated into the prosodic structure at the IP-level, and into the preceding PWd if non-initial.

Likewise, PWds which have been subject to stress reduction (see Chapter

---

[2] See e.g. (10) and (11) in Chapter 9, which show that no tonal movement is associated with the syllable carrying secondary stress.

10.3.2), will be included as weak members of the AP to their left. We may, however, assume two degrees of postlexical stress reduction. Stress deletion with concomitant reduction of vowel length and gemination will result in a fully unstressed syllable which will be incorporated into a prosodic word by cliticization: see Section 11.6 below. Reduction to secondary stress will on the other hand result in accent deletion, while quantity will be retained. In this case, the result will be an unaccented, *postlexical* prosodic word, that is, a PWd that is left-headed, because any prestress syllables belonging to the same *lexical* PWd will have been transferred to the preceding PWd at the postlexical level.

The result of these adjustments will be a string of left-headed PWds grouped into left-headed APs, where each accented PWd will start, and head, a new AP. As seen in Chapter 10.3, APs can then, in accordance with the principles underlying the Trondheim Model, be grouped into right-headed Intonational Phrases, characterized by a focal rise on the final syllable of the rightmost prosodic word.[3] IPs in their turn make up Intonational Utterances, which will normally consist of at least one and at most two IPs. This renders the hierarchy given in (4).[4]

(4) *Prominence-based postlexical prosodic hierarchy*

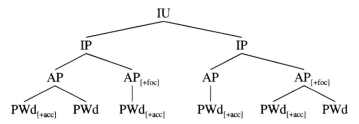

This hierarchy does not only differ from the one assumed by Nespor and Vogel by the fact that it is construed independently of syntactic structure. Since both stress reduction and assignment of [+focal] are governed by pragmatic constraints, any given sentence may be structured in several different ways governed by pragmatic principles, as shown in Chapter 10.3. This makes the prosodic hierarchy of the Trondheim Model radically different from syntax-based hierarchies.

11.2.3 Can the hierarchies be related?

A possible way to bridge the gap between the two hierarchy types can be based on the insight that pragmatics may influence prosodic phrasing—see Cho (1990), Condoravdi (1990) and Kanerva (1990). These authors present evidence that fo-

---

[3] Note that IPs in the Trondheim Model are not coextensive with IPs in the model of Nespor and Vogel (1986). We return to this point below.
[4] This representation is an idealization: it should be kept in mind that the hierarchy will not necessarily respect the Strict Layer Hypothesis, since any constituent preceding the first accented syllable will not be part of any AP. Likewise, final and even medial syllables may be AP-external, as pointed out in Chapter 10.3.5.

cused elements may constitute or delimit prosodic constituents which are not always coextensive with the constituents derived from syntactic structure proper. But these analyses differ from the prominence-based analysis outlined above in that the focused phrases are delimited by word boundaries. A mapping relationship between syntactic structure and pragmatic structure therefore seems to be implied in these analyses, but it is unclear in what direction this mapping takes place. Selkirk (1984: 32), however, is quite clear on this issue. She claims that '. . . intonational phrasing is freely assigned to [syntactic] surface structure, the only structural restriction being that the entire sentence be parsed into a sequence of one or more non-overlapping intonational phrases.' Further, '. . . the syntactic structure of a sentence cannot be said to *determine* its intonational phrasing' (p. 285, emphasis in original). In Selkirk (1986) the IP is excluded from consideration because '. . . intonational phrasing appears to be subject to semantic wellformedness conditions rather than to conditions based on surface syntactic structure . . .' (p. 385). This view is echoed in Nespor and Vogel's assertion (1986: 193) that IPs, even if their basic shape is determined by syntax, may be restructured depending on their length as well as on rate of speech, style and *contrastive prominence* (emphasis added).

This means that at least for the constituent delimited by intonation, the syntax-first models of Selkirk (1986) and Nespor and Vogel (1986) converge with the general pragmatics/semantics-first approach of the Trondheim Model. The unit of the latter that seems to correspond to the IP level of the former models, however, is not the IP but the Intonational Utterance, at least if we base the comparison on Nespor and Vogel's model, where the IP is co-extensive with a 'root sentence'.[5] In the Trondheim Model the typical IU is also equal to a sentence, (an 'S''''); see for example Nilsen (1989: 26, 1992: 33). The IP of the Trondheim Model is therefore a constituent placed one level down in the hierarchy compared to its namesake in the syntax-based models. Comparing the levels mechanically, this should make it equal to the Phonological Phrase of Nespor and Vogel. But the fact that the IP of the Trondheim Model is delimited by the focal Hfoc%, from which FOCUS is transferred to the syntactic representation of a given utterance, while the Phonological Phrase in the frameworks of Nespor and Vogel (1986) and Selkirk (1986) is defined purely in syntactic terms, makes the two constituent types non-compatible. In addition, such a coupling between PPs in the syntax-based models and IPs in the Trondheim Model would lead to a situation where the next level down in the Trondheim Model, the Accent Phrase, would be equal with the PWd in the syntax-based models.[6] Since the Accent Phrase may contain more than one PWd as defined above, APs cannot be seen as equal to PWds. But the PWds in the two frameworks bear a strong resemblance to each other, since both are derived from morphological words. Coupling the levels upwards from the PWd will equal the PP of the syntax-based models with the AP of the Trondheim Model, and the IP of both models with each other.

---

    [5] Given its greater reliance on semantics, the IP as delimited in Selkirk (1984: 286) is more difficult to relate unambiguously to a given level in the TM hierarchy.
    [6] For the moment, I disregard the Clitic Group as a possible constituent type of its own in both models.

In order to obtain a symmetric relationship, we therefore need an extra level in the syntax-based model to match the IP of the Trondheim Model. Such an extra level, which matches the IP of the Trondheim model as a domain limited by focus, is the Focal Phrase proposed in Kanerva (1990), which like the IP of the Trondheim Model is a phrase type that is dependent on pragmatics.[7] If the syntax-based model is enriched as proposed by Kanerva, we obtain the relationship between the two models shown in (5).

(5)   *Syntax-based*   *Intonation-based*
      (Nespor and Vogel)   *(Trondheim Model)*
      Intonational Phrase   *equals*   Intonational Utterance
      Focal Phrase (Kanerva 1990) *equals*   Intonational Phrase
      Phonological Phrase   *equals*   Accent Phrase
      Prosodic Word   *equals*   Prosodic Word

The difference between the two models can now be reduced to one important aspect: the delimitation of boundaries. In the syntax-based model, all boundaries between prosodic constituents coincide with syntactic boundaries, while this is not necessarily the case in the intonation-based model, where all boundaries must coincide with stressed syllables. If both hierarchies are seen as possible candidates for constraining postlexical segmental rules, they therefore render different predictions with respect to the exact domains for these rules. Since the boundaries between the domains in many cases will fall within words in the intonation-based model, postlexical rules that apply between domains, that is, the domain juncture and the domain limit rules referred to in Section 11.2.1 above will not always apply at syntactic boundaries. Given the metrical foundation of the constituency, domain juncture rules will in addition apply only at boundaries between an unstressed syllable followed by a stressed one. This would make them difficult to distinguish from metrically conditioned rules.

A third alternative is also possible, where constituents defined by intonational structure are restructured so that they respect syntactic constituency. This would imply that the Focal Phrase is retained, but unstressed syllables not belonging to the syntactic phrase which contains the FP-head, will be incorporated into the following constituent. Algorithmically, this can be obtained by applying the rules of FOCUS projection of the Trondheim model: see Chapter 10.3.3 and (11) below.

Summing up, this leaves us with three possible models of postlexical prosodic constituency, as summarized in (6).

(6)   (a) Prosodic constituency is derived by rules that refer to syntactic structure only.

      (b) Prosodic constituency is defined by phonological structure (prominence relations as instantiated through tonal structure and syllable quantity) and pragmatics (prominence reduction and assignment of [±focal]).

      (c) Prosodic constituency is defined by phonological structure as in (b), but restructured by rules mapping focus structure onto synctactic structure.

---

[7] See also Cho (1990) and Condoravdi (1990).

As mentioned, these alternatives embody different hypotheses as to at which points in the phonological string we would expect to find edge effects conditioned by domain juncture and domain limit rules. To show this more clearly, we may construe a simple syntactic marker as the one shown as (7).

(7) *Syntactic phrase marker*

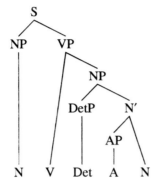

Assume that the words inserted under the lexical categories A, V and N have received stress in the lexicon, while simple determiners such as articles are unstressed. Any sentence with this structure will therefore normally have four stressed (and accented) syllables after lexical insertion. Let us for the sake of simplicity assume that none of these are deaccented and/or destressed for pragmatic reasons.

Consider now the following example sentence, which has the syntactic structure of (7).

(8) [ˈpeː.ri.mi.ˈteː.rə.rɛn.ˈstuː.²rɑː.pə.ˌkɑt]
    Per imiterer en stor apekatt
    'Per imitates a big monkey'

Under alternative (6a) this sentence will receive the prosodic structure shown as (9a).[8] A sentence with more than one IP can be construed by inserting the parenthetical expression *Annes bror* 'Anne's brother' after the subject *Per*, as shown in (9b).

(9)   (a) [[[Per]$_\omega$]$_\phi$ [[imiterer]$_\omega$]$_\phi$ [[en-stor]$_\omega$ [apekatt]$_\omega$]$_\phi$]$_{IP}$]$_U$

     (b) [[[Per]$_\omega$]$_\phi$]$_{IP}$
           [[[Annes]$_\omega$[bror]$_\omega$]$_\phi$]$_{IP}$
           [[[imiterer]$_\omega$]$_f$ [[en-stor]$_\omega$[apekatt]$_w$]$_\phi$]$_{IP}$]$_U$

Within the Trondheim Model, alternative (6b), several constituent structures are possible, depending on how focus is assigned to the sentence. Let us assume that

---

[8] φ denotes phonological phrases. I assume that the determiner will be analysed as a proclitic with respect to the adjective.

the subject and the object noun are focused in the sentence corresponding to (9a), and that *bror* is focused in the separate, nested IU in the sentence corresponding to (9b). This gives us the structures shown in (10).[9]

(10)　(a)　$[[[^1\text{PER-imi}]_{AP}]_{IP}[[^1\text{terer-en}]_{AP}[^1\text{stor}]_{AP}[[^2\text{APE}]_{PWd}[\text{katt}]_{PWd}]_{AP}]_{IP}]_{IU}$

　　　(b)　$[[[^1\text{PER}]_{AP}]_{IP}]_{IU}$
　　　　　$[[^2\text{annes}]_{AP}[[^1\text{BROR}]_{AP}]_{IP}]_{IU}$
　　　　　$[[\text{imi }[^1\text{terer-en}]_{AP}[^1\text{stor}]_{AP}[[^2\text{APE}]_{PWd}[\text{katt}]_{PWd}]_{AP}]_{IP}]_{IU}$

Constituencies in accordance with alternative (6c) can be derived from (10) by applying the rules of Focus Projection cited in Chapter 10.3.3. The simpler sentence will have two focus domains: the subject, since the accented syllable is located here, and the rest of the sentence, which I shall refer to as the VP. These will correspond to the Focal Phrase of Kanerva (1990). In the longer sentence, the parenthetical expression will consist of a Focal Phrase on its own. This gives the constituencies shown in (11).

(11)　(a)　$[[[^1\text{PER}]_{AP}]_{FP}[[\text{imi }^1\text{terer-en}]_{AP}[^1\text{stor}]_{AP}[[^2\text{APE}]_{PWd}[\text{katt}]_{PWd}]_{AP}]_{FP}]_{IU}$

　　　(b)　$[[[^1\text{PER}]_{AP}]_{FP}]_{IU}$
　　　　　$[[[^2\text{annes}]_{AP}[[^1\text{BROR}]_{AP}]_{FP}]_{IU}$
　　　　　$[[[\text{imi }^1\text{terer-en}]_{AP}[^1\text{stor}]_{AP}[[^2\text{APE}]_{PWd}[\text{katt}]_{PWd}]_{AP}]_{FP}]_{IU}$

As can be seen from these examples, the alternatives listed in (6) delimit the prosodic constituents differently. At the U/IU level, the structures are identical. On the next level down, the FPs in (11) are derived by projecting the [+focal] of the IPs of the intonational structure onto the syntax.[10] The IP-boundary which splits the verb *imiterer* is thereby made to coincide with the syntactic boundary between the subject and the verb. In all other respects, the constituents are the same. Going down to the PP/AP level, we find further discrepancies. In the syntax-derived constituency in (9a), three PPs are derived, corresponding to subject-NP, verb and object-NP. The parenthetical NP in (9b) adds a fourth PP. In the phonology-derived constituency in (10), the adjectives constitute APs of their own. In addition to the AP-boundary splitting the verb in the a-version, which corresponds to the PP boundary between the subject and the verb in the syntax-derived constituency, we therefore get boundaries between attributive adjectives and their head nouns which are not derived in the syntax-based model.

In the sections to follow, we shall explore to what extent different post-lexical rules can be seen as being constrained by the domains and boundaries derived by the alternatives stated in (6). To my knowledge, there exist no prior investigations bearing on this question. The conclusions reached will therefore be tentative. To the extent that postlexical rules are automatic and therefore beyond conscious control, a reliability problem is added that can only be solved by under-

---

[9] PWd-boundaries have not been inserted where they coincide with AP-boundaries.
[10] Recall that this level is lacking in the Nespor and Vogel hierarchy.

taking an analysis of a considerable amount of representative recorded speech.

11.3 POSTLEXICAL CORONAL PHONOLOGY

In this section we shall discuss the fate of word-final /r/ in different environments. The first is in front of a vowel, where /r/ will resyllabify and join the vowel as an onset across the syntactic boundary (Section 11.3.1). The next is in front of a non-coronal consonant, where it may delete, subject to a set of additional constraints (Section 11.3.2), and the third is in front of alveolar consonants, where the Retroflex Rule will apply (Section 11.3.3).

11.3.1　Resyllabification of /r/

In Chapter 7.3.2 it was claimed that the domain of continuous syllabification cannot be delimited to the PWd, as has been claimed for other Germanic languages such as English and Dutch. The evidence referred to is the fact that stem-final /r/ will obligatorily syllabify as onset across an internal compound boundary when the second member starts with a vowel, as for example in [²ʋæː.rɔm.ˌʂlɑːg], *vær-omslag* 'change of weather', composed of *vær* 'weather' and *omslag* 'change'.[11]

The evidence that speaks in favour of resyllabification in this example is that if the second compound member is consonant-initial, the /r/ may delete if a set of additional requirements is met, which will be discussed in the next section. Resyllabification explains why /r/ can never be deleted when the following constituent is vowel-initial.

/r/-resyllabification extends into the postlexical phonology, as can be seen from the examples used in the preceding section, repeated here as (12).

(12)　(a) *Per imiterer en stor apekatt*
　　　　　'Per imitates a big monkey'

　　　(b) *Per, Annes bror, imiterer en stor apekatt*
　　　　　'Per, Anne's brother, imitates a big monkey'

In (12a) the environment for the rule is satisfied between the subject and the verb, the verb and the indefinite article *en*, and between the adjective and the following noun. In (12b) the subject and the verb are split by a parenthetical NP. The environment is satisfied across both the left and the right boundary of the parenthetical. The normal pronunciations of the two utterances are given in (13).

---

[11] Resyllabification between PWds is not general, however, and seems to be limited to obligatory application of Onset Formation (Chapter 5.3.3) across boundaries preceded by a consonant and followed by a vowel. One clear case where resyllabification does not take place, is sequences of /s/ after long vowel combined with a voiceless stop across a compound or word boundary. Resyllabification of /s/ would cause the stop to deaspirate, but this does not take place. An example is [²løːs.ˌtʰɛn.nr̩], *løstenner* 'false teeth', composed of *løs* 'loose' and *tenner* 'teeth'.

(13)   (a)   [¹peː.ɾi.mi.¹teː.ɾə.ɾɛn.¹stuː.²ɾɑː.pə.ˌkɑt]

       (b)   [¹peːr | ²ʔɑn.nəs.¹bruːr | ʔi.mi.¹teː.ɾə.ɾɛn.¹stuː.²ɾɑː.pə.ˌkɑt]

We see that resyllabification does not take place across the IP boundaries in (13b), but in all other environments.[12] The rule therefore appears to be a domain span rule bounded by the Intonational Phrase. Boundaries between lower constituents do not block the rule. It applies across the syntactic FP boundary between the subject and the verb, as in (11a). It applies across the PP-boundary between the verb and the article, as in (9a), as well as across the AP-boundary between the adjective and the noun in the object NP, as in (10a). The latter sequence also represents a concatenation of two PWds within both frameworks. Given the fact that IP-boundaries are the same in the three alternative approaches to prosodic constituency in (6), the rule does not allow us to evaluate them against each other. The rule is stated in (14).

(14)   *Resyllabification of /r/*

       Rule type: Domain span
       Domain: Intonational Phrase

11.3.2 /r/-deletion

The fact that motivates the resyllabification rule discussed in the preceding section, is that /r/ will often delete when the segment following /r/ is a non-coronal consonant; see again the discussion in Chapter 7.3.2. This deletion rule, which is discussed in Rykkvin (1946) and Haugen (1948), applies between words in the syntax as well. It is optional, and according to Haugen (1948), subject to sociolinguistic constraints such as rate of speech and the social background of the speaker. In addition there is an intricate set of structural constraints that must be met for the rule to apply. Haugen (1948) sorts out these constraints by identifying three subrules. In all of them stress plays a decisive role. The precise meaning of 'stress' as used by Haugen in this connection will be further discussed below. We shall first look at the three subrules.

---

[12]   In order to simplify the discussion, I shall from now on refer to the highest level of the hierarchy in (5) by means of the term *Intonational Phrase (IP)*, in accordance with the terminology of Nespor and Vogel and Selkirk. This is the Intonational Utterance (IU) of the Trondheim Model. The next level down, the Intonational Phrase in the Trondheim Model, will generally be called the *Focal Phrase (FP)*, in accordance with Kanerva (1990). The FP delimited by syntax of alternative (6c) will be referred to as a syntactic FP, while the prosody-based FP (=IP) of the Trondheim Model will be referred to as an intonational FP. *Phonological Phrase (PP)* will exclusively refer to analyses couched in the syntax-based framework, while *Accent Phrase (AP)* will refer to analyses based on the Trondheim Model.

(I) In the four auxiliary verbs *blir* 'becomes', *er* 'is', *var* 'was' and *har* 'has', /r/ is deleted before non-coronal consonants as well as before vowels when they are pronounced without stress. /r/ must nevertheless be underlying, for two reasons. The first is that /r/ is pronounced before vowels and non-coronal consonants when the same words receive stress, and the second is that when they are combined with a word beginning with a coronal, the Retroflex Rule applies whether the verbs are stressed or not. Since the Retroflex Rule requires /r/ (or a retroflex flap) in the input, its application in this environment can only be explained if an underlying /r/ is assumed.

The following examples show this distribution, where the frame *Det blir* __ *kroner* 'That will be __ kroner' is used with the numerals *to* 'two', *fem* 'five' and *åtte* 'eight' inserted to provide the three relevant environments.

(15)

	Unstressed	*Stressed*
Before coronal consonants	[də.bli.¹ʈuː.²kruː.nɾ]	[də.¹bliː.¹ʈuː.²kruː.nɾ]
Before non-coronal consonants	[də.bli.¹fɛm.²kruː.nɾ]	[də.¹bliːɾ.¹fɛm.²kruː.nɾ]
Before vowels	[də.bli.²ɔt.tə.²kruː.nɾ]	[də.¹bliːɾ²ɔt.tə.²kruː.nɾ]

(II) In other environments where /r/ occurs in unstressed syllables, deletion only takes place before non-coronal consonants, while resyllabification takes place before vowels and the Retroflex Rule applies before coronal consonants. Before /h/ we find variation, presumably due to the fact that /h/ may be deleted word-initially when a word is weakly stressed. /r/ may belong to monosyllabic words that frequently occur without stress, such as prepositions (*for* (id.)), adverbials (*her* 'here', *der* 'there'). Such words *may* occur with stress, however, in which case the rule does not apply. /r/ may also occur in inherently stressless syllables, such as in different inflectional endings. Some examples are given in (16).

(16)   *Monosyllabic words*

[fɔ.²ral.lə] *for alle* 'for everybody'
[fɔ.²maŋ.ŋə] *for mange* 'for many'
[fɔ.²n̩uː.un] *for noen* 'for some'

[hæ.²ran.nə.sn̩] *herr Andersen* 'Mr. Andersen'
[hæ.¹kris.tn̩.sn̩] *herr Kristensen* 'Mr. Kristensen'
[hæ.²tɛl.lɛf.sn̩] *herr Tellefsen* 'Mr. Tellefsen'

Inherently stressless syllables

[də.²gleː.də.²ral.lə] *Det gleder alle* 'It pleases everybody'
[də.²gleː.də.²maŋ.ŋə] *Det gleder mange* 'It pleases many'
[də.²gleː.də.²n̩uː.un] *Det gleder noen* 'It pleases some'

(III) /r/ may also delete before a non-coronal consonant when it belongs to a stressed syllable. In this case two conditions must be met according to Haugen: /r/

must represent an inflectional ending,[13] and the two words involved must not both have 'maximal stress'.[14] These constraints are illustrated in the examples in (17), all of them except (a), (d) and (e) taken from Haugen. The relevant environments are established by means of the present tense *bor* of *bo*, 'to live at, reside' contrasted with the homophonous simplex form *bord* 'table'. Narrow focus, a focused constituent that does not extend to the end of the sentence, is signalled by the head syllable of the focused AP being printed in boldface.

(17) (a) [hɑm.¹buː.²rʉː.tə] *Han bor ute* 'He lives abroad'

    (b) [hɑm.¹buː.²jɛm.mə] *Han bor hjemme* 'He lives at home'

    (c) [hɑm.¹buːr.²jɛm.mə] *Han bor hjemme* 'He lives at home'

    (d) [hɑm.¹buː.¹ʈrɑŋt] *Han bor trangt* 'He lives in cramped quarters'

    (e) [hɑm.¹buː.¹ʈrɑŋt] *Han bor trangt* 'He lives in cramped quarters'

    (f) [hɑm.¹buː.pɔ.hu.¹tɛl.lə] *Han bor på hotellet* 'He lives at the hotel'

    (g) [hɑn.ˌjuː.rə.¹reː.nt.¹buːr.pɔ.hu.¹tɛl.lə] *Han gjorde rent bord på hotellet* 'He won everything (lit. 'made a clean table') at the hotel'

The examples used in the text suggest that Haugen by 'maximal stress' refers to what was termed focus in Chapter 10.3. On this assumption, /r/-deletion is blocked between two primary stressed syllables divided by an FP-boundary. Since primary stress is signalled on the leftmost syllable of an AP, and focus on the final, the first FP must be monosyllabic for such a state of affairs to obtain. If we compare example (c) with (f) we see that this is the case in (c), while it is not the case in (f), since an unstressed syllable intervenes between the two stresses.

Note that the relevant FP-type is the *intonational* FP. If we map focus onto the syntax in (17c and f), the verb would in both cases emerge with narrow focus, rendering the focus structure of the two examples identical, with an FP-boundary between the verb and the following word. I therefore conclude that the data support alternative (6b) above, i.e. that the postlexical sandhi rule in this case is con-

[13] The restriction that /r/ must represent an inflectional ending ought to block the rule from applying in compounds with a monosyllabic first member. Haugen notes this constraint explicitly, using *bordkant* 'table edge' as one example where /r/ cannot be deleted. But this should then also apply to an example that was discussed in Chapter 7.3.2, viz. *værmelding*. If Haugen's rules were exhaustive, deletion should not be possible here. Haugen himself points out that the phenomenon appears to embody the seed of a sound law which eventually may establish itself as a parallel to the linking *r* in some British and American dialects. If we are indeed dealing with an ongoing change, it would not be surprising if the rule has expanded to environments where it was blocked 50 years ago, when Haugen wrote his article. It can in fact be argued that *værmelding* represents an environment that would constitute a 'natural' expansion of the rule. This is due to the fact that [æː] almost only occurs before /r/ and /ʈ/, where it can be interpreted as an allophone of /e/; see Chapter 4.4. The underlying /r/ is therefore indirectly present in the signal, even if the segment itself is deleted. The same is not true for example of *bordkant*, where /r/ does not have any impact on the quality of the preceding vowel. Lacking a larger body of systematically sampled data, this observation must remain speculative, however. In the discussion that follows, we shall restrict ourselves to the environments discussed by Haugen.

[14] Haugen uses the expression 'full styrke', which literally means 'full strength' and which can be related to the Norwegian linguistic term *trykksterk*, lit. 'stress-strong', which simply means 'stressed'.

strained by the same prosodic hierarchy that defines the intonational structure.[15]

/r/-deletion also represents a challenge to the fundamental division between a lexical and a postlexical module of standard Lexical Phonology. It is clearly postlexical, and under the standard view all lexical information should therefore be unavailable when it applies. All the same it has lexical exceptions, viz. the auxiliary verbs mentioned under (I). Positing a separate rule for these words would result in a postlexical rule that applies to a list of specific *inflected* forms. The rule would therefore need access not only to lexical items per se, but to their morphological structure, for instance that /ʋar/ is past tense of *være* 'to be'. The same type of access to morphological structure is needed in order to identify the environment outlined in (III). The rule must know that the final segment in /bur/ represents an inflectional suffix in order to apply. If all morphological brackets are erased at the point where a given word enters the syntax, this information is not available at the point where the rule applies.

/r/-deletion therefore supports the contention that the division between the lexical and the postlexical module cannot be drawn as neatly as envisaged in the early versions of Lexical Phonology: see the discussion in Hargus and Kaisse (1993b). The rule, with its clear connections with lexical structure, rather appears as a P1 rule as defined in Kaisse (1990). One of the characteristics of P1 rules, however, is that they are supposed to be insensitive to intonational phrasing. This is not the case here; Haugen's data suggest that the environment where deletion is blocked in a stressed syllable is before a Focal Phrase boundary. Syntactic constituency seems irrelevant.

The rule can now be stated as in (18).[16]

(18) */r/-deletion*

    Rule type: Domain span
    Domain: Focal Phrase

    Condition: if σ_i bears stress, /r/ belongs to a suffix

As it stands, this rule will delete /r/ before any onset segment, including coronals. However, our featural theory does not allow us to define the set of non-coronals, except disjunctively, so the restriction that the rule only applies to non-coronals is

---

[15] Some speakers of UEN that I have consulted claim that (17f) as well requires that /r/ be realized. If that is the case today, the scale tips in favour of the syntactic FP. Judgements tend to be rather insecure, however, so a corpus-based investigation is clearly called for.

[16] I assume that a separate rule must be stated with respect to the auxiliaries, given the different environments involved.

difficult to state as part of the rule in a simple way. This might seem an argument against the constriction-based theory discussed in Chapter 2.2, which by employing monovalent place features blocks negatively-defined classes such as non-coronals and non-labials. But this putative counterevidence founders on the fact that /r/ is 'deleted' in front of coronals as well, by the Retroflex Rule. We can in other words establish a relationship between the two rules, where /r/-deletion will function as the least specific elsewhere case which applies after the Retroflex Rule. See Kiparsky (1973) for a discussion of the 'elsewhere' concept in phonology.

11.3.3 The Retroflex Rule

In Chapter 4.3.6 it was argued that the Retroflex Rule should be seen as consisting of two subrules, [ap]-spreading and Rhotic Delinking. In this section we shall see that both rules apply at the postlexical level as well, but with slightly different properties. At this level we find evidence that we are indeed dealing with two independent rules. Another postlexical property of the RR is that across PWd and higher order prosodic boundaries, [ap]-spreading remains obligatory from /r/, while it is optional from /ɽ/.

We first turn to the relationship between [ap]-spreading and Rhotic Delinking. In the lexicon, the doubly associated apicals that trigger delinking are all created by spreading of [ap] from an underlying [apical], /r/ or /ɽ/, onto a non-apical coronal. This fact has led earlier analysts to posit one rule. An alternative way that such doubly linked apical structures may arise is through juxtaposition of two underlying apicals across a boundary, with subsequent merger on the [ap]-tier. The occurrence of apicals in morpheme-initial position is severely restricted, however, only /ʂ/ is allowed in underlying forms in this position. In addition, apical /l/ will occur as a free allophone morpheme-initially, as discussed in Chapter 2.1.2.4. Examples involving the sibilant will be used in the discussion, but the conclusions will extend to cases involving apical /l/.

When a word ending in /r/ is combined with one beginning with /ʂ/, the latter is already specified as [ap], and spreading will be blocked. /r/ is all the same deleted, so that sequences of /r#s/ and /r#ʂ/ have identical realizations. This can be seen from the examples given as (19).

(19)　stuːr # ʂek > [¹stuː.¹ʂɛk] *stor sjekk* 'big check'
　　　stuːr # sek > [¹stuː.¹ʂɛk] *stor sekk* 'big sack'

These examples show that Rhotic Delinking takes place also when the following segment is underlyingly specified as [ap]. Since [ap]-spreading does not feed delinking in this case, this constitutes an argument that [ap]-spreading and Rhotic Delinking are independent rules. But in order for delinking to apply, the two segments must merge with respect to the [ap] tier. This can be seen as a typical OCP-effect: adjacent, identical specifications on a given featural tier will merge. This is stated formally in (20).

(20)   [ap]-merger

Cor Cor   Cor Cor
 | | ⇒   \ /
[ap] [ap]   [ap]

If the first segment in the output of (20) satisfies its structural description, Rhotic Delinking will apply. Since the input will be identical with that created by [ap]-spreading onto /s/, the outputs will be identical, as shown in (19).[17]

Another property of the RR that is most prevalent at the postlexical level, but which in fact is a property that is restricted to boundaries from the PWd-level and upwards, is its optionality in flap-clusters. Examples of this across PWd-boundaries in compounds have already been discussed in Chapter 4: the compound section in (22) in Chapter 4.3.6, reproduced here as (21). While we see that the RR is obligatory in r-clusters, alternative surface structures are possible when the first compound member ends in a flap. In addition to the alternation between lateral and flap, caused by the optionality of [post]-linking, as in Chapter 4.3.3, [ap]-spreading appears to be optional from the latter, so that three different pronunciations are possible. This means that the RR is obligatory only *within* prosodic words, irrespective of whether the first member of the cluster is /r/ or /ɽ/.[18]

(21)   *The Retroflex Rule in compounds*

Input	Surface of stem in isolation	Output of RR
/ʋor-tejn/	[¹ʋoːɾ]	[²ʋoː.ˌʈæjn] *vårtegn* 'spring sign'
/ʋor-dag/		[²ʋoː.ˌɖɑːg] *vårdag* 'spring day'
/ʋor-sul/		[²ʋoː.ˌʂuːl̩] *vårsol* 'spring sun'
/ʋor-luft/		[²ʋoː.ˌʟuft] *vårluft* 'spring air'
/ʋor-nat/		[²ʋoː.ˌɳɑt] *vårnatt* 'spring night'
/sul-dag/	[¹suːɽ]/[suːl]	[²suːl.ˌdɑːg] [²suːɽ.ˌdɑːg] [²suː.ˌɖɑːg] *soldag* 'sun(ny) day'
/sul-ʂin/		[²suːl.ˌʂin] [²suːɽ.ˌʂin] [²suː.ˌʂin] *solskinn* 'sunshine'

---

[17] Two problematic cases should be mentioned: combination of flap and lateral and combination of flap and /r/. In the first case, the rule predicts an apical lateral as output, so that e.g. *sollys* 'sunlight' should be pronounced [²suːˌʟyːs], which would be the same as the output of a sequence of two apical laterals, which would merge. When asked, however, native speakers tend to report, in addition to unassimilated cluster, a flap-only pronunciation, that is [²suːˌɽyːs], some even explicitly rejecting [²suːˌʟyːs] as a possible pronunciation if the input contains a flap. The other case is combination of flap and /r/, as in *gulrot* 'carrot' (lit. 'yellow root'). An unassimilated output is perhaps the most common in UEN, but if assimilation takes place, the rules here also predict merger of [ap] and subsequent deletion of the flap, so that the expected outcome would be [²gʉːˌruːt]. This pronunciation is attested, at least for some rural dialects. But we may also find [²gʉːˌɻuːt] (Eric Papazian, p.c.). The two cases held together suggest that when liquids are combined with a flap, the Coronal node itself may spread from the flap, turning /l/ into a flap, and /r/ into a retroflex approximant.

[18] An example of a postlexical PWd where [ap]-spreading has taken place from a flap onto a clitic is the final example in the clitic section of (22) in Chapter 4, [¹stjæːɳ], from /stjel#n/, 'steal it!'.

This difference between r-initial and flap-initial clusters is a pervasive feature of the postlexical application of the RR. While application with respect to flap-initial clusters is heavily constrained by sociolinguistic factors, the use of the RR in r-initial clusters seems to be beyond speakers' active control. This difference can be related to the fact that /r/ is a phoneme, while the flap has semi-allophonic status with a certain degree of sociolinguistic stigma attached.[19]

Let us now examine to what extent the RR is constrained by higher order postlexical constituency by submitting it to the same test as the one we used for r-deletion above, by inserting appropriate lexical items in the syntactic structure given as (7) above. In sentence (22a) we see that the RR applies between the subject and the verb, and between the adjective and the noun in the object NP. If we replace the article with the indef. pl. quantifier *noen* 'some', we get [ˈseː.ɳun.²stuː.rə.²løː.ʋɽ], which shows that the rule applies between the verb and an initial determiner of the following NP as well.

(22)   (a)   *Per ser en stor løve*
             'Per sees a big lion'
             [ˈpeː.ʂeː.ɾɛn.ˈstuː.²løː.ʋə]

       (b)   *Per, Siris bror, ser en stor løve*
             'Per, Siri's brother, sees a big lion'
             [ˈpeːr. | ²siː.ris.ˈbruːr | ˈseː.ɾɛn.ˈstuː.²løː.ʋə]
             ??[ˈpeː. | ²ʂiː.ris.ˈbruː | ˈʂeː.ɾɛn.ˈstuː.²løː.ʋə]

(22b) shows that application of the RR does not seem well-formed across IP-bound-aries. But no matter how the focus structure in (22a) is construed, the rule will ap-ply across the resulting FP-boundaries. The RR in its postlexical version, at least when the triggering rhotic is /r/, can therefore be identified as a domain-span rule whose domain is the IP. In this respect it is parallel with Resyllabification of r.

11.3.4 [ap]-spreading from non-rhotic apicals

In footnote 46 in Chapter 4 it was mentioned that a possible motivation for con-struing the Retroflex Rule as consisting of two independent rules is that the feature [apical] may spread from other segment types than /r/ and a flap without concomi-tant deletion of the segment from which the feature spreads. The example given was the def. sg. of *bart* 'moustache' /baʈ-n/, where the apicality of the stem-final stop spreads onto the nasal suffix, giving [ˈbaʈ.ʈn̩]. There are, however, two argu-ments against collapsing this process with [ap]-spreading as part of the RR. The first is lack of iterativity. If a coronal segment following an apical is turned into a segment phonologically specified as apical, we would expect it to trigger [ap]-spreading itself if followed by yet another coronal. The second argument can

---

[19] Although this would need further investigation, it seems that the stigma is greater on forms where the RR has applied, such as [²suː.ʂin], than on forms with a realized flap, such as [ˈsuːɽ.ʂin].

be based on the fact that in some cases the result of spreading is not identical with the apicals produced by the RR.

Let us first turn to the lack of iterativity. This can be shown by means of patronymic-formation, which is done by means of the suffix /-sn/, written *-sen*.[20] If the stem ends in /r/, the RR will apply, as for example in /per-sn/, *Persen*, which is realized as ['peː.ʂn̩], and where we see that [ap] has spread onto the final nasal. If the stem ends in a single, non-rhotic apical, as in ['jæt̪], *Gjert*, the initial segment of the suffix will be realized at least partly as apical, but not the nasal. Therefore ['jæt̪.ʂn̩] is possible, while *['jæt̪.ʂn̩] is not well-formed. If the *stem* ends in a doubly linked apical, as for instance in [²mɔt̪.t̪n̩], *Morten*, where the apicality of the final segment can be seen as the result of spreading from the previous, underlying apical in underlying /mot̪n/, further spreading is blocked. Hence [²mɔt̪.t̪n̩.sn̩] is the correct output, neither *[²mɔt̪.t̪n̩.ʂn̩] nor *[mɔt̪.t̪n̩.ʂn̩] is grammatical.

The second argument relates to the fact that assimilation does not always result in neutralization between products of the RR and those of spreading from non-rhotic apicals. We would expect this to be the case if the spreading that is part of the RR is the same rule as the latter. In order to show that there is indeed a difference, we must first establish that the output of the RR applied to sequences of /r#s/ is identical with the realization of /ʂ/. This has already been shown in (19) above. In isolation, *sjekk* is pronounced ['ʂɛk] and *sekk* ['sɛk]. When combined with a word which ends in /r/, such as the adjective *stor*, the output is ['stuː.'ʂɛk] in both cases. In *stor sjekk*, the [ap]-specifications of the two segments merge, triggering Rhotic Delinking. In *stor sekk*, [ap] has spread from /r/, followed by Rhotic Delinking.

If [ap]-spreading from non-rhotic apicals is the same rule as the one being part of the RR, we would expect the same type of neutralization between the phrases *kort sjekk* 'short check' and *kort sekk* 'short sack'. Here the final segment of the adjective /kot̪/, *kort* 'short' is an underlying non-rhotic apical. With respect to *kort sjekk*, the apicality of the segments on each side of the word boundary will merge, but no delinking can take place, since the first is neither /r/ nor /ɽ/. If spreading of [ap] onto the initial /s/ of *sekk* were complete, we would expect *kort sekk* to have the same surface form as *kort sjekk*. But this is normally not the case. While there appears to be a fair amount of variability involved, there will normally be some degree of apicality involved in the pronunciation of the /s/ in *sekk*. But full neutralization is very marked, if possible at all.

The analysis should incorporate this difference. While the output of the RR is categorical and obligatory, the output of [ap]-spreading from non-rhotic apicals seems to be gradient and variable. This suggests that the latter should be seen as a phonetic implementation rule in the sense of for example Keating (1996). A characteristic property of this rule type is that the result may be gradient. Closer inspection involving physical measurement of the phonetic properties of outputs of the rule is needed before this conclusion can be established as reasonably secure, but this bipartition of [ap]-spreading into a phonological one, applying to /r/ and /ɽ/,

---

[20] The preceding obstruent will cause the nasal to surface as syllabic; cf. Chapter 5.3.2.

and a phonetic one applying to all apicals followed by a non-apical coronal, seems to capture the differences outlined above in a simple and promising way: the reason why the rule is non-iterative can be related to its non-categorical status—assimilation is not complete.

11.4 NASAL PLACE ASSIMILATION

In this section we shall discuss the process by which a nasal may acquire the Place specifications of a following consonant. This process can be seen to work at two levels, between Place nodes, and within each of these. We shall begin the discussion by looking at the constraints that hold in clusters where the segments have different Place nodes. In Section 11.4.2 we shall look at cases where assimilation takes place within the same Place node. The rule will be referred to as Nasal Place Assimilation (NPA).

11.4.1 Assimilation between Place nodes

In Chapter 3.2.4.1 it was noted that in roots a nasal must agree in place of articulation with a following obstruent if the latter is non-coronal: see the data in (23).[21]

(23)   [¹kɑmp] *kamp* 'battle'   [²kʉn.də] *kunde* 'customer'
       [¹tɛm.pu] *tempo* (id.)   [¹taŋk] *tank* (id.)
       [²ɾum.bə] *rombe* 'rhombus'   [²taŋ.kə] *tanke* 'thought'
       [¹kɑnt] *kant* 'edge'   [¹taŋ.gu] *tango* (id.)
       [²tɑn.tə] *tante* 'aunt'

Before *coronal* obstruents, labial and dorsal nasals occur, however, such as [¹tɔmt], *tomt* 'building ground', [¹gɾums], *grums* 'dregs', [¹puŋt], *punkt* 'point'[22] and [¹diŋs], *dings* 'thing' (coll.). The restriction therefore applies before labial and dorsal segments only.

The constraint seems further to be limited to following stops. The only non-coronal fricative that can be preceded by a nasal is /f/, since /ç/ is phonotactically restricted to stressed onsets. Here we find both labial and coronal nasals, cf. [¹kɑɱ.fɾ], *kamfer* 'camphor' and [¹tɾuɱf], *trumf* 'trump' vs. [in.¹fæː.n̩u], *inferno* (id.) and the obsolete place name *Genf* 'Geneva' and its derived adjectival prefix *genfer-*, which may still be used in the name *Genfersjøen* 'Lake Geneva'.[23]

The establishment of the exact scope of the constraint with respect to what kind of segment the nasal may assimilate to is further complicated by the fact that se-

---

[21] Recall that the Postvocalic *Shared Place Constraint stated in Chapter 3.2.4.1 blocks combinations of nasals and *voiced* obstruents word-finally.

[22] This word may also be pronounced [¹puŋkt]. Clear cases of monomorphemic [ŋt] are hard to find.

[23] Geneva is currently referred to as [ʂɛ.¹neːʋ]. All examples of nasal before /f/ are found in loan words, whether spelled with *m* or *n*.

quences of monomorphemic /n/ + non-coronal sonorants are rare as well. There are no /nm/, /nŋ/. Nor are there clear examples of /nv/ clusters, but if words beginning with Latinate /kon-/ are counted as roots, there are examples such as *konveks* 'convex'. Here we find the same pattern as before /f/: both a coronal and a labiodental nasal are possible. Before /j/, however, only [n] may occur, as in [²lin.jə], *linje* 'line' and [²mœn.jə], *mønje* 'minium'. Here, the nasal cannot assimilate, *[²mœɲ.jə] is impossible.

The conclusion that can be drawn from monomorphemic data is therefore that agreement in place features is obligatory before non-coronal stops, and optional before non-coronal fricatives (= /f/), while the data on sonorants are too limited to allow any clear inferences, except that the Place agreement constraint does not hold before /j/. The basic pattern is that clusters of coronal nasal + a non-nasal, non-coronal stop must agree with respect to Place features. This holds without exceptions in non-derived environments. In order to see whether it holds in general, we now turn to derived environments.

No cohering suffix begins with a non-coronal stop. The only relevant example of a cohering element is the negative clitic /-ke/, analysed in Section 11.6.4 below. This, however, requires a vowel or r-final host, with one exception: it may combine with the modals *kan* and *kunne*, giving obligatorily [¹kɑŋ.kə] and [²kʉŋ.kə]. Even if these forms are best analysed as lexicalized phrases, they still suggest that the constraint on nasal + stop sequences holds within PWds, in non-derived as well as derived environments.

Let us now proceed to compounds in order to test whether it applies *between* PWds. Examples are given in (24), where the compound boundary is marked by a hyphen inserted in the orthographic form. The data show, as we would expect, that only a coronal nasal may assimilate. The rule is not obligatory.

(24) (a) *Stems ending in /m/*
          [²liːm.ˌbɔn] *lim-bånd* 'adhesive tape' (lit. 'glue ribbon')
          [¹liːm.ˌtʉː.bə] *lim-tube* 'a tube of glue'
          [²liːm.ˌkruk.kə] *lim-krukke* 'a pot of glue'
          [²liːm.ˌfɑr.gə] *lim-farge* 'distemper (paint)'
          [¹stɑm.ˌvæj] *stam-vei* 'principal road'
          [¹stɑm.jɛst] *stam-gjest* 'regular guest'

      (b) *Stems ending in /ŋ/*
          [¹sɑŋ.ˌbuːk] *sang-bok* 'song book'
          [¹sɑŋ.ˌstɛm.mə] *sang-stemme* 'singing voice'
          [¹sɑŋ.ˌkuːr] *sang-kor* 'choir'
          [¹sɑŋ.ˌfʉːl] *sang-fugl* 'songbird'
          [¹sɑŋ.ˌvæːɭ.sə] *sang-værelse* 'song room'
          [²uŋ.jɛn.tə] *ung-jente* 'young girl'
          [²uŋ.ˌmœj] *ung-møy* 'young girl' (archaic)
          [²uŋ.ˌnæwt] *ung-naut* 'young cattle'

(c) *Stems ending in /n/*[24]

[²tɑm.ˌbœʂ.tə] / [²tɑn.ˌbœʂ.tə] *tann-børste* 'tooth brush'
[²tɑn.ˌtroː] *tann-tråd* 'dental floss'
[²tɑŋ.ˌkreːm] / [²tɑn.ˌkreːm] *tann-krem* 'tooth paste'
[²vɑŋ.ˌfɑr.gə] / [²vɑn.ˌfɑr.gə] *vann-farge* 'water-colour'
[²tɑm.ˌværk] / [²tɑn.ˌværk] *tann-verk* 'toothache'
[²vɑm.ˌmær.kə] / [²vɑn.ˌmær.kə] *vann-merke* 'watermark'
[²tɑn.ˌjʉːl] *tann-hjul* 'toothed wheel'
[²tɑn.ˌçœt] *tann-kjøtt* 'gum' (lit. 'tooth meat')

The rule also applies across word boundaries. This can be seen from (25), where only stems ending in a coronal nasal are included. The data are NPs consisting of the adjective *sunn* 'healthy, nutritious' combined with appropriate nouns.

(25) [¹sʉm.²pœl.sə] / [¹sʉn.²pœl.sə] *sunn pølse* 'healthy sausage'
[¹sʉn.¹sɑft] *sunn saft* 'healthy juice'
[¹sʉŋ.¹grøːt] / [¹sʉn.¹grøːt] *sunn grøt* 'healthy porridge'
[¹sʉɱ.¹frʉkt] / [¹sʉn.¹frʉkt] *sunn frukt* 'healthy fruit'
[¹sʉɱ.¹viːn] / [¹sʉn.¹viːn] *sunn vin* 'healthy wine'
[¹sʉm.¹mɑːt] / [¹sʉn.¹mɑːt] *sunn mat* 'healthy food'
[¹sʉn.¹jʉːs] *sunn jus* 'healthy juice'
[¹sʉn.¹çɛks] *sunn kjeks* 'healthy biscuit'

While all the forms given above can be seen as fairly uncontroversial, it is difficult to find evidence which throws more precise light on the applicability of assimilation. Speakers' intuitions, my own included, are not as firm as could be wished. Most naive speakers are unaware of the rule, and when confronted with assimilated forms they tend to react with scepticism, but will accept them as possible after some reflection. All that can be established, therefore, is that this is an optional process which is probably influenced by style and rate of speech, but probably not by dialect or social background.

Some examples are regularly mentioned in the sections on assimilation in the standard introductory books on Norwegian phonetics and phonology.[25] But the only attempt at a rule statement that I have come across is Vanvik (1979: 51). A translation of Vanvik's statement is given as (26), with examples omitted.[26]

(26) 1. A dental nasal turns into a bilabial immediately before a bilabial plosive or nasal.
2. A dental nasal turns into a velar immediately before a velar plosive.
3. Phonetically (subphonemically) a dental nasal is often turned into a labiodental before labiodentals.

---

[24] The order of the alternatives does not imply any ranking with respect to acceptability or probability of occurrence.
[25] E.g. Broch and Selmer (1961: 86), Sivertsen (1967: 109) and Jensen (1969: 75).
[26] The examples involve either a word or a compound boundary.

This rule says that assimilation may take place before any non-coronal consonant. But it may be the case that the acceptability of the output varies with environment. In Vanvik (1979) there is no discussion of conditions on applicability. Vanvik's statement in fact gives the impression that the two first subrules are obligatory, but in light of data given in his pronunciation dictionary, Vanvik (1985), this is certainly an oversight. But they suggest that the rule is more prone to apply in some environments than in others.

(27) shows in which environments Vanvik offers alternative pronunciations reflecting Nasal Place Assimilation. Three types of compound stems containing final /n/ are included, the non-cohering prefix /an-/, where a precise meaning cannot be identified, the adverbial *inn* 'in' and a category called Lex. comp., which includes a random selection of n-final stems which are either nouns or adjectives. Several stems have been included in this category because Vanvik does not list more than a few compounds for each stem. The numbers given in the table represent number of stems listed with one or the other alternative. '± ass' means that the stems in question are listed both with assimilated and unassimilated pronunciation, and '–ass' that only the unassimilated form is listed. '–' means that no relevant forms were found. Note that no item was found where assimilated pronunciation was the only possibility listed.

(27)   *Transcription of Nasal Place Assimilation in*
        Vanvik (1985)

	/an-/		/inn-/		Lex. comp.	
	±ass	–ass	±ass	–ass	±ass	–ass
k	2	–	5	–	–	2
g	2	–	6	–	–	3
p	1	–	–	4	–	2
b	1	2	–	11	1	5
f	–	3	–	16	–	5
v	–	2	–	9	–	2
m	–	4	–	4	–	2
j	–	2	–	4	–	1
ç	–	–	–	2	–	–

Disregarding for the moment the variation with respect to stem type, the environment where assimilation emerges as possible in the speech style mirrored in Vanvik (1985) is limited to oral stops.[27] This environment corresponds to that given in the two first parts of (26), except that no examples were found of assimilated /n-m/ clusters. Held together with (26) these data suggest that the probability of application of NPA can be scaled in accordance with the three subrules of (26). It is highest when a dorsal stop follows, lower before labial stops, even lower before labial continuants.

---

[27] Vanvik does not state how the forms given were established.

A question that may be addressed at this stage is whether these properties make NPA a P1 or a P2 rule according to the typology of Kaisse (1990); see the discussion above. Alternatively, it can be evaluated with respect to the distinction between phonological rules and rules of phonetic implementation of Keating (1996), where the phonological rules will correspond to P1 rules and phonetic implementation rules to P2 rules.

NPA seems to lack most of the properties associated with P1 rules, and would therefore seem to be a P2 rule, that is, a rule that may be associated with phonetic implementation more than with the categorical nature of phonological rules proper. Suspending for the moment the question whether it is sensitive to syntactic information, it is neutralizing only when applying before oral (and nasal) stops, since labiodental nasals are not part of the underlying set of segments. It does not seem to be rate-insensitive: the probability of application probably increases with rate. Neither does it have lexical exceptions, at least not in the sense that it is absolutely blocked in some stems.[28] Also speaking against its classification as a P1 rule is that it appears to be gradient (Christiansen (1946–8: 49). Gradience is one of the main features of phonetic implementation rules in the distinction between phonology and phonetics made in Keating (1996).

Another property of phonetic implementation rules according to Keating (1996) is that assimilatory effects may result from masking effects due to temporal articulatory ('gestural') overlap as analysed in a series of articles by Catherine P. Browman and Louis Goldstein: see for example Browman and Goldstein (1990). In principle it could be envisaged that NPA is a phonetic effect of such overlap, in the sense that articulatory anticipation of the place features of the following stop will mask any articulation of the stem-final coronal nasal.[29] But note that such masking by overlap seems possible only with respect to labials, since a coronal articulation can hardly by overlaid by a dorsal one such that the auditory effect will be dorsal. In other words, underlying /tan#krem/, 'toothpaste' can only be perceived as [²taŋ.ˌkreːm] if there is no complete coronal closure involved, while underlying /tan#pasta/, 'toothpaste', heard as [²tam.ˌpɑs.tɑ] may well involve simultaneous coronal and labial closures.[30]

Whether this is indeed the case with respect to NPA to labials cannot be given a definite answer in the absence of better speech data. But if overlap is used as a

---

[28] The fact that Vanvik only lists assimilated forms in some cases cannot be taken as proof of its having lexical exceptions. There may very well be different probabilities of application attached to the different environments listed above, but I very much doubt that specific lexical items can be identified where the rule is absolutely blocked.

[29] Cf. also Myers (1997: 125n), where it is explicitly assumed that postlexical nasal place assimilation in English, which closely corresponds to the process discussed here, results from gestural overlap.

[30] It should be noted that Browman and Goldstein (1990) seem to assume that dorsals may mask coronals acoustically by means of overlap (p. 365). They do not discuss examples where only coronals and dorsals interact, however, and in their only example where a velar is supposed to partially mask a coronal, /ktm/ in 'perfect memory', the X-ray data given show that the most marked difference between the unassimilated and assimilated version is the phasing of the labial closure with respect to the coronal and velar closures.

deciding criterion for the rule being a phonetic implementation rule, only clusters of nasal plus *labial* are potential environments for assimilatory effects created by masking, since in order for the nasal to be heard as dorsal before dorsal consonants, there cannot be a complete coronal closure involved. Masking in this sense is therefore not a viable analysis in this environment. The alternation before dorsal stops should therefore be analysed as spreading instead of masking.[31] This difference between labials and dorsals suggests two rules: a phonological P1 rule (?) applying before dorsals, and a phonetic or P2 rule applying before labials.

While this partitioning of NPA may seem speculative if based on the data in (26) and propensity for masking only, there are in fact additional arguments in favour of it. First, the fact that *all* labial consonants can participate in the rule, while only the dorsal stops and not the dorsal continuants can, now follows if the P1 rule applying in the dorsal environment is assumed to be neutralizing and structure-preserving. This is so because /ŋ/, which is the output if the following segments are /k, g/, is part of the underlying set of consonants. /ɲ/, which would be the output if the rule also applied before /ç, j/, is not, and the rule will therefore be blocked. On the other hand, if assimilation before labials is a P2 or phonetic implementation rule, structure preservation should be irrelevant, and we therefore derive labiodental nasals even if /ɱ/ is not part of the underlying alphabet.

Second, NPA may potentially interact with a rule to be discussed in more detail in Section 11.5 below, *Homorganic Trapping*, by which a stem-final, empty vowel, which in other environments surfaces as schwa, may be filled by spreading from the preceding consonant when the consonants preceding and following the vowel have identical Place features. The agreement marker /-e/ can be phonologically interpreted as an empty vowel. If we combine the adjectives /lam/, 'paralysed' and /laŋ/, 'tall', both inflected with /-e/, with definite forms of /gut/, 'boy' and /pike/, 'girl', the output in casual speech may be [dn̩.²laŋ.ŋ̩.¹gut.tn̩] and [dn̩.²lam.m̩.²piː.kn̩] vs. [dn̩.²laŋ.ŋə.²piː.kn̩] and [dn̩.²lam.mə.¹gut.tn̩].[32] If filling the empty vowel with vowel features is the default case with respect to Homorganic Trapping, and in addition a phonological rule, since it implies manipulation of discrete categories, viz. filling in of phonological features, Homorganic Trapping must also be phonological, since it will precede the default rule.

The assumption that the syllabic position is empty with respect to features also implies that a stem-final nasal will be autosegmentally adjacent to the consonant following the empty position with respect to place features. The structural description of NPA is therefore met as long as the vowel features have not been supplied. If NPA can be shown to apply in this environment, it must therefore apply *before* vowel insertion, which would make it a phonological rule as well. Using the adjective /blin/, *blind* 'blind' as a test case, we would in other words expect

---

[31] There may of course be a split nasal involved, beginning as coronal and ending as dorsal before the velum is raised. This would not involve temporal masking of the coronal either, however, but partial assimilation that should be analysed as spreading as well.

[32] In more careful speech, the empty vowel will be realized as schwa also between homorganic consonants.

?[dn̩²bliŋ.ŋ̩.¹gʉt.tn̩] and ?[dn̩²blim.m̩.²piː.kn̩] to be possible pronunciations of *den blinde gutten* 'the blind boy' and *den blinde piken* 'the blind girl'. If only NPA before dorsals is a phonological rule, we would on the other hand expect only the former to be possible, since NPA before labials as a P2 rule in that case would be ordered after, and therefore be bled by, the filling in of vowel features.

In order to test this prediction, I have polled fellow linguists by explaining the possible interaction between the two rules. Lay people I have tested by inserting [dn̩²bliŋ.ŋ̩.¹gʉt.tn̩] and [dn̩²blim.m̩.²piː.kn̩] into the frame *Ser du ___ der borte?*, 'Do you see ___ over there?'. I pronounced these sentences in a normal to fast tempo, and asked my consultants whether there was something peculiar in the pronunciations. The results were fairly clear in both cases, assimilation is fairly acceptable before a velar, while before a labial it sounds peculiar. For what they are worth, these results therefore support the hypothesis that NPA before dorsals is phonological, while only NPA before labials is a matter of phonetic implementation.

Before we state the two rules, a final point must be addressed, viz. the underlying specification of /n/. The simplest statement of NPA can be obtained if /n/ is assumed to be unspecified for Place. The rule can then be stated as a feature-filling rule (Clements and Hume 1995), that is, as a simple spreading rule that applies to the Place node of the following segment. An argument in favour of the nasals lacking a Coronal node is the fact that apical nasals do not assimilate, as in [¹bæːn̩.kun.vɛn.ˌʂuːn̩], *Bern-konvensjonen* 'the Bern Convention', where assimilation is not possible. This would follow directly if assimilation could only target nasals lacking a Coronal node, since nasals specified as [ap] must have a Coronal node dominating the feature. Under a delinking analysis, it must be specified that Coronal must not have dependent nodes for the rule to apply.

But this solution cannot be reconciled with the assumption made in Chapter 4.3.4 that all coronals are specified as Coronal under the Place node.[33] On this assumption, NPA must be stated as delinking of the Coronal specification and spreading of the content of the Place node of the following segment. In this case the rule would be feature-changing, a more marked type according to Clements and Hume (1995). This might be construed as an argument in favour of placeless coronals, but since both rule types are allowed for in the theory, a simplicity argument in itself is not decisive.

NPA is stated as in (28). In (28b) I have not assumed delinking. The double association that results, which must be assumed to be ill-formed in the phonology, expresses the fact that at the stage where the rule applies, the coronal and labial gestures may overlap.

NPA may also apply to syllabic nasals. Thus *våpengren* 'branch of military service' (lit. 'weapon branch') may be pronounced [¹voː.pn̩.ˌgreːn] or [¹voː.pŋ̩.-ˌgreːn], and *Holmenkollen* (place name in Oslo) as [²hɔl.mn̩.ˌkɔl.ln̩] or

---

[33] Partial assimilation, cf. footnote 31, would also be difficult to account for if the nasal were unspecified with respect to Place, since spreading of Dorsal would presumably block subsequent insertion of Cor, while spreading of Dorsal to a node already specified as Cor, without delinking of the latter, would give us the correct representation without further stipulation.

(28) *Nasal Place Assimilation (NPA)*

(a) *Coronal to dorsal NPA*
Domain: Postlexical, P1
Rule type: Domain span
Domain: Intonational Phrase
Status: Optional

Condition: Coronal must be
empty

(b) *Coronal to labial NPA*
Domain: Postlexical, P2
Rule type: Domain span
Domain: Intonational Phrase
Status: Optional

Condition: Coronal must be
empty

[²hɔl.mŋ.,kɔl.lŋ]. There is, however, one exception. When the preceding consonant is another coronal, assimilation seems to be blocked. Thus *tordengud* 'thunder god' can only be [¹tur.dn̩.,gʉːd], and *kristengymnas* 'Christian secondary school' only [²kris.tn̩.gym.,nɑːs]. This exception follows if we assume that the coronal clusters have a shared Place node specified as Coronal, and at the same time invoke the Linking Constraint of Hayes (1986) which says that association lines must be interpreted exhaustively. The rule stated as (28a) will then be blocked, since only singly linked nasals can be subject to the rule.

The optionality of NPA in all derived environments precludes us from assuming that the rule also applies in roots, where the co-occurrence restrictions expressed by the rule hold without exceptions. If the latter pattern is to be captured by a rule, we would have to assume a separate one that spreads place features from stops onto preceding nasals in roots. This is of course feasible, but this pattern might as well be stated as a lexical redundancy rule that defines the 'ideal' pattern that explains the existence of the two rules in (28) in the sound system of the language.

Finally, we must ask if NPA is constrained with respect to prosodic domains. In the absence of systematic investigations, it is difficult to give a precise answer. Again, appeal to intuitions can only suggest an answer. In (29), two sentences with the syntactic structure of (7) are given, and with lexical items that supply environments where NPA can apply. Again IP boundaries seem to act as barriers against rule application. Within IPs, the rule seems to be able to apply in all environments, irrespective of syntactic phrase type and the internal prosodic structure of the IP. The domain for NPA therefore seems to be the same as that constraining the Retroflex rule, the difference being that the latter is obligatory, while NPA is optional.

(29) (a) *Jon klapper en grønn panter*
'Jon pats a green panther'
[¹juːŋ.²klɑp.pə.rɛŋ.¹grœm.¹pɑn.tɽ]
(or [¹juːn.²klɑp.pə.rɛn.¹grœn.¹pɑn.tɽ])

(b) *Jon, Gunnars venn, klapper en grønn panter*
'Jon, Gunnar's friend, pats a green panther'
['juːn. | ²gɵn.naʂ.ˈʋɛn. | ²klɑp.pə.rɛŋ.ˈgrœm.ˈpɑn.tʃ]
*? ['juːŋ. | ²gɵn.naʂ.ˈʋɛŋ. | ²klɑp.pə.rɛŋ.ˈgrœm.ˈpɑn.tʃ]

11.4.2 Assimilations within Place nodes

In addition to assimilation between Place nodes, we also find assimilation within the labial and coronal place node. Thus an underlying /m/ will normally be realized as a labiodental before /f/ and /ʋ/, and /n/ will be realized as apical before /ʂ/, as in *lunsj* 'lunch' (Vanvik 1979: 51f, Alnæs 1925: 12). These assimilations are different with respect to domain, however. Labial assimilation is clearly postlexical. Its output is allophonic, and it seems to apply across word boundaries in the same way as (28b). Assimilation of nasals to a following /ʂ/ must on the other hand be lexical. It does not apply across word boundaries; note the difference between [²kaɳ.ʂə], *kanskje* 'maybe' and the phrase [də.ˈkan.ˌʂeː], *det kan skje* 'it may happen'.[34] It also has exceptions; Vanvik claims that assimilation is found in a few words only, but he does not give an exhaustive list, only three examples. The rule will spread [ap] from /ʂ/, which is underlyingly specified for the feature, onto the unmarked /n/. The rule is stated in (30). It will for example turn underlying /kanʂe/ into [²kaɳ.ʂə].

(30) *Regressive [ap]-spreading*

Domain: Lexical word
Rule type: Postcyclic

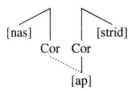

[nas]   [strid]

Cor   Cor

[ap]

11.5 THE REALIZATION OF UNSTRESSED
WORD-FINAL EMPTY VOWELS

In Chapter 2.1.1.5 I argued that the vowel normally realized as unrounded [Coronal: –high, –low] should be analysed as an empty vowel segment in underlying structure. The main argument for this was the fact that we find alternations between [eː, ɛ] in metrically strong positions with zero and schwa in metrically

---

[34] Vanvik lists one example where assimilation crosses a PWd boundary in a compound, viz. the lexicalized and rather opaque [ˈɵɳ.ˌʂyl.lə], *unnskylde*, 'to excuse'.

weak positions, as in [ɑ.ˈpɛl], *appell* 'appeal' vs. [ɑ.pl̩.ˈleː.rə], *appelere* 'to appeal', see also Chapters 6.5.1 and 10.6.2.

In this section we shall look at further alternations that support this analysis. Many words end in schwa when pronounced in isolation, such as the simplex words [²bɑk.kə], *bakke* 'hillside' and [²seː.lə], *sele* 'suspender'. These contrast minimally with monosyllables such as [¹bɑk], *bakk* 'tray' and [¹seːl], *sel* 'seal' (zool.). The final vowel in the first type does not show up in all environments, however. When the def. sg. ending /-n/ is added to these words, which are all masculine, the result is identical segmental structures, and only the tonal accent will show whether the stem has one or two syllables. Thus we get [²bɑk.kn̩] vs. [¹bɑk.kn̩], and [²seː.ln̩] vs. [¹seː.ln̩]. This will follow from the rule Empty Vowel Truncation stated as (32) below.

On this analysis, suffixes may consist of an empty vowel only. The most common suffixes with this structure are the infinitive marker, the suffix marking def. sg. in neuter nouns and the adjectival agreement marker signalling definiteness and/or plural. Examples are [²klɛm.mə], *klemme* 'to hug', [¹toː.gə], *toget* 'the train' and [²lɑm.mə], *lamme* 'lame', compared with the imp. [¹klɛm], the indef. sg. [¹toːg] and the uninflected adjective [¹lɑm].

The empty vowel seems to remain empty into the postlexical phonology, since also at this level, its realization may be influenced by neighbouring segments.[35] This may take place in two environments. The first is when a vowel-initial word follows. The rule responsible for this we shall term *Empty Vowel Truncation*. The other is when the vowel gets 'trapped' between homorganic consonants. This will be referred to as *Homorganic Trapping*. Both are briefly discussed in Alnæs (1925: 20f.).

11.5.1 Empty Vowel Truncation

Consider the examples in (31). In (31a) we see that when the following word begins with a consonant, which must not be homorganic with the consonant preceding the empty vowel (see below), the latter is realized as schwa. If the next word is vowel-initial, on the other hand, the empty vowel disappears, as can be seen from the examples in (31b). As a result, the consonant preceding the empty vowel surfaces as onset for the initial vowel of the second word. This means that the syllable heading the empty vowel must be truncated in order to derive the correct output.

(31)   (a) *Before consonant-initial words*
            [ɔ.²klɛm.mə.¹gʉt.tn̩] *å klemme gutten* 'to hug the boy'
            [ɔ.²klɛm.mə.²tan.tn̩] *å klemme tanten* 'to hug the aunt'
            [¹toː.gə.²stɔp.pr̩] *toget stopper* 'the train stops'
            [¹toː.gə.²brɛm.sr̩] *toget bremser* 'the train slows down'

---

[35] I assume that in metrically strong positions, it is filled with vocalic features as soon as stress is assigned, since the head of a stressed syllable must be a vowel.

(b) *Before vowel-initial words*

    [ɔ.²klɛm.¹muŋ.kl̩n] *å klemme onkelen* 'to hug the uncle'

    [¹toː.¹gɑŋ.ˌkɔm.mɽ] *toget ankommer* 'the train arrives'

The simplest analysis seems to be that a final empty vowel deletes along with its syllable when immediately followed by another syllabic head. If this head is specified as [+son], the rule will also account for the alternation between *bakke* and *bakken* discussed a moment ago. Another example, where it applies within PWds, is when the feminine def. sg. suffix /-a/ is added to the stems [²jɛn.tə], *jente* 'girl' and [²hyt.tə], *hytte* 'cabin'. The results are [²jɛn.tɑ] and [²hyt.tɑ].

    The rule is formalized as (32).

(32) *Empty vowel truncation*

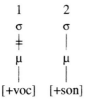

Condition: 1 lacks features below the root node.

After application of (32), the stranded onset of the first syllable will be adjacent to the onsetless second syllable. On the assumption that syllabification is continuous, they will form a new syllable. This will account for the forms given in (31b).

    The rule applies to the empty vowel only. If the stem or first word in a postlexical string ends in any other vowel, truncation does not take place. Thus if we combine the def. sg. *jenta* with a vowel-initial word, as in *jenta elsker* 'the girl loves', the output will be [²jɛn.tɑ.²ɛl.skɽ] and not *[²jɛn.²tɛl.skɽ].

    Since the rule does not supply the empty vowel with features, it does not represent prima facie evidence for the absence of features in the underlying form, but the fact that the rule only targets the vowel that in other environments surfaces as schwa or zero shows that this vowel is special in some way. The next rule to be discussed, Homorganic Trapping, represents such evidence, however.

    There are no data available with respect to postlexical domain constraints. My own intuition is that (32) will be blocked, or at least severely inhibited, by a Focal Phrase boundary. Thus *toget ankommer* with an Hfoc% on the noun is more likely to surface as [¹toː.gə.¹aŋ.kɔm.mɽ] than [¹toː.¹gɑŋ.kɔm.mɽ].

11.5.2 Homorganic Trapping

This rule was briefly mentioned in Section 11.4. Consider the data in (33), some of which are repeated from (31).

(33)   (a) *Heterorganic environment*
         [ɔ.²klɛm.mə.¹gʉt.tn̩] *å klemme gutten* 'to hug the boy'
         [ɔ.²klɛm.mə.²tɑn.tn̩] *å klemme tanten* 'to hug the aunt'
         [ɔ.²çɛn.nə.¹gʉt.tn̩] *å kjenne gutten* 'to know the boy'
         [ɔ.²çɛn.nə.²piː.kn̩] *å kjenne piken* 'to know the girl'
         [ɔ.²riŋ.ŋə.²tɑn.tn̩] *å ringe tanten* 'to telephone the aunt'
         [ɔ.²riŋ.ŋə.²piː.kn̩] *å ringe piken* 'to telephone the girl'

        (b) *Homorganic environment*
         [ɔ.²klɛm.m̩.²piː.kn̩] *å klemme piken* 'to hug the girl'
         [ɔ.²çɛn.n̩.²tɑn.tn̩] *å kjenne tanten* 'to know the aunt'
         [ɔ.²riŋ.ŋ̍ .¹gʉt.tn̩] *å ringe gutten* 'to telephone the boy'

(33b) shows that if the consonant preceding the empty vowel and the initial consonant of the next word have the same place features, the intervening syllabic head
is not realized as a schwa, but as a syllabic extension of the preceding consonant.
The rule is not obligatory, and may be suspended in careful speech. The features
of the preceding consonant are in other words spread onto the empty syllable. In
(33) nasal + stop clusters are used as examples, but it seems that assimilation may
take place between any pair of homorganic consonants. Again no systematic investigation is reported in the literature, so there is no information available about possible differences in applicability according to consonant type. But even between
voiceless stops and fricatives the empty vowel may be trapped in rapid speech, as
for example in *å stoppe posten* 'to stop the mail' and *å kysse sønnen* 'to kiss the
son', which may be realized with a prolonged closing or fricative phase instead of
two consonants with an intervening schwa. Whether we are dealing with a *syllabic*
obstruent in such cases is perhaps debatable. In the absence of clear criteria for
identifying syllabicity in voiceless obstruents I leave the question open.

As was the case with Empty Vowel Truncation, Homorganic Trapping may
apply in the lexicon also, within as well as across PWd-boundaries. Within
prosodic words it applies when the cohering preterite suffix /-et/ is added to stems
ending in coronals. In casual, but not necessarily rapid speech, it occurs when the
stem-final coronal is voiced, such as in /led/, 'lead' and /bad/ 'bathe'. Preterites of
these *may* be pronounced as [²leː.dət] and [²bɑː.dət]. They may also be pronounced
with trapped vowel, which is produced by adding strong voicing to a prolonged
closing phase of the fused stop, followed by a voiceless, aspirated release: [²leː.ɖtʰ]
and [²bɑː.ɖtʰ]. When the stem ends in voiceless /t/, as in /lʉt/, 'to lean', trapping
seems to require rapid speech. It is produced by lengthening of the closure phase
of the stop, giving [²lʉːtː]. Trapping may also occur in rapid speech when the passive marker /-s/ is added to an s-final stem, as in /vis-e-s/, *vises* 'to be shown',
which may be pronounced [²viː.səs], or in rapid speech, [²viːsː].

How can we give a formal account of the rule? If the empty syllable lacks place
features, the rule can be interpreted as an OCP-driven fusion of the place features
of the consonants on each side of the syllable. Note that these will be C-Place specifications; see (14) in Chapter 2. As a possible next step, the shared C-Place node

could also link with the empty syllable, but this will effectively block further insertion of V-Place features, since these will then come to specify the adjacent consonants as well. After the fusion there is therefore no way in which the intervening syllabic head can be realized as a vowel. In order to save the syllable, the only option is to link its mora to the (so to speak) surrounding consonant. There are in other words two steps involved in the rule: Fusion of C-Place features across the empty syllables, and linking of the mora of the syllable with the preceding consonant's root node. The two steps are shown in (34).

(34)   *Homorganic Trapping*

   (a) *Fusion*   (b) *Mora relinking*

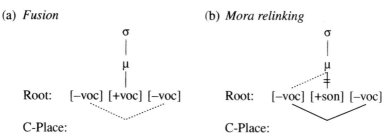

Root: [−voc] [+voc] [−voc]   Root: [−voc] [+son] [−voc]

C-Place: C-Place:

Given the lack of systematic data, it is difficult to determine to what extent Homorganic Trapping is constrained by the prosodic hierarchy. Again, my own intuitions suggest that the rule cannot apply across a Focal Phrase boundary. I therefore tentatively analyse it as a domain span rule delimited by the Focal Phrase.

11.6 CLITICS

Clitics are elements that are independent with respect to syntax but dependent with respect to phonology. This means that they may serve the same syntactic functions as full words and phrases, and therefore be interpreted as morpho-syntactic words from a syntactic point of view. But phonologically they may not constitute stress domains on their own, and can therefore not function as prosodic words. Instead, they are incorporated into a higher order prosodic constituent, often referred to as a *host*, either as proclitics or enclitics. Here we shall discuss only the *phonological* properties of UEN clitics.

11.6.1 Clitic types

I distinguish between cliticization as a process of prosodic incorporation, and clitics as a specific type of lexical items that are obligatorily subject to such incorporation. The phonological form of the cliticized element can in many cases be derived from a corresponding full form of the same element by general rules of reduction. Thus the 3. p. sg. neuter pronoun /de/ *det*, will be pronounced with long vowel, [ˈdeː], when stressed, and therefore a PWd on its own, but with schwa, [də], when cliticized. Forms that are phonologically predictable in this way are often referred to as *simple clitics*.[36] Since these are units which may function as PWds on their own as well as being prosodically incorporated in another PWd, their clitichood is not inherent. As lexical items they should therefore not be classified as clitics *per se*, but as elements which under appropriate circumstances may be subject to cliticization. Their phonological realization as clitics will be predictable from general principles of the phonology.

There are on the other hand lexical elements which can *only* be realized as part of a PWd headed by another lexical item. Most of these will have corresponding full forms, but the phonological relationship between the two is not predictable in the same way as for simple clitics. The relationship between clitic and full form should therefore be analysed as allomorphy rather than rule-governed instantiations of the same underlying form. UEN examples of such *special clitics* (Spencer 1991: 376) are the 3. person sg. masc. and fem. clitics /-n/ and /-a/, which cannot be derived from the full forms /han/ or /den/ (masc.) and /hun/ (fem.) without stipulating ad hoc rules whose domain will be limited to these forms.

Finally there will be clitics which lack a corresponding full form altogether, called *bound words* in the sources referred to above. The possessive marker /-s/ represents an example of this type.[37]

11.6.2   The place of clitics in the prosodic hierarchy

Since clitics are syntactic elements, their phonological properties must be accounted for at the postlexical level. The fact that they cannot function as PWds on their own suggests an analysis where they are interpreted as postlexical syntactic correlates of cohering affixes. This will account for their independent status, and at the same time predict that the result of adjoining a clitic to a given host will be a PWd. In this sense the PWd, as suggested earlier, is interpreted as a prosodic constituent which spans the lexical/postlexical divide.

This approach implies that the prosodic hierarchy in UEN should not include a Clitic Group as a separate constituent—see Nespor and Vogel (1986). In fact, my definition of the PWd as a domain delimited by stress assignment precludes an analysis along the lines of Nespor and Vogel, where clitics constitute separate PWds. Norwegian clitics cannot be stressed, and they therefore cannot form PWds on their own.[38]

The elimination of the Clitic Group as a separate constituent level implies that

---

[36] The division between simple and special clitics assumed here is based on Spencer (1991: 376). It differs somewhat from the one assumed in Zwicky (1985) and Zwicky and Pullum (1983), but the difference is of no consequence in the present context.

[37] This element was briefly discussed in Chapter 4.2.3.1.

[38] In rejecting the Clitic Group as a relevant prosodic category, I follow Booij (1995, 1996) and Wiese (1996), who reach the same conclusion for Dutch and German respectively. Stress as the decisive criterion for rejecting the Clitic Group as a separate prosodic category is also invoked in Peperkamp (1996).

any difference in phonological behaviour between lexical affixes and clitics must now be made to follow from the fact that they belong to different phonological levels, and not from differences in constituency. As noted in Booij (1996), for instance, this represents a simplification of the model, since the number of prosodic constituent types is reduced without complicating the grammar in other respects.

11.6.3 Pronominal clitics

The most commonly discussed class of Norwegian clitics are the personal pronouns, where we find examples of simple as well as special clitics.[39] (35) is an overview of the personal pronouns of UEN, with simple and special clitic forms given for each full form where appropriate.

(35)   *Personal pronouns*

		Full form	Simple clitic	Special clitic
Singular				
1st person	subject	[ˈjæj]		[jæ]
	non-subject	[ˈmæj]		[mæ]
2nd person	subject	[ˈdʉː]	[dʉ]	[rʉ]
	non-subject	[ˈdæj]		[dæ] [ræ]
3rd person	subject, +human, masc.	[ˈhɑn]	[ɑn]	[n̩]
	non-subject[40]	[ˈhɑm]	[ɑm]	[n̩]
	subject, +human, fem.	[ˈhʉn] [ˈhʉː]	[ʉn]	[ɑ]
	non-subject	[²hɛn.nə] [²hɛn.nɽ]	[ɛ.nə]	[ɑ]
	–human, –neuter	[ˈdɛn]	[dn̩]	[n̩]
	–human, +neuter	[ˈdeː]	[də]	[rə]
	Reflexive	[ˈsæj]		[sæ]
Plural				
1st person		[ˈʋiː]	[ʋi]	
2nd person		[²deː.ɽə]	[dɽ.ɽə]	
3rd person[41]	subject	[ˈdiː] [ˈdɛm]	[di] [dɛm]	[ri] [rɛm]
	non-subject	[ˈdɛm]	[dɛm]	[rɛm]

The special clitics in the rightmost column can be divided into three types by phonological criteria. First there is the diphthong reduction in 1st and 2nd person sg.

---

[39] Their syntactic properties are discussed in Fretheim and Halvorsen (1975), Christensen (1985), Johannessen (1989), Hellan (1994) and Hellan and Platzack (1999).

[40] Used in formal and upper-class varieties only.

[41] The form [dœm] also occurs in vernacular speech, as full form as well as simple clitic. A corresponding r-initial form [rœm] occurs as a special clitic.

Nouns and adjectives ending in the same diphthong, e.g. [ˈʋæj], *vei* 'road', do not undergo a similar reduction when unstressed, and the reduced forms are therefore best interpreted as special clitics separately listed as such in the lexicon.[42]

Second, there are the forms beginning with [r], whose distribution is phonologically conditioned in that they occur after vowel-final hosts, as shown in (36a). As with diphthong reduction, it is not possible to derive the r-initial forms by means of a general phonological rule, since there are no other instances of underlying /d/ changing into /r/ between vowels.

(36) (a) [hɑŋ.ˈgɑː.rɛm.²kɑː.kə] *han ga dem kake* 'he gave them cake'
      (b) [hɑn.ˈjiː.rɛm.²kɑː.kə] *han gir dem kake* 'he gives them cake'
      (c) [²hɑː.rʉ.kə.ˈjʉʈ.ʈə] *har du ikke gjort det?* 'haven't you done it?'
      (d) [²hɑː.ræ.ˌʉːt] *ha deg ut!* 'get out' (lit. 'have you out')
      (e) [hɑn.²tuːk.də.ˌmɑː] *han tok dem av* 'he took them off'
           (cf. *[hɑn.²tuːk.rə.ˌmɑː])

We also find forms without /d/ after hosts ending in /r/, as in (36b). Given the fact that rd-sequences in other instances are subject to the Retroflex Rule, the underlying form of the pronoun here cannot be d-initial. (Retroflex *d* is in fact possible, in more formal styles (36b) will surface as [hɑn.ˈjiː.ɖɛm.²kɑː.kə], but in this case the underlying form of the pronoun must be the full form, which is subsequently destressed and cliticized.) We may interpret the clitics as r-initial also after r-final hosts, since the geminate /r/ that results from concatenating the r-final host with the clitic will automatically degeminate when occurring between two unstressed vowels, since non-syllabic prosodic geminates are allowed only after short, stressed vowels. When a geminate arises after a stressed, long vowel, the quantity of the input will be preserved, and the result is again a non-geminate, as in (36c and d).[43] After consonants other than /r/, only the d-initial forms occur, as in (36e), where resyllabification creates an open syllable so that the underlying /e/ may reduce to schwa.

The third type of special clitics consists of /-n/ and /-a/ used as 3rd person sg. pronouns. These are identical with the masc. and fem. def. sg. suffixes on nouns— see (5) in Chapter 3, but have a much freer distribution in that they attach to verbs, prepositions and complementizers. In most cases, they may be interchanged with the corresponding simple clitic forms, but there is a marked sociolinguistic difference between the two. The simple clitics will be used in more formal registers as

[42] The 3. person forms without initial *h* might perhaps have been classified as special as well, since other lexical items beginning in *h* do not lose it due to stress reduction. The reason why they have been interpreted as reduced forms is that *h* cannot start a word-internal, unstressed syllable. A similar argument might have been applied to /ej/, since diphthongs only occur in stressed syllables, but here it is not clear that full destressing would lead to the monophthong [æ]. In fact, when /ej/ shortens in stressed syllables the result is [ɛ]: cf. the alternative pronunciations [ˈbæjst] ~ [ˈbɛst], *beist* 'beast'.

[43] The present tense form in (36c) may also surface with a short vowel and geminate /r/. This might be interpreted as an effect induced by a geminate /r/, but the evidence is not unambiguous, since in other verbs, shortening seems less felicitous. Also, shortening of the imperative in (36d), *[²hɑr.ræ.ˌʉːt], is not possible.

well as in the prestige varieties of UEN, while the special clitics are more common in the vernacular varieties. The examples in (37), which are taken from Hellan (1994), show the same sentence with the simple and the special 3rd person sg. clitics, where the subject, the indirect object, and the direct object are cliticized to the verb. The underlying form of (37b) is assumed to be /ga#n#a#n#ike/.[44]

(37)   (a)   [¹gɑː.ɑ.nɛn.dn̩.ni.kə] *ga han henne den ikke?* 'Didn't he give it to her?'
             (Lit. 'gave he her it not')
       (b)   [¹gɑː.n̩.nɑ.n̩.ni.kə] *ga'n a'n ikke?* (id.)

Note that Sonority-driven Delinking and Nucleus Spreading (Chapter 8.4.1) are applicable here, rendering [¹gɑː.ɑ.nɑ.n̩.ni.kə] as an alternative surface form.[45] Note also that the subject and both of the objects may be represented by the masculine clitic /n/, deriving the rather marked [¹gɑː.n̩.n̩.n̩.ni.kə], 'gave-he-him-it-not?'. It is an open question whether this can be auditorily distinguished from [¹gɑː.n̩.n̩.ni.kə], 'gave-he-it-not?' or even [¹gɑː.n̩.ni.kə], 'gave-he-not?'. Other combinations are also possible, but given the fact that indirect objects may be replaced by a prepositional phrase, it is unclear whether all possible combinations of three clitic clusters of this type are in fact used.

11.6.4   The negative clitic /-ke/

Another special clitic with phonological constraints on its distribution is the negation marker /-ke/, whose full form is /ike/, [²ik.kə]. Its distribution is analysed in Christensen (1985) and Fretheim (1988). The present analysis is based on the latter, but differs from it in substantial ways.

/-ke/ requires an inflected verb as a host, but other clitics, such as the pronominal clitics discussed above, may intervene between the verb and /-ke/. It can only be inserted if the preceding element, be it the host verb or another clitic, ends in a full vowel or /r/ underlyingly, but the latter must be deleted for the surface form to be well-formed, so a phonetically realized /r/ requires the full form. Thus two possible surface forms, [¹tœr.ɾi.kə] and [¹tœk.kə], are well-formed realizations of underlying /tør#NEG/, *tør ikke* 'dares not', where NEG henceforth stands for the allomorphs {[kə]/[ik.kə]}. *[¹tœr.kə] is on the other hand ill-formed as a realization of /tør#NEG/, since the /r/ is phonetically realized, even though no phonotactic restrictions are violated in the form *per se*, cf. [²tœr.kə], *tørke* 'drought'.

Another peculiarity is that the preceding vowel must be short. If the stem vowel is long, as in the present tense form /se-r/, [¹seːr], 'sees', cliticization of /-ke/ will

---

[44] Note that the orthographic form given for this example is not allowed within any of the written norms, but may be encountered in renderings of dialogue in fiction, for example.

[45] The surface form in this case will be identical with the version with the simple clitic /-an/. The difference emerges when the verb contains another vowel than /a/. For example, adding the simple clitic to /stu/, *sto* 'stood', will give [¹stuː.ɑn], while the special clitic results in [¹stuː.n̩] or [¹stuː.un].

cause the vowel to shorten, giving the surface form [¹sɛk.kə]. Adding /-ke/ to the imperative [¹seː], 'look!' gives the same result, [¹sɛk.kə].⁴⁶

The element to which /-ke/ is added may not end in schwa. Thus preterites ending in the /-Te/ suffix always take the full form of NEG, with concomitant Empty Syllable Truncation; see Section 11.5.1 above. Thus underlying /snu-Te#NEG/, 'turn-PRET#NEG' is realized as [²snʉd.di.kə], not *[²snʉd.də.kə] with schwa in the penultimate syllable.⁴⁷

The input constraints that in other words must be satisfied for /-ke/-cliticization to take place are that the preceding segment must be a vowel, though not schwa, or /r/. Further, we must assume two rules, /r/-deletion and vowel-shortening, which conspire to secure that at the surface level, the clitic is always immediately preceded by a short vowel.

If enclisis is limited to contexts where the preceding segment must be [+voc] (optionally followed by /r/), the exception with respect to schwa must be handled by a requirement that the vowel must have vowel features. It then follows that /ke-/-enclisis is blocked as well if the preceding segment is a syllabic sonorant, as in the disyllabic present tense form /send-r#NEG/, 'sends not', which can only surface as [²sɛn.nɾ.ri.kə]. Neither *[²sɛn.næ.kə] nor *[²sɛn.nə.kə] is possible.

Turning now to /r/-deletion, this example also shows that a preceding /r/ can only delete, and thus feed enclisis, if it is non-syllabic. Monosyllabic present tense forms such as [¹jøːr], gjør 'does' therefore allow /-ke/, while it is blocked in disyllabic forms, where the present tense marker is syllabic. The /r/ must also be final on the root tier. An intervening /e/ blocks /r/-deletion, as shown by the preterites [²juː.rə] and [²tuː.rə] of å gjøre 'to do' and å tore 'to dare', respectively. Here, /r/-deletion, and therefore /-ke/, is blocked; [²juː.ri.kə] and [²tuː.ri.kə] seem to be the only possible forms here, as *[²juk.kə] and *[²tuk.kə] are not good.⁴⁸ This means that an /r/ will delete only if it immediately precedes the clitic.

Two problems arise with respect to the proper formulation of /r/-deletion. The first is whether this is an isolated, minor rule triggered by the NEG-clitic only. The answer is no: we have already seen several examples of /r/-deletion before non-coronal consonants. In Section 11.3.2 postlexical /r/-deletion was discussed, in Chapter 7.3.2 we saw an example of /r/-deletion triggered by compounding (/vær-mel-iŋ/ → [²væː.ˌmɛl.liŋ]), and in Chapter 7.2.6 it was mentioned that the final /r/ in the unstressed prefixes /for-/ and /er-/ deletes before a non-coronal consonant. In all these cases, deletion is optional and dependent on style and/or speech rate. This is also the case with /r/-deletion before /-ke/, but in an indirect manner. Here it is the choice between the clitic and the full form that depends on style and speech

---

⁴⁶ Imperatives followed by NEG are somewhat marked, the more common construction being NEG#Imperative, e.g. [²ik.kə.¹seː], ikke se! 'don't look'. But the inverse order is clearly grammatical as well.

⁴⁷ Note that stress is not relevant; /-ke/ may be added to unstressed, full vowels as well, as in the preterite /kast-a#NEG/, kasta ikke 'didn't throw', which is realized as [²kɑs.tɑ.kə].

⁴⁸ For some reason [²juk.kə] does not seem as bad as [²tuk.kə] but intuitions are not at all clear on this point.

rate. The cliticized form is used in less formal style, but once the clitic is chosen, /r/-deletion is obligatory. /r/-deletion as stated in (18) above should therefore be generalized to apply within PWds, in the lexicon as well as postlexically, but in derived environments only. Thus the /rk/-sequence in the simplex word [tœr.kə], *tørke* 'drought' is left unchanged, while underlying /for-klare/, *forklare* 'to explain' may be realized as [fɔ.¹klɑː.rə] or [fɔr.¹klɑː.rə], and /tør#NEG/, *tør ikke* 'dares not' as [¹tœr.ri.kə] or [¹tœk.kə].

The second problem connected with /r/-deletion before /-ke/ is related to the fact that it is clearly output-oriented, in that it can be said to create the environment for enclisis, viz. a preceding vowel. But in input-oriented approaches such as the one underlying this book, /r/-deletion cannot apply until the clitic has been added. With respect to the input, we therefore need a disjunction: the stem to which the clitic is added must either be vowel-final, or end in a non-syllabic /r/. The latter will invariably delete, however, so the output constraint on its distribution is simply that the stem must be vowel-final. The clitic must in other words be able to look ahead in the derivation: it can only attach to an r-final stem in case the /r/ subsequently deletes.

There are two exeptions, one apparent and one real, to this selectional restriction, both connected with modal verbs. The apparent one is that /-ke/ can combine with the present tense forms /vil/, *vil* 'will' and /skal/, *skal* 'shall', both ending in /l/, giving [¹vik.kə] and [¹skɑk.kə] along with the expected [¹vil.li.kə] and [¹skɑl.li.kə]. The reason why these are not true exceptions is that we find l-less realizations of the hosts also in other environments, as in [vi.²kɑn.ʂə], *vil kanskje* 'will maybe' and [skɑ.²kɑn.ʂə], *skal kanskje* 'shall maybe'. This alternation with zero is only found in these modals; a verb like *spille* 'to play' is not subject to deletion. Thus the negated imperative /spil#NEG/ is obligatorily [¹spil.li.kə]. *[¹spik-kə] is as impossible as *[spi.²kɑn.ʂə], *spill kanskje* 'play maybe' instead of [spil.²kɑn.ʂə]. The obvious solution is therefore to assume that these modals each have two lexically listed allomorphs, one with and one without final /l/. The latter will be vowel-final, and therefore an eligible host for the clitic.

A similar analysis is not available for the present tense /kan/ and the preterite /kunne/ of *å kunne*, corresponding to English 'can, could'. Despite the fact that these are consonant-final and schwa-final respectively, the forms [¹kɑŋ.kə] and [²kʉŋ.kə] are well-formed (Fretheim 1988). This raises the question whether it is stem-final /n, ŋ/ or the modal itself that is exceptional. Few forms exist that this can be tested against, but the imperative and preterite of *å synge* 'to sing', [¹syŋ] and [¹sɑŋ], do not seem to accept the clitic, although judgements with respect to the preterite are not completely clear. Leaving a more detailed investigation for future research, I tentatively analyse [¹kɑŋ.kə] and [²kʉŋ.kə] as lexically stored phrases.

We now turn to the fact that the vowel preceding the clitic will always be short, irrespective of vowel length in the input. In Fretheim (1988) this is derived from the assumption that the underlying form of the clitic is /-kke/, that is, that it contains an initial geminate that will force a long vowel in the stem to shorten. This solution is not available within the overall analysis assumed here. In Chapters 5.1.3 and 6.4 I argued that syllable weight is not underlying, but derived when an open syllable is assigned stress. A cohering element with an underlying initial consonant encoded as geminate would therefore be highly marked.

On the assumption that clitics are cohering elements that are attached at the postlexical level, but which in all other respects behave like cohering suffixes, the shortening may now be derived by assuming that the PWd that results from cliticization is subject to the rule of vowel shortening stated in Chapter 8.2.3. This rule shortens a stem-final vowel when a cohering obstruent-initial suffix is added. It accounts for the short vowel in [²rud.də], *rodde* 'rowed', and the right result, [¹ruk.kə], *ror ikke* 'doesn't row', follows if the rule can apply at the postlexical level to the input /ruːr#ke/ as well, as a domain-span rule constrained by the PWd.

In Chapter 8.2.3 it was noted that the rule is only triggered by specific suffixes, other obstruent-initial suffixes such as the passive marker /-s/ do not induce shortening. This will explain why the rule does not apply when any of the d-initial simple clitics in (35) are cliticized to a vowel-final host. The same holds for the s-initial reflexive /sæ/, *seg* 'self'.

It should perhaps also be noted that /-ke/ is more suffix-like than other clitics in that the head of the prosodic word that it attaches to can only be a verb. This distinguishes it from the pronominal clitics, which can combine with verbs, prepositions and, structural constraints permitting, complementizers. In Zwicky and Pullum (1983), the corresponding English element *n't* is argued to be an inflectional suffix. To go all the way and reanalyse /-ke/ as an inflectional suffix in the same manner would be problematic, however, because most of the other criteria listed by Zwicky and Pullum define it as a clitic.[49] For example, pronominal clitics may intervene between the head and /-ke/, as in [²çɛn.nɽ.rɵ.mæ.kə], *kjenner du meg ikke?* 'don't you know me?' (lit. 'know-you-me-not').[50]

But it allows us nevertheless to connect two suffix-like properties that distinguish the NEG-clitic from pronominal clitics, for instance, which neither trigger Vowel Shortening nor combine with only one category of heads. To the extent that this is not a spurious correlation, we may conclude that the theory-driven distinction between inflectional affix and (syntactic) clitic does not allow us to capture all the generalizations that we would like to make concerning the interface between word-structure, phrase structure and prosodic phonology. /-ke/ has properties that would mark it as cyclic, yet being a clitic, it is not lexical.

11.6.5 Directionality of incorporation: Proclisis or enclisis?

In Section 11.2 above I claimed that a restructuring of the PWd takes place at the transition from the lexical to the postlexical level, in that all postlexical PWds (as

---

[49] This possibility is discussed in Johannessen (1989), and rejected for just this reason.

[50] Of the six criteria used by Zwicky and Pullum, /-ke/ is a suffix on two of them: it exhibits a high degree of selection with respect to its host (criterion A), and it shows morpho-phonological idiosyncrasies in the form of vowel shortening (criterion C). On the others, which are gaps in the set of combinations (B), semantic idiosyncrasies (D), possibility of host + /-ke/ of being subject to syntactic rules (E), and the one already mentioned, that it should not be able to attach to clitics (F), it scores as a clitic.

well as Accent Phrases on the next level up) are left-headed, while lexical PWds are right-headed. As shown there, the edges of postlexical PWds will therefore not necessarily coincide with the edges of morpho-syntactic words. For example, the morpho-syntactic string *betále presángen* 'to pay for the gift' consists of two lexical PWds coextensive with the morpho-syntactic words. At the postlexical level, the string is changed into be(tále-pre)(sángen). The motivation underlying this analysis is the intonational system as discussed in Chapter 10.

This assumption has consequences for the analysis of clitics. First, all cliticization will be enclisis, since proclisis will mean that the head syllable will no longer be leftmost. Utterance-initial unstressed syllables, such as the /be-/ in the example, will therefore find themselves outside any PWd and AP, and must therefore be adjoined at a higher level, the Focal Phrase.

11.7 CONCLUSION

In this chapter some aspects of the postlexical phonology of UEN have been discussed. A central theme has been what kind of constituency postlexical rules are constrained by. Given the paucity of reliable data, it has not been possible to decide between the different alternatives outlined in Section 11.2, but we have seen that several of the rules discussed seem to be constrained by the hierarchy derived from stress and intonation rather than the hierarchies more directly derivable from syntactic structure.

12

ORTHOGRAPHIC CONVENTIONS

In this chapter the relationship between letters and sound will be discussed. I assume that most speakers of Norwegian will have a set of correspondence rules that relate each letter to an unmarked sound value. In many cases we will be dealing with universal or near-universal relationships, as for example *m, n, f* = [m, n, f]. In other cases we have a language specific correspondence overruling the universal one, as in *u* = [ʉ]. The emphasis will be on aspects of the orthography where the correspondence is not straightforward in this sense. Since Bokmål is the norm used by the great majority of UEN speakers, the relationship between UEN and Nynorsk will not be considered.[1]

The chapter is organized as follows. Section 12.1 is a short recapitulation of the ideology underlying Norwegian spelling, see also Chapter 1.2. In Section 12.2 the alphabet will be presented. Section 12.3 will deal with the extent to which prosodic features are signalled in writing, while Sections 12.4 and 12.5 will be concerned with vowels and consonants respectively. The chapter will be closed by a brief section on diacritics.

12.1 UNDERLYING ORTHOGRAPHIC PRINCIPLES

As stated in Chapter 1.2, the development of a specific Norwegian orthography started during the latter half of the nineteenth century. Before that, Danish had been used from the late Medieval period, when written Old Norse gradually disappeared due to the political situation at the time. In the development of the two standards, three different types of principles have been invoked, and often been opposed to each other. First there has been much disagreement about which of the spoken varieties of Norwegian an official orthography should be based on. Moderate Bokmål is usually seen as reflecting middle- and upper-class East Norwegian speech varieties. Second, earlier spelling conventions, Old Norse and Danish, have played an important role in the discussion of how find to the proper balance between tradition and reform; see the difference between moderate and radical Bokmål discussed in Chapter 1.2. Less controversial has been the tension between phonetic faithfulness vs. morphological stability where morpho-phonological alternations are involved.

---

[1] The discussion that follows has benefited from Vinje (1987: 124–33).

12.2 THE ALPHABET

The Norwegian alphabet consists of 29 letters, 9 vowels and 20 consonants. The vowels are *a, e, i, o, u, y, æ, ø, å* and the consonants *b, c, d, f, g, h, j, k, l, m, n, p, q, r, s, t, v, w, x, z*. The alphabet is the same in Bokmål and Nynorsk, as are the (unmarked) correspondences between letters and sounds.

The vowel letters *æ* and *ø*, which Norwegian shares with Danish, correspond to German (and Swedish) *ä* and *ö*. In the unmarked cases, they represent a low, front vowel and a mid, central (or front: see Chapter 2.3.1.2) rounded vowel respectively. *Å* is used in Danish and Swedish as well, and represents a back, round mid or low vowel sound (IPA [o] or [ɔ]). The letters *c, q, w, x* and *z* are regarded as foreign, and are used in a few loan words only, such as *celle* 'cell', *quiz* (id.), *weekend* (id.), *taxi* (id.) and *zoologi* 'zoology'.[2] In most cases, these letters are replaced in loan words, such as *seremoni* 'ceremony', *kvart* 'quarter', *maksimum* 'maximum' and *sebra* 'zebra'.

12.3 PROSODIC FEATURES

12.3.1 Quantity and stress

Placement of word-stress is in most cases not marked in the spelling. One exception is stress on final /e/, which is marked by means of acute accent, as in *kafé* 'café'; *idé* 'idea' and *komité* 'committee'. When an *e*-initial suffix is added, this stem-final *e* does not truncate, as in words ending in unstressed *e*. Such forms are therefore spelled with double *e*: as in the indef. pl. *kafeer, ideer* and *komiteer*. Given that the location of stress can be inferred from the double *e*, accent is not supposed to be used in these forms, but one sees it quite often.

As noted for example in Chapter 3.2.3, vowels may be long only in stressed syllables, and no more than one consonant may normally follow a long vowel. This means that a stressed vowel followed by more than one consonant will in most cases be short. Short vowels may also precede single consonants, however, and in that case the consonant is geminated in order to signal the shortness of the vowel. The principle can be stated as follows: a stressed vowel followed by no or one consonant letter is long, a stressed vowel followed by more than one consonant is short. It is illustrated by the forms in (1).

(1) *Short vowel*   *Long vowel*
     bakk [¹bɑk] 'tray'   *bak* [¹bɑːk] 'behind'
     bakke [²bɑk.kə] 'hillside'   *bake* [²bɑː.kə] 'to bake'
     bark [¹bɑrk] 'bark'

There are several exceptions, however. First, there are words spelled with only one

---

[2] They are also often used in names, sometimes as variants. Thus Jacob is used alongside Jakob, Bendixen alongside Bendiksen and Zachariassen alongside Sakariassen.

consonant following the stressed vowel, but which are nevertheless pronounced with short vowel. Second, while a stressed short vowel in most cases is followed by a double consonant (or a consonant cluster), one cannot infer from a double consonant that the preceding vowel heads a stressed syllable. Third, in complex words a long vowel may be followed by more than one consonant: see Chapter 8.2.2.

The rule that a short stressed vowel must be signalled by double consonant in writing, has one principal exception: *m* is never geminated at the end of a word. Here one therefore has to know whether the vowel is long or short, as in *grim* [¹grim] 'ugly' vs. *lim* [¹liːm] 'glue'. If followed by another vowel, however, *m* is geminated after short, stressed vowels; see the effect of adding the agreement marker to *grim* and the def. sg. marker to *lim*, both /-e/, which gives *grimme* [²grim.mə] 'ugly' vs. *limet* [¹liː.mə]. Homographs occur in singular which are distinguished in inflected forms, such as *dom* [¹dɔm] 'judgement' vs. *dom* [¹duːm] 'cathedral'. The def. sg. forms of these are *dommen* and *domen*.

The letter *v* is never doubled. In most cases a preceding vowel is long when *v* is not part of a cluster, but in *støvel* [²stœv.ʋl] 'boot' and *lever* [¹lɛv.ʋɾ] 'liver', for instance, the vowel is short.

Words that are frequent in running text and often realized as unstressed, such as articles, modal verbs, pronouns, prepositions, etc., may also lack double consonant. Thus the indef. neuter article *et* is written with a single *t*, but with double *t* as a numeral, *ett*. When the corresponding masculine article *en* [ɛn], is used as a (stressed) numeral, the vowel lengthens, and this may be marked by means of an acute accent, *én* [¹eːn]. The conjunction *men* [mɛn] 'but' is written with a single *n*. It is homophonous with the plural noun *menn* 'men', but is orthographically identical with the noun *men* [¹meːn] 'harm'. Similarly the personal pronouns *han* [¹hɑn] and *hun* [¹hʉn] (3rd person sg. masc. and fem.) are written with a single *n*, while the nouns *hann* [¹hɑn] and *hunn* [¹hʉn] with double *n* refer to males and females of a given species. This principle is not consistently adhered to, however, the object form of the 1st person pl., *oss* [¹ɔs], is written with double *s*.

In addition, there are lexical exceptions such as *moro* [²mur.ru] 'fun', cf. *Toro* [¹tuː.ru] (brand name) and *goro* [guː.ru] 'kind of cake', *selektiv* [¹sɛl.lɛk.ˌtiːʋ] 'selective' and *valuta* [ʋɑ.¹lʉt.tɑ] 'currency'.Vinje (1987: 130) also lists some words where the vowel vacillates between long and short. These are all written without double consonant. The only consistent principle that therefore can be inferred is that double consonant invariably means that a preceding vowel is short, while a single consonant usually, but not always, signals a preceding long vowel.

Even if vowel quantity can be inferred, stress cannot be inferred from the use of double consonant, since in loan words there are numerous examples of double consonants following unstressed vowels. Examples are *kommando* [ku.¹mɑn.du] 'command'; *apparat* [ɑ.pɑ.¹rɑːt] 'instrument' and *selleri* [sɛ.lə.¹riː] 'celery'. Vinje (1987: 131) notes that these cases are conditioned by spelling of the lending language.[3] There are also rather strange principles of alternation. Words ending in

---

[3] With respect to *selleri*, this means that the word must have been borrowed through German, since French and English have one *l*.

double consonant, such as *fabrikk* [fɑ.ˈbrik] 'factory' retain the double consonant before the stressed suffix /-ere/, but not before other stressed suffixes: hence *fabrikkere*,[fɑ.bri.ˈkeː.rə] 'to manufacture', but *fabrikant* [fɑ.bri.ˈkɑnt] 'manufacturer' and *fabrikasjon* [fɑ.bri.kɑ.ˈʂuːn] 'manufacture (n.)'.

While a double consonant in writing is an unequivocal signal that the preceding vowel is short, a consonant group transmits the same only in simplex words—see the discussion in Chapter 8.2.2. When a consonantal suffix such as the neuter adjectival agreement suffix /-t/ is added to a stem ending in long vowel plus a consonant, such as *ful* [ˈfʉːl] 'sly', and *vis* [ˈʋiːs] 'wise', the orthographic results are *fult* and *vist*. The pronunciation is nevertheless [ˈfʉːlt] and [ʋiːst].[4] A stem-final double consonant is on the other hand usually changed into a single when a consonant-initial suffix is added, as in *vill* [ˈʋil] 'wild' and *krass* [ˈkrɑs] 'crass', whose neuter forms are *vilt* and *krast*. However, when 'degemination' would lead to homographs, as would be the case with *full* 'full' and *ful*, and *viss* 'certain' and *vis*, the double consonant is retained in the neuter as well, giving *fullt* vs. *fult* and *visst* vs. *vist*.

12.3.2 Tonal accents

Tonal accents are not marked as such in the orthography, but at least in one case their distribution is to a considerable degree inferrable. An *e* at the end of a disyllabic word, as in *bakke* 'hillside'; *kjøre* 'to drive', etc., usually signals accent 2 —see Chapter 9.3. Disyllabic words ending in other vowels usually have accent 1, although some names are exceptions. In other cases, especially compounds, tonal accent is unpredictable; there is nothing in the spelling that tells speakers that *ballkjole* 'ball gown' has accent 1, while *ballspill* 'ball game' has accent 2—see Chapter 9.5.

12.4 VOWELS

The relationship between the vowel letters of the alphabet and the phonetic values they may represent is visualized in (2).[5] The slashes between the phonetic symbols, which represent groupings according to phonemic value, show that there is a high degree of correspondence between letters and phonemes. Except for *e* and *æ*, the

(2)   *Relationship between vowel letters and pronunciation*

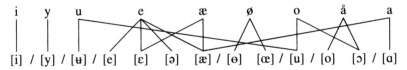

---

[4] Recall from Chapter 8.2.2 that shortening takes place in some lexically marked cases.
[5] Loan words which have retained their original spelling may represent additional types of links. Most of these cannot be considered systematic, however, and have therefore been excluded.

relationship between sound and letter is straightforward with respect to the non-back vowels, plus *a* and *å*, given that the two values for *ø* and *å* respectively represent long and short realizations of the same phoneme.

The relationship between /e/ and /æ/ and the different realizations of /e/ was discussed in Chapters 2.1.1.5 and 4.4. In most cases *æ* represents [æ], but there are a number of exceptions concerning cases where *æ* is used in front of letters other than *r*. Here it is usually pronounced [ɛ], as in *væske* [²vɛs.kə] 'fluid', which is homophonous with *veske* 'bag'. But in names one may hear [æ], as in the family name of a former mayor of Oslo, *Sæbønes*, which is often pronounced [²sæː.bœ.ˌneːs].The letter *a* may be pronounced [æ] in English loan words such as *bag* (id.) and *camping* (id.).

Long and short dorsal vowels have undergone different developments since the Medieval period. The long vowels have been subject to a chain shift, whereby older [uː] was fronted to [ʉː], [oː] was raised to [uː] and [ɔː] to [oː]. The short vowels did not take part in this shift. Instead we find fronting before some, but not all, consonants, most notably of older [u]. This means that short consonants, when not fronted, were left behind with their original phonetic value, while long vowels moved one level up ([ɔː] and [oː]) or from back to central ([uː]). In the orthography, however, the old correspondences between long and short are retained. With respects to long vowels, there is still a one-to-one correspondence between letter and sound, but the sound value differs compared to German, for example.

The letter *u* will therefore always represent [ʉː] when long. Thus [¹hʉːs] 'house' is spelled *hus*, and [²rʉː.tə] 'square' *rute*. Before geminated consonants or before consonant clusters it is pronounced either [ʉ] or [u]. Fronted pronunciation is most common, as in [¹mʉn], *munn* 'mouth' and [²sʉp.pə], *suppe* 'soup'. There is no longer a fully complementary distribution, but especially before the non-coronal nasals we find non-fronted pronunciations, such as *dum* [¹dum] 'stupid' and *tung* [¹tuŋ] 'heavy'.

While the high back vowel *u* underwent the same change whether long or short, leaving only a subset of the short vowels unchanged, the non-high back vowels split in three. The long vowels raised, while the short vowels remained unchanged, raised or fronted. The latter change will be disregarded here, since the end was not a new central vowel, but merger with vowels already part of the system. The interesting distinction is therefore between long vowels, which consistently raised, and short vowels, which vary. Hence the letter *o* is pronounced [u], as in *sol* [¹suːl] 'sun' and *skole* [²skuː.lə] 'school' when long. As a short vowel *o* is often pronounced [ɔ], as in *vott* [¹vɔt] 'mitten' and *kropp* [¹krɔp] 'body'.[6] But in other words it represents a high vowel, as in *fort* [¹fut] 'quickly', *kost* [¹kust] 'brush' (but *kost* [¹kɔst] 'diet'). In yet other words we find variation, such as *lomme* [²lumme] or [²lɔm.mə] 'pocket', etc. To complicate matters further, this pattern (or lack thereof) interacts with the fact that the difference between mid and low is allophonic with

---

[6] Cf. the examples discussed above, *dom* with long and short vowel being realized as [¹duːm] and [¹dɔm] respectively.

respect to the back, round vowels: short non-high vowels are consistently pro-nounced [ɔ]. This means that [ɔ] may be spelt with *o* as well as with *å*. Thus *flott* 'good' and *flått* 'tick' (zool.) are both pronounced [¹flɔt].[7]

In short, the relationship between sound and letter when it comes to short dorsal vowels is so complicated that rules can hardly be stated. Spelling cannot be pre-dicted from pronunciation, nor can pronunciation be inferred from spelling.

12.5 CONSONANTS

12.5.1 Silent consonants

Norwegian spelling is characterized by a large number of 'silent' consonants, that is, consonants which have disappeared on the way from Old Scandinavian to mod-ern Norwegian. It is not always possible to predict when to pronounce them.

A rule that has no exceptions in East Norwegian, however, is that *d* is never pronounced word-finally when it follows *l* or *n*: see Chapter 3.2.4.1. Thus *land* (id.) and *kald* 'cold' are pronounced [¹lɑn] and [¹kɑl]. Neither is *g* pronounced after a nasal; *lang* 'long' can only be pronounced [¹lɑŋ]. It is on the other hand always pronounced after *l* in word-final position, thus [¹sɑlg] for *salg* 'sale', except in imperatives of verbs where the *g* is not pronounced in the infinitive, such as *selge* [²sɛl.lə] 'to sell' and *følge*, [²fœl.lə] 'to accompany', whose imperatives are *selge*, [¹sɛl] and *følg*, [¹fœl].

Between vowels the pronunciation of these sequences varies. In simplex words the stop is pronounced before all vowels except *e*, hence [²rɑn.di], *Randi* (girl's name) [¹sɑl.du], *saldo* 'balance of an account' [¹tɑŋ.gu], *tango* (id.) and [¹tɔl.gɑ], *Tolga* (placename). Before *e* in simplex words we find variation. A telling example is the polysemous *følge*, which may mean 'consequence, result' or 'company'. The former is pronounced [²fœl.gə], the latter [²fœl.lə]. As to *nd*, it is most often pro-nounced [nd], but *ende*, [²ɛn.nə] 'end' is an exception.[8]

The letter *d* is also often silent after a stressed vowel, as for example in *blod*, [¹bluː] 'blood' and *blid*, [¹bliː] 'good-natured'. In other words, such as *blad* 'leaf', it *may* be pronounced, both [¹blɑː] and [¹blɑːd] can be heard. In yet others, such as *bad* 'bath' and *spyd* 'spear', it is obligatory, hence [¹bɑːd] and [¹spyːd] only. The former contrasts with the preterite of the verb *å be*, 'to pray', which is written *bad* (or *ba*), but invariably pronounced [¹bɑː]. The letter *g* is silent in the adjectival suffixes *-ig* and *-lig*, except when superlative /-st/ is added, when it turns up as [k]: see Chapter 4.2.3. It is also silent in a number of other words, such as *fugl*, [¹fʉːl]

---

[7] Words with short *å* are often related to words with long *å*. The neuter form of the adjective *våt*, [¹voːt] 'wet' is *vått*, whose pronunciation, [¹vɔt], is identical with that of *vott* 'mitten'. It is also used before *nd*, cf. *ånd* [¹ɔn] 'spirit', which contrasts with *ond* [¹un] 'evil'.

[8] The stop is on the other hand usually not pronounced in infinitives with *nd*, cf. Chapter 4.2.4. Thus å runde, 'to make round' is pronounced [²rʉn.nə], while the related noun *runde*, which means 'round (of a match, etc.)' is [²rʉn.də]. The stop is not pronounced either in the present participle ending *-ende*, cf. *løpende* [²løː.pn̩.nə] 'running'.

'bird'; *morgen*, [²mɔ:.ɔn̩] 'morning'; *også*, [¹ɔs.sɔ] 'too' and in the conjunction *og*, [o:/ɔ] 'and'. In the latter two, one often hears the *g*, however, probably due to spelling pronunciation.[9]

In the neuter def. sg. suffix *-et* the *t* is not pronounced, as in *huset* [¹hʉ:.sə] 'the house', but one may occasionally hear it in more formal settings, again probably due to spelling pronunciation. The suffix differs from two other homograph suffixes, preterite and perfect participle *-et*, where the *t* *is* pronounced, as in *hakket*, [²hɑk.kət] 'chopped'.

Most of the cases discussed so far concern word ends. Word-initially we also find silent consonants, however. An *h* followed by another consonant (only *j* and *v* are possible) is never pronounced, as in *hjelp*, [¹jɛlp] 'help' and *hval*, [¹ʋɑ:l] 'whale'. Likewise a *g* preceded by *j* is silent, for instance, *Gjert* [¹jæt̩] (man's name).

12.5.2 Consonant clusters corresponding to one speech sound

While some of the silent consonants discussed above also may be said to form consonant groups which correspond to one speech sound, the type that we are going to discuss now consists of clusters where the pronounced sound does not correspond to the sound normally associated with any of the letters forming the group.

The palatal fricative [ç] has developed from Old Norse /k/ followed by a front vowel or from /k/ or /t/ preceding /j/. The origin is still reflected in the spelling; there is no single letter that represents [ç] uniquely. When preceding a high vowel, it is written *k*, as in *kino*, [¹çi:.nu] 'cinema' and *kysse*, [²çys.sə] 'to kiss'. Some recent loan words with this spelling are pronounced with a stop, however, such as *kibbutz*, [¹kib.bʉts] (id.) and *kidnappe*, [¹kid.ˌnɑp.pə] 'to kidnap'. A single /k/ preceding the diphthong *ei* is also usually pronounced [ç], as in *keitet*, [²çæj.tət] 'awkward', but the word *keiser* 'emperor' is an exception, being usually pronounced [²kæj.sʃ]. Before other vowels [ç] is spelled *kj* or *tj*, depending on etymology, hence the homophonous *kjære*, [²çæ:.rə] 'dear' and *tjære*, [²çæ:.rə] 'tar'.[10]

The retroflex sounds [ʈ, ɖ, ɳ] are always written *rt*, *rd* and *rn* respectively. With respect to the clusters with *t* and *n*, the relation is bidirectional: *rt* and *rn* are are always pronounced as retroflexes, also across word boundaries; see Chapter 11.3.3. Written *rd* is on the other hand predictably pronounced as retroflex only when *r* and *d* belong to different morphological or syntactic constituents. In simplex words *rd* has three different realization types. In the first case, *rd* is pronounced as [r] or [ʈ]; see Chapter 4.3.3. In the second, the phonetic output is [rd]. An example of the first type is *bord* 'table', which may be pronounced [¹bu:r] or [¹bu:ʈ], while *bord* 'border (on a garment)' is pronounced [¹bɔrd]. The third possible pronunciation is as retro-

---

[9] This in some cases spills over into the homophonous infinitive marker *å*, which may be heard as hypercorrect [o:g] once in a while.

[10] There are a few exceptions, such as *København*, [çœ.bn̩.¹hɑʋn] 'Copenhagen' and *keramikk*, [çɛ.rɑ.¹mik] 'ceramics'. The verb *tjene* 'to serve' and words derived from it are usually pronounced with [tj], hence [²tje:.nə] and [²tje:.nə.stə] 'service'.

flex [ɖ], which is the case after an unstressed vowel, as in *verdi*, [ʋæ.¹ɖiː] 'value'.

The retroflex lateral may be written *rl*, and sequences of *rl* are always pronounced [ɭ]. But single *l* may also represent a retroflex lateral, as discussed in
Chapter 2.1.2.4.

A much more complicated pattern is found with [ʂ]. The sequence *rs* is invariably
pronounced as [ʂ], but the sound has other origins as well which are reflected in the
orthography. The most important is palatalization of former /s/. If followed by the
palatals /j/ or /ç/, the latter itself the product of palatalization of a velar stop, the
sequence has merged into [ʂ]. The older stage is reflected in the spelling, however,
as in *sjø*, [¹ʂøː] 'sea'; *ski*, [¹ʂiː] (id.); *skje*, [¹ʂeː] 'spoon'. The letter *j* is used before
all vowels except *i*, *y* and the diphthong *ei*.[11] The choice between *sj* and *sk(j)* is
determined by etymology, and therefore arbitrary from a synchronic point of view.

[ʂ] may also be written in other ways, mostly in loan words. *sj* may occur
postvocalically, thus *dusj*, [¹dʉʂ] 'shower' rhymes with *ressurs*, [rɛ.¹sʉʂ] 're-
source'. It is written *sh* for example in *sherry*, [¹ʂær.ri] (id.), *ch* for example in
champagne, [ʂɑm.¹pɑn.jə] (id.) (besides *sjampanje*), *sch* in *schæfer*, [¹ʂeː.fr̩] 'Alsatian (dog)', *g* in *giro*, [¹ʂiː.ru] (id.), and *j* in *journalist*, [ʂu.ɳɑ.¹list] (id.).

12.6 DIACRITICS

Diacritics are used only to a very limited extent, and in most cases in loan words
where they are part of the original spelling, as in *Orléans, Genève, Côte d'Or* and
Citroën. The acute accent is also used consistently to mark stress on a final *e* in
loan words. Grave and circumflex accent may in a few cases be used to distinguish
between words that would otherwise be homographs. One example is the sequence
⟨for⟩. The prefix and the preposition *for*, pronounced [fɔr], are written without
diacritic. The feminine or masculine noun *fòr*, pronounced [¹foːr] and also written
får, means 'furrow', while the neuter *fôr*, pronounced [¹fuːr], means either 'lining'
or 'fodder'. The preterite of *fare* 'to move quickly', written *for*, and pronounced
[¹fuːr], is officially without diacritic, but is sometimes seen as *fór*. A grave accent
may also be used to distinguish between *òg* 'too', which must be pronounced accented, from the usually unaccented conjunction *og* 'and'.

---

[11] There is one word that may have *j* in front of *ei*, viz. the rather rare *kjei*, [¹çæj] 'girl' (coll.), which
may also be spelled *kei. J* is not used before *øy* either, but there are only three words beginning with *køy-*
or *skøy-*, i.e. *køye* 'berth', *skøye* 'have fun' and *skøyte* 'skate' or 'kind of boat'. Only *skøyte* is pronounced with initial [ʂ].

REFERENCES

ABBREVIATIONS

FL   *Folia Linguistica*
Lg.   *Language*
LI   *Linguistic Inquiry*
LR   *The Linguistic Review*
NJL   *Nordic Journal of Linguistics*
NLLT   *Natural Language and Linguistic Theory*
NLT   *Norsk Lingvistisk Tidsskrift*
NTS   *Norsk Tidsskrift for Sprogvidenskap*
Ph.   *Phonology (Yearbook)*
TPS   *Transactions of the Philological Society*

AASEN, I. (1864), *Norsk Grammatik* (Kristiania: P. T. Mallings Boghandel).

—— (1873), *Norsk Ordbog* (Kristiania: P. T. Mallings Boghandel).

ALNÆS, I. (1916), *Norsk sætningsmelodi* (Kristiania: H. Aschehoug and Co.).

—— (1925), *Norsk uttale-ordbok*. 2nd edn. (Oslo: H. Aschehoug and Co.). Introduction reprinted in Jahr and Lorentz (1981), 110–45.

ARCHANGELI, D. (1988), 'Aspects of underspecification theory', *Ph.* 5: 183–208.

—— and D. PULLEYBLANK (1989), 'Yoruba vowel harmony', *LI* 20: 173–217.

—— —— (1994), *Grounded Phonology* (Cambridge, MA: MIT Press).

ARONOFF, M. (1976), *Word Formation in Generative Grammar* (Cambridge, MA: MIT Press).

BASBØLL, H. (1973), 'Notes on Danish consonant combinations', *Annual Report of the Institute of Phonetics, University of Copenhagen*, 7: 103–42. Translated into German and published as chapter VII (122–59) of BASBØLL, H. and J. WAGNER (1985), *Kontrastive Phonologie des Deutschen und Dänischen. Segmentale Wortphonologie und -phonetik.* (Tübingen: Niemeyer).

—— (1985), 'Stød in Modern Danish', *FL* XIX: 1–50.

—— (1991), 'Distinctive features, syllable structure, and vowel space', in Bertinetto *et al.* (1991), 3–17.

BERTINETTO, P. M., M. KENSTOWICZ and M. LOPORCARO (eds) (1991), *Certamen Phonologicum II. Papers from the 1990 Cortona Phonology Meeting* (Torino: Rosenberg and Sellier).

BERULFSEN, B. (1969), *Norsk uttaleordbok* (Oslo: H. Aschehoug and Co.).

BJERRUM, M. (1948), *Felstedmaalets tonale accenter* (Aarhus: Universitetsforlaget i Aarhus).

BLEVINS, J. (1995), 'The Syllable in Phonological Theory', in Goldsmith (1995), 206–44.

BOOIJ, G. (1981), 'Rule Ordering, rule application and the organization of grammars', in W. U. Dressler, O. E. Pfeiffer and J. R. Rennison (eds) *Phonologica 1980*, 45–56. (Innsbruck: Institut für Sprachwissenschaft der Universität Innsbruck).

—— (1993), 'Against Coronal Underspecification: the Case of Dutch', Vrije Universiteit, Amsterdam.

—— (1994), 'Lexical Phonology: a Review', *Lingua e stile* XXIX: 525–55.

—— (1995), *The Phonology of Dutch* (Oxford: Clarendon Press).

—— (1996), 'Cliticization as prosodic integration: the case of Dutch', *LR* 13: 219–42.

—— and R. LIEBER (1993), 'On the simultaneity of morphological and prosodic structure', in Hargus and Kaisse (1993a), 23–44.

—— and J. RUBACH (1984), 'Morphological and prosodic domains in Lexical Phonology', *Ph.* 1, 1–29.

—— —— (1987), 'Postcyclic versus postlexical rules in lexical phonology', *LI* 18: 1–44.

BORGSTRØM, C. H. (1938), 'Zur Phonologie der norwegischen Schriftsprache (nach der ost-norwegischen Aussprache)', *NTS* IX: 250–73.

BOROWSKY, T. (1989), 'Structure Preservation and the Syllable Coda in English', *NLLT* 7: 45–166.

—— (1990), *Topics in the Lexical Phonology of English* (New York: Garland).

—— (1993), 'On the Word Level', in Hargus and Kaisse (1993a), 199–234.

BREKKE, K. (1881), *Bidrag til dansk-norskens lydlære* (Kristiania). Reprinted in Jahr and Lorentz (1981) 17–78. (Page references in the text are to the reprinted version.)

BRIGHT, W. (ed.) (1992), *International Encyclopedia of Linguistics*, vols. 1–4 (New York, Oxford: Oxford University Press).

BROCH, O. (1927), 'Lyden [š] som ekspressivt middel i Oslo-målet', in *Festskrift til Hjalmar Falk*, 1–12. (Oslo: H. Aschehoug and Co.). Reprinted in Jahr and Lorentz (1981), 146–57.

—— (1935), 'Rhythm in the spoken Norwegian language', *TPS*, 80–112. Reprinted in Jahr and Lorentz (1983a), 78–112.

—— and E. W. SELMER (1961), *Håndbok i elementær fonetikk.* 9th edn. (Oslo: H. Aschehoug and Co.).

BROWMAN, C. P. and L. GOLDSTEIN (1990), 'Tiers in articulatory phonology, with some implications for casual speech', in Kingston and Beckman (1990), 341–76.

BRUCE, G. (1977), *Swedish Word Accents in Sentence Perspective* (Lund: CWK Gleerup).

—— (1984), 'Rhythmic alternation in Swedish', in Elert *et al.* (1984) 31–41.

—— (1987), 'How floating is focal accent?', in Gregersen and Basbøll (1987), 41–9.

—— and E. GÅRDING (1978), 'A prosodic typology for Swedish dialects', in Gårding *et al.* (1978), 219–28.

BYE, P. (1996), *Correspondence in the Prosodic Hierarchy and the Grid. Case Studies in Overlength and Level Stress.* Cand. philol. thesis, University of Tromsø.

CHAMBERS, J. K. and P. TRUDGILL (1980), *Dialectology* (Cambridge: Cambridge University Press).

CHAPMAN, K. G. (1962), 'Icelandic–Norwegian linguistic relationships', *NTS*, Suppl. 7.

CHO, Y.-M. Yu (1990), 'Syntax and phrasing in Korean', in Inkelas and Zec (1990), 47–62.

CHOMSKY, N. and M. HALLE (1968), *The Sound Pattern of English* (New York: Harper and Row).

CHRISTENSEN, K. K. (1985), 'Subject clitics and A-bound traces', *NJL* 8: 1–23.

CHRISTIANSEN, H. (1933), 'Gimsøy-målet. Fonologi og orddannelse', *Skrifter utgitt av Det norske videnskaps-akademi i Oslo. II. Historisk-filosofisk klasse*, 1932. (Oslo: Jacob Dybwad)

—— (1946–48), *Norske dialekter* (Oslo: Tanum).

CLEMENTS, G. N. (1985), 'The geometry of phonological features', *Ph.* 2: 225–52.

—— (1988), 'Toward a Substantive Theory of Feature Specification', *Proceedings of the North Eastern Linguistic Society* 18: 79–93.

CLEMENTS, G. N. (1990), 'The Role of the Sonority Cycle in Core Syllabification', in Kingston and Beckman (1990), 283–333.

—— and E. V. HUME (1995), 'The Internal Organization of Speech Sounds', in Goldsmith (1995), 245–306.

—— and S. J. KEYSER (1983), *CV-Phonology. A Generative Theory of the Syllable* (Cambridge, MA: MIT Press).

COLE, J. (1995), 'The Cycle in Phonology', in Goldsmith (1995), 70–113.

CONDORAVDI, C. (1990), 'Sandhi Rules of Greek and Prosodic Theory', in Inkelas and Zec (1990), 63–84.

DALEN, A. (1985), *Skognamålet. Ein fonologisk analyse* (Oslo: Novus).

DANELL, G. (1937), *Svensk ljudlära*, 4th edn. (Stockholm: Svenska bokförlaget).

DIDERICHSEN, P. (1953), 'Bidrag til en analyse af det danske skriftsprogs struktur', *Selskab for nordisk Filologis Årsberetning for 1951–52*, pp. 6–22. Reprinted, with a summary in English, in P. Diderichsen (1966), *Helhed og struktur*, 169–91. (Copenhagen: G. E. C. Gads forlag).

DOMMELEN, W. van, T. FRETHEIM and R. A. NILSEN (1998), 'The perception of boundary tone in East Norwegian', in S. Werner (ed.), *Nordic Prosody*, 73–86. (Bern: Peter Lang).

DRESHER, B. E. and A. LAHIRI (1991), 'The Germanic Foot: Metrical Coherence in Old English', *LI* 22: 251–86.

DURAND, J. (1990), *Generative and Non-Linear Phonology* (London: Longman).

—— and F. KATAMBA (eds) (1995), *Frontiers of Phonology. Atoms, Structures, Derivations* (London: Longman).

ELERT, C.-C. (1970), *Ljud och ord i svenskan* (Stockholm: Almquist and Wiksell).

——, I. JOHANSSON and E. STRANGERT (eds) (1984), *Nordic Prosody III* (Umeå, Stockholm: Almquist and Wiksell).

ELIASSON, S. (1978), 'Swedish Quantity Revisited', in Gårding *et al.* (1978), 111–22.

—— (1985), 'Stress alternations and vowel length: new evidence for an underlying nine-vowel system in Swedish', *NJL* 8: 101–29.

—— and N. LA PELLE (1973), 'Generativa regler för svenskans kvantitet', *Arkiv för Nordisk Filologi* 1973: 133–48.

ELSTAD, K. (1979), 'Det nordnorske cirkumflekstonemet', in Gårding *et al.* (1978), 165–74.

—— (1980), 'Some remarks on Scandinavian tonogenesis', *Nordlyd* (Tromsø University Working Papers on Language and Linguistics) 3: 62–77. Reprinted in Jahr and Lorentz (1983a), 388–98.

—— (1982), *Borgfjerdingsmål 1–2* (Oslo: Novus).

ENDRESEN, R. T. (1974a), 'On the existence of a Retroflex Flap Rule in Eastern Norwegian', *Working Papers in Linguistics*, 5 1974 (University of Oslo: Dept. of Linguistics).

—— (1974b), 'On retroflex segments in Norwegian', *NTS* 28: 73–8.

—— (1976), *Handsaminga av trykk og tonem i generativ fonologi*. Mag. art. thesis, University of Oslo.

—— (1977), 'An Alternative Theory of Stress and Tonemes in Eastern Norwegian', *NTS* 31: 21–46. Reprinted in Jahr and Lorentz (1983a), 362–87.

—— (1985), 'Norske konsonantar. Fonetiske og fonologiske merknadar', *NLT* 3: 65–100.

—— (1990), 'Svar på anmeldelser av *Fonetikk. Ei elementær innføring*', *NLT* 8: 169–92.

—— (1991), *Fonetikk og fonologi* (Oslo: Universitetsforlaget).

ENGSTRAND, O. (1995), 'Phonetic interpretation of the word accent contrast in Swedish', *Phonetica* 52: 171–9.

FAARLUND, J. T. (1974), 'Some remarks on the phonological status of retroflex flap in Eastern Norwegian', *Working Papers in Linguistics*, 6 1974 (University of Oslo: Dept. of Linguistics).

——— S. LIE and K. I. VANNEBO (1997), *Norsk referansegrammatikk* (Oslo: Universitets-forlaget).

FANT, G. (1973), *Speech Sounds and Features* (Cambridge, MA: MIT Press).

FÉRY, C. (1995), *Alignment, syllable and metrical structure in German* (Tübingen: SfS-Report-02-95, Seminar für Sprachwissenschaft).

FINTOFT, K. (1970), *Acoustical Analysis and Perception of Tonemes in some Norwegian Dialects* (Oslo: Universitetsforlaget).

——— and P. E. MJAAVATN (1980), 'Tonelagskurver som målmerke', *Maal og Minne*: 66–87.

——————, E. MØLLERGÅRD and B. ULSETH (1978), 'Toneme patterns in Norwegian dialects', in Gårding *et al.* (1978), 197–206.

FISCHER-JØRGENSEN, E. (1952), 'On the definition of phoneme categories on a distributional basis', *Acta Linguistica* VII: 8–39. Reprinted in E. Fischer-Jørgensen (1979), *25 years' phonological comments*, 90–121 (München: Wilhelm Fink).

——— (1993), 'Stress in compounds and derivatives in 17th and 18th century Danish', in Granström and Nord (1993), 33–47.

FIVA, T. (1983), 'Noen fonologiske regler i norsk med utgangspunkt i Bodø-dialekten', *NLT* 1: 13–40.

FOLDVIK, A. K. (1974), 'Phonetic light on the Endresen–Fretheim controversy', *Working Papers in Linguistics*, 6 1974 (University of Oslo: Dept. of Linguistics).

——— (1977), 'Realisasjonen av r i norsk', *Svenska Landsmål och Svenskt Folkliv* 100: 110–18.

——— (1989), Review of Rolf Theil Endresen: *Fonetikk. Ei elementær innføring*, *NLT* 7: 109–13.

FOLEY, J. (1973), 'Assimilation of phonological strength in Germanic', in S. R. Anderson and P. Kiparsky (eds) (1973), *A Festschrift for Morris Halle*, 51–8. (New York: Holt, Rinehart & Winston).

——— (1977), *Foundations of theoretical phonology* (Cambridge: Cambridge University Press).

FOSSESTØL, B., K. I. VANNEBO, K. VENÅS and F.-E. VINJE (eds) (1984), *Festskrift til Einar Lundeby* (Oslo: Novus).

FRETHEIM, T. (1969), 'Norwegian Stress and Quantity Reconsidered', *NTS* XXIII: 76–96. Reprinted in Jahr and Lorentz (1983a), 315–34.

——— (1974a), 'The Norwegian retroflex flap and the concept of "Natural Class" in Phono-logy', *NTS* 28: 79–85.

——— (1974b), 'Some Cases of Accent Shift in East Norwegian', *NTS* 28: 113–29.

——— (1981a), 'Intonational Phrasing in Norwegian', *NJL* 4: 111–37.

——— (ed.) (1981b), *Nordic Prosody II* (Trondheim: Tapir).

——— (1984), 'så—pro-adverb eller gradsadverb?', *Maal og Minne*: 188–212.

——— (1988), 'Den kontraherte negativpartikkelen: 'ke eller 'kke', *NLT* 6: 73–88.

——— (1990a), 'The Form and Function of Foot-External Syllables in Norwegian Intonation', in Wiik and Raimo (1990), 87–110.

FRETHEIM, T. (1990b), 'Pitch-cued emotive meaning in Norwegian imperatives', *Grazer Linguistische Studien* 33/34: 75–91.

—— (1991), 'Intonational phrases and syntactic focus domains', in J. Verschueren (ed.), *Levels of Linguistic Adaptation*, 81–111. (Amsterdam: John Benjamins).

—— (1992a), 'Themehood, Rhemehood and Norwegian Focus Structure', *FL* XXVI: 111–50.

—— (1992b), 'Om ikoniske og ikke-ikoniske delmelodier i østnorske intonasjonsmønstre', in *Det Kongelige Norske Videnskabers Selskab. Forhandlinger 1992*: 219–34 (Trondheim: Tapir). (Contains a summary in English.).

—— and P. K. HALVORSEN (1975), 'Norwegian cliticization', in K. H. Dahlstedt (ed.), *The Nordic Languages and Modern Linguistics*, 446–65. (Stockholm: Almquist and Wiksell).

—— and R. A. NILSEN (1989), 'Terminal rise and rise–fall tunes in East Norwegian intonation', *NJL* 12: 155–81.

—— —— (1991), 'In Defense of [±foc]', in Y. No and M. Libucha (eds) *Escol '90. Proceedings of the Seventh Eastern Conference on Linguistics*, 102–11 (The Ohio State University).

GABRIELSEN, F. (1991), *Haugesund bymål* (Bergen: Alvheim and Eide).

GÅRDING, E. (1977), *The Scandinavian word accents* (Lund: CWK Gleerup).

——, G. BRUCE and R. BANNERT (eds) (1978), *Nordic Prosody* (Lund: Dept. of Linguistics, Lund University).

—— and M. STENBERG (1990), 'West Swedish and East Norwegian intonation', in Wiik and Raimo (1990), 111–30.

GOLDSMITH, J. A. (1976), *Autosegmental Phonology* (Bloomington: Indiana University Linguistics Club).

—— (1982), 'Accent Systems', in van der Hulst and Smith (1982), 47–63.

—— (1989), *Autosegmental and Metrical Phonology* (Oxford: Blackwell).

—— (ed.) (1995), *The Handbook of Phonological Theory* (Oxford: Blackwell).

GRANSTRÖM, B. and L. NORD (eds) (1993), *Nordic Prosody VI* (Stockholm: Almquist and Wiksell).

GREGERSEN, K. and H. BASBØLL (eds) (1987), *Nordic Prosody IV* (Odense: Odense University Press).

HAGEN, J. E. (1986), 'Bestemthetsbøying i svake substantiv' *NLT* 4: 72–7.

HALL, T. A. (1989), 'Lexical Phonology and the distribution of German [ç] and [x]', *Ph.* 6: 1–18.

—— (1992), *Syllable Structure and Syllable-Related Processes in German* (Tübingen: Max Niemeyer Verlag).

HALLE, M. (1992), 'Phonological Features', in Bright (1992, vol. 3), 207–12.

—— (1997), 'On stress and accent in Indo-European', *Lg.* 73: 275–313.

—— and M. KENSTOWICZ (1991), 'The Free Element Condition and cyclic versus noncyclic stress', *LI* 22: 457–501.

—— and K. P. MOHANAN (1985), 'The Segmental Phonology of Modern English', *LI* 16: 57–116.

—— and J.-R. VERGNAUD (1980), 'Three Dimensional Phonology', *Journal of Linguistic Research* 1: 83–105.

—— —— (1987), *An Essay on Stress* (Cambridge, MA: MIT Press).

HALVORSEN, P.-K. (1983), 'Tone in Norwegian polysyllables', in Jahr and Lorentz (1983a), 351–61.

HANSSEN, E. (1985), '"Kak før ei kron"—Om variasjon i Saltenmålet', in A. Fjeldstad and T. Bull (eds): *Heidersskrift til Kåre Elstad*, 21–36. (Tromsø: Universitetet i Tromsø, Institutt for språk og litteratur).

HARGUS, S. and E. M. KAISSE (eds) (1993a), *Studies in Lexical Phonology* (Phonetics and Phonology 4). (San Diego: Academic Press).

—— —— (1993b), 'Introduction', in Hargus and Kaisse (1993a), 1–19.

HARRIS, J. and G. LINDSEY (1995), 'The elements of phonological representation', in Durand and Katamba (1995), 34–79.

HASLEV, M. (1987), 'Toneme 1 or toneme 2 in certain Norwegian utterance types', in Gregersen and Basbøll (1987), 81–90.

HAUGEN, E. (1942a), 'On the stressed vowel systems of Norwegian', in *Scandinavian Studies. Presented to George T. Flom by Colleagues and Friends* (Urbana: Illinois Studies in Language and Literature, vol. XXIX). Reprinted in Jahr and Lorentz (1981), 196–207.

—— (1942b), 'Analysis of a sound group: *sl* and *tl* in Norwegian', *Publications of the Modern Language Association of America* LVII: 879–907.

—— (1948), 'Mere om r-bortfall i sørøstlandsk', *Maal og Minne*: 117–22. Reprinted in Jahr and Lorentz (1981), 239–42.

—— (1955), 'Tonelagsanalyse', *Maal og Minne*: 70–80. Reprinted in Jahr and Lorentz (1983a), 202–8.

—— (1963), 'Pitch accent and tonemic juncture in Scandinavian', *Monatshefte für deutschen Unterricht, deutsche Sprache und Literatur* 55: 157–61. Reprinted in Jahr and Lorentz (1983a), 277–81.

—— (1967), 'On the Rules of Norwegian Tonality', *Lg.* 43: 185–202. Reprinted in Jahr and Lorentz (1983a), 293–309.

—— (1969), *The Norwegian Language in America: a study in bilingual behaviour*, 2nd edn. (Bloomington: Indiana University Press).

—— (1976), *The Scandinavian Languages*. (London: Faber and Faber).

—— and K. G. CHAPMAN (1982), *Spoken Norwegian*. 3rd edn. (Fort Worth: Holt, Rinehart & Winston).

—— and M. JOOS (1952), 'Tone and intonation in East Norwegian', *Acta Philologica Scandinavica* 22: 41–64. Reprinted in Jahr and Lorentz (1983a), 179–201.

HAYES, B. (1986), 'Inalterability in CV Phonology', *Lg.* 62: 321–51.

—— (1989), 'Compensatory lengthening in moraic phonology', *LI* 20: 253–306.

—— (1995) *Metrical Stress Theory. Principles and Case Studies* (Chicago: University of Chicago Press).

HELLAN, L. (1994), 'A Note on Clitics in Norwegian'. *Eurotyp Working Papers*, Theme Group 8, vol. 6, 80–90.

—— and Christer Platzack (in press), 'Pronouns in Scandinavian Languages', in H. van Riemsdijk (ed.), *Clitics in the Languages of Europe*, 123–42. (Berlin: Mouton de Gruyter).

HOEL, T. (1981), 'An intonation analysis of the Oslo dialect', in Fretheim (1981b), 96–110.

HOFTVEDT, B. O. (1980), 'Noen trekk ved formell og uformell språkbruk i Oslo-mål', *Norskrift* 29: 27–45. (University of Oslo: Institutt for nordistikk og litteraturvitenskap).

HOGNESTAD, J. K. (1997), *Tonemer i en høytonedialekt* (Oslo: Det Norske Samlaget).

HOVDHAUGEN, E. (1970), 'Tonelag og trykk ved avledninger med prefikset u- i bokmål', in E. Hanssen (ed.), *Studier i norsk språkstruktur*, 81–5. (Oslo: Universitetsforlaget).

—— (1971), *Transformasjonell generativ grammatikk*, 2nd edn. (Oslo: Universitetsforlaget).

HOVDHAUGEN, E. (1974), 'A note on the linguistic variability of the retroflex flap in Eastern Norwegian', *Working Papers in Linguistics*, 6 1974 (University of Oslo: Dept. of Linguistics). Reprinted in Jahr and Lorentz (1981), 300–5.

HULST, H. van der (1984), *Syllable Structure and Stress in Dutch* (Dordrecht: Foris Publications).

—— (1995a), 'Radical CV Phonology: the categorial gesture', in Durand and Katamba (1995), 80–116.

—— (1995b), 'Metrical Phonology', *Glot International* 1,1: 3–6.

—— (1996), 'Primary accent is non-metrical', *Rivista di Linguistica* 9.1: 99–127.

—— (1999a), 'Word Accent', in van der Hulst (ed.), 3–116.

—— (ed.) (1999b), *Word Prosodic Systems in the Languages of Europe* (Berlin: Mouton de Gruyter).

——, B. HENDRIKS and J. van de WEIJER (1999), 'A survey of word prosodic systems of European languages', in van der Hulst (ed.), 425–76.

—— and N. SMITH (eds) (1982), *The Structure of Phonological Representations*, vols. 1–2. (Dordrecht: Foris Publications).

HUME, E. (1994), *Vowels, Coronal Consonants and their Interaction in Non-linear Phonology* (New York: Garland).

—— (1996), 'Coronal consonant, front vowel parallels in Maltese', *NLLT* 14: 163–203.

HYMAN, L. (1985), *A Theory of Phonological Weight* (Dordrecht: Foris).

INKELAS, S. and Y.-M. Yu CHO (1993), 'Inalterability as prespecification', *Lg.* 69: 529–74.

—— and D. ZEC (eds) (1990), *The Phonology–Syntax Connection* (Chicago: University of Chicago Press).

ITÔ, J. (1988), *Syllable Theory in Prosodic Phonology* (New York: Garland).

—— (1989), 'A prosodic theory of epenthesis', *NLLT* 7: 217–59.

IVERSON, G. K. and J. C. SALMONS (1995), 'Aspiration and laryngeal representation in Germanic', *Ph.* 12: 369–96.

JAHR, E. H. (1981), 'L-fonema i Oslo bymål', in Jahr and Lorentz (1981), 328–44.

—— (1985), 'Another explanation for the development of *s* before *l* in Norwegian', in J. Fisiak (ed.), *Papers from the 6th International Conference on Historical Linguistics*, 291–300. (Amsterdam: John Benjamins).

—— (1988), 'Social dialect influence in language change: the halting of a sound change in Oslo Norwegian', in J. Fisiak (ed.): *Historical Dialectology—regional and social*, 329–35. (Berlin: Mouton de Gruyter).

—— and O. LORENTZ (eds) (1981), *Fonologi/Phonology* (Oslo: Novus).

—— —— (eds) (1983a), *Prosodi/Prosody* (Oslo: Novus).

—— —— (1983b), 'Innleiing', in Jahr and Lorentz (1983a), 9–29.

JASANOFF, J. H. (1966), 'Remarks on the Scandinavian Word Tones', *Lingua* 16: 71- 81. Reprinted in Jahr and Lorentz (1983a), 282–92.

JENSEN, M. K. (1961). 'Tonemicity. A technique for determining the phonemic status of suprasegmental patterns in pairs of lexical units, applied to a group of West Norwegian dialects, and to Faroese'. Årbok for Universitetet i Bergen 1961. Humanistisk serie nr. 1 (Bergen: University of Bergen).

—— (1969), *Språklydlære*, 2nd edn. (Oslo: Universitetsforlaget).

JOHANNESSEN, J. B. (1989), 'Klitika—en avgrensning', *NLT* 7: 117–47.

KAGER, R. (1993), 'Alternatives to the Iambic–Trochaic Law', *NLLT* 11: 381–432.

—— (1995), 'The metrical theory of word stress', in Goldsmith (1995), 367–402.

KAISSE, E. (1990), 'Toward a typology of postlexical rules', in Inkelas and Zec (1990), 127–43.

—— and P. A. SHAW (1985), 'On the theory of lexical phonology', *Ph.* 2: 1–30.

KANERVA, J. M. (1990), 'Focusing on phonological phrases in Chicheŵa', in Inkelas and Zec (1990: 145–61)).

KAYE, J., J. LOWENSTAMM and J.-R. VERGNAUD (1985), 'The internal structure of phonological elements. A theory of charm and government', *Ph.* 2: 305–28.

KEATING, P. A. (1988), 'Underspecification in phonetics', *Ph.* 5: 275–92.

—— (1996), 'The phonology–phonetics interface', in Kleinhenz (1996), 262–78.

KENSTOWICZ, M. (1994), *Phonology in Generative Grammar* (Oxford: Blackwell).

KINGSTON, J. and M. E. BECKMAN (eds) (1990), *Papers in laboratory phonology I* (Cambridge: Cambridge University Press).

KIPARSKY, P. (1973), ' "Elsewhere" in phonology', in S. R. Anderson and P. Kiparsky (eds), *A Festschrift for Morris Halle*, 93–106 (New York: Holt, Rinehart & Winston).

—— (1979), 'Metrical structure assignment is cyclic', *LI* 10: 421–42.

—— (1982), 'Lexical morphology and phonology', in The Linguistic Society of Korea (ed.), *Linguistics in the Morning Calm. Selected Papers from SICOL-1981*, 3–91. (Seoul: Hanshin Publishing Company).

—— (1984), 'On the lexical phonology of Icelandic', in Elert *et al.* (1984), 135–64.

—— (1985), 'Some consequences of Lexical Phonology', *Ph.* 2: 85–138.

KLEINHENZ, U. (ed.) (1996), *Interfaces in Phonology* (Studia Grammatica, vol. 41). (Berlin: Akademie Verlag).

KNUDSEN, K. (1856), *Haandbog i dansk-norsk Sproglære* (Kristiania: J. Chr. Abelsted).

KRISTOFFERSEN, G. (1982), 'Om progressiv stemthetsassimilasjon i norsk', *Maal og Minne*: 167–84.

—— (1990), *East Norwegian Prosody and the Level Stress Problem*, MS, University of Tromsø: Institut for språk og litteratur.

—— (1991), *Aspects of Norwegian Syllable Structure*. Doctoral dissertation, University of Tromsø.

—— (1992a), 'Cirkumflekstonelaget i norske dialekter, med særlig vekt på nordnorsk', *Maal og Minne*: 37–61.

—— (1992b), 'Tonelag i sammensatte ord i østnorsk', *NLT* 10: 39–65.

—— (1993a), 'An autosegmental analysis of East Norwegian pitch accent', in Granström and Nord (1993), 109–22.

—— (1993b), 'East Norwegian pitch accent', in *Runes and Representations: Proceedings of ScandiLingFest 1, Occasional Papers in Linguistics, The University of Chicago*, 29–50.

—— (1995), 'The Nordic quantity shift and the question of extrametricality', in *Proceedings from the XIVth Scandinavian Conference of Linguistics and the VIIIth Conference of Nordic and General Linguistics*. Gothenburg Papers in Theoretical Linguistics 69, vol. 1: 219–31. (Gothenburg: Dept. of Linguistics, Gothenburg University).

—— (1998), 'Om palataler, men fra en fonologisk synsvinkel', in G. Akselberg and J. Bondevik (eds) (1998), *Ord etter ord*, 179–95. (Bergen: Norsk Bokreidingslag).

—— (1999), 'Quantity in Norwegian syllable structure', in H. van der Hulst and N. Ritter (eds), *The Syllable. Facts and Views*, 631–50. (Berlin: Mouton de Gruyter).

LADD, D. R. (1996), *Intonational Phonology* (Cambridge: Cambridge University Press).

LADEFOGED, P. and I. MADDIESON (1996), *The Sounds of the World's Languages* (Oxford: Blackwell).

LARSEN, A. B. (1894), 'Lydlæren i den solørske dialekt', *Videnskabsselskabets Skrifter. II. Historisk–filosofiske Klasse* 4. Kristiania.

—— (1897), *Oversigt over de Norske Bygdemaal* (Kristiania: H. Aschehoug and Co.).

—— (1907), *Kristiania Bymål* (Kristiania: Cammermeyer).

LASS, R. (1980), *On Explaining Language Change* (Cambridge: Cambridge University Press).

—— (1984), *Phonology. An Introduction to Basic Concepts* (Cambridge: Cambridge University Press).

LAVER, J. (1994), *Principles of Phonetics* (Cambridge: Cambridge University Press).

LEVANDER, L. (1909), 'Älvdalsmålet i Dalarna. Ordböjning ock syntax', *De Svenska Landsmålen ock Svenskt Folklif*, vol. 4.3: 1–129.

LEVIN, J. (1985), *A Metrical Theory of Syllabicity*. Doctoral dissertation, MIT.

LIBERMAN, M. and A. PRINCE (1977), 'On stress and linguistic rhythm', *LI* 8: 249–336.

Lie, Svein (1983), 'Noen fonologiske regler i norsk med utgangspunkt i hedalsmål', *NLT* 1: 3–12.

—— (1984), 'Om noen følger av schwa-bortfall i norsk', *Maal og Minne*: 120–57.

LIND, E. H. (1905–1915), *Norsk–isländska dopnamn ock fingerade namn från medeltiden* (Uppsala: Lundequistska bokhandeln/Leipzig: Otto Harrassowitz).

LINDAU, M. (1978), 'Vowel features', *Lg.* 54: 541–63.

LOMBARDI, L. (1994), *Laryngeal Features and Laryngeal Neutralization* (New York: Garland).

—— (1995), 'Laryngeal neutralization and syllable wellformedness', *NLLT* 13: 39–74.

LORENTZ, O. (1981), 'Adding tone to tone in Scandinavian dialects', in Fretheim (1981b), 166–80.

—— (1984), 'Stress and tone in an accent language', in Elert *et al.* (1984), 165–78.

—— (1990), 'Polytonicity', handout distributed 31 Oct. 1990 at talk given at the conference *Fonologisk uke*, University of Trondheim.

—— (1995), 'Tonal prominence and alignment', *Phonology at Santa Cruz* 4: 39–56.

—— (1996), 'Length and correspondence in Scandinavian', *Nordlyd* (Tromsø University Working Papers on Language and Linguistics) 24: 111–28.

MCCARTHY, J. J. (1988), 'Feature geometry and dependency: A review', *Phonetica* 45: 84–108.

—— (1995), 'Extensions of faithfulness: Rotuman revisited', MS, University of Massachusetts.

—— and A. PRINCE (1986), *Prosodic Morphology*, MS, University of Massachusetts and Brandeis University.

—— —— (1990), 'Prosodic morphology and templatic morphology', in M. Eid and J. McCarthy (eds), *Perspectives on Arabic Linguistics 2. Papers from the Second Annual Symposium on Arabic Linguistics*, 1–54. (Amsterdam: John Benjamins).

—— and Alison Taub (1992), Review of C. Paradis and J.-F. Prunet: *The Special Status of Coronals: Internal and External Evidence. Ph.* 9: 363–70.

MADDIESON, I. (1984), *Patterns of Sounds* (Cambridge: Cambridge University Press).

MALMBERG, B. (1956), 'Distinctive features of Swedish vowels: some instrumental and structural data', in M. Halle *et al.* (eds): *For Roman Jakobson*, 316–21. (The Hague: Mouton).

—— (1967), *Lärobok i Fonetik* (Lund: Gleerup).

MESTER, A. and J. ITÔ (1989), 'Feature predictability and underspecification: palatal prosody in Japanese mimetics', *Lg.* 65: 258–93.

MOEN, I. and H. G. SIMONSEN (1997), 'Kontaktmønstre for apikale plosiver, /t, d/, i østnorsk', MS, University of Oslo: Dept. of Linguistics.

MOHANAN, K. P. (1985), 'Syllable structure and lexical strata in English', *Ph.* 2: 137–55.

—— (1986), *The Theory of Lexical Phonology* (Dordrecht: Reidel).

—— (1991), 'On the bases of radical underspecification', *NLLT* 9: 285–325.

MONRAD-KROHN, G. H. (1947), 'Dysprosody or altered "Melody of Language"', *Brain* LXX: 405–15. Reprinted in Jahr and Lorentz (1983a), 144–53.

MYERS, S. (1987), 'Vowel shortening in English', *NLLT* 5: 485–18.

—— (1991), 'Persistent rules', *LI* 22: 315–44.

—— (1997), 'Expressing phonetic naturalness in phonology', in I. Roca (ed.), *Derivations and Constraints in Phonology*, 125–52 (Oxford: Clarendon Press).

NESPOR, M. and I. VOGEL (1986), *Prosodic Phonology* (Dordrecht: Foris).

NILSEN, R. A. (1989), 'On prosodically marked information structure in spoken Norwegian', *University of Trondheim Working Papers in Linguistics* 7. Trondheim.

—— (1992), *Intonasjon i interaksjon. Sentrale spørsmål i norsk intonologi*. Doctoral dissertation, University of Trondheim.

—— and T. FRETHEIM (1992), 'The East Norwegian "No Big Deal" intonation', in J. Louis-Jensen and H. W. Poulsen (eds) *The Nordic Languages and Modern Linguistics* 7, 453–63 (Tórshavn: Føroya Fróðskaparfelag).

NOREEN, A. (1903), *Vårt språk*, vol. 1 (Lund: C. W. K. Gleerup).

NORSK TERMBANK (1986), 'Bokmål baklengsordliste', *Norske Språkdata* 3. (University of Bergen: Norsk Termbank).

OFTEDAL, M. (1952), 'On the origin of the Scandinavian tone distinction', *NTS* XVI: 201–25. Reprinted in Jahr and Lorentz (1983a), 154–78.

OHALA, J. J. (1974), 'Phonetic explanation in phonology', in A. Bruck, R. A. Fox and M. W. La Galy (eds), *Papers from the parasession on natural phonology*, 251–74. (Chicago: Chicago Linguistic Society).

OOSTENDORP, M. van (1995), *Vowel Quality and Phonological Projection*. Doctoral dissertation, Tilburg University.

—— (1998), 'Schwa in phonological theory', *Glot International* 3.5: 3–8.

PAPAZIAN, E. (1977), 'Om "tjukk l" og andre rare lyder', *Norskrift* 14: 1–56 (University of Oslo: Institutt for nordistikk og litteraturvitenskap).

—— (1984), 'Dokka med snabern', *Maal og Minne*: 223–37.

—— (1994), 'Om sje-lyden i norsk, og ombyttinga av den med kje-lyden', *Norskrift* 83: 1–105. (University of Oslo: Institutt for nordistikk og litteraturvitenskap).

PARADIS, C. and PRUNET, J. F. (1991), *The Special Status of Coronals. Internal and External Evidence* (San Diego: Academic Press).

PEPERKAMP, S. (1996), 'On the prosodic representation of clitics', in Kleinhenz (1996). 102–27.

PERLMUTTER, D. (1995), 'Phonological quantity and multiple association', in Goldsmith (1995), 307–17.

PIERREHUMBERT, J. B. and M. BECKMAN (1988), *Japanese Tone Structure* (Cambridge. MA: MIT Press).

POPPERWELL, R. G. (1963), *The Pronunciation of Norwegian* (Cambridge, Oslo: Cambridge University Press and Oslo University Press).

PRINCE, A. S. (1983), 'Relating to the grid', *LI* 14: 19–100.

—— and P. SMOLENSKY (1993), *Optimality Theory. Constraint Interaction in Generative Grammar*, MS, Rutgers University and University of Colorado.

PULLEYBLANK, D. (1986), *Tone in Lexical Phonology* (Dordrecht: Reidel).

—— (1995), 'Feature geometry and underspecification', in Durand and Katamba (1995), 3–33.

RIAD, T. (1992), *Structures in Germanic Prosody*. Doctoral dissertation, Stockholm University.

—— (1995), 'The quantity shift in Germanic: a typology', in H. Fix, (ed.), *Quantitätsproblematik und Metrik* (Amsterdamer Beiträge zur älteren Germanistik 42: 159–84.) (Amsterdam: Rodopi).

—— (1998), 'The origin of Scandinavian tone accents', *Diachronica* XV: 1, 63–98.

RICE, C. (1999), 'Norwegian', in van der Hulst (ed.), 545–53.

RINGGAARD, K. (1973), *Danske dialekter* (Copenhagen: Akademisk forlag).

RINNAN, G. D. (1969), 'Nok en gang om alveolarene', in *Tilegnet Carl Hj. Borgstrøm. Et festskrift på 60-årsdagen 12.10.69 fra hans elever*, 128–33. Reprinted in Jahr and Lorentz (1981), 273–7.

RISCHEL, J. (1960), 'Über die phonematische und morphphonematische Funktion der sogenannten Worttöne in Norwegischen', *Zeitschrift für Phonetik und allgemeine Sprachwissenschaft* 13: 177–85.

—— (1963), 'Morphemic tone and word tone in Eastern Norwegian', *Phonetica* 10: 154–64. Reprinted in Jahr and Lorentz (1983a), 266–76.

ROCA, I. (1994), *Generative Phonology* (London: Routledge).

ROSS, H. (1895), *Norsk Ordbog* (Kristiania: Cammermeyer).

—— (1905), 'Norske bygdemaal. Fyrste bolken', *Videnskabsselskabets Skrifter. II. Historisk-filosofiske Klasse* no. 2. Kristiania.

RUBACH, J. (1990), 'Final devoicing and cyclic syllabification in German', *LI* 21: 79–94.

—— (1996), 'Shortening and ambisyllabicity in English', *Ph.* 13: 197–237.

—— and G. BOOIJ (1990), 'Syllable structure assignment in Polish', *Ph.* 7: 121–58.

RYKKVIN, O. (1946), 'Om R-bortfall i søraustlandsk', *Maal og Minne*: 144–50. Reprinted in Jahr and Lorentz (1981), 232–8.

SAGEY, E. C. (1990), *The Representation of Features and Relations in Non-Linear Phonology* (New York: Garland).

SANDVIK, O. H. (1979), *Talemål i Rogaland—i går, i dag og i morgen* (Stavanger: Rogalandsforskning).

SANDØY, H. (1994), 'The nature of "overlong syllables" in the Scandinavian languages', in W. U. Dressler *et al.* (eds) (1994), *Phonologica. Proceedings of the 7th International Phonology Meeting*, 233–42. (Torino: Rosenberg and Sellier).

—— (1996), *Talemål*, 2nd edn. (Oslo: Novus).

SCALISE, S. (1984), *Generative Morphology* (Dordrecht: Foris).

SELKIRK, E. (1982), 'The Syllable', in van der Hulst and Smith (vol. 2), 337–83.

—— (1984), *Phonology and Syntax. The Relation between Sound and Structure* (Cambridge, MA: MIT Press).

—— (1986), 'On derived domains in sentence phonology', *Ph.* 3: 371–405.

—— (1991); 'On the inalterability of geminates', in Bertinetto *et al.* (1991), 187–209.

SELMER, E. W. (1920), 'Enkelt og dobbelt tonelag i Kristianiasprog', *Mål og Minne*: 55–75.

—— (1921), *Tonelag og tonefald i Bergens bymaal* (Kristiania: Jacob Dybwad).

—— (1927) 'Den musikalske aksent i Stavangermålet', Avhandlinger utgitt av Det norske vitenskapsakademi i Oslo, II. Historisk-filosofisk Klasse 1927 (Oslo: Jacob Dybwad).

—— (1966), *Fremmedordbok*. 6th edn. (Oslo: H. Aschehoug and Co.).

SIEVERS, E. (1885), *Grundzüge der Phonetik* (Leipzig: Breitkopf and Hartel).
SIGURD, B. (1965), *Phonotactic Structures in Swedish* (Lund: Scandinavian University Books).
SIVERTSEN, E. (1967), *Fonologi* (Oslo: Universitetsforlaget).
SKAUTRUP, P. (1944), *Det danske sprogs historie*, vol. 1 (Copenhagen: Gyldendalske Boghandel).
SKJEKKELAND, M. (1997), *Dei norske dialektane* (Kristiansand: Høyskoleforlaget).
SKÅNLUND, E. B. (1933), 'Saltamålet. Kort oversikt over lydverket', *Bidrag til nordisk filologi av studerende ved Universitetet i Oslo*, vol. X (Oslo: H. Aschehoug and Co.).
SPANG-HANSSEN, H. (1959), *Probability and Structural Classification in Language Description* (Copenhagen: Rosenkilde and Bagger).
SPENCER, A. (1991), *Morphological Theory* (Oxford: Blackwell).
STANDWELL, G. J. B. (1972), 'Towards a description of stress and tone in Norwegian Words', *NTS* 26: 179–94. Reprinted in Jahr and Lorentz (1983a), 335–50.
—— (1975), 'Norwegian Phonology', *Acta Linguistica Academiae Scientiarum Hungaricae* 25: 339–77.
STANLEY, R. (1967), 'Redundancy rules in phonology', *Lg.* 43: 393–436.
STERIADE, D. (1986), 'Yokuts and the Vowel Plane', *LI* 17: 129–46.
—— (1987), 'Redundant values', *Papers from the Twenty-third Regional Meeting, Chicago Linguistic Society*, vol. 2: 339–62. (Chicago: Chicago Linguistic Society).
—— (1992), 'Syllables', in Bright (1992, vol. 4) 106–11.
—— (1995), 'Underspecification and Markedness', in Goldsmith (1995), 114–74.
STORM, J. (1884), *Norvegia. Tidsskrift for det norske folks maal og minder.* Vol. I. (Kristiania: Grøndahl and Søn).
STRANDSKOGEN, Å.-B. (1979), *Norsk fonetikk for utlendinger* (Oslo: Gyldendal).
—— and R. STRANDSKOGEN (1995), *Norwegian: An Essential Grammar* (London: Routledge).
SWEET, H. (1873–74), 'On Danish pronunciation', *TPS*, 94–112.
TANNER, G. A. (1976), 'The use of the retroflex flap among children aged 12–16 in Oslo', *Norskrift* 11: 9–63 (University of Oslo: Institutt for nordistikk og litteraturvitenskap).
TORP, A. (1982), *Norsk og nordisk før og nå*, (Oslo: Universitetsforlaget).
VANVIK, A. (1957), 'Norske tonelag', *Maal og Minne*: 92–102. Reprinted in Jahr and Lorentz (1983a), 209–19.
—— (1958), 'Om regressiv sonorisering i norsk', *Maal og Minne*: 156–8.
—— (1962), 'Three Tonemes in Norwegian?', *Studia Linguistica* 15: 22–8.
—— (1969), 'Norwegian Prosody', *NTS* 23: 71–5.
—— (1972) 'A phonetic–phonemic analysis of Standard Eastern Norwegian. Part I', *NTS*, 26: 119–64.
—— (1973), 'A phonetic–phonemic analysis of Standard Eastern Norwegian. Part II', *NTS*, 27: 101–39.
—— (1975), 'En detalj i oslodialekten', *Maal og Minne*: 65–6.
—— (1979), *Norsk Fonetikk* (University of Oslo: Dept. of Phonetics).
—— (1985), *Norsk uttaleordbok/A Norwegian Pronouncing Dictionary* (University of Oslo: Dept. of Phonetics).
VIKØR, L. S. (1995), *The Nordic Languages: their status and interrelations*, 2nd edn. (Oslo: Novus).
VINJE, F. E. (1987), 'Å forbedre sine språkvaner', in E. B. Johnsen (ed.): *Vårt eget språk*, vol. 3: 34–133 (Oslo: H. Aschehoug and Co.).

VOGT, H. (1939), 'Some remarks on Norwegian phonemics', *NTS* 11: 136–44.

—— (1942), 'The Structure of the Norwegian monosyllables', *NTS* XII: 5–29. Reprinted in Jahr and Lorentz (1981), 208–31.

WEINSTOCK, J. M. (1970), 'A sketch of Norwegian phonology', in H. Benediktsson (ed.), *Nordic Languages and Modern Linguistics*, 572–98. (Reykjavik: Vísindafélag Íslendinga).

—— (1972), 'Redundancy rules and Norwegian vowel alternations', in J. M. Weinstock (ed.), *Saga og språk: Studies in language and literature*, 201–9. (Austin). Reprinted in Jahr and Lorentz (1981), 278–86.

WESSÉN, E. (1970), *Våra folkmål* (Lund: Fritzes).

WESTERN, A. (1889), 'Kurze Darstellung des norwegischen Lautsystems', *Phonetische Studien* II: 259–82.

WIESE, R. (1986), 'Schwa and the structure of words in German', *Linguistics* 24: 697–724.

—— (1996), *The Phonology of German* (Oxford: Clarendon Press).

WIIG, E. H. (1967), *A Comparative Study of Fundamental Frequency Characteristics in East Norwegian and Inland Northern American*. Doctoral dissertation, Western Reserve University.

WIIK, K. and I. RAIMO (eds) (1990), *Nordic Prosody V* (Dept. of Phonetics, University of Turku).

WILLIAMS, E. S. (1976), 'Underlying tone in Margi and Igbo', *LI* 7: 463–84.

WITHGOTT, M. and P.-K. HALVORSEN (1984), 'Morphological constraints on Scandinavian tone accent'. (Stanford: Center for the Study of Language and Information, Report No. CSLI-84-11).

—— (1988), 'Phonetic and phonological considerations bearing on the representation of East Norwegian accent', in H. van der Hulst and N. Smith (eds), *Autosegmental Studies on Pitch Accent* (Dordrecht: Foris).

YIP, M. (1991), 'Coronals, clusters and the coda condition', in C. Paradis and J.-F. Prunet (eds), 61–78.

ZWICKY, A. M. (1985), 'Clitics and particles', *Lg.* 61: 283–305.

—— and Geoffrey K. Pullum (1983), 'Cliticization vs. inflection: English "*n't*"', *Lg.* 59: 502–13.

INDEX